ALSO BY MELISSA DE LA CRUZ

DESCENDANTS
The Isle of the Lost
Return to the Isle of the Lost

THE BLUE BLOODS SERIES
Blue Bloods
Masquerade
Revelations
The Van Alen Legacy
Keys to the Repository
Misguided Angel
Bloody Valentine
Lost in Time
Gates of Paradise

The Ring and the Crown

#1 *NEW YORK TIMES* BEST-SELLING AUTHOR
MELISSA DE LA CRUZ

BASED ON *DESCENDANTS 2* WRITTEN BY
**SARA PARRIOTT &
JOSANN MCGIBBON**

SCHOLASTIC
SYDNEY AUCKLAND NEW YORK TORONTO LONDON MEXICO CITY
NEW DELHI HONG KONG BUENOS AIRES PUERTO RICO

Copyright © 2018 Disney Enterprises, Inc. All rights reserved.
Visit www.DisneyBooks.com and DisneyDescendants.com

Published by Scholastic Australia in 2018.

Scholastic Australia Pty Limited
PO Box 579 Gosford NSW 2250
ABN 11 000 614 577
www.scholastic.com.au

Part of the Scholastic Group
Sydney • Auckland • New York • Toronto • London • Mexico City
• New Delhi • Hong Kong • Buenos Aires • Puerto Rico

Cover design by Marci Senders
Cover art by James Madsen
Hand lettering by Russ Gray

All rights reserved. No part of this publication may be reproduced or transmitted in any form or by any means, electronic or mechanical, including photocopying, recording, storage in an information retrieval system, or otherwise, without the prior written permission of the publisher, unless specifically permitted under the Australian Copyright Act 1968 as amended.

ISBN 978-1-74299-586-1

Printed in Australia by Griffin Press.

Scholastic Australia's policy, in association with Griffin Press, is to use papers that are renewable and made efficiently from wood grown in responsibly managed forests, so as to minimise its environmental footprint.

10 9 8 7 6 5 4 3 2 1   18 19 20 21 22 / 1

For Mattie & Mike,
Always

And for

Heidi, Sasha, and Calista Madzar,

friends & allies, thank you for all your support
and enthusiasm for the series!

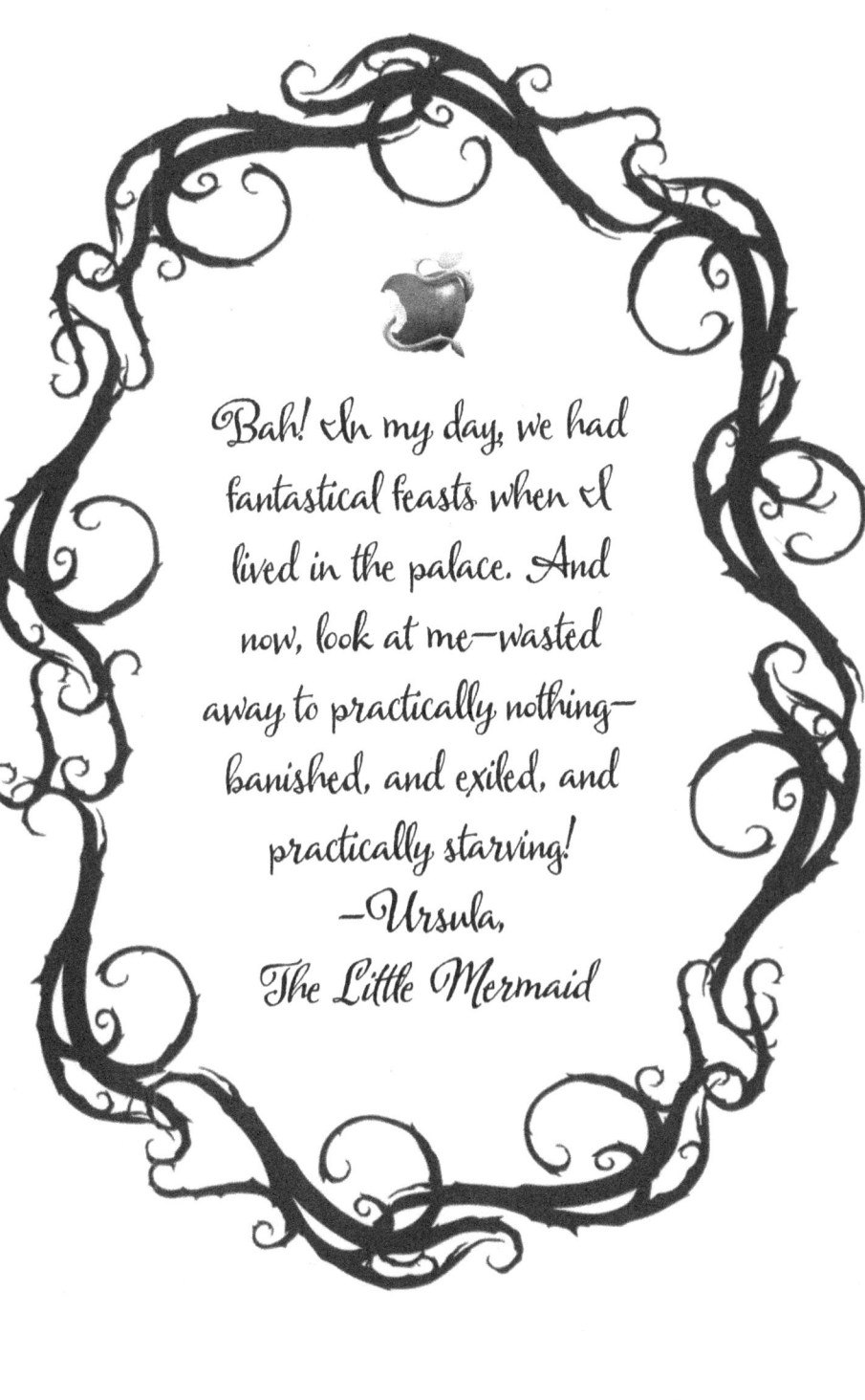

> Bah! In my day, we had fantastical feasts when I lived in the palace. And now, look at me—wasted away to practically nothing—banished, and exiled, and practically starving!
> —Ursula,
> The Little Mermaid

Left Behind

Once upon a time, the offspring of an evil fairy and a sea witch were friends. Mal, daughter of Maleficent, Mistress of Darkness, and Uma, daughter of Ursula, Witch of the Seas, were an inseparable duo, partners-in-petty-crime. Mal had purple hair, flashing green eyes, and a mischievous streak, while Uma had turquoise locks, eyes the colour of the abyss and a wicked sense of fun. Luckily for the poor, unfortunate souls who lived on the Isle of the Lost, they didn't get to see each other very much, since they lived on opposite sides of the island and went to rival schools—Dragon Hall for Mal and Serpent Prep for Uma.

Life on the Isle of the Lost—where all the villain folk had been banished after King Beast united all the good kingdoms and exiled all the evildoers and their snarky sidekicks—was already difficult. For one, an impenetrable dome covered the island and its surrounding waters, keeping out any source of magic, as well as every kind of Wi-Fi network. For another, most of the island's residents subsisted on leftovers from Auradon's mainland along with the goblins' terrible coffee. But life always got a little worse during the summer when school was out, because that was when Mal and Uma could hit the streets together again.

They would rampage up and down the island, terrorising step-granddaughters and traumatising even the most stalwart goons, and no-one would dare voice a peep of annoyance, for fear of something truly frightening—*the girls' mothers*.

One hot day in June, not long after each had turned ten, Mal and Uma were playing on the docks by the water. The two bad little girls were pranking Hook's crew, making tick-tock noises to scare the pirate captain himself, and getting on Smee's already agitated nerves. They giggled naughtily behind some empty barrels as their best trick of all went off without a hitch. One pirate after another tripped and fell on the slippery wooden planks, which they had covered with a nearly invisible slime. It was Mal's idea to coat the decks with bilge and oily, murky scum, and she laughed with glee to see it work so well.

'Here comes Cruella De Vil,' said Mal, spotting a telltale black-and-white bouffant rising from the crowd of pirates. 'Let's get her!'

Cruella was a nemesis of theirs. As one of the only citizens on the Isle who wasn't afraid of Maleficent or Ursula, the Dalmatian-obsessed lady never hesitated to pinch their ears when they tried to make her their victim. They were determined to get her back one of these days, but they'd have to be crafty.

They watched her sauntering down the docks with a ratty spotted fur on her shoulder, glaring at everyone she met.

'What's she doing down here, anyway?' whispered Uma.

'Goblin barge is arriving soon, and she likes to have first dibs,' explained Mal, holding her breath as Cruella sashayed closer and closer to where they were hiding. 'She's always hoping someone's thrown away an old fur coat.'

The girls looked at each other, eyes sparkling with mischief. Mal raced to pour another batch of the disgusting concoction in Cruella's path, but the giant bucket was too heavy for her.

'Hurry!' said Uma, running to grab the bucket's other handle.

'I've got it!' said Mal.

'Let me!' said Uma. 'You did Gaston!'

Mal chuckled darkly at the memory of the big man going bottoms-up on the dock and finally crashing over the railing with a loud roar and splash, his sons slack-jawed at the sight.

Uma pulled the bucket to her side.

'Stop it! Let go!' Mal demanded.

'*You* let go! You're splashing it on me!' whined Uma.

They each yanked on the bucket. As Uma wrenched it away, Mal lost her grip on the handle, overturning the pail and its contents—and she tripped and fell upon their own slippery puddle.

'Mal!' yelped Uma, as her friend skittered down the length of the dock, flailing, all the way to the edge.

'Help! Help me!' Mal screamed, as she attempted to grasp the wooden rails while she sped towards the sea. 'I can't swim!'

But the irony that the mastermind had been caught in her own naughty little prank and the sight of her purple friend sliding down the docks like a flopping wet fish was too hilarious for Uma to resist, and instead of running to help, the little sea witch was doubled up on her knees in laughter.

Mal spun down past the gaggle of pirates, past a confused Cruella De Vil, and disappeared overboard.

That shook Uma from her laughing fit. 'Mal!' she called, rushing to the railing's edge. 'Mal! Where are you? Are you okay?' Uma craned her neck, searching the churning waters for a sign of her friend.

Her heart stopped, for she couldn't catch sight of Mal's purple head anywhere in the waves, and while Maleficent might find it amusing that her daughter had landed in the drink, she would not take too kindly to the news that her one and only spawn was gone forever.

'Mal! Where are you?' Uma cried, a little desperately now.

Uma felt a tap on her shoulder and looked up to see Mal standing there, totally dry. 'You didn't fall in!' she cried in relief.

'I caught a wooden rung right before I fell,' said Mal sweetly.

'You're all right!'

'Yes, I'm okay,' said Mal with a sugary smile that suddenly turned evil. 'But you're not!' she yelled, and before Uma could blink, Mal reached behind her back and dumped a huge bucket of smelly and disgusting baby shrimps all over Uma's head. Turned out Mal had scampered back up on the docks just in time to see the goblins unloading the latest catch from the barge. Furious at her friend for laughing at her bad luck, Mal decided to create a little bad luck herself.

Uma screamed.

And screamed.

And screamed.

Sadly, the smell never quite left Uma's hair, no matter how many times she washed it.

Much worse, Mal's nickname for her caught on, and from that fateful day forward, everyone called Uma 'Shrimpy' behind her back.

Except for Mal, of course, who called Uma Shrimpy *to her face*.

From the sandbox to the doomball courts, the animosity between the two girls festered and bubbled over the years—especially during rival *super-sinister-thirteen* birthday parties, which they scheduled on the same night. Somehow, Mal always ended up on top.

But Uma knew the day would come when she would beat Mal at her own game.

One fine day . . .

Three years later, that day had not yet come. Especially not after the shiny black limousine drove up to the Isle of the Lost. Uma had never seen a car like that—the only means of transportation on the island were rickshaws pulled by goblins, old skateboards and rusty bikes. It was clear limousines were more than just cars; they were moving cocoons of luxury, decked out in buttery leather seats and filled to the brim with sugary drinks and snacks.

So what was it doing here of all places, on this forgotten island of villains?

The young sea witch elbowed her way to the front of the gaping crowd so she could get a better look at what was happening. At 16, she was small for her age, but more than made up for it by cutting a striking figure. She wore her turquoise hair in a river of long braids that fell down her back, and was partial to patchwork leather dresses and low boots decorated with fishing nets and seashells. Truly, Uma was one of the head-turners on the island, not that she cared. Uma had bigger fish to fry—literally, since she worked at her mum's Fish and Chips Shoppe.

The assembled group of louts, toughs and goons (otherwise known as the population of the island) were *ooh*ing and *ahh*ing at the sight of the marvellous automobile. No-one had any idea why it was there, or what it meant, but before a riot broke out among the villainous ranks, the door to Maleficent's castle opened and Evie, Carlos and Jay walked out carrying luggage, followed by their parents.

'Bring home the gold!' yelled Jafar.

'Bring home a puppy!' urged Cruella De Vil.

'Bring home a prince!' Evil Queen cried.

Uma nudged the fellow on the left. 'What's going on?' she asked. 'Are they leaving?'

The henchman nodded, barely concealed envy on his face. 'Rumour has it they're going to Auradon.'

'Auradon? Why?' said Uma, appalled and intrigued at the same time.

'To go to school. Some kind of new proclamation or something. They've been chosen to attend Auradon Prep.'

Carlos, Jay and Evie trooped into the car.

'Is anyone else going?' Uma asked, just as a fourth villain

kid burst through the castle doors. An annoyed-looking Mal handed her backpack to the driver.

Of course Mal had been chosen, too.

Uma watched as Mal looked up to the balcony, where Maleficent raised her staff in goodbye, her green eyes blazing. After a moment, Mal's purple head disappeared into the limousine as well.

Somehow, instead of feeling glee at the sight of the four villain kids' depressed and resentful faces, Uma only felt a spark . . . of envy.

Why wasn't *she* chosen to leave the Isle of the Lost and live in Auradon? Was she not wicked enough? Not special enough? Why was she left behind like a common goblin?

And why was Mal chosen instead?

Uma had to find a way out of the Isle of the Lost. If Mal and her crew were living in Auradon, then *that* was the place to be—the place where *Uma* needed to be. Not here, working day in and day out at Ursula's Fish and Chips Shoppe slinging fish cakes and lost-soul casseroles to the rabble. Uma was special: she was the sea witch's daughter, a force to be reckoned with! She couldn't stay here, lost and unloved and unappreciated!

There was nothing she could do, however. The weeks went by, and the dome was impenetrable. There was no way out of the Isle of the Lost. No matter how much she wanted to leave, there was simply no escape.

Until one day, a few months later . . . one ordinary day, like every other, but unlike every one that came before it, when something different happened.

Uma was getting her hair done at her favourite beauty salon, Curl Up & Dye, watching the television while sitting under the dryer.

'It's the Coronation. Wish we could be there,' the hairdresser said with a sigh, as a handsome Prince Ben bowed his head to accept the king's crown and the duties that came with it.

'Mmm,' said Uma, indifferent to Auradon's pomp and glory. Young Dizzy, the wicked step-granddaughter who was sweeping up tendrils from the floor, was glued to the sight.

On-screen, Fairy Godmother was holding out her wand, but in the blink of an eye, someone else had taken it, and then a huge explosion rocked the whole island.

'What was that?' Uma cried, rushing out of her chair and running outside, just in time to watch a dark shape rising up into the sky, flying like a veritable bat out of hell.

'Magic! The dome is broken!' she heard someone cry. 'Maleficent is gone!'

Like the rest of the island's residents, Uma saw her chance—it was time to go! Time to leave the Isle of the Lost forever! But without a bridge, there was only one way to get to the mainland, so the island's residents were scrambling to the shoreline. Uma followed the crowd rushing down to the docks to find a ship, a boat, a way out—and just as she had clambered on the last goblin rowboat and made it a few miles away from shore, the dome closed again.

They ran smack into the invisible wall.

Wha—? How—?

Uma pressed her nose against the unseen barrier and tried not to scream.

She was still stuck on this witch-forsaken rock. Later that day, she watched with a weary annoyance as Mal and her friends celebrated their victory, dancing around some castle while fireworks went off in the distance.

Mal and her crew.

Crew.

That was it! That was how she was going to get off this island. As much as she didn't want to admit it, she couldn't do it alone. What was that saying? *No man is an island?* Well, no-one should live on an island either, at least not unless they had a choice in the matter.

In any case, Uma vowed then and there to put together a real crew of her own.

Friends don't let friends stay on the Isle of the Lost.

Under the Sea

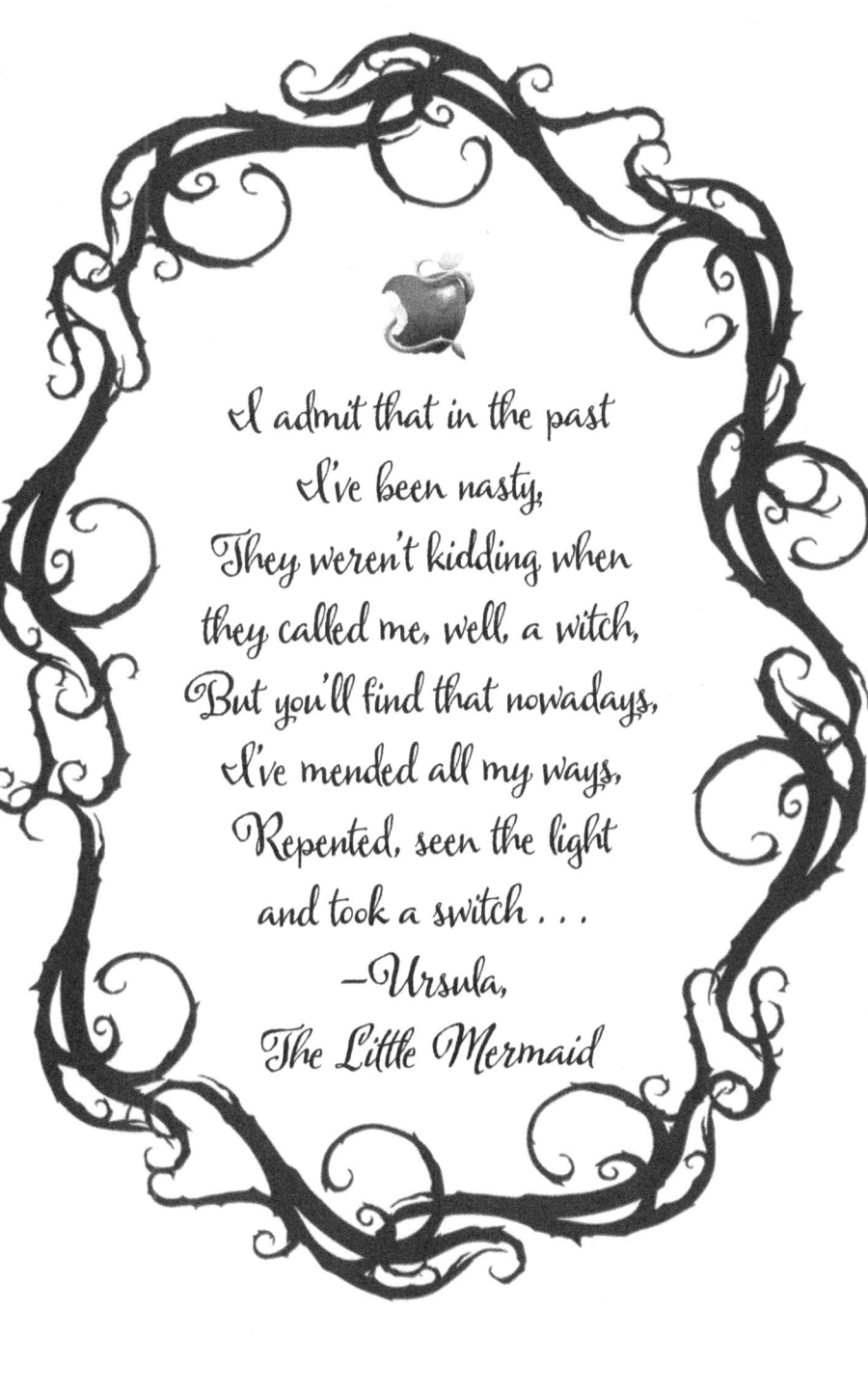

I admit that in the past
I've been nasty,
They weren't kidding when
they called me, well, a witch,
But you'll find that nowadays,
I've mended all my ways,
Repented, seen the light
and took a switch . . .
—Ursula,
The Little Mermaid

chapter 1

A Celebration of Auradon

'And now, please welcome Sebastian and the Seven Wonders of the Sea!' the cheerful announcer, a merman floating above the waves, joyfully declared. A magnificent clam-shaped stage rose from the ocean and slowly opened to display the famous crab and a row of pretty mermaids launching into a rollicking tune. The sandy beachfront in front of Ariel and Eric's castle had been turned into an outdoor stadium, complete with bleachers above the water. Seated high up in the royal box with Ben and her friends, Mal eagerly clapped with the rest of the audience gathered for the start of the annual Seaside

Festival, a daylong celebration of merfolk life. Next to her, Evie was taking zapps on her phone with Arabella, Ariel's niece, who was something of a fashion maven and idolised Evie's style. The two were currently sporting matching V-braids and poison-heart necklaces. Evie had even made Arabella's outfit, a lavender-coloured blouse with a lace bodice along with a distressed leather skirt.

Evie and Arabella couldn't stop giggling. 'What's so funny?' Mal asked.

'Mal, do this filter with us!' Evie said, and Mal obliged, sticking her tongue out at the camera. The image on the phone turned the three of them into mermaids complete with curved green tails.

'That's pretty much what I look like when I swim,' Arabella said approvingly.

'Cool,' Mal smiled.

On the stage, Sebastian was zooming around on his claws, belting his heart out while the mermaids harmonised and splashed, swimming in synchronised patterns around the stage.

'Who knew crustaceans were so talented?' Mal whispered to Ben as Sebastian hit a high note. Ben grinned and squeezed her arm in agreement.

He looked so handsome in his royal coat and sash, the golden crown on his honey-coloured hair. The crowd cheered when they saw him smile, and he waved back from the balcony. 'Come on, Mal, give them a wave,' he urged.

Mal hesitantly raised her hand and waved as well, and another cheer rose from the crowd. She was still getting used to the position of royal girlfriend and all the attention it generated. She never wanted to embarrass Ben, and she was keenly aware of how different she was from his former girlfriend. Audrey was the epitome of an Auradon princess—she looked so perfectly sweet and lovely that birds would perch on her finger, while Mal was definitely a villain kid from the Isle. A reformed villain, for sure, but chirping birds certainly wouldn't be worshipping her any time soon. Unlike Audrey, Mal preferred to wear leather pants rather than pretty dresses. So far the people of Auradon didn't seem to mind, and Mal was grateful they were so accepting.

'How do they fly so high?' asked Carlos, as the mermaids shot into the air to the rhythm of the music and performed dizzying backflips. 'I thought they were mermaids, not fairies.'

'They're jumping, not flying,' said Jay, looking envious. 'It's like water parkour.'

'Oh, like what they do in R.O.A.R. competitions,' Carlos teased, meaning the Royal Order of Auradon Regiment. 'You know, all that sword-fighting, flips and stuff, or as you call it, "jumping."'

'Right, when are tryouts again?'

'After our last tourney game.'

'Cool,' said Jay, adjusting his red beanie over his forehead. Mal shushed the guys as the mermaids finished their song and the clam closed again and disappeared underwater. Next, the orchestra was introduced, showcasing a talented variety of sea creatures playing instruments in a custom-built stage-size aquarium. It was a joyful, dazzling celebration. Growing up, Mal recalled watching (okay, sneering at) the festival coverage on Auradon News Network, but that was nothing compared to seeing it live, to marvelling at the shimmering scales on the mermaids and watching a killer shark pluck harp strings with its fin so delicately. The Seaside Festival was just the first in an annual all-kingdom 'Celebration of Auradon' wherein every kingdom hosted the king with a plethora of festivities that showcased their unique culture.

Suddenly, Mal felt something shift in her pocket and got a glimpse of the Dragon's Egg she had found in the Catacombs of Doom only a few days earlier. The evil talisman had been disarmed, but its surface was crisscrossed with fine green lines, and they were multiplying by the minute.

Mal knew it was dangerous, but she couldn't help keeping the Dragon's Egg with her at all times. It had to be destroyed soon, and Ben kept reminding her about it, but she always had an excuse as to why she couldn't see Fairy Godmother just yet. For some reason, she just wanted to keep the egg a little longer. There was no rush just yet, was there? Besides, the Dragon's Egg was so warm and toasty in her pocket.

'It's nice to be back,' said Mal. 'Even though we were only gone for a day, it felt like we were down in the Catacombs for a long time.'

Ben nodded. 'I'm glad everything worked out.'

'Thanks to you,' she said, since Ben had appeared at the last minute to set everything right on that adventure.

'And you!' he said, nudging her.

'And us!' chimed in Carlos, Jay and Evie teasingly.

'Totally! Group hug?' said Mal, opening up her arms.

'Group hug!' they chorused, and the five of them shared an affectionate embrace. Evie pulled in Arabella too, so she wouldn't feel left out, even though she hadn't braved the Catacombs of Doom with them.

The orchestra finished its performance with a roaring crescendo of percussion by a group of manta rays, just as a proud King Triton rose from the waves. He held his golden trident to the sky and the entire coastline exploded in a dazzling canvas of colour and light and magic. The crowd thrilled at the sight, and Ben put an arm around Mal as the fireworks boomed all around them. She leaned her head against his chest and nestled into his arms, feeling lucky and content—and just a tiny bit guilty about the Dragon's Egg hidden in her pocket.

After the show, the gang wandered down to the exhibitor booths to shop for Seaside souvenirs before the start of the mer-games. Mal and Ben walked hand-in-hand behind their friends, lingering at a stand selling seashell necklaces.

'Pretty,' said Mal, holding up a particularly luminescent piece, a creamy pastel-coloured one polished to a high shine.

'Each one is unique.' The mermaid attending the booth smiled. 'No two are alike in all the world.'

'Do you want one?' asked Ben, reaching for his wallet.

Mal smiled and shook her head. 'No, I just like looking at them.' She handed the seashell necklace back to the mermaid.

'They're not just beautiful,' the mermaid told them. 'Each of them contains a little sea magic. The most famous seashell necklace was Ursula's golden one, of course. Her power almost defeated Triton's, but thankfully it was destroyed.' The mermaid shuddered at the memory.

Mal nodded and took Ben's hand and pulled him away to catch up with the rest of the group. She didn't want any mention of villain history to mar their day, and Ursula's evil actions still cast a shadow on the Seaside community, in the same way that Audrey's grandmother had snapped upon seeing Mal, the daughter of Sleeping Beauty's famous nemesis, attending school in Auradon.

They found their friends in front of a booth selling scoops of Seaside's famous clam-shaped fried ice-cream. Arabella had taken on the role of unofficial tour guide, and was telling Evie, Jay and Carlos which flavours tasted the best and which ones to avoid.

'Plankton is a good choice; it tastes like pistachio,' Arabella said, tapping the glass and pointing to the nearest tub.

'Sounds good, I'll take it,' said Carlos.

Jay leaned over the counter. 'What about that one?' he asked, motioning to a dark-coloured flavour.

'Oh, that's anemone. It tastes like chocolate.'

'Nice, I'll go with that one,' said Jay, nodding to the merman working the counter. He watched as the merman scooped up a hefty roll, placed it between two crusty pieces of bread, closed it up like a clam and tossed the entire thing into the fryer, then stuck it on a Popsicle stick and handed it to Jay to eat.

Jay bit into it and smiled in satisfaction. 'Wow, how does it keep from melting?' he asked.

'Magic,' said Evie. 'Kidding. The bread keeps the heat away from the ice-cream like a shield. It's simple chemistry.'

'Which one do you want, Mal?' asked Ben. 'My treat. Let me guess. Purple starfish!'

'Good guess!' she said, squeezing his hand.

'One purple starfish coming right up,' he said with a smile. 'I'll have the same,' Ben told the clerk.

Mal took a bite. It tasted like lavender and honey. Delicious. Evie and Arabella chose the whitecaps flavour, which Evie reported tasted just like vanilla except with a little more sea salt. The group left the ice-cream counter and slowly made their way through the crowded aisles of booths, admiring colourful pieces of sea glass and scrimshaw sculptures.

'Hey, what about this?' said Carlos, picking up a T-shirt that proudly proclaimed, "I Went to the Seaside Festival and All I Got Was This T-shirt."

'Perfect,' said Evie. 'Especially since it's in black and white.'

'Of course!' said Carlos, tossing the shirt over his shoulder.

The next booth sold CDs of blue-whale songs, and Carlos picked up a set of headphones to listen. 'I wonder why they haven't switched to offering it on a digital streaming service yet,' he said.

'Oh, you know blue whales, they're a little old-fashioned and set in their ways,' explained Arabella. 'But you guys should head back to the aquatic auditorium to catch the start of the one-million-metre butterfly. The mermen swim so fast you can't even see their fins! They're just blurs in the water!'

'You're not joining us?' asked Evie.

'I have to say hi to my family. My grandfather's hosting a reception under the sea,' said Arabella. 'I'll catch you at the free-fin race.'

The mer-games were just as thrilling as Arabella promised, and Mal cheered with the rest of the crowd as the merfolk showcased their speed and strength in a number of races and competitions. Evie decided she liked the synchronised fin dancing best, while the boys enjoyed the underwater boxing matches, which were projected on a screen since the other audience members couldn't actually go underwater to watch them like the mermaids did. The free-fin race was just about to start when a flash of lightning forked the sky and a crash of thunder rolled, booming so loud it echoed all over the open-air stadium.

Ben looked up with a frown at the suddenly dark skies. 'Huh, that's weird. All the weathermen predicted sunny skies for today,' he said.

'But isn't it always sunny in Auradon?' asked Mal.

'Not today,' said Carlos, as seemingly out of nowhere, an angry storm gathered above their heads, turning the clouds black and sending sheets of rain all over the colourful tents and booths and drenching everyone seated in the auditorium. The merfolk dove into the sea while everyone else rushed to the exits.

'Let's get out of here,' said Ben, removing his jacket to use as an umbrella over their heads. 'Follow me to the limo!'

They ran out towards the parking lot, where cars and carriages were gridlocked as everyone tried to get out of the rain and leave the festival at the same time. The five of them piled into the royal limousine, drenched and shaking from the cold, wet droplets soaking the leather seats.

'Where did that storm come from?' said Evie, her fringe

plastered to her forehead. 'There were blue skies just a second ago.'

'Where's Arabella?' asked Carlos.

'She texted me earlier. She said she was going to stay a little longer at her grandfather's party and not to wait,' said Evie, checking her phone again. 'She's with her family.'

'We need to get home before it gets any worse,' said Ben.

Mal agreed. 'Yeah, let's go.' Outside, rain lashed the windows and a furious wind howled, rocking the car. The exuberant celebration of underwater life had ended, literally, with a wash.

'So much for the festival,' said Jay.

'It's too bad,' said Evie. 'They worked so hard to make it special.'

Mal kept silent. In her pocket, the Dragon's Egg throbbed and turned warmer. Was it connected to what was happening outside? She hoped not, but the freak rainstorm made up her mind. As soon as they got back to school, it was time to say goodbye to the evil talismans once and for all.

chapter 2

A Sudden Wild Magic

It stormed for the entire trip from Seaside to Auradon City, but when they finally arrived at Auradon Prep that afternoon, the skies were as blue as ever. As the limousine pulled up to the school, Mal turned to her friends. 'You guys, I think it's time we dealt with the talismans.'

'I was hoping you would say that,' said Evie, making a face as she removed the golden apple—now a tarnished bronze—from her purse. 'I've been carrying this for a few days and it gives me the creeps.'

'I don't know, it's kind of fun having them around; it reminds me of where we came from,' said Jay, unearthing a twisted wooden stick with a cobra head from his pack. Its snake eyes were leering and baleful, even in stasis.

'Well, unlike you, I don't want to be reminded of the Isle of the Lost all the time,' said Evie. 'Do you have yours, Carlos?'

Carlos nodded but looked nervous. 'Yes, unfortunately. I wanted to leave it in my room because I don't like carrying it around, but it felt like too much of a risk.' He showed them the plastic ring he had in his pocket.

'I have mine,' said Mal, removing the glowing Dragon's Egg from hers.

'Great, I'll let Fairy Godmother know we're on our way,' said Ben.

'Right,' said Mal, taking a deep breath as they all got out of the car.

There was only one way to deal with the talismans; only one power in Auradon that was stronger than evil, tougher than wretchedness, and more tenacious than malevolence. A force that could turn a kitchen girl into a princess, tiny mice into a team of king's horses and a simple pumpkin into a wondrous carriage. The most powerful magical artifact in all of Auradon: Fairy Godmother's wand, wielded by the most powerful magic-user in the land: Fairy Godmother.

They entered campus and headed to the main building, where they trooped into the office of the headmistress. The cozy, comfortable place was decorated in shades of princess pink and periwinkle blue, and even the curtains sparkled with starlight. There were cozy plump couches to sit on and many framed photographs of Fairy Godmother and her daughter, Jane.

'Welcome back! How was the Seaside Festival?' asked Fairy Godmother, getting up from behind her desk and smiling at all five of them. 'Did you give King Triton my regards?'

'I did,' said Ben. 'The festival was wonderful as usual, except for this strange storm at the end.'

'I saw on the news,' said Fairy Godmother. 'What a shame.' She nodded to the four villain kids holding out their talismans. 'So there they are, huh? I've been expecting them.'

'Sorry, we got distracted by school,' said Mal.

'Absolutely understandable. It's not as though I were looking forward to this task either,' said Fairy Godmother, shaking her head. 'Oh dear, what a collection. You are all heroes for surviving their temptations.' She shuddered at the sight of the pulsing Dragon's Egg. 'They will have to be destroyed, of course.'

'The sooner the better, Fairy G,' said Ben. 'It's best for the kingdom.'

'I suppose we have no choice,' she agreed. 'These dangerous objects cannot fall into their true owners' hands, but destroying them could unleash a sudden wild magic—a powerful and uncontrollable blast.'

'A necessary blast,' Ben soothed.

'But sometimes, the consequences of using such great magic remain unknown until much later.' Fairy Godmother sighed.

'Can we do it soon?' said Carlos, grimacing.

'What's your hurry?' said Jay with a grin as he twirled the cobra staff like a baton.

Evie shook her head decisively, her dark blue hair bobbing over her shoulders. 'I'll be glad to be rid of mine. I feel like if I close my eyes I can still see all those awful things that Magic Mirror showed me.'

Mal scrunched her nose. She didn't want to admit it, but the reason she had been procrastinating its destruction was because she found it strangely comforting to hold the Dragon's Egg. She understood that it was evil, and why it had to be destroyed—but it was meant for her. It was part of her heritage, part of her mother. And so a part of Mal—a very small part, but there nonetheless—would lament its demise.

'Right, no time like the present,' said Fairy Godmother, and they followed her out of the office. She led the group towards the Museum of Cultural History, where her wand was once again kept safe and secure, floating in a crystal case.

'Bibbidi bobbidi boo,' said Fairy Godmother, and the case disappeared, allowing her to pluck her wand from the air. 'Hold them out, please,' she ordered.

Mal, Evie, Carlos, and Jay stood in a semicircle, talismans balanced on their palms. Fairy Godmother scratched her head with her wand for a minute, thinking hard. Then with a flourish she waved the wand above the talismans, showering glittery sparks all over the room.

> '*Salagadoola mechicka boola,*
> *Send this apple back to its tree!*
> *Salagadoola mechicka boola,*
> *Destroy this ring of envy!*
> *Salagadoola means mechicka booleroo,*
> *Stop this cobra from hissing forever!*
> *And the thingabob that does the job*
> *Says this Dragon's Egg will hatch never!*'

Fairy Godmother pointed her wand, shooting an arc of light over the talismans that wrapped around them like a mini tornado, and as the power grew, the room became hot with magic.

The light turned into a ball of flame that reached into the ceiling, and with a piercing, high-pitched noise that shattered every window in the museum and caused everyone in the room to put their fingers in their ears, the light burst through the roof and out into the sky, and the four talismans erupted in a huge explosion of sparkles that showered everyone in shiny, powdery dust.

When the smoke cleared, Fairy Godmother waved her wand towards the ceiling and fixed the hole, and then turned to the windows.

'Whoa,' said Mal, rubbing dust from her eyes and coughing.

'Do you like my hair this way?' Evie joked, and Mal realised they now all had frizzed hair that stood on end. Carlos' was practically a Mohawk.

'Everyone all right?' asked Ben, wiping the glittery soot from his shoulders.

'Yeah, I guess,' said Jay, who was on the floor looking for his beanie, which had been knocked off his head by the force of the spell.

'I think we're okay for the most part,' said Carlos, coughing and holding his sides.

'Mal, you look a bit woozy,' said Ben, concerned.

In truth, she felt as if she'd just been punched in the stomach by the loss of the Dragon's Egg, but she gave him a brave smile. 'Evie?' she asked, turning to her friend, who was a bit pale.

Evie nodded, but her smile was strained. The loss of their talismans had affected them all.

'Well, let's hope the only damage was to the ceiling and windows,' said Fairy Godmother with an anxious smile. The pink bow around her neck was slightly singed. 'Like I said, you never know what happens when this kind of wild magic is unleashed.'

'I'll ask the council and all the kingdoms to keep an eye out for anything out of the ordinary. Thank you, Fairy Godmother,' said Ben.

Mal straightened her jacket, a troubled look on her face. 'But what about the dome remote control that got left on the Isle of the Lost? If the goblins on the island ever get it to work, Cruella De Vil, Evil Queen, Jafar and all their minions can still get off the Isle.'

'Hmm, that is a puzzle,' said Fairy Godmother.

But Carlos was bouncing on the balls of his feet, his face lit up with excitement. 'I thought of that, and I was worried too, until I remembered something.' He held up a small black electronic device and fiddled with the buttons.

'What did you remember?' asked Jay, curious, and looking over Carlos' shoulder.

'Codes can be reprogrammed. Even if they get the remote to work, they won't have the new code to open the dome,' said Carlos with a grin. 'I already took care of it.'

'Just like magic!' said Evie.

'Nope, just like science,' said Carlos, with a nod to Fairy Godmother, who strongly advocated that the residents of Auradon learn to live without depending on magic.

'So we're safe now, right?' asked Evie hesitantly.

'Safe and sound,' said Fairy Godmother. 'Except for the exams coming up.'

There was a communal groan as Ben and the villain kids remembered. You could save the kingdom, but you still had to pass Magical History.

chapter 2¼

A Sudden Wild Magic, Indeed

The burst of magic that shot through the entire kingdom of Auradon was so strong and so unexpected that no-one on the Isle of the Lost even noticed when the invisible barrier disappeared for a moment. (Well, it *was* invisible, of course.) It frizzed out of existence, and for that glorious minute, everyone who was trapped on that island could have escaped from it. Except no-one knew, and so no-one escaped, because no-one noticed.

Except for the fish down below, who found it odd that something that had previously been on the other side of the barrier had now floated over to the Isle side. The side where the villains lived, the side where evil ruled, the side where, if anyone had any idea that this certain something was now within grasp, the entire ocean would soon fill with scoundrels of all sorts trying to get their hands on it.

And that is exactly what came to pass . . .

Because someone or something . . . *did* notice . . .

Someone with a big mouth.

chapter 3

A Fishy Story

'A pint of pond scum, two brine balls, a bucket of chum and a side of rot,' the old pirate said, perusing the menu with his one good eye.

'Rot: Dry or wet?' asked Uma, all business, pencil poised above her notepad.

The pirate thought about it. 'Wet.'

'Terrible choice,' Uma growled. 'Order in!' she called, placing the ticket on the revolving machine by the kitchen window.

'Order up!' the cook growled back. She was a surly woman in a white chef's hat and red apron who slammed every order on the table with a bang so that half its contents spilled on the floor. The shop's menu was posted on wooden planks over the counter, listing items such as sea slime, spleen and grit, as well as their specials, shell smell and fish guts.

Uma picked up the tray, tucked the pencil behind her ear, and saw to the other patrons in the drafty, perpetually damp tavern that always smelled like fried fish. Long wooden tables and benches were filled with pirates and louts. A seashell throne stood in the far corner; it had been made for her mother and was now Uma's favourite place to sit. She'd been working at the restaurant for as long as she could remember, watching her mother broil offal and roll out the dogfish dumplings. But while Ursula's name was on the sign at the door, she was hardly ever there anymore. These days, Uma's mother spent most of her time at home watching Auradon soap operas on their rusty television and mourning her glorious past when she lived in King Triton's palace. Ursula had been exiled from Atlantica before being exiled again to the Isle of the Lost, a double banishment that she swore to avenge.

Uma was glad to have the place to herself. If Ursula were around, she would only be raging and complaining about why she had been saddled with such an ungrateful and useless daughter. Ursula never ceased to remind Uma how often she'd lost to Mal. When she'd learned Mal had been chosen to go to Auradon, Ursula flipped her tentacles. Uma never heard the end of it.

Uma cleared a few tables and kicked out some pirates for duelling, pointing to the sign on the wall that said NO DUELLING. A few minutes later, she returned to the old pirate's table laden with his meal. 'Pint of scum, brine balls, boiled chum and a side of wet rot,' she said, banging it all down on the table.

The old guy sniffed at the plate of brine. 'This smells a week old,' he said suspiciously.

'It is a week old,' said Uma, her arms crossed.

'Excellent!' he said, and dug into his rather disgusting-looking meal. Uma had no idea how people could eat at Ursula's. *You'll take it how I make it* was the house slogan, and so far, no-one had the courage to complain. Many on the Isle remembered the power the sea witch used to wield.

Uma continued to 'serve'—more like yelling and dumping food in front of a few more patrons—a couple of hungry Huns sharing a plate of moray soufflé and a few rowdy Stabbington cousins fighting over the tastiest pieces of splat. When Uma returned to the pirate's table, his plates were empty and the old sea rat was rubbing his belly in appreciation. 'Hey, you heard the news?' he asked, seeming to be in a talkative mood.

'What news?'

'Goblins have some hot info,' he said, leaning in to whisper.

Uma rolled her eyes. 'Goblins are terrible gossips.' She kept clearing the table, stacking everything on her tray.

'Yeah, that may be, but they sure have an interesting tale to spin this time,' said the pirate. 'Rumour going around the docks is that it's got something to do with the merfolk.'

'Oh yeah?' Uma couldn't help being intrigued. For all intents and purposes, she herself had merfolk blood. *Queens of the seas,* Ursula would lament. *We would be queens of the seas if not for that awful Triton and that terrible Beast.*

The pirate raised his eyebrow and grinned. 'You know that storm we had yesterday? The big one that almost tore down the mast of the *Jolly Roger*?' Uma nodded. 'Something weird about that storm; it came out of nowhere, ripped through all of Auradon and the Isle of the Lost. Goblins say a couple of eels over by Seaside saw a fool mermaid playing around with King Triton's trident and accidentally created that downpour—and lost the trident in the process.'

She pursed her lips. 'Lost trident, huh? I call fish tale,' she said, putting away the tray of dirty dishes and crossing her arms. 'Everyone knows all the magical artifacts in the kingdom are kept in the Museum of Cultural History. Triton doesn't even use his trident anymore. The golden age of magic is over in Auradon.'

The old pirate scratched his silver beard. 'Doesn't he take it out for every mer-festival?'

'He does,' Uma had to agree. She'd seen the sea king on TV, holding up his trident at the opening ceremony.

'And when was the festival?'

'Yesterday,' Uma allowed, recalling the incessant coverage

on the Auradon News Network. They'd even pulled that stupid crab out of retirement so he could sing that song one more time.

'Ended with that big storm,' said the pirate.

'But if Triton's lost his trident, why doesn't he just call it back up?' she asked. 'Can't he do that?'

The pirate smiled a crafty smile. 'He sure can, except he doesn't know it's gone yet. None of the merfolk do. Whoever took the trident isn't owning up to it. No-one knows how, but some goblins swear they saw it right by the edge of the barrier, and that it somehow floated over on our side. Which means it's currently adrift in the waters around the Isle of the Lost!'

'But how did it get here? Through the barrier? Nothing can pass through that thing, not even underwater,' said Uma skeptically.

'Mystery, isn't it? But the goblins swear it's true. Something must have happened over in Auradon,' said the pirate. 'Now everyone's looking for that thing. Including me.' He grinned. 'What would Triton give to have it back, right?'

Uma's eyes narrowed, her thoughts racing. If the goblins were right, and the pirate wasn't lying, then a golden opportunity had fallen into the Isle of the Lost. Triton's trident was one of the most powerful magical objects in all of Auradon. Even if its magic wouldn't work on the Isle, it was still valuable.

A thing like that could change her life. If Uma could get her hands on it, it would mean she wouldn't have to stay here at the fish shop, slinging the house bilge and pouring drafts of slime. Her hand automatically reached for the locket she wore around her neck. Inside was a tiny piece of junk that her mother had given her as a child. 'It's all I have left,' Ursula had said at the time. Uma never understood why a sliver of metal mattered so much, but she liked holding it when she was anxious.

An idea had formed in her wicked little mind. Her mother had taught her about the power of negotiation, or as she'd described it, talking someone out of their greatest treasures and giving nothing of value in return.

If Uma found Triton's trident, she could use it to negotiate her way out of this island once and for all. She could offer it up to King Ben in exchange for release from exile.

How would she get her hands on it, though? It was underneath the waters around the Isle of the Lost, which meant she would have to find a ship and a crew, and a way to retrieve it before anyone else found it.

But for now, there were stacks of dishes to wash (or at least rinse), plenty of grime to collect for tomorrow's brew, and lots of crabgrass to sauté for Crab Surprise. (The surprise was that there was no crab in it!) Until she figured out a way to get to that trident, she was stuck on land, with nothing to show for her life but a bucketful of pond scum.

chapter 4

The Girls from the Isle

The next morning, Evie woke up early to get ready for class. Back at Dragon Hall, professors expected their students to be late, and chided them if they were early. *The early bird catches the worm, but the tardy bird* steals *the worm*, was one of the school's oft-repeated pieces of wisdom. But Evie was in Auradon now, and getting up with the sun suited her. She'd worried her hair wouldn't recover from the shock of frizzing when the talismans were destroyed, but it was her usual lush, cerulean mane after she'd washed and blow-dried it that morning. Evie pulled on her favourite fingerless gloves, stepped into her stacked-heel boots, and looked over with a fond smile to where Mal was still sleeping, her purple locks peeking out from under a pillow that she always placed on her face to keep the light out.

With a satisfied sigh, Evie smoothed the duvet on her bed to make sure it was perfect, admiring her sewing machine sparkling in the sun by her desk. She straightened her garment rack full of dresses for clients and pinned up a picture of Queen Belle's signature yellow frock to her inspirational pin board filled with photos of various princesses. Mal's side was a little messier in comparison, with sketchbooks and paints thrown around the rug and a little graffiti over the headboard to make it feel like home.

Evie left the room, taking care not to wake Mal, and grabbed breakfast and a cup of chirpy-as-your-smile coffee from the happy workers at the cafeteria—a decided improvement from the black-as-your-soul lattes served up by the goblins back on the Isle. After, she headed to her first class: Life Skills without Magic. She saved Mal a seat next to hers, which remained empty even as the bell rang and class began.

Good Fairy Merryweather was writing some numbers on the board when all of a sudden the clock on the wall flew back to the top of the hour and an unexpected wind blew through the room, sending everyone else back to where they had been 15 minutes ago. Evie blinked, and the seat next to her was suddenly occupied. Mal sat there with an innocent look on her face, just as the bell rang, right on time for class.

'Mal,' Evie said in a scolding tone.

'What?' Mal replied, even as she was holding a well-worn brown tome etched with a golden dragon on its cover.

'You're using your spell book again, aren't you?' she said accusingly.

'Hmmm, it appears that time-turning spell needs some work,' Mal muttered, as Evie peered over Mal's shoulder to watch her write *Those with villain blood appear to be immune* in the page's margin.

Evie shook her head. 'Time turning?'

Mal looked sheepish. 'It only turns back time to the top of the hour, and only if it's been less then 15 minutes. More than that and nothing happens, as I discovered the other day, when I was late and got detention,' she said in an aggrieved tone.

Detention at Auradon Prep wasn't meant to be a real punishment like it was at Dragon Hall—but Evie knew that to Mal, an hour of cake baking with Professor Merryweather was as bad as it got.

'Relying on magic can be a dangerous habit,' Evie whispered, as Merryweather started lecturing on points that would be covered in the exams next week. 'That's what Fairy Godmother says. If you solve all your problems with magic, we never learn how to solve problems on our own.'

'But isn't that what magic is for?' Mal whispered back. 'To solve problems? Isn't that what Fairy Godmother did, when she sent Cinderella to the ball in a fabulous dress?

Or when Beast turned from a monster to a handsome prince? Or when Aladdin got on a magic carpet and showed Jasmine a whole new world? Or even yesterday, when Fairy Godmother destroyed the talismans?'

'No,' said Evie, sounding even more convinced than ever. 'I don't want to lecture, but that's not what magic is for. Magic is an expression of the unlimited capacity of mystery and wonder in the world. Cinderella's goodness brought the Fairy Godmother to her, and Belle's love for Beast transformed him, and while Aladdin was able to charm Jasmine with the magic carpet, remember when Genie turned him into Prince Ali and he almost lost it all? A dependence on magic can be a weakness. It's not for skipping a tardy mark. The talismans were a special case.'

Mal chewed her pencil. 'Okay.'

Evie put a hand on Mal's arm. 'I'm just trying to help.'

'I will try next time, Evie, I promise. Tomorrow,' said Mal, putting a hand on top of Evie's and squeezing it.

Evie nodded, satisfied. They turned their attention back to class. The Life Skills exam would test them on the proper way to balance a chequebook without resorting to arithmancy, or even worse, a calculator. Merryweather stood at the blackboard in front of a column of complicated numbers. 'Now pay attention, because this is important. A balanced ledger means the number on this side equals the number over here. The test will have a list of credits and debits for you to balance.'

'What's a chequebook?' Evie whispered.

'A book filled with checkmarks?' joked Mal. On the island, all transactions were done in trade or through the goblins, who kept meticulous records.

They giggled softly together, and Evie was glad that they were both equally clueless about normal Auradon life.

'We've got to get better at this,' said Evie determinedly, copying down the numbers from the blackboard.

'Maybe it's too late for us. We're the girls from the Isle, after all,' said Mal thoughtfully.

'But our future is in Auradon,' said Evie.

'True. But I still know where we came from,' said Mal.

'I do too,' said Evie, as she went through the calculations and balanced her ledgers perfectly. 'But now I'm more interested in where we're going.' She flashed her friend a reassuring smile, which Mal returned.

'Yeah, you're right, you're more Isle Light,' said Mal.

'Isle Light?' teased Evie. 'Is that some kind of drink?'

Mal laughed and they both finished their study sheets. At the end of class, they walked out together, running into Evie's boyfriend, Doug, in the hallway.

'There are my favourite girls,' he said, slinging an arm around both of them.

Mal raised an eyebrow.

'Ahem, I mean, my favourite girl,' he said, gingerly removing his arm from Mal's shoulder and squeezing the one around Evie.

'She's just teasing,' said Evie with a fond smile at Doug, leaning into his embrace.

'Am I?' said Mal archly.

'Hey, be nice to Doug,' said Evie.

'I am,' said Mal, acting offended. 'When am I not nice to Doug?' She turned to him. 'You did really well during the band performance at the tourney game the other day,' she said sweetly. 'I think Evie particularly enjoyed your jazz solo.'

'Thanks, Mal,' he said, beaming.

'Anyway, I should go,' said Mal, hugging Evie goodbye. 'I forgot I have to meet Ben at the royal library opening. Do I look okay?'

Mal was wearing a purple T-shirt and leather pants, not exactly grand-opening, meet-the-public material, but Evie knew she didn't have time to change. 'You look beautiful!' she said, and that was the truth. Mal always looked great, even when she was wearing a preppie punk dress for a royal event.

Mal smiled hopefully. 'Wish me luck!'

'Luck! You'll do great!' said Evie.

'Luck!' called Doug. They watched as Mal sauntered away.

Doug looked fondly at Evie. 'Speaking of luck. How did I ever get so lucky?'

'What do you mean?' she asked.

'Um, band geek on the short side wins hand of Isle princess?' he said lightly.

'All that matters to me is that you're a prince at heart,' said Evie. 'You really think I'm a princess?'

'Your mother is Evil Queen, right? That makes you a princess.'

'Thanks, Doug,' said Evie, blushing. 'I guess I thought it didn't count in Auradon. No-one ever remembers I actually am a princess.' She realised she never got invited to any of the royal functions—she was overlooked for the princess tea the other day, and while Evie would never say a word, she did have bona fide royal roots, as Doug pointed out.

'I remember,' said Doug. 'How can I forget? You're the fairest in the land.'

Evie felt a spark all the way down to her toes. 'Okay, stop, now you're making me blush,' she said. 'And late for my next class.'

They said goodbye, and Evie hurried to Advanced Goodness, when she heard someone call her name. She turned around to see Arabella fiddling nervously with the edge of her shirt. 'Evie, I need help,' she said.

With her messy, uncombed hair and red-rimmed eyes, she was a far cry from the put-together Arabella from yesterday, who had been proudly showing them around Seaside.

'Sure! What's up? Do you need another dress made?' asked Evie. But something in the look on the little mermaid's face told her that this particular problem wouldn't be so easily fixed by a dress with a lace bodice and a leather skirt.

chapter 5

Royal Engagements

'Ah, there you are, Sire,' said Lumiere, handing Ben a pair of gem-encrusted scissors.

Ben thanked his servant and excused himself from the ambassadors from the Bayou de Orleans, who'd come all the way from Grimmsville to attend today's event.

'Is Mal here?' he asked, making his way to the front of the podium, where a polite crowd of students and librarians had gathered, along with the royal press corps, ready as usual with cameras flashing and television microphones.

'No, Sire, not yet,' said Lumiere.

'Let's give her a minute,' he said.

'I think we need to start,' said Lumiere. They were already running half an hour late, and the guests were getting restless. 'I will bring her up when she arrives.'

Ben agreed, taking the scissors and standing in front of the big yellow ribbon that was draped behind him in front of an open doorway. He looked out at the expectant faces gathered around, as well as the television cameras and phones that were held up to record his every word.

'It's a real treat to be here today at the opening of the royal wing of the Auradon Library. As you know, my mother is an avid reader and believes books are passports to a deeper knowledge and understanding of the world,' he said, giving a speech he'd performed so often he could recite it in his sleep. (There were many royal library wings in Auradon.)

After the speech, Ben shook hands and made polite conversation with the dignitaries, keeping one eye on the entrance, looking for Mal. They hadn't seen each other since Fairy Godmother destroyed the talismans yesterday, and he wanted to make sure she was all right. She'd seemed a little green around the edges after the spell had cleared. He hadn't had any time to text her that day yet; his royal schedule was so packed between classes and royal duties that he hadn't even had a second to himself, so he'd been looking forward to seeing her at the library at least.

Ben wondered what was keeping her as he walked over to the buffet table, perusing the hot hors d'oeuvres, pie and pudding flambé. All his favourite foods. He picked up a cup of the flaming pudding and spooned a bite. Ben had learned to take every opportunity to eat at these royal events; he'd been to a reception in Agrabah once where he had passed on food offered at the pre-ceremony, not knowing about the traditional six hours of speechifying that would follow. By the time they finally served dinner at midnight, he thought he'd pass out.

Ben was also looking forward to seeing Mal so he could ask her to be his lady and have her official debut at Cotillion, an Auradon tradition that was coming up in a month or so. He was a little nervous about it, but it wasn't like he was asking her to publicly declare her love for him in front of the entire kingdom. Except, well, he was. Maybe that meant he should make his Cotillion proposal a little more special? But before he could think more on it, he was pulled aside by some older ladies from the Aurora Priory who wanted to have a word.

'How is your dear mother?' asked a duchess, who counted herself among Belle's closest friends and was something of an aunt to Ben.

'She's very well, thank you,' said Ben. 'I think she's looking forward to coming home; she said she's been a bit seasick on the last leg of their cruise.'

'I'm so glad,' said a countess, who was another of his mother's close friends. 'The kingdom has missed them.'

'I've missed them,' said Ben, feeling a bit homesick for his parents. He was proud they trusted him enough to leave the entire kingdom in his hands, but once in a while, he did miss having his family around.

'Oh, sweetheart!' chorused the ladies, who immediately took to comforting him like their own child.

Ben was assuring them he was quite all right when he felt another tap on his shoulder and turned to see Lonnie. 'Ben, can I have a word?' she asked.

'Sure,' he said, relieved to have an excuse to bid goodbye to the well-meaning mother hens. 'What's wrong?'

'I just got a message from the Imperial Palace. There's some trouble in Northern Wei's Stone City, near the Great Wall: a border dispute with Agrabah.'

Ben frowned. 'That doesn't sound good.'

'It's not. The Emperor doesn't want to insult the Sultan, and they're both asking if you can help them come to an agreement,' said Lonnie. 'The villagers on both sides will listen to you as King of Auradon, without anyone from the Imperial Palace or the Sultan's family losing face.'

'Sounds like a plan,' said Ben.

'Will you come now?' she pleaded. 'The Emperor is worried the situation might escalate. So far everyone is being polite, but he thinks it'll be more than that if people don't calm down soon.'

'Yes, of course.' He wiped his mouth with a napkin and

set down the pudding, following Lonnie out the door just as Mal rushed in with that determined look in her eye that he loved.

'Ben!' she cried when she spotted him. She looked as if she'd just been running.

'Mal!' he said, happy to finally see her.

They hugged.

'Am I that late? Are you leaving already?' she said, stricken. 'I'm so sorry! I thought it was at the main library, not the school library. I went to the wrong place!'

'No, it's okay. Don't worry. The event isn't over, but I do have to go,' he said, motioning to Lonnie.

'Oh, hi, Lonnie,' said Mal.

'Hi, Mal,' said Lonnie, fidgeting anxiously with the sword on her hip.

'What's wrong?' Mal asked.

'Trouble between Agrabah and Northern Wei. I've got to broker a peace deal between them and the empire,' said Ben.

'We have to leave immediately,' said Lonnie.

'How long will you be gone?' asked Mal, just as her phone burst into a devilish laugh. *MUAHAHAHAHA. MUAHAHAHAHA.*

'Interesting choice for a text alert,' teased Ben.

'Yeah, I'm not so into the standard chirping bird,' said Mal, looking down at her phone. 'Huh, Evie just emergency-texted me. I should go too.'

'Let me know if you need anything,' said Ben. 'I don't know when we'll get back yet, so keep in touch.'

'I will, don't worry,' Mal promised, looking up at him with her sparkling emerald eyes. 'And good luck.'

They hugged again, and Ben kissed her forehead. 'By the way, remind me, I have to ask you something when I get back.'

'Okay. Why so mysterious?' asked Mal. 'Just ask me now.'

'I want to make it special,' said Ben with a smile.

'Ben, we should really go,' said Lonnie anxiously.

'Go,' said Mal. 'You're needed.'

Ben nodded and gave her a final squeeze, then ran off to follow Lonnie out the door to make the necessary arrangements with Lumiere.

chapter 6

Hooked on a Feeling

'Coming through, coming through,' Harry Hook called, flying down the banister to his next class at Serpent Prep, the tails of his red waistcoat flapping as aspiring henchmen and teenage toughs scurried out of the way, lest they be unfortunate enough to have a chance encounter with Harry and his hook.

The Serpent Preparatory School for the Education of Miscreants, as it was appropriately named, had many terrible students—a host of evil, wicked, scheming, rotten little villains, who were just like their parents. But in all of Serpent Prep, there was only one Harry Hook.

Harry laughed his maniacal laugh and waved his hook merrily, slashing at the air, as a little first-year tripped trying to get out of his way. Harry himself landed on his feet, and with a flourish, tipped his black tricorn hat and bowed to a group of young witches who tittered at the sight of him. '*Hiiiii*, Harry,' they chorused in a melodic singsong.

'Ladies.' He winked, his smirk making them swoon. Dark-haired, with a wicked gleam in his dark eyes that were roguishly lined with guyliner, Harry had all the swagger and swashbuckling charm of a real devil-may-care buccaneer. He was the only boy in the Hook family—right between his older sister, sassy and mean-spirited Harriet, and his younger sister, CJ (short for Calista Jane—the baby—who was always off having grand adventures of her own). Harry prided himself on being wild and unpredictable, off-kilter and a little mad, his one disappointment being that he hadn't come by his hook naturally—he had to suffer the injustice of having to *carry* a hook in either hand.

He'd tried to entice Tick-Tock to take a bite of him once, hanging off the dock and dipping a hand in the water, but the lazy crocodile just opened one eye and went back to sleep.

Entering the classroom, Harry slid into his seat next to Uma, who was already in her usual place in the back of the room. 'Well, *helloooo*,' he drawled.

'Arr,' she grunted, looking irritated.

Harry wondered what was wrong. Uma was his oldest

friend on the Isle. She'd sort of decided to order him around when they were kids, and he sort of fell into the habit of following her orders. They had a lot in common: cruel intentions, awesome pirate outfits, and well-muscled arms. Plus, they were always up for mischief and adventure.

This was their favourite class, Accelerated Piracy: Hostage Taking and Threatening. But today's lesson was all about different pirate flags, which could honestly put any swashbuckler to sleep.

Uma could usually be counted on to cause a little trouble and a little excitement, and Harry wished she would shake herself out of this dark mood she was in. There were goblins to torment, rigging to swing around in, and victims to rough up out there. He couldn't do it alone.

'Want to go see if we can find some first-years to walk the plank?' he asked. 'Or raid Jafar's Junk Shop?'

Uma shook her head. 'Not today. Today I need a ship.'

'A ship! What do you need a ship for?' he asked.

'We're pirates, Harry. What kind of pirates don't have a pirate ship?' she said.

Uma had a point. A pirate's life on the Isle of the Lost was a bit limited. There were no rich galleons loaded with gold to attack, no merchant ships to hold hostage, no ports to raid. If they had a ship, their pirating would still be restricted, true, but the invisible dome that kept the island apart from the mainland fell a little beyond the immediate shores, which meant a ship could still sail from one end of the island to the other, maybe even to the Isle of the Doomed, the haunted island that nobody visited.

'Think of all the awful things we could do if we had a set of sails,' said Uma. 'Especially if we ever got out of the Isle of the Lost. We'd have the freedom to do bad deeds everywhere!'

That did sound promising, thought Harry. Freedom to rampage and adventure—explore the world and steal its finest treasures. 'All right, we need a ship, but where would we get—?' he said, just as he remembered a flyer he'd ripped from the school bulletin board earlier that morning. He unfurled it from his pocket, studying it carefully. 'Look at this,' he said, nudging Uma.

It was a ship, or more accurately, a drawing of a ship. A pirate ship with black sails, flying the Jolly Roger and everything. A real beauty.

'*The Lost Revenge*,' read Uma.

'Good name for a pirate ship,' said Harry approvingly.

They read the rest of the text together.

PIRATE RACE
FIRST MAN TO REACH DEAD MAN'S
COVE FROM THE GOBLIN WHARF WINS
THE *LOST REVENGE* FROM THE ONE
AND ONLY CAPTAIN HOOK
IF IT FLOATS, USE IT AS A BOAT!
TO ENTER: BRING TREASURE!

'This is it!' said Uma, eyes alight. 'I'm winning that ship!'

'You?!' said Harry, almost choking on the word and falling off his chair. 'This is a ship from my dad's fleet! That ship should be mine!' Of course, his father couldn't just *give* him the ship, could he? Instead Captain Hook was using it to amass more bounty. 'And you'll need a crew to sail that thing!'

'I'll get a crew!' howled Uma, slamming her palm on his desk. 'Isle of the Lost? This is more like Isle of the Lemmings! Everyone here is just looking for someone to follow, someone to look up to, someone to fear! Now that Maleficent's a lizard, there's no-one in charge! Why not me? I'll have a crew faster than you can say *octopus*!'

'But you don't even know how to sail!' Harry protested.

'And you do?' sneered Uma.

'Of course I do!' yelled Harry. 'I'm a pirate! You're just a sea witch!'

'I don't care! That ship is mine!' said Uma.

'No, it's mine!' said Harry, as they each took hold of the paper's edge and pulled it towards him- or herself.

Uma let go of the flyer, taking Harry by surprise, and he lost hold of his hook, which rolled to the floor. Quick as Lucifer, Uma pounced on it and held it high. 'It's mine!' she said triumphantly.

'Give it back,' growled Harry, seething.

'Oh, I'll give it back . . . *if*.' Uma said, a dangerous smile creeping on her face. She looked so much like her mother at the moment that it gave Harry chills.

'If?' he squeaked.

'If you or I win this pirate race, I'll give you your hook back,' said Uma.

'And if we don't?'

'If neither of us win, your hook is gone forever. I'll throw it in the ocean. And if I win, you work for me as first mate. I can't sail a ship, but you can,' said Uma.

Harry considered the offer. 'So if you win or I win, I get my hook back,' he said. 'And if you win I have to work for you.'

'Uh-huh,' said Uma with a salty smile. 'Like I said, you'll be the first mate on my crew.'

'If *you* win,' reminded Harry. 'If I win, you'll be *my* first mate.'

'You're not going to win,' said Uma smugly, crossing her arms. 'I always beat you.'

'I might,' said Harry. 'I'm fast.'

'Slippery, more like.'

'Slippery is still fast,' Harry said with a winning smile.

'So it's a deal?' said Uma, keeping Harry's hook behind her back while she held out her hand.

'Deal,' said Harry, shaking it. 'Now tell me why you really need that ship.' He knew Uma well enough to know she wasn't telling him the whole story. They'd been pirating all their rotten lives, and she'd never been interested in a pirate ship until today.

Uma leaned in and told him an unbelievable story about a missing golden trident and how they could bargain their way off the island with it.

Harry listened attentively without yawning or interrupting. But at the end of her story, he did have one question. 'Okay, say we do get that ship. How are we going to find that thing in the water?'

She waved her hand dismissively like Ursula did whenever she had to cast away any doubts in her victims' minds. 'I'll figure it out later.'

'You really think we'll get off this island?'

'If we play our cards right,' said Uma. 'Negotiation is my specialty.'

Harry scratched his cheek with a fingernail, thinking it over. He wasn't sure exactly what he'd agreed to, but however it turned out, he'd probably get his hook back, and he already missed it. 'All right, let's go put some rafts together then,' said Harry, studying the flyer again. 'The race is this afternoon.'

chapter 7

Fairy Goddaughter Casts a Spell

A merman in a gold scale-patterned uniform came flying at him, sending the ball towards the goal, but Carlos blocked it quickly, throwing it back into the melee. Jay caught the ball with his paddle and ran down the field, jumping on shields, dodging every defenceman and cannonball shot in his path, until he successfully sent the ball whizzing into the Seaside goal. *Yes!*

But the Seaside team quickly recovered. Carlos was still celebrating Jay's score when another merman came barrelling towards him, almost certain to score. The ball shot towards the very edge of the goal, and right when it seemed all was lost, Carlos flew up and slammed it away from the net, just as the whistle blew to end the game.

Auradon Fighting Knights 3, Seaside Mermen 2.

It was the final game of the season, and they had just won the championship against the number one seed. Carlos cheered, jumping up in the air and waving his paddle. He pointed at Jay. 'You!'

'You!' cheered Jay, removing his helmet and rushing across the field to thump Carlos in the chest. They laughed and joined their team in a group hug, a sweaty huddle of excitement and adrenaline.

Then, like the good sports they'd learned to be, they joined their teammates in consoling their opponents, who were congratulating them. 'Good game, good game,' Carlos said, high-fiving the defeated mermen as they streamed by the Auradon Fighting Knights.

'Yo! Bomb Goalie!' yelled Herky, a rather large teammate.

'Huh? What did you call me?' asked Carlos.

'Bomb Goalie! You're the goalie, and you're the bomb!'

'Ha! Nice one, thanks,' said Carlos, pounding his teammate's outstretched fist. Herky enthusiastically tapped him back, sending Carlos flying right into the path of the Auradon mascot.

'Oof!' said a distinctly feminine voice from inside the Fighting Knight costume.

Jane! Carlos thought, rushing to see if she was all right.

'I'm so sorry!' he said, helping her stand back up. Jane removed her costume helmet and shook out her hair.

'Are you okay?' asked Carlos.

'I'm fine,' Jane said with a laugh. 'Risks of being the mascot.' Her dark hair was plastered to her cheeks and neck and she was all sweaty, but Carlos thought she looked sweet.

'Okay, good.' Carlos smiled. When she turned the other way, he surreptitiously smoothed down his shock of white hair. He was wearing it combed to the side these days, hoping it made him look older, more serious, and less like a computer geek.

They fell in step together off the field, Jane carrying the helmet under her arm. 'Good game,' she said. 'Poor mermen. They haven't been having the best week.'

'Did you get caught in the rain too?' asked Carlos.

'Yeah, I went with Lonnie. We got drenched,' said Jane. 'It's my favourite of the Auradon celebrations too.'

They passed Audrey and the cheerleaders, who were squealing and holding their pom-poms while congratulating the team. Jane twirled a lock of her hair around her finger and glanced wistfully at them. 'I was thinking of trying out for cheer,' she said. 'But that seems silly, right?'

'Why would that be silly?' asked Carlos. 'You should try out if you want to.'

'But I'm just the mascot,' said Jane. 'Mascots aren't cheerleader material.'

'That's not true. Look at me, I never thought I'd make the tourney team,' he told her, swinging his paddle absently.

'Really?' asked Jane. 'I thought you and Jay were recruited the minute you got here.'

'Jay was,' said Carlos. 'I was more of an accidental addition. Coach saw me running away from Dude and put me on the team. I used to be scared of dogs when I got here.'

Jane giggled. 'That's funny.'

'See, if I can do it, you can.' He smiled.

'But you're, like, brave and all,' she said. 'You guys stood up to Maleficent. You can do anything.'

Carlos tried not to laugh at her assessment. But he had to set the record straight. 'No way, I'm not brave. I was scared the entire time. Ask Jay. Or Mal. Or Evie.'

Jane was surprised. 'Really?'

'Yeah, I'm scared of a lot of things. I'm also scared of heights. And my mum.' He shuddered.

'Aw, come on, *everyone's* scared of your mum.'

'You got that right.' He turned to Jane and smiled. 'But cheerleaders are definitely not scary. Come on, what do cheerleaders do? I'll help you practise. Aren't tryouts for the new season next week?'

Jane nodded. 'Yeah. I was thinking of maybe auditioning.'

Carlos bounced across the field. 'Come on, let's practise flips. I've seen you do them in the mascot costume!'

Jane laughed and stepped out of the rest of the costume,

leaving the outfit in a pile on the grass. She was wearing a T-shirt and shorts. 'Okay! Let's do it!'

She did a bunch of cartwheels and backflips, and Carlos taught her how to do a one-handed cartwheel that he'd picked up from R.O.A.R. training. She taught him the Auradon cheer, and the routine that went with it, and by the end, they flopped together on the grass, red-faced and out of breath. 'That was fun,' said Jane.

'You're really good,' said Carlos, and he couldn't stop smiling.

'You think so?' she asked shyly.

'So you'll try out?'

'Yeah. Why not.' Jane laughed again. She stood up and brushed her knees, her eyes twinkling like stars from her mother's wand. 'Me, a cheerleader . . . I mean, stranger things have happened, right?'

'Like villain kids going to school in Auradon?' said Carlos with a smile.

'I guess so,' said Jane. 'Did you ever think you guys would end up here?'

He shook his head. 'Honestly, it's the last thing we expected. It was a total surprise, and we didn't even want to go.' He recalled that day so vividly, how their parents had schemed and pressured them into going to Auradon as part of their evil plan.

Jane didn't expect to hear that. 'You didn't?'

'No, I mean, we were raised to believe bad is good, and

all we knew was the Isle of the Lost. But our parents were determined to send us here so they could have their revenge.'

'Thank goodness you guys didn't do it,' said Jane.

'Yeah. It's weird. I never thought I'd be over on this side of the barrier, but it feels really natural now,' he said, thinking of all the good things in his life now that he lived in Auradon. His dog, Dude, for one, and his solid gang of friends for another. *Even Jane,* he thought. If he'd never moved to Auradon, he wouldn't have met her.

'What do you want to do when you get out of here? Auradon Prep, I mean,' she asked, as they left the field and walked onto campus.

'What do I want to do when I grow up?' Carlos thought about it. 'I don't know. Something with computers, maybe? What about you?'

'I always thought I'd be like my mum,' said Jane.

'Headmistress?'

'No, I meant like someone who grants people's wishes. But now that magic is discouraged, I guess I have to go back to the drawing board,' said Jane. 'Which is totally fine. Although, I was sort of looking forward to suddenly popping up when people are crying and changing everything so that they get their heart's desire.'

'You like helping people,' said Carlos.

'I guess I do,' said Jane. She smiled and blushed, as if she'd revealed too much of herself. 'Come on, race you back to the dorms. One, two . . .'

But before she even said *three*, Jane was already running, holding her mascot costume in her arms.

Carlos yelped and ran to catch up with her, following the sound of her laughter all the way to the buildings.

Jane had a sweet, lovely laugh, and hours later Carlos discovered he was still thinking about it.

chapter 8

The Little Mer-thief

After saying goodbye to Ben, Mal burst out the library doors and crossed campus, weaving her way through a crowd of students rushing out of their classes, and headed to study hall. Evie deployed the emergency-text option sparingly, so Mal knew it was serious. When she finally arrived back at their room, she found Evie sitting on the bed with Arabella, who was sniffling and wiping her eyes.

'Mal! Thank goblins you're here,' said Evie.

Thank goblins? Things must really be serious if Evie was slipping back into Isle-speak. Mal took a seat across from Arabella and tried to look comforting.

'Tell Mal what you told me,' Evie said to her friend.

Mal thought that maybe Arabella, who was new to Auradon Prep, had some kind of first-year problem. The villain kids all had questions when they'd first arrived too: Was it okay to eat as much food as you could from the refectory? (Jay) Could you take as many classes as you could fit into your schedule—or even take two classes at the same time, if you worked really fast? (Carlos, of course.) Evie had wanted to know if they had to wear uniforms (they didn't), while Mal's only question was where she could acquire purple spray paint (the art studio). Although it had to be more serious than that, since Evie'd texted SOS.

'I have a big problem,' Arabella gulped and wiped her eyes. She was shaking. *Hmmm. Definitely not the usual first-year drama*, thought Mal.

Evie soothed. 'Big problems are Mal's specialty.'

'Okay,' said Arabella. She took a deep breath. 'Remember when I went to my grandfather's reception at the Seaside Festival yesterday?'

Mal nodded.

'So, um, I did something stupid at the party. I took something that wasn't mine,' said Arabella, still sniffling. 'When he wasn't looking, I swiped my grandfather's trident. I just wanted to see if I had enough power in me to use it, like my cousins. I just wanted to prove that I'm one of the king's heirs too, that I could raise the waves like he did. I figured I'd return it right after.'

'Okay, so you took his trident . . .' Mal tapped her chin with her fingers; she could tell where this story was going already. The girl had gotten into some kind of mischief, obviously, but nothing too hard to untangle or fix.

'But . . .' said Evie, prompting.

'But it didn't work out that way,' said Arabella, miserable. 'I didn't just call up some waves. The trident was so powerful that I called up that huge storm. I lost hold of it, and it flew up into the sky—and when it fell, I couldn't find it. It washed away somewhere!'

'So it's gone?' asked Mal, shocked. *That* she hadn't foreseen, although she was relieved to discover that the Dragon's Egg hadn't been the reason behind the storm after all. Even though the talisman was gone forever, she was glad it hadn't caused any more destruction as the result of her delay in taking it to Fairy Godmother.

'It's gone.' Arabella nodded.

'Does King Triton know?' Mal asked. She could only imagine the sea king's rage when he found out. Mal knew all about what happened when powerful beings were bereft of their magical instruments.

Arabella shook her head determinedly. 'No. I didn't tell him. I didn't tell anyone. I was too scared.'

Mal nodded. 'I can imagine.' The sea king's anger could make the very seas boil with rage.

'But isn't he going to find out soon? I mean, it is his trident.'

'I told him I put it back in the case, which he's going to return to the museum tomorrow.'

'Okay.'

'So I only have until tomorrow night to get it back,' said Arabella. 'Before Grandfather finds out it's missing.'

'And you haven't told anybody?'

Arabella shook her head. 'My mum would kill me . . . and so would all my aunts, of course. I saw it shoot into the air, but no-one seemed to notice because of the storm.'

'They probably thought it was just lightning,' said Evie.

'So what exactly do you need us to do?' asked Mal.

'Help me find it?' Arabella said weakly.

'We have to help her,' said Evie.

Mal considered it. Arabella should probably tell her family what happened as soon as possible, but Mal understood wanting to take care of something on your own, or with the help of your friends. Speaking of friends in need, Ben was on his way to Northern Wei, and Mal didn't want to bother him while he was on such an important trip. But she could still rely on the rest of the gang.

'Evie, let's get the boys,' said Mal.

Arabella's face lit up with hope. 'So you guys will help?'

Mal nodded. 'Of course we'll help. Any friend of Evie's is a friend of ours.'

chapter 9

Race to the Bottom

Down by Jailor's Pier the docks were filled with sloops and schooners, brigs and clippers, vessels of all kinds and shapes, some driven by sail, others by paddle. They crammed the bay, anchor lines stretching in every direction, the boats rocking back and forth as the wind caught this one or that one. A galley with 50 paddles rowed past Uma, the men chanting in time, the oars beating the water. Seagulls filled the air with their shrieks, adding to the cacophony of chants and mixing with the hawkers' cries from their stalls. Uma crouched on a makeshift raft she'd fashioned from one of the shop's old tables, a broom handle and a bedsheet. It was seaworthy enough to sail on the bay for a small race, but would not be able to handle more than that. A great cutter sailed past her, and its wake nearly sent her tumbling overboard. Next to her, Harry was bobbing up and down in a bathtub, using a shower curtain for a sail. The wake half-filled his tub, and immediately he had to bail furiously to keep the thing from sinking. Even empty, the tub barely floated. It hung at water level, and each time it tipped, a bit of water ran into it. All in all, he'd done more bailing than sailing, Uma noticed with wicked glee. It was all he could do to keep afloat.

'Let's go over there,' she told Harry, leading them through the assortment of ships. They passed a few goblins on an old junk, one of those ancient boats from Northern Wei, sporting a red sail like the fin of some exotic fish.

'Check that out,' said Uma, as the junk sailed out of their path to reveal a pair of witches sitting in great buckets rowing with giant spoons.

'Where do you suppose you get a spoon that size?' asked Harry. 'And what's it for?'

'Well, it's for eating little boys,' Uma said, coughing up her best impression of a witch's cackle. 'I think your head would fit nicely on that spoon.'

'I see your point. Let's steer clear,' said Harry.

'Already ahead of you,' she replied, sailing the other way. Neither of them wanted to get any closer to the witches or goblins.

'Looks like everyone's after the prize,' said Uma, and

she didn't mean just the pirate ship. The water was full of goblins clad in snorkel gear and thugs flailing around in old fins and rusty scuba apparatuses—all of them looking for the trident, combing every bit of the ocean floor.

'So many,' said Uma, her heart sinking a bit in her chest. News of King Triton's trident had gone out, it seemed, and half the island was looking for the golden spear. Uma watched them nervously. Some had maps and others had formed groups. They were drawing grids across the bay and moving zone by zone, covering every inch. They were all as eager to find it as she was, and that worried Uma. *The whole island's gone mad for the trident*, she thought, *and while I'm trying to win a boat, they're already combing the sea.*

Next to her, Harry whistled at a goblin swimming by the junk. 'Ahoy! What sort of *junk* are you looking to find?' he asked with a grin.

Harry must have been hoping the goblin would take him up on the joke, but he received an honest reply. 'A trident! Haven't you heard?' said the green little fellow.

'That golden thing? I heard the mermen saw it on the other side of the Isle!' Harry said, then winked at Uma. He whispered, 'Thought I'd throw them off the scent!'

'Wonderful,' she replied, rolling her eyes. 'There are hundreds looking for the trident, maybe more, and you've thrown *one* off course.'

'It's a start,' said Harry, shrugging.

Over by the edge of the harbour, Captain Hook had

finally made his appearance. He sauntered down one of the larger docks, the planks creaking beneath his weight, the wind at his back. He wore his characteristic red jacket and an enormous red hat with an even larger white plume dangling over the brim, swaying this way and that as he walked.

'Dad really knows how to make an entrance,' said Harry.

Captain Hook stopped at the end of the dock and stepped onto a soapbox so everyone could see him. All around Harry and Uma, the competition readied itself. Henchmen wrestled with sails, ropes were flung aside or unwrapped from the docks. A great buzz of excitement and preparation built, and Uma stood a little taller in her raft. Hers was one of the smallest boats in the race, but she was confident in her victory. That ship was hers, and so was that trident.

'How are we even going to get out of the harbour?' Harry replied. 'This place is so choked with boats that it'll be an hour before we sail past any of them.'

'Mmm,' said Uma.

Suddenly all oars were in the air and everyone's eyes darted towards the dock. Captain Hook had raised his hooked hand high into the air to indicate that the race was about to begin.

Uma gritted her teeth. She was ready. Captain Hook lowered his hand as Smee fired the starting pistol. The race was on!

A fury of sails and splashing oars overwhelmed the bay.

Sailors were yelling, goblins were giggling, witches were gaggling. It was a terrible ruckus, and the water churned, once more filling Harry's tub and threatening to drag him down if he didn't bail fast enough. 'We'll never be able to sail faster than those ships on these things,' Harry shouted.

'Oh, you just figured this out?' Uma said.

'And you knew that?'

'Yeah, and that's why I'm going to beat you,' Uma said as she coiled a rope around her forearm. She'd fixed a noose at the end and she checked it to make sure it would work.

Then she threw the rope high into the air. It arched over a diver, past a rowboat full of pirates and landed soundly on a cleat attached to a small motorboat. She gave it a little tug to cinch the knot around the cleat, but there was no need. The boat's engine roared to life, and immediately the rope tightened, jerking her little craft forward. If she hadn't moored the rope to the deck of her raft, it would have been yanked from her hands. Even now it threatened to tear her craft apart. The boards moaned and creaked, but the raft held. Soon she was skipping across the waves, bounding up and down like a magic carpet tethered to a rocket.

Before she knew it, Uma was out of the bay and on the open sea. She'd chosen the fastest of the lot to hitch on to, and now they were in the lead. There was just one problem: since she was tethered to the goblins and her rope was fairly long, the *goblins* would likely win the race.

But only if they make it to the finish line, she thought.

Behind her, Harry was paddling furiously, still trying to make his way out of the boat-swamped harbour. He smashed right into one of the great galleys. Then he had to wait as more and more ships passed in front of him. By the time Uma caught sight of him again, half the bay was empty. Harry's shower curtain caught the wind, but it was too late. He was already taking up the rear. *Ha!*

But Uma didn't celebrate long. Harry's bathtub crashed into the nearest sailing ship, and he quickly abandoned it, jumping onto the catamaran. Since the ships were so crowded together, he was able to hopscotch from ship to ship all the way to the front.

Uma watched Harry's progress with narrowed eyes until she remembered she had her own problems. There was a tug on the cord and she swung the sail around just in time to catch sight of a pair of goblins gnawing furiously at the rope she'd attached to their speedboat. Once they finished, she was done, but all that gnawing seemed to be going awfully slowly and the knot was cinched too tightly for them to pull it off the cleat.

And that was when she saw the screwdriver.

She'd forgotten that goblins were clever folk. While one gnawed at the rope, the other started undoing the screws that secured the cleat. They were both in a race to cut her loose, and sooner rather than later one of them would win.

But Uma was not quite ready to lose her chance. She pulled on the rope, yanking on it so hard that it knocked one goblin straight into the water. Uma smiled at the little green fellow as she sped past him. She yanked again, this time harder, pulling her raft closer to the goblin craft. She noticed that when she gave it a good pull, the goblins' boat jerked wildly to one side. So she pulled again as the remaining goblin worked furiously at the screws.

The two were locked in their own race now.

He'd loosened two or three of the screws, and the cleat was hanging halfway off the back of the boat. A few more screws and Uma would be set adrift in the water while the goblin claimed the prize.

Fearless as ever, Uma gave the rope another strong tug, coiling it as much as she could. When it was as tight as she could make it, she let it go, and the rope whipped wildly back into the air, snapping the goblin in the face and sending him tumbling into the water. She cackled as she passed him, just as she realized there was no-one left on the motorboat.

The goblins had tied the steering wheel in place and jammed the throttle into gear while they tended to her rope. This was probably why the boat had veered to and fro when she pulled at it. There was no-one to correct the boat's course. It was hers for the taking.

If she could reach it.

The cleat rattled, and one of the screws flew off. It tumbled through the air and landed with a plunk as it struck the water. Only one screw still held the cleat in place, and it was already halfway out of its socket.

She tugged cautiously on the rope. If she pulled too hard she might yank that last screw loose, but if she waited too long the screw would come loose. Either way, the boat would be gone. And the motorboat was not the only fast ship on the water. All this tugging and swerving had slowed its progress, and she saw now that two or three of the larger sailing ships had caught up to the goblin boat. Even the galley was closing in, its oars beating the water, the oarsmen chanting.

'Yoo-hoo!' Harry called with a broad grin from the top of the sailing ship barreling towards the lead.

Uma could never be his first mate!

She needed to hurry.

One tug. A second.

She pulled and pulled, and that cleat held. It whipped back and forth, pivoting about that last screw, but it was still attached. Fortunately, the force of all the pulling made the screw bend, so it had stopped twisting itself free. But now it looked as though it might break in two.

She gave another tug. One more.

She was closer to the boat. She could try to jump the gap, but it was still too wide. So she gave the line another pull, gently dragging herself towards the stern of the out-of-control motorboat.

The cleat bent. The last screw flew loose.

Uma tugged one last time, pulling herself just a little closer, and just as the whole thing fell apart she leaped through the air, arms outstretched, reaching for the stern of the boat.

She caught it! She was flattened against the back, but she hung on, and with her other arm she reached up and pulled herself aboard.

She did it!

She was at the helm of the fastest boat in the race, except she was no longer winning the race. All that fussing around had allowed three, no, four ships to sail ahead of the goblin boat, including Harry's, which was now in the lead.

Uma hurried to the helm, tore free the ropes holding the wheel in place, and jammed the throttle into gear.

chapter 10

The Jet Set

The journey to Stone City, a small village on the eastern border of the Great Wall, was past the vast forests of Eden and the Lone Keep, so Ben decided the fastest way to get there was on the royal jet. 'We leave for the airport in five,' he told Lonnie, who was already more cheerful now that she'd secured Ben's commitment to fixing the issue plaguing the Imperial Palace.

Ben ran to change out of his formal clothing for travel gear, trading his sash and epaulets for a royal hoodie and jeans. He wished he'd had more time with Mal, but such was the life of a king—he was constantly needed in so many places at once. He envied his parents for the length of time they'd had for courtship. Sure, Beast was hiding in exile and Belle was basically imprisoned, but they'd had all the time in the world to fall in love, right?

He would make it up to Mal, he decided, by making his Cotillion proposal extra-special for sure. He just needed a little help. *But that's what friends are for,* he thought, as he texted Jane the details of his idea.

Lumiere, who had followed Ben out of the library reception and helped get him ready for the trip, doted anxiously on the young king. 'But, Sire, are you certain this is absolutely necessary?' he asked. 'Why not send an envoy? Or at least bring me along.'

'Not necessary,' said Ben, zipping up his hoodie as they made their way out of the royal residence to the front, where the limousine was waiting. 'I'll be fine. I don't want to travel heavy, and with the jet, I'll be back before dinner, if not earlier.' Lumiere would be too concerned with protocol, and settling a border dispute was bound to get hairy. But Ben would be lying if he didn't admit to a small case of nerves.

Lonnie was already out front. 'Thanks for doing this, Ben,' she said.

'At least summon the cavalry?' Lumiere said worriedly. 'They can travel on the royal speed train.'

Ben shook his head, ushering Lonnie inside the car first. 'If we arrive with a show of force, the villagers might not believe we're acting in their best interests. I'd like to resolve this as peacefully as I can, and if they see it's just me and

Lonnie, they'll know I'm there to listen and not force them to do anything they don't want to do.'

Lumiere looked as if he wanted to keep protesting, but he decided against it. His shoulders slumped, as if lights had been extinguished on a candelabra. 'As you wish, Sire.'

'Don't worry, Lonnie's with me,' said Ben with a smile. 'She'll keep me safe.'

Lonnie motioned to the sword strapped on her back. 'Nothing will happen.'

Chip rushed out with a bag of snacks. 'In case you get hungry, Sire,' he said. 'Mum packed you some sandwiches.'

Ben thanked them both, and the driver bowed and closed Ben's door.

'The village elder is meeting us first, then you have a meeting with the representative from Agrabah,' Lonnie told him.

Ben nodded to the driver, and the limousine left campus. A few students looked on, confused as to why the king was leaving in the middle of the school day.

The royal jet zoomed above Auradon City, flying over Charmington and Faraway Cove. 'What gorgeous countryside,' said Lonnie, admiring the rolling green fields dotted with golden haystacks and flocks of sheep that looked like white specks. 'Do you ever think about how lucky we are to be in Auradon?'

'All the time,' Ben said.

They were making good time but had to refuel, so they stopped in Notre-Dame before lunch, almost halfway to their destination. While the pilots took care of the plane, Ben and Lonnie walked over to a little square and stopped at a charming place for hot chocolates to drink with their sandwiches.

The café owners were beside themselves to discover they were waiting on royalty, and insisted the king take the best table in the house, one with a view of the church. 'Please, sit, and enjoy the ringing of the bells,' the waiter urged.

Ben thanked them profusely and remarked that Quasimodo's bell-ringing was indeed the best in the land. When the noonday chimes ended, they resumed their conversation.

'My family really appreciates you doing this,' said Lonnie. 'My mum says she wishes she could have sent us her cricket for good luck.'

'Tell her thanks,' said Ben, taking a sip from his cup. 'I've asked a bunch of councillors to meet us on their side of the Great Wall. The Grand Vizier agreed to meet with me. It's important that they feel their voices are heard as well, since you are travelling with me.'

'Good idea,' said Lonnie. 'I hope they listen to you. It would be a shame if things escalated.'

'I hope so too, but it's more important that I listen to them,' said Ben, thinking of the various issues he'd worked on since taking the throne. Most notably, he had handled the sidekicks' complaints and approved the cost of Camelot reparations after an out-of-control Madame Mim had plagued them earlier in the month.

'Is that what being king is all about?' asked Lonnie. 'Listening?'

'Pretty much. How about you?' he asked. 'Everything going okay?' He'd known Lonnie since they were kids, and they were almost like siblings. He remembered when Lonnie got her first sword at the age of five, and how she'd tried to stab Chip when he pulled her pigtails. Lonnie was there when Ben made his first balcony appearance; instead of waving to the crowd, he'd hidden his face in his mother's shoulder. She'd teased him about it mercilessly.

'Yeah,' she said with a long sigh and fiddled with the sword at her waist.

'That doesn't sound like everything's okay,' he said, concerned.

'You know how you wish you could change things, but there's nothing you can do about it?' she asked.

'Sometimes,' said Ben. 'But there's always something you can do about it.'

Lonnie looked longingly at her sword once more. 'Maybe.'

'What's this all about?' he asked.

She shook her head. 'You wouldn't understand.'

'Try me.'

'Has anyone ever told you that you can't do something

just because of who you are?' asked Lonnie, as the waiter came by to offer them heaping platters of croissants and baskets of delicate pastries.

Ben considered it as he picked up a lemon tart and took a bite, smiling his thanks to the waiter. 'Lots of times, actually.'

'Really?' Lonnie didn't sound like she believed him.

'Yeah. When you're king, you can't just think of yourself or what you want. You have to think of the people, always.'

'Always?' she said skeptically. 'I thought being king meant you always got your way, actually.'

'Maybe a terrible king, yeah—but not if you want to be a good one. Like, sometimes, I just really want to tell someone off, you know? Or lose my temper? Or just say what I mean? But I can never do that, because I'm the king. If I did, it would be a big deal—a yawn or an offhand comment suddenly becomes a matter of state. What I do matters more because of who I am, and so I can't ever really be myself. I have to be the king, always.'

'I never thought of it that way,' said Lonnie, putting down a half-eaten éclair.

'Still, I've found a way to balance being me and being king. I'm the king of Auradon, but I do it my own way,' said Ben, thinking of how he had invited the villain kids to Auradon, over the objections of his parents and a host of disapproving courtiers. 'So whatever it is you want, don't let anyone stop you from dreaming your dreams and following through on them.'

'You sound like your mum,' said Lonnie with a smile.

'I try to,' said Ben, asking for the bill. 'She's a wise woman.'

chapter 11

Biceps to Spare

Some would say it was always *unhappy hour* at the Fish and Chips Shoppe, but during the early afternoon and evening, Tears of Despair and Spoilage Brew were half off, along with discount bowls of gruel and only slightly used dirty candy. A raucous crowd had gathered around a certain table, where an arm-wrestling match was under way between Gil and La Foux Doux.

Gil, just like his father and brothers, was manly, burly, and brawny with muscles to spare, and yes—every last inch of him was covered with hair. Okay, maybe not *every* last inch, but Gil was one of the finer specimens of the Isle of the Lost, with golden hair he kept under his bandanna and that signature cleft chin. He wore a faded leather doublet that showed off his arms, with two sword belts crisscrossing his chest and leather-patched jeans that were artfully distressed in the current 'pirate' fashion.

Right now, Gil was doing what he loved to do: showing off his brute strength to the ladies. He slammed La Foux Doux's arm down on the table in victory, sending the stout boy to the ground.

'What do we say?' said Gil.

'Th-th-thank you!' said the young La Foux. 'Thank you, Gil!'

Gil flexed so that he made two guns with his arms and pretended to kiss each one.

Two witches sitting nearby audibly swooned.

Gil swaggered over to his table, satisfied, and ordered another round of bilge. Life was good when you were the strongest man on the island. Okay, so maybe he wasn't the smartest guy on the Isle of the Lost, but it wasn't the worst way to live.

No matter, Gil had girls to impress and feats of strength to display. He finished his meal, thinking the scum chowder was not as mouldy as usual, and looked around for more entertainment.

'Who wants to see me balance the table on my head again?' he asked, lifting the heavy oak table and setting it upon his noggin. But when he turned around, the room, which had been filled with noisy revellers just a moment before, was empty.

'Where'd everyone go?' he asked, irritated.

'To watch the race,' huffed the cook, pointing out the window and towards the docks.

Gil let the table down with a bang and headed towards the commotion. All week there had been talk about this race. A real pirate race, with a real pirate prize. The harbour was full of onlookers, pirates cheering each other on and bets placed on who would come in first. Gil sauntered over to the front to watch the action, pushing people out of the way.

'Who's in the lead?' he asked.

'Harry,' said one.

'Uma,' said another.

Gil squinted at the horizon, where an assortment of vessels, from homemade rafts made of recovered planks with sheets for sails to a little goblin motorboat, were cresting over by Evil Queen's house. They raced towards the finish line by Dead Man's Cove in Hook's Bay, gaily decorated with old shoes and cans. There was a roar from the crowd as one pulled forward ahead of the rest, a turquoise-haired sailor raising her fist in glory as she crossed the finish line in victorious fashion.

Shrimpy? wondered Gil. *Where'd she get that goblin boat?*

'Uma! Uma! Uma!' chanted the crowd, as Uma docked her boat and stepped up to the platform.

Uma made rude gestures to the crowd to indicate her pleasure. 'Thank you, thank you, thank you, everyone,' she said into the microphone. 'And I'd like to introduce you all to Harry Hook, my first mate!'

She brought Harry up to stand next to her. 'Just like I promised, here's your hook back,' she said, handing it to him.

Harry, who'd looked glum and defeated just a moment ago, lit up with a huge grin. 'My hook!' he said, waving it in the air.

Smee handed Uma the keys to the pirate ship that was docked right behind them, and Harry and Uma happily climbed aboard.

Gil marvelled at the thought of winning a real pirate ship, kitted out with a Jolly Roger flag and everything. Too bad it wasn't a wrestling match, or he'd have entered the competition for sure.

Harry and Uma waved from the top deck of their brand-new (actually old, shabby and holey) pirate ship.

Gil felt a pang at being down at the docks while they were up on the ship's decks. They'd all been inseparable once, he and Harry and Uma. When they were kids, he and Harry used to follow Uma around, doing her bidding. They'd been part of a gang, but over the years Gil had drifted away from them somehow.

He melted back into the crowd and went back to showing off at the fish shop, impressing the ladies and challenging anyone to a fight. But beating his enemies in arm-wrestling matches and bullying La Foux Doux only went so far.

So when someone mentioned that Shrimpy—sorry, *Uma*, he had to remember she went by Uma now, *duh*—and Harry Hook were looking for a few good mates for their pirate crew, Gil decided to meet up with his old not-quite-friends.

'Heard you're looking for muscle,' he said, his white teeth gleaming, as he swaggered up to Harry and Uma a few minutes later. He pulled up his shirtsleeves. 'You're in luck, as I've got some to spare.'

'Yes, we are,' said Harry with a grin. 'Welcome to my crew.'

'*My* crew,' said Uma, patting Gil on the back. 'Now get with the others.'

Gil climbed aboard the pirate ship, excited to find it was already filled with villains like him. Pirates, ruffians, rogues, all seeking adventure, and it looked like they'd found it.

chapter 12

Swordplay

After the last tourney game ended, Jay marched back with the team towards the lockers to change, but noticed that half the guys went straight into another practice, trading helmets for face masks and carrying practise swords.

'R.O.A.R. tryouts,' explained Aziz, Aladdin and Jasmine's oldest son. 'You coming?' he said, tapping Jay lightly on the arm with his sword.

'Yeah, come on,' said Herky, lumbering towards the mats. 'We're short a couple of guys. Ben had to quit since he couldn't fit it into his royal schedule.'

Jay nodded, curious about this other Auradon sport that Carlos had mentioned the other day. He followed his friends into the gym, where a few guys were already suited up, wearing sleeveless blue-and-gold R.O.A.R. uniforms and face masks. There was a spirited duel going on in the middle of the mat, and Jay watched attentively, admiring their graceful swiftness. At last, one of the sword-fighters pinned down the other one.

'I yield!' said the loser.

The fighters removed their masks, revealing their identities. The two opponents shook hands cordially, and Jay was surprised to find the winner was none other than Chad Charming.

Jay chuckled his disbelief and Chad overheard. He looked over at Jay. 'You think you can do better?' he sneered.

'Can't be hard,' Jay said.

'Let's see it, then,' said Chad. 'Suit up.'

Gauntlet thrown and accepted, Jay changed into a uniform, pulled on a face mask, and picked up a sword. The sword was heavier than he expected, and a tad unwieldy as well. But, whatever, it was just Chad. He could beat Chad blindfolded.

Turned out he couldn't beat Chad blindfolded.

Instead of advancing and retreating in a line as Jay had seen fencers do before, Chad unexpectedly bounded into the wall, leaped off of it, and came around behind Jay, tagging him on the back. This caused Jay to fall, and Chad whirled around to face him. The match was over before Jay could even find his opponent.

'Yield?' asked Chad, his sword underneath Jay's chin.

'I yield,' Jay spat. He tossed his mask off in frustration.

Chad laughed and helped him to his feet. 'I've been training since I could walk. What do you think princes do in their spare time?'

'I don't know, sit on tufted pillows?' said Jay moodily.

'Well, that too. But mostly sword practice.'

Chad left the gym, whistling.

Jay tapped his sword on the floor, making one dent after another. He hadn't anticipated such a quick defeat. He hadn't anticipated any defeat at all. He'd thought he would crush the pompous prince—a few strokes and he'd be victorious. But it hadn't gone down like that at all. He'd barely had a chance to raise his weapon and the whole thing was over.

Training—isn't that what Chad had said? The guy had been training his whole life at the sport. Chad wasn't better at this, he was just more experienced. Jay tapped the sword against the floor once more. It was time for him to start accruing a bit of that experience.

R.O.A.R. was half parkour and half fencing, and the two were not easy to mix. There was a reason fencers normally moved back and forth in neat little lines. They had swords in their hands, and even if the tips were blunted they could still do real damage if they struck you. Leaping into the air and bouncing off walls wasn't exactly what a person ought to do with a sword in their hand, but Jay guessed that was the fun of it, the challenge. Jay liked challenges.

He gripped the hilt. It was a sabre, which was a heavier fencing blade, not like one of those flimsy ones that arched at the lightest touch. This one had some weight to it, so if you landed on it wrong it might just slice you, but Jay guessed that was why they wore the heavy jackets. Body armour. And he knew how to do it; he'd done it all the time back on the Isle of the Lost.

But when he tried to run up the wall this time, he fell flat on his face, and just barely missed cutting himself with the sword.

That was the problem with walls. They were rather solid things, and you were generally meant to stand next to them, not on them. He was just out of practise, he decided, so he tried again. He began with a running start, jumped and hit the wall—planning to run up its side—but when he struck the surface, he collided into it with such force that he simply sank to the floor. Actually, he crashed to the floor. Jay turned so both of his shoulders lay flat, his eyes facing the ceiling. He had to try again. He wouldn't give up so easily.

The second jump was worse than the first. He had to toss the blade aside just to keep it from ramming a hole in his neck. This time when he hit the floor he came down hard on his back again. Every bit of him ached when he stood. The third jump yielded similar results. On the fourth he actually abandoned the jump midway through the act. He knew what was coming. He knew he'd have to toss the blade, and he could see exactly how his shoulder was going to strike that floor.

He was learning, but unfortunately, he was learning how *not* to R.O.A.R. He tossed the sword aside and ran up the wall easily. It was the addition of the sword that was the problem.

'You're doing it all wrong,' said a voice, and Jay turned to see Lonnie's older brother, Li'l Shang, holding up a sword. Li'l Shang had graduated from Auradon Prep the year before, and was an assistant coach of the team, taking a gap year before going home to rule his kingdom and launch his hip-hop career. 'Want some help?'

Jay was about to shake his head. His pride was bruised. And it was still hard for him to accept help when it was offered. No-one on the Isle ever helped anyone else out. But he had to remind himself he was in Auradon now, and they did things differently here. Plus, it had been beyond annoying to lose to Chad Charming.

'Yeah, yeah, I guess I do want help,' he admitted.

'Okay, let's start now,' said Li'l Shang. The gym had already cleared.

'Should we grab swords?' Jay asked.

'I don't think you're ready for those just yet.'

'Ouch, that hurts.'

'I'm just being honest.'

'So where do we start?'

'Well, I saw how you lost your fight. Chad made a great jump. You were trying to practise that move—weren't you?'

Jay shrugged. 'Yeah, I mean I used to be able to jump, you know? But not with a sword.'

'Let's practise the basics first. Each time you hit the wall or the floor, you want to lengthen the time of impact, slow it down so your whole body absorbs the force. And don't just kick off with your feet. Try putting a hand on the wall. It'll keep you steady and spread out the force of impact. Same goes for the landing. Move your whole body. You need to bend your back and knees; your arms, too. Remember: slow down the impact, spread it out. That's how to jump.'

'Okay, so slow it down. And use my whole body.'

Jay took one step, two. Li'l Shang stopped him dead in his tracks. 'Take a few more steps, open up your stride and give yourself a little more height so you have time to flex your body while it's still in the air.'

Jay nodded, absorbing the information. He started again. He took three steps, four, five this time—big, long strides. On the last one he leaped, trying not to stay rigid, spreading his arms, spider-like, and letting two hands touch the wall at the same moment that his feet struck it. It was perfect.

He was completely enamoured with himself. Unfortunately, he fell straight down to the floor.

'Good start,' said Li'l Shang. 'Better than I would have guessed for a first-timer, but never get cocky. You hit the wall right, but you need to immediately spring backwards. Take the force of your own impact and turn it around into another leap. Try again.'

He did. He tried twice more, and then a third time. Each was a tad less embarrassing than the previous one. He wasn't sure how many jumps it took, but after a while the landings stopped hurting. It all started to feel natural.

Li'l Shang handed Jay back his sword. Jay accepted it gladly. It was time to move on to the good stuff: swordplay.

He levelled the sabre, ready for a *real* fight.

But Li'l Shang just shook his head.

'The first thing is that you're holding it wrong,' he said, fixing Jay's grip.

Jay was surprised; he thought he knew how to hold a sword.

'You shouldn't hold it that tightly,' Li'l Shang continued. 'You need to keep your wrist loose, keep your grip light so you can move quickly. If you hold it too tightly, you're locked into a position and won't be able to dodge or parry.'

Jay looked down at his fist: he'd gripped his sword so hard his knuckles were strained white. He relaxed just a little bit and found it was easier to hold once he wasn't choking it.

'The next thing you need to remember about making the R.O.A.R. team is that it's all about balance—kind of like the jumps we practised. But now we're using swords. It's almost like a choreographed dance: you'll learn to move on every surface, and use flips and kicks along with sword-fighting,' said Li'l Shang. He sprinted across the gym and launched himself against the wall, running up it diagonally, until he flipped backwards and landed on his feet.

'Nice,' said Jay.

Li'l Shang bowed. 'It's all practise.' He tapped Jay's sword with his. 'En garde!' he called. 'It means, *on your guard*. Every duel starts with it. It's a tradition.'

'En garde!' echoed Jay.

They circled each other around the mat. 'You have to be nimble, and lead your opponent. If you're just reacting to their blows, you're going to lose. You have to set the tone.' He attacked with a series of lunges, moving left and right, then leaping atop a chair to land at Jay's side, pressing his sword to Jay's neck.

'Um . . .' said Jay.

Li'l Shang gave him a generous smile. 'Let's try that again. R.O.A.R. isn't fencing. It's not linear. We aren't simply advancing and retreating. You can move sideways, off a wall, off anything. Think of it as 3-D fencing. Your opponent can literally jump out at you from any direction, so you have to be ready to defend yourself against an attack that could come from any direction.'

'How?'

'In fencing, we protect ourselves from the front, but, like I said, in R.O.A.R. an attacker can approach from any angle. So you need a whole new set of moves. The side-parry, the backward block, the over-the-shoulder cut. These are R.O.A.R. moves. Let me show you.'

Shang went through each one, carefully displaying the move, then helping Jay copy it. Shang had just given him a whole new set of tools, for a whole different kind of fighting. Jay was ready to R.O.A.R.!

This time, Jay was able to not only block his coach's sword but push forwards so that it was his opponent who found himself stepping backwards. Jay kept advancing aggressively, the sword singing through the air as if he'd been born wielding one. He even attempted to run up the wall to dodge a blow. As he fought, his confidence grew, and he flipped, cartwheeling in the air when his coach tried to slash forwards. He landed just as Shang had instructed, bending his whole body, flexing every muscle, one hand touching the floor just as his feet struck it.

'Better.' Li'l Shang nodded. 'Much better. We've worked on your jumps and your R.O.A.R. moves, but you still aren't bringing the two together.'

'But I almost beat you!'

'I was just going easy on you. This is going to take a lot more practise on your part. Keep trying to improve your jumps and don't let the sword be a detriment to your movement. You're still too afraid that you are going to poke yourself with that thing. Use the sword as if it were part of your body. Quit holding it at arm's length. Flex your sword arm when you hit the wall and when you land. And don't separate your jumps from your attacks. Some of the best fighters will strike with their blade midway through a jump, or just as they hit the ground they'll roll into a lunge instead of planting their feet.'

Jay tried a few of these moves. R.O.A.R. was definitely a hybrid sport, and it took fencing to a whole new level, but he felt like he knew the basics now. Unfortunately, he was still back where he'd started: he needed to practise.

'You think I'll make the team?' asked Jay. He knew he was acting a little optimistic, but he'd come a long way in a short time. How much longer would it take to master R.O.A.R.?

'Sure, if you work hard enough,' said Li'l Shang. 'My sister's pretty good at this stuff, too. You should practise with her sometime. She just left for Northern Wei, to help with an issue there, but when she gets back you should ask her.'

'Lonnie?' said Jay. 'I guess I shouldn't be surprised, considering who your mum is. She's on the team?'

But Li'l Shang didn't have time to answer. The gym doors banged open, and Carlos, Evie and Mal entered, calling Jay's name and looking distressed.

'What's up?' Jay asked, putting down his sword. 'You

guys look like someone just told you we had to go to back to the Isle of the Lost.'

'We might have to,' said Mal.

Jay raised an eyebrow and wondered what was wrong now.

chapter 13

How Many Wonders Can One Cavern Hold?

Now that she had a pirate ship and a pirate crew, Uma was in the market for a new pirate hat. Her old one had gotten way too ratty, and there was a hole on the brim that she'd covered up with duct tape. She needed something that told the world she was large and in charge. She puttered about the bazaar shops down by the central market around the Bargain Castle, looking at fedoras and trilbies, boaters and turbans. She'd brought Gil with her, who was trying on a succession of ridiculous headgear.

'What do you think of this?' asked Gil, donning a

black silk top hat. 'Or this?' he said, as he switched it for a feathered creation.

She ignored him, and continued to root through the racks. Maybe it wasn't the greatest idea to let Gil on their crew. He seemed to be about three screws short of a lightbulb, honestly. But then again, he seemed very enthusiastic about doing her bidding, which was never a bad thing.

'Uma! This one, right?' he asked, strutting up in a white ten-gallon cowboy hat.

'No,' she said flatly, trying on a hat of her own and considering her reflection in the shop's mirror.

'How about this one?' he said, putting on a pointy velvet hat.

'No,' she said again, picking through a deep selection of tricorn pirate hats that would suit any aspiring buccaneer. She tried on a couple, but nothing was quite right.

'I think I'll go with this one,' said Gil, placing a brown leather hat on his head. 'Looks good?'

'Not bad,' she had to admit.

'I'll take this bunch,' he told the sales clerk, motioning to a big pile by the counter of all the hats he'd tried on. 'They're on sale. You find anything?'

She shook her head. 'I'll meet you on the ship,' she said.

'Yup, see you there.'

Discouraged, Uma left the shop, annoyed that Gil had been able to find something while she was empty-handed.

'What's wrong, dearie, give us a smile,' barked a goon by the wharf.

'What about I give *you* a smile,' said Uma, removing her cutlass and placing it just under his chin. He yelped in fear and she kicked him away, growling to herself.

Just as she turned the corner, she spotted the hat she'd been looking for. Crushed brown leather with a metal-studded brim and decorated with seashells. Sassy and stylish. It would look mighty fine with her cutlass and sword. 'Yo-ho-ho!' she called. The lass wearing the hat turned.

'What do you want for that hat?' asked Uma.

'This one?' the girl squeaked, pointing to the hat on her head.

'No, not that, the other one you're wearing—of course that one!' Uma snapped, her patience wearing thin.

'Okay . . .' said the girl hesitantly, removing it from her head and holding it out.

Uma studied it, admiring its craftsmanship and detail. It really was a fine pirate's hat.

'You can have it,' the girl said suddenly.

'Oh? What do you want for it?' asked Uma.

'Nothing! I don't want anything from you!' she protested. 'I want to keep whatever I have, my voice, my legs, my soul, my humanity! Here, take it!' She shoved the hat forcefully into Uma's outstretched hand.

'Oh! Good,' Uma said, taking it happily. 'Did you make this?'

'Yes,' said the young pirate, looking sad to have now lost the hat. 'I washed the leather five times and picked all the seashells, then I stitched the band with a grosgrain ribbon. . . .'

Uma shrugged; all her interest had waned now that the hat was hers. She wasn't the type to make conversation anyway.

'Nice hat,' said Harry, when she arrived at the ship.

Uma grinned. 'Nice ship,' she said, watching pirates cut down planks to the right length, nailing boards, and threading the sail.

'Sweet, isn't it?' he drawled, scratching his cheek with his hook. 'At least once we patch up the holes, fix the mast, and see to the anchor, we'll be set to go. I've got the crew working day and night.'

Uma crossed her arms, hoping she appeared as fierce as she thought she did. It was hard work looking this awesome. 'Good job,' she said to Harry.

'Good job, Captain?' he said hopefully.

'As if. You work for me, remember? Do I have to keep reminding you? I'm captain, you're first mate,' said Uma, pointing a finger and stabbing his chest with it.

'First *date* if you're lucky,' said Harry with a wink, pulling on his collar and strutting a little.

'Shut up,' said Uma with a laugh. 'And see to that sail.'

Harry swaggered away chuckling. Uma knew, try as she

might, she couldn't hurt his feelings. It was all part of the game of question-and-rejection they'd played forever. But a few minutes later, Harry swivelled on his boots and returned to her side, leaning in closely. 'Uma, darling,' he said, in his rough brogue. 'I just need to ask again—how *are* we going to find that thing in the water?'

'Leave that to me,' said Uma. 'Just get this ship ready.' She gave him a confident smile, but she was none too pleased by that pesky reminder. How *were* they going to find that trident?

The answer came later that day—at the Fish and Chips Shoppe, no less. Uma was taking a break in the kitchen with Cook, who was feeding Flotsam and Jetsam, the two electric eels who had been Ursula's sidekicks during her glory days. The eels were swimming in their tank, below an old portrait of Ursula that hung in the middle of the kitchen, as if to remind everyone whom they worked for.

'Mama was really something, wasn't she? Back then?' said Uma. Flotsam and Jetsam nodded in their aquarium, slithering over each other.

Cook, a swarthy woman with messy red hair who always wore an ill-fitting white peasant dress with a red collar, had a faraway look in her eye. 'She really was,' she mourned as she cleaned a fish and saved the guts for stew.

Uma wondered what it was like, living under the sea, ruling the waves. 'Those days will come back,' she said.

'You think so?' Cook said hopefully.

Uma nodded decisively. 'I know so. I plan to make it happen. Finish what Maleficent started, get off this island, and wreak vengeance on our enemies!' She stared intently at the golden seashell around Ursula's neck. 'Hey, do you know whatever happened to Mum's necklace?'

Cook squinted at the picture. 'It got destroyed; when Prince Eric defeated your mum it shattered into a thousand pieces.'

'I know that. I mean what happened to it after that?' asked Uma.

'After?' Cook frowned, setting a pot to boil and adding sea slime to the broth.

'It must be gone forever,' said Uma sadly.

'Hold on. I remember now,' said Cook, wiping her hands on her dirty apron. 'It was too dangerous to have a thing like that just lying around, even broken. The pieces were collected and confiscated. They were supposed to go to that museum in Auradon. We heard they found the last two pieces just the other month. But then the embargo happened, so they're stuck here,' said Cook, cutting up more rotten potatoes for curly fries.

Uma was intrigued. 'Here? On the Isle? Where?'

'Who knows? We heard that professor, Yen Sid, was the one in charge of it. If anyone has them, he does,' said Cook with a shrug.

'Professor Yen Sid has the pieces to my mother's seashell necklace?'

Cook nodded.

'Well, what's it matter anyway? There's no magic on the island,' Uma lamented.

Cook considered that. 'True. But just because there's no magic around doesn't mean there's no power left in it.'

'What kind of power could it have?' asked Uma, confused.

Cook whispered in her ear. Uma listened carefully. When she was done, Uma raised her eyebrows.

'You don't say,' she said. What Cook had told her was very interesting indeed. 'Are you sure that would work? If I found the necklace and put it back together?'

'Absolutely,' said Cook.

'Uh-huh,' said Uma. This was it; her mother's seashell necklace was the missing link. She knew exactly how to find the trident now. Ursula's necklace was the answer.

If only she could discover where Yen Sid was hiding it.

chapter 14

Nemesis

'Wow, that's one brave mermaid,' said Carlos when Mal was done sharing Arabella's story with him, Evie and Jay after they'd pulled Jay away from R.O.A.R. practice. They were sitting at a table in the refectory at Jay's insistence, since he didn't like to hear bad news on an empty stomach. 'I would never even dream of touching my mum's furs, and she goes and steals King Triton's trident? That's insane.'

Jay nodded, his mouth full of food. He swallowed loudly to the consternation of the girls. 'I don't mean to be rude, but why is this our problem exactly?' he asked.

'Arabella's a friend, and she came to us,' said Mal defensively. 'She didn't know who else to ask for help.'

'Uh-huh,' said Jay. 'Because she did something naughty, and we're from the Isle of the Lost. But the thing is, we have stuff to do in Auradon now.'

Carlos slowly nodded his head. 'Jay has a point. You have a packed royal schedule, Mal. You don't really have time for something like this. Why does it have to be you—*us*—who have to look for this thing? We didn't steal it. Plus, don't forget, exams are coming up.'

'And what about Ben? Doesn't this fall under his responsibility?' asked Jay.

'Ben's in Northern Wei negotiating some kind of truce between the Imperial City and Agrabah,' said Mal. 'I don't want to bother him with this.'

The boys still looked a little wary.

Mal put her hands on her hips and scowled. 'Okay, this is not the team that returned to the Isle of the Lost and defeated their evil talismans! I'll tell you why it's our problem. Because when a friend's in trouble, what do we do?' she asked fiercely.

'We leave them alone?' joked Jay. He sighed. 'All right, all right.'

'Come on, you guys, we all know what it feels like to have done something wrong,' Evie beseeched. 'And to feel scared and alone afterwards.'

'Of course we'll help,' said Carlos.

'Yeah, we were just playing, what do you call it, devil's advocate,' said Jay with a smile.

'But it seems like the best thing to do is to tell Fairy Godmother so she can alert King Triton,' said Carlos. 'I mean, right?'

'But Arabella asked us to keep it secret,' said Evie.

'We can handle this ourselves,' said Mal. 'Let's not bring Fairy Godmother into it.' Mal didn't want to sit around waiting to have tea with the goddesses from Mount Olympus or laughing at the Sultan of Agrabah's corny jokes again, which took up a lot of her time now that she was the king's girlfriend. She itched to do something meaningful, to be useful instead of simply decorative. 'Are you guys with me?' she asked.

One by one, each of them nodded.

Mal smiled, relieved. 'Obviously, first things first, we need to figure out where the trident is,' she said briskly. 'Any ideas?'

'That's what this is for,' said Evie, removing the Magic Mirror from her purse. She flipped it open and spoke directly into its reflection. *Magic Mirror of seas and skies, show me where the trident lies!*'

The mirror turned cloudy and gray and nothing happened. 'Is it broken again?' asked Carlos.

Evie shook her head. 'It was never broken, it just didn't

work in the Catacombs.' Evie gave it another good shake, and the mirror showed the trident stuck between two rocks under the sea.

'Where is that?' asked Mal, squinting at the screen. 'I wish your Magic Mirror could talk, Evie.'

'It's only the last shard of the mirror; no audio function, sorry,' said Evie apologetically.

'Looks like it's somewhere near the barrier. See that shimmering line? That's the invisible dome,' said Carlos, looking over Evie's shoulder.

'Which means anyone on the Isle of the Lost could grab it, if they know it's there,' said Jay.

'But where exactly is it?' asked Mal, her forehead scrunching in dismay.

Carlos took a closer look at the screen. 'As far as I can tell, it looks like it's right by the Isle of the Doomed. The water's murkier over there. And see those flashes of green in the water? That's goblin slime.'

Mal nodded. It was the same green colour that seeped out of Maleficent's fortress.

'Those goblins would do anything to get their hands on that kind of treasure. Not to mention the pirates if they knew about it,' said Jay.

'Magic Mirror, is anyone else looking for the trident?' asked Evie.

This time, the mirror's surface glowed, and showed villain after villain on the Isle of the Lost searching the surrounding waters for the trident. Witches in scuba outfits, pirates diving off docks, hooligans of all kinds swarming the beaches and picking through seaweed, searching.

'Looks like everyone's looking for it. Word must have gotten out somehow that it's there,' said Carlos.

'Goblins are terrible gossips,' muttered Mal.

'The worst,' agreed Evie.

Jay only shrugged. He had no opinion on goblins other than that they were fun to steal from.

'It's still going,' said Evie, as the mirror showed an image of a crowded tavern.

'What's that?' asked Jay, leaning over for a better look.

'Don't push!' said Carlos, as they all crowded around Evie.

'It's Ursula's Fish and Chips Shoppe,' said Mal, as the mirror zoomed in more closely, until they could make out the blurry silhouette of a figure in the middle of the crowd.

'Who's that?' said Evie, catching sight of thick, ropy strands.

'I can't tell yet. One of the pirates, maybe?' said Carlos. The mirror kept focusing.

'It's a girl,' said Jay decisively. 'Those are braids.'

'That's not a girl. That's a sea witch,' said Mal, tapping on the screen.

'It's Uma!' said Jay.

'Uma!' quaked Carlos.

'Uma.' Evie sighed.

'Ugh. Come on. It's Shrimpy,' said Mal. 'It's always Shrimpy.' She told Evie about her long, nasty history with Uma.

'You know Uma's mostly mad because you said she was too small to be in our gang,' Jay reminded her.

'But she *was* too small to be in our gang,' said Mal defensively.

'She's not *that* small,' said Carlos. 'There was a height requirement?'

'Mal just didn't want to share,' said Jay with a grin.

Mal shrugged, but Jay was right: she hadn't wanted Uma to be part of her crowd. She'd pushed her away, even though Uma was fiercer than Ginny Gothel and much scarier than Harriet Hook. The truth was, Uma was real competition, and Mal hadn't wanted any of that back then.

Evie squinted at the picture of Uma in the Magic Mirror. 'Why do you hate her so much?'

Mal was taken aback. 'I *don't* hate her. Actually, since we've been in Auradon, I'd forgotten all about her. She's the one who's always been obsessed with me.'

Carlos and Jay nodded. 'Uma *loathes* Mal,' said Carlos.

'I mean, I get it, you dumped a bucket of shrimp on her head. You can't be her favourite person,' said Evie. 'But it's also not any different from what people on the Isle do to each other every day. Couldn't she get over it?'

Mal smiled ruefully at the memory of that fateful day. 'I

think it bothered her more because we were close once, best friends actually. But then she . . .'

'She laughed at you,' said Carlos, who had turned away from the Magic Mirror and had zipped open his backpack to get a head start on his homework. 'I was with my mum that day at the docks. I saw what happened. Uma laughed at you when you tripped and fell and slid down the dock.'

'Yeah, I didn't like it,' said Mal, eyes glazing at the memory. 'So I took my revenge. Her hair never smelled the same again. In fact it smelled . . .'

'Shrimpy,' Jay said with a laugh.

Evie shuddered, thinking of how terrible that would be. 'Yikes.'

'I wasn't the nicest person back then,' said Mal, frowning at the image in the Magic Mirror.

'You were only doing what you were taught,' said Evie supportively. 'What we were all taught on the Isle.' She picked up a piece of fruit from Jay's tray and took a bite, glad that it was fresh and not rotten like they were used to on the island.

'But how does she think she's going to find that trident? She doesn't have a Magic Mirror at her disposal, like we do,' said Jay.

'Maybe everyone who's looking for it is working for her?' guessed Evie.

'No, the goblins only work for themselves,' said Mal.

'The only ones who could possibly be loyal to her are the pirates.'

'A bunch of thieves and thugs,' said Jay.

'Harry and Gil? You used to run with them,' Carlos chided. 'Didn't you?'

'I sure did,' admitted Jay. 'That's how I know they're all a bunch of scoundrels.'

'But if any of them found it, they'd definitely give it to Uma,' said Mal. 'They always follow orders. Especially Harry Hook.'

'We don't have much time; King Triton will notice the trident's missing by tomorrow, so we need to get it back tonight,' said Evie.

'And Uma's after it, so you all know what that means.' Mal stood up from the table, ready to take action.

'We need to find it before she does,' said Evie.

'And hurry,' added Carlos.

Jay smiled. 'Here we go again.'

Ocean's Elevens

Just look at the world
around you,
Right here on the ocean floor.
Such wonderful things
surround you.
What more is you
lookin' for?
—Sebastian,
The Little Mermaid

chapter 15

The Sorcerer's Snare

Uma paced the top deck of the *Lost Revenge* confidently. With Harry and Gil at her side, she'd assembled a solid squad—a bona fide pirate ship with a bona fide crew. No matter that Gil was so dim he often forgot not to call her by that horrid nickname; Harry and his wharf rats were ready to cut up anyone who stood in their way. She surveyed the work the pirates were doing to bring the ship up to task.

They were busy provisioning the ship, bringing on food and water from Ursula's as she'd ordered, as well as a whole host of supplies. All sorts of things could go wrong at sea, and you couldn't exactly head home if you had a problem, so they needed extra lengths of rope and sail, boards that could be used to fix the hull, and all the tools and hardware to make those repairs. Plus, Harry insisted that every inch of the ship had to be checked. Every length of rope was inspected for rents or frayed edges. Rats loved to chew on ropes, and they tended to choose the most undesirable places to snack on them. If the pirates didn't check every inch of the ropes, their main sail might just sail free the moment the wind caught it, or their anchor line might snap in two just as it took hold.

The crew went over every length of sail, and they checked all the winches and pulleys as well, making certain that each was sound, replacing a few, fixing others. They checked the mast for cracks and the rudder for soundness, and made certain it worked in proper coordination with the captain's wheel. Things seemed to be coming together. But there was one particular problem that caught Uma's attention. Apparently the *Lost Revenge* had as many holes as the ship had boards. Wooden sailing ships always take on a bit of water, she knew. But the *Lost Revenge* took on water by the bucketful, and when they'd tried to push off the dock the problem had only increased, with more water rising faster, threatening to turn her sailing vessel into a gigantic bathtub.

'So what do we do?' she asked Harry, who, coincidentally, had experience sailing in a bathtub.

'Well,' Harry started, clearly excited that she had decided

to consult him on the matter. 'We should have her lifted out of the water, the hull scraped clean and repainted, then—'

'Stop. That's not happening. We need to do something about the state of this ship, but we don't have time to lift it or do anything major. Be serious.'

'Yeah, I guess. Okay, so then maybe it's just a matter of resealing the boards. When the ship was built, the joints were all watertight, you know, fitted together closely so no water could pass through them. But ships age, and boards flex and rot and chip, and pirate ships have a way of getting rammed into or ramming into things, taking cannon shot, the usual stuff. It ruins the hulls and the boards that make them up.'

'Wonderful history of sailing, thanks, but I have no interest. Get to the point, will you?' she growled.

'We caulk the joints. There's an adhesive that's fitted between the boards and then it's all slathered over with pitch.'

'*Pitch*? As in singing on key?' she asked.

'*Pitch* as in tar or mastic—what we call sludge: that black sticky stuff that water can't penetrate.'

'Gotcha. Get on it,' she said, pushing at his chest.

'Me?' he asked, stumbling back.

She crossed her arms. 'Well, you do seem to be the expert, and I recall seeing a barrel of something black and sticky down there in the hold. I reckon you'll find all the supplies you need down there, so grab a few of the crew and get working.'

'Great. I'll be covered in sludge for days.'

'It beats bailing water every time we sail.'

'It does,' said Harry as he headed down into the hold. 'I'll have this ship watertight in no time.'

When Harry had disappeared out of sight, she headed to the wooden bridges and trudged back to the fish shop. Her shift was up. It was time to put away her captain's hat and put on an apron.

Later that evening, Harry, Gil, and the rest of the crew filed in. There was ferocious Jonas, with his cornrows and scar on his left cheek, Desiree, tiny but vicious in a ragged peasant dress, fierce Gonzo in his red bandanna, long braid and blue pantaloons, crazy Bonny in her torn fishnet shirt and patched dungarees, and a whole host of others—all hardened mercenaries. They took one of the long tables in front of the kitchen window. 'Recap. What do we know about Yen Sid?' asked Uma, drumming her fingers on the table.

Harry dumped a pile of documents on the table, pulled out a notepad, and paged through it with his hook. 'Professor at Dragon Hall, but not a villain. *Volunteered* to live on the Isle of the Lost to, quote, "help the new generation of villain offspring." ' At this Harry snickered. 'What a loser.'

'What else?' said Uma impatiently.

'Let's see,' said Harry, having trouble turning the pages

with his hook. Uma sometimes wished he would give up with the whole hook obsession and just use his hands, but she knew it would never happen.

'Here we go,' said Harry. 'Keeps to himself, amateur lepidopterist.'

'Lepidop-what?' said Gil.

'Studies butterflies,' explained Harry. 'You know, those bugs with the pretty wings?'

'I know what a butterfly is,' growled Gil.

'Really? Well, you learn something new every day,' said Harry with a smirk. He continued to read the list. 'What else, let's see . . . has never set foot in the Fish and Chips Shoppe, but is a regular at the Slop Shop, where he takes his tea.'

'Tea?' Uma made a face.

'Yeah, it annoys the goblins to no end, because they're a coffee shop, and apparently he always insists on chai, which of course they don't have,' said Harry. He kept reading. 'No known acquaintances. No associates. An enigma, shall we say . . .'

'Hold on, what's this?' said Uma, picking a paper off the top of the pile. It was marked with a golden beast-head stamp and signed by Fairy Godmother.

Harry peered over her shoulder. 'Oh, those are transfer documents—for when he moved here to the Isle of the Lost from Auradon. I had one of my boys pull the file.'

Uma pointed to an additional name on the paper. 'Look.'

Harry read the file and caught Uma's eye. They grinned at each other, matching evil smiles. 'This is it. This is how we get in.'

'What?' asked Gil, still oblivious and his stomach growling loudly.

Uma studied the document again. This was all coming together beautifully. She could see the outline of a plan already. Truth be told, she was a little afraid of the esteemed professor. There was a hidden strength and a fortitude to the old guy that chilled her, and the scope of his magical power was legendary. For once she was glad there was a magical barrier to protect them from such wizardry. There was no way they would ever get her mother's necklace back from the sorcerer himself; Uma knew that for a fact. Yen Sid would never let that happen. But here on paper was another way. 'Professor Sid didn't move here alone,' said Uma slowly.

'He brought his apprentice!' added Harry gleefully.

Uma held up the file. 'The Sorcerer's Intern.'

'We just need to find out who he is and where. We'll never get the professor to talk, but this is the weak link. His apprentice is sure to know where he keeps that necklace,' said Harry triumphantly.

Gil studied the grainy, blurry picture. 'She.'

'She?' asked Uma.

Gil nodded in excitement, happy to contribute to the planning. 'I know her, she helps out Professor Sid in class.

Like a teacher's assistant. Sort of quiet, shy, a little mousy even. Always sweeping. Sophie, I think her name is.'

'Great! Let's see, we can threaten, bribe, or intimidate. What do you suggest?' asked Harry gleefully.

'First things first,' said Uma, thinking quickly. 'Gil, invite her to the Fish and Chips Shoppe tonight. Tell her we stumbled on a bit of magic and want to discuss it with her before alerting her boss.'

'Discuss?' Harry asked innocently. 'Is that the word for tying someone up and threatening them with my hook?'

Uma smirked. 'Don't worry, Harry, you'll have your fun.' By the time they were done with her, this Sorcerer's Intern would wish she'd never set foot on the Isle of the Lost.

chapter 16

Lad and Lass

Gil had never had any trouble asking girls to go out with him. In truth, most of them went out of their way to make themselves available. Girls were always dropping schoolbooks in front of him, or giggling uncontrollably in his presence. He was used to a certain amount of admiration from the female species. But when he approached Sophie after class that day, she was wary.

'What do you want, Gil?' she asked, setting down the books she was holding and pulling up the red sleeves on her robe. She had dark hair and a skeptical expression. 'I'm not giving you the answers to next week's test, if that's what you're asking.'

'Oh, too bad,' said Gil, before catching himself. 'Wait, no, that's not what I wanted to ask you.'

'Well, what is it, then? I've got study notes to hand out and quizzes to return to the professor,' said Sophie impatiently.

'Wanted to know what you're doing tonight,' said Gil, throwing her his most dazzling smile. He flexed a bicep for good measure.

'Tonight? I'm refilling the professor's well. Exciting, isn't it?' said Sophie dryly. 'I'll be carrying buckets of water all night.'

'I've got a better idea. You, me and the Fish and Chips Shoppe,' said Gil.

'Huh? Is that like a date?' asked Sophie.

'What, you've never been on one before?' asked Gil.

'I've been on dates!' said Sophie defensively.

'Okay then!' said Gil. 'I'll see you tonight!'

'No. I told you, I'm busy,' said Sophie, turning away.

This was not going as planned, and Gil began to sweat. Uma would not be pleased if he couldn't get Sophie to come out tonight. 'But you have to go!' he whined.

'Why?' asked Sophie.

'Because I really like you?' Gil blurted.

Sophie stared at Gil. 'Really?'

Gil smiled, then slapped his forehead. 'No! I mean yes. I mean, also, Uma's got something magical that she wants to show you.'

'Something magical? There's nothing magical on the island.'

'Well, she has something,' Gil insisted.

But Sophie clapped her hands and suddenly looked delighted. 'Does she have it? We've been looking for it everywhere!'

Gil had no idea what 'it' was, but figured correctly that the right answer was 'Yes!'

Her wan face glowed. 'Great! I'll be there. But she better return it,' warned Sophie. 'I need it back as soon as possible!'

'Okay,' said Gil, relieved it had all worked out. Now Uma wouldn't yell at him. Uma could be scary when she felt like it, which seemed to be always. 'See you there!' he said enthusiastically, hoping that somehow Uma had whatever Sophie was looking for.

chapter 17

Rug Burn

'King Ben is here! King Ben is here!' The villagers of Stone City left their work and dwellings to line the road near where the royal jet had landed. Ben got out and waved to his people, who waved and cheered back. They walked together in a merry parade all the way to the centre of town. After hours of sitting, it was a relief to finally arrive at the peaceful valley in the middle of Northern Wei. Like its name, all the buildings and houses in Stone City were made of rock, and the village itself had been built near a giant mushroom-shaped stone. The Great Wall loomed over the north side of the village, casting a long shadow.

They passed the city gates that led into the greatest

pavilion, and followed the cobblestoned path all the way to the front of the structure, where the town's leaders were waiting to greet them.

Elder Wong, who wasn't a grey-bearded official in a smock, but a young man who wore his dark hair in a ponytail and was wearing a natty suit, bowed upon seeing Ben. 'Thanks so much for honouring us with your presence,' he said.

'Charlie?' Ben asked, delighted. 'You're the elder of this village?'

'Hey, man,' said Charlie, slapping Ben a high five. 'Yeah, went home and took on the role. Looks like you did too,' he said, motioning to the golden circlet that Ben wore as his travelling crown.

Charlie had been a few years ahead of Ben at Auradon Prep, and Ben was glad to find an old friend in unfamiliar territory. Maybe this dispute could be settled easily after all.

'Hey, Lonnie,' said Charlie. 'How's Shang doing?'

'Still coaching R.O.A.R. and trying to get that hip-hop record out,' said Lonnie, giving Charlie a hug.

'Nice,' said Charlie. 'Come on in, let's talk over some bubble tea.'

Ben and Lonnie followed Charlie inside the stone house, which, while ancient and minimal on the outside, was outfitted with the latest gadgets inside. Ben spied a large-screen television on the wall, a roving robot sweeper on the carpet and a high-end security system with a 12-camera display. Charlie led them to a small room with a view of the mountains and a portion of the Great Wall.

Charlie sat cross-legged on the floor in front of a low table that had been set for them with the village's finest china and silver, and Ben and Lonnie did the same.

Instead of diving right into the business at hand, Ben and Lonnie regaled Charlie with the latest news from Auradon.

'Is it true that Audrey's dating Chad?' said Charlie, shock written all over his face. 'Whoa.'

'Yeah, although I hear Audrey's changed her mind about him,' said Lonnie with a laugh.

'Oh no, really?' said Ben, who hadn't heard that rumour. 'Poor Chad! He'll be crushed!'

They talked about the Seaside Festival, and Charlie mentioned the Imperial Palace was looking forward to hosting Ben during their Auradon celebration. 'I hear they've hired acrobats from all over the kingdom,' said Charlie. 'Especially the ones who can do tricks with fire.'

Lonnie smiled. 'The fire dancers were always my favourite.'

'Yeah, I can't wait,' said Ben. 'It's going to be amazing. Too bad Seaside got rained out.'

'It happens,' said Charlie.

'So what's going on here?' asked Ben, accepting a tall

glass of bubble tea from a smiling servant. He sipped the round tapioca balls through the extra-large straw.

'See up there?' asked Charlie, putting down his glass and pointing out the window. 'Those dots in the sky? They're flying carpets. You think they'd be quiet, right? But they fly so fast they can create a sonic boom. So every time one of them flies over the wall to our side, everything in the village shakes. It's horrible. Babies cry, things fall off tables, and see that cluster of trees over there? They're olive trees. They're planted on the Agrabah side of the wall, and when the carpets fly over, they shake the trees.'

'Uh-huh,' said Ben.

'Some of the olives fall over on our side then,' said Charlie. 'So we use them. But our neighbors over there say that the olives are theirs, if not for the wall blocking their ability to harvest them. They want their olives back, and, well, we don't want to give them back. They're on our side of the wall, fair and square. Plus, the carpets are a nuisance—a huge headache. We're sick of it. We've asked them to ground the carpets, but they refuse.'

Lonnie raised her eyebrows and looked to Ben, who scrunched his forehead and chewed a bubble of tapioca before answering. 'Why do they need carpets? They never use them anywhere else in Auradon,' said Ben.

'Because of the wall over here. The carpets are the only way to get over it without having to go all the way around.'

'I see. And you guys eat a lot of olives?'

'Enough,' said Charlie. 'My villagers are doubly annoyed because the branches and leaves of the olive trees shed in the winter, and who has to clean up all the mess? We do, because they fall on our side of the wall. The Sultan's people don't offer to clean it up, do they? No, they just want to fly their carpets and eat their olives without any of the work.'

Ben leaned forwards. 'And what are you guys doing about it?'

'So far, nothing yet. Just shouting from opposite sides of the wall. But we're prepared to do more. We've stationed archers on the wall,' said Charlie defensively.

A servant placed a tray of food in front of them. There was olive bread, olive oil and a fragrant, olive-scented roast beef. Ben reached for a hunk of bread, tearing the loaf, and bit into a piece, just as the entire room began to shake with a boom from a flying carpet. 'This is delicious,' he said. 'And I can see why you find the carpets aggravating.'

Charlie relaxed slightly. 'I'm glad you understand the situation. I was a bit worried about the response from Auradon. To be honest, I wasn't expecting to see the king.'

'Lonnie asked me to take charge personally,' Ben explained.

'Then we have you to thank,' said Charlie to Lonnie, who bowed and smiled.

'Ben will do right by us,' said Lonnie. 'Won't you, Ben?'

Ben wiped the crumbs from his hands with a napkin and rose from the table, grunting a little from the exertion of having to stand from the floor. He was careful not to promise anything without meeting with the other side first. If this issue was going to be resolved, he needed to figure out a fair way to appease both sides.

'Thanks so much for your hospitality,' he said, shaking Charlie's hand. 'I'm meeting with the Agrabah delegation next and then I'll get back to you guys.'

'Great. We look forward to settling this issue once and for all,' said Charlie. 'We know you'll do your best.'

Ben nodded. He meant to be a king for all his subjects, which meant keeping the interests of the villagers from Stone City in mind as well as the grievances of the people of Agrabah when he made his final decision. He hoped they would abide by it.

chapter 18

A Spell for Every Occasion

'We need to steal a boat from the dock,' said Jay. 'How else are we going to get out into the ocean?'

'Steal? No way!' said Mal, who was leery of embarking on a plan that might get them in trouble, especially while Ben was away. They'd been in Auradon for a few months now, and no-one looked at them as villains anymore. They were just regular students like everybody else. She hoped they could solve this the Auradon way and not resort to tactics they'd learned on the Isle of the Lost.

'We'll just borrow one,' suggested Evie. 'Right?'

'But who do we know that owns a boat?' said Jay.

'Um, Ben does,' said Carlos. 'He has the royal fleet at his command.'

'And we only need one boat,' said Evie.

'Okay, let me try him,' said Mal, taking out her phone. Borrowing a boat sounded like an excellent, Auradon-approved idea. Ben would surely allow them the use of one of his boats, and, as Evie pointed out, they only needed one. Mal dialled his number, but instead of ringing, the line gave her a busy signal. She typed a text instead. But it bounced back as well. 'Hmmm. I can't get through. He's over at a village near the Great Wall,' she said.

'Yeah, they don't have good signal in the outer provinces of Northern Wei,' said Carlos. 'I doubt you'll be able to get ahold of him in time.'

'Like I said, we'll just steal one, and once we're done with it, we'll bring it right back,' Jay insisted. 'There's no other way.'

Mal crossed her arms and put away her phone, frowning. 'I guess not.' She still didn't like the sound of it, but there didn't seem to be another alternative. *Goodness is as goodness does*, Fairy Godmother liked to say, and Mal thought that if their intentions were good, that counted for something. Right?

'There really isn't any other way for us to get out there,' Evie said reluctantly.

'Not unless we turn into mermaids,' said Carlos, shrugging.

'Great!' said Jay, clapping his hands together. 'Let's go!'

'But we have to be really careful that we don't get caught,' said Mal, as they hurried out of the cafeteria together.

Jay shook his head. 'Come on, it's me! Just a few months ago I was the best thief on the Isle of the Lost. And did I ever get caught?'

They all had to admit the answer was no.

Jay almost felt nostalgic as they made their way down to Belle's Harbour that night. Getting past the guards stationed at the entrance to the royal marina was easy. They had done enough slinking and scurrying around in the shadows on the Isle of the Lost that they were experts in hugging walls, crouching, and scampering when someone was looking the other way. They ran down the gravel path towards the water, coming to a stop right at the gate before the dock.

'It's locked,' said Mal, tugging on the handle.

'Not a problem,' said Jay with a smile, as he held up his trusty pin. He was enjoying being able to indulge in his old bad habits once more. But as much as he twisted and turned and shook the pin inside the lock, it wouldn't open. 'Huh,' he said. 'That's never happened before.' He removed his beanie in frustration.

'Let's just climb over it,' said Jay, already scampering up the iron mesh. The rest of them tried to do the same, but the gate was too tall, and the steel cut painfully into the palms of their hands. Even Jay had to quit halfway up the gate.

Carlos slid down with a yelp, and Evie almost twisted her ankle trying to get a foothold.

'This isn't going to work,' said Mal, trying to stop the bleeding on her knuckles.

Jay kicked at a pebble, frustrated.

Mal looked around to make sure there was no-one around. 'Step aside, I'll just spell it open.' She removed her mother's trusty spell book from her pack and paged to the right incantation.

'Toad's breath and vampire's tickle, open up this door a little!'

The gate swung open an inch, and Mal smiled.

'Nice work,' said Jay, pushing the door open. 'After you, ladies.'

Evie looked concerned as she stepped through the gate. 'Mal, you're really using that spell book more than you should.'

'I'll stop after today, I promise,' said Mal, as Jay and Carlos followed after them and ran ahead to check out the different kinds of boats.

'Which one do we want?' asked Jay, as there were sailing and motor vessels of all kinds. He rubbed his hands in glee at all there was for the taking. There were cabin cruisers, sleek sailing catamarans, fishing trawlers complete with outriggers, and even a hydroplane.

'I don't know, just something that will get us there fast,' said Mal.

'How about this one?' asked Jay, whistling at the sight

of the crowning glory of the royal collection, a fancy two-hundred-foot yacht complete with a helicopter pad on the top deck.

'We're not taking that,' said Mal.

'Why not?' Jay asked, annoyed. He was already picturing himself in the captain's seat, and he would bet there was a sweet royal Jacuzzi up there.

'It's the royal yacht,' said Mal. 'It's saved for only special occasions. Ben would kill us.'

'Fine,' he said, sulking.

'Hey guys, how about this one?' Carlos called from farther down the dock.

They rounded the corner and found Carlos grinning from a sleek black speedboat with the royal insignia on the side. BEAST'S FURY was carved in gold on the stern.

'It looks fast,' said Jay, hopping on.

'Faster than a pirate ship, hopefully,' said Mal. 'Uma cannot have that trident. Who knows what she'd want for it!'

'She'll want to get off the island for sure,' said Evie.

'And we cannot have her rampaging around Auradon,' said Mal. 'Think of the trouble she'd stir up.'

'Just one problem,' said Jay, glancing around the dashboard of the elegant boat. 'We don't have the keys to this thing.'

'Again, not a problem,' said Mal, consulting her spell book once more. 'Hmmm, what kind of spell do you think would work? Key-making spell? Boat spell?' She flipped through the pages. 'Oh! How about this one? My mum's notes said she used it all the time before she came to the Isle to turn on the microwave when it didn't work.'

Mal held her hand up and pointed to the boat. *'Lizard's tongue and demon's spawn, make this blasted thing turn on!'*

The boat's engine purred to life. Jay grinned and gave her a thumbs-up.

'Just one problem,' said Carlos. 'None of us actually know how to drive a boat. And I'm not sure there's a spell for that.'

'Hmm, maybe not,' said Mal. 'But let me check.'

'I think that's probably enough spells for the day,' said Evie delicately.

'But we'll need the spell book to get through the barrier, and then to call up the trident,' Mal reminded her.

'Need what to do what?' a voice called, just as a bright light shone upon them on the shadowy dock, temporarily blinding all of them.

Mal frantically motioned to Jay to cut the engine, and the four of them froze in place, barely daring to breathe.

'Who's there?' called the increasingly familiar voice. 'Show yourselves!'

Mal shielded her eyes and looked up past the light to the person holding the spark. She knew that wand.

'Oh no! It's Fairy Godmother!'

chapter 19

The Sorcerer's Secret

Uma had worked at the Fish and Chips Shoppe her entire life, from when she was so little she could barely see above the counter, until she was old enough to wear an apron, carry a tray, and take an order. She recognised most of their regulars, and when new customers walked in, Uma always paid attention. So when the Sorcerer's Intern entered on Gil's arm, Uma spotted her right away.

She and Harry were whispering by the counter when they arrived. Uma nodded to Gil, who waved back and signalled for Uma to come over. She shook her head. She wanted Gil to talk to Sophie for a little bit, soften her up before Uma went in for the kill.

Harry slunk away and Uma went back to work, slamming down trays and yelling at patrons who dared not to tip, pointing to the sign—TIP OR ELSE!—that hung by the exit. After an hour, Gil sidled up to the counter that Harry was leaning on and Uma was wiping with a rag. 'Are you ready to talk to her yet?' he asked Uma, a desperate tone in his voice.

'Why, are you out of conversation?' Uma asked.

'Almost! We've been sitting over there forever. I did what you said. She thinks we're on a date. Keeps asking me about my hobbies and whether I enjoy long walks on the beach. I've seen a lot of pictures of her cats,' he groaned. 'I told her you wanted to chat now.'

'Fine. Harry, stay close in case I need you.' Uma squared her hat on her head and walked over to the table, to where a young woman in a red wizard's robe was seated, sipping bilge and snacking on a side of fried clams. 'Hi, Sophie?'

'Hey, Uma,' said Sophie. 'These are great! What do you guys put on them?' she said, motioning to the plate of clams and wiping her mouth with a napkin.

'You don't want to know,' said Uma frankly. 'I mean . . . Cook has a fabulous recipe.' She realised that buttering up the clams, so to speak, was the way to get what she wanted from this girl. 'Did you guys have a nice dinner?'

'We did,' said Sophie. 'I've never been here before.'

'Come back again,' said Uma. 'On Fridays we have the weekend special.' The weekend special was everything that didn't sell over the week, but Uma didn't say that.

'Okay, I will,' said Sophie. 'I don't really get to go out too much.'

'The sorcerer keeps you busy?'

'Yeah, there's always papers to grade and research on his experiments. But I have nights and weekends off. It's just a bit far from where we live.'

'I see,' said Uma. 'I heard you're not from here, like we are.'

'Yeah, I'm not. My family's from Eden, actually,' said Sophie. 'We live in the middle of the forest.'

'Do you miss it?'

'Sometimes. It's so green back home and so . . . well . . . not green here.' Sophie shrugged.

'You don't have to say,' said Uma. 'We know what the Isle is like.' She whistled to a server. 'Bring us two pints of the best swill.'

'Oh wow,' said Sophie.

'My pleasure,' said Uma. 'Gil is handsome, isn't he?'

Sophie's eyes flicked to Gil, who raised his bilge glass to her with a goofy smile. 'Yeah, I guess, if you like brawny.'

'Who doesn't?' said Uma.

Sophie giggled self-consciously. 'Belle, I guess. Although she married Beast.'

Uma decided it was time to get down to business. 'Anyway, you have a second?'

Sophie nodded and put away her napkin. 'Gil said you had something magical for me,' she said, in a professional tone.

'He did?' Uma was confused for a moment until she remembered it had been her idea to tell Sophie that she had something for her. 'Oh, right, I do.'

'You really have it?' Sophie asked, her neck tensing at the question. Whatever it was that she thought Uma had, it was clear it was incredibly important to her.

Like Gil, Uma decided the best answer was a definitive, 'Yes. I have it.'

'Oh, thank wizards!' said Sophie, smiling in relief. 'I've been looking for it everywhere! Where'd you find it?'

'Around,' said Uma vaguely.

'I mean, I can't believe the shop gave me a witch's hat back!' Sophie grumbled.

'Right . . .'

'I just took it there because the brim was fraying,' said Sophie. 'I should have just fixed it myself. I'm sure they sold the sorcerer's hat to someone else.'

'The hat! You're looking for the sorcerer's hat!' said Uma.

Sophie was suddenly not as friendly. She frowned. 'Yeah, and you said you had it.'

'Pointy blue one? With all those stars and moons on it?

What's so special about it?' asked Uma. She would never understand the ways of wizards.

'Nothing!' said Sophie abruptly.

'Nothing?' said Uma suspiciously.

'The professor doesn't like to be without it,' Sophie finally admitted. 'He's a little sensitive about his bald spot.'

Uma raised an eyebrow. 'That can't be all it is.'

'Fine! Whoever wears the hat is able to use his power, except there's no magic on the Isle, thankfully,' said Sophie. 'But I still need to get it back. So, out with it. Do you have it or not?'

Uma slammed a palm on the table. 'Of course I have it! And it can be yours *if*—'

'What do you mean *if*?' asked Sophie.

'If you give me something in return,' said Uma with a wicked smile. 'Can't get something for nothing, you know. Ursula's rule. And you're on our turf now.'

Sophie's eyes narrowed. 'What do you want for it?'

'Tell me where Yen Sid keeps my mother's necklace,' said Uma.

'You want Ursula's necklace?' asked Sophie.

'Are you deaf? Yes, I want her necklace—the seashell one!' growled Uma.

'But it's broken; what would you need it for . . . ?' said Sophie.

'I don't care, I want it. It was my mother's, and I want it back,' said Uma. 'Sentimental value, shall we say.'

'You? Sentimental? As if!'

'It was my mother's!' said Uma. 'It's rightfully mine.'

Sophie stuck her nose in the air. 'Be that as it may, it's the property of the kingdom now. It belongs in the museum,' she said in a superior tone. 'The only reason it's still on the Isle is—'

'The embargo,' said Uma. 'I know.'

'I'm not telling you where it is,' said Sophie.

'Fine, then no hat,' said Uma.

'You don't have it,' said Sophie.

Uma grunted in frustration and motioned for backup.

'Sophie,' said Harry, stepping up to the table from the shadows. 'You're surrounded. There are many of us and only one of you, and you don't have any magic at your disposal. You're going to lose. We don't want to hurt you. But we could.'

She trembled. 'I'm not afraid.'

Uma glared at her. 'You should be.'

'Okay, so if I tell you where the necklace is, you'll give me the sorcerer's hat back,' said Sophie.

'Precisely.' Harry smiled and nonchalantly wiped his hook on the front of his shirt, so she could see how sharp it was.

'I can't tell you where it is,' said Sophie. 'I just can't.'

'Why not? I'll give you whatever you desire,' said Uma, trying a different tack.

'How? There's no magic on the island, and last I checked

you're not Ursula, and I don't need to sell you my voice for a pair of legs.'

'Not interested in princes, are you?' said Uma.

'Princes are boring. Have you even met Chad Charming? That's all you need to know,' said Sophie.

'There are other things a girl might want. I don't need magic to help you,' said Uma. 'Tell me, there's got to be something you need that you can't have. A way out of your internship? A better apartment down at the Knob? Maybe even another date with Gil? Pirates over princes every time, am I right?'

Sophie shook her head. Uma and Harry exchanged a look and left the table—Uma ostensibly to serve other customers; Harry had no excuse but followed Uma anyway. 'She won't budge,' said Uma.

'You're losing your touch,' said Harry.

'Oh, stuff it,' said Uma. 'You couldn't get her to spill either.'

Harry shrugged. 'The Uma I know could talk the hat off a wizard.'

'If only we had the sorcerer's hat,' said Uma. 'Or if we could come up with something else she wants that I can give her.'

'Or else?' said Harry, holding up his hook with a wicked grin.

'If it comes down to that, yes. But hold on.'

Uma returned to the table empty-handed. 'I don't think you have it,' said Sophie, taking a last sip of her drink and gathering her things.

'Are you sure?' Uma smiled mysteriously.

Sophie hesitated, considering the odds. 'I'm pretty sure . . .' She crossed her arms over her chest and seemed to have come to a decision. 'We're done here,' she said, getting up. 'Tell Gil next time he should take me to the Slop Shop instead.'

'Wait, where are you going?' roared Uma.

'Home,' said Sophie. 'I don't need anything from you but the sorcerer's hat, and you don't have it.'

'How can you be so sure?'

'Because. I've looked everywhere and so has Professor Yen Sid. If we can't find it, no-one can.' She regarded Uma with hostility. 'Just admit you don't have it already!'

'But I do!' said Uma.

'Prove it!' said Sophie.

'I will!' said Uma hotly, annoyed to be questioned. She stood from the table, her mind racing. Sophie mentioned losing it in a hat shop, which rang a bell . . . Why? Where had she seen a hat like the sorcerer's? She knew she'd spotted it somewhere . . . But where?

Then she remembered.

'Gil!' she said, finding him throwing darts at the poster of King Ben on the wall. 'Do you have those hats you bought from the shop the other day?'

'I do!' said Gil with a big smile. 'But you said they didn't look good on me.'

'I don't need you to wear them, I need you to bring them back here.'

Gil ran off and came back carrying a big sack. 'This one?' he said, showing her his white cowboy hat. 'Or this one?' He held up a black top hat.

'No, the pointy one,' said Uma impatiently.

Gil reached into the bag once more and before he could say anything, Uma had already grabbed it out of his hand.

Uma ran back to the table, holding the pointy velvet hat aloft. 'Is this what you're looking for?' she asked Sophie triumphantly.

'Where on earth did you find it?' said Sophie, shocked and happy.

'Bought it at the hat shop, of course,' said Uma, dangling the hat with the tips of her fingers and walking dangerously close to the open flame in the centre of the room. 'Now tell me where Yen Sid is hiding my mother's necklace. Or I'll throw it into the fire.'

chapter 20

Desert Pride

Since the Great Wall blocked the direct way to the desert kingdom, Ben and Lonnie had to take the jet, despite the short distance of the trip. Ben could see why the people of Agrabah insisted on the flying carpets. Without air rights in the area, they'd have to go completely out of their way to get to Stone City. Once Ben and Lonnie set foot in Agrabah, they were met with as much fanfare and joy on that side as in the village.

The Sultan's nephew, the Grand Vizier, awaited them at the bottom of the mountain. While it had been cold and damp in Stone City, Ben found he was already sweating in his regiment coat after a minute in the hot desert sun.

'Welcome, welcome!' said the Grand Vizier, walking towards them with his arms outstretched, the golden bells decorating his elaborately embroidered sandals tinkling with every step. Like the citizens of Northern Wei, residents of Agrabah wore both traditional and modern garb; the Grand Vizier wore a shiny tracksuit and a pair of noise-reducing headphones around his neck. He embraced them warmly and kissed them on both cheeks, in keeping with the native custom.

The Sultan's people kept watch over the royal jet while the Grand Vizier led them towards a pair of camels for their journey to the palace. The desert kingdom hadn't changed much from the days when Aladdin prowled the souk in the middle of the city with his pet monkey. The place was buzzing with merchants and tourists haggling with each other, arguing over the prices of spices and rugs.

Ben found the camel ride a bit bumpy, but soon enough they were sitting comfortably on rugs in the Grand Vizier's great room, while a succession of mouthwatering dishes were presented for their nourishment—lamb tagine with stewed prunes and apricots, great bowls of couscous, eggplant pastries and aromatic saffron rice.

'Is this our third lunch?' Lonnie asked, amused at all the feasting the trip had brought.

'I stopped counting,' said Ben, piling his plate high with food from every dish presented in front of him.

'How are things in Stone City?' asked the Grand Vizier,

when they had finished eating. 'I know you stopped there first. I hope you have time to listen to our side of this sorry tale.'

'I do have time, that's why I'm here,' said Ben, taking a sip of sweet-smelling tea served in an ornate silver cup. 'I understand it's a question of air rights over the Great Wall in regard to the use of flying carpets.'

'Yes,' said the Grand Vizier, his face darkening. 'The Great Wall keeps us out of Stone City, and so the flying carpets are our only means of transport to reach what has always been a trading partner for us.'

'I understand,' said Ben.

'And they've told you about our olive situation as well, yes? Our farmers plant and nurture the trees, but the wind carries the fruit over the wall, and the imperials are the ones who benefit from our hard work. Now I ask you, is that fair?'

Ben demurred from answering just yet.

'The leaves from the trees also blow over to the Stone City, and they have to clean it up,' said Lonnie hotly. 'Agrabah doesn't offer to help clean up the mess, but only demands the villagers return the fruit without payment.'

'We don't have to pay for something we create ourselves!' said the Grand Vizier, just as hotly.

Lonnie jumped to her feet, a hand on her sword. The Grand Vizier did the same, a hand on his scimitar, and the guards in the room followed suit, ready to attack on the Grand Vizier's command.

'Now, now,' said Ben, holding out his hands in a pacifying gesture. 'We don't have to fight. We're here to find some peace between the two kingdoms. You have both been good neighbours for centuries, and you can still continue to be good neighbours for centuries more.'

'What is your solution?' asked the Grand Vizier.

'A compromise,' said Ben, trying to catch Lonnie's eye. But she was looking at her feet, seemingly still angry at the Grand Vizier.

'Compromise?' said the Grand Vizier, shaking his head. 'There is no compromise. We need to fly our carpets! And we want our olives back! Nothing else!'

'Grand Vizier, what would it take for you to listen to my proposed solution?' asked Ben.

The Grand Vizier shook his head, and it appeared all hopes of a truce had disappeared, when Lonnie unexpectedly knelt before the Grand Vizier like a supplicant, and offered him her sword, holding it lengthwise and balanced on the edge of her fingertips. 'Forgive me, Grand Vizier, for my rudeness earlier,' she said, her head bowed low.

The Grand Vizier looked shocked. 'The imperial favourite's daughter, bowing to me?'

'Yes, my lord,' said Lonnie, her eyes on the floor. 'I took advantage of your hospitality and should never have acted in such a hostile manner in your presence. Normally I wouldn't do something like that. I'm not sure what came over me, but my mother taught me that honour is about admitting when you are wrong, and I was wrong.'

The Grand Vizier looked thoughtful for a moment. 'I accept your apology,' he said. 'Please, rise.'

Lonnie stood up. Ben tensed, wondering what was going to happen now. But the Grand Vizier smiled kindly. It appeared he had been moved by Lonnie's humble gesture.

'I will listen to you, King of Auradon,' he said. 'Because if someone of such high imperial blood can admit their mistake, the people of Agrabah are not so proud that we cannot do the same. Perhaps we can work with them as we have before.'

'I am glad to hear it,' said Ben, grateful that Lonnie had insisted she come along on this task and proud that she had changed the mind of the Grand Vizier without having to resort to battle—even if she had acted a bit more rashly than he'd had in mind.

'If you please, tell me the Auradon compromise,' said the Grand Vizier. 'I find I am quite excited to hear it.'

Ben took a deep breath and explained his idea. Now all he had to do was convince everyone that his solution was the answer to their problem.

chapter 21

Thieves in the Night

'Who's down here?' asked Fairy Godmother, holding her wand high in the air like a torch and walking closer and closer to the speedboat.

'Quick, hide!' said Mal, and the four of them scrambled to find the nearest hiding place. Jay and Carlos dove under the seats, while Mal and Evie crouched behind a few containers.

'Do you think she saw us?' Carlos whispered worriedly. His heart was pounding rapidly under his black-and-white leather jacket.

'I hope not,' said Mal, crouching down even lower in the shadows.

'I swear I heard something,' said Fairy Godmother, sending beams of light everywhere.

The light arced over the boat they were hiding in, but no-one moved, so it danced over to the next boat. Carlos breathed a small sigh of relief.

'I guess I was wrong,' muttered Fairy Godmother, and she walked back towards the shuttered yacht club at the end of the dock and began waving her wand again, making the windows sparkle and giving the building a new coat of paint.

'What's Fairy Godmother doing down here anyway?' Evie whispered.

'It looks like she's working on the royal yacht club,' said Mal. 'Ben's parents are returning from their cruise, and I think that's where they're planning to hold the welcome reception. I heard the work on getting the place up to snuff was behind schedule.'

'How long is she going to be here? My legs are getting cramped,' complained Jay.

'Shush!' said Mal.

They watched as Fairy Godmother unfurled giant banners with the Auradon crest and gave the yacht club sign a little more sparkle.

'There,' said Fairy Godmother. 'That should do it.' She began walking away from the dock and back to the harbour entrance.

Carlos found he could breathe again. If they'd been caught stealing the royal speedboat, they would be in so much trouble. It felt as if his stomach had dropped into his shoes ever since he heard their headmistress' voice.

Mal poked her head up to check, and there was no sign of Fairy Godmother anywhere. 'I think she's gone,' she said, stepping out from behind the boat's containers. The rest of them came out from their hiding places, Evie hugging herself with her arms and Carlos still looking uncertain. Only Jay appeared unfazed.

'Let's give it a little more time,' suggested Evie.

'Good idea,' said Carlos, who was not in any rush to get moving.

They waited a little while longer, sitting in the dark and listening to the waves slosh gently against the sides of the boat. When Mal was satisfied Fairy Godmother had left the harbour, she nodded to the team.

'Okay, let's go,' she said, tapping the steering wheel as she muttered the words of the spell, and the boat's engine roared to life once more.

Alas, a second later, the entire dock was flooded with light, and this time, Fairy Godmother caught them boat-handed.

'Aha! I knew there was someone here!' said Fairy Godmother triumphantly. She walked down the narrow dock, pointing her wand at the perpetrators. 'Mal, Jay, Carlos and Evie! What are you four doing down here? And with the royal speedboat?' She gasped. 'Are you *stealing* it?'

It certainly looks that way, thought Carlos.

'Fairy Godmother! We can explain!' said Mal.

'Yes! We were, uh . . .' said Carlos, as he vainly tried to come up with a plausible explanation as to why they had trespassed onto the royal dock.

But Fairy Godmother shook her head, her lips a tight line. She kept the wand trained on the four of them and herded them away from the shoreline. 'Shush, I don't want to hear it till we're safely back at school!'

She bundled all the four villain kids into her van and drove them to Auradon Prep. They sat in silence in the backseats, miserable and scared.

'What do you think's going to happen to us?' whispered Carlos from the third row.

'A lot of detention?' Mal whispered back. 'That can't be too bad, right? We'll just have to bake a lot of cakes?'

'Hopefully, she won't send us back to the Isle of the Lost,' said Jay.

Evie squeaked. 'She wouldn't do that, would she?'

'She could,' said Mal.

'Oh no,' said Evie. 'I don't want to go back there.'

'But it's home,' said Mal, trying to soothe her friend. 'It won't be that bad.'

'Mal, don't you understand? Auradon is my home now,' said Evie, looking out the window at the array of lights from the sparkling castles that dotted the landscape.

Carlos nodded. He couldn't go back to the Isle of the Lost, not after everything they'd seen and done in Auradon.

The thought filled him with a heavy dread. He couldn't go back to scrubbing his mother's bunions. He wouldn't.

'No talking back there!' said Fairy Godmother from the driver's seat. 'And no talking on your phones either!' With a flick of her wand, all their phones disappeared.

When they got back to campus, Fairy Godmother marched them in front of her, holding the wand at Jay's back at the end of the line. The hallways were full of students heading to dinner. Carlos thought longingly of his life in Auradon, convinced this was the end of the tale. He hadn't even been able to say goodbye to Dude. The school would not look kindly on thievery. Or was it grand larceny? Marine larceny? Worse, it was exactly what the good people of Auradon expected from a few villain kids. Except they weren't villains anymore, not at all, and they were only stealing the boat so they could help a friend. But what was that saying? About the path to darkness? It was paved with good intentions . . .

A few students looked at them curiously, but no-one said hello, as Fairy Godmother had a very angry look on her usually cheerful face.

One student wasn't deterred, however—Jane spotted them on the way to Fairy Godmother's office.

'Mum!' she said, stopping in her tracks. 'What's going on?'

Carlos' heart lurched once more, this time with hope.

Maybe Fairy Godmother would listen to Jane! Jane could make her understand they weren't doing something evil.

He was about to answer her, but Fairy Godmother didn't give him a chance. 'Nothing, dear, get out of the way,' said Fairy Godmother, brushing off her only child, and striding to the front of the pack. 'This doesn't concern you.'

But Jane wouldn't be dismissed so easily. She fell in step with the four friends. 'What happened?' asked Jane. 'Why's my mum so mad?'

Jay looked glum. Mal shook her head. 'I don't want to get you in trouble, too,' she said.

'Evie? What's wrong? Are you crying?' asked Jane, as they kept walking up the stairs.

Evie sniffled but didn't answer.

They reached the landing and Fairy Godmother unlocked the door to her office. She tapped her wand and motioned the villain kids to enter.

Jane caught Carlos' sleeve before he disappeared behind the door. 'Carlos? What's the matter? What did you guys do?'

'Help us,' Carlos whispered urgently. 'I think we're going to be kicked out of here.'

'Kicked out?' said Jane, so aghast that she almost dropped her books. She stared at Carlos, shocked and wide-eyed at the very idea. 'But you guys can't leave!'

'We don't want to,' he said, feeling as terrible as he looked.

'I'll figure out something, I promise,' said Jane. 'You guys aren't going anywhere.'

He smiled his thanks and reached for her hand. Jane gave it a squeeze, but had to let go as Fairy Godmother pulled Carlos into the room.

It was too bad their little Auradon experiment was ending already, thought Carlos. He would have really liked to spend more time in Jane's company.

chapter 22

A Pirate's Life

Outside on the dock, Harry was gathering the pirates together, slapping backs, readying the crew for the voyage ahead. Their merry band was ready, polishing swords and greedy for treasure. Once they found that trident and they were off the Isle of the Lost, there was all of Auradon to pillage! The thought brought them all much wicked glee.

'I heard in Agrabah there are warehouses full of the Sultan's gold,' said Desiree.

'Don't forget the jewels we'll find in the Summerlands by the dwarf mines,' growled Gonzo, his eyes going starry at the thought.

'Olympus is mine!' said Bonny.

Pirates. Harry smiled. They were itching for adventure. First, the trident; after, the world was theirs for the taking.

Inside, from the window of her small apartment above the fish shop, Uma felt a grim satisfaction as she looked at her reflection in the mirror. The time had come. It was so close, she could feel it—this was the start of her revenge, the start of her ascendancy. No more tiny room, no more apartment drenched in fish stink. She didn't need a fancy limousine to fetch her off the island, she would do it herself, cut her own deal, make her own way.

'I'm leaving, Ma!' she yelled, and a slender blue tentacle crept around from behind the door and splashed her with a few drops of water. It was the only goodbye she expected, the only one she needed. She was off to find herself; her past would soon be nothing more than a memory.

She clambered down the stairs, saying goodbye to it all: to that step that wobbled, and that patch of mould that could never be washed from the ceiling corner. She strode through the door and out onto the dock. Her ship lay waiting; the crew snapping to attention when she arrived in their midst.

Uma regarded them with pride. Just that morning she'd had nothing but slow-burning frustration and a jealous rage. But tonight she had so much more—she was captain of a ship, with a first mate and muscle to boot, as well as a crew of the toughest pirates on the island. Her name was Uma, and before long, everyone in Auradon would know who she was when she lifted that trident and demanded her freedom.

The first part of her plan had already worked perfectly. Sophie had crumbled like a piece of cake once Uma had threatened to set fire to the sorcerer's hat, and she had given up the necklace's secret location as soon as the flames had licked the brim.

'Ready?' Uma asked Harry.

In response, Harry gave her the usual pirate salute—which was no salute at all. He cocked an eyebrow and grinned. 'Ready.' He raised his hook, which had been polished to a high shine. It gave him an air of malevolence that she quite liked.

'Gil?' she said.

'Yes, Shrim—Uma,' said Gil. 'And, um, do you think we can grab dinner after this? I'm hungry.'

'Let's go,' said Uma, ignoring him and leading the way.

The motley crew headed down the wharf towards the *Lost Revenge*. They shambled past the rope bridge and towards the decks of the pirate ship, setting about unfurling the sails, hoisting up the jib, and removing the ropes that held it to the deck so it would be ready for launch.

Uma climbed the steps of the forecastle and turned to face the heavy wooden rail. The foremast stood at her back, ropes flanking her on two sides. The crew gathered on the main deck. The ship was ready to sail.

She drew her sword from its scabbard, the blade flashing yellow and orange in the evening light. This was her crew, her people. Time to put them in order. 'Pirates! Somewhere on the Isle of the Doomed is a treasure chest that holds the pieces of a necklace that belonged to my mother! If we find it, I can call that fool Triton's trident from the sea and use it to win our freedom from this island prison! Are you with me?'

'*Arrrr!*' cried the pirates. A few grunts followed and a shrug or two. In pirate terms, it was a good enough reception.

Uma slashed the air with her sword. 'We ride with the tide!' she cried.

'We ride with the tide!' roared Harry, raising his sword just as high.

'We ride with the tide?' said Gil. He shrugged his shoulders, removed his cutlass, and waved it in the air like the rest of them. The rest of the pirates joined in, raising their blades and cheering in unison.

Harry took hold of the wheel and kicked off the motor that would power the ship until the wind took hold. The *Lost Revenge* solemnly pulled out of the dock and into the dark waters beyond. A curious crowd gathered by the harbour to watch as it pulled away, some tossing rotten tomatoes at the ship's bow in the usual Isle send-off.

Harry steered the ship out past the shattered lighthouse, and through the fog he could make out the barrier over the Isle of the Lost and the waters surrounding it. But they had room to move, and when they reached the Strait of Ursula, the wind blew and the sails plumped at last. But the ocean waves were choppy and high, slamming the ship's hull. They ran right into one, sending a spray of water onto deck, but Harry laughed as he peered through the mist and the crew seemed to take it all in stride.

At last, they were off.

Uma smiled, for once utterly gratified with how her life had turned out. She had her ship and her crew, and they were sailing to find their freedom.

chapter 23

Sail Away

Contentment didn't last long. 'Um, Harry? Is this as fast as we can go?' she asked. The *Lost Revenge* had only sailed a few yards, and the dock was still in view. They had inched up the archipelago, but were still miles from where they needed to be. She paced the deck impatiently. First the necklace, and then the trident was theirs for the taking, if only they could get there faster.

'It only goes as fast as the wind will take it,' said Harry. 'Sorry.'

'Right,' said Uma. 'I get it: the wind hits the sails and off we go.' She looked up at the billowing white cloth. A single swatch of linen fluttered in the wind, held there by four ropes and tied to the foremost mast. But just behind it were not just one but two others. 'What do you call those other masts?' she asked, acting a bit coy.

'Oh, yes,' he replied, a bit sheepish, 'that's the mainmast just behind the foremast, and the one in the back is called the mizzen.'

'I see. And these masts have sails as well?' she asked, still acting coy. The boy had to know exactly where this was going, right? He told her he knew how to sail, didn't he?

'Yes, I mean technically we do have three masts,' he allowed.

'And each one has a sail or two?'

'Three, actually.'

'So why in the world aren't we using them all!' she yelled.

'Well, it's the waves, you see; with all of this rocking it would be quite difficult—no, dangerous, to go up there and unfurl the rest of the sails.'

'So you're telling me we could be going two, three times this speed, and all we have to do is climb up there and unroll the rest of the sails?'

'Something like that,' said Harry. 'It's not as easy as it sounds. Try climbing 50 feet into the air while the boat is pitching to and fro, and see if you can hold on. These things—'

'I think I will.' She was headed towards the second mast before he could make any further attempt to dissuade her from climbing it and wrestling with the sails.

How hard can it be? she thought. *Climb the mast, untie some ropes, and it's done.*

She looked at Harry with disdain as she raised her foot and caught hold of the first peg. She grabbed one and then another, and soon she was seven, eight feet in the air. The ship rolled and her face promptly collided with the mast; her hand slipped from one peg, her leg from the other, and she reeled. Were it not for that fact that her shirt had caught on yet another of the pegs she would have fallen onto the deck. Or worse, she might have landed in the ocean itself.

Harry snickered.

'I suppose this is that moment when you mutter *I told you so?*' she asked.

'I might have,' said Harry. 'But now you've gone and ruined it. I suppose I'll have to come up there and help you out. It does take two to unfurl a sail. You know that, don't you?'

She didn't. She hadn't the faintest idea of how any of this worked. She only wanted to get to the trident as quickly as was possible, and if that meant a bit of mast-climbing, she'd do it. She'd already made it past the hard part, right?

The boat leaned again, answering her question. This time she was ready, though, and wrapped her arms tightly around the mast. She wasn't going to let her feet slide from the pegs a second time.

Harry was snickering again.

She had half a mind to stab him when he reached her.

He held one peg tightly, balancing himself. 'You're going to squeeze that mast in two if you hold on to it any tighter,' he said.

She immediately loosened her grip and regained her composure.

'So tell me how all of this works,' she ordered. Each time the ship rocked, the mast swayed wildly, hurtling them through the air. *Like being launched from a slingshot*, she thought, her hands wrapping a bit more tightly around the pegs again. At this height, there were rope ladders too—a great number of ropes actually, all of them running back and forth between the mast's various arms. There was more to grab on to, more to catch if she fell. She supposed she was a little safer at this altitude, but who knew.

'See that rope?' Harry pointed to a tightly wound bit of cord. 'Unwrap it on your side, and I'll do the same on mine. Just hold the last little bit. Don't let the whole thing loose . . .' he said, but she had already unwound the rope. It was easy enough. She simply pulled the rope from the sail and cast it off.

Unfortunately, Harry hadn't even started to unfurl his end of the sail. So the end she had set free caught the wind, jerking the boat towards its starboard side, which was a boating term that Harry would not stop using. *Isn't it just called the right side?* she had thought over and over again, but now the word was in her head and *she* was using it.

'This would have been a bit easier if you had waited,' Harry said grumpily.

'Got that,' she said. The boat was turning rapidly to one side, threatening to pull them off course, but Harry was quick, his fingers nimble. The sail pulled at the ropes, tightening them, but somehow he managed to get the rope unwound, and the entire sail billowed gorgeously into the air.

The ship righted itself.

'Next time we do it together!' he exclaimed, and Uma made no argument. She was eager to get to the necklace and the trident, but she'd already twice seen where a bit of overeagerness got her. She'd nearly fallen into the drink (as pirates called the sea) and partially driven them off course. *I think it's time to listen to directions*, she thought.

Uma *hated* directions. She gave orders; she didn't follow them.

But she climbed to the next sail as Harry directed. This one had a plank behind it and a rail, so it was easier to balance as she undid the ropes.

'Wait,' said Harry.

'I know. I'm not an idiot.'

He raised an eyebrow.

'Now!' he cried, and they both let loose the next sail. This one blossomed into a perfect half circle, snapping tight in the wind. They undid one more and then moved to the rear, where there were three more sails to unfurl. All in all, it was a lot of work, but each time a sail caught the wind, she felt their speed increase. By the time they'd unfurled the last of them, they were moving at quite a clip—the boat dashing across the waves, sometimes almost skipping from peak to peak.

'See, that wasn't so bad,' she said as they climbed down the last mast, the *mizzenmast*, as he'd called it.

'You did nearly fall into the ocean,' Harry reminded Uma. 'Twice.'

The boat rocked once more, as if it too were reminding her of what happened. It swung back in the other direction, and both of them spun, catching each other and holding on to the mast to avoid falling to the deck. The increased speed had also added a bit more instability to their ride, making it slightly more dangerous. When the boat rocked, it did so with incredible force. It pitched again, and even Harry went fumbling for something to hold on to. Fortunately, sailing ships are webbed with ropes. He caught one or two and steadied himself.

'Lost your sea legs?' Uma asked.

'Even a good sailor needs a handhold every now and then.'

She nodded as if she didn't believe a word he'd said.

'Oh, stop it—don't we have a treasure chest to find?' Harry pointed out.

They did. She'd almost forgotten about it.

Uma stared out over the ocean. She knew the trident was

there, and she also knew she was not the only one looking for it. But they were moving faster now, and she had to hope that they would find it first.

'That's all the sails?' she asked.

'That's it. I can throw an oar in the water if you want to paddle?'

'I'll let you do that,' she replied.

'I'm sailing this ship,' Harry said—and indeed he was moving back and forth, checking all of the ropes that wound from the gunwale to the masts, from mast to mast and from mast to sail. And all the while he had to make certain the rudder was set in the right direction. He'd fastened it in place with a lash, but it needed constant correction. 'If you don't head straight into these waves they can knock you over, leaving you on your side. And then you're done,' he said. 'The sea is growing rougher: the waves are certainly higher, and the wind's stronger. I hope this trident of yours is worth all this effort.'

'It is—trust me,' said Uma. 'With that trident, we can buy our ticket out of here.'

Harry shrugged. 'I hope so. We're all counting on it.'

chapter 24

Building a Compromise

'You think this will work?' asked Lonnie, as she and Ben watched a group of strongmen from Agrabah take sledgehammers to the Great Wall. The stone crumbled underneath their blows, and soon enough, there was a hole big enough to see through to the other side, where a similar group of imperial soldiers was doing the same thing.

'I hope so,' said Ben, waving to Charlie, who waved back from his part of the wall.

When the hole was big enough to walk through, Ben crossed from the desert kingdom into Northern Wei's territory, the Grand Vizier by his side.

'Welcome to Stone City,' said Charlie, bowing to the Grand Vizier.

'It is an honour to be here,' said the Grand Vizier, bowing low as well. The two shook hands, and Charlie motioned for the group to take a seat on his porch, where they could watch the construction from a safe distance.

Ben had sent a pigeon to carry a message over the wall after he had convinced the Grand Vizier of his plan. Charlie then forwarded the message to the Emperor for approval. The Imperial City had sent its response—a white dove that meant the plan was approved.

And so, for the first time in the history of the Great Wall, there was going to be a door to Stone City on the other side. The people of Agrabah would no longer need to fly their carpets over the wall in order to get access, and the people of Stone City would no longer be aggravated by the noise from the pesky things.

'After all, we are not enemies,' said Charlie. 'We are neighbours and friends, and have been for thousands of years. The wall was built for one purpose, but now must serve another.'

'Not enemies at all,' agreed the Grand Vizier, slurping his bubble tea and chewing noisily on the tapioca balls. 'What *is* this amazing concoction?'

Charlie explained the provenance and the ingredients that went into the making of bubble tea, and the Grand Vizier declared he would press the Sultan to serve it during their festival, which was coming up in a month or so.

Ben laughed, glad to see that the dispute had been resolved amicably.

The two kingdoms also agreed that the olive trade would be overseen by foremen from both sides of the wall, and that the Stone City and Agrabah would both take care of harvesting the olives and pruning the trees. The desert farmers even offered to teach the villagers how to nurture and care for the trees, and in turn the villagers offered to trade recipes and other spices. A few Stone City farmers even suggested planting olive trees on their side of the wall, although the Grand Vizier told Ben in confidence that he wasn't sure that was a feasible idea, since the climates of the two kingdoms differed greatly. Olive trees were a desert fruit, and the Stone City's mountainous terrain would not be conducive to its flowering. But who knew? Ben reminded them they lived in Auradon after all, where the impossible had a way of becoming possible: where street rats married Sultans' daughters, and awkward girls grew up to be great warriors.

Ben and Lonnie bade their goodbyes to Charlie and the Grand Vizier. 'You must come visit us again, especially during harvest season,' said Charlie.

'I will.'

'See you at the Agrabah Festival,' said the Grand Vizier.

'I look forward to it.'

'And thank you again, young lady, for being brave

enough to change an old man's mind,' said the Grand Vizier to Lonnie.

Lonnie bowed low in appreciation.

'They're bringing your horses now,' said Charlie. 'Safe journey back.'

Ben thanked them again, and watched as Charlie and the villagers retired to their side of the wall and the Grand Vizier and his entourage exited to their side. But a few workers from both cities stayed at the site, finishing up the construction of the Great Wall's first Great Door.

'Where did you get the idea to apologise like that?' Ben asked Lonnie, when their new friends were out of earshot.

'From my mother,' said Lonnie. 'I realised not every dispute has to be resolved with a sword. She said that sometimes a good apology can also do the trick. Mushu is always apologising, by the way.'

'Of course he is,' said Ben, chuckling.

They headed towards the royal jet, when all of a sudden a strange whirlwind surrounded Ben.

'Don't be afraid!' a voice boomed. 'Just stay still.'

'Ben?' Lonnie called fearfully. 'What's happening?'

'I don't know,' he replied, as the whirlwind around him twirled faster and faster. 'But I think it's okay.' He recognised that voice, so he remained still and wondered where this next journey would take him.

chapter 25

Doom and Gloom

'Foggy,' said Harry, as he steered the ship away from the Isle of the Lost and towards the Isle of the Doomed, where the treasure chest containing Ursula's necklace was supposed to be buried. 'I don't recall ever seeing this much fog in the bay.'

'Do you think it's a bad sign?' asked Uma, who was still perched against the rail, gazing out at the bowsprit. A gorgeously carved mermaid adorned the long wooden pole. Sculpted with almost lifelike detail, it was painted in shades of teal and coral, the colours of the sea.

'I don't think it's any sign at all. Sometimes a fog is just a fog,' Harry shrugged.

'I'm sure you're right, but it still gives me the chills. I know there's no magic here, but it's not much of a start. How we will navigate through all this fog?' Uma asked. They had sailed into a dense patch of grey. It was all around them, on their arms and in their noses. It left a cool, damp feeling on her face, like cold perspiration.

'I don't mind, and there are many ways to sail in the fog. Leave the navigation to me,' Harry continued. 'There are far worse things in the sea than a grey sky. Try sailing through ten-foot waves or one-hundred-mile-an-hour winds.'

'I see your point.'

Harry was trying to sound optimistic. He was the one with the sea legs. He wasn't supposed to be afraid, not out here. But it wasn't the sea that bothered him. Their destination was another matter. The Isle of the Doomed wasn't exactly a paradise. That was probably why Yen Sid had hidden the broken necklace in a treasure chest on the smaller island in the first place. No-one from the Isle of the Lost ever visited the Isle of the Doomed—not if they could help it. It was rumoured to be haunted, and Maleficent's fortress loomed, tall and forbidding, over its desolate landscape. The island's only inhabitants were the descendants of goblins loyal to the evil fairy. *There must be some reason they call it the Isle of the Doomed*, Harry thought. But he wasn't sure he wanted to find out what it was—or if the rumours he heard about it were true.

Even with the fog, they sailed smoothly. The winds were light, but the ship moved at a respectable clip, cutting through the waves, edging ever closer to the shore.

'I wish the fog weren't so dense. I'd like to get a better sense of the beach before we set anchor. There could be rocks or . . .' said Harry. Then he stopped.

'What?' asked Uma.

'I don't know. This is a forbidden place. There could be anything hiding in those waters and this fog isn't helping. There could be spikes—iron ones, submerged below the waterline—obstacles to keep boats from landing on the island. This might not be as easy as we expect, Uma.'

Harry thought about what else could be out there. Goblins swarming over that beach, or traps, or who knows what. Anything could be hiding in a fog this thick.

'Let's stop here,' Harry announced. 'We'll drop anchor and row out in small boats. We'll make a smaller target, harder to spy on, and if there's anything in the water we'll be able to see it more easily.'

Uma protested at first. She didn't like his suggestion. It would only slow things down. She was ready to be bold and take chances, and she told him so. But she went along with Harry, for now. 'Fine,' she said at last. 'We'll do it your way.'

So they rowed out with the crew in small wooden boats, hugging the sea, creeping towards the dark beach, their hulls grinding against the sand as they made shore. Uma was the first out of the boat, her feet falling into the cold water. It drenched her up to the knees. The sand here was grey, like the sky and the fog that still choked the air. Goblin Beach was dark and deserted, ghostly under the moonlight.

'At least it's empty. No goblins,' said Uma.

'Not yet,' Harry said.

'All right, Sophie said Yen Sid left some sort of clue, a trail,' said Uma.

'Like a path?' asked Harry.

'Maybe, but I don't think it's anything that obvious,' said Uma. 'I'm certain it's as hidden as the chest itself.' She eyed the distant fortress, tall and dark, its black stones wreathed in angry thorns. And she swore it glowed a strange colour—something like purple, but at times it shifted, turning to shades of green, like the photos Uma had seen of the aurora borealis. But the colours were gone as soon as she glanced at it, vanishing as if they had never been there at all. 'Let's head towards the castle.'

'Are you sure?' said Harry. 'That place is filled with goblins. We don't want those little guys to find out we're looking for something valuable, or they're bound to try and steal it.'

'We're only heading towards it, dummy. I didn't say anything about crossing the moat.'

'Good, as I'm more of a seafaring adventurer, less of an evil-castle explorer.'

'We all are,' mumbled Gil.

The pale sand of the fog-shrouded beach gave way to

a forest of grey thorn-infested trees. Their trunks wound every which way, growing in seemingly unnatural patterns, curling in upon themselves or twisting into odd spirals, as if some mad gardener had tortured them, forcing their limbs to twist into tangled bunches. It made for slow going, and more than once Harry was forced to draw his cutlass and hack through the thorns and the trees. Even the ferns were dense, and he hacked at those as well.

'At least there's no goblins,' he said as he slashed at a thorn tree, slicing clear through its base, sending it tumbling to the side. The dense forest at the shoreline thinned as they drove deeper into it. It soon cleared, and they were walking around in low grass. Harry sheathed his blade.

'Now that Harry has graciously led us through the thorns, I think we can spread out,' said Uma.

'What do we do if we find anything?' asked Harry.

'Just yell,' said Uma, brazen as ever.

'But that might draw the attention of you-know-what.' He eyed the imposing fortress.

'Live a little,' said Uma. 'And quit your worrying. 'We've come this far, haven't we?'

Gil *humphed* and Harry rolled his eyes.

The crew dispersed, fanning out in all directions—eager to search for treasure, but always aware of the fortress, which seemed to watch over them, its tower looming in the distance.

Harry went towards what looked like a jungle. Desiree

lingered at the thorny grove, while Uma and Gil headed towards the castle's base, where smaller trees grew amidst tumbled stones.

Harry hacked his way into the jungle. They were looking for a trail. Most of those were on the ground, he thought, but the earth here was covered in a thick layer of underbrush, and the trees grew so closely together he had to press each branch aside with his shoulders while he hacked at the ferns with his cutlass, his hook gathering up what was shorn and tossing it aside. Each time he cleared a patch of ferns or some other jungle plant, there was nothing resting beneath it—nothing that looked like a path, at least.

He turned to see if Uma and Gil had made any progress, but they had disappeared into the rocks. He wiped the sweat from his brow and wondered if this was all just a waste of time. The jungle was too dense; they'd never find a trail here. Maybe they needed a new strategy. He turned, following the path that he had already cut through the forest, hoping to find Uma and the others.

On his way back, he hacked at a particularly old and tangled branch, one he had pushed aside when he'd first come through. The branch fell, leaving a slender stump dangling from the face of the tree. There was a cut below the stump, and at first Harry mistook it for the stroke of his own blade. But he had been making slender cuts that went from side to side. This was something altogether different. It was a carving. When the clouds cleared and a bit of light shone through the canopy, he noticed that it formed a distinct pattern.

'I've found something!' he called out, loudly but not too loudly, still concerned he might draw the goblins' attention. A moment passed. He glanced up at Maleficent's fortress, wondering if hundreds of the crafty little creatures were watching him.

chapter 26

Secrets and Lies

Mal shifted her weight from foot to foot as the four of them stood on the rug in Fairy Godmother's office, where just yesterday they had surrendered their evil talismans. They definitely weren't those heroes anymore. She had a sinking feeling in her stomach. This was the exact opposite of what she had intended to happen when she'd taken on Arabella's problem. She'd only meant to help a friend, but she'd gotten them all in trouble in the process.

'I'm sorry, guys,' Mal whispered.

Evie put an arm around Mal. 'It's okay.'

'We're all in this together,' said Jay. 'We go down as one.'

'I just hope we're not really going down,' said Carlos.

Fairy Godmother finished locking the door and stood in front of the group. She stared at each of them in turn with a frosty glare. 'What is the meaning of this? Outside of school property and past the security gate down at Belle's Harbour! The rules are there to keep you kids safe, you know.'

Mal grimaced as Evie and Carlos looked chagrined, but Jay tried for a winning smile. 'You see, Fairy G, we were—'

'Hush!' said Fairy Godmother, putting up her palm.

'We were just—' said Mal softly.

'Hush!' said Fairy Godmother again.

They all began to talk all at once. 'We were night-swimming!' said Jay.

'We saw in the Magic Mirror that . . .' said Evie.

'Auradon is in danger,' said Carlos.

'Uma can't win!' cried Mal.

'One at a time!' said Fairy Godmother.

Once again, they all started to speak at the same time.

'You go ahead,' said Mal to Evie.

'No, you go,' said Evie to Carlos.

'You explain,' said Carlos to Jay.

'I will,' said Jay. 'Well, you see, Fairy G, it's like this . . .' he began.

'Stop,' said Mal. 'I know what you're about to say.' Jay was an experienced and practised liar, and no doubt he'd already come up with a good story and was fabricating some details in his mind.

'You do?' asked Jay.

'Whatever it is, it's not the truth. And I think we need to tell the truth tonight,' said Mal, sticking her hands into her jacket pockets, her shoulders slumping in defeat.

'Are you sure?' said Jay.

'I would prefer the truth,' said Fairy Godmother, sounding amused for the first time that evening.

'I'm sure,' said Mal.

Fairy Godmother nodded. 'Also, I must inform you that this is a very serious offence indeed. Stealing something that doesn't belong to you goes against every rule we have in Auradon. I'm afraid if you are found guilty of such a crime, you will all be expelled from Auradon Prep and sent back to the Isle of the Lost.'

'Sent back!' cried Evie.

Carlos went pale.

Jay gulped.

Mal balled her hands into fists, frustrated. They were only trying to help. Uma was out there, and the trident was within her reach—not to mention the reach of all the other villains who were searching for it.

'So, yes, I dearly hope you have a good explanation for this.' Fairy Godmother crossed her arms, still holding her wand like a weapon.

Maybe it was time to come clean, and confess all—Arabella's mischief, the missing trident, and their plan to recover it.

'You see, Fairy Godmother . . .' said Mal. She was just about to admit everything, when who should burst into the office but the King of Auradon himself.

Ben entered the room wearing a dusty regiment uniform, Jane at his heels. Before Mal could say anything more, Ben held up his hand. 'What's going on here?' he asked. 'Mal? What happened?'

'Oh! Ben,' said Fairy Godmother. 'I'm so glad you're here! We have a situation.'

'I can see that,' said Ben mildly. 'Someone care to tell me what it is?'

'Fairy Godmother caught us in a restricted area by Belle's Harbour,' said Mal. 'On the royal speedboat.'

'I see,' said Ben, frowning.

'They were in the middle of stealing it,' said Fairy Godmother, her voice rising an octave. 'This is exactly what we feared when we let villains into Auradon.'

I can explain, Mal mouthed when the headmistress wasn't looking.

Ben held his elbow with one hand and scratched his chin with the other. 'Actually, Fairy Godmother, they were doing nothing of the sort. They weren't breaking any rules. They were down at the harbour because I sent them there.'

'Right, we'll put them on the first boat back to the Isle of the Lost . . . wait, what?' said Fairy Godmother. 'Excuse me? What did you say?'

'They weren't doing anything wrong. Mal, Evie, Jay and

Carlos were on a secret mission for me, which is why they were on the royal speedboat. Because I told them to take it,' said Ben firmly. 'And that's why they couldn't explain what they were up to: because they knew it was confidential.'

'They were on a secret mission for you? Did I hear that correctly?' Fairy Godmother cupped an ear.

Ben yelled into it. 'Yes!' He exchanged a meaningful look with Mal.

'Ben, you don't have to do this,' she whispered.

'Of course I do,' he said. 'I can't let you guys get in trouble when you were only doing this for me.' He turned away before Fairy Godmother could get suspicious.

'See, Mum?' said Jane. 'I told you they weren't doing anything wrong!'

'And may I ask what the secret mission is . . . ?' Fairy Godmother still looked unconvinced.

'Unfortunately, it's council business,' said Ben. 'Top secret information that could compromise the safety of the kingdom. You do understand.'

Fairy Godmother sighed and finally relented. 'Of course. If you say so.'

'You have my word,' said Ben. He walked over to Mal and slung an arm around her shoulders. 'I don't know what I was thinking, sending you guys on such a dangerous assignment alone. We'll do it together.'

'I'm so sorry I meddled,' said a contrite Fairy Godmother. 'But I'm so relieved as well. I was quite distressed about expelling you,' she told the four friends. 'I couldn't believe my eyes when I found you.'

'It's all right,' said Jay with a grin.

'Don't worry, Fairy Godmother. All is well,' said Ben.

'I'm glad to hear it. I hope I didn't disrupt your, um, mission,' said Fairy Godmother, still mystified.

'Not at all,' said Ben.

She turned to the four villain kids. 'Well, then. It appears I owe you four an apology. I'm so sorry to have assumed the worst.'

'Quite all right,' said Evie. 'It looked bad.'

'So bad!' said Carlos.

'The very worst,' said Jay. 'Speedboats are expensive, aren't they?'

'We're sorry we couldn't tell you the truth,' said Mal. 'Are we dismissed?' she asked hopefully.

Fairy Godmother nodded. 'If the king agrees,' she said.

'I do,' said Ben.

'Dismissed,' said Fairy Godmother.

The six of them left the headmistress' office, but no-one said a word until they were safely in Ben's study. Mal found she could breathe again when they were inside the plush, opulent suite, with its magnificent desk against the window and the gym equipment in the corner. Jay wiped his forehead and flopped down on the nearest couch. 'Phew! That was close!'

'Too close,' said Carlos, taking a seat next to him.

'I agree,' said Evie. 'Thanks for rescuing us, Ben.'

'How'd you get back here so fast?' asked Mal.

'Jane called Merlin and told him to zap me back here immediately. At first, he was worried about using such dramatic magic, but she was able to convince him that it would be my wish given the circumstances,' said Ben with a smile. 'That felt weird, I've got to say. Not sure I have all my molecules back. Am I missing any part of me?' he asked, patting himself down.

'You look complete to me,' said Mal, laughing in relief. She turned to Jane. 'You are awesome,' she said, giving Jane a quick hug.

'Thanks,' said Jane, shrugging. 'But I knew whatever it was my mother was mad about, it was probably just a misunderstanding. You guys can't be sent back to the Isle of the Lost!' Mal noticed Jane sneak a look at Carlos as she said this and Carlos beamed.

'Did you get your work done, though?' Mal asked, turning to Ben. 'Were you able to get the villagers on both sides of the wall to agree to the terms of the truce?'

'Yes, thanks to Lonnie,' he said. 'We were just about to return to Auradon when I was pulled away. She's taking the jet home in a bit. So fill me in. Why were you guys taking the boat in the first place?'

'It's my fault, I was the one who suggested we steal it. Never again,' said Jay. 'From now on, I'm going to follow every rule to the letter. I'm walking the straight and narrow path!'

'Well, now that we don't have to steal the boat, can we get back there, actually?' said Mal. 'Ben, I'll fill you in on the way. But right now we've got a trident to find.'

chapter 27

Treasure Hunt

Uma would never admit it, but the Isle of the Doomed gave her the creeps just as much as it did Harry. She'd lost him somewhere around the forest of thorns, but heard his call and made her way back to where she saw him last, finally coming upon him in the middle of a clearing.

'Tell me you've found the trail,' she said, Gil right behind her.

'Nope, nothing like that,' said Harry.

'Oh, so you got bored and gave up, did you?' she accused.

'Stop grouching. Follow me.' Harry led them to what

he'd found. There, carved into the bark, a symbol glimmered in the evening light.

'What is it?' said Uma.

'A crescent,' said Harry.

'Or maybe it's a moon,' Gil added.

'A crescent *is* a moon,' Harry snapped. He traced the mark with his finger. 'The professor didn't make a map, Sophie said, because he thought it would be too dangerous to leave around. But he had to have some way to figure out where he'd kept it.'

'You think this is it? This mark?' Uma asked.

'Shall I grab the shovels?' Gil asked.

'I don't think this symbol marks the treasure. Remember, we're looking for a trail. The path isn't on the ground. It's written on trees. If I'm right, there are more of these markings. Follow them, and we'll find the treasure,' said Harry.

'Or we'll find out where two lovers carved a heart in some tree,' said Uma.

'Are you trying to tell me something?' Harry joked.

'That I'll cut you if you don't find the treasure chest?' Uma snorted. 'There's nothing here that says *trail* to me.'

'Fine, you've got a better idea on how to find this thing?' Harry said.

Uma shook her head reluctantly. 'It's just there are a lot of trees, and it's not exactly easy to get a look at their bark.'

'I know, I had to hack off a branch to find this one, but

I think that's the point. The trail is hidden. It's not *supposed* to be easy to find.'

And it wasn't. They searched trees and shrubs, rocks, and moss. They cut aside branches and sheared the leaves off of bushes.

'I'm beginning to feel like a lumberjack,' Gil whined.

'And I'm—' Uma stopped.

'What is it?' Harry asked.

'About to give up. That was what I was going to say, but look here.'

Her toe had hit a rock. A small sun—a rough circle, ringed by radiating lines—graced its surface. 'I think our professor had a chisel,' said Uma. 'It's a sun, and I think that last one *was* a moon. This might be a trail after all,' she said. Now her spirits were lifted. The impossible suddenly seemed a tad more possible, though they had found only two symbols. It wasn't exactly a trail, but it was a good enough start.

'Two points make a line,' said Uma, 'so let's look this way and that and see if there is another marker that aligns with these first two.' She stood at a spot midway between the two marks and pointed in either direction. Gil went one way, Harry the other, hacking his way into the jungle as he went.

The third mark was easier to find than the second. It wasn't exactly in line with the first two, but it was close enough, so Harry found it relatively quickly.

'It's a star,' said Uma when she caught up to him.

'We're on the right path,' said Harry. 'Three marks: the sun, the moon and a star. Just like the symbols on the wizard's hat. It cannot be a coincidence.'

As the crew drove deeper into the jungle, the marks were more difficult to unearth, hidden as they were among tangled branches or scratched on stones half covered by clumps of moss. And the trail bent in every direction, not following a straight line, but curving to and fro, making it difficult for the pirates to judge where they might find the next mark.

Branch after branch fell to the earth. Stones were overturned. They made a royal mess of the island, but there was no-one there to complain about it. And Uma doubted the goblins would mind, although she still hoped they wouldn't notice all the noise. They followed the celestial markers. There were stars of all different types, and even a few constellations carved into the trees and rocks, but at last one symbol stood apart from the rest.

'This is it!' said Harry. He was kneeling in a clearing, brushing away some scattered leaves from the earth as Uma approached. Over his shoulder she read the words TOPS EHT SKRAM X deeply scrawled into the hard-packed dirt.

'Is it telling us to scram?' asked Harry, reading the text.

'I do feel like getting out of here. That fortress gives me the creeps.'

Uma shushed him. 'It must be here. This is the spot. There's an *X*! Pirates love them. It's highly piratical.'

'Yen Sid is a sorcerer, not a pirate. And this is a bit clichéd, if you ask me,' Harry said.

'I didn't ask you,' Uma replied, looking around, trying to discern what import the message held.

Harry stood and put away his sword.

Gil wandered over from the other side of the clearing and looked at the message upside down and backwards. '"X MARKS THE SPOT"!' he declared.

'You're a genius!' said Harry.

'Let's not go that far,' said Uma. 'It's written backwards. Even brats can figure out this code.'

'But you guys didn't,' Gil pointed out.

'Who cares? It was hard enough just finding this thing—let's start digging,' said Harry, removing the shovel that he'd strapped to his back. He whistled for the rest of the crew, who came running, clanking through the jungle, picks and shovels at the ready. 'We found it!' he told them. 'Dig!'

'Where?' said Gil.

'On the *X*, just like it says,' said Harry. 'Makes sense, right?'

They dug, shovelling dirt and stone, and the pit grew larger and deeper. Harry and Gil were down in the hole as it grew in width as well as depth, but they didn't find a treasure chest.

'I knew this was too easy,' said Harry as he climbed his way out of the hole. They had dug exactly on the spot the *X* had marked, but they'd found nothing. 'There must be more to it. I mean, any random goblin could wander through the forest, find the *X*, and dig this thing up.'

'You're right,' Uma acknowledged. 'The professor would never have done something so obvious. He hid his symbols well, so clearly he hid the chest just as well.' She looked down at the symbol. 'Wonder why he wrote the words backwards. I mean, it's not much of a code.'

'What if it's not a code?' Harry offered.

'What do you mean?'

'I mean, what if it's a direction of some sort,' said Harry.

Gil was already ahead of them. He had turned around backwards and walked to a place where two trees grew at strange angles. One tipped to the right and the other to the left. Together they formed an *X*.

'There it is!' Uma saw the *X* formed by the trees. If she turned so the hole was at her back, this tree was exactly in line with where the carving had been. So once more, they drew shovels and thrust them into the earth, digging as fast as they could.

chapter 28

Twisted Mysteries

Harry dug furiously by the X-shaped trees, forming a pit that was too small for anyone else to stand in when the sound of steel striking wood echoed in the hole. 'I think I found it!' he crowed, his entire body covered with mud.

Uma ran to the edge of the pit, Gil at her shoulder. 'You found it?' she asked, sounding as if she didn't quite believe it.

'I did!' he said, hitting the shovel on the ground again, this time with an extra-strong wallop. That was when the ground gave way underneath his feet and he tumbled down into the darkness.

Harry flailed in the air, barely hanging on to his hook. He was falling, the wind blowing in his face. He nearly retched. His stomach heaved. He was weightless and then he wasn't. With a great splash, he struck water. He had fallen a good distance, and he did not hit the water lightly.

'It might as well have been concrete,' he mumbled, splashing around.

He was in a great underground lagoon, black as night and as still as ice on a frozen lake. Harry frantically tried to keep his head above water. A pair of light trousers and a thin shirt would have been useful in such circumstances, but pirates wore neither, and Harry's heavy clothes threatened to draw him down. He threw off his jacket and paddled to the shore. At least he *did* know how to swim.

Harry checked for injuries—water can break bones after a fall from such heights—but he was intact. His back stung from when he'd struck the surface, but that pain would fade. Only his pride was truly damaged—he'd landed in the ultimate belly flop. Luckily, no-one had been around to see it.

His eyes slowly adjusted to the darkness, but there wasn't much to see. He could not even make out the far side of the lagoon. Harry looked up and found only an enveloping darkness.

He was trapped. 'Help!' he cried. 'Help! I'm down here!'

But there was nothing but silence. Where was everybody?

He reached an area of rocks at the edge of the lagoon

and tried to get some kind of hold on the muddy walls surrounding him, to find some kind of footing, but it was too slippery, and he fell back in the water every time. 'Hey! Anyone up there? Help!' he called again.

Ominously, from the darkness, he heard a sound that was all too familiar.

Tick-tock, tick-tock.

Maybe after all this time, Harry would get his real hook at last. He found he wasn't looking forward to that possibility as much as he'd imagined.

'Get me out of here!' He scrambled against the slick mud walls, trying to use his hook for leverage, but it kept slipping off the surface. Harry was about to panic. It was dark and the lagoon was deep. He could not see the far side, so he dared not try to swim across it. He was stuck here at the rocky edge of the water, clambering for a foothold.

Tick-tock, tick-tock.

Once old Tick-Tock got a taste of him, he was sure to want more.

He fumbled over more rocks, tripped, and hit the water. He stood and tried again, feeling his way through the darkness.

Tick-tock, tick-tock.

Closer and closer.

Harry ran backwards, splashing across the narrow edge of the lagoon, but the sound only got louder. It was all around him. There was no use in running. Nowhere to hide.

Nowhere to go. So he did the first thing that came to mind: Harry shut his eyes and prepared to be chomped.

A moment passed.

Tick-tock, tick-tock.

That terrible ticking persisted, but no crocodile arrived. He waited for the titanic jaws to close around his head, for the forelegs to clamp his neck, but nothing touched him. There was only darkness, the water, and the rocks.

He stepped back, and his foot touched sand. It was dry and sturdy. The hole he'd fallen in was larger than he'd realised. Out of the water, he followed a sandy beach, stumbling in the dark, hoping his head wouldn't smash into some unseen wall.

Tick-tock, tick-tock.

The sound hadn't been coming from the water: it was out on the sand somewhere. Harry had a good idea what was making it, so this time he ran towards it.

The cave opened into a wider space where a hole in the distant ceiling sent shafts of light streaming into the cavern like golden spears. They faintly illuminated a great pile of discarded objects, including an old alarm clock.

'So that's what made all that ticking,' he said, though there was no-one else within earshot. Now that he thought about it, the tick-tock had been a bit too loud to be the tick-tocking of the clock the old croc had swallowed.

Harry rooted through the pile, finding glass canisters

full of strange and wondrous items: NEWT'S SPLEEN read one, EAGLE EYES another. There were candlesticks and candelabras, silver snuffboxes, crystal balls, iron cauldrons, and bloodstained tarot cards. He threw each and every piece aside until at last, beneath all that junk stood a treasure chest, exactly as Sophie had described.

He grabbed it and tucked it under his arm, just as he heard his name being called.

'Harry!' Uma said, materialising in the darkness, holding a torch above her head. He almost jumped out of his boots at the sound of her voice.

'You all right?' said Uma. 'We didn't know where you went. All we saw was this crumbling hole in the ground. It collapsed just after you fell through it, but we dug it out again. We tried calling to you, but you didn't answer, so we just climbed down after you.'

Harry grinned. 'Yeah, I'm all right. Thanks, Captain.'

She smiled, and Harry realised it was the first time he'd fully acknowledged that she was captain and meant it.

Behind her was the rest of the crew, ropes coiled around their shoulders. 'Ooh, what's that?' Gil said, seeing a skull in the assemblage of magical items.

'Don't touch it!' cried Uma, but it was too late.

A whirling red cloud shot out of the skull, and the pirates cowered, fearing the worst. But the red mist only turned into a butterfly and dissipated.

'Phew,' said Gil.

'Don't touch anything else!' barked Uma. 'Leave it all alone!'

'Look,' Harry said. 'I found it.'

'The treasure chest!' Uma cried. 'Open it.'

Harry set the treasure chest on the ground gently. All of them gathered around it, Harry and Uma, Gil, and the rest of the pirates. They'd come far and risked much to find this little chest. All of them were eager to see its contents.

'Ready?' Harry asked.

'Ready,' said Uma. 'Show me my mother's necklace.'

Harry pried the lid of the treasure chest and it opened with a great creak.

And that's when all the skeletons appeared.

chapter 29

Rivals

Ben didn't argue against Mal's urgent assessment of the situation. Whatever it was, it had to be dire if Mal wanted them to hurry like that. 'You guys go,' urged Jane. 'I'll keep an eye on things over here and make sure my mum doesn't meddle again.'

'Thanks, Jane,' said Carlos. 'You saved us.'

'It was the least I could do,' she said, flushing pink. 'Now go, run. Go do what you need to do.'

Ben commandeered the royal racer, the fastest car in all of Auradon, and they all crowded into it, which was kind of a problem since it was built for two and the backseat was designed for carting either dogs or picnic baskets, and certainly not three friend-size bodies.

'You guys all right back there?' he asked, taking the wheel with Mal in the passenger seat.

'Sort of,' said Evie, who had the advantage of being small and flexible, while the boys contorted themselves to fit in the space.

'Not really!' said Carlos. 'Please hurry!'

'That's my neck!' said Jay, who had pretzelled himself behind the driver's seat.

Ben drove them back to the marina, and Mal filled him in as promised on the loss of the trident and the Uma situation.

'Everyone on the Isle is really looking for this?'

'That's what Evie's mirror showed,' said Mal. 'And if anyone could find it, it's Uma. Knowing her, she won't give up until she's got it.'

'Why does she want it so badly?' Ben wondered aloud.

'I don't know, probably because she thinks she can finish the job I was supposed to do, with Fairy Godmother's wand I mean. You know, get rid of the dome and free all the villains,' said Mal. 'She's probably even taken over my old territory by now.'

'Your old territory?' asked Ben, amused. 'What were you, some kind of boss lady?'

'Not some kind,' interrupted Jay. 'THE boss lady of the Isle.'

'Shush,' said Mal, a bit embarrassed about her past as one of the most feared villains on the island. 'That was before.'

But Ben looked at her admiringly. 'Of course you were the best boss lady. I wouldn't expect anything less.'

She had to admit it had been fun, terrorising the citizens of the Isle of the Lost, Jay and the rest of the thugs by her side. 'Let's just say everyone avoided getting on my bad side,' Mal said proudly, feeling just a tiny bit nostalgic about the old days.

'Or else!' said Jay, raising his fist and hitting the roof with his head. 'Oof!'

When they arrived at the harbour, the royal speedboat was just as they'd left it, as if waiting for their return. Ben jumped off the deck and onto the speedboat's helm, helping Mal and Evie aboard. The boys followed right behind.

Jay bowed and motioned towards the wheel. 'Your Highness,' he said jokingly, but with a hint of seriousness as well.

'You can drive this thing, right?' Mal asked Ben.

Ben nodded. 'I should, I've been taking lessons all my life.'

'Princes,' Jay said, rolling his eyes. 'So many lessons.'

'Archery, horseback-riding, sailing, boating, swords-and-shields, dancing, manners, etiquette, statesmanship,' said Ben, counting them off in his head.

'Is there anything you can't do?' asked Carlos, curious.

'I'm sure there's a tonne of things I can't do,' said Ben.

'I sort of doubt it,' said Carlos.

'Where are we headed?' asked Ben, as Carlos and Jay saw to pulling off the ropes that secured the boat to the dock.

'Evie?' asked Mal.

Evie pulled out her Magic Mirror. 'Yup, it looks like the trident is still under the waters by the Isle of the Doomed, over on the far side of Goblin Beach. I can see the dome shimmering.'

Ben nodded and the boat pulled out of the harbour. The waters were calm by Auradon Bay, but became rockier and harder to navigate once they reached the Strait of Ursula.

A fine mist coated the Isle of the Lost, and everyone had to hold on to the handles on the side on the boat, lest they be thrown into the water by the increasingly large waves. 'Over there?' asked Ben, as they came closer and closer to the foggy mist.

'Yes! To the left!' said Carlos, yelling to be heard above the crashing waves and the distant roar of thunder.

'How are we going to slip through the barrier?' asked Evie.

'We're not going to,' said Mal. 'Ben, just get us as close as you can.'

Ben steered towards the edge of the mist.

'I see Goblin Beach!' called Jay. 'Right through there.'

'Evie, how are we doing?'

Evie checked the mirror. 'We're getting closer. But I'm worried someone else could get to it first.'

'Hurry,' urged Mal, as Ben accelerated and zoomed forwards. The speedboat jumped through the waves.

'We'll get there just in time!' said Carlos, navigating with Jay.

Mal felt the usual excitement and adrenaline of a well-matched competition. This was just like when she used to race her toad against Uma's for all the dirty candy in Ursula's shop. Except this time, the winner didn't get toad pee all over their hands.

chapter 30

Skeleton Island

The skeletons came out of the darkness, descending from the sky like ghosts, their calcium-white bones glistening in the light of Uma's torch. They danced in the black, their limbs making herky-jerky motions up and down, bobbing as they walked.

Gil screamed and fell backwards, splashing water everywhere. Uma thought one of the skeletons might have struck him with its sword. Harry bent to check for wounds, while the skeletons drifted closer, dipping up and down, their feet hardly touching the ground.

What magic was this? Uma was confused. How was

this all happening? And now there were more skeletons, descending from the dark reaches of the cavern's ceiling, a place so distant that not even her torchlight could reach it.

The crew formed ranks, drawing their swords and readying one another for the fight, but their faces were as white as the skeletons. This was a hardened crew, but none of them had ever seen anything like this, not even Uma.

'Gil's okay,' said Harry.

'Just a bit of wounded pride,' said Gil as he shook the water from his hair, stumbling backwards to avoid the approaching skeletons. They were all retreating, but the lagoon was at their backs, so with each step they took, they were forced to walk deeper into the water. This could only go on for so long before they'd need to stop and fight.

But the skeletons didn't pass the water's edge. They hung there, waiting, their twirling swords and nodding heads tempting the pirates into battle. Uma had never been one to turn down a fight, so she rallied her crew and stormed the beach. 'At my back, you cowards.'

Shamed by her courage, the pirates called out battle cries and emerged from the water, splashing onto the beach.

Uma swung at the nearest skeleton with all her fury, hoping to nick a bone or perhaps to break a rib or two but instead its entire rib cage shattered, sending bones flying in all directions, landing in the water with a hundred different splashes.

Encouraged by her success, she struck the next skeleton, this one at the neck. The spinal cord popped in two, the body falling limply to the sand, but the head stayed where it was, bobbing in the air. It *had* to be some kind of magic, but she could barely make out anything besides the skull floating in the air. She struck it with her sword and it just rolled to one side, swinging back and forth like a pendulum, rocking like a child on a swing.

'It's on a rope,' she said. Uma slashed at the darkness above the skull, severing the cord, sending the head tumbling onto the beach. A quick inspection revealed a whole series of thin black ropes that were tethered all over the skeletons. Some mechanism must have been jerking them up and down, back and forth, like marionettes on a string.

'They're not alive!' Uma said. 'It's not magic! It's just a trick! Keep moving!'

'There must be some machine up there, embedded in the cavern's ceiling,' she said. The black strings were nearly invisible in the dark cave.

Harry nodded. He was going over the fallen skeleton, inspecting the ropes, some of which were still connected to the machine. A severed hand leaped upward from the beach, dangling in his face, sword still in its grasp. Harry slashed at the cord and the arm fell limply to the sand, but the whole thing was unnerving.

By now, the rest of the pirates were all slashing at the ropes. But they could only cut so many, so the dead continued their dance. Pieces of broken arms and legs kept jerking about in the air.

'I never thought they were alive,' said Harry, as he pushed against a skeleton, sending it swinging away. But it swung right back, hitting him so hard it knocked him to the ground.

'Maybe, but they don't need to be alive to take you down,' Uma joked.

Even if these were mechanical skeletons, their blades were real enough that they could still do damage.

'Be careful,' she cautioned her crew. 'Cut the ropes, watch out for the swords, and someone fetch me that torch. We need light!'

One of the crewmen retrieved the still-flaming torch that Uma had dropped near the water's edge. He held it high above them all, revealing at last an elaborate web of strings and cables, all of them disappearing upward towards the cavern's ceiling.

In spite of their increased illumination, Harry got his hook wrapped up in a skeleton hand. He twisted to and fro before finally getting so caught in the cables he fell to the sand. Gil was doing a little better, having wrestled one of the skeletons to the ground and stomped all over its bones. He slashed the ropes when he was finished. The rest of the crew howled their battle cries, as they took down the cables.

Uma growled, annoyed that it was taking them so long

to escape. It was a booby trap. Which meant there were others.

'Keep cutting strings!' she ordered. 'And try to do it with a bit more organisation.'

Taking her advice, the pirates went about cutting the ropes in a more coordinated manner, moving down the line, slashing just above the heads so the skeletons would fall limply to the beach in a single cut. One after another they dropped to the sand, a great pile of bones and cords forming at their feet.

As the last skeleton fell to the ground at last, a low thrum echoed in the darkness.

'What was that?' she cried, as an arrow struck the stone next to her. An inch to the right and it would have split her head in two.

The soft whistle of bowstrings reverberated in the darkness. All the pirates had hit the sand after seeing the first arrow, flattening themselves as best they could as the barrage sailed over their heads.

'When we cut that last skeleton it must have triggered some new part of the mechanism,' said Harry.

'I guessed as much,' said Uma. The real question was, what was coming next? It was clear the sorcerer had no intention of letting anyone take what was in that treasure chest. Some of the pirates had already stood, but Uma heard a distant clicking—and a winding sound.

'Duck!' said Uma, and the pirates slammed once more onto the sand, covering themselves with their hands, or whatever else they could use for shields, from a new assault of arrows.

'The machine rewound itself,' said Uma. 'It paused after the first volley, just to trick anyone who was clever enough to avoid the first, before it sent out another attack.'

'So what do we do now?' asked Gil. 'I can't stay here with my face pressed in the muck.' Indeed the boy's knees were sunk in the water, and his face was dabbed with mud. Most of the pirates weren't in much better shape. All of them were wet. And only half had made it fully out of the water before they'd had to drop.

'Listen,' said Uma.

'To what?' asked Harry.

'To the silence. The machine stopped.' She motioned for everyone to stand. One by one they lifted themselves from the muck, their feet making terrible slurping sounds. They were wet and dirty but alive.

Uma took a deep breath. The machine had stopped, but she doubted they were out of danger yet. 'Come on!' she said, leading them towards a narrow finger of light in the distance, indicating a way out of the cave.

She took a step towards it, and felt something tense and release beneath her foot as the earth shifted. From a distance, she heard an ominous rumbling.

'I think I triggered something,' said Uma. 'The machine's going again.'

Dust sifted downward from the ceiling, followed by a low thunder that nearly shook her to her knees. Rocks fell from the cavern ceiling, and they could hear stones breaking all around them.

'The cavern's collapsing!' Uma cried, but by then they'd all figured it out. This must be the final trap, the one that would seal them in the cave with the treasure chest forever.

The sorcerer had obviously been serious about the safety of these formerly magical objects. Even without magic at his disposal, he had successfully created obstacles that would deter even the hardiest and greediest goblin.

But Uma was no goblin, and she was determined to leave the Isle of the Doomed with the only inheritance she would ever receive from her mother's past.

'Run!' she called.

'Already there!' said Harry, at her side, Gil puffing not far behind.

Uma waved her cutlass in the air. 'Follow me!' she said, leading the crew towards the light. All around them, stones pelted their heads. The air was already filled with dust, but a light shone faintly in the distance so they ran towards it. The very earth beneath their feet was collapsing as they went, and the walls were falling behind them.

Uma was the first to make it to the cave's mouth, but she

stayed there, waiting for each member of her crew to pass. The captain was always the last to leave, after all, the one who went down with her ship. She would not budge until the last pirate was out. Luckily the pirates were a frightened bunch, so they ran like children, tumbling over one another to get out of the cave as quickly as possible. Uma stepped out of the cavern just as the last stone broke, and the ceiling collapsed entirely, forever trapping whatever was left in there.

'We made it,' she muttered, stating the obvious, as she stumbled out onto the sand, her hair caked with dust and tiny stones. Harry brushed a rock off her shoulder.

In a panic, she looked around. All she saw were pirates, shaking the mud from their hair and brushing it from their clothes.

'Where is it? The treasure chest?' she demanded. In all the confusion—in their sheer desire to get out of there—had they left the one thing they had come to find?

Harry tapped her on the shoulder.

What did he want? He didn't have it either!

But he reached underneath his arm and revealed what he had been carrying the entire time. The treasure chest.

Without hesitating, Uma flipped open its wooden lid. There was an old yellowed envelope inside. Uma pulled it out.

'"Ursula," ' she read, examining the spiky handwriting on the envelope.

Then she shook out the contents onto her palm. There it was, her mother's seashell necklace, except it was in a hundred tiny little pieces. 'I forgot it was broken.'

'Nothing a little island sludge can't put back together,' said Harry. 'Come on. We've got a bucket of the stuff back on the ship. It's stronger than glue; it'll work.'

chapter 31

Pirate's Booty

Fitting each of the pieces of the broken seashell together was like trying to put together a puzzle without any reference as to what it should look like. They knew it was a shell, but they had no idea where this ridge or that one should fit. It took patience and attention to detail, and they'd just fought a band of skeletons, dodged arrows, and escaped a disintegrating cave. No-one was in the mood for a bit of jewellery repair. But there was no time to waste, so they set themselves about the task—clearing a great table and making certain it was clean before Uma placed the envelope's contents upon it.

'How do we know we even have all the pieces to this thing?' said Uma, frustrated.

'We don't,' agreed Harry. 'But if we give up now, we'll never find out.'

'Shush,' said Gil, who was placing each piece back together with a delicacy the others hadn't known he was capable of. They had to trace the edges of each piece, looking for ridges and bumps that matched another piece or a streak of colour that ran from one fragment to the next. It was subtle work, almost impossible. Harry threw up his hands more than once, and Uma twice had to take a walk out on the deck to let loose a bit of frustration. They all took turns at the task, but it was Gil, oddly enough, who stuck with it, supervising the whole thing. The work was painstaking, until Gil finally made an announcement. 'Okay,' he said, 'we're missing one piece.'

'Honestly?' muttered Uma.

'It might have fallen under the table,' said Harry. 'Everyone look!' He stood and knelt on the floor to see if he could find a tiny gold piece. Gil, Uma, and the rest of the crew did the same. They looked everywhere and even sent some of the crew back to the beach to see if one of the pieces had fallen out when Uma first opened the envelope. They found nothing.

Perhaps it was lost in the sea, thought Uma.

She recalled her mother telling her about that final

battle. How Ursula had called the great waves, urging them to skyscraper-like heights, and how she had blown up to a thousand times her size—a large, laughing octopus, larger than the ship, loud as thunder. How she had cursed them all, wreaking havoc on Prince Eric's ship, and aiming to drown all aboard.

Except Prince Eric had taken the wheel and rammed his ship right into her heart, right into her necklace, scattering its pieces all over the ocean. Uma always held her breath at that part of the story, wondering how it was that her mother had survived such a battle. Because even though she'd lost, she'd survived. Prince Eric hadn't destroyed her completely.

And here was the necklace.

Here was hope.

A way out of this island prison.

A way out of stagnation and broken dreams, endless routine, and a future that went nowhere.

Harry was shaking his head. He slammed his fist against the nearest table, sending the plates and cups jumping. 'It's not here.'

He'd given up, and Uma felt the same pain run through her. It just wasn't fair, to come this close only to be missing one miniscule little piece.

Uma took the seashell in hand and looked at it carefully. 'Maybe we don't need the missing piece,' she said. It was a chip barely larger than a hairline crack. That was all.

'I don't know,' said Harry. 'It looks incomplete.'

'What about your locket?' asked Gil. 'Didn't you say there was something in there?'

Uma gasped. She'd almost forgotten about the locket she always wore. What had her mother said when she'd given it to her? *It's all I have left.* All Ursula had left of what? They were about to find out. Uma swung the chain over her head and held it out so everyone could see it. Then she carefully pried open the top with her fingernail. It flipped up with a snap, revealing a sliver of gold.

'That's it!' said Harry.

'I think it just might be the last piece,' said Uma. It looked to be the right shape, but she wouldn't be sure until they'd fit it into place. Her heart skipped a beat as she lowered it into the opening.

It fit perfectly. 'Gil, sludge me.'

Gil handed her the bucket of sludge, and they all watched, holding their breath, as Uma glued the final piece onto the shell. She could have sworn there was even a flash of light, but maybe it was just the gold reflecting off the moonlight through the window.

It was done. The shell was complete.

'There,' Uma said with satisfaction. 'I think that's it.' She studied her handiwork. The shell glittered in her palm—history, legacy, and tragedy in each curve of its shape. She held it up for everyone to see. 'Ursula's necklace!' she cried.

'Put it on,' said Harry.

She nodded, undid the clasp, and draped the necklace over her collarbone. The gold was warm against her skin, and she felt a faint echo of its former power. It had the sense and shape of her mother's wrath. One of the greatest treasures of the sea, and it was in her hands.

'All right?' said Harry.

Uma nodded. 'I can feel it,' she said, holding the gold seashell between her pointer finger and thumb. 'It's almost like it's alive.'

'Excellent,' said Harry. 'Where to, Captain?' he asked, a hand on the wheel.

Uma whispered to the seashell, 'Find me the trident.'

She felt the shell tilt slightly to the right, like a compass, just as Cook told her it would. The necklace and the trident, as the most powerful objects from the underwater kingdom, were linked. Drawn to each other like magnets.

'West,' she said. 'It's due west of us.'

'West it is. To the trident!' cried Harry. 'Avast, me hearties! Flip up the jib! Haul anchor! Let's go!' he ordered, rushing around.

'To the trident!' cried Gil. 'Um, what's a trident?' he asked.

Uma took the scope and looked through the lens. In the distance, she could see Auradon, the mainland. *Soon*, she thought. Soon she would have Triton's trident, and she and her crew would be off this cursed island forever.

Showdown

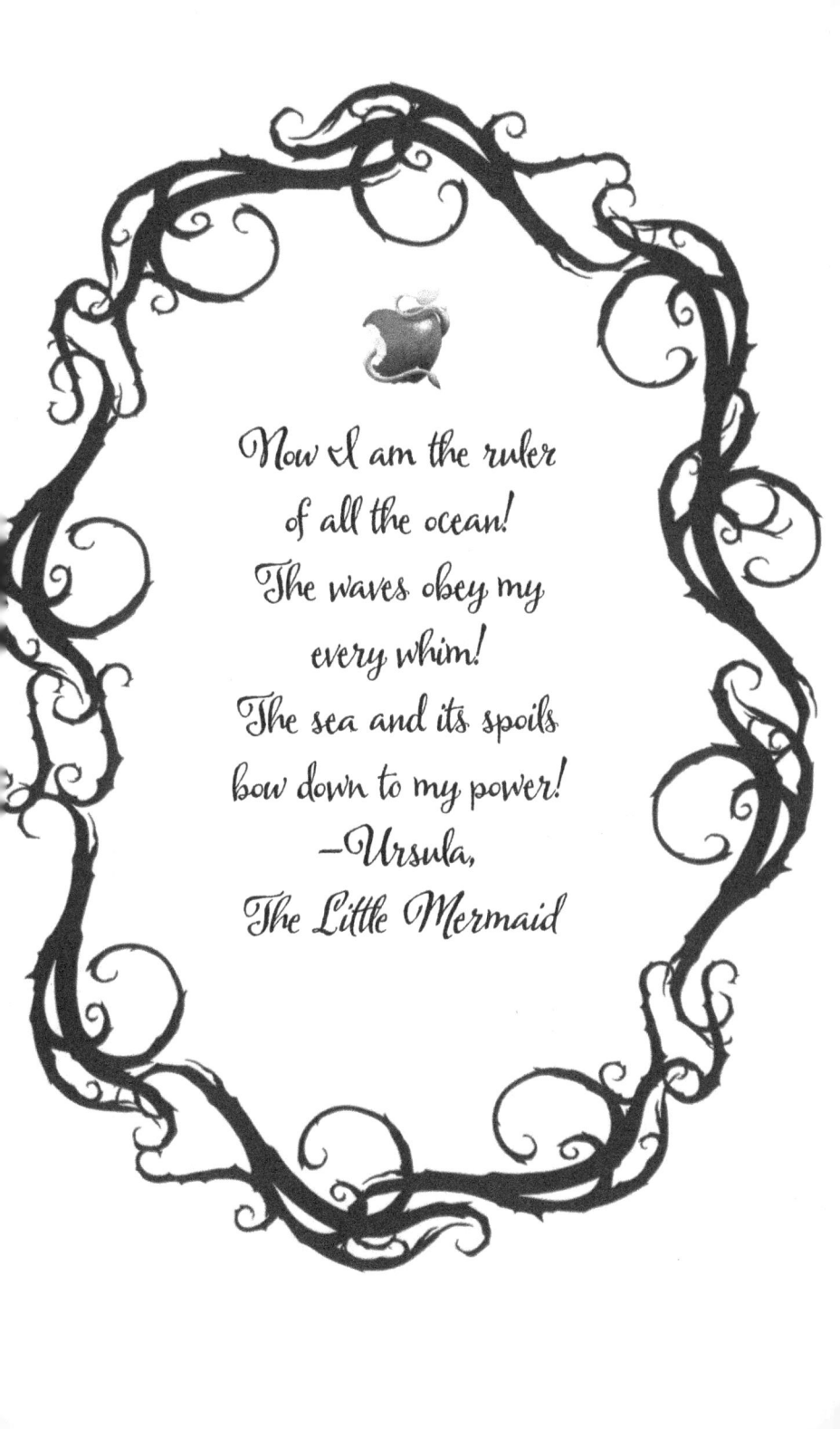

Now I am the ruler of all the ocean! The waves obey my every whim! The sea and its spoils bow down to my power!

—Ursula,
The Little Mermaid

chapter 32

Into the Deep

Uma scanned the horizon. Countless waves dotted the sea, crashing higher and higher, curling into whitecaps, the wind catching the water and throwing it into the air. The sky was dark with clouds, but even so, she thought she saw something in the distance, headed towards them from the opposite side of the bay—the Auradon side. She thought it might be driftwood at first, but it was moving quickly against the wind. 'Do you see something over there?' she asked, focusing on a small dot that she could barely make out through the wind and fog.

Harry picked up a telescope. 'Yeah, I see it. It's on the other side of the barrier, and it's heading towards us.'

Uma gnashed her teeth, annoyed at this unexpected arrival from an unknown party. 'What does it look like?'

'I don't know. We'll need to get closer, but it must be some sort of boat,' said Harry.

'They're moving against the wind, which means they've got a powerful speedboat of some kind,' said Uma.

'But why are they here and why now? Fishing? No-one ever comes this close to the Isle of the Lost. All the Auradon folks like to stay on their side of the channel,' said Harry. 'They know what's good for them.'

'I don't think they're out here to fish,' said Uma. 'It's not exactly fishing weather.' The waves were taller now, and each time they struck them, the ship was cast upward, then quickly set down again, loudly thumping into the gap between the waves before the next one hit and sprayed the deck with water. All in all, it was miserable progress, but at least they were moving quickly. Just not quickly enough for comfort. Uma took to the telescope to monitor the progress of the boat they'd spotted. She had a bad feeling about this.

Worse, it began to pour. The skies cracked with thunder and all around them the air darkened as raindrops pelted the ship.

'Harry! Can't you make us go faster?' she ordered. The

necklace kept tugging towards the right, and it appeared the trident was somewhere close by. But Goblin Beach was almost endlessly long.

'Aye, aye, Captain,' said Harry. 'I believe we've done all we can, short of throwing over any excess cargo. A light ship is a fast ship, if either of you would care to jump over the side? Or maybe I can make the wind blow a bit harder?'

'Well, if anyone can do it, you can,' said Uma.

'I'm on it,' said Harry, raising his chin and mockingly blowing towards the sails. 'There,' he said. 'Now I've done everything.'

Uma balled her fists in annoyance. In truth, she knew Harry had done everything possible to get them moving as quickly as their sails would allow. They were cruising at a considerable clip to the other side of the island, but so was the other ship—and there was no doubt now that they were both headed to the same place. Plus she didn't need the telescope to know it was moving faster than they were.

'It's below there,' said Uma, as the necklace in her hand began to heat up. 'I can feel it. We're at the right place. Can you get us closer?'

Harry squinted, measuring the distance. 'Too many rocks for this big a ship, and with all the sails unfurled we're moving too fast to navigate those waters. We'll have to anchor and take out the rowboat.'

He stowed the sails as quickly as possible, while Gil

tossed out the anchor. They had to fiddle with it a bit, waiting until the great hook caught hold of the sea bottom. The rope snapped tight, and they were moored.

Harry indicated a small boat with only a pair of paddles. 'That's our ride, if you want your trident. It's the only way into those rocks,' he said.

It didn't look promising, but it was all they had, so Uma, Harry and Gil clambered into the rickety boat, and Harry and Gil rowed Uma closer to the edge of the beach. The rocks made it difficult to navigate, and since both of the boys were facing the wrong direction, they had to rely on Uma to tell them which way to go.

'Right!' she exclaimed, but the boat went left. 'My right, you idiots,' she said, correcting them. 'Left now, just a bit. Now right again.' Uma had to stand at the bow and push off the rocks to keep from colliding with them. It was a veritable maze and they were forced to go this way and that, back and forth. At points the rocks were so dense they had to stop paddling altogether. All Harry and Gil could do then was push off manually against the stones.

'Come on, faster,' said Uma. 'This is taking too long.'

'You're welcome to get out and pull us,' huffed Harry, straining with exertion.

Uma frowned, but she got up and pushed against the rocks as well until they were clear, finding themselves in a circle of clear blue water not far from the beach. She stood and glanced down into the depths, spotting something gold glinting through the seaweed.

King Triton's trident!

Her heart leaped with wicked glee. 'This is it!' she said, readying to dive down and take it.

The trident was hers!

chapter 33

Power and Glory

The Isle of the Doomed loomed larger and larger through the mist as they got closer to their destination. Mal had forgotten how foreboding the mysterious island looked, especially with Maleficent's fortress built right on the top of the tallest cliff, casting gloomy shadows everywhere.

'Hurry!' said Mal urgently, as Evie checked her mirror.

Jay scanned through the fog, just as it began to rain. 'Look!' he yelled, as a huge pirate ship came into view on the other side of the beachhead.

'Uma!' cried Evie. 'She's already here!'

'Ben! Faster!' urged Mal.

'I'm trying,' said Ben. But it was hard to navigate the three-foot-tall waves, and all of them were drenched.

'Turn left again!' said Carlos, tracking the trident's possible location on the map and attempting to navigate the rough waters.

Ben steered the boat left, and they all leaned forwards and tried not to fall off.

'Uma's found it!' yelled Evie, as she watched Uma stand up from the little rowboat. 'She's diving for it!'

'No!' cried Mal. 'She can't have it! Ben, come on!'

Ben zoomed the boat over to an inlet by the Isle of the Doomed. They couldn't see anything in all the fog and rain, and as he turned the boat, it crashed against the barrier. 'This is as close as I can get us,' he said, trying to keep his eyes open against the howling wind and rain.

'Mal, do it now!' said Carlos.

'Jay, take the wheel,' said Ben, as he jumped to the boat's hood, balancing himself as it was rocked by the waves. He offered a hand to Mal. 'Come on!'

Mal climbed up from the dashboard next to Ben, holding her spell book tightly. Waves lashed against the boat, and it was hard to stand upright. She stumbled, but Ben caught her. 'I've got you,' he said, his hands steady against her waist.

She shot him a quick smile and opened the book to the spell she needed. A simple one—even a child could use it. *'Spark and fire, elf and gnome, open up this invisible dome!'* she cried. For a moment nothing happened; then a small, pinprick-size hole appeared in the invisible barrier. It grew larger and larger until Mal was able to thrust her arm through the unseen wall.

'It worked!' she said, laughing in relief.

'Get the trident!' yelled Ben.

'Too late!' cried Evie, watching the mirror. 'Uma's got it!'

Mal wanted to curse, until she realised creating a hole in the dome meant that she could use a little magic within the barrier for a change. And a little magic was all she needed. She checked her watch; it was not yet 15 after the top of the hour.

'Time and tide, wind and night! Turn the clock back to the top!' she chanted, and time went backwards for everyone else just enough to give Mal time to grab the trident before Uma could lay her hands on it.

'Whoa, what just happened,' said Carlos, confused.

'Mal turned the time back; it's okay, you'll get used to it,' said Evie. 'Mal, now! Uma's back on her boat, she doesn't have the trident yet!'

Mal opened her palm. She'd written the spell on her own, and hoped it would work. *'Demon heart and all things abhorrent, bring me the sea king's missing trident!'*

But no trident appeared, only more sheets of rain.

What was going on?

It turned out a little bit of magic was all her opponent needed as well, and with the hole in the barrier still open, Uma was tapping into a power of her own. She stood on the rowboat and held a golden seashell necklace, which glowed in the darkness.

'Uma's using Ursula's necklace—it's pulling on the trident, too!' said Evie, watching the mirror intently.

Mal's spell and Uma's necklace each drew the trident, causing a magnetic force that roiled the seas, angering and confusing the waves. The wind lashed with fury, and rain stormed on the water.

Mal wiped her hair from her eyes. She was soaking wet and shivering in her leather jacket. Lightning struck the skies, thunder rolled, and the waves got bigger and bigger, threatening to overpower the speedboat. They wouldn't last out here much longer. She had to get that trident away from Uma.

Evie was almost thrown overboard, but Carlos caught her hand in time. 'One hand for you, and one hand for the ship,' he advised, as the skies cracked open overhead once again.

'Bring me King Triton's trident!' Mal called, her arm straining across the barrier. She felt the power of the spell through her body as she bent her will towards recovering that trident from the ocean floor.

From afar, she could see the golden trident as it wavered in its rise towards her enemy. It stalled, floating in the ocean, then slowly began to wrench towards her.

'It's working!' yelled Evie.

The energy around their boat crackled as the necklace

and the spell fought for supremacy over the trident and the trident moved towards the speedboat.

'To me!' Mal cried, using every last ounce of her will and magic to bring it forwards.

It jerked towards their boat, just a hairbreadth away.

But at the very last second, the trident twisted around, moving closer to the Isle of the Lost, closer to Uma.

chapter 34

Evil Enchantment

Magic! What was this? There was magic in the air. It crackled with furious energy. Uma could feel it emanating from the seashell necklace and pervading the very atmosphere around her. She had no idea why it was there, or how it happened, or why she had a strange, vague memory of swimming down to the bottom of the sea and actually placing her hands on the trident, but she could feel magic all around her and she knew exactly what to do.

Uma held up her mother's necklace. 'Bring me Triton's greatest treasure!' she called, and she held up the necklace a bit higher. For a moment, she felt the wind swirl, picking up the necklace and twirling it around her fingers. The sky darkened to a deeper shade of grey and the boat pitched back and forth. Water splashed the deck.

There was a loud *boom* as thunder rolled. Lightning lit the sky with streaks of white and blue. A cool wind swept the boat, and Uma felt the presence of something otherworldly. The necklace and the trident called to each other. She felt the pull; it was all around her.

The very air vibrated with power, and the seashell became hot in her hand, glowing fiery through her clenched fist. Light emanated from the shell, turning her face a pale shade of orange, making her fingers glow. The wind blew her hair off her shoulders.

'What's happening?' said Gil, as the orange glow of the seashell grew brighter and the power Uma sought drew nearer. Soon all of them were lit in shades of red and orange. The light pulsated, washing over them in waves.

'I can feel it!' Uma called. 'It's coming up!'

A vortex formed in the water, a churning, swirling funnel, and there was something at the bottom of it.

Harry peered over the side of the boat into the dark depths. 'There!' he cried.

Uma looked down, and she could almost see it, the tip of the trident emerging from the bottom of the vortex. There it was, twinkling gold . . . just out of her reach . . .

Closer . . .

Closer . . .

Closer . . .

The trident was rising now, flying out of the water. It was nearly within their grasp. The wind howled, and the rain poured down. The water spun in a furious circle, threatening to draw them down into it, just as the trident came near. The boys whooped in victory. Against the wind and the current, they paddled towards the trident, but the boat pitched violently, side to side, dipping and leaning as the wind and waves cast them to and fro.

'Grab it!' cried Harry. 'I can't keep this up much longer. In a minute, we'll capsize and then we'll be swimming.'

'Or sucked down into that vortex,' said Gil.

Uma ignored their pessimism. The trident was all she cared about. The shell glowed wildly; the trident rose. They were close now, terribly close—but as Harry warned, they were just as close to falling into the water as they were to catching hold of the trident. Uma wouldn't celebrate until that golden staff was safely on board. None of them would.

'Do it!' Harry cried again. This time they were finally at the trident. They rowed as near as they dared, fighting the current, trying to stay upright as the wind whirled and the water twisted around the mighty golden spear.

'This is it,' said Harry.

'We're close enough,' said Uma. Through the dark fog she could make out the shape of a speedboat on the other side of the barrier. She was sure its occupants had come for the trident too, but they were too late.

Uma had reached it first.

There it was, rising, like a phoenix from the ashes. Triton's greatest treasure. It would be hers!

She reached out—it was only a few more feet away . . . inches . . . All she had to do was grasp it . . .

chapter 35

All for One

Mal felt the prize slipping away from her, but at the very last second, she chanted the spell again, forcing her immense will on the trident. Suddenly, it hurtled towards her like a missile.

Mal gasped as the trident slammed into her palm, and she clenched her fist around it. It jerked and twisted in her grasp, and Mal could see powerful energy waves around it, attempting to pull it in the opposite direction. Mal tried to hold it with both hands, but the energy from Uma's necklace pulled off her left glove, sending it soaring away.

Mal yanked the trident through the hole in the barrier. 'I've got it!'

'The barrier!' Carlos reminded her.

'Elf and gnome, close this dome!' she yelled, and the hole in the invisible barrier shut with a snap. The magnetic energy around the trident immediately disappeared, and her hand dropped suddenly as the tension vanished. The shock of it sent her flying into Evie, who fell overboard.

Mal clutched the trident and crouched on top of the boat, searching the churning ocean. 'EVIE!' she screamed. 'EVIE, NO!'

Jay steered the boat around the waves as they frantically searched for their friend.

'EVIE!' called Jay.

'Evie, come on!' yelled Carlos.

Come back to me, Mal thought fiercely, hanging on to the edge of the railing. *Come back, Evie.* She wished so hard, she thought her head would explode; still there was nothing but the raging sea and the crash of thunder and lightning.

'You guys,' said Jay. 'The storm is just getting stronger. We're going to sink.'

'I think I saw her over there!' yelped Ben. 'Circle around!'

'EVIE!' Mal cried. 'Where are you?'

But still there was nothing. The largest wave they'd ever seen rose from the ocean and slammed hard onto the boat, throwing them against each other.

'I can't keep us afloat much longer!' Jay cried.

Just when it seemed they were going to capsize, Evie emerged from the water, her arms flailing. Mal was spent from using her magic, and fell limply against the railing. 'Help her! I don't know what to do,' she cried, keeping a tight grip on the trident.

But her friends picked up the slack, moving with precise urgency. 'We're too far away for her to swim,' said Ben. 'Quick, Carlos, grab a life ring. Jay, you have the best arm, throw it to her!'

Ben took the wheel of the speedboat while Jay tossed the orange floatie as far as he could. 'EVIE! GRAB IT!'

Evie caught the ring with one hand and held on, keeping her head above the waves.

'PULL!' yelled Ben, steering the boat as Jay and Carlos tugged mightily on the rope, bringing Evie back despite the waves and the rain, inch by inch, until at last she was floating by their side.

'Evie! I thought we'd lost you!' Mal cried joyfully, tears of relief falling down her cheeks and mingling with the rain as she leaned over to help Carlos and Jay haul her back onto the boat. 'Are you okay?'

'You're okay, you're okay,' said Carlos, smacking Evie's back to help her cough up seawater.

'Here,' said Jay, handing Evie a warm towel he'd run to grab from belowdecks and helping Carlos drape it over her shoulders.

Evie leaned on Mal, still shaky on her feet. 'I'm okay, thanks to you guys.'

Mal gave Evie a tight hug. 'I don't know what I would do without you! Don't ever scare me like that again!'

'You scared all of us,' said Ben, letting Jay steer the boat once more. 'That was intense. But you got it, Mal?'

'I got it,' she said, handing him the trident.

'We did it,' Ben said.

'We did it,' she said, not quite believing it, as Ben held the golden trident in his hands.

'We did it together.' He nodded. Then he turned to Jay, who was back at the wheel. 'Come on, let's get out of here before we sink.'

chapter 36

Lost Revenge

'Where did it go?' yelled Uma, as the trident disappeared right before her eyes, and she was thrown backwards onto the rowboat, falling hard on her back. Her hat tumbled off her head, and she scrambled to catch it before recovering her balance. 'Where's the trident?' she screamed, looking for it on the floor of the boat, even though she knew it was gone.

Lightning flashed overhead, and waves crashed against the boat, dumping water all over them. The necklace's chain had snapped, and she almost lost hold of it. The rain was relentless, and the whirlwind doubled its speed, spinning them around in a dizzying spiral, obscuring their vision.

'Do you have it!' cried Harry. 'Uma! Where's the trident?!'

Uma scanned the waters frantically but saw nothing. 'It was mine!' she howled. 'I almost had it! It was right there!'

'Where?' yelled Harry. 'I don't see anything!'

'I don't know!' she yelled back.

'Do you have it or not?' screamed Harry, as six-foot waves roared and crashed over the little dinghy. He had to fight to hold on to the oars and steer the boat back to the *Lost Revenge*.

But Uma was too dazed to answer; she was still trying to get back up and resume her balance.

'Gil!' Harry cried, just as the boat lurched upward and slammed back down, throwing Gil overboard.

'Where's Gil?' yelled Uma, trying to be heard above the whistle of the wind.

'I don't know! He fell over!' cried Harry, as he lunged to grab an oar that had slipped from its hold, before it could be lost to the sea as well.

Without hesitation, Uma jumped off the boat and into the churning water to save Gil.

Harry saw a brown hat bobbing up and down in the froth. 'He's over there!'

'Help!' screamed Gil, scrambling in the waves. 'Help!'

Gil went under, and Harry feared the worst—but suddenly, Uma's turquoise head appeared by his side. Slowly but surely, she swam them back to safety.

When they reached the dinghy, Harry leaned over and hauled them both back aboard. Gil coughed and choked and spewed water all over the deck.

'Ew,' said Uma. 'You're welcome.'

That was too close. They needed to get back to the ship if they were going to survive, so she motioned for the boys to start rowing. Fighting against the thundering waves, the pouring rain, and the howling winds, they finally reached the *Lost Revenge*, where the other pirates threw a rope ladder down the side.

'Captains first,' Harry said, giving a hand to help Uma climb the rope.

Uma nodded and hoisted herself up. Gil went up next, and Harry last.

The crew was vainly trying to keep the ship upright as it lurched wildly from side to side, at the mercy of the roiling, angry sea. Uma, Harry, and Gil ran to the decks, helping to hold the sail, while trying to stay away from the boom—which was swinging wildly with the wind—as well as all three masts, which were threatening to break and splinter. The storm raged around them, pouring rain all over everyone and everything.

'Let's get out of here!' yelled Harry. 'We need to go back! The storm's too strong!' He took the wheel of the ship and brought it around, making for the Isle of the Lost.

But as the *Lost Revenge* reached its destination, the waves pounded against the hull, finally sending the mast crashing onto the deck, and the sails tore as it slammed right against the dock, tearing up the deck plank by plank.

Shipwrecked.

When the storm had passed, and the ship was still, the pirates groaned and assessed the wreckage. It was clear to Harry that the *Lost Revenge* would never sail again. The damage to the hull was too great.

A fine, light rain continued to fall, adding to the gloom.

Harry sighed and removed his black tricorn hat to squeeze the water from it. But he was too exhausted to be angry, and too relieved to still be alive to feel disappointment.

He looked up to see Uma standing in front of him, a confused and shocked look on her face. 'I had it. I saw it, Harry. It was right there. I almost held it in my hands. The necklace worked, and there was this huge surge of magic for a moment—almost as if something had opened a hole in the dome.'

'So what happened?' asked Harry.

'There was someone else there, some kind of magic,' she said. 'That's the only explanation.'

'You're holding something,' said Harry. 'In your hand.'

'I am?' said Uma, wonderingly. She looked down, surprised to find that Harry was right. She was holding on to something she hadn't noticed in all the commotion.

'Yeah, what've you got?' asked Gil.

Uma looked stunned to find she was holding a purple

fingerless glove with a dragon symbol embroidered on the kidskin. It could only belong to one person.

'MAL!' Uma raged, when she realised it had been none other than her fiercest rival who had been on that speedboat.

Harry had no idea why or how Mal was there at the same time they were, but there was no denying it. Mal had Triton's golden trident now, and Uma had nothing but a purple glove.

'MAL! You don't always get to win!' Uma screamed in fury.

'I think she just did,' said Gil. 'Didn't she?'

'Shut up, Gil,' said Harry, sighing as he put his black tricorn hat back on his head.

chapter 37

No Place Like It

It was almost dawn when they returned to Auradon Prep, and Mal thought she'd never seen a sight more beautiful than the grey stone towers of the school turning pink in the sunrise. No matter that Auradon still didn't feel one hundred percent like home, she *was* home in Ben's arms. 'Thanks for being there for me,' she whispered.

'Always,' he said, nuzzling her hair.

He gave her one more hug, then went to help the boys dock the boat in the harbour as they pulled into the bay. Evie went over to where Mal was seated and leaned her head on her friend's shoulder. 'Thanks for being there for me,' she said, echoing what Mal had said to Ben just moments before.

Mal leaned her purple head against Evie's and told her what Ben had said in return: 'Always.'

'That was close,' said Jay, as he helped them climb out of the boat. 'I didn't think we would make it.'

'But we did,' said Mal.

Jay flashed her a rueful smile. 'You know it,' he said, giving Ben a fist bump.

'Um, guys? I think we want this, right?' said Carlos, who'd gone to fetch the trident they'd left in the back of the boat.

Ben asked Arabella to meet them at his office, and the little mermaid practically burst into tears when she saw the trident leaning innocuously against a bookshelf.

'You did it!' she said to Ben, obviously not quite believing it was true. 'You got it back!'

'We all did,' said Ben with a smile, offering his hand to Mal.

Mal took it and offered her hand to Evie, who linked hands with Carlos, who took Jay's hand too. 'Ben's right, we all played a part,' she said. 'I couldn't have done it without any of these guys.'

Arabella thanked them profusely. 'I'll make sure it gets back to Grandfather and the museum right away.'

Ben turned to her with a serious look on his face. 'Arabella, I hope you already know what I'm about to say to you.'

She blushed as red as her hair. 'I know, King Ben. I know. I'll never steal anything again, I promise. Fairy Godmother's right, magic is too dangerous to use.' Humbled, she curtsied to Ben and left, holding the trident tightly in her hands.

'Arabella will be okay,' said Mal. 'I don't think she'll ever get near that trident again.'

'Speaking of the museum. You guys do know that all magical artifacts belong there for safekeeping,' Ben said with an embarrassed cough.

'You mean even my Magic Mirror?' said Evie, looking worried.

'And my spell book?' said Mal. The two girls looked askance at each other.

'I guess we should hand them over,' said Evie reluctantly. 'I do keep reminding Mal that we're not supposed to depend on magic.' She removed the mirror from her purse and handed it to Ben.

'I'll make sure the curators get this and keep it somewhere safe,' he promised. He turned to Mal expectantly.

Mal shrugged. 'I left my spell book in my room,' she told him. 'But don't worry, I'll make sure it gets to the museum.'

'Great,' said Ben. 'I don't know about you guys, but I think I'm going to sleep for the entire day.'

'We'll get out of here,' said Mal, and Ben hugged each one of them as they left, holding Mal extra tightly. She closed the door behind her with a smile.

When they were walking down the hallway, Evie nudged Mal. 'He's a good king,' said Evie.

'The best,' said Carlos.

'You know it,' said Jay.

'Yeah, I think I'll keep him around,' said Mal. She and Evie said good night to the boys and headed over to the girls' dormitory.

Mal sat on the edge of her bed, chewing her thumbnail. 'What's wrong?' asked Evie.

Mal sighed. She was glad Auradon was safe once more, and that they had defeated Uma, but she was still embarrassed about almost getting all of them kicked out of school and sent back to the Isle of the Lost. She'd seen the horror and fear in her friends' eyes, and while she might still feel the tug of home, she knew they felt otherwise—especially Evie, who loved Auradon. She also had to take her position as Ben's girlfriend more seriously. What she did reflected on him, on his reputation, and on his ability to govern the kingdom.

She wasn't the girl from the Isle anymore. She wasn't

just Maleficent's daughter, tagging King Beast's posters with spray paint and generally kicking up a ruckus. But she wasn't an Auradon princess either, who knew exactly how to act at every royal occasion.

If she wasn't Mal from the Isle anymore, who was she?

Later that afternoon, Mal grabbed Maleficent's spell book from her locker. She intended to walk it over to the Museum of Cultural History at some point before classes started the next day. She flipped through its well-worn pages, softly caressing each spell.

It was one of the only things she had left of her mother's, and she was loath to part with it. There was so much knowledge and wisdom in its pages. The time-turning spell had helped them retrieve the trident after all. Plus, there were so many more that she loved to use. Hair spells, which had proven popular with the female segment of Auradon Prep, love spells, and anti-love spells. There were spells that brought luck or great fortune, and even a few that could turn a girl from the Isle into an Auradon princess, or a close facsimile of one. Spells for every aspect of life, truly. And while Mal understood why it had to go to the museum, that didn't mean she wanted to surrender it.

Still, she had promised Ben, and if Evie, who cherished her Magic Mirror as much as Mal treasured her spell book, could voluntarily give that up, then she could give up her book. Mal tucked it under her arm, determined to head to the museum before she changed her mind.

But as she walked across campus, Mal realised that while she still wasn't sure exactly who she was, she did want to make Ben happy and explore the kingdom by his side—even if the idea of all the royal events coming up made her feel just a little ill. She turned on her heel and ran all the way to her room.

'E?' she said, bursting through the door and glad to find Evie at her sewing machine as usual.

'Yes, M?' asked Evie, looking up from her task.

'I think I need some help,' she said. 'I've got a kingdom to meet.' She counted herself lucky to have Auradon's most promising young fashion designer as her best friend and roommate. Mal decided she wanted to make a splash, and not the watery kind that left her looking like yesterday's yams.

'Do you think you could make me look more like them?' Mal asked, motioning to the wall of princesses on Evie's pin board. She wanted to look as smart as Belle, as beautiful as Cinderella, even as sweet as Aurora—but she wanted to maintain something of herself as well.

'Ooh! Yes!' said Evie, clapping her hands. 'I have so many ideas. Plus, I want to show you this fabulous dress I made you for Cotillion.'

'Great!' said Mal, picking up a thick fashion magazine and riffling through the pages. 'When's Cotillion?'

'Oh!' said Evie. 'Ben hasn't asked you yet?'

'Asked me what?' said Mal.

Evie smiled mysteriously. 'You'll see.'

chapter 38

Something There That Wasn't There Before

Over at his homeroom, Carlos leaned back in his seat, his exams arranged on his desk. All of them boasted A-pluses, as well as effusive praise from his teachers in the margins. *Brilliant!*—Professor Merryweather. *Astounding*—Genie. Even crotchety old Grumpy, who was teaching a seminar on Cooperation, had drawn a happy face on Carlos' paper.

Carlos smiled in satisfaction at a job well done. He was looking forward to the next semester. There were so many new elective classes to take: Language of the Stars, Enchanted Oceanography and the Politics of the Palace, just to name a few. After having the usual fight with the registrar over his need to take over the maximum amount of classes allowed for the term, he bumped into Jane, who was wearing a brand-new blue-and-gold Auradon cheer uniform.

'You did it!' he said. 'You made the team! That's awesome! Congratulations!'

'I did! Thanks so much!' Jane said, a huge smile on her face.

'What did I do?' asked Carlos.

Jane punched him in the shoulder. 'You're the one who said I should try out and not give up!'

'Aw, shucks. Anyone would have told you the same thing,' he said, looking down and shuffling his feet as his ears turned pink.

'But you did,' said Jane. 'So thank you. Are you heading that way?' she asked. 'I have to meet Ben in a few minutes.'

Carlos, who had been heading in the exact opposite direction, said 'Yes,' just so he could walk with her a little more.

'So everything worked out okay?' asked Jane. 'With that secret mission?'

Carlos nodded. 'Yeah, it did.' He wished he could tell her all the details, but he knew it was safer for everyone if only the five of them plus Arabella knew what had happened. 'It all worked out okay.'

'Good.' Jane looked up from behind her fringe and

smiled at him, and Carlos felt something in his heart that hadn't been there before. Something more than friendship. He couldn't stop smiling; his cheeks started to hurt.

But before he could say anything about it, Audrey ran up to them. The bossy princess looked harried. She was carrying a huge cardboard box in her arms. 'Jane! Just the person I've been looking for!' she declared.

'Oh, hey, Audrey,' said Jane.

'I'm so glad I found you. I need a lot of help,' said Audrey.

'What's up?' asked Carlos.

In the background, they could hear Chad sobbing. 'Audrey! Audrey, don't do this!'

'Ignore him, he'll be fine,' said Audrey, rolling her eyes. 'Jane, we're really glad to have you on the team, and you're sure you can handle Cotillion duties, too?'

'For sure!' said Jane.

'Great,' said Audrey, and she dumped the box on Jane. 'That's all the planning we've done so far. You're going to have to work closely with Mal, since it's her big debut. Although hold on, I don't think Ben's asked her yet, so she probably has no idea she has to do all this. So maybe remind Ben he's got to formally ask her.'

'He's working on it as we speak,' said Jane.

Audrey didn't respond, and tapped her pen against her forehead, thinking. 'What else? Oh, and do you have a date yet? Just curious.'

'No,' said Jane. 'Not yet.'

Carlos blushed and tried to look somewhere else. He'd heard vaguely about Cotillion, but hadn't realised that it was a date type of situation. So far at all the balls and parties, everyone went as a group, even Mal and Ben.

'Oh,' said Audrey, looking condescendingly at Jane. 'It's okay if you don't.'

'I know it's okay,' said Jane, rolling her eyes and struggling under the weight of the box. 'Carlos?'

'Yes!' he said hopefully, standing at attention.

'Will you help me bring this box back to my dorm?' she asked sweetly.

That was so not what he expected to hear, and Carlos' smile wavered a little. But he rallied. 'Of course!'

Jane doesn't have a date for Cotillion.

One day at a time, he thought.

chapter 39

Oh Captain, My Captain

It was the afternoon of the final R.O.A.R. tryouts. Carlos had already won his spot on the team, and now it was Jay's turn. The field was whittled down to the last four guys, and Jay crushed them all in quick succession. If he did well in the final round, he would make the cut, too.

'Ready?' said Chad, suiting up.

'Believe it,' said Jay, examining his sword.

'We'll see,' Chad said with a smirk, but he didn't have his usual overconfident tone and his curls appeared a tad wilted.

'Something wrong, man?' asked Jay.

Chad shrugged. 'Nothing. Audrey dumped me. Whatever.'

'Oh, that's too bad,' said Jay. 'Sorry about that.'

'It just doesn't make any sense!' wailed Chad, adjusting his face mask.

The coach blew his whistle to start the match. Chad tapped his sword against Jay's. 'Let's go!'

'En garde!' said the referee. *'Prets. Allez!'* On guard. Ready. Go.

'Allez,' said Jay, pulling down his face mask. He raised his sword as Chad did the same. On the balcony circling the courtyard, a group of cheerleaders and random students gathered to watch the match.

Chad came out swinging, literally, and Jay feinted and parried, advanced and attacked. If the breakup with Audrey had affected Chad, he didn't show it. Years of lessons had turned him into a graceful and formidable swordsman. But Jay held his ground, executing riposte after riposte.

'You've gotten better,' said Chad. 'But not good enough.'

Jay snorted. Chad moved left, seeing an opening, and Jay feinted right. But at the very last moment, he struck towards the left, his sword coming up underneath Chad's chin in a decisive victory. 'Touché!' Jay called triumphantly, breathing hard from exertion.

The whistle blew, signalling the end of the match.

Chad removed his face mask in annoyance. 'You cheated!'

Jay hesitated, but the coach was clapping his hands, and

there were cheers from the balcony. Jay looked up and saluted Mal, Evie and Carlos, who had come to support him.

'It's a legal move,' said the coach. 'He won fair and square. Good job, Jay. Welcome to R.O.A.R.'

Chad threw his sword and shield down on the mat in disgust.

'Thanks,' said Jay, grinning widely.

'You beat the captain of the team,' said the coach.

'Chad was captain?'

'Not anymore,' said the coach. 'Now you are.'

Chad stormed off in agony. He'd lost his pride and his captaincy all in one fell swoop.

'Good job,' said Lonnie, who'd been watching from the balcony.

'Thanks,' said Jay, pleased with how everything had turned out. He smiled when he realised he hadn't even had to steal anything to get what he wanted. He'd done it all by playing by the rules.

chapter 40

Evie's 4 Hearts

'Turn around, let me see it twirl,' said Evie, as Arabella stood in the middle of the room in her Cotillion dress. Arabella spun, and the dress floated gracefully around her ankles.

'It's gorgeous!'

'You're gorgeous in it,' said Evie, and she took a few pins, adjusted the pleats on the neckline, and fluffed the sleeves.

The dress was an exact replica of Ariel's dress, a pale lavender colour with silver accents, but with a few Evie touches—brocade instead of plain silk, a few more layers of taffeta to accentuate the waist and lace instead of satin ribbon around the sleeves.

Arabella was back to her old fun self now that the trident had been returned to the museum, and her grandfather had no inkling of the danger she had brought to the kingdom. 'What are you wearing to Cotillion?' she asked, still admiring herself in the mirror.

'I haven't even started on my dress,' said Evie. 'I haven't had any time for myself, I've had so many orders to fulfill for all the other events coming up first.'

'How did you learn to sew so well?' asked Arabella, as she removed the garment and changed into her jeans and T-shirt.

'Back on the Isle,' said Evie, putting Arabella's dress in a garment bag and zipping it up, 'I was castle-schooled. I spent a lot of time at home, and I had to amuse myself.'

'The Isle of the Lost must have been good for something, then,' said Arabella with a smile.

'Yeah, I guess it was,' said Evie. 'I'm never going back, though.'

'Of course not.' Arabella shuddered. 'Who would ever want to go back there?'

Evie nodded. The past was past, and it was time to concentrate on what the future would bring. She escorted Evie out of the door just as it opened again.

'Hi-ho,' said Doug, who'd shown up to take her to dinner.

'Hey, Doug.' She gave him an affectionate hug. 'I'll be ready in a sec, I just have to make a few more adjustments to this dress,' she said, taking out the beautiful blue-and-gold dress that she'd hidden from Arabella.

Doug took a seat at her desk and saw all the messy receipts, calculations, and dress orders. 'Is this how you're keeping track of all your clients?' he asked.

Evie glanced over and looked embarrassed. 'I've been meaning to get organised, I just haven't had time. Orders keep piling up, and I need all my free time to sew.'

'Here, let me do it,' said Doug, taking his laptop out of his backpack. 'I'll make a spreadsheet and keep track of payments.'

'You will?' she asked.

'Yeah, dwarfs are really good accountants. We have to be, with all the diamonds and jewels in the mine,' he explained.

'That would be such a great help!' she enthused, watching as he began to plug numbers into a column.

They worked side by side for a moment, Evie on the dress and Doug filing away all the order slips. When he was done he showed her the invoicing system he'd set up. 'So you just enter the name here, and then the dress here, and the amount here,' he explained.

'You are a lifesaver!' she said. 'Oh, and I came up with a name for my label.'

'Yeah?'

'Evie's 4 Hearts. You like it?' she asked. 'I got it from

Mal's spell. You know, the one that says "The Power of Four Hearts Are Better than One."'

Doug smiled. 'I love it.'

Evie sat back down at her sewing machine. Doug watched her thread a needle. 'Oh, and Evie?' he said finally.

'Yes?' she asked, the needle in her teeth.

'I've been meaning to ask, will you be my date for Cotillion?' he said nervously.

'Me?' she said coyly.

'Um, I don't see any other princesses in the room?' he said. 'Unless you'd rather go with a prince?' His shoulders slumped.

'Why would I do that when I have you?' Evie said warmly. 'Of course I'll be your date. I'm honoured. I was wondering when you would ask me, actually.'

Doug mopped his forehead in relief. 'I still can't believe you're real, that we're real. It's like a fairy tale.'

'Fairy tales come true,' said Evie with her sweetest smile.

'By the way, where were you guys?' asked Doug. 'I was looking all over for you the other day.'

Evie put away the dress and grabbed her purse. 'Oh, let's just say we had a little excitement under the sea. But we've got to hurry. Ben wants us all there in five minutes. So I'll tell you all about it at dinner.'

'Great. Oh, and I wanted to warn you, we're eating with

my dad and Uncle Sneezy tonight. I'll try and make sure you're not sitting next to him.'

'Does he always have a cold?' asked Evie wonderingly.

'Allergies,' said Doug.

chapter 41

A Second Chance to Make a First Impression

Mal's final class of the day was her favourite: Freestyle Painting, where she could do whatever she wanted. She was looking forward to working on her self-portrait, which covered an entire wall in the studio. When Mal turned the corner, she was surprised to find the classroom not only empty of other students and the usual mess of paints and canvases, but also sparkling clean and overwhelmed with dozens of flower arrangements.

'Um, what is happening?' she said, just as Ben stepped out from behind a garland.

'Mal,' he said, taking her hand with a look of adoration

in his eyes. 'Remember I wanted to ask you something?'

'Sort of?' she said, not quite sure what was happening, as her heart began to pound painfully in her chest. But as she glanced around the room, she got a better look at the flowers. It was sweet of him to have remembered that her favourites were black dahlias and bat orchids. The room was bursting with their sweet-but-spicy scents.

'Mal, will you be my lady at Cotillion?' he asked.

She looked at Ben. 'Um, okay?' she said. Ben looked so sweet and sincere kneeling before her, and of course she would do whatever he needed her to do.

'Great!' he said, folding her into his arms.

Mal smiled, looking deep into his eyes, just as hundreds of balloons fell from the ceiling and the paparazzi came out of their hiding places, dozens of cameras flashing.

'Ben, I'm so sorry, I tried to keep it a secret, but they followed you guys in here,' said Jane, wringing her hands.

'It's all right,' said Ben. 'I'm sorry they're here. I wanted this just to be our moment,' he added to Mal.

'It's okay. You're the king. Everyone wants to know what's going on with your life,' Mal said, glad that she had changed out of her torn jeans and leather jacket and worn a cute dress that Evie had loaned her as part of the beginning of her makeover.

'Oh!' she said, shielding her eyes from the glare of the flashes. She tried to pose prettily.

'Hooray!' said Evie, rushing out to give Mal a hug, followed by Jay and Carlos, who were holding even more flowers. Jane appeared to have begun berating one of the journalists in attendance.

Mal smiled at all of them, feeling as if she had just won something that she didn't quite ask for. Ben pulled her into a hug and she whispered in his ear, 'By the way, what's Cotillion?'

'It's a dance,' said Ben, waving to the cameras with kingly grace. 'You get introduced to the kingdom and officially become Lady Mal.'

Ben looked completely happy, but now it was Mal's turn to be nervous. Lady Mal? That sounded . . . fancy and serious. She'd never had a title before. Unless you counted Mal the Worst, which is what she'd been called back on the Isle of the Lost. There were so many ways to be wicked; she could dream up so many if she tried . . .

'Oh,' she said again. 'When is it?'

'Soon, but there are all these events leading up to it first, sort of wrapped up with the Celebration of Auradon. We're going to tour the kingdom, make sure you meet all our subjects,' said Ben.

Mal gritted her teeth in determination. She could do it. She would be perfect from this day forward, all the way up to Cotillion. She would play the part of royal girlfriend to the hilt. 'Ben, can I ask you something?' she said.

'Sure. Anything,' he said, kissing her hand.

'Can I move my mum out of the library and into my room? I don't think she's a threat to the kingdom as a lizard.'

Ben thought about it and smiled. 'Yeah, I think that can be arranged.'

'Thanks, Ben.'

Mal took a deep breath. Cotillion was not too far away, plus she had all those Celebration of Auradon events to accompany Ben to. Agrabah's festival was next on the calendar, so a royal visit to Aladdin and Jasmine was in the works. She was going to do her best, she promised herself, thinking of the spell book temporarily hidden back in her dorm room.

She just had to make a few changes here and there . . .

chapter 42

The Villains of Our Story

Uma, Harry and Gil stood on the deck of the shipwrecked *Lost Revenge*. Their clothes were almost dry from the storm, and they were no worse for wear. But the ship was another story altogether. The mainmast was broken, there were holes in the hull, and it was clear she would never sail again. She would be a permanent addition to the dock from now on. The three of them leaned over the railing on the topmost deck, watching the colourful, messy lives of pirates and villains unfold in the rickety wooden tenements right across from the bridge.

Uma stared moodily at the lively scene in front of her without seeing anything. She still couldn't understand what had happened out there on the Isle of the Doomed. She definitely swam down to the ocean floor and grabbed the trident—that was a memory, not a dream, she was sure. But how was it that she had ended up back on the rowboat without the trident, using her mother's necklace to call it up? And why had she lost to Mal, of all people? Mal, who wasn't even a proper villain anymore, but an Auradon turncoat. Mal, who wasn't worthy of her mother's name, let alone her legacy. Mal, who had gone soft and was dating the king of Auradon—gross. Mal, who'd beaten her once again.

It was way too painful to dwell upon, so Uma decided she'd been robbed, not beaten. That trident had been rightfully hers, but Mal had done something, used some horrible Auradon magic, and cheated Uma out of her victory.

'So what now?' asked Gil.

'Rough up goblins?' suggested Harry.

'Ooh, or taunt first-years and make them walk the plank!' said Gil.

'Uma?' asked Harry. 'Captain's choice?'

She shook herself out of her reverie. She still had Mal's glove in her pocket, but she planned on burning it in the kitchen fire soon enough. 'I've got a better idea,' said Uma.

She led them out across the bridge and into the bazaar. The stalls were full of hawkers, and she and her pirates had a fun time swiping scarves, taking things that weren't theirs, and causing the usual chaos and mayhem.

'Look,' she said, stopping in front of a puke-inducing poster of King Ben and Mal. 'Spray paint,' she ordered, holding out a palm, and Harry slapped a canister in her hand.

'Let's give him a nice little mustache and horns, shall we?' she said, drawing them over Ben's head and face.

The pirates snickered. 'There's more over there,' said Gil.

The crew vandalised every poster of King Ben that they could find, especially ones that depicted him and that Isle traitor Mal. It was a petty victory, but it did make Uma feel better, especially when she scrawled the pirates' motto all over their faces: *WE RIDE WITH THE TIDE.*

Uma examined her handiwork with a smile. Once she was satisfied that there wasn't a poster of the king that wasn't defaced on the Isle of the Lost, they headed back to their ship.

'Still, it's too bad we lost,' said Gil, leaning back on the railing with a frown. They were facing the other way now, looking out into the ocean at Auradon in the distance.

'Lost? We didn't lose!' said Uma. 'We never lose!'

But Harry's sly pirate's face burst into a grin. 'Exactly! We never really had a chance anyway!'

'Huh?' Gil looked confused, but Uma had an inkling of what Harry was trying to say.

Harry's smile grew wider. 'Come on. We're trapped here. Look up there!' he said, pointing to the sky. 'That invisible barrier? It's impossible to get off the Isle of the Lost. The deck was stacked against us from the beginning.'

Uma raised her fist to the sky in annoyance. Harry was right. They were playing long odds, betting against the house, and the house always wins. She knew that, since she and Harry ran a dice game at the fish shop every other Thursday.

'Listen, we might not have the trident, and we might not have a way off this island,' said Harry. 'But we've got a serious crew here.'

Uma looked around at the pirates on the ship—Desiree, Jonas, Bonny, even Gonzo. They were hers. A real crew.

'We've got a lot to do,' said Harry. 'So much trouble to start, eh?' He slung an arm around Uma, and another around Gil.

'Ugh,' said Gil. 'You smell like shrimp.'

'Um, that's me,' said Uma.

'No, it's me,' said Harry with a wiggle of his eyebrows. 'I just had breakfast.'

But the three of them stood there for a bit, with their arms over each other's shoulders, looking out to the ocean and to the distant skyline of Auradon. Because Harry was right. They might not have much, but they were each part of a pirate crew. And on the Isle of the Lost, that was more than something—it was everything.

'One day, when those Bore-a-don snobs least expect it, we'll pounce,' promised Harry. 'They'll make a mistake, maybe even wander into the wrong neighborhood. Fall into our net! And you know what we'll do then!' he said, making a slashing motion across his neck with his hook.

'Um, what will we do?' wondered Gil.

'We'll have our revenge,' Uma declared, her eyes glittering with malice. 'Mark my words. This isn't the end of our story. It's only the beginning.'

Don't miss the other books in the series:

acknowledgments

As ever, a huge, heartfelt, sliding-in-right-before-the-deadline thank you of gratitude and relief to my main peeps who help make these books happen: my editors Julie Rosenberg and Emily Meehan, my publicist Seale Ballenger, and our faithful compatriots at Disney Channel: Naketha Mattocks and Carin Davis. Thanks for believing!

Thank you to everyone at Disney Publishing and Disney Channel including Andrew Sugerman, Raj Murari, Mary Ann Naples, Gary Marsh, Jennifer Rogers-Doyle, Adam Bonnett, Laura Burns, Kate Reagan, Hannah Allaman, Mary Ann 'MAZ!' Zissimos, Elena Blanco, Kim Knueppel, Sarah Sullivan, Jackie De Leo, Frank (Frankie BOOM!) Bumbalo, Dina Sherman, Elke Villa, Andrew Sansone, Holly Nagel, Alex Eiserloh, Maggie Penn, Sadie Hillier, Marybeth Tregarthen, Sara Liebling, Guy Cunningham,

Dan Kaufman, David Jaffe, Meredith Jones, Marci Senders, James Madsen, and Russ Gray.

Thank you to the talented stars of *Descendants 2* who are so inspiring and always fun to watch—Dove Cameron, Sofia Carson, Cameron Boyce, Booboo Stewart, Mitchell Hope, Brenna D'Amico, Dianne Doan, Jedidiah Goodacre, Zachary Gibson, and the awesome new pirates China McClain, Thomas Doherty, and Dylan Playfair.

Thank you, Kenny Ortega, for making another fun movie!

Thank you to Richard Abate, Rachel Kim, and everyone at 3Arts. Thank you, Talia Hurst and Candy Ford for everything you do at home to keep it running.

Thank you to my family—Mum, Steve, Aina, Nicholas, and Joseph Green; Chito, Christina, Sebastian, and Marie de la Cruz, Terence, Trina, and Olivia Lim; Odette and Christina Gaisano; Clarke, Isabel and, Cailyn Ng; Sony and Badong Torre; Melanie, Maj, and Mica Ong/Calangi, and everyone in the extended DLC-Ong clan!

Thanks to Marg and Raf always.

Big love and thanks to the YallCrew: Shane Pangburn, Tori Hill, Spencer Richardson, Jonathan Sanchez, Tahereh Mafi, Ransom Riggs, Marie Lu, Kami Garcia, Brendan Reichs, Sandy London, Veronica Roth, Holly Goldberg Sloan, Patrick Dolan, and Emily Williams.

Thank you my CH crew: Heidi and Andy McKenna, Jill Lorie and Steve Stewart, Cole Hartman, Tiffany Moon,

Dan and Dawn Limerick, Carol Koh and Tony Evans, Sean Curley and Bronwyn Savasta, Gloria Jolley and Scott Johnson, Fatima Goncalves and Auggie Ruiz, Mike and Betty Balian, Saher and Bassil Hamideh, Ava and Ron McKay, Nicole and Chris Jones, Bob and Carolyn Holmes, Celeste and Patrick Vos, Jenni and Adam Gerber, and Molly and Chad Ludwig.

Huge thanks to all the rotten little Descenders!

Thanks most to everyone on our Netflix account: especially Mike, who stopped working on his book to help with mine, Mattie, the light of our lives, Mimi, loyal hound, and Summer, who's still alive (she's a beta). Mama can hang out again.

MELISSA DE LA CRUZ

(www.melissa-delacruz.com) is the author of the #1 New York Times best sellers *The Isle of the Lost* and *Return to the Isle of the Lost*, as well as many other best-selling novels, including all the books in the Blue Bloods series: *Blue Bloods, Masquerade, Revelations, The Van Alen Legacy, Keys to the Repository, Misguided Angel, Bloody Valentine, Lost in Time,* and *Gates of Paradise*. She lives in Los Angeles with her husband and daughter.

Escape from the Isle of the Lost

ALSO BY MELISSA DE LA CRUZ

DESCENDANTS
The Isle of the Lost
Return to the Isle of the Lost
Rise of the Isle of the Lost

THE BLUE BLOODS SERIES
Blue Bloods
Masquerade
Revelations
The Van Alen Legacy
Keys to the Repository
Misguided Angel
Bloody Valentine
Lost in Time
Gates of Paradise

The Ring and the Crown

Escape from the Isle of the Lost

A DESCENDANTS NOVEL

#1 *NEW YORK TIMES* BEST-SELLING AUTHOR
MELISSA DE LA CRUZ

BASED ON *DESCENDANTS 3* WRITTEN BY
**JOSANN MCGIBBON &
SARA PARRIOTT**

SCHOLASTIC
SYDNEY AUCKLAND NEW YORK TORONTO LONDON MEXICO CITY
NEW DELHI HONG KONG BUENOS AIRES PUERTO RICO

Copyright © 2019 by Disney Enterprises, Inc.
Visit www.DisneyBooks.com
and www.DisneyDescendants.com

Published by Scholastic Australia in 2019.

Scholastic Australia Pty Limited
PO Box 579 Gosford NSW 2250
ABN 11 000 614 577
www.scholastic.com.au

Part of the Scholastic Group

Sydney • Auckland • New York • Toronto • London • Mexico City • New Delhi
Hong Kong • Buenos Aires • Puerto Rico

Cover design by Marci Senders
Cover art by James Madsen
Hand lettering by Russ Gray
Designed by Marci Senders

All rights reserved. No part of this publication may be reproduced or transmitted in any form or by any means, electronic or mechanical, including photocopying, recording, storage in an information retrieval system, or otherwise, without the prior written permission of the publisher, unless specifically permitted under the Australian Copyright Act 1968 as amended.

ISBN 978-1-76066-556-2

Printed in Australia by Griffin Press.

Scholastic Australia's policy, in association with Griffin Press, is to use papers that are renewable and made efficiently from wood grown in responsibly managed forests, so as to minimise its environmental footprint.

For Mattie

And the

C.H. Class of 2025

who were there from the beginning.
Love you kids.

And for the Shallmans:

Ariana Rose
Nina Juliette
Benjamin Joseph
Jonah Samuel

Thanks for all your support!

Some Time Ago...

Rude Awakening

Once upon a time in ancient Greece, there lived extraordinary heroes and powerful gods, and the most powerful of them all was *Hades*. Yes, you read that right: *H-A-D-E-S*. Hades gazed over his divine kingdom from high above on Mount Olympus with a smug smile. Life was good. Nope, life was better than good. Life was great! No more working himself to death down in the Underworld. No more living near the smelly River Styx, no more listening to the obnoxious wails and cries of torment from the floating dead all around him. No more living in caves with demons. He had won! He was the greatest god who had ever breathed life into a flying horse! Okay, so he hadn't actually done that yet. But he would soon!

For now, he was more than content to eat plump, juicy grapes fed to him by beautiful nymphs, listen to tinkling music played on lyres and harps and lounge on a puffy cloud, while his back pocket was full of lightning bolts he could use against anyone who dared oppose him.

He sighed in satisfaction and took a bite from the nearest grape.

Then he spat it out.

'DEAR ZEUS, WHAT ON EARTH WAS THAT?!' he said, choking and gasping for breath as he looked around for water. He took a huge gulp from a dirty mug he found next to him. That wasn't a grape he'd eaten. It was a disgusting, withered raisin that was way past its expiration date! And he wasn't lounging on a cloud at all, but lying on garbage bags! The horror! The humiliation! What was this?! Where was he?!

Hades blinked his eyes. He looked all around. He was in the middle of a crowded bazaar, filled with ruffians of all kinds hawking their sordid wares. There was a tent filled with broken electronics, and another selling old furniture, the merchant sitting in a cracked bathtub. This was no Mount Olympus! Not even close!

He groaned in despair, realising he had once again dozed off and dreamed he was back where he belonged. He should be up in the sky with his fellow deities—hanging out with vain Apollo, snarky Hermes and beautiful Aphrodite . . . But in reality, he was still here. *Trapped.* Stuck on the Isle of the Lost—which certainly sounded like a region in the Underworld if he'd ever heard one—living among a bunch of filthy mortals. (Some of them might *look* like scruffy demons, but they were definitely human.)

The island was surrounded by an invisible barrier that kept him and everyone else there barred from the mainland and unable to use their powers. How long had he been here? Too long! No matter, no matter. He would take care of that soon enough. He had found something among his meagre possessions just that morning.

He might not have a pocketful of lightning bolts like his annoying brother Zeus, but he still had his ember. His greatest weapon. An ember that, once sparked, could unleash the fires of doom. He reached into his back pocket, checking to make sure it was still there. Yep. There it was, just a plain lump of coal. He had a plan. He was going to escape, and he was going to escape today.

He felt smug at the proposition. While these filthy losers had to stay here, he would be out among the gods once more! This neglected, remote island was certainly no place for someone who was practically a rock star! He was meant to be worshipped, feared and admired! Not stepped over and pushed aside by ruffians trying to get to the market before it ran out of brown bananas.

Hades left the crowded bazaar and walked all the way

out of town, to the edge of the coastline. In the distance, he could catch a glimpse of Auradon's gleaming skyline. Somewhere, over there, was his true home. Somewhere, over there, were magic and power and freedom.

He held up his ember. 'RELEASE ME!' he yelled to the skies.

The skies did not thunder. Lightning did not strike. Nothing happened.

A few residents of the Isle of the Lost walked by, but they gave him no notice. No-one even cared to watch. But Hades would show them! He was just out of practice. He warmed the ember in his hands and then held it up again.

He could feel one of his raging tantrums building. His face began to turn red all the way to the roots of his hair. He needed to get out *right now*. It was time to blow this joint. He was the god of fire and rage, a ruler of souls, one who had brought the mighty Hercules to his knees! (Well, not really—but he *almost* brought Hercules down. Almost!)

'RELEASE ME!' he commanded.

Nothing.

He tried again . . .

Nothing.

His face turned an even darker shade of crimson and he screamed his anguish towards the sky, throwing curses and hexes every which way.

But still nothing. Hades' shoulders slumped. He was out of breath and out of energy. His blue Mohawk wilted.

He looked down at the ember in his hands. It was dead. It was a piece of coal. It did not glow, nor did it burn with divine fire. It was useless.

Try as he might, and as hard as he wished it otherwise, the reality was that there was no magic on the island. And while that barrier stood, there never would be. Zip. Zilch. Nada. Which meant he had to accept it. On the Isle of the Lost, Hades was no longer a god.

He was just a blue-haired dude in a leather jacket.

Heroes and Villains

'We were so close! So close we tripped on the finish line.'
—Hades, Hercules

chapter 1

The Lady is a Villain Kid

Mal made her way across the sparkling campus of Auradon Prep, taking in the sound of chirping birds, the warmth of the sun against her face, and the sight of the tall castle walls shining with early morning dew. Although Mal wasn't about to burst into song at any moment like some of the princesses and princes who filled this place, she might as well have been singing in her heart. They'd made it! Mal, Evie and Jay were seniors now—Carlos, who was a junior, still had one more year to rule the school—and in a few months, they would graduate. They would be free to make their own futures, forge their own paths—the world was their pearl-bearing oyster.

As Mal greeted her friends who were milling about the lawns, she recalled their days on the Isle of the Lost. Not so long ago, Mal had spent her free time spraying graffiti on posters featuring King Beast's face with her signature tag: **evil lives**. Not so long ago, she had been proud of the many, many ways she was wicked. At Dragon Hall, she had been famous for her pranks, locking first-years in their Davy Jones lockers, starting epic spoiled-food fights in the cafeteria, and threatening everyone with Maleficent-style curses if they dared defy her. But it turned out that being evil meant feeling small and petty, while being good meant being brave. It meant facing your fears and standing up for the people who depended on you. Being good was so much harder and so much more satisfying than being bad. It *felt* good to *be* good. Who knew?

Now Mal was Auradon's hero and protector, ready to transform into her dragon self to defend the kingdom against any villain or monster that would threaten its shores. Life had been calm since Uma had disappeared during Cotillion. There had been no sign of that turquoise-haired sea witch so far. Mal's childhood rival had dived deep into the waves, and had not been seen since. But Mal liked to keep watch anyway. You never knew where or when the enemy would strike.

'Any sign of her?' she asked the guard, who had been stationed by the coastline to check.

'Not today,' the guard replied.

'Good,' said Mal.

When she arrived at the meeting for the Royal Council, she was the first one there. Today she was dressed simply in a matching black-and-purple shirt and skirt, her long purple hair tucked behind her ears. Gone were the days when Mal would stomp into class or any meeting place at the last minute, snarling and annoyed. She was the future Lady Mal now—bad fairy heritage, irreverent attitude, battered thick-soled boots and all. She wanted to make Ben proud of her, and, in turn, show the kingdom she was proud to wear his school ring.

Still, Mal's unexpectedly prompt appearance seemed to surprise Lumiere, who was still fluffing cushions and helping Cogsworth and Mrs Potts set out the tea service.

'Oh! Mal! You're early!' said Lumiere with a bit of a frown. As the head of the king's household, he didn't like to be caught with his candelabras down, so to speak.

'Don't mind me,' said Mal. 'Anything I can do to help?'

'No, dear. Please, be our guest,' said Mrs Potts, bustling over with two heaping plates of scones and pastries, almost dropping them in her haste.

'Here,' said Mal, taking one of the plates away from the overburdened cook and placing it in the middle of the table.

'Thank you, dear,' said Mrs Potts with a relieved smile.

'We don't have much time!' fretted Cogsworth, who was opening drapes and letting light into the conference room. 'The kings and queen will be here shortly! And Fairy Godmother runs a tight ship. She'll turn us all into pumpkins—or worse, back into furniture—if things aren't perfect!'

'Oh, Cogsworth, you worry too much!' Mal laughed as she helped Chip pour tea into everyone's cups. She knew Cogsworth was simply being his normal, nervous self—Fairy Godmother was far too kind to turn anyone into furniture. After they were done with the tea, she helped Chip fold the napkins the way Lumiere taught them, so they resembled ladies' fans on the plates.

At last, the room was ready and at the appointed hour, Mal took her seat as Cogsworth held the door open for King Beast, Queen Belle, King Ben and Fairy Godmother, who all filed in. They were already deep in discussion.

'I think it's a wonderful idea,' Ben was saying. 'She'll be so thrilled.'

'I thought she might,' said Fairy Godmother, who looked as polished as ever in her pink ruffled shirt and powder-blue suit.

Ben grinned and took his seat next to Mal.

'Oh, the tea looks lovely, Mrs Potts,' Fairy Godmother said, as she picked up her cup. Cogsworth audibly sighed in relief.

'One lump or two?' asked Chip, appearing at her elbow, as Mrs Potts beamed behind him.

'What's going on?' whispered Mal to Ben.

'You'll see,' he promised, reaching for a scone.

King Beast and Queen Belle, who had recently returned from another all-kingdom cruise—they had become very fond of those—looked deeply tanned and relaxed. Ever since handing over the reins of government to their son, the retired king and queen were only brought in to consult with the Royal Council. Ben had the final word on every decision.

Ben let the assembled group eat and chat for a moment before calling the meeting to order. 'Mal, I'm sorry we started this discussion without you, but it's come to my attention that some members of the Royal Council would like for you to do some diplomatic visits around all the kingdoms of Auradon,' he explained. 'I think you would do an amazing job. What do you think?'

'Oh!' said Mal, sitting up straighter. 'That sounds . . . exciting!'

'I thought you would say that!' Ben smiled at her, but then his brow creased. 'Although it *does* mean a lot of travel,' said Ben. 'And frankly, I'll miss you.'

In the back, Mrs Potts swooned while Chip giggled.

'Ben,' said Mal, taking his hand at the table. 'I'll always come back to you.'

Ben smiled back and squeezed her hand. He had grown up so much since the crown was first placed on his head.

He was their leader, fair and firm, and so handsome that she still blushed when he looked her way. 'I'll be waiting,' he promised.

Fairy Godmother cleared her throat. 'It's important that our future *Lady* Mal see as much of the kingdom as she can. She didn't grow up in Auradon, and it would be good for her to observe the customs of the country.'

'I agree,' said Queen Belle. 'The people are curious about Mal and excited to show her how much they appreciate all she's done for Auradon. I know in Northern Wei, they're planning a dragon dance parade in her honour. And in Corona, a festival of sky lanterns.'

King Beast beamed. 'What wonderful news! Dear, do you think our next cruise could take us to Northern Wei as well? I've never even seen a dragon dance myself!'

'I'll make sure of it,' said Queen Belle.

'Then it's settled,' said Fairy Godmother. 'I hope it's not too distracting from your studies, my dear. But here is a list of kingdoms for your itinerary.' She pushed a piece of paper across the table in Mal's direction.

Mal felt her heartbeat speed up in excitement. It was true—she hadn't seen very much of Auradon at all, and the chance to travel the world sounded thrilling after a childhood spent trapped on a remote island. So many things to see! So many people to meet!

She glanced at the list.

Agrabah, Camelot, Northern Wei, Olympus, East Riding, Corona... and everywhere else, from Tiger's Head to Triton's Bay. So many wonderful places to visit! She couldn't wait to eat beignets with Princess Tiana's family and sip nectar and honey with the gods and goddesses in their palace in the sky. Every kingdom and region in Auradon was represented on her itinerary.

Every region, that is, except one.

Mal looked up from the paper. 'Did we forget to add the Isle of the Lost to this list?' she asked.

'The Isle of the Lost?' echoed Fairy Godmother, as if she couldn't quite believe her ears.

King Beast and Queen Belle shifted uncomfortably. King Beast coughed, and Queen Belle added two more lumps of sugar to her tea. When she brought the cup to her lips, it rattled against the saucer she held underneath it.

'The Isle of the Lost is Mal's home,' Ben reminded everyone.

'Yes, it is,' said Mal. It was her duty to represent the island as much as she could, to remind everyone that there were noble hearts everywhere, and that even villain kids could grow up to be good. 'And the Isle is part of Auradon, right?'

'Technically,' Fairy Godmother admitted.

'Unfortunately,' groused King Beast.

'Now, now, dear,' said Queen Belle.

'Then shouldn't I visit the Isle as well?' she said. 'Shouldn't I go there as part of my official itinerary? I don't want them to think they've been forgotten.' It was already so easy to dismiss the kids who were imprisoned on the island, punished for their parents' evil deeds. If Ben hadn't felt sympathy for them in the beginning, when he made his first proclamation as king, who knew where she would be now? Certainly not in a plush room in the palace eating warm scones on a porcelain plate. Most likely scrounging for leftovers in back alleys like every other Isle kid.

'Of course not,' said Ben. 'We can't forget the Isle of the Lost.'

'Let's not make a hasty decision just yet,' said Fairy Godmother. 'Why don't we discuss it again at the next meeting of the Royal Council? Give us a little time to think it over.'

'Absolutely,' said Ben with a smile. 'Besides, I'd take any excuse to have more tea and scones from Mrs Potts.'

chapter 2

Arabian Knight

Jay and his opponent battled up and down the mat, crashing against the walls and over every obstacle. Once the slyest thief in all the Isle of the Lost, Jay had found that it was just as much fun to score a goal in tourney or win a battle at R.O.A.R. as it was to swipe a scarf from a merchant on the plaza. Maybe even more fun, since no-one chased him around angrily afterwards. Whenever he put on his team's yellow-and-blue face mask or picked up his sword for another round of swords-and-shields practice, he forgot that he had ever spent his childhood in a junk shop on a remote island. All he cared about was victory, his world narrowing to the points he scored against his fearsome opponents.

He leapt and attempted a strike, but was deflected. His opponent rushed forwards and made a hit. The referee called the score. Now Jay was behind.

They went back to their places on the mat, and this time, Jay waited and let his rival come to him. He didn't have to wait for long, and was on the defensive again, blocking strikes and cleverly dodging any attack.

At last, he found his advantage, twirled around and landed a direct hit. The buzzer sounded, signalling that time was up, and the referee blew his whistle. 'That's the game,' the ref called. 'It's a tie!'

'Good one!' said Lonnie as she took off her mask and let her long black hair fall on her shoulders. She shook his hand.

'Thanks, Captain.' Jay grinned as he removed his mask and gloves.

There was a round of applause from a group lined up along the courtyard, watching them. 'Excellent work!' said one. 'Brilliant!' said another. 'Bravo!' said the third.

Jay squinted in their direction. He hadn't noticed them at the start of the match. He'd been playing for himself, not to impress anyone. 'Who are they?' he asked, as he put his equipment away.

'Coaches,' said Lonnie. 'It's college visiting day, remember?'

Jay did not remember. He never kept track of dates or

read announcements or emails. Life was too short, and he had too many fun things to do, like play video games and eat pizza.

'Go over there! They definitely want to meet you,' said Lonnie, gently pushing him in their direction.

The first coach was a muscular gentleman in a black-and-gold vest, voluminous white pants and gold shoes with curled tips. He wore a grand white turban with a ruby in the middle and a gold stripe running around it. 'Jay!' he said heartily, as if they were old friends. 'I am Coach Razoul, formerly captain of the guard at the Sultan's palace. But now I head up the athletics program at ASU—Agrabah State University.'

'Nice to meet you,' said Jay, bowing to the coach.

The coach bowed in return, seemingly pleased that Jay remembered Agrabah's customs. 'You must come and visit us sometime. Have you decided where you will continue your education? Would you consider coming home?'

Jay startled at that. While his father was from Agrabah, Jay's home was the Isle of the Lost. But he didn't want to embarrass Coach Razoul. 'To be honest, I haven't given it much thought yet.' Graduation was still a few months away. He didn't have to decide where to go to college yet, did he? Definitely not.

'Jay!' said the next coach, a big bear of a guy who wore the green livery of Robin Hood's men. 'Coach Little John here, from Sherwood Forest University. We'd love to see you play for the Arrows.' He handed Jay a card. 'We're ranked number one in the league.'

'For archery,' said Coach Razoul, wagging his finger. 'Not R.O.A.R.'

'Not yet, maybe,' admitted Little John. 'But with players like you, we will be.'

Coach Razoul gave the archer a condescending smile. 'In Agrabah, your dormitory will be a palace! Every meal is a feast and if you rank first in your class, a genie will grant you three wishes!' He pressed a gold-foil-covered catalogue into Jay's hands.

Meanwhile, Little John handed Jay a tote bag filled with Arrows merchandise—a water bottle, a bow and arrow, and a sweatshirt with the school's motto—**steal from the rich; give to the poor**—embroidered on the front. The bearlike coach smiled affably. 'Stealing was your hobby, wasn't it? You'll fit right in!' he said.

'Stealing? Well, in the past maybe. Not anymore. But thank you so much,' said Jay, as he accepted the loot.

Not to be outdone, Coach Razoul presented Jay with a treasure chest of riches—robes with the Agrabah State University crest, new golden slippers and a genie lamp. 'It's just an oil lamp, no genie in it,' said Coach Razoul with a laugh. 'Yet!'

'Don't listen to them,' said the third coach, a cheerful apple-cheeked woman in powder-blue wizard robes with a pink bow that tied the hood under her chin. She looked vaguely familiar. 'Hello, Jay! My sister tells me so much about you! You must consider playing for us! Everyone knows MIT is the best college in Auradon. Our alumni include Professor Yen Sid, as well as Flora, Fauna and Merryweather!'

Magical Institute Training was the top college in the kingdom, taking only the best and brightest from Auradon Prep. Students needed an almost-perfect SAT (Salagadoola Abracadabra Test) to be considered.

'MIT!' said Jay. 'I'm not sure I have the grades?'

'Oh, we work miracles at MIT, don't worry,' said Fairy Godmother's sister. She waved her wand, and a small white carriage loaded with treats—athletic duffel bags, sneakers and a new face mask, sword and gloves—appeared next to the treasure chest and tote bag.

'Think about it.' She winked.

'Come home to Agrabah,' said Coach Razoul, shaking Jay's hand once more.

'Join our merry band,' said Coach Little John, slapping him on the back. 'Come to visiting day and hang out with the team.'

'Visiting day?' asked Jay. 'What's that?'

'Oh, you go on a little adventure with the students, see what Sherwood is like, check out the scene,' said Little John. 'I think you might enjoy it.'

'I think I just might,' said Jay with a grin.

'Great! I'll send you the information,' promised Little John.

At last, the coaches left to talk to other players. Jay gathered his stuff and jogged back to Lonnie. 'Do you want any of this?'

'I'm good. I met with them last week,' said Lonnie. 'They even spoke to my parents.' She picked up the tote bag. 'Let me help.'

They walked out of the training courtyard together, Jay straining under the weight of the treasure chest and the carriage full of treats. 'Did you decide where to apply?' he asked.

'I'm not sure yet if I will. I might play R.O.A.R. professionally instead. But if I do decide to go to college, I'll definitely choose one that would prepare me to join my mother's army. I'm going to be a general like her one day,' she said proudly.

'Cool,' said Jay. The only inheritance he'd receive from his father was a decrepit junk shop on the Isle of the Lost. But Jafar had been the Sultan's grand vizier once, the power behind the throne. Perhaps one day Jay could have that same kind of stature, but without the greed and the obsession with Aladdin's lamp.

As if she had read his thoughts, Lonnie asked, 'What about you?'

'Me? I'm just glad I didn't have to steal any of this,' he said truthfully. Until this moment, he hadn't really given much thought to his future. It felt like he had just arrived at Auradon Prep. He was sad to think that soon there would be no more tourney games, no more living with his friends and seeing them every day. Sherwood sounded like a fun prospect—he would definitely have to visit, see what it was like.

They were all growing up so fast. Time was speeding along too quickly. One day he was just a street rat from the Isle of the Lost, and the next he was a top recruit at MIT. Wait until he told his dad! Except Jafar would probably insist that Jay steal all the school's magical secrets. Some things never changed.

chapter 3

Once, There Was a Princess

As Evie sat at her trusty sewing machine and worked on a gorgeous graduation gown for herself, she felt a flutter of sadness in her chest. When she was a kid growing up all alone in a damp and mouldy castle, Evie had wanted nothing more than to have a group of friends—to play with, to laugh with, to depend on. But Mal, Jay and Carlos were more than friends—they were family. Even though their parents had been just as successful at raising children as they had been in executing their evil schemes (read: total failures), the four of them had always been there for each other. But now high school was ending, and graduation would be here before they knew it. It felt like they were all going their separate ways.

Mal had told Evie about her official tour the other day—she would soon be travelling all over Auradon to learn more about the various kingdoms and their people. Jay was always off training with his R.O.A.R. team, and when Carlos wasn't studying, he spent most of his time with Jane. Evie missed her friends.

She felt a tear come into her eye and almost pricked her finger on the needle. She sighed and put the gown away. It was going to be a deep sapphire blue to complement her hair, with a red ruby heart in the middle. Usually the joy of dreaming up and creating a beautiful dress to wear for a fancy event filled her spirit, but today she just felt melancholic.

'What's wrong? Are you crying?' asked Doug, looking up from Mal's desk, where he was practising his trumpet.

She smiled sweetly at him and brushed away her tears. 'No, not really. I was thinking that everything is happening so fast. Didn't I just arrive at Auradon Prep? Now we're graduating.'

'Time certainly flies,' he said. 'Even my hair is longer!'

She chuckled. Doug had been growing out his hair so that it was shaggier than usual. 'It really is!'

'Do you not like it?' he asked worriedly.

'I love it!' said Evie, clasping her hands. 'You look very dashing. But . . .'

'But . . . ?' Doug asked, setting down his trumpet.

'But things are ending,' said Evie. She hung up her graduation gown and admired its sweetheart neckline and puffed sleeves. Just a few more flourishes on the sash and the dress would be done. 'I don't even know where I'm going to live when I graduate. I just realised I don't have a home here. Where am I going to go?' She couldn't return to the Isle of the Lost, of course, but after she left her room at the school dorms, there wasn't anywhere else she could go.

Doug shook his head. 'Auradon is your home.'

'I know,' said Evie. 'But I'm not like the other kids. I'm not from here.'

'We'll think of something,' said Doug, a serious look on his face.

Evie nodded. 'I would love to have a place of my own. But who knows what next year will bring?'

'Hopefully not Uma,' said Doug.

'Roger that,' said Evie, shuddering. 'But I *am* hoping next year brings more villain kids to Auradon. You know, to study. Like the four of us.'

Doug smiled. 'Isn't Ben doing that?'

'Sort of,' said Evie. 'He definitely wants to recruit more kids from the Isle to apply to Auradon Prep. Except . . .'

'Except?'

Evie smoothed the fabric on her gown. 'Well, we're just not getting the response we thought we would.'

'How many people have applied from the Isle of the Lost so far?' asked Doug.

Evie turned back to him. 'How many?'

'Yeah.'

'One.'

Doug's mouth quirked in amusement. 'One?'

She nodded. 'Just Dizzy, who was invited to apply, and actually still has to be selected by the admissions committee before her registration can be confirmed.' Evie was sure Dizzy would be accepted, but of course nothing was guaranteed until Fairy Godmother sent the enrolment letter.

Doug crossed his arms against his chest. 'Just Dizzy? Really?'

Evie let out a rueful chuckle. 'I know. Isn't that sad? There's got to be a way to get more kids from the Isle to apply.'

'How many spots are open?' asked Doug.

'Good question. I'm not sure, but I think Auradon Prep would take more than one, since they want more students from the Isle to apply.'

'Then what you need,' said Doug, putting his trumpet away in its case, 'is a recruitment strategy.'

Evie looked at him thoughtfully. 'Intriguing. Go on.'

'The kids from the Isle of the Lost will probably be too intimidated to apply, unless they get encouragement from kids like them who are already doing well in Auradon.'

'Kids like us, you mean?' asked Evie, her mind whirling with ideas.

'Exactly. Once they hear more about how you, Jay, Carlos and Mal have grown at Auradon Prep, they'll be inspired to join you guys. Maybe it won't be so scary if they know they'll be welcome here.'

'You're right,' said Evie, clapping her hands. 'So let's show them! I've got to find Carlos, Jay and Mal!'

Evie ran from the room, excited to get started. She was halfway down the hall when she realised she'd forgotten something.

Just as quickly, she ran back into her room and kissed Doug on the forehead. 'You're a prince. Thank you!'

'Just a dwarf, really, but I'll take it,' he said, hugging her back.

chapter 4

Look Out for Carlos De Vil

The last bell of the day had finally rung, and the weekend beckoned. Carlos packed up his books and followed the crowd out of the classroom. There was a lively chatter in the air as people made plans to meet up at Camelot Grill for dinner and darts games or to hang by the Enchanted Lake. He craned his neck and spotted Jane, who had her Advanced Wish-Fulfillment class right next door to his History of Heroism seminar. Carlos was still getting used to the idea that she *liked-him* liked him. He had been so nervous to ask her to Cotillion, she hadn't even understood what he was asking her until it was almost too late. But now, when she saw him, it was like everyone and everything else melted away.

'Hey!' she said, her bright eyes shining. Her dark hair was pulled away from her face with a light-blue headband, and she was wearing a matching ruffled dress. With him in his black jacket, white button-down shirt and black-and-white pants, they made a handsome pair, if he did say so himself.

They smiled shyly at each other. 'Happy Friday!' he said, because seeing her always made him happy.

'Happy Friday to you,' she said. They reached for each other's hands at the same time, causing Jane to giggle. 'So, is everything set for you-know-what next week?' she asked, lowering her voice in case one of the seniors could overhear them.

'I've got the list and I've alerted the proper authorities,' said Carlos. 'Everything should be ready.'

'Amazing,' said Jane. 'It's going to be such a fun night!'

'The best!' he enthused. They had really pulled it together. It had been a little difficult getting all the parents to agree to their plans—Rapunzel, for one, didn't want to let down her hair too much—but in the end they'd all agreed to help. Carlos was no longer the scared little boy who'd arrived at Auradon Prep, shaking at the sight of a puppy. He had grown taller, leaner and much more confident in the time he'd spent away from the Isle of the Lost. Without his mother's haranguing and constant criticism, he had truly come into his own—especially since he no longer had to fluff her wigs and take care of her furs.

Everything was going happily-ever-after—he was doing well in his classes, he had a very cute girlfriend, and next year, once Jay and Ben had graduated, he was going to be the BMOC: Big Man of the Castle. Maybe he could even run for Class King! He ruffled his crop of black-and-white hair, thinking about how everything would truly be perfect. Except for just one thing—he would miss his friends.

The others would be going their own ways after graduation—that was for sure. Jay was going to be some big R.O.A.R. star, Evie would probably expand her fashion business and Mal had her duties to Auradon—after all, she was the future Lady Mal now. Carlos felt a tad nostalgic for how it used to be, when the four of them were just a bunch of Isle of the Lost misfits, stumbling and scheming their way through Auradon.

Which was why he was doubly glad he and Jane had coordinated this very special supersecret project next weekend that was part of the traditional graduation activities at Auradon Prep.

'See you tomorrow?' she asked.

'At the Auradon City Mall,' he replied with a grin. 'Seven o'clock.'

'They just installed new dancing fountains—trained by the Sorcerer's Apprentice!' she said. 'It'll be so cool!'

'Can't wait.'

He walked her back to her dorm, where she gave him a quick kiss goodbye. 'Tomorrow,' she promised.

'Tomorrow,' he echoed with a smile, still feeling the sweetness of her kiss against his cheek.

As Carlos walked back to the boys' dorm, he texted the group chat nicknamed 'VKs':

> **C-Dog:** *Hey! It's Friday! Let's hang! Want to grab eats at Charming's Chili?*
> **Malevolent:** *Sounds SO FUN, but Ben and I have a dinner with Aziz and his new princess tonight. So sorry!!!*
> **It'sJay:** *Rain check? Kinda sore from practice, spending night in.*
> **PrincessEvie** . . .

Carlos was waiting for Evie's reply when she ran right into him, still typing a response on her phone.

'Carlos!' she said joyfully.

He broke into a smile; Evie was always so cheerful. She was like a big sister to him. 'Evie! What's up? Want to go to Charming's Chili?' he asked.

'I'm so sorry, I can't. Doug's band is playing at the Wishing Well later,' she said with an apologetic smile. 'Want to come with?' While Doug was a member of the marching band in the daytime, at night he whistled a different tune.

Carlos would usually be happy to join her, except Doug's music was just a tad too *EMO* for him. (Extremely Moody Orchestrations, that is.)

'Next time,' Carlos promised, as they fell into step together.

'But do you have time now?' asked Evie. 'I'm actually going this way.' She motioned back to the main castle.

'Now?' he asked, following her lead.

'Yeah, I was about to go and find Mal and Ben to talk about the VK program—you know, the initiative to bring more villain kids to Auradon?' she asked, as she opened the doors and they stepped through.

Carlos nodded. It sounded vaguely familiar, although he hadn't been paying much attention. Mostly he'd been wrapped up in his new relationship with Jane. 'Uh-huh?'

Evie led the way to Ben's private wing of the palace. 'I was thinking maybe we should go back to the Isle of the Lost and get more kids interested in applying!'

'We should?' he asked, paling to the roots of his black-and-white hair. Even though they'd returned to the Isle of the Lost before, it always felt like a dicey proposition. In the back of his mind, he was always a little worried he'd end up stuck there again, and he really didn't want to be trapped in his dingy room in Hell Hall.

'Yeah, we should!' said Evie, who seemed very intent on this idea. 'That way, they can see Auradon is a great place, even for villain kids. Don't you think? Because, so far, no-one's applied to the program except for Dizzy.'

'Oh.' That did seem odd. Carlos would have guessed there would be more kids who might want to escape the island. For starters, he remembered the kids from the Anti-Heroes club were pretty keen on Auradon.

'Yeah.' Evie shrugged. 'Doug thinks that maybe they're scared or intimidated somehow. Or maybe they think it's some kind of trap. You know how it was, back on the Isle. There's always some kind of angle.'

He certainly did. Carlos drummed his fingers on his chin. He was warming up to the idea. 'You know what would help? If we brought peanut butter!'

Evie laughed. 'Um, okay. I was thinking we should meet with the kids personally to talk about Auradon. But that works, too!'

'Perfect. Let's find Jay and Mal first, then go talk to Ben,' said Carlos. He always found safety in numbers.

chapter 5

Everyone's Favourite King

Ben bent over the paper on his desk, his brow creased as he read the latest safety report from Genie, who kept an eye on all the kingdoms. The news was the same—no sign of Uma or her tentacles. Ben was writing a note advising Genie to keep an eye on the oceans, when the door to his study burst open. He was surprised but happy to find Mal, Evie, Jay and Carlos talking excitedly to each other as they made their way to the front of his desk.

'We could tell them about tourney!' said Jay.

'And chocolate chip cookies!' said Carlos. 'Oh, and hot showers!'

'We could stress how *good* the classes are. Pun definitely intended,' said Mal with a droll smile.

'And how nobody locks you up in a tower if you forget your homework!' said Evie.

'Ben! Wait till you hear this idea!' said Mal, coming to perch on the side of his desk.

'What is it?' asked Ben, grinning and leaning back on his chair, glad to have a distraction. It was his duty as king to read every document presented to him and make certain he was prepared for meetings. He liked to be just as informed as his councillors, if not more so. But sometimes, even kings needed a break. 'What's the big idea?'

'You know the VK program?' Evie asked. 'The one that's going to bring over some more villain kids to study at Auradon Prep? Well, I was looking at the applications we've received, and aside from Dizzy, there aren't any.'

Ben raised his eyebrows. He hadn't heard that it was quite that big a failure. 'Really?'

'Yeah, really,' said Carlos, taking an empty seat across from Ben's desk. Jay took a place by the windowsill, and Evie sat on a chair near to Mal.

'Isn't that awful?' said Mal. 'I think they're scared to apply.'

'Or maybe they don't know about it,' said Jay. 'The Isle is a little . . . isolated.'

'So we need to drum up more interest,' said Evie. 'I was

thinking I could take some photos of us, and we could use them to make posters and put them all over the island. Kind of aspirational! Like, 'You, too, could grow up to be Mal!'"

Ben smiled. He was pretty sure Mal was one of a kind, but he understood where Evie was going. 'Okay, posters. I like it! Maybe we could put them up all around the mainland too, prove to people that anyone can be a great student here.'

Mal nodded. 'We need to show them that *everyone* can come to Auradon Prep,' she said meaningfully.

'Everyone?' asked Ben.

'Well, yeah,' said Mal. 'Right, Evie?'

'Right,' said Evie.

'We'll definitely give everyone a chance to apply,' Ben said. 'But we can't take everyone from the Isle of the Lost. Where would they live? And who would mentor them? We need to figure out exactly how many kids we can bring over. There's a lot to plan before this happens.'

'But we can't waste another day,' said Evie.

'I agree,' said Ben. 'We'll get to work on those posters as soon as possible.'

Carlos leaned over. 'That's a good start'—he turned to Evie—'but didn't you say you wanted to meet with kids to talk about the program? That the four of us should go to the Isle of the Lost?' His tone was hesitant.

'Well, yes, as long as Ben thinks it's all right,' said Evie hopefully. 'I just think if we could tell them exactly how wonderful it is here and answer their questions, we'll be able to get a lot more of them interested in applying.'

'The four of you? Back to the Isle?' Ben pondered the idea. The last time they had gone back to the Isle, things hadn't gone so well. As in, getting kidnapped by Uma, and then being tied to the mast of a pirate ship and menaced by some pirate holding a hook in his hand. Ben had sympathy for the kids on the Isle, but he wasn't sure he really wanted his friends to go back there. Wasn't it too dangerous?

He said as much.

'Dangerous? Not to us,' scoffed Jay. 'We know every trick in the book.'

'Because we wrote it,' said Mal.

'Danger is my middle name,' said Carlos. 'I'm serious. Ask my mum. Or Dude. Or neither. Neither might be preferable.'

'We can handle it,' said Evie. 'Nothing will happen.'

But there was also Fairy Godmother to think about. 'Auradon Prep discourages student travel during the school year,' said Ben.

'But not if it's part of my diplomatic visits . . .' mused Mal. 'That's it! My diplomatic visits!' She turned to Ben, her eyes sparkling. 'We both agreed that the Isle of the Lost should be included on my official itinerary. And if I'm using my visit to promote the VK program at the same time, Fairy Godmother won't be able to say no. It's the perfect opportunity!'

'And we'll all come, too!' said Evie.

'Definitely,' said Jay. 'You'll need all the help you can get.'

'Yeah,' said Carlos. 'I don't want to see my mother. But I guess I'm in.'

'Good,' said Mal, who smiled at Evie.

Ben finally nodded. 'It does make sense. We'll present it at the next council meeting!'

chapter 6

They Weren't Kidding When They Called Her, Well, a Witch

Uma seethed as she swam under the waves, thinking about all the ways she had been wronged. For a brief moment, back at the Auradon Cotillion, she had been a princess; she had stood on the deck of a magnificent ship, and Ben was hers. He had looked in her eyes with love—sure, he had been spelled, but who really cared? Except in the end, that's all it was—a brief moment. As always, Mal had messed things up for her, and Uma was left floundering in the waves, alone.

What was it Ben had said to her that night? *I know you want what's best for the Isle. Help me make a difference.* He had offered his hand, but she hadn't taken it. Instead, she had returned his ring and swum away. But her rage had not diminished.

Mal! Daughter of Maleficent. Meddlesome, annoying, heroic Mal.

It was always Mal.

Still, Uma had to admit, it wasn't all that bad spending this much time in the ocean. At least, not at first. She'd never had the chance before when she was trapped on the island, behind that invisible barrier. Now the world was hers to explore—the undersea world, that is. She had ventured to the deepest depths, seen ancient creatures of incredible size and swum with fish so big that she spent days lounging on their backs, feeling the sun in her hair and the salt spray on her cheeks. But eventually she'd grown listless and bored.

After all, how many coconuts can one person eat?

(Five hundred and twenty-seven. She had counted.)

Uma missed her pirates, she missed their camaraderie, she missed Harry's smart mouth and his sly banter, she missed Gil's goofy appetites. She had been alone too long, under the sea, in the water, with only sharks for company. And sharks were only entertaining for so long.

She could go anywhere she wanted on Auradon, but Uma found herself drawn back to the Isle of the Lost. She didn't belong among the fresh-faced, good-hearted residents of the mainland. She wanted to be back at Ursula's Fish and Chips Shoppe, making jokes with her crew and scheming to free everyone from the island once and for all. And maybe, just maybe, she wanted to go home. Home was a place where when you showed up, they had to take you in, right? She'd seen something like that embroidered on a random pillow in Auradon, so it had to be true.

Uma spent many days swimming around the waters surrounding the Isle, searching for a hole in the invisible barrier. Days turned into weeks, until she lost count. But Fairy Godmother's spell was too strong. Still, there had to be a way to break it, wasn't there? Uma was a witch; she had her mother's seashell necklace and the powers of the sea in her blood.

She drew herself up to her greatest height, transforming into a giant octopus with eight arms, and tried to cast her spells. 'BREAK BEFORE ME!' she screamed. She felt the magic pulse in her throat and in her veins. The very skies above the island cracked with lightning and thunder.

'I COMMAND YOU TO BREAK!' she raged.

Nothing happened.

The barrier around the Isle of the Lost stood firm. The villains, including her pirate crew, would be trapped behind that dome forever. There was no way out or in.

Uma returned to her human form and swam away.

Once in a while, she glimpsed a few pirates at the coastline and tried to call to them. One afternoon she even spied Harry, stealing another fisherman's catch.

'Harry!' she called. 'HARRY!'

But he didn't notice. He just unhooked that unfortunate soul's line and stole away with the bounty.

Another day there was Gil, skipping stones on the beach. 'GIL! I'M RIGHT HERE! GIL!' she yelled.

Gil looked into the distance. 'Uma?' he asked. He looked down and found a large seashell. He put the conch to his ear.

'YES! I'M RIGHT HERE!'

But he didn't seem to hear her. Eventually, he set the conch down.

The next time she saw the boys on the deck of her ship, she didn't even bother to call out to them. There was no use. It was as if she were as invisible to them as the barrier.

Uma dived down into the depths again. Maybe if she swam deep enough, she would find a place where the barrier ended.

It felt like she had been swimming forever, down and down, cutting across currents and into the dark deep below. And still the barrier held. There was truly no way through the spell.

Except . . .

What was that?

That sound . . .

Was she dreaming, or was it . . . rock music? Coming from the depths below?

chapter 7

Once Upon a Dance

It had been a few days since Mal, Evie, Carlos and Jay had approached Ben to discuss the VK program, and Mal was starting to feel a little impatient. Every moment on the Isle of the Lost meant neglect, filth and abandonment for the kids who lived there. The sooner they got more kids to apply to Auradon Prep, and the sooner they got them off the Isle, the better those kids' lives would be. Evie had brought it up again the other night, and Mal had promised she would ask Ben about it today.

They were at their ballroom dancing practice. And even though Mal wished they were training with swords and shields instead, she kept it to herself. Since she had been announced as the future Lady Mal, she and Ben were expected to lead many dances in countless royal balls around Auradon. There were so many styles to learn—the fox-trot, the waltz, the Viennese waltz (who knew there were two kinds of waltzes?) the quickstep, the mambo, the cha-cha.

Ben was already in the palace ballroom with Merryweather, their instructor. The good fairy was wearing her usual blue gown, blue hat and blue cape. She eyed Mal's purple dress and smiled.

'Good morning, good morning, King Ben, Mal,' she said. 'Are we ready for our lesson?'

'We sure are,' said Ben heartily. Kingly duties took up so much of his schedule, and Mal knew he was glad for any excuse to spend more time together. Even if that meant learning complicated formal dances. 'Shall we?' he asked, offering Mal his hand.

'We shall,' she said, her eyes sparkling as she took it.

He swept her into his arms and they began counting the steps to the waltz.

Ben was concentrating hard on his footwork, and Mal had to make sure she kept in time with the beat. So it was only when Ben swung her around and dipped her that she was able to catch his attention.

'Pardon?' he asked, as Merryweather tapped her wand and music filled the room.

'I was saying—about the VK program—I was thinking we should bring as many kids as possible to Auradon Prep,' she told him.

'Wouldn't that be too many?' said Ben, spinning her around.

'What's too many?' she asked, trying not to feel dizzy.

Ben shrugged as his hands drifted back to her waist for the next step. 'It's a delicate situation. We need to handle it correctly.'

Merryweather tapped them with her wand. 'Ben, chin up! Mal, please don't hold your skirt that way.'

They adjusted accordingly. 'I just wish we could bring them all over,' said Mal, as they picked up the dance again.

'I know. I do too,' said Ben. 'Honestly, I didn't realise the impact of my decision on the kids who weren't originally chosen. I didn't know they took it so personally—like Uma.'

Mal made a face. 'There's only one Uma,' she said.

'I don't think Auradon can handle more than one,' he said mildly.

'I agree,' said Mal, as Ben twirled her around. 'So how many then? How many kids will be accepted into the program?'

Ben whispered, 'Name a number.'

'Ten!'

'Two,' he replied teasingly.

She snorted. 'Six.'

'Three.'

'Four,' said Mal as she curtsied to him at the end of the waltz.

'Done,' said Ben, bowing low with a smile.

'Exactly!' said Merryweather as the music ended with a flourish.

Four more villain kids. It was hardly everyone, but it was a start. She smiled at Ben. 'Perfect.'

'Oh!' Merryweather clasped her hands together. 'You are both lovely dancers!'

chapter 8

A Thrilling Chase

Jay knew that graduating from Auradon Preparatory School was no small feat. And over the years he'd discovered the school offered an array of traditions for its graduating seniors to celebrate the achievement. There was the Senior Tea, presided over by a beaming Mrs Potts. There was the Senior Ball, rivalling official royal balls in pomp and majesty. There was the Senior Crown Ceremony, where first-years placed golden crowns on the seniors' heads. There was Senior Ditch Day, when everyone left class and spent a day at the water park in Triton's Bay. (Jay had practically stuffed himself full of Scuttle's churros!) There was even an upcoming class trip to the Enchanted Wood and a fancy

Senior Dinner two weeks before the last day of school.

No-one ever made a big deal of anything back on the Isle of the Lost. Once you graduated from Dragon Hall, they kicked you out the door. (Literally.) In comparison, senior year at Auradon Prep seemed like one big celebration. The school did its best to make everyone's last year special and more memorable, and Jay found he was enjoying every minute of it.

But there was one tradition that had absolutely nothing to do with the administration, and if Fairy Godmother ever caught wind of it, she might wave her wand in annoyance and end the entire practice. So every senior kept quiet about it.

This tradition was called the Senior Quest. (Also known as the Senior Scavenger Hunt, but traditionalists liked to call it by its formal name.)

Ben had spent one afternoon at tourney practice filling Jay in on all the details. All participating seniors met at the tourney field at twilight to get the list of objects and tasks. Whoever completed the quest first would go down in Auradon Prep history—and win a trophy, along with a hundred-dollar gift certificate for a meal at Ariel's Grotto.

The Senior Quest was famous for its daring triumphs over the years: Genie had been made to grant three wishes; the statue of King Beast had been stolen from the commons and placed on the roof; the sword had been pulled from the stone. Even more shrouded in legend were its winners:

Prince Charming was said to have charmed his way through it. Prince Philip had slain a dragon (an illusion crafted by Merlin, of course). Princess Merida had shot the highest arrow up in the sky. A student named Wendy was famous for bringing back pixie dust from Never Land. But one thing was certain: Only the best of the best were named champions.

Once Jay had heard about the quest, he couldn't wait. He wanted his name in the history books. As well as that gift certificate—all the fish fingers he could eat!

When he arrived at the tourney field right at sunset—on his motorbike, no less—all the teams were already gathering. Aziz was at the wheel of his Magic Carpet, a tricked-out car with a superfast engine. Chad was on a white horse, alone. Evie and Doug were hanging out with six of Doug's cousins, waiting for the game to start. Doug's cousins were a fun bunch: Cheerful, Shy, Crabby, Snoozy, Doc the Second, and Gesundheit, who was called Gus for short. Crabby was annoyed he had to be on a team with Gus, who was always blowing his nose, but then, Crabby always lived up to his name. Evie was wishing them all good luck.

Jay didn't see Mal and Ben anywhere, but he knew they wouldn't miss this.

Carlos and Jane were standing at the head of the group. It was tradition for the juniors to coordinate and judge the quest, so while Jay was sad Carlos couldn't participate, he knew his friend had had a blast putting everything together.

He'd heard Carlos and Jane laughing over the list many times leading up to this night.

'Okay!' said Jane, holding up a hand to get everyone's attention. 'You guys know the rules. There are no rules! First one back to the goalpost with everything on the list wins!'

Jay pulled his motorbike up next to Lonnie's horse. They had agreed to work together as a team. 'What's on the list?' he asked.

'Um, let me see,' Lonnie replied. 'First: 'Bring back a shard from Cinderella's glass slipper.' That's in the museum, isn't it?'

'No, that's the whole one. We need a piece from the one that broke,' said Jay. 'That would be in Cinderella's castle.'

'Yes!'

Groups of seniors were already beginning to break away from the tourney field, laughing and cheering as the quest began in earnest, while Jay and Lonnie continued working on their game plan. Chad's parents, Cinderella and Prince Charming, lived in a castle in nearby Charmington, Jay remembered. It wouldn't be too hard a ride, although Jay was starting to think that maybe a horse and a motorbike weren't the best modes of transport.

'Should we drive instead?' asked Lonnie.

'For sure,' said Jay with a grin. 'I know where they keep the royal limo.'

They dismounted and bolted to the car. Once Jay

was at the wheel, they sped out of the school grounds, a motorcade of electric carriages filled with rowdy seniors right behind them.

'So, do you know what you're going to do after?' Jay asked as they zoomed up the main road.

Lonnie was still studying the list. 'After we win this thing?'

'No, after graduation.'

'I think I'm doing a gap year,' she said as she folded the map.

'Is that some Northern Wei thing?'

'No, silly. It's an Auradon thing. Some kids delay going to college to see the world.'

'Oh, cool.'

'This is our exit,' she said, pointing to the sign. 'Anyway, I'm still not sure if I'm going to college or going pro.'

'Pro?'

'There are some professional R.O.A.R. teams coming to recruit at Auradon Prep soon. You should meet them too!' she said. 'That way you'll know all your options.'

Jay considered it. He hadn't counted on his hobby becoming a profession, but it sounded like a worthy idea. 'When will they be here?'

'Next week. Will you remember this time?'

'I'll try,' he said. 'Will you remind me?'

She laughed. 'Fine. And I think we're here,' she said, as they pulled up to a towering castle in the woods.

chapter 9

With New Horizons to Pursue

The next meeting of the Royal Council didn't involve scones, mostly because it was after dinner, but Ben's disappointment was assuaged when he noticed that Mrs Potts was serving dessert instead. Pies and pudding en flambé. *Yum.* He shared a conspiratorial wink with Mal.

His parents were already at the table with Fairy Godmother. After exchanging a few pleasantries and going over the notes for the upcoming trade meeting, Ben steered the conversation back to the decision about Mal's official itinerary.

'Do we really need to discuss this right now?' King Beast yawned.

'Yes, we do,' said Ben. They were already late for the Senior Quest, and if this meeting didn't wrap up soon, he and Mal had no shot at the trophy—or bragging rights.

'Sending Mal to the Isle of the Lost doesn't seem like a terrible idea,' said Queen Belle gently. 'She is from there, and they are our people, too.'

Fairy Godmother scraped up the last bit of her pudding en flambé. 'I agree with Belle,' she said. 'It's not a terrible idea—I just worry it might be a dangerous one.'

'Mal will have her friends with her. She'll be perfectly safe,' said Ben.

'I promise, nothing will happen,' said Mal. 'In fact,' she continued, looking to Ben for encouragement, 'I would like to use my trip to help with the initiative of bringing more VKs over to Auradon. I think hearing it directly from me and my friends will help these kids understand how their lives can really change for the better.'

'I totally agree,' said Ben. 'It's time to bring more kids from the Isle to the mainland, and Mal can help us do that.'

'The longer they stay isolated and influenced by their parents' evil deeds, the harder it will be for them to ever acclimate to life on Auradon,' said Mal. 'I should know. When we were brought here, our parents tried to get us to steal Fairy Godmother's wand.'

'How can we forget?' said Fairy Godmother.

'But now Mal, Evie, Jay and Carlos are some of Auradon

Prep's top students,' Queen Belle reminded them. 'The others will be like them.'

'I still have my doubts,' said Fairy Godmother.

'Please, trust us,' said Mal.

'Trust her,' said Ben. 'As king, I believe this is the right thing to do.' He checked his watch. If they made it out of here in the next few minutes, they still had a fighting chance at winning the quest.

'The king has decided, then,' said King Beast. 'Hear, hear. Mal will be visiting her homeland.'

Fairy Godmother nodded. 'Hail to the king. And congrats, Mal. I know you'll have a wonderful trip.'

'Good job, son,' said his mother. 'And well done, Mal.'

Ben was relieved they had reached consensus so quickly. 'Great! Now that we've all agreed, I've outlined the plan,' he told them. 'Mal and her team can meet with Dr Facilier of Dragon Hall and liaise with him to drum up interest in the program. Once we receive all the applications, we'll select four new worthy candidates.'

Fairy Godmother pulled out a feathered pen and began scribbling notes. 'We'll have the royal press issue a proclamation with the dates of Mal's visit.'

'Excellent,' said Ben.

'Mal, remember that this time, you will be travelling as Auradon's representative,' said Fairy Godmother.

'I won't fail you,' said Mal.

Ben looked at the dates Fairy Godmother proposed. 'Oh!'

'What?'

'That's the same weekend that we're having the meeting to discuss the new NAFFA trade agreement,' said Ben.

'That's right. The National Association of Far Far Away,' said King Beast. 'Everyone from Agrabah to Camelot will be there.'

Ben turned to Mal. 'I won't be able to come to the Isle of the Lost with you. I'm so sorry.'

'Don't worry about it,' Mal said, giving him an understanding look.

'No-one said ruling was easy,' Ben said with a sigh.

'That's okay,' said Mal with a wicked smile. She lowered her voice to a whisper. 'You know what *is* easy?'

Ben raised an eyebrow.

'Winning the Senior Quest! We have to move. The first teams are already at Cinderella's castle! Let's go!'

As Mal and Ben zoomed out of the room, Fairy Godmother turned to the king and queen. 'Senior Quest? What's that?'

But Belle and Beast only smiled mysteriously. There were some traditions that were best kept secret.

chapter 10

Hold Your Breath, It Gets Better

'Come on,' said Evie, tiptoeing along the castle walls. She and Doug had crossed the moat by bringing down the drawbridge. Now all they had to do was get inside.

Evie picked the lock and swung the door open.

'You do that so well,' said Doug, a little nervously.

'You can take a girl out of the Isle, but you can't take the Isle out of the girl,' said Evie with a smile. She was never embarrassed about where she came from.

They went inside. The castle was empty, since Cinderella and Prince Charming had agreed to let the kids use their castle for the scavenger hunt and were away visiting Prince Charming's father—the King—and the Grand Duke. The servants had been given the day off in preparation as well. Even though Evie and Doug were sneaking in, it was mostly to avoid the other senior teams. Cinderella just asked that everyone take their shoes off at the entry.

Doug led the way up the grand stairs, the two of them padding lightly in their socks, and quickly found Cinderella's closet. Evie stopped to admire the light-blue gown that Cinderella had worn to that famous ball, where she captured the heart of her prince. She touched its silk folds reverently. 'Did I tell you?' she asked Doug. 'I had an idea to expand my business. I'm going to design everyone's caps and gowns for graduation.'

'That's perfect! Everyone is going to want an Evie's 4 Hearts original,' Doug said, kneeling down to look at rows and rows of boxes of glass slippers.

'I hope so!' said Evie, admiring Cinderella's many tiaras.

'You can't graduate without one!' said Doug with a smile. He held up one of the shoe boxes. 'Where do you think she keeps the shards of the original shoe?'

Evie tried to think. If she were Cinderella, where would she keep her mementos? They searched everywhere, going up to the attic filled with her old brooms and the basement where the castle cooks kept the cauldrons. But there was no sign of the broken shards of the original glass slipper.

'Maybe we should move on to the next item on the list?' asked Doug.

'Hold on!' Evie said excitedly, as she realised the twist. 'Cinderella doesn't have the shards of the slipper. She's not sentimental. After all, she sent the remaining one to the museum. Prince Charming was the one who picked it up when she left it at the ball. I bet it's in *his* closet!'

They ran to Prince Charming's closet . . . But another quest team had already beat them there.

Ben was looking through the shelves while Mal was pulling out the cape rack. 'Oh, hey!' said Mal. 'You guys are here, too!'

'Slipper shards?' asked Doug.

'Nothing yet,' said Ben.

Mal turned to Evie. 'Guess what? The Royal Council approved my visit to the Isle! We're all going back to recruit more kids to come to Auradon!'

Evie squealed, and the two of them hugged.

'You know, when the new kids come over, we should do something fun, truly celebrate them. Maybe not just the marching band, but an entire parade. A really big welcome!' said Evie.

'That's a great idea,' said Doug.

'I like it,' said Ben. 'Certainly for their first day of school. But we're going to bring the new kids over during the summer, so that they have time to get used to Auradon.' He turned over a treasure chest full of medals. 'No shards here.'

Mal and Evie looked through the prince's collection of crowns. 'But where will they stay? The first-year dorms are being remodelled this summer,' said Mal.

'We'll find a place!' said Evie cheerfully. She picked up one of the golden crowns and checked underneath it. 'Except we can't seem to find any shards of glass.'

Mal peeked beneath an ermine coat, where she discovered a safe. 'Look!'

The safe was already open, and there was a note on the floor in Jay's handwriting. '"Left you some shards, but the crown is ours!"' Mal read. 'He got here first, that thief!'

She reached into the safe and found the velvet bag where Prince Charming kept the shards of his true love's glass slipper. Mal picked up a shard and carefully put it in a plastic pouch. Evie did the same. Then the two teams went their separate ways. Now they just needed to steal a banana from Tarzan's pal Terk's refrigerator . . .

chapter 11

An Endless Diamond Sky

It was close to midnight. Carlos and Jane sat at the edge of the tourney field near the goalpost, a plastic trophy between them. He checked the list he and Jane had put together for the quest, and wondered how much longer it would take for the teams to arrive. He was starting to get a little hungry.

'Don't worry, they'll be here soon. It's not an impossible quest,' said Jane with a reassuring smile.

They had spent months talking to all the respective parties, negotiating use of locations, and making sure everyone was in on the joke, while keeping things secret from the school administration. Jane had sent long letters to every prince and princess in the kingdom, begging them for access to their treasures, reminding them of their own glory years at Auradon Prep, while Carlos had been the one to keep track of the number of teams playing and make sure that there were enough objects for everyone to collect.

He looked down at the list again:

Collect a shard from Cinderella's glass slipper.
Pluck a flower from Aurora's rose garden.
Cut off a lock of Rapunzel's hair.
Steal a banana from Terk.
Bring back one of Rajah's collars. (Jasmine's tiger had quite a collection.)
Pick an apple from Snow White's orchard.
Take a slice of birthday cake from Mad Hatter's tea party.
Grab a thingamabob from Ariel's collection.
Bake a beignet using Princess Tiana's recipe.
Kiss a prince.
Hum 'Be Our Guest' when you get to the finish line.

'I think I hear something. They're here!' said Jane excitedly. She stood up and craned her neck.

Mal and Ben burst out of Ben's carriage. Mal was holding up a fork while Ben was balancing a plate of beignets in one hand and carrying his backpack in the other. The two of them were humming loudly to the tune of 'Be Our Guest.'

At the same time, Evie and Doug raced to the goalpost from the other side. Evie was holding up a rose while Doug held a satchel of scavenger-hunt objects. They were humming just as loudly, with Evie occasionally bursting into giggles.

It looked like first place would come down to these two teams, but at the last minute, Jay and Lonnie burst from the hedges. Lonnie was carrying a basket with all the items on the list, apples and bananas piled high on top.

All the teams reached the goal line at the same moment, and Mal noticed Evie and Lonnie bolting towards Ben, which reminded her that she, too, needed to fulfill the second-to-last item in front of the judges: Kiss a prince. All three girls hurriedly leaned in to kiss Ben on the cheek almost at the same time. Almost, that is, because Mal kissed him first. 'We win!' said Mal, cheering. 'Yay, us!'

Carlos shook his head. 'Nope, you all lose.'

'What?' they chorused. Mal did a double take, Evie looked affronted, and Lonnie frowned and looked as if she were about to go into battle.

But Jane only laughed and motioned to Chad, who was right behind them. Chad was kissing his own hand. 'DONE!' he crowed.

'Ben is a king,' said Jane. 'The quest is to kiss a *prince*. And well, Chad is kissing a prince, all right.'

The group groaned in unison, and Carlos handed Chad the trophy and the gift certificate. 'Try the grey stuff. It's delicious,' he joked.

'I don't think they serve that at Ariel's Grotto,' said Jane. 'I think that's Mrs Potts's recipe.'

'Oh, right,' said Carlos. 'Congratulations, Chad!'

Chad screamed in delight and danced around the goalposts, hoisting the trophy up in the air as they all looked on with amusement. The rest of the teams arrived, singing and showing each other the treasures they'd scored.

'Congratulations, everyone!' said Jane. 'You are all winners!'

'Midnight eats from Snow White's Snack Shack?' Carlos suggested, as his stomach was growling now.

A cheer went up from the crowd of seniors, and they all piled back into their carriages, laughing and high-fiving as they went.

Over the late-night meal, they relived the highlights of the quest. Evie and Doug showed off the scratches on their arms from the thorns from the rose garden, while Jay and Lonnie laughed about how loudly Jay screamed when Rajah caught him sneaking away with one of the tiger's jewelled collars.

When the laughter died down and the crowd at Snow White's trendy new restaurant began to disperse, Mal cleared her throat and leaned in towards her friends. 'So, the Royal Council said we can go back to the Isle of the

Lost next weekend to talk to the kids there. Sound good to everyone?'

'Oh! Wonderful!' said Evie.

'Back to the Isle? For sure!' said Jay, who was always up for an adventure.

Only Carlos looked hesitant.

'Carlos?' asked Mal.

'In,' he said with a nervous smile. 'Always.'

'It'll be okay,' said Evie, placing an arm around his shoulder. 'This is just what you wanted—for everyone to hang out and make the most of our time together.'

'Right, thanks for reminding me,' said Carlos.

Jane looked a bit worried, but he squeezed her hand. 'It'll be all right,' he said. 'Maybe my mum will be at the spa.'

'By the way, it was the best Senior Quest yet! Thanks, you guys, for putting that together,' said Evie to Carlos and Jane.

'Wait till you see what we have prepped for graduation!' said Jane.

'We have something planned for graduation?' asked Carlos.

'You'll see!' said Jane.

Carlos beamed. Jane was the best. And, actually, her birthday was coming up in a few months . . . He'd organise something! She was always doing nice things for everyone else, and he wanted to do the same for her. He'd think of something special—he knew he would.

chapter 12

Where There's Smoke, There's Fire

Yes, that was definitely rock music coming from under the depths of the sea. Loud, angry rock music. Uma swam closer to the sound. She recognised it. There was only one resident of the Isle of the Lost who liked playing music at those ear-shattering decibels.

She swam around, looking for the source. But all she could see was grey rock, furry with algae and coral. She swam the length of the rock, where the sound was loudest. *There.* She found a crack, just the smallest crevice. She swam closer. If she could squeeze herself through it, she would be able to get back inside the island. Underground, of course, but still—back on the Isle of the Lost!

Well, she considered, if she could make herself large, she could probably also make herself small. With that, Uma transformed into a tiny squid and slipped through the crack.

When she was back to her human self, she looked around, realising she was standing on her own two feet once more. It was good to be on dry land again. She was in a tunnel of some sort, an abandoned mine shaft. There were tracks leading deeper underground, where the music was even louder.

Uma followed the tracks all the way down.

All of a sudden, the music was interrupted by the voice of a news anchor from Auradon News Network. 'There's been a formal announcement from the palace. As part of her itinerary around the kingdom, the future Lady Mal will be going on an official visit to the Isle of the Lost.'

Lady Mal.

Hmpf.

Uma kept walking, her rage growing stronger within her, a plan forming in her head. And then she snuck into his little cave, where the god of the Underworld preferred to spend his days now that he was a prisoner on the Isle of the Lost.

Hades was playing air guitar, pretending he was performing in front of thousands of screaming souls. Or fans. Whatever you wanted to call them.

Uma tapped him on the shoulder and cleared her throat.

Hades jumped and almost hit his head on the cave

ceiling. 'Oh! You! What are you doing here? And what's your name again?'

'Uma!'

'Uma? Why did I think it was Shrimpy?' he asked, confused.

She frowned at the reviled nickname. No-one called her Shrimpy. *No-one.* It made her furious at Mal all over again.

'Hades. You still have that ember of yours, right?'

chapter 13

Pro Tip

The night after the Senior Quest, Lonnie suggested that she and Jay go see one of the professional R.O.A.R. games at the Auradon Arena. Her home team, the Great Wall, was fighting against the Summerland Sevens.

Once they arrived at the stadium, they made their way to a private suite that belonged to Coach Yao, one of the Great Wall's team owners, where a full buffet was laid out. It was complete with burbling chocolate fountains and towering ice sculptures in the likeness of the Great Wall's best player, Lonnie's brother, Li'l Shang. Li'l Shang used to coach R.O.A.R. at Auradon Prep, but had turned pro a few weeks ago.

'Great seats,' said Jay, as they filled their plates with an array of delicacies.

'Thanks,' said Lonnie with a wink. 'I know the owner.'

Today's game was tournament-style, which meant pairs of fencers squared off, and whichever team won the most matches won the tournament. The arena showed several matches at the same time. The Summerland Sevens had taken an early lead, with Happy's eldest son, Hap, scoring the most points by the break. The ferocious dwarf had defeated one of the best imperial players. The Summerland Sevens had the advantage of being physically much smaller than the Great Wall team, which meant there were fewer places to hit them at swordpoint.

But Li'l Shang was up next, against Doug's brother Derek. Derek was a hulk of a dwarf, with rippling muscles underneath his R.O.A.R. uniform. He came out swinging, slashing his sword to and fro and racking up points quickly. But Li'l Shang came rushing back, and soon didn't let Derek score another point.

Jay and Lonnie stood and cheered. Jay was so excited he threw his popcorn everywhere. He admired both teams' grit and finesse. Watching Li'l Shang take a flying leap off the edge of the arena to win the match point was positively thrilling.

The players came to the owner's suite after the game, and Li'l Shang grinned when he saw his younger sister and his protégé. 'I hoped you guys would be here! What's been going on? How's Auradon Prep?'

'Great! We lost the Kingdom Cup, but we came really close,' said Jay, referring to the championship R.O.A.R. game the Auradon Prep team had played several weeks before. 'How's life on the pro circuit?'

'Can't complain,' said Li'l Shang. 'We travel by first-class carriage all the way. Thousands of fans screaming in packed arenas.' He pulled open his R.O.A.R. jacket to show Jay a T-shirt with his face on it, **Shang Life** written in huge letters on the front. 'Look! I'm famous!'

Jay laughed. 'Dude, you made it!'

'Been trying to get my sister here to join the team, but she says she still hasn't made up her mind whether to go pro or go to college.' Li'l Shang rubbed Lonnie's head. 'Suit yourself, sis.'

Li'l Shang and Lonnie introduced Jay to Coach Yao, who had been a soldier in Mulan's army, along with his partners, Ling and Chien-Po.

'Jay, son of Jafar, of course! I've heard you're one of the best at R.O.A.R.!' he said, shaking Jay's hand. 'Ever think of going straight to the pros?'

'Skipping college?' asked Jay.

Yao nodded. 'You could be playing in this arena in a few months!'

'You'll have to sign him first,' Lonnie reminded him.

'Right, right,' said Coach Yao. 'And see your moves. We'll be at Auradon Prep next Saturday. We'll check you out.'

'Next Saturday?' asked Jay with a frown.

'Is there a problem?'

Jay scratched his head. 'Yeah, I'm pretty sure I have . . . a conflict.' He never remembered important dates, but he knew this one.

'Oh,' said Coach Yao.

Lonnie frowned. 'You do?'

'Yeah, I'm supposed to go back to the Isle of the Lost with Mal, Evie and Carlos. We're going to try to get more kids to apply to Auradon Prep,' he told them sheepishly.

'Do you have to?' asked Lonnie. She took Jay aside. 'I mean, if you want to be considered for a pro team, this is the only day they'll come to Auradon Prep. It's kind of a big deal.'

Jay thought about it. If he missed the recruiting session, Coach Yao wouldn't see him play, and Jay would be passing up the chance to play professionally. He looked around at the arena. He could just imagine it thundering with a thousand fans calling his name. He could do this. He was one of the best. His future was open.

But he couldn't let his friends down. Time with his friends was precious, and it would be even rarer after graduation. They had to stick together. Plus, he wasn't even sure if he wanted to play professionally; there was still college to consider.

'I don't know,' said Jay. 'I don't really know what I want to do yet.'

Lonnie nodded. 'I understand. You'll figure it out.' They went back to the party.

'Jay?' asked Coach Yao. 'Shall we put you down on our list? Will we see you next Saturday?'

'No, you won't. I'm so sorry, but I have other commitments,' said Jay.

'No problem. There's always next year,' Coach Yao said. 'You've got a lot of time to decide.'

Jay smiled. The coach was right. He was no longer trapped on the Isle of the Lost. In a few weeks, he had visiting day to look forward to at Sherwood Forest University; the itinerary included a lot of merrymaking. He had all the time in the world right now, and he wanted to spend a good chunk of it with the friends who helped him become the person he was today.

chapter 14

Trade Secrets

The week flew by, and finally it was time for Mal, Evie, Jay and Carlos to head back to the Isle of the Lost. Mal and Evie had packed so heavily for their short trip that Ben had to help Lumiere and Cogsworth carry their trunks to the royal limousine.

'You know you're only going for the weekend, right?' he asked, grunting under the weight of one particularly large case. 'You're only there for two nights.'

'Two nights! Oh my! Thank you for reminding me! I almost forgot my second alternate evening gown!' said Evie, who flew back into her room.

Mal smiled. 'I'm sorry. Most of it is Evie's.'

Carlos and Jay walked right behind them, each boy holding one small backpack. 'I travel light,' said Jay.

'No baggage,' quipped Carlos with a grin. 'At least not anymore.'

Mal threw her arms around Ben. 'Thanks for doing this. Letting us go back to talk to the kids, I mean.'

'Yeah, man, we're so pumped that more kids like us are going to be able to go to Auradon Prep!' said Carlos, bumping fists with Jay.

'I am too,' said Ben. He really was glad, although he was still a bit worried about where the new VKs would stay over the summer.

Evie rushed back, wheeling another trunk.

'Wait, these things have wheels?' asked Ben as Lumiere and Cogsworth staggered beside him.

'Yes, if you set them down the right way,' said Evie. 'How do you think I travel?' She chuckled.

They walked out of the school's front doors and loaded their bags into the car. Evie and the boys said their goodbyes to Ben and settled into their seats.

Mal lingered, a wistful smile on her face. 'I wonder if there'll be a day when we can bring every villain kid over to Auradon.'

'There will be. We just need to take it one step at a time. It's too risky right now, especially with Uma still out there.'

'Uma,' said Mal with a grimace.

'You take care,' he said.

'I will. You too. Are you okay?' she asked, putting a hand on his cheek.

'A little nervous about the NAFFA trade meeting. No-one can seem to agree lately! I have so many competing proposals to sort out.'

'I know you'll make it work. Say hi to the dwarfs,' she said, getting into the car.

Evie popped her head out. 'Give them my love!'

'I will,' said Ben, waving them off. He stood watching by the entrance until the royal limousine disappeared out of sight.

Just as Ben had predicted, every kingdom represented at the trade council argued that their goods were the most valuable.

'They're diamonds,' said Grumpy. 'We need to be able to charge top Auradon dollar!'

'Diamonds they might be, but our magic potions from Camelot are far more valuable,' argued Merlin.

'Everyone will look withered without our age-defying lotions,' Eugene Fitzherbert reminded them. 'The sun-drop golden flowers only grow in Corona.'

'We might not have magic flowers or magic potions or diamonds in the bayou,' said Princess Tiana. 'But we have the best food, and we should be compensated fairly.'

Ben listened to every kingdom's representative make their case, and then he spoke his piece: 'Just as Auradon Prep has become open to taking more students from the Isle of the Lost, Auradon must remain open to trade between all our united kingdoms. Diamonds, potions, lotions and beignets are equally important. Surely we can find a solution that would satisfy everyone here.'

The meeting continued, and eventually, all parties were satisfied by the trade agreement. Grumpy didn't even look that grumpy in the end. Ben began to put his papers back into his folder and a few delegates began to leave the room when Aquata, Ariel's oldest sister, who was representing Atlantica, came up to Ben, rolling her bathtub-like contraption forward. 'Can I ask you something?' she said, looking worried and splashing a little.

'Of course, anything for a princess of the sea,' said Ben with a charming smile.

'We hear from our people that Uma has been seen underwater. She's out there, free to wreak havoc and do whatever she wants.'

Ben brushed his hair off his forehead and nodded. 'We are aware and have stepped up security. Genie mentioned seeing something near the Isle of the Lost that looked like it could have been a giant octopus. I'll make sure to send more reinforcements to your area if she's seen there,' he said, trying to sound reassuring.

'Thank you,' said Aquata, sounding a tad relieved. 'It's just, her mother . . . her mother almost destroyed my family.'

Ben nodded. 'I'll make sure everywhere on Auradon is safe, even underwater.'

'We're not safe, not anywhere, as long as there's a villain out there,' said Aquata, shuddering. 'I heard you were going to let more of those people from the Isle come to Auradon. I hope that's just a terrible rumour. Do say it isn't true!'

'Actually, it is true,' said Ben. 'We'd like to give more people a chance, especially the children, who are innocent. Everyone deserves a chance to be good, don't you think?'

Aquata frowned, and her cheeks flushed. It was clear she did not agree. 'I hope you know what you're doing, for all of our sakes.'

Ben kept a diplomatic smile on his face. 'My main priority, always, is the safety of everyone in Auradon. Now, if you'll excuse me.'

Aquata splashed away in a huff, but Ben let it go. He knew it was an almost impossible task, to bring the people of the Isle and the people of Auradon together to live peacefully once more, but he had to keep trying. He had to unite his kingdom somehow. That's what a king was meant to do.

chapter 15

Two of a kind

Uma and Hades faced each other. She crossed her arms and Hades crossed his. He glared at her. She glared back. It was like they were looking into a mirror; they were both blue-haired villains with a score to settle against their enemies.

'Did I hear you right? Did you ask me if I still have my ember?' said Hades.

'Yes, or are you deaf from all this loud music?' said Uma. 'Your ember. Do you have it or not?'

'Why do you ask?' he said imperiously.

'It could be useful,' she said, leaning against the wall of

his cave as if she didn't care a whit whether he still had it or not.

Hades frowned. His blue hair stuck up from his forehead like a rock star's, but he had lines around his eyes. Like Uma's mother, Ursula, he'd been on the Isle of the Lost for more than two decades. Uma thought that Hades' life on the Isle of the Lost was probably not all that different from his former life in the Underworld—there was no sunlight down here either.

'Aren't you tired of living underground?' she asked. 'In this damp and dreary cave?'

'Is it any better up there?' he scoffed. 'On Auradon?'

'You fool! You know it is! I was there! The place is a fairytale land!' she told him. 'And we should be part of that fairytale.'

Hades yawned. 'I'm more of a myth guy.'

'Whatever you are, you're not content here. How could you be?' said Uma. 'You used to be a god! Don't you guys live on nectar and honey?'

Hades sniffed. 'We do have delicate constitutions. Not that you'd know anything about that, being an octopus.'

'Sea witch,' corrected Uma.

Hades looked suspicious. 'By the way, how did you get in here?'

'There was a crack in the tunnel. A tiny one.'

'And you fit through it?'

Uma waggled her eyebrows. 'I have my ways.'

Hades nodded. 'Shape-shifter. I get it. So why are you here? Why aren't you out there with your pirates?'

Uma studied her fingernails, affecting insouciance. 'I don't want to let anyone know I'm around until my plan is in motion.'

'You've got a plan?'

'I do,' she said with a crafty smile.

Hades picked up his real guitar and began to pluck a few discordant notes. 'Fine. Tell me.'

'We should team up, you and I. Together we could bring down the stupid barrier that holds everyone here. Then we could all be free!'

Hades listened. Then he smiled. Then he grinned. 'Bring down the barrier, huh?'

'Yes. And I would finally beat Mal.' That's all Uma wanted: to show Mal that she could beat her, that Mal didn't get to win every time. So Mal had won the trident, and Ben's heart, but Uma would have this. She would show her old friend, her forever rival, that Uma would have her revenge. Mal would never forget her name, or who freed the Isle of the Lost: UMA.

'Think about it. Once the barrier is down, you could go anywhere and do anything you wanted!' said Uma.

'You don't say?' said Hades. He played a chord and let it echo around the cave.

'I do say,' said Uma. 'How long have you been here? Twenty years? And how long were you in the Underworld?

They don't remember you up on Olympus anymore. Hades? He's over. He's *nothing*. That's what they say.'

'Is that so?' He waggled his eyebrows in frustration.

'I'm afraid so,' said Uma with a faux-sad frown. 'No-one remembers you. All they talk about is Hercules. I've met his kid, Herkie. He's huge as a bull and even more famous than his father.'

Hades threw off his guitar and paced the rocky cave floor. Soon he would overturn the lamp and kick the television set. His bad temper was as predictable as the weather.

'And Zeus, well, he's just having a ball up there on Mount Olympus. Every once in a while he throws down his lightning bolts just to remind everyone who's in charge,' said Uma. At this point she was completely spitballing. She had no clue what they were doing on Mount Olympus. But Hades didn't have to know that.

'But *I'm* the boss!' cried Hades. 'ME!'

'Then help me. Show them,' said Uma. 'Show them who's boss!'

'I will!' he said, his eyes lighting up. But Uma thought she saw something else flickering there, until he went on, 'I'll go back to ruling the world and causing destruction. We must take down the barrier and escape from the Isle of the Lost!'

'Now you're talking,' said Uma. She held out her hand. 'You know, you're not too bad for a has-been.'

Hades cackled. 'You ain't seen nothing yet!'

Some Time Ago...

Hole in the Sky

Hades paced on the beach and considered his situation. He was not without options. He had to try *something*. He couldn't just rot on this island forever. Come on, were they kidding? He was the lord of the Underworld, the god of the dead! In Olympus, they would be laughing if they saw him looking like some washed-up little minion. Yesterday he'd been offered the most disgusting stew, made by some deluded she-octopus at some little shack. And yet he had forced himself to choke it down, because he was hungry. He had no choice. But he vowed he would not spend one more day on this gods-forsaken rock.

He had an idea.

If there was an invisible barrier around the island, there had to be an end to it, right? It couldn't go on forever, could it? While there were rumours it was a dome, it seemed like it was basically a fence, which meant that he just had to find the top so he could jump over it into freedom! And if it was a dome, maybe the top would be weaker somehow—since the air was thinner up there and maybe the magic was, too.

He had corralled a bunch of pirates and promised them treasure chests full of gold if they helped him. Once they were convinced, he had ordered them to build a ladder using some old ships' masts tied together with rope and assorted pieces of wood they found in junk piles. Somehow, they made it work.

The ladder was so long it went almost the entire length of the beach. All they had to do now was set it upright. Then Hades would climb it all the way to the top, punch a hole in the dome with his little invention that he was carrying in a bag strapped across his chest, scale the barrier, and then slide down. He was a god. *Immortal.* Even if he fell from a great height he'd survive. Probably.

'On my count!' he told the crew.

'One, two . . . THREE!'

They heaved the ladder upright. Hades was delighted. 'That's what I'm talking about! Now hold it still.'

And then he began to climb.

He got dizzy and tried not to look down.

He kept climbing.

He saw mountain peaks in the distance. He spied ravens' nests in their crags. At one point he was so high up that his throat began to tighten from lack of oxygen until he remembered—duh, he was a god. He kept climbing.

He felt like he was practically as high as Olympus! Could he see it from here? Should he call out for Zeus or Athena? Nah, he'd give them a nice surprise when he was on the other side and had all his powers back.

Finally, he reached the end of the ladder. The pirates down below were just a bunch of dots. Hades removed a transistor radio from Jafar's junk shop that he'd been tinkering with; he'd carried it all the way up in his bag. He had this idea to shoot a bolt of electricity at the invisible barrier, sort of like using Zeus's bolts of lightning.

He pressed a switch and sent a huge jet of power blasting at the top of the invisible dome. The dome was supposed to shatter and fall, and everyone would be free. Including Hades!

But nothing happened. It didn't work.

The barrier was still there.

Hades raged. He screamed. He turned red—everywhere but his electric-blue hair, that is. If there had been magic on this side of the barrier, he would have burst into flames.

But instead, in his rage, he just fell off the ladder, back onto the island, hitting the ground with a *thump*.

The pirates looked over. 'You all right, dude?'

'I'm alive! I'm alive!' he said. (After all, he'd never been dead.)

Hades picked himself up and looked at the deep crater he'd created. Hmmm. Maybe he was going the wrong way. Maybe he should have been digging instead of climbing all along . . .

'Pirates!' he called. 'I've got a new idea.'

No Place Like Home

'My mother's not a barrel of laughs when she doesn't get her way. Just ask Snow White.'
—Evie, Descendants

chapter 16

Isle Alumni

One thing you could say about the Isle of the Lost was that it never changed. Mal wasn't sure if she loved or loathed that about the place. When Mal, Evie, Carlos and Jay arrived in the middle of the busy market, everything was exactly as they remembered it. The decrepit tenement buildings covered with peeling paint and graffiti on the sides, the lines of wet, ragged laundry that crisscrossed the plaza, the tin sheds, the hay carts, the vendors hawking everything from holey scarves to varnished trinkets. The sky was gloomy, and everyone looked filthy and sad. This was where they had come from, the neglected island prison where villains were trapped for their crimes against the people of Auradon.

Granted, the four of them had returned to the Isle not so long ago to fetch Mal and then rescue Ben from Uma's clutches. But, just the same, it was still a shock to see it.

Mal glanced up at her mother's old balcony. Her entire childhood had been spent in those shabby rooms above the Bargain Castle that sold wizard robes half price. She used to sit on that balcony and look wistfully over at the mainland, wondering when her life would change. Sometimes Jay came to join her and they would split a bag of stale cheese puffs, their fingers turning as orange as the sunset.

'Come on,' said Evie, taking Mal by the arm. 'Let's go to our old hideout.'

'Hideout?' asked Carlos. 'Isn't this an official visit from the palace? Don't we have any other place to stay?'

Evie smiled at him indulgently. 'You're cute.'

'You'd rather go to your house?' teased Mal.

'Never,' said Carlos. 'Lead the way.'

'There aren't any five-star castles on the Isle of the Lost,' Jay chided.

'I just remembered that,' said Carlos, smacking his forehead. 'If anyone asks, I didn't pack my spa bathrobe, okay?'

A few curious onlookers spotted them in the crowd, but most left them alone. Mal's fearsome reputation tended to keep people away. But even though it seemed like people still feared her, she wondered if they would ever look up to her as a true leader, someone to follow and admire and respect, especially now that she was on official business from Auradon. She tried smiling magnanimously at a street urchin who scurried past them, but the kid just squealed and sped up. Mal sighed. This wasn't going to be easy.

Once they arrived, Carlos found the hidden latch, and Jay threw his shoe at it. The iron door opened, and they walked up to the loft. It was just as they'd remembered, with graffiti on the walls, lumpy mattresses, and trash everywhere.

'Home, sweet hideout,' said Evie, wrinkling her nose. Mal knew she was thinking of their pretty room back at school, with its comfortable beds, fat fluffy pillows, neat rows of bookshelves and lush carpeting. Carlos grimaced at the sight, and Jay looked just as bummed. It was seriously grimy. There was soot on the windowsill, and there were streaks of dirt on the floor.

'It's only for a few days,' said Mal, trying to sound comforting.

'I know, I just . . . I always forget what it was like,' said Evie.

'Who wants to remember?' Jay smiled. 'Dibs on the couch.'

Carlos accidentally kicked a trash can, overturning its contents, and one of Harry's hooks rolled out. 'Pirates were here. Ugh. No wonder this place is such a dump,' he said, his frown deepening.

Jay glared at the mustaches and assorted doodles the pirates had drawn on the portraits of the four of them that Mal had painted on the walls. 'Animals!' he pronounced, and went to look for a rag.

They made the place as habitable as they could, sweeping up the trash and scrubbing the floors. Evie put clean sheets on the beds and unpacked the pillows she'd brought from Auradon. 'Thank goodness you don't travel light,' said Carlos, looking relieved.

'Never,' promised Evie, removing a vase and flowers from the bottom of her trunk. She looked around at the newly clean and brightened space. They had brought a little Auradon to their old pad. 'Better.'

'Let's get going,' said Mal. She felt a rush of energy. 'I want to make the announcement as soon as possible.'

They left and locked the hideout, and Mal led them out through the crowded bazaar back to her old castle. Inside, everything was covered with a thick layer of dust, from Maleficent's old throne to the green refrigerator that still held goblin slime from two years ago. For a moment, Mal felt sad about her mother, who was still trapped as a lizard—wherever she was now.

Mal braced herself to go out on the balcony and address the crowd.

'Hold on,' said Evie, brushing Mal's hair from her forehead and pulling up her jacket collar. 'Better.'

'Thanks,' said Mal, trying not to feel too nervous.

'You've got this, okay? It's a great plan, and I know you're going to do Auradon proud,' reassured Evie.

'I just really want this to work,' said Mal, taking a deep breath.

'I know. Me too,' said Evie.

'You're gonna be great!' said Carlos. Jay grinned and clapped Mal on the shoulder for encouragement. She smiled and stepped onto the balcony.

Mal took her place and raised her hands to signal for attention. Jay, Carlos and Evie walked behind her, fanning out so that everyone could see them. Mal hoped they looked like a power squad, and not like a bunch of kids who didn't know what they were getting themselves into.

A hush fell over the crowd as the people of the Isle of the Lost spotted them. But whatever Mal had expected their reaction to be, it wasn't this. The audience shrank back, whispering wildly and gesturing with fright towards the four of them. Some people even seemed to be trembling! A few of the little ones were outright crying. Mal looked around in confusion and disbelief. She knew she had a reputation, but how scary did they really think she was?

Evie crept up beside her. 'Um . . . Mal?'

Mal stage-whispered back, 'What's going on? Why do they look so freaked-out?'

Carlos cleared his throat. 'Well, we're kind of standing in the shadows,' he said, gesturing to the overhang that was cloaking them in darkness. 'I think that they think you're, well, your mum.'

It was only then that Mal could make out the fervent, terrified whispers from the crowd. 'Maleficent!' they were saying. 'She's back!' Someone in the crowd shrieked and ran away.

Mal tugged down the collar of her jacket—which might have looked a bit cape-like in silhouette, she realised. But, come on, it's not like she had *horns*. She stepped out of the shadows and into the sunlight.

'Guys, guys,' she said, waving her hands. 'It's me, Mal!' *And my mum is like, eating leaves and lying on a rock somewhere,* she wanted to add, but didn't.

A murmur rippled through the crowd as terror turned into something that resembled relief, but a relief that was definitely still tinged with terror. *Mal! She's back! Mal's going to curse us! Why is she here? Who's that behind her? Why, it's the four of them! They're all back! I like Evie's dress! What's Mal going to do to us?!*

'I hope my mother doesn't find out I'm here,' muttered Carlos, standing next to Evie.

'Shhh,' said Evie, who was waving to the crowd and blowing kisses like a true princess. 'Everyone calm down! We have good news!' called Evie, but the crowd ignored her and continued to churn with nervous energy.

Jay stepped forwards. 'Settle down, settle down!' he commanded. 'Go on, Mal, tell them.'

Mal raised her hands once more for silence. This time, she got it.

'Hi,' she started again, then took a breath and squared her shoulders. 'I have an official announcement from the kingdom of Auradon. Auradon Prep is taking more applications from the Isle of the Lost!' Mal paused, glancing around for applause or gasps of excitement. But they were only staring up at her silently. 'Four new kids are going to be selected to attend the school, just like we were. I promise you, this is the opportunity of a lifetime, and I hope you'll all consider applying. Join us on the mainland!'

Mal finished her announcement with a grin and waited. But the villains were just shaking their heads. They grumbled to each other: *School? Who wants to go to school? Auradon? Why would we want to go there? This is stupid. Homework? Ew.*

The crowd began to disperse, muttering and shaking their heads. Evie rushed up next to Mal, her arms outstretched. 'Wait! Hear us out! Please!'

'Please?' Mal heard one of the kids scoff. No-one ever used common courtesies like *please* on the Isle. Mal thought that most of them must have been shocked into complying, though, because they all seemed to pause.

'Yes, listen!' said Carlos. 'We've had a great time in Auradon! There are so many delicious things to eat that aren't even rotten or expired. And so many awesome desserts!'

'There's this game called tourney,' said Jay. 'Where you can really beat someone up!' Evie shot him a look and he shrugged. 'You have to give them what they want to hear.'

Mal nodded. Jay was right. They would never be able to explain the appeal of Auradon to people who only knew life on the Isle of the Lost. But she had to try.

'I was like you once,' she said. 'I just wanted to live a wicked life, full of treachery and evil deeds. But Auradon changed me. I realised there's more to life than being wicked.'

'Like what?' sneered a snaggletoothed witch.

'Well . . .' said Mal, searching for something the crowd would respond to. 'There's strawberries—these amazing fruits that burst with flavour on your tongue!'

'And there's this stuff called peanut butter!' said Carlos. 'It's . . . like butter! Made from peanuts!'

'They don't know what butter is except that it's rancid,' Evie reminded him in a whisper. 'Let me try.' She stepped up to the railing. 'Like Mal said, there's more to life than being evil. There's loyalty and friendship.' The four of them linked hands and smiled at each other.

'You will find friends who will do anything for you,' said Carlos.

'You'll discover that you're more than what you thought you were,' added Jay, and they lifted their hands to the sky in unison.

'And there's love,' said Mal, feeling tears come to her

eyes. She was Maleficent's daughter, born and bred to hate, to plot, to scheme, to command minions to do her bidding. Mistress of Darkness. Queen of the Isle of the Lost. But all she felt for this ragged, unruly crowd was deep empathy and affection. Mal wished they could all understand that there were greater things to live for than revenge or violence or pettiness, greed and corruption.

The crowd still didn't look too convinced, but Mal thought it was a good start. She had to give them time. Even the four of them took a while to discover they were better off in Auradon than the Isle of the Lost.

chapter 17

Big, Bad Voodoo Daddy

The next morning, they all headed back to their old stomping grounds at Dragon Hall. Evie felt a momentary rush of nostalgia for the place. Even though it was no Auradon Prep, she had always loved coming to Dragon Hall—especially after all those isolated years of castle-schooling. The front steps of the mausoleum were full of students tripping each other and pushing their way up the stairs in the usual morning chaos. Once again, the kids stared as they noticed Mal, Jay, Carlos and Evie in their midst.

The whispers buzzed through the crowd. *Isn't that Mal?*

What's she doing here? Did you hear she turned her mother into a lizard? Don't stare or she'll turn you into one!

Evie saw that Mal was trying to smile at them, but when she did, the kids ran from her. 'How am I ever going to connect with them if they can't see past my old reputation?' she asked Evie with a sigh. 'I'm not my mum. It seems like people in Auradon finally get that. But maybe everyone on the Isle will always think of me as the old Mal.'

'They'll come around,' Evie said firmly, as she looped her arm through Mal's.

'And if they don't, Mal will burn them with her dragon fire,' said Jay with a laugh.

The girls glared at him. 'Not the point, Jay,' said Mal.

He held up his hands in surrender. 'I was just kidding!'

A trembling LeFou Deux awaited them at the entrance of the school. 'Welcome back to Dragon Hall. Please follow me. Dr Facilier is expecting you.' He grovelled, bowing so low his forehead almost touched the floor.

LeFou Deux led them to the headmaster's hidden office in the Athenaeum of Secrets. Dr Facilier was seated at his faded velvet chair, but he stood when they entered. 'Welcome back,' he said with a terrifying grin. He was as tall and slender as ever—almost as thin as his mustache. He shook their hands with his long, bony fingers. Dr Facilier never failed to strike fear into the hearts of Dragon Hall's pupils, and Evie knew the four of them were having difficulty remembering that they were no longer under his supervision. They were Auradon Prep students now, and protected by Fairy Godmother, she reminded herself.

'Now, what brings the four of you here?' he asked as they all sat down. 'Not looking to come back, I presume? Or are you?' He laughed heartily at his own joke.

Evie shot the other three a nervous smile. 'Planning to trap us here, Dr Facilier?' she asked lightly.

'Oh, no, no,' he said, with a wave of his hand. 'As much as I would enjoy trying, I don't think that would be beneficial to anyone.'

Mal cleared her throat and sat up straight. 'Auradon Prep is expanding its program to bring more students from the Isle of the Lost over to the mainland,' she told him. 'So we were hoping you could distribute these applications and encourage kids to sign up. And as you discussed with the Royal Council, tomorrow we will be available to talk to students and answer any questions they might have about Auradon.'

Carlos opened his backpack and handed over a stack of papers to their old headmaster. 'Here you go,' he said.

Dr Facilier picked up one of the documents. 'And how many kids from the Isle of the Lost is Auradon Prep accepting?'

'Four,' said Jay.

'I see,' Dr Facilier said, as he continued to study the forms. 'And if I do this for you, what's my cut?'

Mal blinked. 'Your cut?'

'Excuse me?' asked Evie, as Carlos hesitated to remove more application forms from his backpack.

'Your cut,' said Jay, deadpan. 'Your bribe, you mean.'

The headmaster of Dragon Hall leaned back on his chair, put his feet up on his desk, and took a moment to admire his shiny shoes. 'Exactly. What do I get in return for sending students to your program?'

'The joy of knowing they're learning and well cared for!' Evie said indignantly.

'Dr Facilier, that's not really how it works,' said Mal sharply. 'We don't do kickbacks or deliver bribes. Especially not in Auradon.'

Dr Facilier chuckled, sending shivers up their spines. 'Let me remind you, you're back on the Isle of the Lost now.'

'What do you want?' Jay asked bluntly.

'Yeah, spill it,' said Carlos.

Evie looked at the boys, alarmed, but Mal nodded. 'I suppose it's the price of doing business,' she said. Mal gave Evie a look that said, *Just trust me.*

'I'm glad we're in agreement,' said Dr Facilier with a smug smile. 'I don't ask for much. You know my younger daughter Celia, don't you?'

Mal narrowed her eyes. 'I don't think we've met, no.'

'She feels very left out when she hears all the stories that her sister Freddie has been telling her about Auradon. Very left out indeed,' said Dr Facilier meaningfully.

Mal and Evie exchanged a glance. 'We're not on the admissions committee,' said Evie.

'But I'm sure you could put in a good word,' said Dr Facilier.

Mal raised an eyebrow. 'We'll take that under advisement,' she said. 'That is, if you honour your end of the bargain.'

'You see that you do,' said Dr Facilier. 'So, for tomorrow, you will be speaking with students at some kind of roundtable discussion?'

'Yes,' said Mal. 'We're going to tell them all about Auradon Prep! I believe we've been given the study hall for our presentation.'

Dr Facilier sighed. 'Fine, I don't see how I can stop you, since I've been ordered by Fairy Godmother to let you in.'

Mal nodded. The four of them began to stand up to say their goodbyes.

'Also,' said Evie, 'we're going to be sending over posters—marketing materials, to encourage the kids to apply. It would be great if we could put up some here at Dragon Hall as well.'

Dr Facilier shrugged. 'I suppose we could agree to that,' he said.

'Great,' said Mal.

'Just remember her name: Celia.'

'Of course,' said Mal. 'We'll do our best.'

The four of them shook Dr Facilier's hand. Evie knew

they weren't in the business of taking bribes; if Celia deserved to get in to Auradon Prep, she would. But it would be on her own merit, not because the VKs swayed the committee. They left the application forms at the headmaster's office and reminded him of the deadline.

'A pleasure doing business with you,' said Dr Facilier, ushering them out of his office. 'Oh, and here's Celia now. Celia, come meet these fine folk.'

Celia jumped back. It was obvious to Evie that she had been eavesdropping at the door. 'Oh! Hi, Dad,' she said. She wore a red dress and a little top hat that matched her father's, and she was holding a deck of cards.

'Celia, this is Mal, Evie, Carlos and Jay. They used to be my top students here, but unfortunately they go to Auradon Prep now.'

'Nice to meet you,' said Celia. 'Want to hear your fortune?'

Dr Facilier smiled proudly. 'That's my girl.' He closed the door, and the four VKs were left in the hallway with Celia.

They all hesitated, but it was clear Celia was intent on reading someone their cards.

'Sure, tell me my fortune,' Evie relented. She could humour the kid, right?

'We're going to talk to a few more teachers to make sure they tell kids about the Auradon Prep roundtable tomorrow,' said Mal. 'I don't trust Dr Facilier to get those applications out. Maybe Lady Tremaine can help, since Dizzy really wants to go to Auradon.'

'Sounds like a plan,' said Carlos. 'Jay, you go find Coach Gaston in PE, and I'll hit up Madam Mim.'

'I'll go meet Professor Gothel and catch up with you guys at the hideout after hearing my fortune,' said Evie.

They nodded and went their separate ways.

Celia led Evie to a quiet desk in the library. She offered the cards to Evie to shuffle. Evie closed her eyes and shuffled them. Celia took the cards back and laid them out in three piles. Then she revealed the top card of each deck. 'These three cards represent the past, the present and the future,' she told Evie. 'The first card is the Tower. It means you came from a difficult past. You were trapped and in danger.'

'Pretty much. I mean, I am from the Isle of the Lost,' said Evie. 'I was exiled to our castle with my mother, the Evil Queen.'

'Dangerous indeed,' said Celia.

'When I missed our usual Friday face mask, she wanted to murder me,' said Evie with a roll of her eyes. In truth, she did miss her shallow, beauty-obsessed mother just a little bit. Still, she would rather keep her distance while they were on the Isle; it just wasn't worth it when her mother would never understand the things Evie wanted to accomplish. 'On Thursdays we practised smiling and waving.'

Celia snorted. She pointed to the second card on the

table. 'The Ten of Pentacles. This is your present. It means you have strength behind you. That you belong to a group of people who have your back. They bring you a lot of luck.'

Evie smiled. 'I have an amazing group of friends.'

'And the third card is your future. Oh,' said Celia staring at the card. 'It's dark.'

'It is?' asked Evie nervously.

'Very. This is the Judgment card. It means change, mostly for the worse. This card means disaster is on the horizon. Something terrible is about to happen. Aaaaaaand'—Celia drew out the word, quirking her eyebrows at Evie—'if you want to know how to prevent it, you'll have to buy another session.'

'Another session?! How much was this one?' asked Evie. 'I didn't realise you charged.'

'Of course I do. Nothing's free in this world.' Celia smirked and named her price.

'Okay,' said Evie, opening her purse and handing over a few gold coins. 'But I'm not paying for another one.'

'Really? I don't advise that. You should really find out how to avoid whatever it is the Judgment has foretold. Or you should at least try to discover who is conspiring against you guys.'

Evie knew a hustle when she saw one. 'Nice try, but I'll take my chances,' she said with a sweet smile.

'Suit yourself,' said Celia, putting her cards away.

Evie shook her head. She was far from superstitious and

was highly sceptical that the future could be divined from a few fortune cards. She wondered about Celia's chances with the Auradon Prep admissions committee. So far, all Evie could see was a trickster through and through. But, of course, that didn't mean there wasn't more to Celia—after all, there had been more to Evie and her friends. It was going to be interesting to see if Celia ended up at Auradon, that was for sure.

chapter 18

This Little Light of Mine

The same day that Mal and her friends were meeting with Dr Facilier at Dragon Hall, Uma returned to Hades' lair. The blue-haired ex-god of the dead was snoring on his couch, a little line of drool dripping from his open mouth. He woke up with a start when Uma cleared her throat.

'You again?' said Hades, rubbing the sleep from his eyes. 'I thought we had a deal. You agreed to leave me alone,' he groused.

'That wasn't our deal,' said Uma, annoyed. 'And did you ever think of doing any housekeeping around here? This cave reeks.'

Hades looked affronted. 'I'm sorry my league of demons are more interested in preying on souls than vacuuming. Anyway, did you hear that Mal was spotted on Maleficent's balcony last night? I thought it might interest you, given our agreement.'

Uma looked furious. 'She's back on the Isle of the Lost, is she?'

'That's right,' said Hades, a strange look on his face. Uma thought she caught something that almost looked like regret there. But regret for what?

'Ugh! I can just picture it. Mal and her little minions, strutting around thinking they're so great, as if they own the place, when all they did was abandon it!' said Uma, who could never stand the way Mal and her friends acted like the Isle was their territory. The Isle of the Lost was *her* turf. She ached to reveal herself to Mal and show them exactly who was the real lady of this island. But she had to stay focused on the plan. If she showed her hand too quickly, she might lose her advantage. She had to be patient. And she had to have Hades on her side.

'Okay, so?' said Hades, who was now looking through his record collection to find something to play on his ancient record player.

Uma raised an eyebrow at the albums Hades picked up. They never got anything good on the Isle, only Auradon castoffs that no-one on the island really wanted. *Sebastian the*

Crab's Greatest Hits. Genie Sings the Blues. Eugene Fitzherbert and His Polka Band.

She shook her head impatiently. 'So we need to get to Mal. If we can get to Mal, I can get hold of the remote control that opens the barrier. Click—open and out.'

'Sounds simple enough,' said Hades.

'Except I can't get that close. She knows I'll cause trouble for her, so if she sees me, she'll run the other way. I need her to come to me, where she won't be able to escape.'

Hades barked a laugh and gave up searching for a decent record. He grabbed a copy of his own band's last album instead. 'She's a smart one to avoid you, then.'

'Obviously,' said Uma. 'But we can't give up just yet. You said you still have your ember, right?'

'Yeah, but I hate to break it to you, kid, it doesn't glow anymore. It's useless.' Hades flopped down on one of the broken recliners in his cave and opened an expired canned coffee drink from the Slop Shop. He took a big gulp and grimaced. 'Black as my soul indeed.'

Uma shook her head. 'Do you see all these cracks in the tunnel?' she asked, pointing to the fissures on the cave wall and ceiling.

'Yeah? So what?'

She leaned over so she was almost in his face. 'I think these cracks might let in a little magic. We're so far beneath the island that Fairy Godmother's spell is weaker down here.'

Hades perked up. 'A little magic? Is that so?' He put away his coffee.

'There's only one way to find out, isn't there? Bring it out,' she ordered. 'Let's see if it still works.'

Hades sighed and got up to fetch the ember. 'I usually keep it in my sock drawer . . .' he said. 'Hmm. When was the last time I had it? Ah, here we go.' He strode over to his desk and grabbed it from where it had been holding down a stack of papers.

'It's dead; I was using it as a paperweight,' he said, showing it to Uma. In his hand was a grey rock. It was just a hunk of coal, nothing more. No spark.

'Try it,' Uma urged.

He waved a hand above it. Nothing happened. He waved his hand once more. Still nothing. 'I told you, it's useless . . .'

'THERE!' yelled Uma.

A minuscule, almost imperceptible spark of blue light shone in the centre of the grey stone. It was barely there, but still—it was definitely glowing.

Uma hooted. 'I told you!'

Hades gazed at his ember with what looked like love. It wasn't enough magic to get them out of there, but it was magic. He wasn't powerless after all.

'You need Mal to come to you, right?' he asked thoughtfully.

'Right.'

'Leave it to me. I'll take care of Mal.'

'Perfect. And, Hades? Don't fail me. Or I'll feed you to my mother,' Uma threatened with a toss of her turquoise braids.

'That would improve her stew, if you ask me,' said Hades. 'Now scram!'

chapter 19

The Walls Have Ears

Dr Facilier would've been proud to know that, at that very moment, his daughter Celia was cutting class and sneaking around the Isle of the Lost instead of sitting through another boring lecture about the history of evil. After failing to sell Evie on another fortune reading, Celia had snuck out of Dragon Hall through the basement, which led to an underground tunnel system that snaked all around the island. It was an easy way to get around without being seen.

The tunnels were dark and damp, and rumour had it that magic had once run wild down here, creating wondrous lands underneath the island, along with a pathway that led to Auradon itself. That is, until Mal and her friends had shut off the entrance to the Catacombs and the magical barrier was reinforced once more, Celia recalled glumly. Now there was just the one underground channel, through a leftover mine shaft.

Celia was winding through the mine shaft and approaching Hades' cave when she heard a new voice inside with him. Hades hardly ever had visitors. It was why she ran errands for him sometimes. So who was there now? The voice sounded highly annoyed. Celia strained her ears until she recognised it with a start. That could only belong to one surly pirate queen: *Uma*. Uma was back! What were they talking about? Celia tried to press her ear to the wall, but she couldn't make out much. Something about the barrier, it sounded like. 'Click—open and out,' she heard Uma say, but it was hard to hear the rest.

'I'll take care of Mal,' she heard Hades say. There was more murmuring, and then Hades boomed, 'Now scram!'

That she heard loud and clear.

The door to the cave opened with a bang, and Celia pressed herself against the tunnel walls, hoping Uma wouldn't see her. But Uma never appeared. She definitely wasn't in Hades' cave anymore, though. After his outburst, Hades' lair had gone silent.

Take care of Mal?

Click—open and out? What was that?

What were Hades and Uma planning?

It had to be an escape of some sort. A way to get off the Isle of the Lost. That was all Uma—and every other villain on the Isle—had ever wanted.

Celia felt her heart beat loudly in her chest. She bolted out of the tunnel and ran all the way back up to Dragon Hall, where she bumped into Dizzy, who was leaving her Introduction to Scheming class. She and Dizzy had become good friends ever since Dizzy had designed her the little hat she wore—at least, as good friends as anyone could be on the Isle. Celia *loved* her hat. 'Dizzy!' she called, trying to push her way through the crowd of villains in the hallway.

'Yes?' asked Dizzy, pushing up her glasses.

Celia looked around the halls to make sure no-one was listening. 'Want to hear the craziest thing?' She liked being the first to know and share gossip around the Isle.

'Um . . . I guess so?' said Dizzy, looking wary.

'They're going to let four more kids from here go to school in Auradon,' said Celia. 'Just like Mal and her friends!'

Dizzy yelped in glee. 'They are? Do you think they'll finally take me?'

'You were invited. Of course they'll take you! But this

means three more kids will get to come, too. Maybe I'll be one of them!' said Celia.

Dizzy squealed. 'That would be wicked! Wicked good, you know.'

'And I could finally hang out with my older sister Freddie, too. She owes me some money from when I read her fortune before she left.'

'Oh, Celia,' said Dizzy. 'You never change.'

'I know.' Celia drummed her fingers together and smirked. Dizzy gave her a look that said she didn't approve of whatever Celia was scheming. But Celia just laughed. Then she remembered the next part of her news. 'Oh, and . . .' She was about to tell Dizzy more, but the second bell rang and Dizzy had to run.

Celia shrugged. Uma and Hades were definitely planning to bring down the barrier somehow and let everyone out. Except, hmm . . . Uma and Hades hadn't succeeded at anything yet, and probably wouldn't succeed at this either. The only thing they would achieve would be getting everyone on the Isle of the Lost in trouble.

And if everyone on the Isle of the Lost was in trouble, then no-one would be allowed to go to Auradon. That would definitely cut into her plan of bringing her card-reading gig to Auradon. Not ideal, since they were so very trusting over there.

She began to shuffle her cards like she did when she

was feeling anxious. Was this the bad fortune she always predicted for everyone when she read them their cards?

Should she do something about it? Like warn Mal and her friends, maybe?

Maybe.

chapter 20

Blasts from the Past

Wherever Mal went in Dragon Hall, it was like her old life was mocking her. She had her work cut out for her to convince everyone that she was straight and true, that was for sure. It was hard for them to believe she was really Mal of Auradon now. To them, she would always be Maleficent's rotten little spawn. Or worse, if they did believe she was good, they were disappointed in her. That much was clear when she went to meet with Lady Tremaine, who had once taught her Advanced Evil Schemes. The evil stepmother was less than thrilled to see her best student fall into the 'clutches of good', as she put it.

'Oh, Mal, how far you've fallen,' sighed Lady Tremaine. 'And now you've corrupted my little Dizzy as well.'

'I'm proud of Dizzy,' said Mal. 'She's a great kid.'

Lady Tremaine waved her hand dismissively. 'I suppose I should rest my hopes on my other grandchildren. I know why you're here.'

'You know about the VK program? And the Auradon Prep roundtable tomorrow?'

'Yes, yes, yes, we received the royal proclamation and heard about your . . . shall we say, *ineffective* balcony announcement,' said Lady Tremaine, sniffing. She picked up the application form that Mal had placed on her desk and read it out loud: '"Mal and King Ben ask you to be truthful and sincere, and to always speak from the heart."' The steely-eyed professor looked over at Mal through her pince-nez glasses. 'Where on earth do you think you'll find students who will act that way? Not here.'

Mal flushed. 'We need to find them, to unite our divided kingdom.'

'Good luck,' said Lady Tremaine dryly.

'I know there are students at this very school who have the courage to join us in Auradon. I was one,' said Mal. 'I just didn't know it back then.' She tried to sit straighter and project some kind of authority. Ben always seemed to be able to command the respect of the room in his council meetings. Why couldn't Mal convince just this one person to take her seriously?

Lady Tremaine drummed her fingers on her desk. 'The Mal I knew excelled at evil pranks; the Mal I knew spelled a boy to force him to fall in love with her. The Mal I knew is just biding her time to rule the kingdom.' She winked. 'That *is* what you're doing, isn't it?'

Mal was about to protest when she nodded. If she couldn't beat 'em, she would at least pretend to join 'em. In the end, she just wanted to make sure the kids came to the discussion tomorrow and had access to the applications, even if she and Lady Tremaine couldn't see eye to eye. 'Exactly.'

'Excellent. I will be happy to find such students to send you tomorrow,' said Lady Tremaine.

Coach Gaston was running doomball drills when Jay interrupted to talk about the new VK program. Gaston looked the same as he always did: dark-haired, aggressively handsome with his swell cleft of a chin, and still as large as a barge. 'You want me to talk to the kids about going to school in Auradon?' he asked, scratching his incredibly thick neck. 'And send them to some event you have planned tomorrow?'

'Would you, Coach?' asked Jay.

Gaston shrugged. 'What do they have in Auradon that's so great, anyway?'

'For starters, they can have five dozen eggs for breakfast if they want,' said Jay, who knew the way to Gaston's heart was through his breakfasts.

'We have that here,' said Gaston. 'Rotten, of course, but you get used to the taste.'

'Right,' Jay said with a sigh. 'I'll leave the forms here, just in case.'

Madam Mim was in between teaching classes in alchemy when Carlos arrived. 'Shut the door!' she screeched when he entered. 'You're letting in too much sunlight! Bah! I hate sunlight!'

'Okay! Sorry!' said Carlos. 'How are you, Professor?'

'As bad as can be,' moaned Madam Mim. 'Ever since they closed off the Catacombs I've been terribly hungry.' Madam Mim used the old tunnels to poach sheep and wildlife from the farms surrounding Camelot. She had quite a large appetite when she was in her dragon form. She narrowed her eyes suddenly. 'Weren't you one of the kids responsible for shutting them down?'

'W-well, um . . .' Carlos stammered. Then he shook his head. His mother might be terrifying, but he wasn't going to let himself be intimidated by Madam Mim. 'Sorry about that,' he said. 'But that's not what I'm here to talk about today.'

'Then what's this all about? That Auradon program, is it?' Madam Mim sniffed.

'Yes! Would you mind distributing these forms to your students? And reminding them that four of us from Auradon Prep will be taking questions tomorrow during study hall?' He deliberately didn't call it a *roundtable*, so as not to upset Madam Mim with bad memories of Arthur and his knights.

'I suppose I could,' said Madam Mim, taking the stack of papers from him. 'Although why anyone would want to stay in Auradon for that long, I don't know. It's always sunny there.'

Evie had always been Mother Gothel's favourite student during her time at Dragon Hall; Evie had excelled in her Self-Interest, Selfishness and Selfies classes. Mother Gothel was trying out another age-defying skin cream when Evie found her in the faculty lounge.

'Evie! Your skin! It's glowing!' said Mother Gothel jealously. 'What's your secret?'

'Fresh air, exercise and a healthy diet,' Evie replied with a smile.

'Bah!' said Mother Gothel. 'Who wants to do that?'

'Try it, you might like it,' said Evie cheerfully. She set a bunch of applications in front of her former professor. 'I wanted to drop these off with you, to give to your students. Did you hear about the VK program?'

'Who hasn't?' said Mother Gothel, curling her lip. 'You know we're all gossips here on the Isle.'

Evie's smile faltered a little. 'Well, the four of us are going to be taking any questions tomorrow during a roundtable at study hall. If anyone's curious about Auradon

Prep, they can come and talk to us. It would be great if you could let people know.'

Mother Gothel shrugged. 'People make their own decisions around here.'

'Please,' said Evie. She opened her purse and removed a tiny jar of moisturiser and pushed it across the table. 'From me, as a token of my appreciation.' If it would help get a few kids to apply to Auradon Prep, was it truly that bad?

Mother Gothel snatched it up greedily without a word of thanks, but, of course, Evie hadn't expected any.

The four friends met back up in the loft at the end of the day. They were hungry for dinner, so Evie opened her trunk again and set out a full meal, pulling out a picnic blanket, a cooler full of icy drinks, and hot containers of fried chicken and mashed potatoes. 'Bless you,' said Carlos, awed by the incredible spread in front of them. 'I thought we'd have to go to Ursula's Fish and Chips Shoppe to eat.'

'Or the Slop Shop,' said Jay with a shudder. 'Goblin cuisine. Blegh. I used to get the worst stomach-aches.'

'Preparation is the key to success,' said Evie, spooning out braised greens and yams.

'And Mrs Potts,' added Mal.

'Hear, hear,' agreed Evie, handing out napkins and utensils. They helped themselves and murmured their thanks to the benevolent school cook.

'So how'd it go?' Evie asked. 'Do you think we'll get

more applications? And anyone to come to the roundtable tomorrow?'

'We tried,' said Mal. 'Hopefully.'

'Who knows?' said Jay. 'They'd be silly to miss out on Auradon Prep.'

Carlos shrugged. He was too busy eating.

There was a knock on the secret door, and Evie went to answer it. 'Oh, hey, Celia,' she said. 'What's up? I don't think anyone else is interested in having their fortune read.'

'No, I'm not here for that,' said Celia, flushing a little.

'Okay,' said Evie, ushering her inside. 'Come and have a bite to eat with us, then.'

Celia's eyes grew wide at the picnic spread. For a moment, the four VKs felt guilty for the bounty they shared. No-one ate this well on the island. 'Here, have a doughnut,' said Carlos.

'Thanks,' said Celia, and took a big bite.

'So, what's up?' asked Mal.

Celia put down the doughnut and fidgeted with the sleeve of her dress. 'I came to tell you guys: Uma's back. She's definitely on the Isle of the Lost somewhere. And I think she's coming for you, Mal.'

Mal wiped her mouth with a napkin. 'Uma hasn't been seen anywhere, Celia,' she said reassuringly. 'I promise, Ben and I have been taking the security of both Auradon and the Isle very seriously. Anyway, if she were back, she'd be with her pirates.'

'But my cards foretell doom and disaster,' said Celia.

Jay cocked his eyebrow. 'Do they, now?'

'I wouldn't believe everything the cards say,' said Evie, shaking her head and starting to put things away, folding up the picnic blanket and saving the leftovers in plastic containers.

'Whatever it is, we can take care of it,' said Carlos. 'Don't worry about us.'

'But I heard Uma's voice! And we all know Uma is *dangerous*,' said Celia defensively. 'She already attacked you guys once!'

'We're leaving the day after tomorrow,' said Mal. 'We'll be fine. And we will watch out for Uma, I promise.' But Evie saw something flicker in Mal's eyes. Was Mal worried? Were they safe from Uma? Evie shook away her thoughts. Everything was fine. They were just here to do a job. Nothing bad was going to happen!

'Okay,' said Celia finally. 'Don't say I didn't warn you.'

'We won't,' said Mal. 'Thanks for coming by.'

'If something happens, you owe me for predicting it correctly,' said Celia with a smirk. 'I take gold coins. Lots of them.'

'How can we forget?' said Jay dryly.

They said goodbye to Celia, and Evie sent her off with the leftovers. Mal locked the door behind her.

'Do you really think Uma's back on the Isle?' asked Carlos, when it was just the four of them.

'Anything's possible,' said Mal. 'We'll keep watch.'

'Okay, I'll take the first shift,' said Jay.

'Uma again,' said Evie with a sigh. She supposed that, on an island full of villains, they should be glad there was only one to worry about, but it was a fitful night's sleep nevertheless.

chapter 21

Square Pegs in a Round Table

When he lived on the Isle, Jay used to sleep in until noon, but now that he was an Auradon kid, he was up bright and early the next day—even if he had been up all night keeping watch for anything suspicious. There was too much to do to stay in bed! The four of them had to get ready for the roundtable event they'd planned for study hall. 'Do you think anyone will show?' asked Carlos, yawning as they made their way back to campus.

'I hope so,' said Evie, looking determined. She had made a slideshow and everything, even giving it a sound track.

'They will,' said Mal. 'If only out of curiosity.'

'Curiosity killed the cat,' Jay reminded them with a grin. 'But in this case, curiosity will send people to Auradon!'

When they arrived, they discovered to their dismay that the room used for study hall was covered in dust and cobwebs, and it made Jay sneeze. 'We forgot,' said Evie. 'No-one actually *goes* to study hall.'

'Because no-one studies,' said Carlos. 'It's Dragon Hall.'

They set about clearing the cobwebs and putting the chairs in a semicircle. Then they waited for students to arrive. Minutes ticked by. Mal fiddled with her notes. Evie took out her journal and sketched some dresses. Carlos did homework. Jay paced the room, unable to keep still.

'You guys, I don't think anyone is coming,' he said.

'Maybe we should have met with Yen Sid? You know, and his secret Anti-Heroes Club?' said Evie. 'They were helpful in shutting down the Catacombs that time, remember?'

'Yen Sid is on a sabbatical. He's actually back in Auradon—I checked yesterday after meeting with Coach Gaston,' said Jay. 'And the Anti-Heroes Club was disbanded by Dr Facilier when he found out it was actually a pro-heroes and anti-villains club. I think those kids are a bit freaked out.'

'Bummer,' said Carlos. 'They would have been great candidates.'

'Shhh,' said Mal. 'I think someone's here.'

The door creaked open. Ginny Gothel, who used to be one of Mal's friends on the island, entered. 'I think I'm in the wrong place. This isn't the world-domination seminar, is it?' she asked.

'No!' said Mal. 'But it could be. I mean, you could learn about how to dominate the world for good.'

'Why would I want to do that?' sneered Ginny with a toss of her curly black hair.

'It would mean getting out of here,' said Jay. 'For one.'

Ginny thought it over and took a seat. 'Okay.'

Jay shot Mal a triumphant grin. Mal grinned back.

'We're going to wait for a few more students before we get started,' said Mal.

Jay hoped there would be a few more, but he wasn't counting on it. Then the door opened again, and Anthony Tremaine walked inside. Anastasia's son was as fastidiously dressed as ever; even though his jeans were patched, they were still immaculate. He raised an eyebrow when he saw Jay. 'Oh, it's you,' he said in a haughty voice.

'You,' Jay said with a menacing tone. Then he smiled happily. 'I was hoping I'd run into you! Here you go.' He handed Anthony his wallet. 'I've been holding on to it for a while, I stole it a long time ago. Sorry.'

Anthony took it back with a dubious look on his face. He opened the wallet and counted the bills inside.

'It's all in there,' said Jay.

'*Quelle surprise*,' said Anthony, who liked to make people feel inferior by speaking in French. 'My grandmother sent me.'

He sullenly took a seat next to Ginny Gothel, just as LeFou Deux walked in. The squat little boy looked nervously at the older kids in the room. 'Coach Gaston forced me to be here,' he explained. 'I'm too scared to go to Auradon.'

The last student was Mad Maddy, one of Madam Mim's granddaughters. She had her namesake's wild hair and fierce expression. She too, looked balefully at the four Auradon representatives. 'This is the roundtable thing, right? About getting into Auradon?'

'Yes, it is!' said Evie. 'Please, take a seat.' She glanced nervously over at Mal, and it seemed like Evie was wondering if Mal would be upset at seeing her old-friend-turned-enemy. But Mal just smirked and shrugged.

Mad Maddy took the other seat next to Ginny Gothel, and the two of them were soon whispering and cackling. Anthony looked bored and LeFou Deux kept fidgeting.

'I think this is it,' said Jay, whispering to Mal. 'We need to start, or we'll lose them too.'

'Evie, did you want to start?' asked Mal.

'Sure!' said Evie, running up to the chalkboard to pull down a screen, which was also covered in dust. Once she stopped coughing, she turned to her friends. 'Jay, the lights? Carlos, can you run the projector?'

'Since we can't bring you guys to Auradon Prep, we thought we'd bring Auradon Prep to you,' said Evie, hitting **play** on her computer to begin her slideshow. A photograph of the main castle building came on-screen, and the school song began playing in the background. The next slides showed earnest Auradon kids in classrooms, learning how to be good, the homecoming and tourney championship games, the marching band and the cheer squad, along with various shots of ordinary life—students laughing, eating and hanging out.

Jay turned the lights back on and was discomfited to find their entire audience had fallen asleep. He and Evie shared a distressed glance, and Carlos looked practically indignant.

'Is it over?' LeFou Deux blinked.

'Oh, thank Maleficent,' said Ginny Gothel.

'What a snore,' hissed Mad Maddy.

Anthony Tremaine was still asleep, his dark head resting on his arms on the table.

'Anthony, wake up, it's done,' said Ginny Gothel, poking him awake.

Evie's smile faltered. 'I just thought you might want to see what it's like,' she said.

Jay patted her arm in consolation.

Mal crossed her arms and called the room to attention. 'Thanks, Evie, that was really a wonderful peek into Auradon life, and I wish you guys had been paying attention.' She narrowed her eyes at their audience. '*Anyway*, we wanted to talk to you guys about the VK program, and to see if you had any questions about Auradon.'

Mad Maddy raised her hand immediately. 'Oh! I have one! Can we use magic?'

'Yes!' said Mal, looking relieved that it was an easy question. 'But it's discouraged and regulated.'

Maddy's face fell. So did Ginny Gothel's. 'What's the point, then?' asked Ginny.

'The point is to learn how to be a good person without having to resort to using magic. Magic makes people lazy and irresponsible,' said Evie.

'Hmpf,' said Ginny, who didn't look convinced. 'Sounds dreary.'

'So, what's Auradon Prep like?' asked Anthony Tremaine. 'Why would we want to go there?'

'It's great! There are so many advanced classes, and it really prepares you for college,' said Carlos.

'And so many extracurricular activities,' said Evie. 'What are you guys interested in?'

'Embezzling,' said Anthony Tremaine.

'Poisons,' said Ginny Gothel.

'Revenge,' said Mad Maddy.

LeFou Deux just continued to look nervous. 'Anything you guys think I would be interested in,' he said, resorting to his usual flattery.

The rest of the discussion went the same way, frustrating both groups at the roundtable. At the end of the period, not one of the villains took an application form.

When they had the room back to themselves, Jay said what was on all their minds. 'Well, that went well. *Not*.'

'Was the slideshow that boring?' asked Evie.

'It was the best! You even got Dude in there,' said Carlos supportively.

'They don't understand. I thought they would if we came and spoke to them and they saw how we'd changed,' said Mal. 'Or maybe this is all a mistake. Maybe we're just wasting our time.'

Evie turned to Mal and put both of her hands on Mal's shoulders. 'Helping people and showing them another way to live—it's always worth our time. We can't give up yet. We'll figure out how to make them understand—how to make them *want* Auradon.'

'Oh, they'll want it, I assure you,' said Jay. 'Evie's right, we'll figure it out. It's just that right now all they know is evil.'

'So we have to sell them good,' mused Carlos. 'Show them how amazing it is.'

chapter 22

Around the Island

After the meeting, the four of them split up—Evie to see if she could find the remaining members of the Anti-Heroes Club and convince them to apply, Jay to follow up with Coach Gaston after practice, Carlos to scout some locations for the Auradon Prep posters and Mal to take a few pictures of the island to show Ben how things were faring there. Except Mal didn't take a camera with her. She didn't want to alarm her friends, but she was truly worried about Celia's warning. She decided to do a security sweep of the island to see if there was any place in the invisible barrier that might have been weakened by Uma.

As she walked around the island, Mal checked her pocket to make sure she still had the remote that opened the barrier and called up the bridge to the mainland. She felt a little spooked that this one small key could open up the island just like that, but that was the way its magic worked. Ben trusted her with it, too. Still, though she had never worried about it before, she found that she kept making sure it was there.

So far, nothing seemed amiss on the island. There were no signs of any illicit magic around, and while she did find a trail of tentacle slime, it only led to Ursula's cottage, where Ursula was watching her 'stories', aka the soap operas she watched on an old DVD player. The old sea witch was annoyed to see Mal at her doorstep.

'What do you want?' she rasped.

'Oh, hey, I was just wondering—Uma hasn't been around, has she? You haven't seen her?' asked Mal.

'No, last I saw her was on the news when she was blasting you with her magic!' Ursula laughed. 'Good for her!'

'Um, yeah,' said Mal. 'Okay, just wanted to check.'

'What do you want to see her for, anyway? Thought you guys weren't friends anymore,' said Ursula suspiciously.

'Oh, nothing,' said Mal. 'Just curious is all.'

She backed up, hoping Ursula wouldn't take a swipe at her with her tentacles. Ursula closed the door with a bang.

Mal was heading away when she realised she had no idea where she was going or where she had been. That was odd, wasn't it? It almost felt like she was daydreaming. She was standing on the sidewalk, a confused look on her face, when she bumped into Carlos.

'Hey, Mal!' said Carlos. 'What's up? You all right?'

She shook off the weird feeling. Maybe she was just spooked to be back on the Isle of the Lost. Too many bad memories. 'Yeah, I'm okay. What are you up to?'

'Oh, just figuring out the best places for the posters. I thought we should put up some Auradon Prep billboards, too. Really inundate the place.'

'Cool,' said Mal.

'What about you? What are you doing so far from the hideout?' asked Carlos.

'Nothing,' said Mal. She couldn't remember. What had she been doing? Maybe it wasn't important—that's why she couldn't remember.

'Well, I've got to check out a building over there. I think we can paste over your old "Down with Auradon" signs,' said Carlos apologetically. 'See you later.'

'Yeah, see you back at the hideout,' said Mal. 'Be careful.'

'I will,' promised Carlos.

Carlos watched Mal walk away. She seemed a bit off, but maybe she was just concentrating on something. She was Mal, and she could take care of herself. He didn't have to worry, did he?

Like Mal, Carlos hadn't been completely straight with

the gang. Sure, he was scouting locations for posters and billboards, but he was also testing a system he had invented. Part of the graduation surprise he and Jane had cooked up. It had mostly been Jane's idea, but Carlos was the technical part of the operation.

He took out his phone and opened the new app he'd put on it. He studied the screen and grinned as it began to work.

Excitedly, he texted Jane.

> **C-Dog:** *I think your surprise is going to work!*
> **Jaaaaane:** *If you're texting me, it sure is! How's everything over there?*
> **C-Dog:** *Okay. Glad we're going home soon. Isle kids don't really get the appeal of Auradon.*
> **Jaaaaane:** *Maybe we need to make a bigger deal out of them.*
> **C-Dog:** *?*
> **Jaaaaane:** *Like a day to really celebrate the villain kids.*
> **C-Dog:** *Oh like a VK Day!*
> **Jaaaaane:** *Yes!*
> **C-Dog:** *Evie will LOVE that idea. You're a genius!* ☺
> **Jaaaaane:** *Okay I have to go. See you soon!*
> **C-Dog:** *Counting down the minutes!*

She sent him a heart. Carlos looked at it for a long time, then put his phone away.

If Mal had noticed Carlos was being cagey earlier, she didn't give it much thought. She was too worried about the strange gap in her memory. She was walking through the bazaar, lost in her thoughts, when she bumped into Harriet Hook.

'Hey, Harriet,' said Mal.

'Mal!' said Harriet. 'Oh, I heard about your roundtable at study hall. My sister, CJ, kept bugging me to go, but I had a big test, and you know the Queen of Hearts threatens to chop off our heads if we fail.'

'It's okay,' said Mal. 'You probably know all about Auradon from CJ.'

Harriet gave Mal one of her rare smiles. 'So, how did it go?'

Mal shrugged. 'Not our finest hour,' she admitted. 'We couldn't get anyone to realise how great it is. Maybe they didn't want to hear it. Not everyone will get to go, after all.'

'That's never stopped a determined bunch of villains before,' said Harriet.

'You're right,' said Mal. 'Maybe we have the wrong approach . . . Thanks!'

'No problem,' said Harriet.

Mal began to walk away, but Harriet stopped her.

'Mal?' Harriet said. 'You were headed that way,' she said, pointing her fake hook in the opposite direction.

Mal startled. 'I was?'

'Yeah. I'm the one going this way.'

'Oh,' said Mal. 'Thanks!'

Mal twirled around, trying to hide her embarrassment. What was going on? Why was she acting like this? And why did she have a feeling it had something to do with Uma?

chapter 23

Pied Piper

That night, Mal lay in bed, thinking of Celia's warning and the strange gaps in her memory earlier that day. Was Uma out to get her? Of course she was. Uma was *always* out to get her. Uma had never forgiven Mal for, well, being Mal. Being the best at everything. At first, that meant being wicked. Then she hated Mal for being good and for being Ben's choice. But if Mal kept worrying about Uma, she would never go to bed. She tossed. She turned. She tossed again. Jay was sitting by the window, keeping watch. If anything happened, they would know. Mal relaxed, and slowly she went to sleep.

She dreamed she was back in her old home, sitting on

her bed. She was younger than she was now. She was a kid: maybe four, five years old. Her mother was in the kitchen, a cauldron was bubbling on the stove, and goblins were cowering at Maleficent's words because they had brought back the wrong ingredients for the soup. It could have been any other ordinary day.

Mal hadn't thought of her childhood in a long time. Why was she dreaming about it now?

Then the dream changed, and she was standing in front of the classroom at Dragon Hall. She was still a little kid, but now she was in third grade. She had just won the Wicked Prize. It was an award given to the most dastardly student of each grade level, and since kindergarten, Mal had always won. She was the baddest of the bad. Her mother had been so proud of her!

The little Mal in the dream went home to show her parents her prize.

That's our bad little girl.

Mal.

That voice.

That voice was so familiar. It was a voice she hadn't heard for a long time. *Mal...*

Mal sat up. Was she dreaming? Had she just heard a voice or was she just imagining it? She fell back on the lumpy mattress. She wasn't hearing anything. It was completely silent in the hideout.

She closed her eyes and began to drift off once more.

Then she heard it again. *Mal . . . Hey, Mal . . . you know where to go. Come on.*

Mal's arms locked against her sides. Something was happening—something was compelling her to leave. But she wouldn't go.

Mal. Get up. That's an order.

Mal's eyes snapped open, a glazed look to them. She got up quietly. Her friends, including Jay, who was snoring by the windowsill, didn't stir. She had to go. *Now.*

chapter 24

A Dream Is a Wish Your Heart Makes?

Carlos shrank back from his mother in fear. Cruella De Vil was annoyed, and when she was annoyed, watch out. She paced the length of their ballroom, her high heels clomping on the floor as her minions, Jasper and Horace, cringed in front of her. Cruella hadn't seemed to notice Carlos yet, but it was only a matter of time. 'Where are the puppies?!' she demanded. 'Where are they?'

'They're gone! They've disappeared!' Jasper said, quaking, while Horace hid behind him. Carlos curled tighter into himself from where he was crouched against the wall.

Cruella paced the room, her fur coat trailing behind

her as she waved her long cigarette holder and dusted the furniture with ashes. 'Those puppies are mine! Mine, I tell you! Find them!' she raged. 'Bring me ALL THE PUPPIES! OR ELSE!'

Horace shook in his boots and wrung his hat. 'We tried!'

'But they're nowhere!' said Jasper.

'They're gone!'

'Nooooo!' screamed Cruella. 'CARLOS! CARLOS! CARLOS!'

Carlos woke up drenched in sweat, fully expecting to find himself back at Hell Hall, the family estate, his mother looming over him, her diamond bracelets rattling in his face, her lips set in a perpetual scowl as she puffed smoke rings in his direction.

But it was only Evie and Jay, looking concerned. 'You had a nightmare,' said Evie. 'You were yelling.'

'You woke us up,' said Jay.

Outside the window of the loft, two people were arguing over a trinket they'd found on the street. 'That's mine!'

'No, it's mine!'

'MINE!'

'Nooooo!'

The sounds of people squabbling always reminded Carlos of his mother, he realised. She would never stop haunting his dreams.

It was only when his heart had stopped pounding that

he realised that there were just three of them in the hideout. 'Where's Mal?' he asked.

Jay and Evie glanced around. 'What?' said Jay.

'Omigosh!' Evie gasped. 'I was asleep until I heard you, Carlos. Did either of you see her?'

They shook their heads. Evie dashed frantically around the room, overturning pillows and blankets. Mal's jacket and boots were missing too. Carlos scratched his head. 'She's gone?'

Jay flushed. 'I was supposed to be keeping watch!' he said. 'But I was exhausted.'

'It's not your fault,' Evie said. 'Don't blame yourself.'

'But where would she have gone? And why didn't she tell us where she was going?' asked Carlos. An uneasy feeling crept over him.

'I don't know,' said Evie. 'It's not like her to do this. She knows we would worry.'

Carlos looked around the dark loft. 'Did she leave a note?'

'Let's check,' said Evie, and the three of them searched the entirety of the loft. Jay even picked through the trash, which was still full of rotten pirate debris. But they didn't find anything. Not a word.

Carlos sighed. This was why he had been reluctant to go back to the island in the first place. He knew something like this would happen. It always did.

Then he heard Evie gasp. 'Guys, check this out!' She pointed at the floor.

It was Mal's boot print, leading towards the door. But there was something strange about it. It seemed to have the slightest glow. Almost . . . blue.

'Uma,' said Jay, his eyes narrowing. The others nodded in agreement. Whatever this was, it wasn't good. But at least it looked like there were tracks to follow.

Carlos pulled on his black-and-white leather jacket. 'What are we waiting for?' he said. 'Let's go. We've got to find her.'

chapter 25

Once Upon a Dream

This way, Mal.
  Come on.
Hurry.

Mal followed the deep, strangely familiar voice that urged her out of the hideout into the deserted streets of the Isle of the Lost. She walked by the Slop Shop, down Mean Street and past Gaston's cottage. She wandered in a daze, unsure if she was still dreaming and asleep on the mattress or actually outside in the cold night air. She heard the crunch of gravel beneath her feet. Her head felt foggy. She was compelled to follow the voice, no matter what.

'Keep going,' said a new voice, and when Mal looked up she saw Dizzy Tremaine, with her signature pigtails and oversize glasses, standing on the deserted sidewalk.

'Dizzy? What are you doing here?' asked Mal. What was she doing out here so late and so far from her home on Stepmother's Island? Dizzy shouldn't be out at this time of the night.

'Don't worry about me,' Dizzy said with a laugh. 'You just keep going, Mal. That way!' Dizzy threw her head back and cackled, and something glowed around her neck. She reminded Mal of someone. Who laughed like that? The answer was in the back of her mind, but she couldn't access it. It was like she was sleepwalking. Maybe she was.

'Where am I going?' she asked.

'You'll see,' said Dizzy mysteriously. 'You're almost there.'

Mal bent down to tie her shoelace, and when she stood up Dizzy had disappeared. Had that even been Dizzy? What was going on? But she felt that she was going the right way. She had to continue.

She walked to the intersection of Pity Lane and Bitter Boulevard, a route she had travelled countless times when she was a denizen of the Isle of the Lost. She remembered knocking down garden gnomes, pushing over mailboxes, tagging walls.

Then suddenly there was Gil, leaning against a wall, eating a rotten apple. 'Oh, hey, Mal, keep going.'

This was Mal's territory. What was a pirate doing here? It was like he appeared out of nowhere.

'Going where?'

Gil rolled his eyes. 'Jailor's Pier. Where else?'

'What are you doing in my dream?' she asked.

'It's not a dream,' said Gil. 'It's real.' Then he giggled maniacally. Mal thought he didn't sound like himself . . . He sounded like . . .

But she couldn't finish the thought, so instead she kept walking towards the pier. When she was a little girl, she liked to play tricks on people there. She would throw a bucket of slime on the wood slats, making them slippery and sending unsuspecting villains sliding down the length of the pier and into the water. Mal hoped no-one played a prank on her tonight. Seagulls lined the deck, picking at leftover trash. She walked to the end of the pier, where she came upon Harry Hook fishing, his line dangling out into the water. 'Harry?' she asked hesitantly.

'Oi! Mal, there you are.'

'Why am I here?' she asked, still not sure if this was really happening or even if that was truly Harry in front of her. Like Dizzy and Gil, there seemed to be something glowing around his neck.

'You should never have left,' he said solemnly. 'You should never have left the Isle of the Lost.'

'What? And stay here with you?' Mal smirked.

'What's so terrible about that?' asked Harry, attempting to look wounded.

'Everything,' Mal growled.

'Ouch.' Harry disappeared in a blink. Mal stepped back. What just happened? Where did Harry go? And Gil? And Dizzy?

She ventured to the outskirts of town, right to the middle of a forest, in the deep dark heart of the woods, where a glowing blue orb floated in the middle of the darkness. And it spoke with a familiar voice.

Mal . . .

She turned away from the orb and kept walking through to the other side, and now she found herself at the opposite edge of the forest, close to the pier and there was Dizzy again.

'Mal! What are you doing out here?' asked Dizzy.

Mal was confused. Didn't she just see Dizzy earlier? How did she get here so fast? She told Dizzy about walking out into the woods and seeing this blue orb.

'It spoke with a voice . . . and it sounded crazily like my . . .' *Dad?* Mal shook her head. 'No, that's impossible,' said Mal. 'But what are *you* doing out here?'

'We were supposed to meet up at Curl Up and Dye hours ago, remember?' said Dizzy.

'We were?' Mal didn't remember making this plan.

'It's okay, I was just excited to . . .' Dizzy said, and then she stopped and looked disoriented for a moment, as if unsure of where she was and what was happening.

'Dizzy? Are you okay?' asked Mal.

Dizzy jumped. 'Of course I'm okay!' she said with a too-cheerful smile. 'There's just so much glam to add in so little time!' She picked up Mal's hands. 'Just because they're cuticles does not mean they're cute!' she said, and then stopped as if something was choking her.

Mal leaned over and gasped. 'Dizzy! Why are you glowing?'

'Glowing?' asked Dizzy, and then she held her chest in pain.

There was something glowing around Dizzy's neck. Mal reached over and lifted the source of the light. It was a seashell necklace.

'Dizzy! Why are you wearing Uma's necklace?' she asked.

Dizzy looked down at the necklace, confused, but when she looked back up at Mal, there was a crafty smile on her face. It wasn't Dizzy's smile. Mal knew that smile.

'I wouldn't say that Dizzy's wearing my necklace,' said a voice that was definitely not Dizzy's. 'It's more like my necklace is wearing Dizzy!'

'Uma!' Mal said angrily. 'This is so low! Your fight is with me, not Dizzy! And she's a child!'

'Oh, I can go lower, princess,' said Uma as Dizzy. She took off Dizzy's glasses and stomped on them. 'Oops!' She shrugged. 'Just you wait.'

Mal scoffed. Uma didn't scare her. 'Am I supposed to be frightened?'

Just then Harry and Gil appeared out of nowhere and flanked Dizzy/Uma. Both of them had similar glowing lights at the bases of their throats.

Harry waved his hook in Mal's face. 'You're not welcome on the Isle anymore!'

But Mal was simply amused. 'Really? And what are you going to do about it, pal? Mr . . . Coat Hanger?'

'His name is Harry,' Gil said smugly. Then he realised. 'Oh, I get it . . . because it looks like . . . That's pretty funny, Mal!'

Mal smirked. 'Thanks. I'll be here all week.'

'Uma's going to have the last laugh, though,' said Gil, as the three of them began walking closer to Mal, and she had to walk backwards, closer to the pier. 'I wouldn't want to be you right now, Mal.'

'I wouldn't want to be her ever,' sneered Dizzy with Uma's voice.

The three of them kept inching forward as Mal kept walking backwards, edging onto the pier, but now she was annoyed. 'What makes you think this is going to be any different from every other time that I've beaten you?'

Now Harry spoke in Uma's voice. 'Those were measly little battles. There's a war coming!'

'And in this war, I will triumph, I'll have everything— the Isle and Auradon!' said Gil in Uma's angry voice.

Uma was definitely getting worked up, wherever she was.

'And you, princess—I'm coming for you, Mal,' said Uma menacingly through Dizzy.

Mal stood her ground, even as Harry unsheathed his sword and the three of them kept edging towards her in a threatening manner. 'Mal . . . Mal . . . Mal . . .' they whispered, as they glowed with the light from Uma's seashell necklace.

'Oh yeah?' Mal said, curling her lip. She wasn't afraid of them, not now and not ever. 'Not if I come for you first!'

With that, she turned away from them and began running down the pier. If Uma wanted a fight, Mal would bring it to her. She ran to the very end of the dock, determined to fight and vanquish Uma once and for all.

She leapt gracefully, throwing herself up in the air.

Then Mal heard a different voice shriek her name, but it was too late to turn around.

chapter 26

Underground Secrets

After trying to warn Mal and her friends, Celia decided to go back down the mine shaft to see what Uma and Hades were up to. Holding on to her hat, Celia ran to the basement tunnels until she reached the one that led to the mine shaft and Hades' cave.

She grabbed a torch and hopped onto an old rusty bicycle that was on the train tracks. She began pedalling furiously. Surely Mal would figure out some way to thwart Uma's plans after Celia had warned her about the danger. Celia hadn't realised just how much she wanted to go to Auradon Prep until the prospect had been put in jeopardy. She had to get off the Isle and make a name for herself somewhere it would matter. And she wanted to see the world beyond the barrier! There were so many places she had heard of, but had never been . . .

One day, she would fly to Never Land and meet the pixies and the fairies of the hollow. Or she would tour the castles in the Auroria Priory and see how they compared to the ones in Cinderellasburg. But best of all, she would travel to the bayou, to dance with an alligator who played trumpet in a jazz band. After hearing her dad's stories all those years, she was desperate to get a glimpse of it herself.

The VK program was her one shot to get everything she'd ever dreamed of. There was no future on the Isle of the Lost. Her cards always said so.

Her cards . . . She felt around for them in her pockets and realised she'd dropped them somewhere in the tunnel. She got off the bicycle and began to search, sweeping her flashlight to and fro, but they were nowhere to be found. She'd have to retrace her steps.

But just then, the flashlight sputtered out—she had forgotten to replace the battery! Celia shook it in annoyance. To her surprise, she realised that without the beam, she could see light peeking in through tiny little cracks in the cave walls. She'd never noticed them before, but then, the flashlight had always worked before.

'Where are my cards?' she asked herself, and, almost like magic, her cards flew to her hand.

Almost like magic? she wondered. *Or magic itself?*

There was something going on down here. She could feel it in the darkness, in the pinpoints of light, in the way her cards hummed in her hands.

Hades. It had to be Hades. He still had some kind of power down here, magic that was getting in through the cracks. She could feel it vibrating in the air. Not enough magic to escape from the Isle of the Lost, but enough to do some kind of harm, she was sure. Even a little magic can cause a lot of problems. That's what her dad always said, with that evil grin of his.

Celia put a hand to the nearest crack in the wall. It was so deep that the light coming through was almost blinding. Little dust motes filled the air, and Celia felt her cards tremble in her hands. *Magic.* Celia could barely comprehend it, but it had to be true. How else had Uma been able to get in and out of Hades' lair without being seen?

If there was magic on the Isle of the Lost, what kind of mischief was afoot?

Chapter 27

Search Party

They had been looking for Mal for what felt like hours, following her boot tracks, and now Evie was beginning to really worry. They had questioned every person they'd bumped into on the street—goons, thugs, witches and goblins alike—but no-one had seen Mal. They had walked the length of the island, from Hook's Bay to Troll Town to Doom Cove, using the Ricketty Bridge to get across the coastline. But there was no sign of her. And the last boot print they found had been several blocks away.

It was as if Mal had suddenly disappeared. 'Guys, I think we need to call the palace and let Ben know that

Mal's missing,' said Evie. 'We can't keep it from him. What if something terrible has happened to her?' If something terrible really had happened, Evie would never forgive herself.

'We can't. At least not yet. We'd have to go back to Auradon to tell him, which means leaving Mal here,' said Jay. 'Remember? There's no signal on the Isle. It's completely cut off.'

Carlos was about to say something when Jay interrupted him. 'Hey, look, the Slop Shop's open,' he said, as they walked past the storefront. 'Come on, let's ask if she stopped in here.'

They walked into the goblin-run establishment. A few of Maleficent's minions had retired from their lives as henchmen to run a coffee shop. 'Well, look who's back,' said the head goblin barista as he polished some cups. 'What are you guys doing here?'

'We're looking for Mal,' said Carlos. 'Have you seen her?'

'I thought you were here for that Auradon business,' said the goblin cagily.

'Well, yes, but—' began Jay, but the goblin cut him off.

'Trying to get more kids to apply to Auradon Prep, huh?' he said. 'What about goblins?' He wiped the counter with a dirty rag, making the surface even dirtier.

'Um . . .' said Carlos. 'No, not yet, sorry.' Jay picked up a plastic-wrapped scone that was hard as a rock. Evie gave him a look, and he set it back down.

'Our dwarf cousins said they'd put in a good word for us with the king. Guess they forgot about us,' complained the goblin, shaking his green head.

'Okay, focus,' said Evie with a strained smile. 'Have you guys seen Mal? Did she go this way?'

'Yeah, she was here. Not in the shop, but I think a couple of demons mentioned that they saw her outside. Pain! Panic!' he called. 'Come over here.'

Two short demons ambled over. One was slurping a Sloppacino with a green straw. The other one was wearing what looked like slightly scorched plastic sandals with Hercules's face on them. 'What's up?' Pain asked.

'Didn't you say you saw Mal?' asked the goblin.

'Yeah. She was talking to herself.'

'What?' Carlos demanded.

'I know, I thought it was weird, too! It was like she was talking to someone who wasn't there,' said Panic. 'Totally freaky.'

'She looked like she was in a dream state, like sleepwalking,' said Pain. 'The way they do in the River Styx. Like they're dead—you know, when they float around all dead-eyed. That's what she looked like.'

Evie looked alarmed. 'Did you wake her?'

Pain and Panic shook their heads vigorously and hopped up and down. 'Of course not! Are you kidding? Wake Mal? She'd curse us!' they protested. 'Who would do such a stupid thing? Not us!'

'You guys, Mal really isn't like that anymore. Trust me,' said Evie. 'She wouldn't harm a fly . . . or a demon.'

'Well, we weren't going to take any chances,' said Pain stubbornly. Panic nodded vigorously.

'Which way was she going?' asked Carlos.

Panic pointed east. 'Kind of down thataway, towards the harbour.'

They walked towards the direction the demons pointed, down Mean Street, past the bazaar and Frollo's house, but the streets were empty. Jay was starting to think that the demons had deliberately sent them the wrong way.

'Mal doesn't sleepwalk,' said Evie. 'She's been my roommate for years. I've never seen her do that.'

'They said she looked dead-eyed. You think maybe she was under some kind of spell?' mused Carlos.

'But if there's no magic on the Isle of the Lost, how could that be?' asked Evie.

'Maybe someone figured out how to get past the barrier,' said Carlos, as Jay suddenly stopped and knelt to examine something on the path.

'Look,' he said, pointing past an upturned barrel to a mark on the dirt road. It was a perfect print of a boot with a serpent coiled around the heel mark. The same prints they had been following all evening. There was another one not too far away, and then the tracks picked up again. The three of them hurried to follow.

They followed the tracks all the way to Jailor's Pier. 'The demons weren't lying after all. She was headed to the harbour,' said Jay. He glanced towards the end of the dock and then broke out into a flat-out run.

'What's going on?' asked Evie.

'There's MAL!' said Carlos, pointing to the edge of the dock.

chapter 28

All Washed-up

Jay froze in place for a moment, then bolted towards Mal, with Evie and Carlos close behind him. Mal was facing towards them, but it seemed like she was arguing with someone. Jay thought he heard her say, 'Not if I come for you first.' But what did that mean? Who was she speaking to?

'MAL! What are you doing?' screamed Evie.

'MAL!' Jay yelled. He had to wake her up. She was definitely sleeping or dreaming, or something weird was going on. That wasn't the Mal they knew. He was blaming himself for anything that might have happened; he was supposed to be here to protect his friends. Sure, they could all take care of themselves, but he was the one with the swords-and-shields expertise; he was supposed to try to keep everyone safe. Even Mal, who had never needed any help. But she sure did now.

Because it was like Mal didn't—couldn't—hear them. She turned on her heel and sprinted towards the end of the pier.

'MAL!' The three of them were screaming now. 'MAL, STOP!'

But it was too late. Mal threw herself off the pier and plummeted all the way down into the sea.

Jay dived into the water right after her, spinning around in a complete circle, searching for any sign of his friend. The sea was a brilliant shade of blue, which was rare for Isle water. He had expected it to be almost completely murky, but it was crystal clear. He should have been able to spy her the moment he jumped in.

But Mal was nowhere to be found. It was as if she had jumped into the ocean and out of this world. Suddenly, a great swarm of fish surrounded him, dark as the night, obscuring his vision.

He could hardly see the hand he held out in front of his face. There were thousands of the little fish, each one twisting and turning, going this way and that, making it impossible to see anything at all. Jay got the feeling someone was trying to stop him from finding Mal. Most likely the same person who had compelled her to jump off the pier.

Jay held his breath and swam as deep as he could go, but

the fish followed, surrounding him like fog, hindering his ability to see. *Useless*, he thought. Someone was determined to keep him from finding Mal. Jay swam back to shore, gasping for air when he broke the surface.

Evie and Carlos looked down at Jay from the edge of the pier, panic on their faces. 'Where is she?' asked Evie.

'Couldn't find her. Just needed to take a breath,' he said. 'I'll go back down and search again.'

'Hold on,' said Evie. 'I've been thinking of what Carlos said. About how Mal might be under a spell.'

'Yeah, it's like she was enchanted,' said Carlos.

'A spell?' asked Jay. 'Here? On the Isle? Impossible.'

'I know, but when has the impossible ever been an obstacle for magic?' said Evie. 'Someone must have found a way around the barrier and is using their magic against Mal.'

'If there's magic here, it's definitely working against us, too,' said Jay. 'A school of fish was blocking my vision down there. That's probably not a coincidence.'

'Yeah, I don't think you'll be able to find her if you dive back down,' said Evie.

'So what are we going to do about it?' asked Jay, climbing the makeshift rope ladder at the end of the pier.

'Already on it,' said Evie, as Carlos reached out a hand and helped pull Jay back onto the pier. He shook the water from his long hair and wrung it from his jacket.

'What's the plan?' Jay asked.

'We're going home,' said Evie. 'To my castle. If there's magic on the Isle, I think I know how to fight it.'

'Um, your castle is also the home of Evil Queen. I've heard she doesn't like guests,' said Carlos.

'Where did you hear that?' teased Jay.

'From Evie,' said Carlos.

Evie brushed their jokes aside as they walked down the pier. 'Oh, don't worry about Mum. It's game night, when she plays Apples to Apples with her friends. Actually, I think they call it Rotten Apples to Rotten Apples. Or maybe it's Poisoned Apples to Poisoned Apples? I can't remember.'

'Charming,' said Carlos. 'So the castle's empty?' he asked, looking greatly relieved.

'Like a schoolroom after last bell,' said Evie. 'We'll be all alone, but we better hurry. Mum doesn't stay out late. She likes her beauty sleep.'

chapter 29

Under the Sea

Mal heard her friends calling her name, but it was too late. She had already jumped. She fell straight down into the sea, so deep that a wave of bubbles washed up all around her. She opened her eyes and gasped, fearing she would drown, but no water entered her throat. The person who had led her down there wanted her alive.

Uma.

Mal should have known to take Celia's warning more seriously. She should have known that Uma would go to any length to get revenge. Mal didn't know how she had done it, but Uma had managed to get back to the Isle of the Lost, and she'd somehow accessed enough magic to lure Mal away from her friends and trap her under the sea. Mal couldn't believe Uma would stoop so low as to use Dizzy, Gil and Harry to fool her, though. Actually, it was Uma. Uma might not have gotten the crown she'd always wanted, but she was the queen of reaching new lows.

Mal tried to swim to the surface, but she discovered she had landed in the middle of a school of fish. They swam around her like a floating wall, keeping her from getting her bearings. When they disappeared she was alone, underwater and in the dark.

She kept falling deeper and deeper, until she was at the bottom of the sea, standing on what appeared to be the wreck of some old pirate ship.

Mal whirled around, and, sure enough, her old nemesis was standing in front of her.

Uma threw her head back and cackled wildly. 'There you are! Exactly where I want you!'

She was standing across from Mal, but she wasn't really there. It was as if Mal were looking into a mirror, except instead of seeing herself, she saw Uma reflected back at her.

Mal pursed her lips and crossed her arms. She wasn't about to play these games. 'Uma, next time you want to talk to me, maybe you can just send a text? You do know they have those waterproof phones now, so even fish folk like you can have civilised conversations with the rest of us.'

'This isn't a joke,' said Uma.

Mal smirked at her old-friend-turned-enemy. 'Oh, Uma, maybe you've just lost your sense of humour. Defeat has that effect on people.' Mal's eyes glittered dragon green. She could sense the magic all around, but how was it possible so close to the Isle of the Lost? What had Uma done? And what did she want?

'She who laughs last, laughs longest,' vowed Uma, as the pirate ship buckled underneath Mal's feet.

Uma's laughing face appeared in every bubble that rushed up around her, mocking Mal.

The deck cracked in two, a few boards tearing loose, and Mal flew back before they smacked into her. 'Nice try,' she said. 'But you didn't really think it would be that easy, did you?'

Uma seethed. 'Let's try this again, then, shall we?' she said through gritted teeth. With a whirlwind of force, she transformed into her octopus self. Her tentacle arms reached out for Mal, wrapping around her as if they were searching for something. One tentacle darted towards Mal's pocket.

What's she looking for? What does she want? Mal wondered. Then she realised: *She's looking for the key.* The remote that would open the barrier and call up the bridge to Auradon. Jay usually carried it as he sometimes drove the limo, but he didn't this time, because Mal wanted to keep it close to her for safekeeping. It was part of the new security protocols.

So that's what Uma was after. Uma has always wanted

the same thing—freedom from their island prison. Freedom to do as she pleased, to rampage and rage and spread her evil and her malice across the innocent kingdoms of Auradon.

Well, Uma would have to think again. It wasn't happening—not now, not ever. Especially not if Mal had anything to do with it.

'Really, Uma?' she said. 'You're never going to beat me. What makes you think you're going to win this time?'

'I wouldn't be so cocky, Mal,' Uma replied. 'And let's evaluate for just a second. Who's the one with the upper hand here?' She grinned and waved a tentacle in Mal's face.

With a sudden burst of energy, Mal twisted away from Uma's grasp. She felt her eyes flash bright green again, and then she transformed into a great and towering dragon. Her arms became wings, and her fingers sprouted mighty talons. Her teeth turned to fangs, scales replaced her skin, and her long purple hair became a row of fierce spikes down her back.

Uma sneered and drew herself up again, her tentacles reaching out for Mal, but Mal flew back, using her wings to push herself through the water and narrowly avoiding being caught in Uma's grasp.

Uma spun, transformed back into her human form, and lurched away from Mal. Mal swam, chasing Uma, but Uma kept disappearing, changing from a squid to an octopus to a girl, darting into coral reefs and then transforming back into a humongous sea creature. *She's trying to lead me somewhere*, thought Mal. *But where? And why?*

Then Uma was back on the deck of the pirate ship, appearing suddenly in her human form and wielding a sword. Mal transformed back as well and landed on the ship. There on the ground was a discarded sword, and Mal lunged for it and grasped it in her hands. She faced Uma, her blade raised.

'So, we're doing this?' asked Mal.

'Oh, it's on,' vowed Uma.

They battled up and down the deck, steel against steel.

'Just give me the key,' said Uma. 'And I'll let you go.'

'You're not holding me anywhere,' said Mal.

'One word and you'll drown,' threatened Uma.

'Say it then!' said Mal. 'Do it!'

Uma backed away as Mal relentlessly pushed forward, slashing and fighting so strongly that she forced Uma to drop her weapon.

Mal brought her sword under Uma's chin. 'Are we done now?' she growled. But Uma suddenly disappeared, and her image appeared in a golden mirror that materialised on the deck.

Uma laughed at Mal's confusion.

Then Mal was back on the deck of the sunken pirate ship, standing in front of a door with a brass handle.

'UMA! FACE ME!' Mal demanded, reaching for the handle as the ocean reverberated with Uma's laughter.

chapter 30

With a Little Help from Her Friends

It was impossible to imagine that Evil Queen's castle could appear scarier and more foreboding than it already was, but somehow, it had managed to pull off this feat. It loomed above the crag, its dark tower rising to the skies. Evie remembered her lonely childhood spent inside its confines, her only company a mother obsessed with outward appearances. Evie knew every cosmetic trick, every fashion tip, but had been bereft of true support and affection. But this was no time for bad memories or a pity party. Mal was lost under the ocean, trapped by some evil force, and they had to help her.

The VKs made their way towards the castle, fighting

through a row of hedges and vines that surrounded its walls.

'Ouch,' said Jay, as he pulled a particularly large barb from his leg.

'Sorry,' said Evie. 'Mum prefers thorns and cuts off the roses.'

'Of course,' said Carlos. 'Why are we here again?'

'If there's wicked magic on the Isle, then we need to fight it with similarly strong magic. And there's no magic stronger than in my mum's Magic Mirror.'

'Isn't it broken?' asked Carlos.

'The glass is broken, and I have a tiny shard of it in my compact. But the frame still stands, and something tells me the glass was mostly for display. It's made of magic. And if there's magic on the Isle, it'll work.'

They reached the drawbridge, passed over the moat, and stood in front of the main door. Evie felt in her pockets for the key and realised she'd left it back in her room on Auradon. She hadn't planned on visiting home.

'Guys, I have bad news,' she told them. 'I didn't bring the key.'

'What now?' asked Carlos.

'Break in? Can't be that hard,' said Jay with a shrug.

Evie shook her head. 'Mum has massive security on this thing. Remember? This isn't Auradon. If we pick the lock and open the door without the right key, a steel trap will spring, and we'll all fall into a basement full of hungry alligators.' It was the Evil Queen's castle, after all.

'Okay, so let's not do that,' Carlos said with a shudder.

'Mum keeps a spare key in the vultures' nest, over there,' Evie said, motioning to a ledge high in the air where they could just make out a shadow of a large bird's nest.

'Easy enough to climb,' said Jay, starting to find a foothold in the castle walls.

'No!' screamed Evie, and Jay slid back to the ground.

'Sorry,' she said. 'The vultures will peck you to death. We'll just have to convince them I'm my mum.'

Jay picked himself up and dusted off. 'How're we going to do that?'

Evie smiled. 'Makeup.'

Evie knelt at the doorway, set down her purse, and began to remove assorted cosmetics from its depths—a dizzying array of lipstick, foundation, blush, eyeliner and every conceivable beauty instrument known to humanity. She turned her back to the boys and began the transformation.

The eyebrows were easy, since she and her mother had the same dark brows. Evie just had to colour them in so they looked more menacing. Then she covered her face in a pale powder and darkened her lips to bloodred. As a final touch, she fashioned a black scarf she found in her bag into a black cape.

When she turned to Jay and Carlos, the two of them staggered back.

'Whoa!' said Carlos. 'You are way too good at that.'

'Who are you, and what did you do with Evie?' said Jay.

Evie cackled like her mother and held out an apple she'd packed as a snack. 'One bite and all your dreams will come true!' she purred in her best Evil Queen voice.

'Seriously, stop it!' yelled Carlos.

Evie giggled and sounded like her normal self. 'Okay, fine.' She fluffed up her cape and checked her appearance in her phone's camera. 'I look like Mum, right? Enough to fool those old vultures?'

'Totally,' said Jay.

'Could've fooled us,' said Carlos.

She began to climb up the castle walls towards the vultures' nest, lifting herself up inch by inch. When she reached the ledge she smiled sweetly at the hungry birds of prey. Her mother's favourite pets.

'Hello, my dearies,' she said in her best mimicry of her mother's voice. 'I seem to have forgotten my keys! Now let me just . . .' She reached into the nest. The closest vulture lunged, snapping at her fingers.

Evie frowned. It looked like she would have to channel more of her mother after all. She couldn't just put on the makeup and expect the vultures to let her have the key. She had to *be* Evil Queen. The vultures began to shriek and caw at her.

'SILENCE!' she demanded. 'You know the penalty if you fail to give me the key!' She glared at them as her mother would.

She looked so frightening and so much like her mother at that moment that the vultures squawked and flapped their wings, flying away from her as fast as they could.

'Sorry, birdies,' Evie whispered as she reached back into the nest and grabbed the key to the front door.

She slid down, Jay and Carlos giving her a hand as she made it back to the front steps. In a blink, they were finally inside.

It was the same as it ever was, dark and shadowy and full of cobwebs. They tiptoed past the kitchen. 'This place gives me the creeps,' said Carlos. Jay nodded silently.

'Oh, it's not that bad,' said Evie. 'It's worse when Mum's around.'

They made their way through the dark corridors up to the bedrooms, where Evil Queen kept her legendary Magic Mirror. Evie opened the door, half expecting her mother to scold her for letting in a draft. But it was as empty as expected. Mum never missed a night out with her hags.

The mirror's shards clung to the edges of the frame, but when Evie stepped up to it, it was almost as if it were whole again.

'Magic,' whispered Evie. 'I can feel it coming from below, from deep underground, somehow. It's weak, but it's working.'

She gazed into the largest fragment. She noticed she was still wearing her Evil Queen disguise, which might turn out in their favour.

'Magic Mirror, from the furthest space, through wind and darkness, I summon thee!' she called.

For a moment, the mirror remained foggy and dark, but slowly it began to shift and reveal something else: a face in the mirror. The face *of* the mirror.

'What wouldst you know, my queen?' asked the mirror in a deep, sonorous voice that echoed throughout the castle.

It worked! Evie tried to keep her composure.

'Magic Mirror on the wall,' she said, addressing the mirror by its full, true name. 'Show me the dark fairy named Mal.'

The clouds swirled once more. Then they parted to reveal deep blue depths. A sunken pirate ship. A great school of fish, swimming in a circle.

'Where is she?' said Evie, searching every image in the mirror. 'SHOW ME MAL!' she commanded.

Carlos gasped. 'Look!'

Through the bubbles and the murk, they saw their friend walking dazedly on the deck of the ship. Mal was walking towards a door, as if compelled towards it.

She had a glassy look in her eyes as she reached for the handle.

'Mal! Stop! Don't open that door!' yelled Evie.

chapter 31

Open and Out

Back in Hades' cave, Uma had suddenly returned, and was dripping water all over the floor. She was back from her battle with Mal—but the most important part was still to come.

'Hey! Watch it!' said Hades grumpily.

'I got her where I want her!' said Uma. 'See!' She touched her seashell necklace and pointed towards the broken television, which sprang to life. It showed Mal under the sea, on the deck of a pirate ship, heading to a locked door.

'She thinks she won, but when she opens that door,' said Uma gleefully, 'I'll appear right in front of her, and then I'll take the key to our freedom! She's walking right into my trap!'

'She is?' asked Hades.

'Of course she is! I confused her, then spelled her and now she's on the verge of letting all of us out!' Uma laughed in glee.

'How'd you do that?'

'I'm a sea witch,' said Uma smugly. 'I own these waves.'

'Right!' said Hades, who appeared to finally catch on that their plan was working.

Uma plopped down on the couch and leaned back. 'All she has to do is open that door.'

Hades squinted at the screen. 'What door?'

'That door!' said Uma, pointing to the door on the pirate ship, annoyed that she had to explain it again. 'She opens that door and I pop out!'

'Really?' Hades asked, not quite convinced. 'But you're here.'

'When she opens the door, I'll be there! Sheesh, you're so slow. I think you spent too much time in the Underworld,' said Uma.

'So you pop over there, and then what happens?'

'I grab the key to our freedom!' screeched Uma. 'Click— open and out!' She glanced sideways at him. 'What's wrong? You don't seem excited to leave.'

'Oh, I am! I really am!' he said. But there was something else in his voice that Uma couldn't quite place.

Then Hades' face broke into a malicious grin. 'Wait till I surprise my brother Zeus. He won't see me coming!'

'And I'll have my pirates back!' said Uma. She jumped off the couch and knelt by the television screen, her face inches from Mal's pixellated one.

'Come on, Mal!' she said.

'Mal, do it!' said Hades, joining her.

'MAL! OPEN IT! OPEN THAT DOOR!' they chorused.

chapter 32

Friendly Force

Through the mirror, Mal's friends watched in horror as she reached for the door handle.

'NO!!!' Carlos screamed, just as loudly as Evie. 'MAL! DON'T OPEN IT!!!' He was sure they didn't want to know what was behind that door. And he was even more certain that Uma was behind this . . . whatever this was. Maybe Uma was even *literally* behind it. He wouldn't put it past her.

'We need to stop her!' yelled Jay.

'The mirror!' said Evie. She ran up to its frame and thrust an arm into it, bracing herself for a shattering of glass. Carlos sucked in his breath, and Jay lunged for Evie to pull her back. But her arm disappeared beyond the glass. Carlos could feel the water as it splashed out from the frame, cool and wet against his skin.

'Hold on, Mal! We're coming to get you!' Carlos said, as Evie climbed into the mirror and half of her body disappeared through it.

'Evie! Be careful!' said Jay, right behind her.

'Mal!' Evie cried as Mal reached out towards the handle of the door. 'Don't open it!'

But Mal didn't hear. She just kept walking closer and closer to the door, and finally she pushed it open.

Now Uma stood in the doorway, cackling. She had a gleeful look on her face. 'Give it to me!' she ordered, reaching for Mal's pockets.

Uma was fast, but Evie was even faster. She shoved her entire body through the mirror, through time and space. She became a force in the water that pushed Mal away from Uma as hard as she could.

All of a sudden, Mal shot back up to the surface, away from Uma, out of danger.

Uma screamed in anger and turned around, just as Evie's entire body fell through the mirror and appeared underwater, on the deck of the ship. Uma's face darkened. She extended a tentacle, grabbed Evie's wrist, and began to pull her into the abyss.

'Help!' cried Evie.

Carlos lunged into the mirror, grabbed Evie's legs, and started pulling her back, so that she was halfway in and halfway out of the mirror. Jay grabbed Carlos and pulled both of his friends backwards, trying to drag them back into the castle and out of the water.

Uma was strong, but they were stronger.

Together, the three of them pulled with all their might.

They pulled so hard that they went tumbling backwards, out of the mirror, landing with a splash on the floor of Evil Queen's castle.

'Mal!' yelled Evie, jumping to her feet. 'She got away!'

'We did it!' Carlos shouted. Jay whooped.

Evie cheered and then glanced around the room. They were covered in seaweed. 'Are you guys all right?'

Carlos nodded, trying to catch his breath. 'I think so.'

'Yeah, I'm good,' said Jay, getting up from the puddle.

'Um, guys, what just happened?' said Carlos.

'The door . . .' started Evie, but then her eyes began to glaze over. Suddenly Carlos felt his memory slipping away. He blinked, confused, and touched his soaking-wet hair. What had Evie been about to say to them? And why were they all dripping with water?

'Yeah, what are we doing here?' asked Jay. 'Where are we?'

Carlos and Evie stared back at him with matching blank expressions. 'I have absolutely no idea,' said Carlos. He felt like he had just woken up from an extremely vivid dream.

'Something with . . . the Magic Mirror, maybe?' Evie guessed, since they were standing right in front of it.

Carlos stared at the Magic Mirror. It was dark and broken. And it felt like he had been looking into it. Had he imagined that he had seen something there? But that couldn't be right—the mirror needed magic to work.

'We're in my home. But why?' Evie continued.

'We were looking for Mal? I think?' Carlos said, his forehead scrunching.

'Did we find her?' asked Evie.

'I hope so,' said Jay.

'We've got bigger problems, boys,' said Evie, as they heard the front door creak open. 'We need to get out of here. My mum's home!'

chapter 33

Fortune-Teller

The more Celia stared at the cracks in the cave wall, the more she was certain they weren't just fissures in the stone. There was a rip in the fabric of their world—this was a broken seam, spilling magic into the tunnels underneath the Isle of the Lost. Uma and Hades must have been counting on this tiny bit of magic to take Mal and her friends by surprise. *If only Dizzy were here,* Celia thought despairingly. She could help her figure out what to do.

Celia traced the spiderweb of cracks along the cave wall. There were so many of them, and it looked like they were spreading. What could she do? How could she fix a spell? She was nothing but a two-bit hustler, making up fortunes for people silly enough to pay for them. She couldn't help Mal and her friends.

She shuffled and reshuffled her cards out of habit. Then she realised—if there really was magic down here, she could use it. She sat down on the cold cave floor, cutting and shuffling her cards. She would read her own fortune, to guide her hand and find a solution. For once, her tricks might actually work.

How do I fix the cracks? she asked the cards as she shuffled them again and again, her hands shaking from nerves.

Celia placed three cards in front of her.

The first card was the Magician. Her past.

The next was the Queen of Wands. Her present.

The third was the Hermit. Her future.

What did it mean? The Magician was her past. A strong presence—her father, she thought. The great manipulator, a true magician. The second card represented who she was: the Queen of Wands, a sorceress in her own right. Someone dependable. A person others could count on. The third was the Hermit—an inward-looking card, one that represented a person's inner life.

Then she realised: It meant the ability to fix this rested within her. She didn't need anyone's help. She had the power all along.

Celia was her father's daughter. Dr Facilier wasn't just the headmaster of Dragon Hall—he was a powerful witch doctor who had friends on the other side, including one particular friend who was very close indeed. She knew what she had to do.

A spell to fix a spell.

She called on her shadow, the creature that lived in her. Her shadow peeled itself away from Celia and turned to her. 'What is your command, mistress?'

'Seal the spaces in between; weave the fabric of the barrier's spell back to its rightful strength; and where there is light, let darkness rule,' Celia ordered. 'Cast yourself wide and dark and deep.'

Her shadow nodded, and then leapt onto the wall. It grew until it covered the cave in darkness, and one by one, every thread of light in the cave blinked out.

Celia held her cards. They did not tremble, nor did they call. The magic was snuffed out like a candle, by a shadow.

Celia felt herself gasp with relief, and she hugged her cards to her chest. Then, just as quickly, she brushed herself off and stood, pulling herself back together. *After that, I better get picked to go to Auradon Prep,* Celia said to herself as she worked her way back through the tunnel. *Imagine what I could do with real magic at my fingertips!*

chapter 34

Mermaids and Makeovers

Like a curtain closing on a stage, everything suddenly disappeared—the bubbles, the pirate ship, the door—at the same time that an invisible force pushed Mal away and sent her flying off to safety.

'Face it, Uma, I'll always be stronger than you!' said Mal as the waves carried her away.

She could hear Uma's cry of rage from deep below echoing in the waves. 'You, strong enough? In your dreams!!!' screamed Uma.

Mal shut her eyes.

When she opened them, she was standing at the pier again, and it was as if she had never fallen into the water.

Her memory was fading as well. She fought to hold on to fragments of images—the school of fish that had surrounded her, Uma's face laughing in all the bubbles, the pirate ship, a mirror and that strangely compelling door.

Uma! Uma had been standing at the doorway, and she wanted something. Something Mal had.

Mal checked her pocket for the remote. It was still there. She sighed in relief.

Who had pushed Mal away from the door and brought her back to safety? It could only be some kind of friend or ally. She dimly recalled hearing Evie's voice calling to her, along with Jay and Carlos yelling.

Her friends had helped her. They had her back somehow. They had carried Mal away from Uma. She didn't know how they'd managed it, but deep in her heart, she knew they were the ones who'd gotten her to safety. If only she could remember what had really happened down under the waves. Yet, as she stood on the dock, she had already begun to forget what she was trying to recall.

She was standing on the dock when Dizzy appeared in front of her once more.

'Dizzy?' she asked uncertainly.

'Yeah, who else would it be? Are you okay?' asked Dizzy.

'It's the strangest thing. I was walking through the woods, and I came across this glowing orb thing and . . .' Had she told Dizzy this already? Why did she feel such déjà vu? 'And you were Uma—you were speaking in Uma's voice. Then I was underwater, but I could swim.'

Dizzy frowned. 'Ohhhhkay, maybe you shouldn't go back to Auradon just yet. I could give you a makeover! That'll make you feel better.'

Mal was still confused. Then she saw something in Dizzy's hand. She reached for it and studied it.

'You like?' asked Dizzy, offering it to Mal.

It was a seashell necklace.

'Actually, no, I think it might clash with your outfit,' said Dizzy, taking it back.

Then that familiar voice whispered from the woods. *Mal...*

This time, Dizzy heard it too. 'Did you hear that?' she asked nervously.

Mal looked all around, chills running up and down her spine. She knew that voice. 'Dizzy, I think we might want to get out of here,' she said. 'There's danger coming. I can feel it. And I think it might be headed for Auradon.' She took Dizzy's hand and led her away from the shoreline.

Then Mal took the seashell necklace from Dizzy, threw it on the ground, and stepped on it.

Chapter 35

What Villains Want

When Evie, Jay and Carlos arrived back at the hideout, Mal was already there, safe and sound. Evie felt a huge rush of relief at the sight of her friend. She hadn't realised she was so worried until the weight of it fell away. She ran up to Mal and gave her a quick hug.

'Where were you guys?' Mal asked, returning Evie's hug with a grateful expression.

'Looking for you!' said Jay, giving her a fist-bump. 'We went around the whole island!'

'Your hair!' said Evie, pulling away to look at it from an objective distance. 'You got a haircut?'

Mal patted her new wavy locks, now cut into a long bob. 'I ran into Dizzy.'

'That girl is a genius,' said Evie admiringly.

'You like?' asked Mal.

'Love,' affirmed Evie.

'A haircut? At this time of night?' asked Carlos. 'I'll never understand women.'

The girls laughed. Then Mal turned to Evie and stared at her closely. 'Um, Evie? You know you really look like your mum?' asked Mal.

Evie ran to the nearest mirror. 'I do! Isn't that weird? I never wear my makeup this way. I should get it off before I frighten any children.'

'Well, we're glad you're safe. That we're all safe,' said Jay.

'Safe on the Isle of the Lost. Now that's new,' said Carlos with a grin. 'Oh, by the way, I have an idea on how to get more kids to apply to Auradon Prep.'

'You do? What is it?' asked Evie.

'I think we're going about this all wrong. What do villains like?' asked Carlos.

'Fame,' said Mal.

'Riches,' said Jay.

'Attention,' said Evie.

'Exactly! So we have to sell it to them as a way to get all those. Not learning how to be good or being part of a team—they're not interested in that. Not yet. But they'll understand the appeal of a celebration.'

'VK Day!' said Evie.

'Funny, that's what I called it too!' said Carlos. 'But Jane's the one who came up with the idea.'

'I knew there was a reason why I always liked her,' said Evie. 'Anyway, we'll tell Dr Facilier that there'll be a huge party, and that the four kids who are chosen will be famous!'

The four of them turned to each other with just-slightly-wicked smiles on their faces. They knew this would work.

The next morning, they met with Dr Facilier at Dragon Hall once more.

'Before we leave, we just wanted to share with you a new development concerning the VK program,' said Mal.

'Oh? A new development, is there? Pray tell,' said the witch doctor with his frightening smile.

'Tell him, Evie,' said Mal.

Evie leaned forwards, her voice a little breathless. 'The four chosen kids will be celebrated with a huge, kingdom-wide feast that will be bigger and more spectacular than anything anyone has ever seen.'

'We'll have a marching band, the royal family . . . It will be an amazing welcome,' said Mal.

'Talk about rolling out the red carpet,' said Jay.

'The gold carpet,' Carlos said with a wink.

Dr Facilier nodded, and his eyes shone with greed. 'I will make sure to tell the students of this new, very exciting development.'

'See that you do. We'll be back in a few weeks to collect applications and announce the selected kids,' said Mal.

chapter 36

Trickster Sister

A royal limousine flying blue-and-gold Auradon flags was waiting for them when they walked out of Dragon Hall, and a group of students were milling about, gawking at it. Mal felt a bit self-conscious at the sight of the luxurious vehicle, but tried not to show it. They had already picked up their trunks from the hideout, so they were ready to go. All they had to do was open the barrier and call up the bridge, and they would be back in Auradon in no time.

'Home, Jay,' Mal said to her friend with a wink as she climbed into the limo. Jay slid into the driver's seat, grinning.

'Finally,' said Evie, climbing in next to her.

'Ditto,' said Carlos.

'Let's blow this joint,' said Jay, honking the horn. 'Isle of the *Get Lost*.'

Mal nodded. 'I'm glad we're on our way. I have this weird feeling that we need to be back in Auradon as soon as we can. I might even have Ben cancel the rest of my official visits. I want to be on guard,' she said, a determined look on her face.

'It'll be fine. You're just spooked because we're back here,' Carlos said. 'Evil lurks in every corner on the Isle. Really, I think I just saw Claudine Frollo over there.'

'Nah, Mal's right. It's good we're heading back now. Besides, we have to get ready for graduation,' said Jay.

'Graduation!' cried Evie. 'Finals are coming up! And I still have to make all the caps and gowns!'

Jay was about to roll up the window when they saw Celia emerge from a manhole cover, top hat first.

'Oh, hi,' she said, nonchalantly, as if she often emerged from subterranean levels.

'Hey, what's up?' said Mal. She stared at Celia. There was something odd about her, but she couldn't quite place it.

'Everything okay?' called Evie.

'I think so,' said Celia. 'You guys are fine, right?'

'We are,' said Mal. She still wasn't sure what had happened the night before, but she knew she had faced and survived some sort of danger.

'Good.' Celia leaned over to talk to Evie through the window. 'That last card I told you about?' she said. 'When I read your fortune?'

'Yes?' asked Evie warily.

'It doesn't just mean disaster. I mean, it doesn't mean disaster at all. It just means change,' said Celia. 'Sorry I made it sound like a bad fortune.'

Evie brightened. 'Change, huh? So change is in my future?'

'Pretty much,' said Celia.

'Well, I am graduating in a few weeks,' said Evie. 'So there's going to be a lot of change happening.'

Celia yelped. 'I was right? I predicted it correctly? That's so cool!'

Evie laughed. 'You did. Thanks, Celia.'

Celia rewarded Evie with a huge smile. Then she turned to face all of them. 'Headed back to Auradon now?' she asked wistfully.

Mal nodded. 'Yeah.'

'But we'll be back,' said Evie.

'Soon,' added Carlos.

'We promise,' said Jay.

'I hope so,' said Celia, tipping her hat to them.

They waved to Celia until she was just a dot on the horizon and the car was speeding on the bridge back to the mainland. Carlos raided the treats in the limousine, happy to find it was still stocked with as much chocolate and candy as always. Mal looked out the window as the island grew smaller and smaller in the distance.

'I'll call it. This was a success,' said Carlos. 'We got the applications out. Now we just wait to see them come in.'

Jay smiled at them in the rearview mirror. 'They will. Dr Facilier was practically drooling at the thought of VK Day.'

'To villains!' said Carlos with a cackle. He put out his hand. 'Come on, make the pile,' he said to Mal and Evie.

One by one, they put their hands on top of one another's. Jay met their eyes in the mirror and nodded.

'The Isle of the Lost will always be home,' said Evie. 'It's where we're from.'

'But we're also from Auradon now,' said Mal. She had grown up a child of the Isle of the Lost, a mean-spirited, selfish little sprite, but now she was a defender of Auradon, a lady and a dragon. She wasn't only Maleficent's daughter or King Ben's girlfriend. She was also just Mal.

'I'll always be just Mal,' Mal murmured.

'"Just Mal"?' asked Evie. 'That's more than enough.'

They took back their hands and beamed at each other. As long as the four of them were friends, anything was possible. The future was waiting.

'It was weird,' said Mal. 'There seemed to be something off about Celia.'

'What?' asked Evie.

'Didn't you notice?' said Mal thoughtfully. 'For a minute, it almost looked like she had no shadow.'

Some Time Ago....

Lord of the Underworld

Okay, so maybe life on the Isle of the Lost wasn't too bad. There were still demons to do his bidding—fetch his coffee, run his errands, pick up his dry-cleaning. Sure, there wasn't any magic on the island, but henchmen abounded. Even Pain and Panic were there! And there was still food—spoiled and stale, of course, but edible. Oh, dear Athena, what was he saying? This place was a dump! A total nightmare! A low-rent establishment where even centaurs wouldn't stay! And they lived in *stables*!

He should be on Olympus, feasting on grapes, with nymphs hanging on his every word and laughing at all his jokes! Not scrounging for scraps in the back of an alley, just to have some uppity wicked fairy who thought she ran the place chastise him for being in her way.

Hades fumed until his face was red. His hair no longer burst into flame, which was probably a good thing, because nothing on the Isle was fire-retardant. He *had* to get out of here! He just had to find a way.

If he couldn't burst through the invisible barrier that surrounded the Isle of the Lost, or climb over it, there was only one way left: dig underneath it. After he'd fallen off the pirate-mast ladder, he had set his crew of demons, goblins and pirates to digging as deep as they could, creating a maze of tunnels underneath the Isle of the Lost. Hades went down to see how the work was going.

'Any luck?' he asked. 'Have we hit Auradon yet?'

'No,' said a sweaty pirate, wiping his forehead with his bandanna and resting on his shovel. 'Nothing.'

'Maybe this way?' said Hades, gesturing over to the other direction.

'No, I think I hear water trickling from this way,' argued the pirate.

'Hmmm. Okay,' said Hades. (In fact, he had just missed the fork that led into the Endless Catacombs of Doom, which would be discovered and explored by a crew of young villains one day. But that's another story.)

Instead, they kept digging until they dug around in a complete circle. It was officially official: There was no way out of the Isle of the Lost.

Hades raged. He kicked the cave walls. He took his ember and began banging it on the walls of the tunnel, creating a single tiny crack. For a moment, a minuscule blue spark glared weakly from deep within the crack, but it died out before Hades even noticed.

'BY ZEUS, THIS IS IMPOSSIBLE!' he screamed.

Then he called the biggest and strongest demons back and made them clean up the largest part of the tunnel that he would take as his cave. If he was going to be stuck here, he might as well be comfortable. Every good villain needed a lair.

Caps & Gowns

'My heart is telling me that we are not our parents.'
—Mal, Descendants

chapter 37

Auradon or Auradon't

On Monday morning, the students of Dragon Hall gathered for their regular assembly in the crumbling auditorium before classes began. Except there was nothing regular about this morning's assembly at all. In fact, it was completely *irregular*, because no-one had ever actually adhered to the morning schedule, instead just showing up late or causing trouble in the hallways. So when an announcement boomed in the overhead speakers that attendance was mandatory, the students knew something was up.

Dizzy and Celia found seats in the front and waited to hear the news with the rest of the school. Dr Facilier slunk into the room, and a hush fell over the crowd. Some of the younger first-years began to shake and tremble. The witch doctor headmaster was downright frightening sometimes, with his eyes that seemed to see through your soul. Celia should know—it was the look he gave her when she used up the last bit of expired milk in the morning and then put the jug back in the fridge.

'Good morning, villains,' Dr Facilier greeted them when he stepped up to the microphone, a sneering Professor Tremaine and a clueless Coach Gaston behind him. 'I have some special news.'

He surveyed the crowd. 'Transfer applications to Auradon Prep will be available today. These students will be able to leave the Isle of the Lost this summer and continue their studies in Auradon.'

Auradon!

Wasn't this what Mal was saying the other day? From the balcony? That was real? It wasn't a trap after all? And that roundtable discussion they had invited everyone to (except almost no-one went) . . . that was also legit?

'The students who are chosen will be celebrated throughout the land and enjoy a spectacular welcome feast at the school, complete with a parade. Your names will be immortal, and you will be known throughout the kingdom as the Isle's finest villains,' said Dr Facilier, playing directly to the crowd.

'Remember, only the wickedest of you will be chosen,' he added with a laugh. 'Auradon representatives will be back in a few weeks to announce their selections for the VK program. Now go forth and do your evil deeds.'

Celia and Dizzy turned to each other, almost unable to contain their excitement. They were really taking applications! They could really go to Auradon Prep! They clasped hands and headed to the front, where the application forms were stacked.

'My dad said they're going to take four kids,' said Celia.

'Only four?' asked Dizzy. 'That's not that many.'

'There are only two of us!' said Celia. 'We'll make it.'

'Evie said they're going to come back to the Isle again in a few weeks,' said Dizzy. 'That must have been what your dad meant when he mentioned the Auradon representatives. Maybe they'll bring us back then!'

'Maybe.'

'And the celebration sounds amazing,' said Dizzy. 'A welcome feast!'

'I hope it's a warm welcome,' Celia said with a snicker.

There was a bevy of students fighting over the applications.

'You're applying?' Dizzy asked, as she saw her cousin Anthony Tremaine take a form.

'Why not?' said Anthony, raising an eyebrow. 'At least in Auradon there's better hair gel.'

Ginny Gothel walked up with her friend Harriet Hook. 'I'll take one,' said Ginny, her curly black hair flowing down her back. 'There's magic in Auradon. Even if it's regulated, I want to see what I can do there. What about you, Harriet?'

'My sister CJ likes it there, so I'm a little curious,' said Harriet. 'But Harry would never move to Auradon, not without his pirates.'

Ginny nodded. She couldn't imagine Harry without his crew. He was practically miserable without his captain, Uma. 'So are you going to apply or not?'

'I'm not sure,' said Harriet. 'Maybe. Fine, I'll take one. Actually, give me three, I'm babysitting for the Smees tonight. Maybe their kids want to apply.'

By the time the bell rang for the first class, almost all the applications had been taken.

chapter 38

Building a Brand

It was a few weeks after their return from the Isle of the Lost, and things were starting to gear up for graduation, which was coming faster than Cinderella's carriage trying to get home before midnight. During the debriefing, Ben asked the four of them if they thought the visit was a success, and they had unanimously agreed that they had done their best. Ben had assured them that was all he had hoped for, and Mal, Evie, Carlos and Jay went back to focusing on enjoying the last days of the school year.

Just as Doug had predicted, almost all the graduating seniors of Auradon Prep wanted an Evie's 4 Hearts original cap and gown for the ceremony. Between finals and trying to get all the gowns ready, Evie was so busy that Doug had to step in and help as business manager.

A line of girls stood in the hallway leading to Evie and Mal's room, waiting for their appointments. Doug walked out with a clipboard. 'Okay, who's next? Oh, Ally, come on up.'

Ally of Wonderland ran over. 'Is it ready?' she asked upon entering the room, which resembled a high-end boutique.

'Almost,' said Evie with a smile as she brought out Ally's blue-and-white gown. 'Let's see it on you.'

Ally popped into the changing room and walked out, radiant. 'I love it!' she said, looking in the mirror. The gown's colours complemented her bright blue eyes and fair hair. 'It's even perfect for a tea party!' she said, clapping her hands.

Jordan was next, and she approved her flowing, midriff-baring graduation gown with its matching silk cap. She modelled it for Evie and did a little dance. 'It's gorgeous,' Genie's daughter said. 'Thanks, Evie.'

'*You're* gorgeous,' said Evie. 'It's the girl, not the gown!'

'I can't believe we're finally graduating,' said Jordan sadly. 'I'll miss this place.'

'Me too,' said Evie. 'It's not just a school—it's a home.'

'What are your plans for after?' asked Jordan.

'More of this, I think,' said Evie. 'Designing. Maybe doing a fashion show or two. There's so much to think about. What about you?'

Jordan shrugged. 'I'm not sure yet. I'll probably travel the world with my dad for a while. Maybe leave my lamp somewhere and see if I feel like granting wishes.'

'Good luck,' said Evie, hugging her close.

'You too,' said Jordan.

Ariana Rose, Audrey's snooty cousin, swanned in, casting a sceptical eye at Evie's establishment. 'The three good fairies were supposed to make my graduation gown, but of course they're too busy with Audrey's,' she said. 'Audrey, Audrey, Audrey.' She rolled her eyes in annoyance. 'I mean, who cares about Audrey? She's not even dating Ben anymore. Or Chad.'

'Did you want the blue or the pink?' Evie asked, holding up two gowns.

Ariana put her hands on her hips and almost stomped her feet. 'Both, remember?'

Evie forced a smile. 'Audrey doesn't have to date a prince to be happy.'

'Wow, you're naïve,' said Ariana. 'Only a prince would make me happy!'

Evie wrapped up her gowns. 'I used to think that too,' she said.

'And now?'

Evie pressed the brown paper package holding the blue and pink gowns into Ariana's hands. 'I'm just happy to have someone who cares about me.'

Ariana sniffed. 'Hmmpf.'

Mal entered the room just as Ariana was leaving. 'Oh, hey,' said Mal. She wasn't a very popular person with Ariana's family.

Ariana merely brushed by Mal as if she didn't exist.

'You know how your mum cursed someone to sleep for a thousand years?' asked Evie.

Mal nodded.

'I totally get it now.' Evie laughed.

Mal laughed with her, and for a moment, it felt fun to be just a little wicked.

Freddie was by far Evie's favourite client. Her graduation gown was red with black stripes. She adored the little top-hat cap that Evie had made her, complete with bone necklace. 'This is bomb,' said Freddie, looking at herself in the mirror. 'You are a real magician, Evie.'

'Thanks,' said Evie modestly.

'Heard you guys saw my little sister Celia when you guys were back on the Isle,' said Freddie. 'How is she?'

'Good,' said Evie. 'She tried to read my fortune.'

'Ha! Did you let her?' asked Freddie. 'I hope not!'

Even Lonnie stopped by. Evie explained that her gown had pockets for her swords and a sheath for her bow and arrow too. 'I wanted the gowns to be both fashionable *and* functional,' said Evie.

'Extraordinary,' said Lonnie. 'I'll show my mum. Maybe she'll put in an order for the rest of the army.' She drew Evie in for a hug. 'I'm going to miss you,' said Lonnie. 'I can't believe we're all going to be separated so soon.'

'I know, I'll miss you too,' said Evie. 'We won't be too far away, right? You'll come visit?'

'It's about a four-day carriage ride from the Imperial Palace to Auradon City,' said Lonnie. 'So we can't just pop in. But yes, I'll definitely come visit.'

Evie promised she would too. Still, she knew that Lonnie was right—their visits would be few and far between. As much as she hated to admit it, this phase of their life was coming to a close. It was time to forge their own paths now.

Once more, Evie felt a rush of gratitude that she had been able to leave the Isle of the Lost and come to Auradon. Evie hoped that one day every little kid who grew up on that island would have the same opportunity.

Lonnie left and Jane knocked on the door. She was holding her trusty clipboard.

'Hey,' said Evie. 'I have your dress ready.'

Jane didn't need a graduation gown, but Evie had made her a new dress for the occasion anyway. She brought it out—a silvery-blue cocktail dress with a pretty lace collar.

'Evie, it's beautiful,' said Jane in an awed voice. 'It's the most beautiful dress I've ever seen.'

Evie blinked back tears. 'I'm so glad you love it.'

'We'll miss you guys so much,' Jane said, enveloping Evie in a deep hug.

'We'll be back tonnes,' said Evie. 'You'll be sick of us.'

'Really, really sick, okay?' cried Jane. 'So sick we have the flu.'

'Promise,' said Evie.

At the end of the week, Doug showed Evie his spreadsheet. 'Look how much you earned! You are a queen!'

'Oh my fairest!' said Evie. 'I can finally afford what I've wanted all this time!'

chapter 39

The Future's So Bright...

Two weeks before the very last day of school was the annual Senior Dinner, hosted by the royal family in honour of the graduating class. Ben came to knock on Mal's door to escort her to the event. He looked particularly dashing in a new blue-and-gold tuxedo that matched his crown. 'Are you ready?' he asked.

Mal tucked her hair behind her ears and took one last look in the mirror. She was wearing a new purple dress trimmed with black lace that Evie had made her and had combed her hair just the way Dizzy had taught her. She hoped she had gotten it right. Doug and Evie had already left for the event just a few minutes earlier. When she turned to Ben, his smile widened.

'You look beautiful,' he said.

'You don't look too bad yourself,' she teased.

She took his arm and they made their way out of the dorms towards the main lawn, which had been set up with a majestic white tent for the night. Their fellow seniors milled around in their finest formal wear. Lonnie and Jay were standing by the buffet table, sampling the canapés. Jay was wearing his rust-coloured Agrabah-style leather jacket with the epaulets. Carlos and Jane were talking to Fairy Godmother. Doug and Evie were once again saying hi to Doug's many cousins. (His dad did have six brothers.)

'Did I ever tell you how glad I am that nothing bad happened on the Isle this time?' said Ben, as he walked her to their table.

'About that,' said Mal.

'Something bad happened?'

'Yes,' she said. 'Except I don't remember exactly what it was. We did get away. But we need to be vigilant. Something wicked this way comes . . .'

Ben raised his eyebrows. 'I'll double security right now.'

'And we really did our best to try to convince kids to apply here,' said Mal.

'I know you did.'

'I just hope it was enough.'

'What's the event you're planning with Evie? VK Day? That sounds pretty cool,' said Ben.

'I hope it works,' said Mal.

'We'll be inundated with applications. You'll see,' said Ben.

King Beast and Queen Belle arrived, and everyone took their seats. Mrs Potts had outdone herself: there was hearty beef ragout, a bubbling and airy cheese soufflé, luscious and crispy roast chickens, mashed potatoes that had little pools of melted butter. It was the most decadent and delicious meal they ever had.

She was glad that Carlos and Jane had joined them, even though, technically, they were juniors. But as Carlos said, *technically*, Jane had planned the entire thing, down to the six-course dessert menu, so it was only fair that they got to attend.

Ben—who, in addition to being Auradon's king, was also the Class King—stood up to make a toast. 'To the best Auradon Prep class ever!' he said. 'My family wishes you all a wonderful future.'

'To the future!' said Jay, smiling at Lonnie.

'The future!' said Evie, clinking glasses with Doug.

'The future!' said Mal, who feverishly hoped it brought only peace and no threats from her homeland.

'To your future!' said Carlos, nudging Jay while he took a big sip from his glass.

'My future indeed!' said Jay. 'I'm going to check out Sherwood Forest University this weekend for visiting day.'

'You've decided?' asked Lonnie.

'Not yet. I want to check it out, but I'm excited to see what it's all about.'

'Take care,' said Ben. 'They get pretty merry over there. But I'm sure you can handle it.'

Over dessert, Evie told them her good news. 'So, you know how I've been making caps and gowns for everyone? I earned enough money to buy a place of my own. A home in Auradon,' she said.

'Oh, Evie!' said Mal, reaching across the table to give her friend a hug. 'That's amazing!'

'Wow, your own pad, huh? Sweet,' said Jay, looking a bit jealous.

'It's perfect! We found this tiny little adorable cottage in the woods,' said Evie.

'We?' said Mal with a raised eyebrow. She elbowed Ben, who covered a smile with his goblet.

'Doug helped me find it! His uncle was the listing agent,' said Evie quickly. 'Who knew Doc wasn't a doctor? He's in real estate.'

'Is he, now?' asked Jay, who raised his glass in Doug's direction while Doug blushed and coughed.

'What?' Evie asked with wide eyes.

'Mmm-hmm,' said Mal with a smirk.

Evie ignored her friends' teasing, and Doug tried to look somewhere else, even as his ears turned crimson.

'Evie, ignore them,' said Carlos, reaching to hold Jane's hand.

Evie nodded. She was all business. 'Anyway, as I was saying, this solves our problem! The four new villain kids can stay with me over the summer. There's a tonne of space.'

Carlos stole a bite of Jane's cake. Then he turned to Ben. 'Hey, I just realised—Jane and I will still be here at school next year. So we can mentor the new villain kids!'

'Can we?' said Jane.

'It'll be like having a bunch of little brothers and sisters!' said Carlos.

'Okay.' Jane laughed. 'Whatever you want.'

'It's all settled, then,' said Mal. 'They'll stay with Evie this summer, and Jane and Carlos will help them out.'

'Perfect,' said Evie, looking very pleased.

'Now we just need four kids to apply,' Jay reminded them.

Ben pushed his slice of cake over to Carlos so he would stop eating Jane's. 'Don't worry, they will.'

chapter 40

Decisions, Decisions

When Jay arrived at Sherwood Forest University, he was greeted by a friendly student dressed in the green livery of the school. 'Hey, man, I'm Bobby Hood,' he said. 'Welcome to Sherwood.'

'Your dad is a legend,' said Jay, bumping his fist. 'You're a student here?'

'My first year,' said Bobby with a grin. 'Come on, let me show you around.'

Bobby gave Jay the campus tour—taking him to the archery fields, the student centre and the academic buildings. 'And here's the R.O.A.R. gym,' he said. 'It's where you'll be playing.'

It was a gleaming indoor gymnasium, filled with R.O.A.R. athletes in green uniforms, leaping off the walls and practising with their swords and shields. Jay grinned. 'Excellent.'

Next, Jay sat in on a few lectures. The history classes were mostly concerned with the medieval and Renaissance periods, and an economics class showed how taking money from the wealthy aided the less fortunate.

'But of course, the best thing here is the merrymaking,' said Bobby. 'Come on.'

He led Jay to the middle of the forest, where a few students were strumming guitars, playing games, and generally goofing off. There was a group of merry men who looked like a cheeky, irreverent bunch. And they definitely seemed like they were good with their bows and arrows.

'So, what do you think?' said Bobby.

'It's awesome,' said Jay. If he chose to enrol at Agrabah State University, he would be burdened by his father's legacy. Magical Institute Training was prestigious, but sounded way too academic and, well, magical for him—and he wasn't very good at magic. Sherwood Forest U seemed like the perfect fit.

'Good luck,' said Bobby, shaking his hand. 'Hope to see you here next year!'

Jay realised with a start that he still had to get in. Even though he was recruited and invited, nothing was set in stone until he received his admission scroll. Suddenly, he knew exactly how Dizzy felt about her Auradon application.

• • •

At last, it was the very end of school. Final grades had been posted and graduation was only a few days away. It was also the week in which college decisions would go out to those who had applied. Some people had applied early and already knew where they were headed. Lonnie was going pro, joining her brother on the Great Wall team. Evie was expanding her fashion line. Mal was going to help Ben with his royal duties and learn the ropes of palace life.

But Jay still hadn't heard back from all of his schools.

Early digital acceptances, as well as fat envelopes from both MIT and ASU, had arrived. Jay had his heart set on Sherwood Forest University, though. Yet ever since he'd returned from visiting day the other week, there had been no word from the school or the coach.

Now he had to wait with everyone else in the library, staring at a computer, refreshing his screen to see if he had been accepted to the school of his choice.

Jay drummed his fingers on the desk nervously. He never thought he'd ever graduate from high school, let alone go to college. Growing up on the Isle of the Lost, he didn't think he had much of a future. But all that had changed when he came to Auradon. His whole life was ahead of him now. In the end, he told himself, it would be okay if he didn't get into Sherwood. There were other schools. What was important was that he was going to get to do something that he loved, no matter where he ended up.

He refreshed the screen.
There it was. There was a message!

click here for application decision

Jay hit the button and bit his thumb. He never had to wait for anything in his life. For so many years, if he wanted something, he just took it, or stole it, or talked his way into it. If he got in, this would be one of the first times he had actually earned something.

jay of agrabah, congratulations!
you have been accepted into sherwood forest university's merry band of students . . .

It was even signed by Robin Hood himself.
He leapt to his feet and yelled, 'I'm going to college!'
Carlos came over and slapped him on the back. 'Congratulations, man! Dude and I are so happy for you!'
'Go, Jay!' said Evie, who had been sitting with Doug. Doug was still waiting to hear whether he had gotten into one of the top seven schools in the kingdom. They both stood up and hugged Jay.
'You did it!' said Mal, jumping up and down with Ben, as other kids began to scream out their acceptances.
It was a frenzy of excitement and relief. Students tossed their books and notebooks around and danced on the tables.

'I'm sad you're not going pro with me,' said Lonnie. 'But I'll come visit you.'

'Thanks. And I'll come see you when you guys play at Sherwood Arena,' said Jay.

'Perfect,' said Lonnie.

Jay grinned. His future gleamed brighter than all the gold in the world.

chapter 41

Ways to Be Wicked

Even at Auradon Prep, senior year meant a certain loosening of the rules. Fairy Godmother didn't look askance at seniors slouching in late to classes, or leaving their spells unchecked. Earlier in the year, when Mal heard of another secret tradition, the Senior Prank, she decided that the four former villains had to mastermind this operation.

'It's the Senior Prank, and we're from the Isle of the Lost!' she told Evie, Jay, Ben and Carlos, who was helping too.

'Oh, we've got this,' said Jay, punching a fist into his palm in excitement.

'We'll make sure they'll never forget us!' said Evie.

'After we pull this off, they might want to,' said Carlos.

'What exactly do you have in mind?' asked Ben, who couldn't help but look a little worried.

So on the very last day of school, when Auradon students left the dorms for the academic buildings, they found a carriage crashed into the front of the school entrance. The carriage was half in and half out of the wall, and part of it was made of pumpkin. It looked like something terrible had happened.

People gasped until they read what was written on the back of the carriage window, where Mal had scrawled **Seniors Rule**!

But there was more. All the vending machines were stocked with water bottles that just happened to have goldfish inside of them. The hallways were either filled with balloons or covered in plastic wrap. Every chair in the cafeteria had been switched out for a throne and turned upside down. A New Orleans jazz band followed Fairy Godmother around all day.

'Senior Prank,' the professors said with a sigh.

The seniors laughed.

Jay and Carlos hoisted up a large **For Sale** sign on top of the school's roof, while Evie and Mal drew a colourful chalk mural depicting all the seniors on the front concrete steps.

Mal put the finishing touches on Ben's crown and looked at Evie. 'I can't believe it's over.'

'Me neither,' said Evie. 'We had so much fun.'

'Remember when we first got here? How nervous we were?' said Mal.

'Audrey was so mean to you!' said Evie, shaking her head.

'All we wanted to do was wreck the place,' said Mal.

'I'm so glad we didn't,' said Evie.

'Yeah, me too,' said Mal.

The boys slid down from the roof and admired the mural. 'Nice picture of Dude,' said Carlos happily.

'Dude is definitely a senior,' said Mal.

'Yeah, he's graduating with us,' said Evie. 'Even if you're staying.'

'You guys, it's over,' said Carlos, his voice hoarse. 'You're leaving Auradon Prep. What are we going to do without you?'

Mal felt tears come to her eyes. 'We'll always be friends,' she said, slinging an arm around Evie.

'Always,' said Evie, embracing her back.

'Always,' said Jay, putting an arm around both of them.

'I'm not going anywhere,' said Carlos. 'I have one more year!' Then he laughed and joined the group hug. 'Always.'

chapter 42

Pomp and Circumstance

Mal couldn't believe it was finally here: Graduation Day! The tents had been set up, and the parents and grandparents and friends and sidekicks had arrived. So many carriages had rolled up to Auradon Prep that morning, it had caused a bit of a traffic jam. Aladdin and Jasmine were there, looking proud of Aziz. Cinderella and Prince Charming were taking many pictures of Chad, who kept blinking in every photo. The whole Rose family came too: Queen Leah, Princess Aurora, Prince Philip, all fussing around Audrey, who looked radiant, while her cousin Ariana pouted next to her.

Carlos stood at the entrance, looking handsome in

his black-and-white morning suit, handing out programs. 'Welcome to Auradon Prep.'

The first strains of the baccalaureate song played: *Auradon, fair and true . . . Auradon, gold and blue . . . Auradon, for me and you . . .*

The seniors walked in, led by Ben in his cap and gown, holding Mal's hand. Evie was next, with Doug and Jay falling in step behind her.

Carlos held up his camera. 'Say hi to the Isle!'

'The Isle?' asked Mal.

'Yes! Surprise!' said Jane, holding up a microphone. 'This is the surprise we were working on! Everyone on the Isle can watch you guys graduate!'

'To inspire every little villain kid! We wanted them to be able to see that they can grow up to do amazing things one day, just like all of you have,' said Carlos.

'That's awesome!' said Mal. She turned to Ben. 'Did you know about this?'

He grinned. 'I helped set up the streaming signal.'

Mal waved to the camera. 'Hi, everyone! Apply to Auradon Prep! We'd love to have you!'

The graduating seniors took their seats, and Fairy Godmother welcomed everyone. 'Students, parents, princes and princesses, fairies and sultans, kings and queens. We are so proud of this class!' she said. 'We have been through a lot together, and now we celebrate your accomplishments! This is a momentous day for you all. Now I'd like to introduce someone who makes us all proud to live in Auradon—King Ben!'

A huge storm of applause rained down from the crowd as Ben came up to the podium. He smiled at his subjects. 'Thank you, Fairy Godmother! I'm so proud to welcome you all here today, to our graduation. I'm not just your king—I'm also a new graduate. I'm proud to call you all my friends, and I'm even prouder to introduce the person who was voted this year's class speaker. Mal, of the Isle of the Lost!'

There was another roar of applause. Evie, Jay, Carlos and Doug jumped to their feet and gave Mal a standing ovation as she walked to the stage.

Mal stepped up to the microphone. 'When I first arrived at Auradon Prep, I was definitely its worst student. I used my magic for selfish reasons. I even cast a spell on Ben because I wasn't sure if he liked me.'

Ben leaned over and whispered, 'I always liked you.'

Mal smiled. 'That wasn't all. My friends and I even tried to steal Fairy Godmother's wand, so that we could free everyone on the Isle of the Lost, including our parents.'

There was a slight titter from the crowd. Fairy Godmother shifted in her seat, but gave Mal an encouraging smile.

Mal continued. 'But being a student here at Auradon Prep, I learned that good is better than evil. I learned to make friends. I learned to love. I learned I don't have to be a certain kind of person because I was born in a certain part of the world. I can be anyone I want to be. I can be strong, and I can be weird, and I can be myself. That's what I learned in Auradon—that I can change for the better. We all can. Change is good. Because we are all in it together, and only together can we change the world and make it a better place. We are now alumni of Auradon Prep. Let's go out there and make some magic!'

This time, the entire audience gave Mal a standing ovation.

'I'm so proud of Mal,' said Jane, wiping away tears. 'I'm so proud of all of them!'

'You did an amazing job planning the entire thing,' said Carlos. 'Your birthday's coming up, right?'

'It was yesterday,' said Jane.

Carlos paled. 'It was?!'

Jane laughed and gave him a hug. 'I'm only kidding. Yes, it's coming up soon.'

Carlos sighed in relief. He had some planning of his own to do.

chapter 43

Auradon Alums

At last, it was time for the main event. Fairy Godmother called up each student one by one to hand them their diploma. King Beast shook each graduate's hand, and Queen Belle handed them a gold-embossed Auradon Prep pin in the shape of a book. Ally of Wonderland was first, then Arabella, King Triton's granddaughter. The Rose girls were next: Ariana and Audrey, who wore matching pouts, followed by a cocky Aziz.

'King Ben,' called Fairy Godmother with a proud smile.

'Congratulations, son,' said his father, with a firm handshake.

'We're so thrilled,' whispered his mother, giving him a kiss on the cheek.

Ben grinned and walked off the stage, showing his pin to Mal, who helped fasten it to his lapel.

Doug was next. He waved his diploma up in the air and whistled as he walked back to his seat.

'Evie,' called Fairy Godmother.

Evie curtsied to the dignitaries before joining her friends back in the audience.

Jay was next, and he raised his fist in victory upon receiving his diploma, and ran up the walls before jogging off the stage.

'And now we present the commencement awards,' said Fairy Godmother. 'For most improved student: Mal.'

Mal blushed as she received her award. 'Me?'

'Who else?' said Fairy Godmother with a wink. The next award was for best athlete, which went to Jay, who did a backflip upon receiving it.

'The award for diligence goes to none other than Evie,' said Fairy Godmother. Doug cheered the loudest when Evie walked up to receive it.

The ceremony concluded, and the seniors filed out of the auditorium to a fireworks show.

'What's next?' wondered Jay, as they stopped to admire the fiery display that lit up the sky over Castle Beast.

'Everything,' said Ben, with his arm slung around Mal. 'Anything.'

'Maybe we could travel Auradon together,' said Mal.

'That could be arranged, my lady,' said Ben.

'We still need to keep an eye out for Uma,' said Mal.

'We will,' promised Ben. 'We'll keep Auradon safe, together.'

Carlos and Jane walked up to join them. 'What a big day!' he said.

Evie sighed happily, hand in hand with Doug, but at Carlos's words she straightened. 'No! The big day is coming up soon!' said Evie.

'What's bigger than graduation?' asked Jay.

'VK Day!' said Evie. 'It's going to be huge!'

'That's right,' said Ben. 'Fairy Godmother said they're inundated with applications from the Isle of the Lost.'

Mal, Evie, Jay and Carlos turned to each other with gleeful smiles.

'More villains, huh?' said Mal. 'Are you sure Auradon can handle them?'

'More than sure,' said Ben. 'We've got you guys to show them the ropes!'

'We've got to get ready to welcome them!' said Evie.

'Don't worry. We'll make sure to roll out the purple carpet,' said Mal.

Then together, they made their way to the graduation reception to celebrate their hard-earned accomplishments.

Once upon a time, four villain kids from the Isle of the Lost came to Auradon with wicked intentions, but today, they were graduating as some of the kingdom's bravest and best subjects.

Mal squeezed Ben's hand, thinking she was the luckiest girl in the world, especially when she looked over at her friends—sweet Evie, strong Jay, smart Carlos. She wouldn't be where she was without them. They were all in this together. They had all grown up so much, and now they were ready for whatever else was in store.

Rotten to the core? Maybe not so rotten anymore!

epilogue

Ocean Pollution

The force that propelled Mal up and out of the waves had also pushed Uma away from the pirate ship, sending her crashing against the rocks. She couldn't remember what had happened next, only that she had been rescued by her mother's loyal pets, Flotsam and Jetsam, who nudged her awake.

They swam away once they saw her eyes flutter open.

But Uma was confused. Where was she? What was she doing?

What just happened?

She had come so close to winning something, but what? Why couldn't she remember? Her head was throbbing.

Then she heard it: loud, blaring rock music.

Hades!

Now she remembered: She and Hades had a deal. They were going to go after Mal. Bring her down, bring the barrier down, win their freedom, and escape from the Isle of the Lost once and for all!

Uma swam up to the cave, looking for the fissures in the stone where she had slipped inside the tunnel. But everything was plugged up with a dense, solid material, dark and shining. It repelled her touch, sending her back into the water.

'*Hades!*' Uma screamed. '*Hades!* Let me in!'

But there was no answer.

There was no way for Uma to shape-shift into a form that would allow her to slip through the cracks, because there were no cracks anymore.

That washed-up rock god had double-crossed her! But why? Was he on Mal's side now? What was that all about?

'*Hades!*' Uma raged. 'You'll pay for this!'

This was all Mal's doing! She had won again. But one day, Uma vowed, she would have her revenge. She would show that purple-haired punk once and for all. Mal would never forget the name of the person who ruled the Isle of the Lost. The one who would bring Auradon to its knees.

Uma!

acknowledgments

A huge Auradon-style thank-you to my amazing editors, Hannah Allaman and Emily Meehan, for their faith and patience. Thank you to my family at Disney Publishing Worldwide, especially Guy Cunningham, Meredith Jones, Dan Kaufman, Seale 'Eddy' Ballenger, Dina Sherman, MAZ!, Elena Blanco, Kim Knueppel, Elke Villa, Holly Nagel, and Andrew Sansone. Thank you to our Disney queen, Tonya Agurto.

Thank you to our partners at Disney Channel, especially Gary Marsh, Jennifer Rogers-Doyle, and Miriam Ogawa. Thank you to the director and stars of *Descendants 3*: Kenny Ortega, Dove Cameron, Mitchell Hope, Sofia Carson,

Cameron Boyce, Booboo Stewart, Brenna D'Amico, Zachary Gibson, Sarah Jeffery, and Jedidiah Goodacre.

Thank you to my 3Arts family, Richard Abate and Rachel Kim.

It's been such a fun ride. Thank you to my two favorite people on the planet: my husband, Mike, and our daughter, Mattie, for putting up with the late nights and grumpy days. Thank you to my DLC family, especially my nephews Nicholas, Josey, and Seba, and my niece Marie. Thank you to all my dear friends, especially those who were so nice every time I had to cancel plans because I was on deadline.

Thank you to all the amazing Descenders and the people who maintain the Descendants Isle of the Lost books Wiki. WOW! You guys were an amazing help every time I had to look up something in the earlier books!

So much love, your loyal scribe,

Melissa (Mel) de la Cruz • February 2019

Los Angeles, CA

MELISSA DE LA CRUZ

(www.melissa-delacruz.com) is the author of the #1 *New York Times* best-selling Descendants series, as well as many other best-selling novels, including all the books in the Blue Bloods series: *Blue Bloods, Masquerade, Revelations, The Van Alen Legacy, Keys to the Repository, Misguided Angel, Bloody Valentine, Lost in Time* and *Gates of Paradise*. She lives in Los Angeles, California, with her husband and daughter.

Don't miss the other books in the series!

the Isle of the Lost

ALSO BY MELISSA DE LA CRUZ

DESCENDANTS
Return to the Isle of the Lost
Rise of the Isle of the Lost

THE BLUE BLOODS SERIES
Blue Bloods
Masquerade
Revelations
The Van Alen Legacy
Keys to the Repository
Misguided Angel
Bloody Valentine
Lost in Time
Gates of Paradise

The Ring and the Crown

The Isle of the Lost

A DESCENDANTS NOVEL

MELISSA DE LA CRUZ

SCHOLASTIC
SYDNEY AUCKLAND NEW YORK TORONTO LONDON MEXICO CITY
NEW DELHI HONG KONG BUENOS AIRES PUERTO RICO

Copyright © 2018 Disney Enterprises, Inc. All rights reserved.
Visit www.DisneyBooks.com and DisneyDescendants.com

Published by Scholastic Australia in 2018.

Scholastic Australia Pty Limited
PO Box 579 Gosford NSW 2250
ABN 11 000 614 577
www.scholastic.com.au

Part of the Scholastic Group
Sydney • Auckland • New York • Toronto • London • Mexico City
• New Delhi • Hong Kong • Buenos Aires • Puerto Rico

Cover design by Marci Senders
Cover art by James Madsen
Hand lettering by Russ Gray

All rights reserved. No part of this publication may be reproduced or transmitted in any form or by any means, electronic or mechanical, including photocopying, recording, storage in an information retrieval system, or otherwise, without the prior written permission of the publisher, unless specifically permitted under the Australian Copyright Act 1968 as amended.

ISBN 978-1-74299-583-0

Printed in Australia by Griffin Press.

Scholastic Australia's policy, in association with Griffin Press, is to use papers that are renewable and made efficiently from wood grown in responsibly managed forests, so as to minimise its environmental footprint.

10 9 8 7 6 5 4 3 2 1   18 19 20 21 22 / 1

For Mattie,
without whom this book would not be possible.

And for the two baddest ladies in the biz,
*Emily Meehan and
Jeanne Mosure,*

who offered me a chance to work on
an island full of villains and believed in me—
thank you, ladies, for everything.

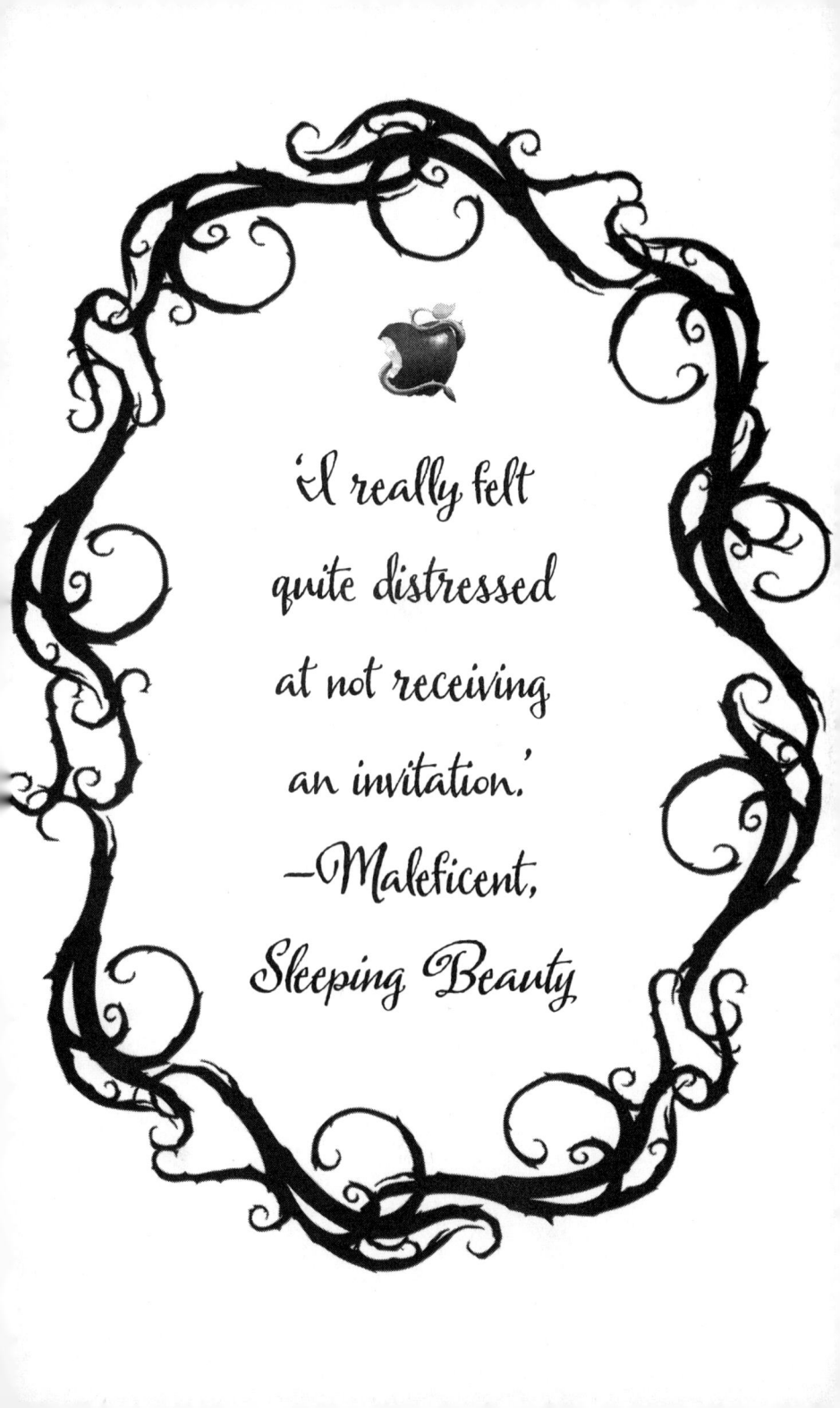

'I really felt quite distressed at not receiving an invitation.'
—Maleficent, Sleeping Beauty

prologue

Once upon a time, during a time after all the happily-ever-afters, and perhaps even after the ever-afters after that, all the evil villains of the world were banished from the United States of Auradon and imprisoned on the Isle of the Lost. There, underneath a protective dome that kept all manner of enchantment out of their clutches, the terrible, the treacherous, the truly awful and the severely sinister were cursed to live without the power of magic.

King Beast declared the villains exiled forever.

Forever, as it turns out, is quite a long time. Longer than an enchanted princess can sleep. Longer, even, than an imprisoned maiden's tower of golden hair. Longer than a week of being turned into a frog, and certainly much longer than waiting for a prince to finally get around to placing that glass slipper on your foot.

Yes, forever is a long, long, long time.

Ten years, to be specific. Ten years that these legendary villains have been trapped on a floating prison of rock and rubble.

Okay, so you might say 10 years isn't *such* a long time, considering; but for these conjurers and witches, viziers and sorcerers, evil queens and dark fairies, to live without magic was a sentence worse than death.

(And some of them were *brought back* from death, only to be placed on this island—so, um, they should know.)

Without their awesome powers to dominate and hypnotise, terrorise and threaten, create thunderclouds and lightning storms, transform and disguise their features or lie and manipulate their way into getting exactly what they wanted, they were reduced to meagre lives, eking a living selling and eating slop, scaring no-one but their own minions, and stealing from each other. It was hard even for them to imagine they once had been great and powerful, these poisoners of forest apples and thieves of undersea voices, these usurpers of royal powers and owners of petulant mirrors.

Now their lives were anything but powerful. Now they were ordinary. Everyday.

Dare it be said? Dull.

So it was with great excitement and no small fanfare that the island gathered for a one-of-a-kind event: a six-year-old princess' wickedly wonderful birthday party. *Wicked* being something of a relative term under a dome that houses a bunch of powerless former villains.

In any event, a party it was.

It was the most magnificent celebration the isolated island and its banished citizens had ever seen, and tales of its gothic grandeur and obnoxious opulence would be told for years to come.

The party to end all parties, this lavish occasion transformed the ramshackle bazaar and its rotting shopfronts in the middle of the island into a spookily spectacular playground, full of ghostly lanterns and flickering candles.

Weeks before, a flock of vultures had circled the land, dropping invitations on every shabby doorstep and hovel so that every grubby little urchin from every corner of the island would be able to partake in this enchanting and extraordinary event.

Every little urchin on the island, that is, *except for one malicious little fairy*.

Whether her invitation was lost to the winds and torn to tatters or devoured by the hungry buzzards themselves—or—gasp!—*never even addressed* in that looping royal scrawl, as was suspected, we will never know.

But the result was the same.

Above the tumultuous bazaar, up high on her castle balcony, six-year-old Mal pulled on the locks of her thick, purple hair and pursed her lips as she observed the dark and delicious festivities below. What she could make of them, at least.

There she saw the tiny princess, the fairest of the (is)land, sitting on her rickety throne, her hair as blue as the ocean, eyes as dark as night and lips as pink as roses. Her hair was pulled back from her face in a pretty plait and she laughed in delight at the array of marvels before her. The princess possessed a darling giggle that was so entrancing, it brought a smile to haughty Lady Tremaine's face, she of the thwarted plans to marry her daughters to Prince Charming; the ferocious tiger Shere Khan was practically purring like a contented kitty; and for old times' sake, Captain Hook bravely stuck his head between Tick-Tock's open jaws, if only so he could make her laugh and hear that lovely peal again.

The princess, it would seem, could make even the most horrible villains smile.

But Mal wasn't smiling. She could practically smell the two-storey cake made of sour apples, sinfully red and lusciously wormy; and try as she might, she couldn't help but overhear the screeches of the parrot Iago as he repeated, over and over again, the story of talking caves that held riches beyond measure, until the assembled villagers wanted to wring his feathered neck.

Mal sighed with green-eyed jealousy as the children gleefully tore into their baddie bags. The crumpled containers held a variety of evil sidekicks to choose from—pet baby moray eels akin to the slinky Flotsam and Jetsam swimming in tiny bowls; little spotted, cackling hyenas who were no quieter than the infamous Shenzi, Banzai and Ed; pouncing and adorable black kittens from Lucifer's latest litter. Their badly behaved recipients screamed with excitement.

As the party escalated in feverish merriment, Mal's heart grew as black as her mood, and she swore that one day, she would show them all what it meant to be truly evil. She would grow up to be greedier than Mother Gothel, more selfish even than Cinderella's stepsisters, more cunning than Jafar, more deceptive than Ursula.

She would show them all that she was just like her—

'Mother!' she yelped, as the shadow of two looming and ominous horns made their way towards the balcony and her mother appeared, her purple cape fluttering softly in the wind.

Her mother's voice was rich, melodious and tinged with menace. 'What is going on here?' she demanded as the children below tittered at the sight of a highly inappropriate shadow-puppet show put on by the frightening Dr Facilier.

'It's a birthday party,' sniffed Mal. 'And I wasn't invited.'

'Is that right?' her mother asked. She peered at the celebration over Mal's shoulder and they both took in the sight of the blue-haired princess giggling on a moth-eaten velvet pillow as Gaston's hairy and handsome young twin sons, Gaston Jr. and Gaston the Third, performed feats of strength—largely balancing their enormous booted feet on each other's squashed faces—to impress her. From the sound of things, it was working.

'Celebrations are for the rabble,' her mother scoffed. Mal knew her mother despised parties of any kind. She despised them almost as much as she did kings and queens who doted on their precious babies, chubby little fairies with a knack for dress design and obnoxious princes on even more obnoxious valiant steeds.

'Nevertheless, Evil Queen and her horrid progeny will learn soon enough from their spiteful little mistake!' her mother declared.

For her mother was the great Maleficent, Mistress of Darkness, the most powerful and wicked fairy in the world and the most fearsome villain in all the land.

Or at least, she had been.

Once upon a time, her mother's wrath had cursed a princess.

Once upon a time, her mother's wrath had brought a prince to his knees.

Once upon a time, her mother's wrath had put an entire kingdom to sleep.

Once upon a time, her mother had had all the forces of hell at her command.

And there was nothing Mal desired more in her heart than to grow up to be just like her mother.

Maleficent stepped to the balcony's edge, where she could see out to the whole island all the way to the sparkling lights of Auradon. She raised herself to her full height as thunder and lightning cracked and boomed and rain began to pour from the heavens. Since there was no magic on the island, this was just wickedly good coincidence.

The party came to a halt and the gathered citizens were paralysed at the sight of their leader glaring down at them with the full force of her wrath.

'This celebration is over!' Mal's mother declared. 'Now, shoo, flee and scatter, like the little fleas you are! And you! Evil Queen and your daughter! From now on, you are dead to the entire island! You do not exist! You are nothing! Never show your faces anywhere ever again! Or else!'

Just as quickly as it had gathered, the group dispersed, under the wary eye of Maleficent's frightening henchmen, the boar-like guards wearing aviator caps pulled down low over their hooded eyes. Mal caught a last glimpse of the blue-haired princess looking fearfully up at the balcony before being whisked away by her equally terrified mother.

Mal's eyes glittered with triumph, her dark heart glad that her misery had caused such wondrous maleficence.

Ten Terrible Years Later...

'Magic Mirror on the Wall, who is the fairest of them all?'
—Evil Queen, Snow White

chapter 1

This is the Story of a Wicked Fairy...

It has to be a dream, Mal told herself. *This couldn't be real.* She was sitting by the edge of a beautiful lake, on the stone floor of an ancient temple ruin, eating the most luscious strawberry. The forest all around her was lush and green and the sound of the water rushing at her feet was soothing and peaceful. Even the very air all around her was sweet and fresh.

'Where am I?' she asked aloud, reaching for a plump grape from the gorgeous picnic set before her.

'Why, you've been in Auradon for days now and this is the Enchanted Lake,' answered the boy seated next to her.

She hadn't noticed him until he spoke, but now that she had noticed, she wished she hadn't. The boy was the worst part of all this—whatever *this* was—tall, with tousled honey-brown hair and painfully handsome, with the kind of smile that melted hearts and made all the girls swoon.

But Mal wasn't like all the girls and she was starting to feel panicked, like she was trapped here somehow. In *Auradon*, of all places. And that it might not be a dream—

'Who are you?' she demanded. 'Are you some kind of prince or something?' She looked askance at his fine blue shirt embroidered with a small golden crest.

'You know who I am,' the boy said. 'I'm your friend.'

Mal was instantly relieved. 'Then this *is* a dream,' she said with a crafty smile. 'Because I have no friends.'

His face fell, but before he could answer, a voice boomed through the peaceful vista, darkening the skies and sending the water raging over the rocks.

'FOOLS! IDIOTS! MORONS!' it thundered.

Mal awoke with a start.

Her mother was yelling at her subjects from the balcony again. Maleficent ran the Isle of the Lost the way she did everything—with fear and loathing, not to mention a healthy supply of minions. Mal was used to the shouting, but it made for a seriously rude awakening. Her heart was still pounding from her nightmare as she kicked off the purple satin covers.

What on earth was she doing dreaming of Auradon?

What kind of dark magic had sent a handsome prince to speak to her in her sleep?

Mal shook her head and shuddered, trying to blink away the horrid vision of his dimpled smile, and was comforted by the familiar sound of fearful villagers begging Maleficent to take pity on them. She looked around her room, relieved to find she was right where she should be, in her huge, squeaky, wrought-iron bed with its gargoyles on each bedpost and velvet canopy that sagged so low, it threatened to fall on top of her. It was always gloomy in Mal's room, just as it was always grey and overcast on the island.

Her mother's voice boomed from the balcony and the floor of her bedroom rattled, causing her violet-lacquered chest of drawers to suddenly spring open, disgorging its purple contents on the floor.

When Mal decided on a colour scheme, she stuck to it, and she had been drawn to the layers of gothic richness in the purple continuum. It was the colour of mystery and magic, moody and dark, while not being as commonplace in popular villainswear as black. Purple was the new black, as far as Mal was concerned.

She crossed the room past her grand, uneven armoire that prominently displayed all of her freshly shoplifted baubles—trinkets of cut glass and paste, shiny metallic scarves with trailing strands, mismatched gloves and a variety of empty perfume bottles. Pushing the heavy curtains aside, from her window she could see the whole island in all its dreariness.

Home, freak home.

The Isle of the Lost was not a very large island; some would say it was but a speck or a blight on the landscape, certainly more brown than green, with a collection of tin-roofed and haphazardly constructed shanties and tenements built on top of one another and more or less threatening to collapse at any moment.

Mal looked down at this eyesore of a slum from the tallest building in town, a formerly grand palace with soaring tower spires that was now the shabby, run-down, paint-chipped location of the one and only Bargain Castle, where *slightly* used enchanter's robes were stocked in every colour and *slightly* lopsided witch's hats were always 50 per cent off.

It was also the home of some *not-so-slightly* bad fairies.

Mal changed out of her pyjamas, pulling on an artfully constructed purple biker jacket with a dash of pink on one arm and green on the other, and a pair of torn jeans the colour of dried plums. She carefully put on her fingerless gloves and laced up her battered combat boots. She avoided glancing at the mirror, but if she had, she would have seen a small, pretty girl with an evil glint in her piercing green eyes and a pale, almost translucent complexion. People always remarked how much she looked like her mother, usually just before they ran screaming the other way. Mal relished their fear, even sought it. She smoothed her lilac locks with the back of her hand and picked up her sketchbook, stuffing it into her rucksack along with the spray-paint cans she always carried with her. This town wasn't going to graffiti itself, was it? In a perfectly magical world it would, but that wasn't what she was dealing with.

Since the kitchen cupboards were bare as usual, with nothing in the fridge but glass jars full of eyeballs and all sorts of mouldy liquids of dubious provenance—all part of Maleficent's ongoing efforts to whip up potions and conjure spells like she used to—Mal headed to the Slop Shop across the street for her daily breakfast.

She studied the choices on the menu—black-like-your-soul coffee; sour-milk latte; crusty barley oatmeal with a choice of mealy apple or mushy banana; and stale, mixed cereal, dry or wet. There were never many options. The food, or scraps more like it, came from Auradon—whatever wasn't good enough for those snobs got sent over to the island. Isle of the Lost? More like Isle of the Leftovers. Nobody minded too much, though. Cream and sugar, fresh bread and perfect pieces of fruit made people soft. Mal and the other banished villains preferred to be brittle and hard, inside and out.

'What do you want?' a surly goblin asked, demanding her order. In the past, the disgusting things had been foot soldiers in her mother's dark army, ruthlessly dispatched across the land to find a hidden princess; but now their tasks were reduced to serving up coffee as bitter as their hearts, in tall, grande and venti sizes. The only amusement they had left was to ruthlessly misspell each customer's name, written with marker on the side of each cup. (The joke was on the goblins since hardly anyone could read Goblin; but that never seemed to make any difference.) They kept blaming their imprisonment on the island on their allegiance to Maleficent, and it was common knowledge that they kept petitioning King Beast for amnesty, using their flimsy familial ties to the dwarfs as proof they didn't belong here.

'The usual, and make it snappy,' said Mal, drumming her fingers on the counter.

'Room for month-old milk?'

'Do I look like I want curds? Give me the strongest, blackest coffee you've got! What is this, Auradon?'

It was like he'd seen her dreams, and the thought made her ill.

The runty creature grunted, wiggling the boil on his nose and pushed a dark, murky cup towards her. She grabbed it and ran out of the door without paying.

'YOU LITTLE BRAT! I'LL BOIL *YOU* IN THE COFFEE POT NEXT TIME!' the goblin shrieked.

She cackled. 'Not if you can't catch me first!'

The goblins never learned. They had never found Princess Aurora either, but then again, the dimwits had been looking for a baby for 18 years. No wonder Maleficent was always frustrated. It was so hard to find good help these days.

Mal continued on her way, stopping to smirk at the poster of King Beast admonishing the citizens of the island to be good! because it's good for you! with that silly yellow crown on his head and that big grin on his face. It was positively nauseating and more than a little haunting, at least to Mal. Maybe the Auradon propaganda was getting to her head, maybe that's why she had dreamed she was frolicking in some sort of enchanted lake last night with some pretentious prince. The thought made her shudder again. She took a gulp of her scalding, strong coffee. It tasted like mud. Perfect.

In any event, she had to do something about this blister on the wall. Mal took out her paint cans and sprayed a moustache and goatee on the king's face and crossed out his ridiculous message. King Beast was the one who had locked them all up on the island, after all. That hypocrite. She had a few messages of her own for him, and they all involved revenge.

This was the Isle of the Lost. Evil lived, breathed and ruled the island, and King Beast and his sickly sweet posters cajoling the former villains of the world to do *good* had no place in it. Who wanted to make lemonade from lemons, when you could make perfectly good lemon grenades?

Next to the poster she sprayed a thin, black outline of a horned head and a spread cape. Above Maleficent's outline, she scrawled *EVIL LIVES!* in bright green paint the colour of goblin slime.

Not bad. Bad*er*. And that was *much* better.

chapter 2

A Wily Thief...

If Mal lived above a shop, Jay, son of Jafar, actually lived *inside* one, sleeping on a worn carpet beneath a shelf straining under ancient television sets with manual dials, radios that never worked and telephones that had actual cords attached to them. His father had been the former grand vizier of Agrabah, feared and respected by all, but that was a long time ago and the evil enchanter was now the proprietor of Jafar's Junk Shop, and Jay, his only son and heir, was also his sole supplier. Jay's destiny had once been to become a great prince, but only his father remembered it these days.

'You should be on top of an elephant, leading a parade,

waving to your subjects,' Jafar mourned that morning as Jay prepared for school, pulling a red beanie over his long, straight dark hair and choosing his usual attire of purple-and-yellow leather waistcoat and dark jeans. He flexed his considerable muscles as he pulled on his black studded gloves.

'Whatever you say, Dad!' Jay winked with a mischievous smile. 'I'll try to steal an elephant if I come across any.'

Because Jay was a prince, all right. A prince of thieves, a conman and a schemer, whose lies were as beautiful as his dark eyes. As he made his way through the narrow cobblestone streets, dodging rickshaws manned by Professor Ratigan's daredevil crew, he took advantage of their frightened passengers ducking under clotheslines weighed down by tattered robes and dripping capes to filch a wallet or two. Ursula chased him away from her fish-and-chips shop, but not before he had managed to grab a handful of greasy fries. He took a moment to admire a collection of plastic jugs of every size and shape offered by another shopfront, wondering if he could fit one in his pocket.

Every manner of Auradon rubbish was recycled and repurposed on the island, from bathtubs to door handles, as well as from the villains' own formerly magical accoutrements. A shop advertised USED BROOMS THAT DON'T FLY ANY MORE BUT SWEEP OKAY, and crystal balls that were only good as goldfish bowls these days.

As vendors laid out rotten fruit and spoiled vegetables under tattered tents, Jay swiped a bruised apple and took a bite, his pockets bulging with pilfered treasures. He waved a cheerful hello to a chorus of hook-nosed witches gathered at a slanted balcony—Madam Mim's granddaughters, who, while relieved to be out of his sticky fingers' reach, swooned at his greeting nonetheless.

Maleficent's henchmen, large boar-like men in leather rags with the familiar aviator-style caps pulled down over their eyes, snuffled an almost unintelligible hello as they passed him on their way to work. Jay deftly took their caps without their noticing and shoved them down the rear of his trousers, planning to sell them back to the guys the next day like he did every week. But he resisted the urge to trip them up as well. There just wasn't time to do everything in one day.

Looking for something to wash down the sour taste of the apple, Jay caught sight of a familiar face taking a sip from a paper cup bearing the Slop Shop logo and grinned.

Perfect.

'What in Lucifer's name?' Mal cried as the cup disappeared from her fingers. She hesitated for a second before realisation hit. 'Give it back, Jay,' she said, hands on her hips, addressing the empty space on the pavement.

He snickered. It was so much fun when Mal was mad. 'Make me.'

'Jay!' she snarled. 'Make you what? Bruise? Bleed? Beg? Thief's choice, today.'

'Fine. Jeez,' he said as he slunk out from the shadows. 'Mmm, pressed hot mud, my favourite.' He handed her back her cup, feeling wistful.

Mal took a sip and grimaced. 'Actually, it's disgusting, you can have it. You look hungry.'

'Really?' He perked up. 'Thanks, Mal. I was starving.'

'Don't thank me, it's particularly awful today. I think they threw some raw toads into the brew this morning,' she said.

'Bonus! Extra protein.' Amphibians or not, Jay drained it in one shot. He wiped his lips and smiled. 'Thanks, you're a pal,' he said in all honesty, even though he and Mal weren't friends, exactly, although they were partners in crime.

Like his, Mal's jeans and jacket pockets were stuffed with all manner of junk, shoplifted from every shopfront in town. A knitting needle was sticking out of one pocket, while the other contained what looked like a sword handle.

'Can I trade you a teapot for that old sword?' he asked hopefully. Everything his father sold was stuff Jay had stolen from somewhere else.

'Sure,' she said, taking a rusty kettle in exchange. 'Look what else I got,' she said. 'The Captain's hook.' She waved it in the air. 'I nabbed it this morning when the old pirate waved hello.'

'Sweet.' He nodded. 'All I got was a handful of fries.'

Jay and Mal were in a constant competition for who was the more accomplished thief. A clear winner would be hard to call. You could say they had bonded over their love of swiping things, but they would tell you that bonds of any kind were for the weak.

Even so, they fell into step on the walk to school. 'Heard the news?' he asked.

'What news? There's no new news,' she scoffed, meaning nothing new ever happened on the island. The island's old-fashioned fuzzy-screened televisions only broadcast two channels—Auradon News Network, which was full of do-gooder propaganda, and the DSC, the Dungeon Shopping Channel, which specialised in hidden-lair décor. 'And slow down, or we'll get there on time,' she added.

They turned off the main road, towards the uneven, broken-down graveyard that was the front lawn of Dragon Hall. The venerable school for the advancement of evil education was located in a former mausoleum, a hulking grey structure with a domed ceiling and a broken-down colonnade, its pediment inscribed with the school's motto: IN EVIL WE TRUST. Scattered around its haunted grounds, instead of the usual tombstones, were doomstones with horrible sayings carved into them. As far as the leaders on this island were concerned, there was never a wrong time to remind its citizens that evil ruled.

'No way, I heard news. Real news,' he insisted, his heavy combat boots stomping through the root-ripped graveyard terrain. 'Check it out—there's a new girl in class.'

'Yeah, right.'

'I'm totally serious,' he said, narrowly avoiding stumbling over a doomstone inscribed with the phrase IT IS BETTER TO HAVE NEVER LOVED AT ALL THAN TO BE LOVED.

'New girl? From where, exactly?' Mal asked, pointing to the magical dome that covered the island and shrouded the sky, obscuring the clouds. Nothing and no-one came in or out, so there wasn't ever a whole lot of *new*.

'New to us. She's been castle-schooled until now, so it's her first time in the dungeon,' said Jay as they approached the wrought-iron gates. The crowd gathered around the entrance parted to let them through, many of their fellow students clutching their rucksacks a little more tightly at the sight of the thieving duo.

'Really?' Mal stopped in her tracks. 'What do you mean, "castle-schooled"?' she asked, her eyes narrowing suspiciously.

'A real princess too, is what I've heard. Like, your basic true-love's-kiss-prick-your-finger-spin-your-gold-skip-the-haircut-marry-the-prince-level princess.' He felt dizzy just thinking about it. 'Think I could lift a crown off her somewhere? Even a half-crown . . .?' His father was always talking about The Big Score, the one fat treasure that would free them from the island somehow. Maybe the princess would lead them to it.

'A princess?' Mal said sternly. 'I don't believe you.'

Jay wasn't listening any more. 'I mean, think of the loot she'd have on her! She's got to have a ton of loot, right?

Hope she's easy on the eyes! Better yet, on the pockets. I could use an easy target.'

Mal's voice was suddenly acid. 'You're wrong. There weren't any princesses on the island, and certainly not any who would dare to show their faces around here . . .'

Jay stared at her and in the back of his mind he heard alarm bells and had a faint memory of an awesome birthday party concerning a princess . . . and some sort of scandal that involved Mal and her mother. He felt bad, remembering now that Mal hadn't received an invitation, but he quickly suppressed the icky emotion, unsure of where it came from. Villains were supposed to revel in other people's sadness, not empathise!

Besides, when it came down to it, Mal was like a sister, an annoying, ever-present pest and a pain in the—

Bells. Ringing and echoing through the island from the top of the tower, where Claudine Frollo was tugging the rope and being pulled up along with it as she rang in the official start of the Dragon Hall school day.

Jay and Mal shared a smirk. They were officially late. The first thing that had gone right all morning.

They passed through the crumbling and moss-covered archway and into the main tomb, which was buzzing with activity—members of the Truant Council putting up signs for a Week-Old Bake Sale; the earsplitting sounds of the junior orchestra practising for the Autumn Concert, the sea witches leaning over their violins.

Frightened students scrambled to get out of their way as Mal and Jay walked past the dead ivy-covered great hall towards the rusting double doors that led to the underground class-tombs. A tiny first-year pirate who ran with Harriet Hook's crew got lost in the shuffle, dropping his textbooks and blocking their path.

Mal came to a halt.

The boy slowly lifted his head, his eye patch trembling.

'S-s-so s-s-sorry, M-m-m-mal,' he said.

'M-M-M-MOVE IT,' Mal said, her voice high and mocking. She rolled her eyes and kicked the torn textbooks out of her way. The boy scampered towards the first open door he saw, dropping his fake hooked hand in his haste and sending it rolling away.

Jay kept his silence, knowing to tread lightly as he picked up the hook and stuffed it inside his jacket. But he couldn't help asking, 'Why not just throw a party of your own instead of sulking about it?'

'What are you talking about?' said Mal. 'As if I care.'

Jay didn't reply; he was too busy hugging himself tightly and wishing he'd thought to bring a warmer jacket instead of a waistcoat as the temperature dropped the usual 20 degrees as they ventured down the cold marble stairs to the damp basement gloom of campus.

Mal had gone silent for a moment and Jay assumed she was still brooding on what had happened 10 years ago, when she suddenly snapped her fingers and said, with a wicked gleam in her eyes, 'You're absolutely right, Jay. You're a genius!'

'I am? I mean, yes, I am,' replied Jay. 'Wait—what am I right about?'

'Having a party of my own. There's a lot to celebrate, after all. You just said there was a new princess in our midst. So I'm going to throw a party.'

Jay goggled at her. 'You are? I mean, I was just kidding. Everyone knows you hate . . .'

'Parties.' Mal nodded. 'But not this one. You'll see. It's going to be a real howler.' She grinned. 'Especially for the new kid.'

Jay smiled back weakly, wishing he had never mentioned it. When Mal got like this, it usually had terrible consequences. He shivered. There was a definite chill in the air—a new wild wind was blowing and he was smart enough to worry about where it would lead.

chapter 3

A Beautiful Princess . . .

In the Castle-Across-the-Way lived a mother-and-daughter duo very different from Maleficent and Mal. Unlike the shabby Victorian confines of the Bargain Castle, this one was full of soot and dust, with broken chandeliers and spiders' webs in the corners. It wasn't so much a castle as a cave—yet another prison within the prison of the island. And for 10 years, this mother and daughter had only had each other for company. Banishment to the far side of the island had made Evil Queen a little odd and Evie couldn't help but notice how her mother insisted on making declarations, just like some legendary 'Magic Mirror'.

'Magic Mirror in my hand, who is the fairest on this island?' Evil Queen asked as Evie was getting ready that morning.

'Mum, you're not holding *anything* in your hand. And anyway, is that really the *first* thing on your mind? Not breakfast?' asked Evie, who was starving. She perused the day's offerings—hard croissants and watery coffee from the basket the vultures left on their doorstep every day.

Your daughter has grace but should take better care of her face to be the fairest,' her mother declared in sombre tones that she called her 'Magic Mirror' voice.

Fairest, prettiest, most beautiful. The thickest hair, the fullest lips, the smallest nose. It was all her mother cared about. Evil Queen blamed all her troubles on not being more beautiful than Snow White, and it seemed no matter how well Evie did her hair or put on her make-up, she would never be beautiful enough for her mother. It made Evie sick to her beautiful stomach sometimes. Like mother, like daughter—or so she'd always been told. The poison apple never fell far from the tree.

And even if Evie suspected there *might* be more to life than being beautiful, that wasn't something she could ever say to her mother. The woman had a one-track mind.

'You didn't put on enough blusher. How will you ever win a handsome prince, looking like that?' her mother scolded, pinching her cheeks.

'If only there was one around here,' said Evie, who dutifully took out her compact and reapplied. There were no princes to be found on the island, as all the princes lived in Auradon now. That's where *all* the world's royalty lived—and that's where *she* should live, too. But it was not to be. Like her mother, she would be trapped on the Isle of the Lost forever.

Evie checked the hallway mirror one last time and adjusted her blue cape around her shoulders, the back of it embroidered with a crown in the middle. Her poison-heart necklace winked red in between the soft blue folds. Her raggedy black skirt with the splashes of red, white and blue paint went well with her forest-print-like, black-and-white leggings.

'Your hair!' Evil Queen said with despair, tucking a loose strand back into her daughter's neat V-plait, which swept her hair off her forehead. 'Okay, *now* you're ready.'

'Thanks, Mum,' said Evie, whose only goal was to survive the day. 'Are you sure it's safe to go to school?'

'No-one can keep a grudge for 10 years! Also, we're all out of wrinkle cream! Pick up some from the bazaar—I don't trust the vultures to send the right one.'

Evie nodded and hoped her mother was right.

But when she stepped out of their castle gates, she froze. Maleficent's curse echoed in her ears. But nothing happened and she kept going. Maybe, for once, the wicked old fairy had forgotten about it.

When Evie arrived at school that morning, everyone stared at her as she walked through the halls. She felt a bit self-conscious and wondered if she'd ever fit in. She was supposed to check in with Dr F, the headmaster, when she arrived. But where were the offices? Evie wondered, whirling round in a full circle.

'May I help you?' a handsome if somewhat hairy and very large boy asked when he saw her.

'Oh—I'm looking for the headmaster.'

'Follow me,' he said with a broad grin. 'Gaston, at your service . . . and this is my brother, Gaston.' He pointed to his identical twin, who gave her the same beaming, arrogant smile.

'Thank you, uh, Gastons,' Evie replied. The boys led her down the hall to the administrative-tombs.

'Dr F, you got a visitor,' Gaston said reaching for the door handle.

'I want to open it,' his brother said, elbowing him away. But the first Gaston punched him without even a backwards look. 'After you, princess,' he offered grandly, as his brother slithered to the floor, holding his jaw.

'Um, thanks, I think,' said Evie.

Dr Facilier looked up and gave the three students a huge smile. 'Yes? Oh, Evie, welcome to Dragon Hall. It's a delight to see you again, child. It's been too long. Ten years, is it? How is your lovely mother?'

'She's well, thanks.' Evie nodded politely but hurried to

get to the point. 'Dr Facilier, I just wanted to see if I could swap my Wickedness class for Advanced Vanities that meets at the same time?' she asked.

The shadowy man frowned. Evie batted her eyelashes. 'It would mean so much to me. By the way—" She pointed to his bolo tie, with its unfortunate silver chain. 'That is so cool!' she said, thinking exactly the opposite.

'Oh, this? I picked it up in the Bayou d'Orleans right before I was brought here.' He sighed and his frown softened into a real smile. 'I suppose Vanities is a better fit for your overall schedule. Consider it done.'

'Good, I'm in that class,' the Gastons chorused. 'On Tuesdays, it's right after lunch.'

'Lunch!' Evie slapped her forehead.

'What's wrong?'

'I forgot to bring mine!' In all the excitement about finally leaving the castle, she'd left her basket at home.

'Don't worry,' the twins replied. 'You can share ours!' they added, holding up two huge baskets of food. A giant block of some particularly smelly cheese poked out, along with two loaves of brown bread speckled with mould and several thick slices of liverwurst.

Evie was touched they had offered to share, even though they looked like they could eat a horse-and-a-half between them, with or without the mould.

They led her down the winding hallway. The stone walls were covered in the same pea-green moss as outside, and seemed to be leaking some sort of brown liquid all over the dusty concrete floor. Evie felt something furry circling her ankles and found a fat black cat with a smug grin looking up at her.

'Hi, kitty,' she cooed, leaning down to pet it.

'That's Lucifer,' said one of the Gastons. 'Our mascot.'

Several yelps from first-year students could be heard from inside the rusty lockers that haphazardly lined the corridor. With only a few lightbulbs flickering overhead, Evie nearly walked into a giant cobweb woven over a heavy steel door. A spider the size of a witch's cauldron sat in its centre. *Cool.*

'Where does that lead to?' she asked.

'Oh that? That's the door to the Athenaeum of Evil,' the other Gaston said.

'Come again?'

'The Library of Forbidden Secrets,' he explained. 'Nobody is allowed down there, and only Dr F has the key.'

'What kind of secrets?' asked Evie, intrigued.

'Forbidden ones, I guess?' Gaston shrugged. 'Who cares? It's a library. Sounds pretty boring to me.'

Finally, they arrived at the classroom's arched wooden door. Evie stepped inside and made her way to the nearest empty desk, smiling at those who came to gather curiously around her. Everyone was looking at her with such awe and admiration, she seemed to be making waves.

The desk she'd chosen had a remarkably large cauldron and a great view of the professor's lectern. She took a seat and there was a gasp in the crowd. Wow, these kids sure were easy to please.

Evie was feeling pretty good about her first day until she heard the sound of a throat clearing.

When she looked up, there was a pretty, purple-haired girl standing in front of her cauldron, staring at her with unmistakable venom. Her mother's "mirror" would have had a few choice words about this one, that's for sure. Evie felt a cold dread as the memory of a certain infamous party came flooding back. Maybe if she played dumb and flattered her, the girl wouldn't remember what had happened 10 years ago. It was worth a shot.

'I'm Evie. What's your name?' Evie asked innocently, although she knew exactly who was standing in front of her. 'And by the way, that jacket is amazing. It looks great on you—I love all the patchwork leathers on it.'

'Girl, that's her cauldron. You should bounce,' a student Evie would find out later was named Yzla whispered loudly.

'Oh, this is yours . . .?' Evie asked the purple-haired girl.

The purple-haired girl nodded.

'I had no idea this was your desk, I'm so sorry! But it has such a great view of the lectern,' Evie said with her trademark bright smile, so blinding it should have come with sunglasses. Evie finally realised why the students had been staring at her. They had been watching a disaster about to happen.

'Yes, it does,' the purple-haired girl replied, her voice soft and menacing. 'And if you don't move your blue-haired caboose out of it, you'll get some kind of view, all right.' She snarled, brusquely brushing past Evie and noisily plonking her rucksack down into the middle of the cauldron.

Evie got the message, grabbed her things and found an empty cauldron at the back of the classroom, behind a column where she couldn't see the blackboard.

'Is that who I think it is?' she asked the small boy seated next to her, whose hair was black at the roots but white at the tips. Actually, everything he wore was black and white with a splash of red: a fur-collared jacket with one black and one white side and red leather sleeves, a black button-down shirt with streaks of white, and long shorts with one white and one black-and-white leg. It was a pretty cool look. For a skunk.

'If you mean Mal, you're right, and I would stay out of her way if I were you,' he said.

'Mal . . .' Evie breathed, her voice trembling nervously.

'Yeah. Her mum's the Big Bad around here. You know—' He made horn signs with his hands on either side of his head. You didn't need to have lived on the Isle for long to know exactly who he was talking about. Nobody dared speak her name, not unless absolutely necessary.

Evie gulped. Her first day and she'd already made the worst enemy in school. It was Maleficent who had banished Evie and her mother 10 years ago and caused Evie to grow up alone in a faraway castle. Her own mother might be called Evil Queen, but everyone on the Isle of the Lost knew that Maleficent wore the crown in these parts. From the looks of it, her daughter did the same in the dungeons of Dragon Hall.

Magic Mirror on the wall, who's the stupidest of them all?

chapter 4

A Smart Little Boy...

Carlos De Vil looked up from the contraption he was assembling and shot the new girl a shy smile. 'It'll be okay. Mal just likes to be left alone,' he said. 'She's not as tough as she seems. She only talks a big game.'

'She does? What about you?' asked the blue-haired princess.

'I don't have a game. Unless you consider getting beat up and pushed around a game, which in a way I guess it is. But really it's not that entertaining, unless you happen to be the one doing the beating and the pushing.'

Carlos turned his attention back to the mess of wires in front of him. He was smaller and younger than the rest of the class, but smarter than most of them. He was an AP student: Advanced Penchant (for Evil). It was only right, since the infamous Cruella was his mother. His mother was so notorious, she had her own song. He hummed it under his breath sometimes. (What—it was catchy!) Sometimes he would do it just to send her into hysterics. Then again, that wasn't so difficult. Cruella's witch doctors believed she was sustained by pure metabolic fury. Privately, Carlos thought of it as her Rage Diet: no carbs, just barbs—no hunger, just anger—no ice cream, just high screams.

His thoughts were interrupted by his friendly new seatmate. 'I'm Evie. What's your name?' she asked.

'Hi, Evie, I'm Carlos De Vil,' he said. 'We met once before, at your birthday party.' He'd recognised her the minute she walked in. She looked exactly the same, just taller.

'Oh. Sorry. I don't remember much about the party. Except how it ended.'

Carlos nodded. 'Yeah. Anyway, I'm also your neighbour. I live just down the street in Hell Hall.'

'You do?' Evie's eyes went wide. 'But I thought no-one lived there but that crazy old lady and her—'

'Don't say it!' he blurted.

'Dog?' she said at the same time.

Carlos shuddered. 'We—we don't have dogs,' he said weakly, feeling his forehead begin to perspire at the very thought. His mother had told him dogs were vicious pack animals, the most dangerous and terrifying animals on Earth.

'But she's always calling someone her pet. I thought you were a d—'

'I told you, don't say it!' warned Carlos. 'That word is a trigger for me.'

Evie put up her hands. 'Okay, okay.' Then she winked. 'But how do you fit in the crate at night?'

Carlos only glared.

Their first class was Selfishness 101, or 'Selfies' for short, taught by Mother Gothel, who took way too many self-portraits with an old Polaroid camera.

The photos were littered around the classroom: Mother Gothel making a duck face, sleepy-eyed Mother Gothel in an "I woke up like this" pic, Mother Gothel in "cobra" pose. But Mother Gothel herself was nowhere to be found. She was always at least half an hour late, and when she finally arrived, she was irritated to find the students there before her. 'Have I taught you nothing about being fashionably, annoyingly late to every engagement?' she asked, letting out an exasperated sigh and collapsing dramatically into her chair, one hand fanned over her eyes.

For the next half hour or so they studied Portraits of Evil, comparing the likenesses of the most famous villains in history, many of whom lived on the island and some of whom were their parents. Today's class just happened to feature Cruella De Vil.

Of course.

Carlos knew the portrait by heart, whether or not he was looking at it.

His mother. There she was in all her finery, with her tall hair and her long red car, her eyes wild and her furs flying in the wind.

He shuddered again and went back to tinkering with his machine.

Class ended, and students began to file out of the classroom. Evie asked Carlos what his next subject was, and looked happy to discover they both had Lady Tremaine for Evil Schemes. 'That's another advanced class—you must have a really high EQ,' he told her. Only those who boasted off-the-charts evil quotients were allowed to take it. 'It's this way,' he said, motioning up the stairs.

But before they could get too far, a cold voice cut through the chatter. 'Why, if it isn't Carlos De Vil,' it said behind them.

Carlos would know that voice anywhere. It was the second-most terrifying on the island. When he turned, Mal was standing right behind him, next to Jay. Carlos automatically checked his pockets to make sure nothing had disappeared.

'Hey, Mal,' he said, trying to appear nonchalant. Mal never spoke to anyone except to scare them or to complain that they were in her way. 'What's up?'

'Your mum's away at the Spa this weekend, isn't she?' Mal asked, elbowing Jay, who snickered.

Carlos nodded. The Spa—really just a bit of warmish steam escaping from the crags of rock in the ruined basement of what had once been a proper building—was Cruella's one bit of comfort, her one reminder of her luxurious past.

How far the De Vil's had fallen, just like the rest of the Isle.

'Y-yes,' he said uncertainly, unsure if that was the correct answer, even though it was the truthful one.

'Right answer,' Mal said and patted him on the head. 'I can't exactly give a party at my place without my mother yelling at everyone, not to mention the whole flying crockery issue.'

Carlos sighed. Like the rest of the Isle, he knew parties brought out Maleficent's worst behaviour. There was nothing she hated more than people openly having fun.

'And we can't have it at Jay's because his dad will just try to hypnotise everyone into being his servants again,' Mal continued.

'Totally,' agreed Jay.

Carlos nodded again, although he wasn't sure where this was leading.

'Great. Perfect. Party at your house. Tonight.'

Party? At his house? Did he hear that right?

'Wait, what? Tonight?' He blanched. 'I can't have a

party! I mean, you should understand, my mum doesn't really like it when people come over—and, um, I've got a lot of work to do—I have to fluff her furs, iron her undergarments, I mean—' He gulped, embarrassed.

Mal ignored him. 'Spread the news. Hell Hall's having a hellraiser.' She seemed to warm to the thought. 'Get the word out. Activate the twilight bark, or whatever it is you puppies do.'

'Bow-wow,' barked Jay with a laugh.

Carlos glared at the two of them, in spite of himself.

'There's a party?' Evie asked shyly. Carlos had forgotten she was standing right next to him, and he jumped at the sound of her voice.

'Eavesdrop much?' Mal said, snarling at her, although it was obvious Evie couldn't help it, as she was standing right next to them.

Before Evie could protest, Mal sighed. 'Of course there is. The party of the year. A real rager, didn't you hear?' Mal looked her up and down and shook her head sadly. 'Oh, I guess you didn't hear.' She mock-winced, looking at Carlos conspiratorially. 'Everyone's going to be there.'

'They are?' Carlos looked confused. 'But you only just told me to have it—' He quickly got the message. 'Everyone,' he agreed.

Evie smiled. 'Sounds awesome. I haven't been to a party in a long, long time.'

Mal raised an eyebrow. 'Oh, I'm sorry. This is a very exclusive party, and I'm afraid you didn't get an invitation.'

With those parting words, Mal went ahead of them into the classroom—she was in their next class too, of course (her EQ was legendary)—and left them to each other.

'Sorry,' Carlos mumbled. 'I guess I was wrong, Mal doesn't just *talk* a big game.'

'Yeah, me too. The party sounds like fun,' Evie said.

'You want to see what I'm making?' he asked, trying to change the subject as they settled into their seats. He took a black box out of his bag, with wires and an antenna poking out from one side—the same contraption he'd been fiddling with earlier. 'I made it from some old magician's stuff.'

'Sure.' Evie smiled. 'Hey, is that a power core? It looks like you're making a battery, right?'

Carlos nodded, impressed. 'Yeah.'

'What does it do?'

'Can you keep a secret?' he asked, whispering.

Evie nodded. 'I keep them from my mum all the time.'

'I'm trying to poke a hole in the dome.'

'Really? Can you do that? I thought it was invincible.'

'Well, I thought I could maybe try to get a signal with this antenna here. It's actually an old wand, and I think if I hit the right frequency, we might be able to bring some of the outside world into the dome, and we can watch something other than that hairy old beast king telling us to be good, or that channel that only sells shackles.'

'I sort of like the Auradon channel,' Evie said dreamily. 'Especially when they feature the Prince of the Week. They're so dreamy.'

Carlos snorted.

She looked from the boy to the battery. 'Frequency? But how?'

'I'm not sure, but I think if I can break through the dome, we'd be able to pick up Auradon's radio waves—you know, internet and Wi-Fi signals. I'm not exactly sure what the frequency is, but I think that's how they get all those channels and stuff.'

Evie sighed again. 'What I'd give to go to Auradon. I've heard that everything is so beautiful there.'

'Um, I guess. If you're into that kind of thing,' Carlos said. He didn't care about princes or enchanted lakes or chirping animals or cheerful dwarfs. What he did care about was discovering more of the online world, a safe virtual refuge, where he'd heard you could even find people with whom you could play video games—that sounded like fun, as he never had anyone to play with.

There *had* to be something more to life than bowing down to the cool kids, organising his mother's fur coats and hiding from her tantrums.

There *had* to be. Although right now it wasn't just his mother he had to answer to. If Mal was serious, which it looked like she was, in the next few hours he somehow had to work out how to throw the party of the year.

chapter 5

And a Handsome Prince Who Lived Far, Far Away

Meanwhile, across the Sea of Serenity, which separated the Isle of the Lost from the rest of the world, lay the USA—the United States of Auradon, a land of peace and enchantment, prosperity and delight, which encompassed all the good kingdoms. To the east lay the colourful domes of the Sultan's seat, where Aladdin and Jasmine lived, not far from where Mulan and Li Shang guarded the imperial palace. To the north was Charming Castle, owned by Cinderella and her king, next door to 'Honeymoon Cottage', the 40-bedroom palace that Aurora and Phillip called home. And to the south, one could spy the lanterns of Rapunzel and Eugene Fitzherbert's divine domicile, near the spot on the coast where Ariel and Eric had made their under-and-over-the-sea royal residence at Seaside.

But right in the centre was the grandest castle in all of Auradon, with lavish turrets and balconies, its highest towers flying the proud blue-and-gold banner of the good old USA. Inside the magnificent building were many ballrooms, great rooms and state rooms, a formal dining room that could seat hundreds, where everyone was made to feel like a pampered guest, and a wondrous library that held all the books that were ever written.

This was all fitting, of course, because this was Castle Beast, home of King Beast and Queen Belle, the seat of Auradon. Twenty years ago, King Beast united all the fairy-tale lands into one under his crown, and for the past two decades he had ruled over its good citizens with strong and fair judgement, and only occasionally a tiny bit of his beastly temper.

Belle had a calming influence on the hot-headed Beast: she was not just the love of his life but the pacifier of his moods, the voice of reason in a gathering storm and the mother of his only child.

The jewel in the crown was their handsome son, 15-year-old Prince Ben. There had been no fairies at his christening to bestow gifts, perhaps because he did not need any. Ben was as handsome as his father, with his strong brow and chisel-cut cheekbones, but he had his mother's gentle eyes and keen intellect. He was a golden boy in every way, with a good heart and a winning spirit—captain of the tourney team, friend to all, destined to rule Auradon one day.

In short, he was the very sort of person that the people of the Isle of the Lost despised. And, as on the Isle of the Lost, magic was no longer a factor in daily life in Auradon, either. King Beast and Queen Belle valued scholarship above enchantment, exhorting the young people to work hard instead of relying on fairy spells or dragon friends for help. Because Beast was the most powerful figure in all the kingdoms, when he proposed the new work ethic, nobody argued against him. It was indeed a new (once upon a) time for the people of the fabled fairy-tale lands.

But even without magic, life in Auradon was close to perfect. The sun always shone, the birds always chirped, there was never more than a five-minute wait at the DFMV (Department of Formerly Magical Vehicles); and if everyone wasn't happy *all* the time (it's not as if this were *heaven*—get a grip, people), everyone was content.

Except, of course, when they weren't.

Isn't that always the way?

The kingdom's various short or fluffy or furry or miniscule—and sometimes animal—sidekicks were causing problems again. Sidekicks United, they called themselves, and they were far from happy. They were, in a word, disgruntled.

'Well, then, how can we help you today? Let's see . . .' Ben wasn't talking to anyone but a piece of paper—or a thousand pieces. He stared down at the documents in front of him, tapping them with his pen. His father had asked him to lead the Council meeting that morning, part of the training for becoming king in a few months.

As was tradition, the firstborn child of the royal household would take the throne of Auradon at 16 years of age. Beast and Belle were ready to retire. They were looking forward to long holiday cruises, early-bird dinners, and playing golf (Beast), bingo (Belle) and generally taking it easy. Besides, Belle had a stack of unread bedside reading so high it threatened to topple over on a huffy Mrs Potts when she came to take away the breakfast tray every morning.

The complaint wasn't the only thing on his mind. Ben had woken up that morning from a bit of a nightmare. Or it felt like a nightmare—and it certainly looked like one. In the dream, he was walking around a strange village full of shabbily dressed, miserable people who ate rotten fruit and drank black coffee. No cream. No sugar. No coffee cake to dip in it. The horror! And he had fallen into some kind of ditch, but someone had helped him out.

A beautiful, purple-haired girl who looked nothing like anyone in Auradon . . .

'Thank you,' he said gratefully. 'And who are you?'

But she'd disappeared before he could catch her name.

He went back to the papers in his hand and tried to forget about her.

Ben studied the Sidekicks United complaint—the first of its kind—and his heart beat a little faster at the thought of having to talk to all these people and convince them that there was no need for this level of discontent.

He sighed, until a familiar voice interrupted his reverie.

'Be careful about the sidekicks, son. Sooner or later they steal the spotlight.'

Ben looked up, surprised to see his father standing in the doorway. King Beast looked like he always did, as smiling and happy and fulfilled as on his posters. All over Auradon, they read *Good job being good! Keep it up! King Beast roars his approval!*

His father motioned to the stack of papers on Ben's desk. 'Looks like you're working hard.'

Ben rubbed his eyes. 'Yeah.'

King Beast clapped his paw of a hand on his son's shoulder. 'That's my boy. So what is it that they want, exactly?'

Ben scratched behind his ear with his pen. 'It seems they're a bit upset, as they do all the work around here and are hardly compensated for their efforts. If you think about it from their perspective, they have a point.'

'Mmm.' King Beast nodded. 'Everyone gets a voice in Auradon. Although you can't let too many voices drown out reason, of course. That's what it means to be kingly,' he said, perhaps a little more forcefully than was necessary.

'If you keep raising *your* voice, my darling, you're going to crack all the china, and Mrs Potts will never allow you either a cup of warm milk or a warm bath again.' Ben's mother, the goodly Queen Belle, arrived in the room and slipped her hand under her husband's muscled arm (yet another Beastly quality the king still seemed to possess— the strength of a wild creature in the form of a mere man). She was as beautiful as the day she had come upon Beast's castle, and resplendent in a pretty yellow dress. If there were laughter lines round her eyes now, no-one seemed to notice; and if anything, they only served to make her look more appealing.

The second he saw his mother, Ben found himself more at ease. He was shy and quiet, his mother gentle and understanding; Ben and Belle had always been like two peas in a castle-garden pod—always preferring to have their noses in books rather than affairs of the state.

'But half the castle staff has signed this petition—see, there's Lumiere's scrawl and Cogsworth's,' Ben said, his forehead wrinkling. Injustice of any kind was upsetting to think about, and it bothered him that the very people on whom his family depended to keep their lives in running order believed that they had cause for complaint.

'Lumiere and Cogsworth will sign anything anyone asks them to sign. Last week they signed a petition to declare every day a holiday,' his father said, amused.

Ben had to laugh. King Beast had a point. The fussy Frenchman and the jolly Brit would agree to anything so they could get back to their work. Chip Potts, who was known to make a little mischief around the castle, had probably put them up to it.

'That's the ticket. Listen to your people, but assert your right to rule. Lead with a gentle heart and a firm hand. That's the way to be a king!'

King Beast extended his own fist, and Ben just stared at it. He gazed down at his own hand, which looked like a small child's in comparison to his father's.

Beast pulled Ben up by the arm, closing his hand round his son's. 'There. Strong. Powerful. Kingly.'

King Beast's hand was so enormous Ben found he could no longer see his own.

'Strong. Powerful. Kingly,' Ben repeated.

Beast growled, then slapped his son on the back, almost sending him flying into the nearest decorative lamp. The floor shook as he strode out of the room, still chuckling.

Queen Belle looked relieved; Beast was not above making a joke at his own expense—though he was much less forgiving when anyone else attempted the same line of humour. She put her arms round her son, drawing him close.

'Ben. You don't have to be another King Beast. Just be yourself—it's more than enough.'

'That's not what Father says.'

Belle smiled. They both knew there was no use trying to explain away his father's logic and she didn't try. 'No matter what, your father and I believe in you. That's why we wanted you to start meeting with the Council. It's time for you to learn how to rule. You will make a wonderful king, all on your own. I promise.'

'I hope so,' Ben said, uncertainly.

'I know so,' Belle said, kissing his cheek.

As the feather-light steps of his mother faded away, Ben took up his pen and turned back to his pages. This time, though, all he could see was his fist, with the same golden beast-head ring that his father wore.

Strong. Powerful. Kingly.

He clenched his fingers harder.

Ben swore he would make his father proud.

chapter 6

Mean Girl

'Well, you look very pleased with yourself,' said Jay as Mal settled into her front-row seat and propped her feet up on the desk next to her.

'I am,' she said. 'I just taught that little blueberry what it means to feel left out.'

'Carlos looked like he was going to have a cow when you told him he was hosting your party.'

'You mean a dog?' Mal laughed, even though the joke was getting old.

Jay elbowed her with a wink before melting away to his desk at the back of the room.

Mal was in a good mood. This class was her favourite:

Advanced Evil Schemes and Nasty Tricks, taught by Lady Tremaine, otherwise known as the Wicked Stepmother. Mal was particularly fond of Mean-Spirited Pranks.

'Hello, you dreadful children,' Lady Tremaine said, entering the room with a swish of her petticoats and casting a bored look at the class in front of her. 'Today, we will embark on our annual class project: Crafting the Ultimate Evil Scheme.'

She turned towards the blackboard and wrote in ear-splitting cursive: *The Cinderella Story: Once Upon a Broken Glass Slipper.* 'As you well know,' she said, as she turned back to the students, 'my manipulation of Cinderella was my greatest evil deed. For years I kept her in the attic and treated her as a virtual servant. If not for some horrid meddling mice, one of my daughters would be the queen of Charming Castle right now, instead of that ungrateful girl. And so, the goal of every teacher at Dragon Hall is to train the new generation of villains not to make the same mistakes we did. You must learn to adapt, to be faster, more cunning, and wickeder than ever before. You will spend this year working on an evil scheme of your choosing. The student with the best nasty trick will win Dragon Hall's Evillest of the Year award.'

The class nodded their heads in unison, each filling with a variety of ideas for awful tricks. Mal scratched her nose with the end of her purple-plumed fountain pen, wondering what her year-long scheming project would be. She looked around the room at her fellow students scribbling away on notepads, brows furrowed, some cackling softly under their breaths. Her mind was racing with horrid ideas, each more horrid than the last. *Lock all the first-years in the dungeon?* Been there, done that. *Fill the hallways with cockroaches?* Child's play. *Let a stampede of goblins loose in the slop hall?* That would be just a regular Tuesday . . .

Across the room, Mal heard a soft giggle. She looked over her shoulder to find that annoying new girl Evie chatting cheerfully with Carlos De Vil as they played with some sort of black box on his desk. Ugh. That girl had nothing to be happy about. Why, hadn't she, Mal, just told her she couldn't come to the howler of the year? Mal was slightly disconcerted for a moment, until she realised: the evil scheme of the year was right in front of her.

A twisted smile formed on her lips, and she chewed her fountain pen for a moment before scribbling a page's worth of notes.

She would show that blue-haired princess a thing or two.

Of course, she'd already told Evie that she couldn't come to the party, but that wasn't *enough*. It was too simple, too blunt. Mal had to be sneaky, like Lady Tremaine had been, pretending to be working in Cinderella's best interests when she had been doing exactly the opposite.

Mal realised that she'd been waiting years for this chance, whether or not she'd consciously known it. The memory of the "lost" invitation—if indeed it had ever existed in the first place (it was still unclear what had truly happened)—grated on her feelings as sharply today as it had when she was six years old.

A day like that can only happen once in 16 years.

A day like that changes a person.

A day like that was never going to happen again.

Not if Mal could help it.

And to be honest, Mal wanted to do more than ruin Evie's day, she wanted to ruin her *year*. On second thoughts, maybe keeping Evie out of the party was the wrong move. If Evie wasn't there, then Mal wouldn't have the opportunity to torture her to her heart's delight.

Mal finished writing down her plans just as the bell rang and caught up with Jay, who was all cheer and charm—and by the time they reached the door, his pockets were full of much more than that.

'Hold up,' Mal said as she spotted Carlos and Evie coming towards them.

Evie looked genuinely fearful and Carlos wary as they approached Mal, who blocked the doorway.

'Hey, Evie, you know that party I'm having?' Mal asked.

Evie nodded. 'Um, yeah?'

'I was only kidding earlier,' Mal said with the sweetest smile she could manage. '*Of course* you're invited.'

'I am?' Evie squealed. 'Are you sure you want me there?'

'I don't want anything more in the world,' said Mal grandly, and truthfully. 'Don't miss it.'

'I won't,' promised Evie with a nervous smile.

Mal watched her and Carlos skitter away with satisfaction. Jay raised an eyebrow. 'What was that all about? I thought you didn't want her there,' he said, as he deftly stole a rotten banana from a first-year's lunch box.

'Plans change.'

'An evil scheme, huh?' Jay waggled *both* eyebrows.

'Maybe,' Mal said mysteriously, not wanting to give anything away. It wasn't like Jay could be trusted. "Thieves' honour" meant neither of them had any.

'Come on. It's me. The only one you can stand on this island.'

'Don't flatter yourself,' she said, only half smiling.

'Don't you hate parties? You didn't go to Anthony Tremaine's kickback the other week, and you missed my cousin Jade's "Scary 16th". They were off-the-hook, as the pirate posse would say.' He smirked.

'Those were different. Anyway, you need to hop to it. Carlos can't throw my party alone.' She grabbed his arm. 'We need jugs of spicy juice, bags of stale chips, sparkling slop, the works.'

Jay peeled the banana and took a bite. 'Done.'

'And make sure it's the good stuff from the wharf, from the first boats. I've got a reputation to uphold.'

He saluted and tossed the banana peel on the floor and they both watched gleefully as a fellow student slipped and fell. Things like that never got old.

Mal smiled, her green eyes glittering a little more like her mother's than usual. 'Let's go. I have a party to throw.' *And someone to throw it at.*

chapter 7

Hellraiser

Carlos never shied from a mission, and if Mal wanted a howler, there was no alternative but to provide one. There was nothing he could do about it, AP Evil Penchant or not. He knew his place on the totem pole.

First things first: a party couldn't be a party without guests. Which meant people. Lots of people. Bodies. Dancing. Talking. Drinking. Eating. Playing games. He had to get the word out.

Thankfully it didn't take too long for everyone he crossed paths with at school, and the minions of everyone *they* crossed paths with, to spread the word. Because Carlos didn't so much issue an invitation as deliver a threat.

Literally.

He didn't mince words, and the threats only grew more exaggerated as the school day wore on. The rumours spread like the gusty, salty wind that blew up from the alligator-infested waters surrounding the island.

'Be there, or Mal will find you,' he said to his squat little lab partner, Le Fou Deux, as they both dissected a frog that would never turn into a prince in Unnatural Biology class.

'Be there, or Mal will find you and ban you from the city streets,' he whispered to the Gastons as they took turns stuffing each other in doomball nets in PE.

'Be there, or Mal will find you and ban you and make everyone forget you, and from this day onwards you will be known only by the name of Slop!' he said almost hysterically to a group of frightened first-years gathered for a meeting of the Anti-Social Club, which was planning the school's annual Foul Ball. They turned pale at his words and desperately promised their attendance, even as they trembled at the thought.

By the end of the day, Carlos had secured dozens of RSVPs. Now, *that* wasn't too hard, he thought, putting away his books in his locker and releasing the first-year who'd been trapped inside.

'Hey, man.' Carlos nodded.

'Thanks, I really have to pee,' squeaked the unfortunate student, running towards the toilets.

'Sure,' Carlos said, scrunching his nose. 'Oh, and there's a party. My house. Midnight.'

'I heard, I'll be there! Wouldn't miss it!' the first-year said, raising his fist to the air in excitement.

Carlos nodded, feeling mollified and more than a little impressed that even someone who'd been trapped inside a locker all day had heard the news about the party. He was a natural! Maybe party planning was in his blood. His mother certainly knew how to enjoy herself, didn't she? Cruella was always telling him how boring he was because all he liked to do was fiddle with electronics all day. His mother declared he was wasting his time, that he was useless at everything except chores, and so maybe if he threw a good party, he could prove her wrong. Not that she would be around to witness it, though. She'd probably be enraged to discover her Hell Hall crawling with teenagers. Still, he wished that one day Cruella could see him as more than just a live-in servant who happened to be related to her.

He made his way home, his mind awhirl. With the guests secured, all he had to do was get the house ready for the blessed event—and that couldn't be too hard, could it?

A few hours later, Carlos took it all back. 'Why did I ever agree to have this party?' he agonised aloud. 'I never wanted to have a party.' He raked his fingers through his curly, speckled hair, which made it stick up in a frazzle, a lot like Cruella's own do.

'You mean tonight?' A voice echoed from the other end of the crumbling ballroom, from behind the giant, tarnished statue of a great knight.

'I mean *ever*,' sighed Carlos. It was true. He was a man of science, not society. Not even *evil* society.

But here he was, decorating Hell Hall, which had seen better days long before he'd been born. Still, the decrepit Victorian mansion was one of the grandest on the island, covered in vines more twisted than Cruella's own mind, and gated with iron more wrought than Cruella's own daily hysterias.

The main ballroom was now draped in the sagging black-and-white crepe paper and partly deflated black-and-white balloons that Carlos had pilfered from a sad stack of dusty boxes stashed in his building's basement. Those few boxes, stamped *De Vil Industries*, were all that remained of the former De Vil fashion empire—the merest scraps of a better life that had long since faded away.

His mother, of course, would be furious when she saw that Carlos had got into her boxes again—'*My stolen treasures*,' she'd scream, '*my lost babies!*'—but Carlos was a pragmatist, and a scavenger.

Why his mother had ever been obsessed with black-and-white Dalmatian puppies, he had no idea. He was terrified of those things, but she had been prepared to own 101 of them, so there was a lot of stuff to scavenge.

Over the years, he'd repurposed more than a few empty crates—*scientists requiring bookshelves as they did*—abandoned leashes—*nylon withstanding the elements as it did*—and unsqueaked squeaky toys—*rubber repelling electricity as it did*—that had fallen by the wayside when his mother's plans were foiled.

An AP Evil scientist and inventor like Carlos couldn't afford to be choosy. He needed materials for his research.

'Why did you agree to this party? Easy. Because Mal asked you to,' Carlos' second-best friend Harry said, shaking his head as he wiggled his fingers, tape dangling from each one. 'Maybe you should try, for your next invention, to build something that would free us all from her mind control.'

His third-best friend, Jace, tried to take a piece of tape but only succeeded in taping himself to Harry. 'Yeah, right. No-one can stand up to Mal,' said Jace. 'As if.'

Harry (Harold) and Jace (Jason) were the sons of Horace and Jasper, Cruella's loyal minions, the two blundering thieves who had attempted to kidnap the 101 Dalmatian puppies for her and failed miserably. Just like their fathers, Harry and Jace tried to look like they were more capable and less nervous than they actually were.

But Carlos knew otherwise.

Harry, as short and fat as his father, could barely reach to fasten his side of the ebony streamer. Jace, taller even than his own tall, scrawny father, didn't have that same problem but, as previously mentioned, couldn't manage to figure out the tape dispenser. Between them, they didn't exactly constitute a brain trust. More like a brain *mis*-trust.

Carlos wouldn't have chosen them as his friends—his mother chose them for him, just like she did everything else.

'They're all we've got,' Cruella would say. 'Even when we have nothing else, we'll always have . . .'

'Friends?' Carlos had guessed.

'Friends?!' Cruella had laughed. 'Who needs friends when you have minions to do your bidding!'

Cruella certainly ruled Jasper and Horace with an iron lead, but one could hardly say that Harry and Jace did Carlos' bidding. They only seemed to hang around because their fathers made them, and only because they were all scared of Carlos' mother.

Which was why he considered them only his *second-* and *third*-best friends. He didn't have a *first* best friend, but he knew enough about the concept of friendship, even without having any proper ones of his own, to know that an actual best friend would have to be able to do something more than follow him around, tripping over his feet and repeating his not-worth-saying-the-first-time jokes.

All the same, it was good to have some help for the party, and it was Harry who nodded sadly at him now. 'If Mal doesn't like this party, we're doomed.'

'Doomed,' echoed Jace.

Carlos surveyed the rest of the room. Every piece of broken-down old furniture was covered in a dusty white linen cloth. Every few metres of plaster wall was punctured by a crumbling hole that revealed the plywood and plaster underneath.

The overachiever in him bristled. He could do better than this! He had to. He rushed upstairs and dug out his mother's antique brass candelabras and rigged them up around the room. With the lights off, the candles glimmered and flickered as if they were floating in mid-air.

Next, was the chandelier swing—a staple at any Isle party, or so he'd heard. He had Jace climb up a makeshift ladder and tie a rope swing to the light fixture. Harry jumped off from one of the sheet-covered sofas to test it out, which caused a cloud of dust to settle over the whole room.

Carlos approved—it kind of looked like a fresh snowfall had been sprinkled over the hall.

He picked up the rotary phone and called his cousin Diego De Vil, who was the lead singer in a local band called the Bad Apples.

'You guys want a gig tonight?'

'Do we ever! Heard Mal's having a full-moon howler!'

The band arrived not too long after, setting up the drum-set by the window and practising their songs. Their music was loud and fast, and Diego, a tall, skinny guy who sported a black-and-white Mohawk, sang out of tune. It was marvellous. The perfect soundtrack for the evening.

Next up, Carlos dug out an old-fashioned instant camera he'd found in the attic. He fashioned a private booth by removing the sheet from a sofa and rigging it on a rod in a secluded corner. 'Photo booth! You take their photo,' he said to Jace. 'And you hand it to them,' he told Harry.

Carlos admired his handiwork. 'Not too shabby,' he said. 'Now we're talking.'

'And it's about to get a whole lot better,' said an unfamiliar voice.

Carlos turned to see Jay entering the room holding four huge shopping bags filled with all manner of party snacks: stinky cheese and withered grapes, devilled eggs (so appropriate) and wings (sinfully spicy), and more. Jay pulled a bottle of the island's best spicy juice out of his jacket and dumped it into the cracked punch bowl on the coffee table.

'Wait! Stop! I don't want things to get out of hand,' Carlos said, trying to grab the bottle and cap it. 'How did you get your hands on all of that sugar!'

'Oh, but that's where you're wrong,' Jay said, grinning. 'Better your party gets out of hand than Mal gets out of sorts.'

Jay sank to the sofa, putting his combat boots up by the punch bowl. The minions shrugged, and Carlos sighed.

The guy had a point.

As the clock struck midnight, Mal's guests began to arrive in force. There were no gourd-like carriages or rodent-like servants to be seen, not anywhere. Nothing had been transformed into anything, especially not what anyone would consider a cool ride.

There were only feet, in varying degrees of shoddy footwear. Perhaps because their feet were the largest, the Gastons arrived first, as usual. They never risked a late entrance, so as not to miss a buffet table full of food they might swallow whole before anyone else got a taste.

During the awkward silence that followed the Gastons head-butting their hellos and slamming pitchers of smuggled root beer, a whole ship's worth of Harriet Hook's pirate crew came marauding through the door.

As Carlos leaned against the faded wallpaper nursing his spicy punch, the Gastons and the pirate posse busied themselves with chasing the next group of guests through the house. This happened to be an entire cackling slew of evil step-granddaughters, festooned with raggedy ribbons and droopy curls, elbowing their way round the corners at top speed. 'Don't chase us!' they begged, just waiting to be chased. 'You're horrible!' they screamed, horribly. 'Sto-o-o-o-o-o-p,' they said, refusing to stop.

Their cousin, Anthony Tremaine, followed them into the room, rolling his eyes.

The band struck up a rollicking tune. Dark-haired Ginny Gothel arrived with a bushel of wormy apples, and a game of bob-for-the-wormiest-apple broke out in the tub.

Everybody wanted a turn on the chandelier swing,

and the rest of the guests were engaged in a serious dance-off over by the band. All in all, it was shaping up to be a wicked good time.

More than an hour after the party had officially started, there was a sharp knock on the door. It wasn't clear what made this knock different from all the others, but different it was. Carlos leaped to his feet like a soldier suddenly called to attention. Jay stopped dancing with a posse of evil step-granddaughters. The Gastons looked up from the buffet table. Little Sammy Smee held an apple between his teeth questioningly.

Carlos steadied his nerves and opened the door. 'Go away!' he yelled, using the island's traditional greeting.

Mal stood in the doorway. Backlit by the dim hall light, in shiny purple leather from head to toe, she appeared to have not so much a halo as a shimmer, like the lead vocalist of a band during a particularly well-lit rock concert—the kind with smoke and neon and bits of sparkly nonsense in the air.

Carlos half-expected her to start belting a tune with the band. Perhaps he should have felt excited that such an infamous personality had decided to come to his party.

Er, *her* party.

There would be no unplugging this party like one of his rebuilt stereos, not once it had begun, especially not the sort of party Mal seemed to have in mind.

'Hey, Carlos,' she drawled. 'Am I late?'

'Not at all,' said Carlos. 'Come in.'

'Excited to see me?' Mal asked with a smile.

He nodded yes. Except that Carlos wasn't excited.

He was *terrified*.

Somewhere, deep down, he even wanted his mummy.

chapter 8

Only Human

'Toad's-blood shots!' declared Mal, leaping into the room as if she were just another guest. 'For everyone!'

And just like that, the party began again, as quickly as it had stopped. It was like the entire room exhaled in one relieved breath. *Mal isn't mad. Mal isn't banning us from the streets. Mal isn't renaming us Slop. Not yet.*

Mal could see the relief on their faces and she didn't blame them. They were right. The way she'd been feeling lately, it was certainly something to celebrate.

So the crowd cheered, and toad's-blood shots splashed across the room by the cupful, and Mal, in a show of generous sportsmanship, chugged a slimy cup right along with the rest.

She circled the party, pilfering a wallet from one of the Gastons, stopping to share a mean giggle with Ginny Gothel about the dress Harriet Hook was wearing, ducking under an overenthusiastic pirate swinging from the chandelier, taking a bite out of someone else's devil dog and grabbing a mouthful of dry popcorn. She walked into the hallway and bumped into Jay, who was out of breath after winning the latest dance-off.

'Having fun?' he asked.

She shrugged. 'Where'd Carlos go?'

Jay laughed and pointed towards a pair of black shoes poking out from behind a sheet covering the biggest of the bookcases. 'Hiding from his own party. Typical.'

Mal knew how Carlos felt, though she'd never admit it. Truly, she'd rather be almost anywhere on the whole Isle than at this party. Like her mother, she hated the sights and sounds of revelry. Fun made her uncomfortable. Laughter? Gave her hives.

But a vendetta was a vendetta, and she had more planned for this evening than just Deep, Dark, Secret or Death-Defying Dare.

'Come on,' said Jay. 'They're playing pin the tail on the minion over there, and Jace has, like, 10 tails. Let's see if we can make it a dozen.'

'Maybe in a minute. Where's Princess Blueberry?'

Mal asked. 'I did a whole loop of this party, and I didn't see her anywhere.'

'You mean Evie? She's not here yet. Nobody seems to know if she's coming or not.' Jay shrugged. 'Castle kids.'

'She has to come. She's the whole point. She's the only reason I'm even having this stupid party.' Mal hated when her evil schemes didn't go exactly as planned. This was the first step in *Operation Take Down Evie, Or Else*, and it *had* to work. She sighed, staring at the door. Pretending to be having fun at a party when you hated parties was the most tiresome thing in the world.

Mal had to agree with her mother on that one.

'What are you two doing?' asked Anthony Tremaine, Lady Tremaine's 16-year-old grandson, a tall, elegant boy with dark hair swept off a haughty forehead. His clothes were as worn and ragged as everyone else's on the Isle, but somehow he always looked as if he was wearing custom tailoring. His dark leather coat was cut perfectly, his jeans the right dark wash. Maybe it was because Anthony had noble blood, and would probably have lived in Auradon except for his grandmother's being, you know, evil and banished. At one point he'd tried to get everyone on the Isle to call him Lord Tremaine, but the villain kids had all just laughed in his face.

'Just talking,' said Mal.

'Evil plotting,' said Jay.

They looked at each other.

Something about Anthony's handsome face brought to Mal's mind another handsome boy—the prince from her dream. He'd said he was her friend. His smile was kind and his voice gentle. Mal shuddered.

'Do you want something?' Mal asked Anthony coolly.

'Yes. To dance.' Anthony looked at her expectantly.

She looked at him, confused. 'Wait—with *me*?' Nobody had ever asked her before. But she'd never really been to a party before, either.

'Well, I didn't mean *him*,' Anthony said, looking awkwardly at Jay. 'No offence, man.'

'None taken.' Jay grinned broadly, knowing how uncomfortable this made Mal. He found it hilarious. 'You two kids go have fun out there. Anthony, make sure you pick a slow song,' he said, as he slid away. 'I have a step-granddaughter waiting for me.'

Mal could feel her cheeks turning pink, which was embarrassing, because she wasn't afraid of anything, least of all dancing with snotty Anthony Tremaine.

So why are you blushing? she thought.

'I'm not really a dancer,' she said lamely.

'I can show you,' he said with a smooth smile.

Mal bristled. 'I mean, I don't dance with anyone. Ever.'

'Why not?'

Why not, indeed?

Mal thought about it. Her mind flashed back to earlier that evening. She'd been getting ready for the party, trying to choose between violet-hued holey or mauve patchwork jeans, when her mother had made a rare appearance at her door.

'Where on this dreadful island could you possibly be going?' Maleficent asked.

'To a party,' Mal said.

Maleficent let out an exasperated sigh. 'Mal, what have I told you about parties?'

'I'm not going to have *fun*, Mother. I'm going so I can make someone *miserable*.' She wanted to share *Operation Take Down Evie* right then, but thought better of it. She would tell her mother once she had completed it successfully, lest she disappoint her once more. Maleficent never failed to remind Mal that sometimes it just didn't seem like Mal was evil enough to be her daughter. *At your age I was cursing entire kingdoms* was a phrase Mal had grown up hearing.

'So you're off to make someone miserable?' her mother cooed.

'Wretched, really!' enthused Mal.

A slow smile formed on Maleficent's thin red lips. She crossed the room and stood in front of Mal, reaching out to trace a long nail along Mal's cheek. 'That's a nasty little girl,' she said. Mal swore she saw a glimmer of pride flicker in her mother's cold, emerald-green eyes.

Mal snapped back to reality as the band finished a punk rock number with clashing cymbals and a drum roll. Anthony Tremaine was still staring at her.

'So why don't you dance, again?'

Because I don't have time to dance when I have evil schemes to hatch, Mal wanted to say. *One that will make my mother proud of me, finally.*

She turned up her nose. 'I don't have to have a reason.'

'You don't. But that doesn't mean you don't have one.'

He caught her by surprise, because he was right.

Because she did have a reason, a very good reason to stay clear of any kind of activity that might hint at or lead to romance. Her missing father. Otherwise known as He-Who-Must-Not-Be-Named-in-Maleficent's-Presence.

So Anthony had her there. Mal had to give him that. But instead, she glared at him. Then she glared at him again, for good measure. 'Maybe I just like to be alone.'

Because maybe I'm so tired of my mother looking at me like I'm weak, just because I came from her own moment of weakness.

Because maybe I need to show her that I'm strong enough and evil enough to prove to her that I'm not like my weak, human father.

That I can be just like her.

Maybe I don't want to dance because I don't want to have anything human about me.

'That can't be it,' Anthony said, picking lint off his jacket. His voice was uncommonly low and pleasant, which once again brought back to Mal's mind the handsome prince by the enchanted lake. Except that Anthony wasn't quite as handsome as the boy in her dream had been, not that she thought that boy handsome, *mind you*. Not that she thought about him *at all*. 'Nobody likes to be alone.'

'Well, I do,' she insisted. It was true.

'And besides, everybody wants to dance with a lord,' he said smugly.

'Nope, not me!'

'Fine, have it your way,' Anthony said, finally backing away, his head held high. In a matter of seconds, he had already asked Harriet Hook to dance, and she'd accepted with a delighted shriek.

Mal exhaled. *Phew.* Boys. Dreams. Princes. It was all too much for one day.

'Mal. Mal. Earth to Mal?' Jay waved a hand in front of her face. 'You okay?'

Mal nodded but didn't answer. For a moment she had been lost in the memory of that awful dream again. Except that this time it didn't seem so much a dream as a premonition. That one day she might just find herself in Auradon. But how could that be?

Jay frowned, holding out a cup of juice. 'Here. It's like you've powered down, or something.'

Mal realised that she hadn't moved from the front hall. She'd been standing there, stupidly frozen, ever since Anthony had left her side. That was three songs ago, and the Bad Apples were playing their current hit, 'Call Me Never'.

She perked up, not because of the juice or the catchy song but because, out of the corner of her eye, she spotted Evie through the floor-to-ceiling window in the foyer. She was coming down the road in a brand-new rickshaw, her pretty V-plait gleaming in the moonlight. *She thinks she is so special. Well, I'll show her,* Mal thought. Her eyes wandered over the room and rested upon a familiar-looking door.

It was the door that led to Cruella De Vil's storage wardrobe. Mal only knew it was there because she and Carlos had once accidentally come across it when they were working on a skit about evil family trees in sixth grade, and Mal had been bored and had decided to go poking around Hell Hall. Cruella's wardrobe was not for the faint of heart.

Mal would never forget that day. It was the kind of wardrobe that would get the better of anyone. Especially a princess who was making her way up the steps to the front door and would appear at any moment now.

'Jay,' she said, motioning to the front door. 'Let me know when Evie arrives.'

'Huh? What? Why?'

'You'll see,' she told him.

'All part of the evil scheme, huh?' he said, happy to do her bidding. Jay was always up for a good prank.

But Carlos went white-faced when he saw where Mal was heading. 'Don't—' he shouted. He shook off his sheet, almost tripping over the fabric in an attempt to get to the door before Mal could open it all the way.

It slammed shut. Just in time.

But Mal crossed her arms. She wasn't backing down from this one. It was just too perfect. She glanced out of the window again. Princess-Oh-So-Fashionably-Late was at the front door now.

Mal raised her voice. 'New game! Seven Minutes in Heaven! And you've never played Seven Minutes if you haven't played it in a De Vil wardrobe.'

The words were barely out of Mal's mouth before most of the evil step-granddaughters practically trampled her to get to the door. They loved playing Seven Minutes and were enthusiastically wondering with whom they would end up inside. A few of them puckered their lips and powdered their noses while fluttering their eyelashes at Jay, who was stationed by the front door like a sentry.

'Who wants to go first?' Mal asked.

'Me! Me! Me!' yelped the step-granddaughters.

'She does,' Jay called, holding a very recognisable blue cape.

'I do? What do I want to do?' asked the cape's owner.

Mal smiled.

Evie had arrived.

'Evie, sweetie! So glad you could make it!' Mal said, throwing her arms theatrically round the girl and giving her a giant and fake embrace. 'We're playing Seven Minutes in Heaven! Want to play?'

'Uh, I don't know,' said Evie, looking around the party nervously.

'It'll be a scream,' said Mal. 'Come on, you want to be my friend, don't you?'

Evie stared at Mal. 'You want *me* to be your friend?'

'Sure—why not?' Mal led her to the wardrobe door and opened it.

'But doesn't a boy go in here with me?' Evie asked as Mal shoved her inside. For someone castle-schooled, Evie sure knew her kissing games.

'Did I say Seven Minutes in Heaven? No, you're playing *Seven Minutes in Hell*!' Mal cackled as she slammed the door closed. She couldn't help it. This was going to be so much fun.

The crowd around the hallway had scattered in fear after it was clear Mal had no interest in having other people join the game—or Evie—inside the locked room.

But Carlos remained standing, his face as white as the tips of his hair. 'Mal, what are you doing?'

'Playing a dirty trick—what does it *look* like I'm doing?'

'You can't leave her in there! Remember what happened to us?' he asked, motioning angrily to his leg, which had two distinct white scars on the calf.

'I do!' Mal said gleefully. She wondered why Carlos was so concerned about Evie. It wasn't as if they'd been taught to care about other people.

But Carlos soon made clear that he wasn't being altruistic. 'If she's not able to get out on her own, I'm going to have to clean up the mess! And my mother will freak out! You can't leave her in there!' he whispered fiercely, anxiety about Cruella's punishment written all over his face.

'Fine, go get her,' said Mal with a sly smile on *her* face, knowing full well that he wouldn't.

Carlos quaked in his scuffed loafers. Mal knew there was nothing he wanted to do less than go back in there again. He remembered all too well what had happened to him and Mal in sixth grade.

There was a scream from behind the door.

Mal wiped her hands. 'You want her out? You get her out.' Her job was done.

Her evil scheme had worked. This was going to be a real howler.

# Chapter 9

Let the Fur Fly

The first thing Evie thought when the door unceremoniously closed with a bang behind her was that she had worn her prettiest dress for nothing. She had been looking forward to the party all day, had run home to go through every outfit in her wardrobe, holding up dress after dress to see which shade of blue looked best. Azure? Periwinkle? Turquoise? She had settled on a dark midnight-blue lace mini-dress and matching high-heeled boots. She'd been extremely late to the party, as her mother had insisted on giving her a three-hour makeover.

Not that it mattered, because she was now locked in a wardrobe alone. She wasn't just imagining it—Mal really *was* out to get her, most likely for not having been invited to Evie's birthday party when they were six years old. But it wasn't as if it was her fault! Evie'd been just a kid. It had been her mother who hadn't wanted Mal at the party for some reason. Mal couldn't hold it against *her*, could she? Evie sighed. Of course she could. Evie still remembered the hurt and anger on six-year-old Mal's face, looking down from the balcony. Evie supposed that she'd probably feel the same way—not that she could see it from Mal's point of view, or anything. *There's no* me *in empathy,* as Mother Gothel liked to say.

In the end, Evil Queen probably should have dropped her grudge against Maleficent and invited her daughter to the celebration. It certainly hadn't been fun being cooped up in their castle for 10 years. Evie wasn't even sure why her mother had decided that now was a safe time to leave, but so far, other than Evie being locked in this wardrobe at the moment, nothing too bad had happened. Yet.

Besides, the darkness of the wardrobe didn't bother her. Evie was her mother's daughter, after all, and used to the horrors of the night—from dark, hidden things with yellow eyes glittering in the shadows, to candles dripping over skull candleholders, to the flash of lightning and the fury of thunder as they rolled across the sky.

She wasn't scared. She wasn't scared in the least bit.

Except . . .

Except... her foot just struck something hard and cold... and the quiet of the wardrobe was broken by the loud, echoing snap of steel meeting steel.

She screamed. *What was that?!* When her eyes adjusted to the dim light, she saw fur traps littered all over the floor, lying in wait for the next animal to wander through. There were so many of them that one wrong step would mean a trap would snap her leg in two. She turned back to the door and tried to open it, but it was no use. She was locked in there.

'Help! Help! Let me out!' she yelled.

But there was no answer, and the band was playing so loudly, Evie knew no-one would hear her, nor care.

It was hard to see, so Evie felt her way tentatively in the darkness, sliding her left foot on the floor first. How many were there? Ten? Twenty? A hundred? And how big was this room, anyway?

Her foot came in contact with something cold and heavy, so she retreated. How was she going to get out of this place without losing a limb? Was there another door on the other side, maybe? She squinted. Yes, that was another door. There was a way out.

She headed slowly to the far end, the floorboards creaking ominously under her feet.

Evie shifted to her right, hoping to avoid the trap, to move around it, but her foot struck another, and she jumped back as it too snapped shut with a bang, springing into the air and barely grazing her knee. Her heart thundered in her chest as she slid around the next trap, careful not to strike the metal for fear that it might close round her ankle. As long as she missed the trap's centre, she would be fine.

She could do this. All she had to do was move slowly, carefully. She edged around another one. She was getting better at this; she could find her way to the back of the room and possibly another door. She cleared one and then another, moving more quickly, sliding one foot in front of the other, searching for and avoiding the traps. Faster. A little faster. The door must be close, then—

She struck a trap and it suddenly popped up with a snap. She jumped away, and as the trap fell on the floor, it hit another trap, which sprang up and hit the one next to it, all in succession—and this time, Evie saw that she couldn't move slowly but that she had to *run*.

The chorus of snapping metal jaws rang through the darkness, steel blades against steel blades, as she ran screaming towards the back door. The traps slammed shut, *BAM BAM BAM*, one after another, one a hairbreadth away from her tights while another almost caught her heel as she turned the door handle, left the room, and shut the door behind her.

But just as she thought she was safe, she realised she had plunged right into a dark, furry presence.

Was it a bear? A horrible shaggy monster? Had she got out of the frying pan only to fall into the fire? Evie twisted and turned, but only succeeded in wrapping herself deeper in fur—dense, thick, woolly fur—*with two armholes?*

This was no bear . . . no monster. She was trapped in a fur coat! Evie tried to shake it off, tried to shrug it off her shoulders, but she was bang in the middle of dozens of coats, all of them black or white or black *and* white, made of the thickest, lushest hides—there was spotted ocelot and dip-dyed mink, silky sable and shiny skunk, all of them packed in like sardines, so full, so fluffy, so thick. This was Cruella De Vil's fur wardrobe, her wondrous collection, her obsession, her greatest weakness.

And those fur traps back there were her security system, just in case anyone got too close to the stuff.

Evie finally managed to untangle herself and push aside the wall of fur, just as a hand grasped her wrist and pulled her through to the other side.

'You okay?' It was Carlos.

Evie took a deep breath. 'Yes. I think so. Do I win the game?' she asked dryly.

Carlos laughed. 'Mal's going to be annoyed you survived.'

'Where are we?' Evie looked around. There was a lumpy mattress on the floor next to an ironing board and a washbasin, along with a dressing table that held dozens of white-and-black wigs.

When Carlos looked embarrassed, she realised it was his bedroom. Cruella's fur wardrobe opened on to a dressing room, where her son slept.

'Oh.'

Carlos shrugged. 'It's home.'

Even if her mother annoyed her sometimes, at least Evil Queen was obsessed with Evie's good looks; and when she wasn't worried that perhaps Evie might not be the fairest of them all, she treated her daughter like the princess she was. Evie's room might be dark and musty, but she had a real bed, not a makeshift one, with a thick blanket and relatively soft pillows.

'It's not so bad in here, really!' Evie said. 'I'm sure it's cosy and, hey . . . you'll never catch a cold. You can just use one of her fur coats for a blanket, right?' It was awfully draughty in the room; like her own home, Hell Hall wasn't insulated for winter.

Carlos shook his head. 'I'm not allowed to touch them,' he said, trying to put the furs back in order. They were so heavy, and there were so many of them. 'I'll fix them later. She doesn't come back till Sunday.'

Evie nodded. 'This is all my mother's fault. If she hadn't tried to challenge Maleficent's leadership when they first came to the Isle, none of this would have happened.'

'Your mother actually *challenged* Maleficent?' Carlos goggled. It was unheard of.

'Well, she is a queen, after all,' Evie pointed out. 'Yeah,

she was angry that everyone on the island decided to follow Maleficent instead of her.' She walked over to the dressing table and began to fix her make-up, delicately powdering her nose and applying pink gloss to her full rosebud lips. 'And now here we are.'

'Mal will get over it,' he said hopefully.

'Are you kidding? A grudge is a grudge is a grudge. She'll never forgive me. Didn't you listen in Selfie class? I thought you were so smart.' Evie smiled wryly. 'Oh well, I should just face it. Go back to our castle and never come out.'

'But you're not, right?'

'No, I guess not.' Evie put away her compact. 'Hey,' she said softly. 'I have an old doona I never use . . . I mean, if you get cold and you can't . . . Oh, never mind.' She'd never had any siblings, so she had no idea what having a little brother would be like. But if Evil Queen had ever stopped looking at herself in the mirror long enough to have another kid, Evie thought it would be tolerable to have a little brother like Carlos.

Carlos looked as if he didn't know what to say.

'Forget I said anything,' said Evie in a rush.

'No, no, bring it. I mean, no-one's ever cared whether I'm warm or not,' he said, blushing red as his voice trailed off. 'Not that *you* care, of course.'

'I certainly don't!' agreed Evie. Caring was *definitely* against the rules at Dragon Hall and could turn anyone into a laughing stock. 'We were going to throw it out.'

'Excellent, just consider my home your rubbish tip.'

'Er, okay.'

'Do you think you might have a pillow you were going to toss out, too? I've never had a pillow.' Carlos turned red again. 'I mean, I've had *tons* of pillows, of course. So many! We have to keep throwing them away. I get so many pillows. I mean, who's never had a pillow in their life? That's preposterous.'

'Yeah, I think we were going to throw away a pillow,' Evie said, turning just as red as Carlos, even as a warm, sunny sensation had taken over her chest. She changed the subject. 'Still working on that machine of yours?'

'Yeah, wanna see?' he asked.

'Yeah, sure,' Evie replied, following Carlos out of the room towards the back of the house, away from the party. Carlos slipped outside, holding the door open for Evie.

'Where are we going?'

'To my lab,' Carlos replied, pulling out a matchbox and lighting a candle to lead the way into the weedy garden.

'Your what?'

'My science lab. Don't worry, I don't, like, sacrifice toads or anything.'

Evie let out a hesitant laugh.

They approached a huge, gnarled tree with a rope ladder. Carlos started climbing up it. 'I have to keep it all in my tree house. I'm afraid my mum is going to get some big ideas and turn my chemicals into make-up and hair products.'

Evie scrambled up the ladder behind him. The tree house was more elaborate than any she'd ever seen, with miniature turrets and a tiny balcony that looked out on to the dark forest below. Inside, Evie spun round, gaping. The walls were lined with shelves of glass beakers, vials and jars containing various neon-coloured liquids. In the corner sat a small, old television with about 15 different antennae strapped to it.

'What is all this?' Evie asked, picking up a jar of something white and snowy.

'Oh, that's from Chem Lab. It's sodium polyacrylate—I was trying to see if I could use it as a sponge when mixed with water,' Carlos said. 'But here, this is what I wanted to show you.' He pulled out the wire-box contraption he'd been working on in class. 'I think I got the battery to work.'

Carlos fiddled with a few buttons and flicked a few switches. It sputtered to life, then died. His face fell. He tried again. This time, it emitted a high-pitched squeal before dying.

He looked up at Evie sheepishly. 'Sorry, I thought I had it.'

Evie looked at the black box. 'Maybe try connecting this wire to that one?' she suggested.

Carlos peered at the wires. 'You're right, they're in the wrong place.' He switched the wires and hit the switch.

A powerful electric burst shot out of the box, sending

Carlos and Evie flying back against the wall and falling to the floor. The beam of light burst up towards the plywood ceiling, blasting a hole in the tree-house roof and up to the sky.

'Maleficent!' Carlos cursed.

'Oh my goblins!' Evie screamed. 'What just happened?'

They both scrambled out onto the tree-house balcony and stared up at the sky, where the light was streaking all the way up, through the clouds, up, up, up, all the way to the dome!

The light seared through the barrier as easily as it had burned a hole in the tree-house roof.

Lightning flashed, and the very Earth shook with a supersonic rumble. For a second they could see through the dome and directly into the night sky. The black box began to emit a strange beeping noise.

Carlos and Evie scrambled back inside, and Carlos picked up the box. It was making a sound neither of them had ever heard before.

And for a brief moment, there was something on the television in the room, which had burst to life all of a sudden.

'Look!' Evie cried.

The screen was flashing with so many different scenes it was dizzying. For a moment they saw a talking dog (Carlos screamed at the sight); then it switched to a pair of twins who were nothing alike (one was boyish and athletic and the other was sort of a diva, and they both sort of looked like Mal, except with yellow hair); then it switched again to two teenage boys who seemed to be running a hospital for superheroes.

'Look at all these different television shows!' Carlos said. 'I knew it! I knew it! I knew there had to be other kinds!'

Evie laughed. Then the screen flickered and went dark again, and the box in Carlos' hands went dead. 'What happened?'

'I don't know. I think maybe it worked? It penetrated the dome for a second, didn't it?' he asked, approaching the box fearfully and touching it with the end of one finger. It was hot to the touch, and he pulled his hand away quickly.

'It must have,' Evie said. 'That's the only explanation.'

'Promise you won't tell anyone about what happened, especially about the dome. We could get in real trouble, you know.'

'I promise,' said Evie, making an X with her fingers behind her back.

'Good.'

'You want to go back to the party?'

'Do we have to?' she asked, unwilling to find herself trapped in another wardrobe.

'You have a point. And that show you like on Auradon News Network, the one that features the Prince of the Week, is going to be on in five minutes.'

'Excellent!'

Unbeknown to the two villain children, far off in the distance, deep in the heart of the forbidden fortress, hidden behind a grey misty fog on the other side of the island, a long black sceptre with a jewel on its end came back to life, glowing green with power again. The most powerful weapon of darkness had been awakened for a moment.

Next to the hidden staff, a stone statue of a raven began to vibrate, and when the bird began to shake its wings, the stone crumbled into dust, and in its place was that black-eyed fiend, that wicked fairy's familiar, the one and only Diablo, Maleficent's best and first friend.

Diablo shook his feathers and gave a throaty, triumphant cry. Evil would fly again.

Evil lives . . .

chapter 10

Council of Sidekicks

Ben nervously fiddled with the beast-head ring on his finger as he waited for the Council members to come in and take their seats around the king's conference table later that morning.

His father's advice rang in his ear. *Keep a strong hand. Show 'em who's king.*

He flexed his own fingers, thinking of his father's fist. His father didn't mean it literally, but Ben was worried nonetheless. He supposed he would just have to improvise.

'Ready, sire?' Lumiere asked.

Ben took a breath and tried to sound as serious as possible. 'Yes, let them in, thank you.'

Lumiere bowed. Even though it had been a long time since he had been enchanted and turned into a candelabrum, there was something about him that still resembled one, and for a moment, Ben could easily imagine two small flames flickering on his outstretched palms.

Lumiere knows who he is—and he's happy being Lumiere. Is it really so much more complicated to be a king than a candelabrum?

The thought was, for a moment, comforting to Ben. But then the Council entered the room—and there was nothing comforting about the sudden sight of the royal advisers.

In fact, they're pretty terrifying, Ben thought.

He didn't know why. They were chatting amiably enough, discussing last night's Tourney scores and whose Fantasy Tourney League was winning. Seats were taken, gossip exchanged, goblets of spiced juice passed around, as well as a plate or two of the castle kitchen's sugar cookies.

Representing the sidekicks were the usual Seven Dwarfs, still wearing their mining clothes and stocking caps. Seated next to the dwarfs (or rather, sitting along the edge of a book of *Auradon's Civic Rules & Regulations* that lay on the table nearest them, because they were much too small to take any seat at all) were the very same mice who had helped Cinderella win her prince—wily Jaq, chubby Gus and sweet Mary. The rodent portion of the advisory board tended to speak in small, squeaky tones that could be hard for Ben to understand without the communicator in his ear, which translated everything that the animals said in the meeting.

Everyone at the table was wearing one of the clever hearing devices, one of the few magical inventions allowed in the kingdom. The mice's squeaks, the Dalmatians' barks and Flounder's burbling were all translated so that they could be understood.

Beyond the mice, a few of Ariel's sisters (Ben could never remember which was which, especially as their names all started with A) and Flounder splashed along in their own copper bathtub, wheeled in by a very unhappy Cogsworth, who grimaced every time the slightest bit of water sloshed over the edge.

'Mind the splashing, please! I only just had this floor mopped. You do know this isn't a beach resort, do you not? Precisely. It's a *council* meeting. A *rrrrroyal* council,' the former clock trumpeted, rolling his r's with great fanfare. Andrina—or was it Adella?—only laughed and flicked him with her great wet fins.

Rounding out the other side of the table were the three "good" fairies, Flora, Fauna and Merryweather, looking cheery in their green, red and blue hats and capes, seated next to the famed blue Genie of Agrabah. They were comparing holiday notes. The fairies were partial to the forest meadows while the genie preferred the vast deserts.

'I guess we should get started?' Ben ventured, clearing his throat.

No-one seemed to hear him. The mice roared with laughter, falling onto their backs and rolling across the

Auradonian law book. Even Pongo and Perdita of the freed De Vil Dalmatian contingent joined in the laughter with a little lively barking. All told, it was a friendly group, or so it seemed. Ben began to relax.

And why shouldn't he? Unlike the infamous villains trapped on the Isle of the Lost, the good citizens of Auradon looked as if the last 20 years hadn't aged them one bit. Ben had to admit it: every one of the royal councillors looked just like they had in the photographs he had studied of the founding of Auradon. The mice were still small and cute, the Dalmatians sleek and handsome. The mermaids—whatever their names—remained as fresh as water lilies, and the good fairies burst with good health. Even the infamous Genie of Agrabah had toned down his usual hyper-manic performance. Dopey was still his mute, charming self, and while Doc may have had a few more white hairs than before in his beard, Grumpy looked almost cheerful.

Except for one thing—

'What—no cream cakes?' Grumpy grabbed a sugar cookie, glaring at the plate.

'It's a meeting, not a party,' Doc said, harrumphing.

'Well, it's certainly not a party now,' Grumpy said, examining a cookie. 'There isn't even a raisin or a chocolate chip! What, are we discussing budget problems today?'

'As I was saying,' Ben said, moving the plate of cookies away from Grumpy, 'welcome, welcome, everyone. I hereby declare this meeting of the King's Council officially open. Shall we begin?' asked Ben.

Heads nodded around the table.

Ben glanced down at the notecards he had hidden beneath his right hand. Hopefully, he was doing this correctly.

He coughed. 'Excellent. Well, then.'

'Don't we need to wait for your dad, kid?' Genie asked, putting his feet up on the table. Now that magic was discouraged in Auradon, the genie had taken physical form and was no longer a floating cloud.

'Yeah. Where's King Beast?' Flounder piped up.

'Isn't your father joining us today, Ben?' Perdita asked, gently.

Colour crept into Ben's face. 'No, sorry. My dad—I mean, King Beast—has uh, asked me to run the meeting this morning.'

Everyone stared. The mice sat up. Grumpy let the cookie drop.

'Anyway.' Ben cleared his throat and tried to affect a confidence he did not feel. 'On to business.' He was stalling.

He looked at the stack of papers in front of him. Petitions and letters and applications and motions, from sidekicks from every corner of the kingdom . . .

Show them who is king. That's what my father said.

He tried again. 'In my role as future king of Auradon, I've studied your petitions, and while I appreciate your suggestions, I'm afraid that . . .'

'Our petitions? Are you talking about the Sidekicks Act?' Grumpy sounded annoyed.

'Er, yes, I'm afraid that we cannot recommend granting these petitions as—'

'Who's we?' asked Mary.

Dopey looked confused.

'I guess, I mean *me*? What I mean to say is, I've taken your suggestions for change but it doesn't look like they can be approved as—'

One of the mermaids tilted her head. 'Not approved? Why not?'

Ben became flustered. 'Well, because I . . .'

Doc shook his head. 'I'm sorry, son, but have you ever even set foot outside this castle? What do you know about the whole kingdom? For instance, our goblin cousins on the Isle of the Lost would like forgiveness—they've been exiled for a long time.'

All around the table, the councillors began to murmur in low tones. Ben knew the meeting had taken a turn for the worse, and he desperately began to review his options. There was nothing on his notecards about what to do in the case of council revolt.

One. What would my dad do?
Two. What would my mum do?
Three. Could I run for it? What would that do?

Ben was still evaluating option number three when Grumpy spoke up. 'If I may interrupt,' Grumpy said, looking the exact opposite of, well, Happy, who sat next to him. 'As you know, for 20 years we dwarfs have worked the mines, gathering jewels and diamonds for the kingdom's crowns and sceptres, for many a prince and princess in need of wedding gifts or coronation attire.' Ben turned even redder, looking at the polished gold buttons on his own shirt. Grumpy glared at him pointedly, then continued. 'And for 20 years we have been paid zilch for our efforts.'

'Now, now, Mr Grumpy,' said Ben. 'Sir.'

'It's just Grumpy,' huffed Grumpy.

Ben looked at the mice. 'May I?'

'Be my guest,' said Gus, hopping down.

Ben pulled the Auradon law book free from beneath the mice, sending a few rodents rolling. He turned to a chart in the appendices at the back of the thick book. 'Okay, then, Grumpy, as a citizen of Auradon, it looks like you and the rest of the dwarfs have been granted two-month holidays . . . 20 days off . . . and unlimited sick days.' He looked up. 'Does that sound right?'

'More or less,' Doc said. Grumpy folded his arms with another glare.

Ben looked relieved, closing the book. 'So you can't say you've been *working* for exactly 20 years, can you?'

'The maths is beside the point, young man—or should I call you, young *beast*?' Grumpy shouted from behind Doc, who was doing his best to shove his own stocking cap into Grumpy's mouth.

'Prince Ben will do,' Ben said, with a thin smile. No wonder the dwarf was called Grumpy; Ben had never met such a cantankerous person!

'If I can interject, and I don't mean to offend, but we're a bit tired of being without a voice and without a contract,' Bashful spoke up. At least, Ben thought that was his name, if only from how red he turned as he spoke.

'You're here now, aren't you? I don't believe you can call that being 'without a voice', can you?' Ben smiled again. *Two for two. Maybe I'm better at this king stuff than I thought.*

'But what will happen to our families when we retire?' Bashful asked, not looking convinced.

'I'm sure my father has a plan to take care of everyone,' Ben said, hoping it was true.

A voice squeaked up from the table. Ben leaned forwards to listen. 'And has anyone noticed that we sidekicks do all the work in this kingdom? Since the Fairy Godmother frowns on magic, we mice make all the dresses!' Mary said indignantly. The little mouse had climbed back up on the law book to make herself heard. 'By paw!'

'That's very—' Ben began, but he was cut off. He was no longer in charge of the room. That much was clear.

'Not to mention the woodland creatures who do all the housekeeping for Snow White,' added Jaq. 'They aren't too happy about it, either.'

Mary nodded. 'Plus, Snow White needs a whole new wardrobe as she's reporting on the Coronation soon! *Your* coronation, I might add!'

Ben searched desperately through the papers in front of him. 'Every citizen has the right to file—to file a—'

'I still collect everything for Ariel,' burbled Flounder. 'Her treasures have grown, but what do I have to show for any of it?'

Ben tried again. 'You have the knowledge that what you do is very much appreciated—'

Flounder kept going. 'And the mermaids give undersea tours all year round without taking a penny. Even in the busy season!'

Ariel's sisters nodded indignantly, their shimmering tails splashing water from the bathtub all over the table. Cogsworth slapped a hand over his eyes, while Lumiere squeezed his arm in support.

Ben nodded. 'Well, that is certainly something worth further consid—'

'And if I might add, living without magic has taken a toll on our nerves,' sighed Merryweather. 'Flora can't sew, Fauna can't bake, and I can't clean without our wands. You'll find our petition at the end there, dear boy.' Flora shoved it into Prince Ben's face, and he sat back in his chair, surprised.

Fauna chimed in. 'While we appreciate all that the Fairy

Godmother has done, we can't see why just a little magic might not be useful?'

'But is there really any such thing as a little—' Ben began.

Pongo sat up. 'And not to sound weary, but Perdy and I are a bit fatigued after caring for 99 Dalmatians,' said Pongo in that rich, elegant voice of his.

'If only there were 99 hours in the day.' Perdy yawned. 'I could at least sleep for five of them. Imagine that.'

Mary the mouse nodded sympathetically, patting Perdy's paw with her own.

A blur of blue appeared in Ben's face. 'To put it bluntly, Prince Ben, this blows,' said Genie, who blew him a mocking kiss.

The dwarfs applauded wildly.

Ariel's sisters tittered, and now the water in the tub was roiling like a small tsunami. Cogsworth left the chamber in a huff, and even Lumiere motioned for Prince Ben to cut the meeting short.

If only Ben knew how.

The room began to dissolve into absolute chaos, as the sidekicks and dwarfs began to shout at one another, while the good fairies kept on complaining about the back-breaking work even ordinary chores now entailed, and all the rest of the company advocated for relief from their own grievances.

It was hard to pick out one from the next, Ben thought, as he slunk down in his chair, trying not to panic.

Breathe, he told himself. *Breathe, and think.*

But it was impossible to think amid the ruckus in the room. The mermaids complained that the tourists left their rubbish everywhere; the dwarfs whined that no-one liked to whistle while they worked any more; Pongo and Perdita barked about the stress of having to pay for 99 college educations; and even Genie looked bluer than usual.

Ben covered his ears. This wasn't a meeting any more. It was an all-out brawl. He had to shut it down, before people started throwing things—or mice.

What would my father do? What does he expect me to do? How could he put me in this situation and expect me to know what to do?

The more he thought about it, the angrier he got. Finally, Ben stood up. No-one cared.

He climbed on top of his chair—and still nobody noticed him.

That's it!

His father had told him to be kingly, and kings were heard!

'ENOUGH!' he yelled from the top of the table. 'THIS MEETING IS ADJOURNED!'.

A shocked silence filled the room.

Ben just stood there.

'Why! I never . . .' growled Perdy. 'How rude! To speak to us in such a way!'

'Impertinent and ungrateful, that's for certain,' sniffed Flora.

'Why, that does it!' said Grumpy. 'Where's King Beast? We're not deaf! Don't you know your manners, son?'

'My word, we've never been treated so poorly!' Merryweather fluttered.

The dwarfs and sidekicks left the room, shooting Ben wary glances as they filed out. The mermaids huffed and made a point of sloshing water on the floor, as Lumiere was left to drag them away, shaking his head. The mice turned their noses up as they walked past without so much as a squeak; the Dalmatians held their tails high; and even Dopey gave the prince a silent, hurt look.

Ben hung his head, embarrassed by his actions. He had tried to lead like his father, and he had failed. He hadn't been able to table the petition, and he hadn't been able to inspire confidence in the King's Council. If anything, he had made the situation worse.

Which is why I would make a terrible king, Ben thought, as he climbed down from his father's council-room table.

He hadn't proven himself.

He'd only proven one thing—

That Prince Ben wasn't fit to wear the royal beast-head ring that was currently on his finger.

chapter 11

Evil Lives?

Mal was standing alone in the corner, nursing her spicy juice, when she noticed two figures trying to sneak their way towards the buffet table to grab a couple of cans of expired fizzy drinks. It was Carlos, of course, and Princess Blueberry. Evie didn't look any worse for wear after spending time in Cruella's wardrobe. She wasn't even bleeding! There wasn't a scratch on her or even a run in her tights. Ugh. Carlos must have helped her somehow, the ungrateful little twerp.

Mal sighed.

Foiled again.

Just like her mother, whose own curse had failed.

Were they destined for failure forever?

This party was a bust. It was definitely time to go. Even the evil step-granddaughters looked tired of pretending to hate being chased by the rowdy pirates.

Mal tossed her empty cup on the floor and left without a backwards glance. She spent the night rearranging her neighbours' overgrown lawns, swapping lawn gnomes, postboxes and outdoor furniture. She amused herself doing some light redecorating by toilet-papering a couple of houses and egging a few rickshaws. Nothing like a little property damage to make her feel better. She left her mark on each house with the message *Evil lives!* spray-painted on the lawn, to remind the island people exactly what they stood for and what they had to be proud of.

Feeling as if she had salvaged the evening, it was with some surprise and not a little shock that when she rolled home to the Bargain Castle, she found her mother awake and awaiting her.

'Mother!' Mal yelped, startled to see Maleficent sitting on her huge high-backed green chair in front of the stained-glass window. It was her throne, as it were—her seat of darkness.

'Hello, dear,' Maleficent's cold voice said. 'Do you know what time it is, young lady?'

Mal was confused. Since when had Maleficent imposed a curfew? It wasn't as if her mother cared where she went or when she came home, now—did she? After all, the woman wasn't called Maleficent for nothing. 'Two in the morning?' Mal finally guessed.

'I thought so,' Maleficent said, pushing up a purple sleeve and correcting the time on her wristwatch. She pulled the sleeve down and looked at her daughter.

Mal waited, wondering where this was going. She hadn't seen her mother in a while, and when they had come in contact, Mal was often taken aback by how small her mother looked these days.

The Mistress of Darkness had literally shrunk with the reduction in her circumstances. Whereas once she had been towering, she was now almost a miniature version of her former self—petite, even. If she stood up, one could see that Mal was taller than she was by a few centimetres.

Yet the distinctive menace had not abated, it just came in a tinier package. 'Where was I? Oh yes, *Evil lives!*' Maleficent hissed.

'*Evil lives*—exactly, Mother.' Mal nodded. 'Is that what you want to talk to me about? The tags around town? Pretty good, right?'

'No, you misunderstand me, dear,' her mother said, and it was then that Mal noticed that her mother was not alone. She was petting a black raven that was perched on the arm of her chair.

The raven croaked, flew to Mal's shoulder and nipped her ear.

'Ouch!' she said. 'Stop that!'

'That's just Diablo. Don't be jealous, my little friend; that's just Mal,' Maleficent said dismissively. And even if Mal knew that her mother couldn't care less about her (Mal tried not to take it personally, as her mother couldn't care less about *anyone*), it still stung to hear it said aloud so bluntly.

'Diablo? That's Diablo?' said Mal. She knew all about Diablo, Maleficent's first and only friend. Her mother had told her the story many times: how, 20 years ago, now, Maleficent had battled Prince Phillip as a great black fiery dragon but had been struck down, betrayed, by a weapon of justice and peace that some irritatingly good fairies had helped aim right into her heart. Maleficent had believed herself dead and passed from this world, but instead she had woken up the next day, alone and broken, on this terrible island.

The only remnant of the battle was the scar on her chest where the sword had struck, and every so often she would feel the phantom pain of that wound. She had told Mal many times how, when she woke up, she had realised that those awful good fairies had taken everything away from her—her castle, her home, even her favourite pet raven.

'The one and only Diablo,' purred Maleficent, actually looking happy for once.

'But *how*? He was frozen! They turned him into stone!' said Mal.

'Yes, they did, those horrid little beasts. But he's back! He's back! And *Evil lives*!' Maleficent declared, with a witch's cackle for good measure.

Okay. Her mother was getting just a *wee* bit repetitive.

Mal gave her mother her best eye-roll. To the rest of the fools, minions and morons on the island, Maleficent was the scariest thing with two horns around, but to Mal, who had seen her mother put goblin jam on toast and drop crumbs all over the sofa, polish her horns with shoe polish and sew the raggedy hemline of her purple cape, she was just her mother, and Mal wasn't *that* scared of her. Okay, so she was still scared of her mother, but she wasn't like *Carlos*-scared.

Maleficent stood from her chair, her green eyes blazing into Mal's identical ones. 'My Dragon's Eye—my sceptre of darkness—Diablo says it has been awakened! *Evil lives!*— and best of all, it is on this island!'

'Your sceptre? Are you sure?' Mal asked sceptically. 'Hard to believe King Beast of Auradon would leave such an impressive weapon on the Isle.'

'Diablo swears he saw it, didn't you, my sweet?' Maleficent purred. The raven cawed.

'So where is it?' asked Mal.

'Well, I don't speak Raven, do I? It's on this blasted piece of rock somewhere!' Maleficent fumed, tossing her cape back.

'Okay, then. But so what?'

'So what?! The Dragon's Eye is back! *Evil lives!* It means I can have my powers back!'

'Not with the dome still up,' Mal pointed out.

'It doesn't matter. I thought those three despicably good fairies had destroyed it, but they had only frozen it, like they had Diablo. It is alive, it is out there somewhere, and best of all, you—my dear—will get it for me!' Maleficent announced with a flourish.

'Me?'

'Yes. Don't you want to prove yourself to me? Prove that you are worthy of being my daughter?' her mother asked quietly.

Mal didn't answer.

'You know how much you are a disappointment to me, how when I was your age, I had armies of goblins under my control, but you . . . what do you do—put your little drawings all over town? You need to do MORE!' she seethed. Diablo flapped his wings and cawed in agreement.

Mal tried not to show her feelings. She'd thought those tags were pretty cool. 'Fine! Fine! I'll go get your sceptre!' she agreed, if only to stop her mother from raging.

'Wonderful.' Maleficent touched her heart, or the hole in her chest where it should have been. 'When that sword pierced my dragon hide, and I fell off that cliff 20 years ago, I was sure I had died. But they brought me back to suffer a fate worse than death, much worse. But one day, I will have my revenge!'

Mal nodded. She'd heard the spiel so many times, she could chant it in her sleep. Maleficent took her hand, and they chorused, *'Revenge on the fools who imprisoned us on this cursed island!'*

Maleficent urged Mal closer so that she could whisper a warning in her ear.

'Yes, Mother,' said Mal, to show she understood.

Maleficent grinned. 'Now, get out of here and bring it back, so we can be free of this floating prison once and for all!'

Mal trudged up to her room. She'd forgotten to tell her mother about the mean trick she'd pulled on Evie at the party, not that it would have been evil enough for the great Maleficent, either. Nothing was. Why did she even bother?

She climbed out of her window and onto the balcony where could see across the entire island and the shining spires of Auradon glimmered in the distance.

A few minutes later, she heard the sound of jingling trinkets, which meant Jay had dropped by to annoy her or to steal a late-night snack.

'I'm out here,' she called.

'You left before the fun really began,' he said, meaning the party. 'We turned the ballroom into a mosh pit and crowd-surfed.' He joined her on the balcony, a bag of smelly cheese curls in his hand.

She shrugged.

'What's with the rude raven?' he asked, chomping noisily on the snack, his fingers turning a fluorescent shade of orange.

'That's Diablo. You know, my mum's old familiar. He's back.'

Jay stopped chewing. 'He's *what*?'

'He's *back*. He got unfrozen. So now Mum thinks the spell over the island might be unravelling somehow.'

Jay's eyes grew wide.

Mal looked away and continued. 'That's not all. Diablo swears the Dragon's Eye is back, too. That he saw it glow back to life. You know, her sceptre, her greatest weapon, the one that controls all the forces of evil and darkness, blah blah blah. She wants me to find it, and use it to break the curse over the island.'

Jay let out a loud laugh. 'Well, she's really gone off the cliff into the deep end to take a swim with the killer alligators, then, hasn't she? That thing is hidden forever and ever, and ever and ever and—'

'Ever?' Mal smirked.

'Exactly.'

Mal turned away, wanting to change the subject. 'Do you ever think about what it's like over there?' she asked, nodding towards Auradon.

Jay scoffed. 'Yeah, horrible. Sunny, and happy and . . . horrible. I thank my unlucky stars every day that I'm not there.'

'Yeah, I know. But, I mean—you never get sick of this place, like you want a change?' she asked, brooding.

Jay looked at her quizzically.

'Never mind.' Mal didn't think he would understand. She continued staring into the night. Jay continued munching on his cheese curls and fiddling with some newly stolen costume jewellery.

A memory came flooding back to Mal. She was five years old and was in the marketplace with her mother when a goblin tripped and fell, spilling his basket of fruit everywhere. Without thinking, she had started picking up the fruit, helping the goblin gather it all. One by one, she picked up the apples, dusted them off on her dress, and placed them back in the basket. Suddenly Mal had looked up from where she was crouched. The market had gone silent, and everyone, including her mother, who was rotten-apple red and fuming, was staring at her.

'Get up this instant,' her mother had hissed. Maleficent kicked the basket, and the apples all fell out again.

Mal obeyed. When they got back home, her mother locked her in her room to think about what she had done. 'If you're not careful, my girl, you'll end up just like *him*—just like your father—weak and powerless. AND PATHETIC!' Maleficent had bellowed through the locked door.

Little Mal had stared into the dingy mirror leaning precariously on her dressing table. Fighting back tears, she vowed never to disappoint her mother again.

'We have to find it,' Mal said to Jay as an icy wind whipped up from the sea below and pulled her from her memory. 'The Dragon's Eye. It's here.'

'Mal, it's not poss—'

'We have to,' Mal said.

'Eh,' Jay replied, shrugging his shoulders and turning towards the window to go inside. 'We'll see.'

Mal took one last look out at the horizon to the bright, sparkling speck in the distance. She felt a pang in her gut, like longing. But what for, she couldn't say.

'Miserable, darling, as usual, perfectly wretched.'
—Cruella De Vil,
101 Dalmatians

chapter 12

Score One for the Team

Jay left the Bargain Castle behind him. It was the very end of night, the time when it was just turning towards morning—when it was still dark, but you could already hear the mournful call of the vultures scavenging their way across the island. He shivered, retracing his steps through the grim backstreets and alleyways of the town, past the eerily bare trees and broken-shuttered buildings that looked as abandoned and hopeless as everyone who lived there.

Jay quickened his pace. He wasn't scared of the dark; he depended on it. Jay did some of his best work at night. He'd never get used to the way the island felt in the darkness, though. Jay picked up on it most when everyone else was asleep, and he could see the world around him clearly, for what it was. He could see that this town and this island and these bare trees and these broken shutters were his life, no matter what other life his father and his peers had known. There was no glory here. No magic and no power, either. This was it—all they would ever have or be or know.

No matter what Mal thinks.

Jay kicked a rock across the crumbling cobblestones, and an irritated cat howled back at him from the shadows.

She's so full of it.

Mal wouldn't admit it—their defeat—especially not when she was in a mood like tonight. Mal was so stubborn sometimes. Practically delusional. In moments like these, Jay had clearly seen the effects of a raised-by-a-maniacal-villain upbringing. He couldn't blame Mal for not wanting to tell her mother 'no'—nobody would—but really, there was no way that Maleficent's sceptre was somewhere on the Isle of the Lost, and even if it was, Jay and Mal would never find it.

Jay shook his head.

Eye of the Dragon? More like, Eye of Desperation.

That raven is bonkers, probably from being frozen for 20 years.

He shrugged and rounded the corner to his own street. He tried to forget about it, half-expecting (and half-hoping) Mal would probably do the same. She had her whims, but they never seemed to last. That was the good thing about Mal; she would get all worked up about something, but totally drop it the next day. They got along because Jay had learned to just ride out the storm.

When he finally made his way through the last of the puzzle of stolen locks, chains and deadbolts that guarded his own house (thieves being the most paranoid about burglary), he pushed the rotting wooden door open with a creak and crept inside.

One foot at a time. Shift your body weight as you step. Stick close to the wall . . .

'Jay? Is that you?'

Oh no.

His father was still awake, cooking eggs, his faithful parrot, Iago, on his shoulder. Was Jafar worried about his only son being out so late? Was he worried about where he'd been, or who he'd been with, or why he hadn't come home until now?

Nah. His father had only one thing on his mind, and Jay knew exactly what it was.

'What's tonight's haul?' Jafar asked greedily, as he set his plate of food down on the kitchen table, next to a pile of rusty coins that passed for currency on the island. The table was where Jafar practised his favourite hobby: counting his money. There was a good-sized pyramid of coins on the table, but Jay knew it wouldn't satisfy Jafar's greed.

Nothing did.

'Nice pyjamas.' Jay smirked. The trick with his father was to keep moving, to stay on your toes, and above all else, to avoid answering the question, because none of the answers were ever right. When you couldn't win, you shouldn't give in and play. That was just setting yourself up for disaster.

I mean, my dad's best friend is a parrot.
Enough said.

'Nice pyjamas!' Iago squawked. 'Nice pyjamas!'

Jafar was wearing a faded bathrobe over saggy pyjamas with little lamps printed all over them. If 20 years of being frozen could turn a raven cuckoo, 20 years of life among the lost had done just as much to diminish the former Grand Vizier of Agrabah's infamy, along with his grandeur and panache (at least, that was how his father thought of it). Gone were the sumptuous silks and plush velvet jackets, replaced by a uniform of ratty velour sweatsuits and sweat-stained vests that smelled a little too strongly of their shop's marketplace stand, which was located, rather unfortunately and quite directly, across from the horse stalls.

The sleek black beard was now raggedy and grey, and he had a rather large gut. Iago had taken to calling him 'the sultan', since Jafar now resembled his old adversary in size; although, in all fairness, Iago himself looked like he was on a daily cracker binge.

In return, Jafar called his feathered pal things that were unrepeatable by any standard, even a parrot's.

Jay hated his father's pyjamas: they were a sign of how

far their once royalty-adjacent family had fallen. The flannel was worn so thin in places you could see Jafar's belly roll beneath it. Jay tried not to look too closely, even now, in the shadows of the early morning light.

His father ignored the pyjama insults. He'd heard them all before. He wolfed down his midnight snack with relish without offering Jay a bite. 'Come on, come on, get on with it. What'd we get? Let's have a look.'

Jay eyed his carpet roll at the end of the room, beyond the table—but he also knew there was no way of getting past his father now. He reluctantly unpacked his pockets. 'Broken glass slipper, got it from one of the step-granddaughters. With some glue, we could get a good price for it.' The cracked, heel-less slipper shattered into a pile of glass shards the moment it hit the table. Jafar raised an eyebrow.

'Um, superglue?' Jay kept going. 'One of Lucifer's collars, Rick Ratcliffe's pistol keychain—and look, a real glass eye!' It was covered in lint. 'It's only a little used. I got it from one of the pirates.' He held it up to his own eye and peered through the glass—then jerked it away, wrinkling his nose and fanning his face with his hand. 'Why don't pirates ever bathe? Hello, it's called a *shower*. It's not like they're even out at sea any more.' With that, he rolled the eyeball across the table to his father.

Iago squawked curiously while Jay waited for the inevitable.

Jafar waved a dismissive hand over the items and sighed. 'Rubbish.'

'Rubbish!' Iago shrieked. 'Rubbish!'

'But that's all there is on this island,' Jay argued, leaning against the kitchen sink. 'This is the Isle of the Lost, the Isle of the Leftovers, remember?'

His father frowned. 'You went to the De Vil place, and you didn't score a fur coat? What were you doing in there all night? Slobbering over Maleficent's girl?'

Jay rolled his eyes. 'For the ten-thousandth time, *no*. And it's not like *I* was the one locked in the wardrobe.' As he said it, he wondered why he hadn't thought of that.

'You need to try harder! What about that princess? The one who's just come out of the castle?'

'Oh yeah, her. I forgot.' Jay dug into his jeans pocket and brought out a silver necklace with a red poisoned-apple charm on it. 'That's all she had on her. I'm telling you, even the castles around this place are dumps.'

Jafar put on a pair of spectacles and examined the jewellery, squinting first with one eye, then with the other. His eyesight was going, and his back ached from the extra work of carrying around his own sweatsuited belly; even villains were not spared the perils of ageing. 'Paste and glass. In my day, a *servant* wouldn't have worn that, let alone a princess. Not quite the big score we're looking for.' He tossed the bauble aside, sighing as he stopped to feed Iago another cracker.

'Score,' said Iago, gleefully spitting cracker crumbs. 'Big score!'

Jay's shoulders slumped.

The big score.

It was his father's dream: that one day his only son would find a cache of loot so big, so rich, so laden with gold, that Jafar would no longer have to preside over a junk shop, ever again. No matter that the Isle of the Lost was a floating rubbish heap, somehow Jafar believed the big score was always right round the corner—a bounty that could transport him back to his rightful place as a sorcerer, with all its power and trappings.

Talk about delusional.

Even if it did exist, could such a treasure take any of them back in time to a better day, or free them from a lifetime of imprisonment? As if an object or a jewel or any amount of gold coins could fix the mess that people like Jafar had got them all into, in the first place?

The big score. His father was as crazy as Mal had been tonight. Jay shook his head.

And then he just shook. Because he'd thought of something.

Hang on.

What had Mal told him tonight? That the raven believed Maleficent's sceptre, the Dragon's Eye, was hidden somewhere on this island? If Diablo was telling the truth, and Jay was able to find it, it would be the biggest score of the year. Of the century! He thought it through. Was it possible? Could it be *that* easy? Could his father have been right to hold on to the faintest hope for something better, even after all these years?

Nah.

Jay rubbed his eyes. It had been a long night. There was no way that thing was on the Isle of the Lost. There was nothing of power here—not when it came to people, and not when it came to their stuff.

And even if it *was* here—however unlikely that might be—the dome over the island kept all magic out. The Dragon's Eye was just a fancy name for a walking stick now. Like he'd told Mal, it was a useless enterprise. They were better off trying to hijack a boat out of the Goblin Wharf back to Auradon. Not that any of them would want to live there.

Maybe we belong *on the Isle of the Lost, Leftover and Forgotten. Maybe that's how this story is supposed to go.*

Only, who's going to break the news to my dad?

Jay watched as his father returned to stacking the coins in neat piles. Counting coins gave him peace in some way his son would never understand. Jafar was whistling, and looked up when he saw Jay staring at him.

'Remember the Golden Rule?' his father purred as he caressed the money with his hands.

'Totally. 'Night, Dad,' Jay said, heading to the worn carpet underneath the shelves in the back, where he slept.

Whoever has the most gold makes the rules. It's what his father believed, and while Jay had never seen any gold in his life, he'd been taught to believe it too.

He just wasn't sure that he believed there was any gold to find. Not on the Isle of the Lost. Still, as he curled up on the hard bit of carpeted floor that was his bed, he tried to imagine what it would feel like to find it.

The Big Score.

He fell asleep dreaming of his father bursting with pride in a pair of pyjamas made of gold.

chapter 13

Aftershocks

Cruella was going to kill him if she ever found out he'd thrown a party while she was away. People on the island kept telling him Cruella had mellowed with age, that she was rounder and less shouty, but they didn't have to live with her.

Cruella De Vil's son knew his mother better than anyone. If his mother had any idea that he'd let a bunch of people come over . . . and even worse, let anyone even come *near* her fur wardrobe—let alone *inside* it—let alone be tackled in a pile of full-length grade-A–pelt coats—well, let's just say it wouldn't be a puppy she would be trying to skin.

But thankfully his mother was still at the Spa and hadn't

returned unexpectedly as she was wont to do sometimes, if only to keep her son and Jasper and Horace on their minion-y toes.

Carlos stumbled out of bed and found a few bleary-eyed guests wandering around Hell Hall, smelling like last night's spicy juice. 'You're probably looking for the bathroom. This way. No problem!' He shoved them out of the front door before they could realise what was happening. As he did, Harry and Jace, the two young, second-generation De Vil minions who had helped him decorate for the party, stumbled out of the ballroom with crepe paper in their hair.

''Morning,' said Carlos, his voice still froggy with sleep. 'Why are you wearing the party?'

'I told him not to get me tangled up in his stupid streamers,' Harry said, still surly.

'*You* told me? You were the one playing tag all night, dragging half the decorations around after you.'

'I was entertaining guests.'

'Then why was no-one playing *with* you?'

As usual, there was no hope of real conversation with either of them. Carlos gave up.

His cousin Diego De Vil gave him a thumbs-up from the sofa. 'Great party. Total howler!' The rest of the band was packing up their gear.

'Thanks, I think.' Carlos wrinkled his nose. The gloomy morning light made everything look sadder and more sordid. Even the chandelier's candles had burned down to stubs, and someone had broken the rope swing so that it swayed gently, brushing the floor.

'We'd better get out of here so you can clean up.' Diego grinned. 'Or did your mum say to leave it for her to do when she got home?' He burst out laughing.

'Very funny.' Carlos ignored his cousin, pushing his way through the swinging door that led to the kitchen. He was hungry, his head hurt, and he hadn't slept well—dreaming anxiously of keeping the party a secret from his mother, but also of the dazzling light that had emanated from his machine and hit the dome.

Did that really happen?

For a moment there, Carlos thought he had felt something in the air. Something wild and electric and thrumming with energy. *Magic? Could it be?*

He wondered if he could make the machine do it again.

After breakfast.

He poked his head into the kitchen, which looked like a party bomb had exploded. Every counter and surface was sticky and littered with cups, bowls, bits of popcorn and crisps, rotten devilled eggs, uneaten devil dogs and empty bottles of juice. His feet stuck and unstuck with every step on the floor, ripping up and down with a noise that was part Velcro, part Pseudopod. He took a broom and began to sweep and clean, just enough so that he could get to the fridge and the shelves.

'Hey, uh, can I just . . .' Carlos said, pushing a snoring

Clay Clayton away from the kitchen counter to grab his breakfast. Clay was the son of the Great Hunter who'd almost captured Tarzan's gorilla troop (*almost* being the operative word: like every villain on the Isle, each one's evil schemes had ultimately ended in failure).

Carlos filled a bowl with some congealed, lumpy oatmeal and grabbed a spoon just as the Gastons stuck their heads inside.

'Hey, man! What've you got there? Breakfast? Don't mind if we do.' The burly brothers high-fived him as they stole his cold porridge from under his nose on their way out of the door. Being the Gastons, they were the last to leave and the first to steal all the food, as usual.

'I guess I wasn't hungry, anyway,' Carlos said out loud, although only he was listening. 'We should get busy and clean this place up before my mum gets home.'

He sighed and picked up the broom.

There was way too much to clean. But he was Carlos De Vil, boy genius, wasn't he? Surely he could figure out a way to make this task easier? Yes, he would. He just had to put his mind to it. He would take care of the clean-up later. First, he had to go to school.

Back at her own castle, Evie hadn't been able to sleep any better than Carlos had. Perhaps her dreams weren't plagued by Cruella De Vil or the cracking dome, but they were tormented by endless mazes of dark rooms and snapping traps—and she had woken up in a full sweat just as one was about to clamp down on her leg with its steel jaws again.

I can't go back to school, she thought. *Not after last night.*

The thought of having to face Mal again made her stomach queasy.

Besides, what was wrong with staying home? Home was, well, home. Wasn't it? So maybe it wasn't nice here, but it was safe. *Relatively.* Cosy. *In a not-exactly-traditionally-cosy way.*

Or not.

Okay, so it was cold and musty and basically a cave. Or a prison, as she had come to think of it during her years of castle-schooling. And today, like most days of her life, Evie could hear her mother talking to herself in her imaginary 'Magic Mirror' voice again.

But at least at home there were no traps and no purple-haired wicked fairies angling for revenge. There were no confusing frenemies, if she and Mal were even that.

I don't know what we are, but I know I don't like it.

And here I thought once I got to a real school, my life was going to be so much better.

Evie got up and went to her desk, which had a few of her old textbooks from her years of castle-schooling. She picked up her favourite, a worn leather grimoire, the Evil Queen's personal spell book.

Of course, it was useless on the Isle, but Evie still liked reading all the spells. It was like a catalogue of her mother's finer days, of a time before she spent hour after useless hour rattling around the empty rooms of the castle doing the Voice. It made Evie feel better sometimes. To remember that things hadn't always been like this.

She flipped through the spell book's worn yellow pages like she had when she was a little girl. She had pored over them the way she imagined the princesses in Auradon pored over their stupid fairy tales. She studied them the way other princesses studied, well, other princesses.

There were truth spells involving candles and water, love spells that called for flower petals and blood, health spells and wealth spells, spells for luck and spells for doom. Trickster spells were her favourite, especially the Pedlar's Disguise, which her mother had used to fool that silly Snow White. That was a good one.

A classic, even.

'Hi, sweetie,' Evil Queen said, entering her bedroom. 'You're looking pale again! Let me blush!' She removed a big round brush and began to work on Evie's cheeks. 'Pink as an apple blossom. There. Much better.' She looked down at the book in her daughter's hand. 'Oh, that old thing? I never understand. Why would you want to get that out again?'

'I don't know. Maybe because I just can't picture it. I mean, did you really do this spell? You?' Evie somehow couldn't imagine her mother as a frightening old hag. Sure, she was plump and middle-aged and no longer resembled the formidable portrait of her that hung in the main gallery, but she was far from ugly.

'Oh, yes! It was a scream! Snow Why-So-Stupid? was completely fooled! What a dope.' Evil Queen giggled. 'I mean, hello? Door-to-door *apple* sales hag? In the middle of the forest?' She sighed. 'Ah. Good times.'

Evie shook her head. 'Still.'

Her mother fussed with her hair. 'Wait. Why are you here? Shouldn't you be in school?'

'I don't feel like going,' Evie confessed. 'I'm not sure it's right, after all. Going to a big school. Maybe I should just stay in the castle.'

Evil Queen shrugged. 'Who needs an education, anyway? *Pretty is as pretty is*—remember that, darling.'

'Don't worry. You don't let me forget.'

'It's attention to the little things. You have to work for it, and you have to want it. Your eyelashes aren't going to curl themselves, you know.'

'Nope. You're going to curl them for me, even if I don't want you to.'

'That's right. And why? So that one day you can have what's rightfully yours, even if you are stuck on this miserable island. It is your birthright, to be the Fairest. Of. Them. All. Those aren't simply words.'

'I'm pretty sure they are, actually.'

'It's a responsibility. Ours. Yours, and mine. With great beauty comes great power.'

Evie just stared. When her mother got like this, it was hard to talk her down.

'I can't want this more than you do, Evie.' Her mother sighed, shaking her head.

'I know,' Evie said, because it was true. 'But what am I supposed to do? What if I don't know what I want? Or how to get it?'

'So you try harder. You reapply. You add that extra layer of gloss over your matte lip stain. You use your blusher and your bronzer, and make sure you don't confuse the two.'

'Bronzer on the bone, blusher on the cheek,' Evie said, automatically.

'You know which mascara makes your eyes pop.'

'Blue for brown. Green for gold. Purple for blue,' Evie recited, as if these were her family's version of maths facts.

'Exactly.' Evil Queen clasped her fingers round her daughter's in a touching, if rare, maternal gesture. 'And please, my darling girl. Never forget who you really are.'

'Who am I?' Evie asked, squeezing her mother's hand. She felt so lost—more than anything, it was all she wanted to know.

'Someone who needs to use elixir on her hair, or it looks too frizzy.' With those parting words, Evil Queen left the room, gathering up her dark skirts behind her. 'Mirror! Magic Mirror!'

Yeah, Evie thought, she could stay here, reading her old books and watching Auradon News Network, just like before. Later, if she was really lucky, her mother would come into her room to give her yet another interesting hairstyle, even though Evie had told her millions of times she preferred the plait.

This is my life when I'm in the castle.

Plaiting and blushing and bronzing.

That was the thing about leaving home, she guessed. Once you'd made your way out into the world, once you'd left the darkness of the cave, it was hard to go back.

Even to make your hair smooth and your eyes pop.

The more Evie thought about it, the more she knew she couldn't stay in the castle one more second. She'd read all the books and watched all the shows and there was no-one to talk to other than her mother, who was only obsessed with the latest cosmetics that arrived on the rubbish barges— the used tubes of lipstick and opened jars of cream that the Auradon princesses tossed when they didn't want them any more.

Even school has to be better than this.

Besides, she could deal with Mal, couldn't she? She wasn't scared of her.

Not *that* scared of her.

Okay, so maybe she was. But Evie was more terrified of rotting in a cave forever. And she was far too young to start working on her own 'Magic Mirror' voice. She shook her head at the thought.

Pretty is as pretty is?

Was that what my mother said?

But what was the point of being pretty if there was no-one there to see how pretty you were?

Even the crack on her ceiling was starting to look like the Dragon's Eye.

Mal stared up at it from her bed, transfixed. She had woken up extra early—even earlier than Carlos and Evie—as she couldn't sleep, thinking of the quest her mother had all but immediately dispatched her on. Maleficent was like that: once she had an idea in her head, there was no stopping her. It didn't matter if it was her daughter or one of her minions—she expected everyone to stop and drop and risk everything to do her bidding.

That was the Maleficent way.

Mal knew there was no exception made for daughters, not when you were one of the all-time most villainous villains of the Isle of the Lost. You didn't get to be number one by being merciful, or even reasonable.

Not when you were one of the evil elite.

Maleficent wanted the Dragon's Eye back, which was great and all, and Mal totally got it; but actually trying to find out *where* it was on the island—now that was something else entirely.

So, yeah.

It wasn't as if Diablo were any help. All the raven did was caw when Mal poked it. 'Where is it, huh, D? If you're back to life, then it can't be far, right? But where?' He'd poke her eyes out if she got close enough to let him. That stupid bird had always wanted her mother all to himself, and to him, Mal wasn't even a threat as much as a nuisance.

Still, it was more than just a bird that was haunting her now.

Maleficent's threats were hard to shake. As always, her mother knew exactly where to strike. She could find her daughter's soft spots as easily now as when she had been a baby with one on the top of her own head.

Don't you want to prove yourself to me?

Prove that you are worthy of the name I bestowed on you, Maleficent!

Mal turned over in her hard, squeaky bed, restless.

Yes, Mal was named for her mother, but her mother liked to say that since Mal had shown so far that she was only a tiny bit evil, Mal could only have a tiny bit of her real name until she proved herself truly worthy of her dark fairy heritage. Which was ridiculous, really, if you thought about it. Mal didn't exactly have an army of evil resources at her command. She made do with what she had to work with— stolen paint cans, hapless high-school kids, a wardrobe full of old mink coats and fur traps. Sure, maybe she wasn't encasing whole castles in hedges of thorns, but then every villain had to start somewhere, didn't they?

And if she had let Evie off the hook at the end of the night, that wasn't her fault either, was it? It wasn't like you could put a timeline on this kind of thing. Good scheming took a little planning, didn't it?

Mal turned over again.

It was still quiet in the Bargain Castle, which meant Maleficent hadn't gone out on the balcony yet to harangue and humiliate her subjects. When Mal finally slid out of bed, slithered into today's purple everything, and tiptoed out of her bedroom, she noticed that the door to her mother's room was locked, which meant Maleficent was not to be disturbed under any circumstance. She was adamant about getting eight hours of 'evil sleep' and recommended a healthy diet of nightmares to keep the claws sharp.

It had worked for her so far, hadn't it?

Mal brooded on her mother's warning as she hurried down the crumbling staircase.

The Dragon's Eye was cursed, as Maleficent had told her, which meant that anyone who touched it would immediately fall sleep for a thousand years. That had always been her mother's specialty—putting people to sleep against their will. Of course, that hadn't exactly worked out during the Sleeping Beauty debacle, but that didn't mean that the Dragon's Eye staff would be any less powerful now. When Mal found the sceptre she would have to take care not to touch it, and then to figure out a way to somehow bring it back without awakening the curse.

If it still works.
If I find it.

If it exists at all.

As Mal picked up her rucksack, she only felt worse. Even dumping an extra spray can into her bag didn't lift her spirits.

Maybe Jay was right.

Maybe this whole quest was too silly to even embark on. She didn't know where to begin to find her mother's lost weapon, no matter how powerful it once had been.

Who was she to think she could find something that had been lost for so long? Maybe she should just forget about it and go back to her usual routine of tagging and shoplifting.

Besides, it wasn't as if anything Mal could do would change how her mother saw her. Even if she did succeed in finding the Dragon's Eye, Mal knew she couldn't help who her father had been, and in the end that was what Maleficent could never forgive nor forget.

The one thing Mal herself could never fix.

So why bother?

Why try?

Maybe she should just accept it and move on. That's what her mother expected from her, anyway.

To fail. To disappoint. To give up. To give in.

Just like everyone else in this place.

Mal pulled open the castle door and set out for school, trying not to think about it.

chapter 14

Evil Enrichments

Like many nerds before him, Carlos liked school. He wasn't ashamed to admit it—he would have told as much to anyone who bothered to ask. Since no-one did, however, he reviewed the argument himself.

He liked the structure and the rules of school. He liked the work, too—answering the kinds of questions that had answers, and exploring the ones that didn't. While there were parts of school that were torture, like when he was forced to run the length of the tombs in gym (why practise *fleeing on foot* when they lived *on an island*?) or when he had to work with assigned partners (usually the kind who teased him for not being able to run the length of the tombs in gym), the other parts more than made up for it.

Those were the good parts—the parts where you actually used your brain—for which Carlos liked to think he was better equipped than the average villain.

And he was right.

Because Carlos De Vil's brain, by way of comparison, was almost as big as Cruella De Vil's fur-coat wardrobe.

That's what Carlos tried to tell himself, anyway, especially when people were making him run the tombs.

His first class today was Weird Science, one he always looked forward to. It was where he'd originally got the idea to put his machine together, from the lesson on radio waves. Carlos was not the only top student in the class—he was tied, in fact, with the closest thing he had to a rival in the whole school: the scrawny, bespectacled Reza.

Reza was the son of the former Royal Astronomer of Agrabah, who had consulted with Jafar to make sure the stars aligned on more than one nefarious occasion, which was how his family had found their way to the Isle of the Lost with everyone else.

Weird Science was the class where Carlos always worked the hardest. The presence of Reza, who was every bit as competitive in science lab as he was, only made Carlos work that much harder.

And as annoying as everyone found Reza to be—he always had to use the very biggest words for everything, whether they were used correctly and whether he was inserting a few extra syllables where they might or might not belong—he was still smart.

Very smart. Which meant Carlos enjoyed besting him. Just the other week they had been working on a special elixir, and Reza had been annoyed that Carlos had figured out the secret ingredient first.

Yeah, Reza was almost as smart as he was irritating. Even now he was raising his hand, waving it wildly back and forth.

Their professor, the powerful sorcerer Yen Sid, ignored him. Yen Sid had been sent to the Isle of the Lost from Auradon by King Beast to teach the villain kids how to live without magic and learn the magic of science instead. Carlos remarked once that it must have been a huge sacrifice for him to give up Auradon, but the crotchety old wizard shrugged and said that he didn't mind and that he had a responsibility to teach all children, good or bad.

Yen Sid resumed their lesson by quoting his favourite phrase, 'Any sufficiently advanced technology is indistinguishable from magic.' The secretive magician smiled from his lectern, his bald head glowing under the light, and his large grey beard covering half his chest. He had traded his sorcerer's robes for a chemist's white coat, now that there was no market in magic, and . . . well, no magic to speak of.

Reza raised his hand again. Once again, Yen Sid ignored him, and Carlos smiled to himself.

'Just because there is no magic on the Isle of the Lost does not mean we cannot make our own,' Yen Sid said. 'In fact, we can create everything we need for a spell right in this classroom. The answer to our situation is right in front of us. From fireworks to explosions, everything can be made from . . . *science*.'

'Except, science is boring,' said one of the Gastons.

'And also, what's that smell?' said the other Gaston, slapping his brother on the head. 'Because—you know—beans are the magical fruit.'

'Shut up,' Carlos hissed. He wanted to listen.

Reza's hand shot up again. *Me, me, me.*

'I'm talking about the *magic of science*,' Yen Sid said, ignoring both Gastons and Reza.

'Excuse me. Excuse me, professor?' Reza couldn't contain himself any longer. He was practically squeaking in his seat. Carlos snorted.

The professor sighed. 'What is it, Reza?'

Reza stood up. 'Irregardless, the irrelevancy of my classmates' simplistical commentation bears no meaningfulness to this experiment, in point of fact.'

'Thank you, Reza.' Yen Sid understood, as Carlos did, that Reza had just said the Gastons were stupid. Which was news to no-one at all.

Reza cleared his throat.

'If science is in fact magic, i.e., per se, could one then correspondingly and accordingly posit the postulate that magic is thus, ergo, to wit, also science, quid pro quo, *quod erat demonstrandum*, QED?'

Yen Sid rolled his eyes. Muffled snorts and snickers came from the rest of the class.

'Yes, Reza. Science could be described, in fact, as magic. From certain perspectives. But you don't have to take my word for it. Why don't you start today's experiment and find out for yourself—'

Reza's hand shot up again. The whole class started to laugh.

Yen Sid looked at him sternly. '—like your classmate Carlos here, who, instead of wasting time with more talk, is halfway done with the assignment?' He raised an eyebrow at Reza.

Reza's face turned red. The class laughed harder.

Today's lesson focused on engineering. Carlos' heart warmed as he bent over his desk and applied himself to the task of learning how to make a robotic broom that swept by itself.

It was the solution to his earlier problem. With this invention, he would be able to clean Hell Hall in a jiffy. He even had a name for it: the Broomba.

The Gastons grumbled, but Carlos couldn't even hear them. Not when he was working. He tightened a screw on the motor of his broom.

This was the *real* magic.

By the end of the first lesson, it wasn't just Carlos who was happy to be back in school. Evie was glad she had decided to show up as well. For one thing, she didn't see any sign of Mal, and for another thing, it was empowering to realise that while her mother might never think she was pretty enough, she was certainly pretty enough for her Selfies Seminar, which only a few students from Selfies 101 were allowed to take. As it turned out, she could have taught the class herself.

'These are amazing!' Mother Gothel gushed as she looked over Evie's homework. The class had been ordered to produce a series of self-portraits, and Evie had spent the hours before Carlos' party hard at work on her portfolio, taking pictures of herself. Beauty required effort, didn't it? Wasn't that what her mother always said?

And, since her mother had made her so aware of every angle and every trick of light and cosmetics, Evie had the best photographs. (Truthfully, this class was nothing; by the time Evie could hold a hairbrush, she had known how to make herself seem 10 times more beautiful than she really was.)

It's all smoke and mirrors, she thought, wincing at the word *mirror*. That's how you get to be the fairest of them all.

She tried to ignore the other girls in the class, the step-granddaughters especially, who looked daggers at her.

'It's as if you spend *every second* staring at your own

reflection!' Mother Gothel marvelled. 'Now, that is a feat of self-centredness!'

Evie smiled. 'Why, thank you. I do try.'

'Your mother must be so proud,' Mother Gothel said, handing back the photos.

Evie only nodded.

After failing his Evil World History exam, Jay ducked to hide from an evil step-granddaughter, who waved to him coquettishly, making him late for his Enrichment class. He slipped into the shadows behind a statue in the stairwell.

Oh no.

It wasn't as if he hadn't enjoyed dancing with her last night; he liked dancing with her fine, and stealing girls' hearts was practically a hobby. But it wasn't as fun as stealing other things, since hearts came with too many strings attached. And it certainly didn't pay as well.

Besides, Jay liked his freedom.

'Jayyyyyy,' her voice sing-songed down the hall. 'Oh, Jayyyyy, I think you might have something of my grandmother's that I need back. I'm very, very angry at you, you bad boy,' she said, not sounding angry at all.

But Jay wouldn't come out of his hiding place behind the statue of Evil Dragon Maleficent. The stone monstrosity, commissioned by Maleficent herself, took up more than half the landing between the school's second and third basement levels, and had become one of Jay's most reliable hiding spots. Soon his predatory dance date gave up the search.

'Phew, that was close.' He slid out of hiding and fell into step with Carlos, who frowned at him without looking up from his book as he walked.

'Closer than all the other times?'

'Yeah . . . no. Not really.' Jay sighed.

Carlos turned the page, and the two boys headed into Enrichment without saying another word.

Enrichment was literally about enriching oneself by taking from others. The class studied lock-picking techniques, shoplifting secrets—which meant it was Jay's favourite class for the obvious reason, being a thief and all—and today's guest lecturer was none other than the school's creepy headmaster himself, Dr Facilier.

'There are many kinds of thieves,' Dr Facilier said in his silky whisper. 'One can shoplift at the bazaar, or burglarise a home, or steal a rickshaw. But these are, of course, petty exercises. Mere child's play.'

Jay wanted to argue. After all, he had Dr Facilier's tie in his pocket, didn't he? *What are you calling child's play, old man?*

'But a true villain has larger ambitions—to steal an identity, a fortune—someone's entire life! Can someone give me an example of such villainy? Such great enrichment?' The good doctor surveyed the room. 'Yes, Carlos?'

'My mother wanted to steal 101 puppies!' Carlos said, almost in a yelp. 'That was large.'

'Yes, and that was an extravagantly evil dream.' Dr Facilier smiled and everyone in the room shuddered at the sight. 'Anyone else? Examples?'

'My mother stole Rapunzel's magic to keep herself young?' Ginny Gothel offered. 'Rapunzel had really . . . large . . . hair?'

'You have a point there. A very good example surely, of enriching oneself through the abuse of others,' Dr Facilier said, nodding. He walked over to the blackboard. 'Now, I understand that the advanced students among you have your project for Evil Schemes due.'

A few heads nodded, including Jay's and Carlos'.

'My own evil scheme was the height of enrichment. Does anyone know it?'

The room was silent. Dr Facilier looked insulted. He muttered something about "kids these days" and resumed his lecture.

'For my evil scheme, I turned Prince Naveen into a frog, and voodoo'd his valet to look like him. My plan was for his valet to marry Charlotte La Bouff, and once he did, I would kill her father and take his fortune. If I had succeeded, I would have stolen a man's identity and another man's fortune. A stroke of enrichment!'

The class clapped. A beaming Dr Facilier bowed, stiffly and quickly.

'Except you failed,' Carlos pointed out, when the room was silent again.

'Yes,' Dr Facilier brooded, his face falling. 'That's true. I failed. Disastrously, unfortunately and decidedly. I was a complete and utter failure. I won neither the princess nor the fortune. Hence, the founding of Dragon Hall, where we must learn from our failures and teach the next generation of villains to do what we were not able to do.'

Harriet Hook raised her hand. 'What's that?'

'Prepare! Research! Be more evil! Work faster! Think bigger!' Dr Facilier urged. 'So that when the time comes, when the dome falls, and magic is returned to us—and it will be, my children, it will be; evil like us cannot be contained—you will be ready.'

Jay scribbled on his notepad. *Be more evil. Think bigger.*

The big score.

Once again, his thoughts went back to the Dragon's Eye. It was Maleficent's sceptre, and the quest for its recovery was Mal's mission. It wasn't his quest, and it wasn't his problem.

But what if it was?

What if it should be?

Mal had asked him to help, and he had blown her off. But what if he told her that he *would* help her? And what if, when they did find it, he stole it right from under her nose? He would be stealing a fortune and her identity as Maleficent's heir all in one swoop, just like Dr Facilier.

And what if, by chance, it still worked?

His father would finally have his big score. Jay would have his evil scheme. Between the two of them, they'd find a way off the Isle of Lost, Leftover and Forgotten.

They didn't belong there any more, did they?

Jay smiled. He would enrich himself, all right. All the way to becoming the Master of Darkness.

By lunchtime, the rest of the school was still talking about last night's epic howler at Hell Hall, but Mal had no interest. The party was the past; she'd moved on.

She had bigger things to worry about now. All she could think about was how her mother wanted the Dragon's Eye back. And how Maleficent wouldn't see her as anything other than her father's daughter—in other words, a pathetic, soft human—until Mal could prove her wrong.

Mal kept reliving last night's conversation over and over, so that she missed her first few classes and sleepwalked through the rest. She arrived for her one-on-one after-school seminar with Lady Tremaine still feeling anxious and out of sorts.

'Hi, Professor Tremaine, you wanted to see me about my year-long evil scheme?' she asked, knocking on the open door to the faculty tombs.

Lady Tremaine looked up from her desk with a thin smile. 'Yes, come in and shut the door, please.' A full thermos of curdled wine sat on the desk in front of her, which didn't bode well. Lady Tremaine only drank sour wine when she was in a sour mood.

Mal knew she was in trouble, but she did as she was told and sat across from her teacher. 'So what's up?'

Lady Tremaine snorted. '"What's up" is this . . . sad excuse for a year-long evil scheme. A grudge against one girl? Party tricks? Pranks? This is beneath you, Mal. I expected more from you. You're my best student.' She reached for her wine and sipped it, making an appropriately disgusted face.

You expected more? You and everyone else on this island, Mal thought sullenly. *Get in line.*

'What's wrong with my evil scheme?' she asked.

'It's just not evil enough,' sniffed Lady Tremaine.

Mal sighed.

Lady Tremaine glared. 'I need you to really put your dark heart and foul soul into it. Come up with a truly wicked scheme. One that will bring you to the depths of depravity and heights of wicked greatness of which I know you're capable.'

Mal kicked the desk and frowned. She'd thought her evil scheme was pretty wicked. 'Like what? And how do you know what wicked greatness I'm capable of, anyway?'

'You are Mal, daughter of Maleficent! Who doesn't know that?' Lady Tremaine shook her head.

You'd be surprised, Mal thought.

Lady Tremaine continued to sip her wine. 'I'm sure you'll come up with something, dear. You are your mother's daughter, after all. I expect something truly horrid and legendary for your evil scheme. Something that will go down in *history*,' Lady Tremaine said, returning Mal's paper to her. 'I'll give you a minute to brainstorm, if that helps.'

Mal looked down at the proposal she'd originally written. At first, she bristled at the criticism. She didn't want to hear it.

What was wrong with this? It was evil, pure evil. And it was *bad*, wasn't it? Taking down a princess—that wasn't exactly a nice thing to do. She was going to make Evie pay, wasn't she?

And a vendetta, that was a time-honoured evil scheme, wasn't it?

Classic villainy? What was wrong with that?

Mal wanted to crumple the paper in her hand. She didn't have time for this. She had other things on her mind . . . her mother and the Dragon's Eye, for one, that stupid cursed sceptre . . .

Hey, wait a minute . . .

What did my mother say about the Dragon's Eye?

Whoever touches the sceptre will be cursed to fall asleep for a thousand years.

Maleficent had only cursed Aurora's kingdom to fall asleep for a *hundred* years after Sleeping Beauty had pricked her finger on a spinning wheel. This curse put the victim to sleep for a *thousand*.

That was like, 10 *times* more evil, unless her maths was off. Anyway, *much* more evil. *Plus or minus a few zeroes.*

Maybe she should embark on this quest, after all.

And if somehow, along the way, she made it happen that *Evie* was the one who would touch the Dragon's Eye . . .

Well, that would be the nastiest, wickedest plan the Isle would ever witness! A two-for-one! No, a triple play—

She'd take out the princess and win her own mother's respect—as well as the school's evil-scheme competition—all at once.

Lady Tremaine was right. All these little petty tricks she had planned to play on Evie were nothing compared to *this*. If Mal sent Evie to sleep for a thousand years—well, what could be nastier than that? Or, more to the point, *who*?

'I've got it!' Mal said, jumping up from her chair and giving the startled Lady Tremaine a big hug, despite her better judgement (and Lady Tremaine's breath). 'Something *so* evil, no-one has seen it before—or ever will again!'

'Wonderful, child! It makes me so happy to see you so wicked,' sniffed Lady Tremaine, bringing a hankie to her eye. 'It brings me hope for our future. Except for, you know, that *hug*.'

Mal smiled triumphantly. Even a sappy hug couldn't get to her now. She couldn't wait to get started. Evil waited for no-one. Her mind started turning.

She couldn't very well embark on an evil quest alone. If she were going to look for a needle in a haystack, or the

Dragon's Eye on the island, she would need minions, her own henchmen to command, just like her mother had. She would have to put together a strike team—plus, it would be easier to get Evie to come with her if she were part of a group.

But where would she get minions of her own? Of course, there were always Maleficent's henchmen's kids. Except those boar-like guys stank too much; and as for the goblins and jackals—well, who would run the Slop Shop? Also, as she'd noted before, she didn't speak Goblin. Besides, her mother kept harping on about how useless they'd been during the whole Curse-Sleeping-Beauty mission.

Pass.

Mal would have to find her own team. Her own crew of right-hand-men and one yes-woman in particular.

Where to start?

She'd need someone who knew the island back and forth, upside down and sideways.

Someone who could be counted on if they met any trouble, being a whole lot of trouble himself. Someone who knew how to get his hands on what he wanted.

She just had to convince him to join her.

Maybe she could promise him some kind of reward or something.

It was already dark when she left school and went straight to Jafar's Junk Shop.

chapter 15

Thick as Thieves

Mal tossed pebbles on the junk shop's window so that they clattered on the sill. 'Jay! Are you there?' she shout-whispered. 'Jay! Come out! I want to talk to you!' She hurled a few more stones again.

'Who's making that infernal noise? Doesn't anyone know how to ring a doorbell these days?' Jafar demanded as he pushed the window open and stuck his head out. He was about to unleash a string of curses when he saw who was standing outside. 'Oh, my dear Mal,' he said, his voice still as silky as when he had been advising the Sultan. 'How may I be of service?'

Mal was about to apologise when she remembered dark fairies are *never* sorry. 'I'm looking for Jay,' she said, trying to sound as commanding as her mother.

'Why, yes, of course,' Jafar said. 'I will let him know. Please, come inside.' There was a pause, and then Jafar bellowed in a booming voice, 'JAY! MAL WANTS YOU!'

'THERE IN A SEC!' Jay yelled back.

'What's the deal with villains and birds?' asked Mal, entering the junk shop and finding Iago on Jafar's shoulder. She thought of how Maleficent showered Diablo with so much affection.

'Excuse me?' Jafar asked, while Iago narrowed his beady eyes at Mal.

'Nothing.'

Jay appeared. 'Oh, hey, Mal, funny you're here, I was just about to head over your way. We should talk more about that—'

'That homework assignment,' Mal said, shooting dagger looks at him. Nobody else could know about the Dragon's Eye.

'Right, yeah. Homework. Thanks, Dad, I'll take it from here,' Jay said, indicating pointedly for his dad to leave.

Jafar pulled his robe round him and huffed, Iago squawking and flying behind him.

'Is there somewhere we can talk?' Mal asked when she and Jay were finally alone.

Jay motioned to the junk shop. 'What's wrong with here?'

Mal looked around the messy shop, noticing a few things that were hers in the pile and taking them back without comment. She supposed it was as good a place as any—and, seriously, what was she hiding, anyway? It wasn't as if anyone else would steal Maleficent's Dragon's Eye. Who would be dumb enough to do that . . .?

She squinted at Jay, who was inspecting a beaker that he'd pulled from his pocket. His dark eyes shone with mischief.

'Where'd you get that?' she asked. 'What is it?'

'I dunno. Reza had it in his bag. He was all protective about it, so I took it,' Jay explained with a sly smile.

Mal made an impatient gesture. She couldn't wait to get started and couldn't afford to get distracted. 'Listen, I know you don't think we can, but we need to figure out how to find that Dragon's Eye. I mean, it does command all of the forces of darkness when it works. And, who knows? Magic might return to the island one day.'

Jay raised his eyebrows. 'Yeah—I was just about to say the same thing.'

'Really?' she asked, shocked that he had taken so little convincing. She began to get a tad suspicious.

Jay blew on his nails. 'Yeah. I mean, come on, if it's really here, we need to get our hands on it. But are you sure your mother's right? I mean, she is a little crazy in the horn-head.'

Mal rolled her eyes. 'You can't deny Diablo's back. He was frozen in stone, but he's alive now. He's already eaten almost everything in our cupboards.'

'Whoa.'

'I know, right?'

'Iago's the same. I think he eats more than me and Dad combined.'

They shared a chuckle.

'Okay, great—I was hoping to start searching as soon as possible,' Mal said, willing to overlook the possibility that Jay was only agreeing to help for his own selfish motives. She could handle him.

Jay was about to say something when he turned round, his reflexes swift and suspicious. 'What's that noise?' he asked, just as the door to the back room crashed down and Jafar tumbled through, Iago sitting on his stomach.

'I told you that you were too fat to lean on that door!' Iago scolded.

Jafar made a valiant attempt to take back his dignity, and pulled himself up to stand and brush the dust and detritus from his hair. 'Oh, we were just about to ask if the two of you wanted dinner, weren't we, Iago? But we couldn't help but overhear . . . forgive me if we are wrong, but did you say that Maleficent's Dragon's Eye sceptre is lost somewhere on this island?' Jafar asked, his dark eyes gleaming.

Mal narrowed her eyes at Jay, mentally berating him for not having found a suitable place for them to talk privately. But it was clear that it was too late, and Jafar already knew everything.

Jafar looked solemnly at the two teenagers in front of him. 'Follow me, it's time we had a real conversation.'

He led them to his private sitting room in the back of the shop, a cosy den full of jewel-toned curtains and Oriental rugs, tufted satin pillows and brass lamps and sconces that gave it a mournful, exotic, desert air. Jafar took a seat on one of the long, low sofas and motioned for them to make themselves comfortable on the ottomans. 'When I was released from my genie bottle and brought here to this cursed island, while I was whizzing through the air, I saw what looked at first like just an ordinary forest but upon closer observation was actually a black castle covered in thorns.'

'Another castle?' Mal asked. 'Covered in thorns, you say? But that would mean . . . that's . . .'

Her mother's true castle. The Bargain Castle was a rental. It wasn't their true home. *The Forbidden Fortress.* Wasn't that what her mother's real home was called? Mal had never paid enough attention, but it certainly sounded familiar. And where else could it be but the Isle of the Lost?

Jafar pulled on his raggedy beard. 'Yes. But I'm afraid I can't be sure of exactly where it is, though. This island is far larger than you think, and you could look forever and never find it, especially if it is hidden in the forbidden zone.' *Nowhere*, as it was called by the citizens of the Isle.

'Never!' repeated Iago with a ruffle of his feathers.

Jay nodded. 'That's what I said.'

'I had completely forgotten about seeing the fortress until now, when you mentioned Diablo's return and his testimony that he saw the Dragon's Eye himself,' said Jafar. 'And if the fortress is on the island, perhaps it's not all that's hidden in the mist.'

'But why would it be here?' Jay asked, leaning forwards on his knees and looking at his father intently.

'These things were too dangerous to keep in Auradon. And with magic made impossible by the dome, they are harmless now. But if we were to take back what is rightfully ours, perhaps we might have a chance against that invisible barrier one day.'

'Diablo swears the Dragon's Eye has sparked back to life. Which means that maybe the shield is not as impenetrable as we thought,' said Mal. 'But we're still stuck with not knowing exactly where it is. There's not exactly a map to Nowhere.'

'We can try the Athenaeum of Evil,' said Jay promptly.

'The Anthe-what of Evil?'

'The Library of Forbidden Secrets in Dragon Hall—

you know, that locked door that no-one's supposed to go into. The one with the big spider guarding it.'

Mal shook her head. 'You really think that's anything? I always thought it was just a way to keep the first-years out of Dr Facilier's office.'

'Well, we have to start somewhere. And I remember Dr F mentioning in Enrichment that the library contains information about the history of the island.'

'Since when do you pay attention in class?' Mal asked disgustedly.

'Listen, you want my help, or not?'

Jay had a point. It was a start, and she'd learned more about the island in one evening at the junk shop than she had in 16 years. 'All right.'

'We'll go tomorrow, bright and early,' Jay said cheerfully. 'Meet at the bazaar for supplies first, as soon as the market opens.'

Mal made a face. She hated getting up early. 'What's wrong with tonight?'

'The orchestra's playing a concert tonight, there will be too many people around. Tomorrow's Saturday: no-one will be there. Easier.'

Mal sighed. 'Fine. By the way, thanks for your help, Jafar.'

'My pleasure,' Jafar said with a crooked smile. 'Goodnight.'

• • •

When Mal had gone, Jay felt his father slither up to him and dig his fingers into his sleeve. 'What's up?' he asked, even though he already knew.

'The Dragon's Eye,' Jafar cooed.

'I know, I know.' Jay nodded. It would be the biggest score of the year.

'I would hate to think you're betraying your friend,' Jafar said with a sorrowful look on his face.

'Don't worry, Dad. None of us has any friends,' Jay scoffed. 'Least of all, Mal.'

As they'd agreed, the next morning Jay met Mal at the crowded marketplace so they could 'pick up' (read *swipe*) supplies for their journey to find the fortress. Jay hung back and snatched a bunch of fruit from a couple of tents while Mal stopped at a fortune-teller's stand and traded a stolen pair of only *slightly* chipped earrings for a tattered pack of tarot cards.

'What are those for?' Jay asked.

'No-one's allowed into the library, right? Where all those documents are locked up and sealed . . .'

'And the only person who has the key is Dr F, and he loves tarot cards.'

'Glad to see you're awake,' Mal replied.

'So, how sure are you about this whole thing? I mean, a little sure? A lot sure? Just-want-something-to-do sure?' asked Jay, juggling a few bruised peaches.

'I don't know. But I have to at least *try* to find the fortress, especially if the Dragon's Eye is there. Also, don't you think it's weird that we've never left the village? I mean, this island's pretty small, and we've never even *tried* to look around.'

'What's there to look at? You said it yourself—we're probably heading for Nowhere.'

'But if somehow there's a map of the island in the library, we'll know exactly *where* in Nowhere we should be heading to find the fortress. There's something out there, beyond the village. I know it.'

'But say we do get a hold of the Dragon's Eye and it can't *do* anything?' Jay asked.

'Diablo swears that it sparked to life!'

'But how? There's no magic on the Isle. Nada.'

'Well, maybe there's a hole in the dome, or something,' said Mal.

'A hole?' scoffed Jay.

'I told you, I don't know; all I know is that the raven swears he saw it spark, and my mother wants me to fetch it, like I'm an errand girl. If you're too chicken to come with me, then go back and steal some more stuff for your junk shop,' Mal said, annoyed.

'I'm not chicken!'

'Yeah—more like a parrot,' said Mal.

Jay sighed. She had him there. 'Fine,' he grumbled. 'Maybe you're right: maybe there *is* a hole.'

chapter 16

Lifelong Frenemies

Mal's and Jay's squabbling voices carried throughout the marketplace, and Evie couldn't help but overhear. She was at the bazaar for her first-ever shopping trip. Since nothing had befallen Evie for having left the castle and gone to school, Evil Queen was more convinced than ever that Maleficent had forgotten about their banishment, or at least didn't care that they had returned. Evil Queen was so excited to be back in the village, she was running from shopfront to shopfront, saying hello to everyone and filling her cart with all sorts of age-defying elixirs and new beauty regimens.

Evie squinted at their faces. Mal was scowling and Jay looked annoyed, as per usual. Was she imagining it, or did she hear them say something about a hole in the magical barrier? The memory of that burst of light that had shot out of Carlos' invention the night of the party came to her quickly.

'Are you guys talking about a hole in the dome?' she asked, coming up to the two of them.

Mal looked up suspiciously, but when she saw Evie, her voice turned thick as honey. 'Why, Evie! You're just the person I've been looking for,' she said.

'She is?' Jay asked, confused.

'Yes, she is,' Mal said definitively. 'Now, what were you saying about the dome?'

Evie wondered if she should tell them what she knew. She knew she couldn't trust Mal, and she had an inkling that Jay was behind her missing poison-heart necklace. She hadn't seen it since the party and suspected he'd lifted it when he'd taken her cloak that evening.

'Nothing,' she said.

'Tell us,' urged Jay, crossing his arms.

'Why should I?' Evie sniffed. Mal had trapped her in a wardrobe! And Jay wasn't any better, really—the little thief.

'Because,' Jay said. Then he was stumped. 'Um. Because if you don't, Mal will curse you?' he added, even though he didn't sound convinced himself.

'If you haven't noticed, there's no magic on this island,' Evie said huffily.

'Not yet,' said Mal. 'But there may be one day.' She took Evie's arm in hers and whispered, 'Look, I know we didn't start off on the right foot, but I think we should let bygones be bygones. It's a small island, and we shouldn't be enemies.'

'Really?'

'Totally,' said Mal with her sweetest smile.

Evie knew Mal wasn't being sincere, but she was intrigued enough to play along with it.

She was about to tell her what she knew about the dome when Evil Queen burst out of Bits and Bobs, wearing a jet-black velour tracksuit with QUEEN embroidered across her derriere. 'Evie! I've got some new eye shadow for you! Oh!' she said, when she saw Evie wasn't alone. 'If it isn't Mal!' she added nervously. 'How are you, dear? How's your mother? Is she here? Is she still mad at me?'

'Uh . . .' Mal blinked.

Evie wished her mother would stop talking, but of course that was a fruitless wish. Her mother continued to babble on nervously. 'Tell your mother to come round and see me sometime. I'd be happy to give her a makeover! I've seen her photos in the paper. She's looking a bit green lately. She needs a stronger foundation,' Evil Queen said.

'I'll, uh, let her know,' Mal said.

'You do that, sweetheart! And if I may say so, your

purple hair is fabulous! It really brings out your cheekbones!' Evil Queen gushed.

'Thank you? I guess?' said Mal, who looked distinctly uncomfortable.

Jay laughed. 'Take the compliment, Mal. Sorry, Evil Queen, Mal isn't used to compliments. You know Maleficent has no interest in beauty unless it can be used to persuade someone into doing her will.'

'Right. Let's go, Evie,' said her mother.

'Oh, can Evie hang out with us?' asked Mal with a syrupy smile. 'We were just about to grab a few unhealthy snacks from the Slop Shop.'

Evie was torn. On the one hand, she knew she should stay away from Mal if she wanted to be safe, but on the other, she never got to hang out with kids her age.

Evil Queen nodded. 'Sure! I'll see you at home, sweetie.' As she left, she mouthed, 'Reapply your lip gloss!'

When her mother had disappeared into the crowd, Evie picked up the conversation where they had left off. 'You guys want to know about the hole in the dome or not?'

Mal and Jay exchanged glances. 'Of course we do,' they chorused.

Evie shrugged. 'Well, something happened the night of the party that may have something to do with the dome.'

'Is that right?' asked Mal with a raised eyebrow.

'You need to talk to Carlos,' said Evie. 'He knows what

happened.' She shivered from the memory, at the bright light that had emanated from that little machine. For a second there, she had worried that they had broken the universe somehow. She still remembered the vibrant, sharp feeling of electricity in the air. It had felt like . . . magic.

'Carlos? Why? What does he have to do with anything?' Mal demanded as they passed a tent selling colourful scarves, and Jay practised his parkour by running across the walls and rooftops.

'Because he was the one that did it,' said Evie.

'Did what?'

'Punched a hole in the dome.'

Jay barked a laugh and dropped down next to them. 'Yeah, right—as if that little guy can punch anything. Come on, Mal. We've got work to do.' He began to turn away.

Evie stared at Mal. Mal stared at Evie.

'I'm not lying,' she said to Mal.

'I didn't think you were,' said Mal, her green eyes flashing. Evie met them with her calm blue ones. Finally Mal said, 'Okay.'

'You actually believe her?' Jay gawked, sounding right then like Iago.

'I think we need to check it all out,' said Mal.

'But we're heading to Dragon Hall,' said Jay.

'No, we'll head towards Hell Hall first. I want to talk to Carlos,' Mal decided. 'And you're coming with us, Evie.'

Evie didn't argue with that. Something big was going down. Something had started, the night that Carlos had turned on that machine. And against her better judgement, Evie wanted to see how it would end.

So, onwards to Hell Hall they went; but now the twosome was three.

chapter 17

Do You Believe in Magic?

One more day of freedom before his mother came home. Carlos surveyed his domain. Considering that it had been the headquarters of a rather epic party earlier in the week, it didn't look too bad. The Broomba had worked wonders. Then again, the place always was a bit of a wreck, so who would notice?

The iron knight who towered over the staircase was as solid as ever, the curtains just as heavy and dusty, the faded wallpaper and the holes in the walls lending just that ruined touch that other decorators on the island tried to copy, to no avail.

Carlos was enjoying the rare, relative peace in his house when it was shattered by the sound of the front door knocker pounding so hard, he was sure its booming echo could be heard across the entire island.

He opened the door, then slammed it shut when he saw who was on his doorstep. 'Go away, Mal—haven't you done enough?' he yelled from inside the house.

'Open up! It's important!' Jay demanded.

'No!'

'Carlos!' That was Evie's voice. 'Something happened with that machine of yours the other night. Something big!'

Wait—what? Evie had told them about his invention? But she had promised! He cracked open the door the tiniest bit so that only his left eye was showing. 'You told them what happened?' he said accusingly. 'I trusted you!'

Evie pleaded, 'Come on, open up! I brought you a pillow!'

Carlos opened the door grudgingly. 'Fine. You guys can come in. But don't even think of locking anyone in the wardrobe this time, Mal!' He turned to Evie. 'Is it made of goose down?' he asked excitedly. He hadn't really believed she would bring him one.

'Yup, the vultures who brought it said the goblin who found it swore it's from one of the Auradon castles,' Evie said, handing him a pillow in a blue-silk pillowcase with a royal insignia.

He accepted the pillow and led them into the sitting room, pushed some deflated black balloons off the sofa, and glowered at them. 'Well, what did my machine do?' he asked.

Mal raised an eyebrow, and he immediately regretted his tone of voice. 'I mean, care to enlighten me?' he asked.

'Evie?' prompted Mal.

Evie took a deep breath. 'Okay, so the night of the party, Carlos switched on this machine he's invented—it's a box that looks for some kind of signal that lets you watch other TV shows—right, Carlos?'

Carlos nodded. 'And music, and lots of other things, through radio waves.'

'So when he turned it on that night, it let out this huge blast of light!' she said breathlessly. 'And it burned a hole right through the tree-house roof! Then we saw it go right through the dome!'

Carlos nodded.

'And the TV suddenly came alive with all these colours! And there were a bunch of new shows! Not just the usual *Dungeon Deals* and *King Beast's Fireside Chats*!'

'But how does that prove it broke through the dome?' asked Mal, who looked sceptical, and Carlos couldn't blame her. He hardly believed it himself.

'Because we've never seen those shows before! Which means the signal didn't come from the relay station on the

Isle of the Lost. Which means it had to have come from a forbidden network on Auradon . . .' said Evie.

'Which means . . .' Carlos prodded.

'The blast broke through the dome. For a second,' Evie finished triumphantly.

Mal turned to Carlos. 'You really think that your machine did that?'

'It might've,' he admitted.

'Do you think there's a possibility it let magic in, and not just radio waves?'

'*Magic* in? I don't know. Why? Do you know something we don't?' There had to be a reason Mal was here. She had to have some kind of angle on this. Mal never paid any attention to anyone unless she wanted something. What did she want?

He could see her weighing her options. Would she tell them? She didn't know him very well except to tease him, and from what he'd observed so far, Mal wasn't fond of Evie in the least. Jay might be in on it—he had to be, otherwise *he* wouldn't be here.

'Fine. I'll tell you guys,' Mal said finally. 'Jay already knows. But this has to stay between us. And, Evie, no hidden backsies.'

Evie put up her hands in protest.

'Okay, so the night of the party, my mother's raven, Diablo—who'd been turned into stone by the three so-called "good" fairies 20 years ago—came back to life. And Diablo swears he saw the Dragon's Eye, my mother's missing sceptre, spark to life as well.'

Carlos stared at her and no-one spoke for a moment.

'But that would mean . . .' Carlos said, his eyes blinking rapidly as if he couldn't believe what he was hearing.

'Magic! That magic had been able to penetrate the dome for a second!' Jay said excitedly. He had been silent until now, looking around Hell Hall most likely to see if he had missed pocketing anything good from the other night.

Carlos himself was still trying to process what Mal had told them. It was one thing to get to watch new television shows, but it was quite another to hear that *magic* had penetrated the invisible barrier, and that Maleficent's missing sceptre—the most powerful dark weapon in the universe—had been brought back to life.

'Yes,' said Mal. 'Diablo swears it's true. And so now my mother has tasked me with getting the Dragon's Eye back. Just in case it happens again, the magic returning. So that *this* time, she'll be ready.'

Jay coughed. 'And so, um, we should get on the road, Mal, before it gets too late,' he said. 'You know I hate to miss a meal.'

Carlos could sympathise with that, especially since meals came so rarely.

'Wait a minute. Before we go, I want to see this box of his,' Mal said, motioning to Carlos.

Carlos was about to argue but decided it was wiser to let Mal have her way. 'All right,' he said. 'Let me go get it.' He ran through the safe way into his mother's wardrobe and returned with the machine.

He handed it to Mal, who inspected it closely. She shook it, put it up to her ear, and shrugged. It looked just like a regular box to her, nothing special, and certainly not powerful enough to break through the dome.

'Can you make it work again?' she asked.

'I haven't tried.'

'Try.'

He hesitated for a moment, then fiddled with a few knobs and looked fearfully up at the ceiling. 'Okay. Here we go.' He pressed the switch.

Nothing happened.

He tried again.

Again, nothing.

He shook his head. 'Sorry. Maybe it was just a one-time deal.'

Mal crossed her arms, looking stymied. Carlos knew that look—it meant she was about to explode. What if Mal thought they were just pulling her leg? Letting her think they had made a discovery, when all along they were just making fun of her? He had to think of something . . .

'Wanna see the hole in the ceiling?' he offered. If Mal wanted proof, he could give her proof.

Mal thought about it for a minute. 'Sure, why not?'

Carlos took them to his tree house, and the four of them inspected the ceiling. It was definitely there, a perfectly round, tiny black hole.

'Rad,' pronounced Jay, bumping fists with Carlos.

Carlos grinned proudly. He was still hugging his new pillow. He was looking forward to trying it out soon. Would he actually sleep through the night for once without tossing and turning?

Mal peered up at the ceiling. 'I don't know how much I believe your little invention actually blasted a hole in the invisible dome, but Jay's right—we should get going.'

Carlos sighed, unsure of whether to be relieved or distressed. Mal was about to leave the room when the black box on his desk suddenly began to beep.

Beep.

Beep.

Mal turned round and stared at it. 'Why's it doing that?' she asked.

Carlos ran over to check. 'I don't know, but it's been beeping on and off since it blew a hole in the roof and the dome.'

'Maybe it's looking for a signal?' said Evie excitedly. 'Maybe it senses something.'

'Like what?' he asked, looking down at his invention with something like awe. He never thought it would really work. But if Diablo was right, then this thing of his might have actually broken the magical barrier. And now Evie was hinting at something more? He'd only hoped to get a glimpse of the outside world, not bring magic back into the island.

'Yeah, what do you mean, Evie?' asked Mal.

'Like maybe now it senses the Dragon's Eye! You said it's never done this before. Maybe it's because that's never happened before. It's never had anything to talk to,' Evie said, rather astutely.

'You think it could be communicating with the Dragon's Eye?' asked Mal.

'Like a compass. Or a homing beacon,' said Jay. His eyes gleamed as he studied the machine hungrily, and Carlos put a protective hand on his invention. Jay was most likely already calculating how much he could get for something like it at the shop.

'Could be,' said Evie.

'She might actually have a point,' said Carlos.

'A homing beacon,' echoed Mal.

'I was just guessing,' said Evie. 'I don't know anything about anything.' Carlos wanted to tell her that she was selling herself short, when he realised that he always did the same thing.

'No, you don't,' said Mal sharply. 'But you're still coming with us.'

Evie jumped back. 'With you? Where? I agreed to come to Carlos', but . . .' She shook her head and tugged her cloak tightly round her shoulders. 'I'm not going anywhere.'

'No way, you have to help us find the Eye,' said Mal.

'You're a natural at this. You're so good at it. I need help, and you want to help me, don't you? Don't you want to be my friend? I want to be yours, Evie.'

'Oh I—I don't know . . .'

'Shush! It's settled. And I'll take this, thank you very much,' Mal said, reaching for the box.

'No way!' Carlos said, as Mal tried to pull it from him.

Mal tugged it to her side. 'Let go, Carlos!' she growled.

He yanked it back. She was not taking it. He'd made it himself!

Mal glared. 'I mean it! Let go, or you'll be sorry!'

Carlos shook his head, trembling all over.

'Fine. You win. Keep the box, Carlos, but you have to come with us if you do!' Mal ordered.

'Come again? Go with you—where?' No way. He wasn't going anywhere. Especially anywhere dangerous.

Mal told him about the Forbidden Fortress hidden on the island and where it might be and how they had to find it.

'Nope, I'm not going to Nowhere! I'm staying right here,' Carlos said, crossing his arms.

'You'll do what I say, you little . . .' threatened Mal.

Carlos opened his mouth to argue, but thought better of it. In the end, it was *Maleficent* who wanted to reclaim her sceptre, not just Mal, and if word ever got back to the Mistress of Darkness that he had opposed or hindered the search in any way, he might as well *start* calling himself Slop, because that's what he would be.

'Okay fine, I'll go. But only if Evie goes too,' he said.

'Evie?' asked Mal. 'You're coming, aren't you, lovely?'

Evie sighed. 'Fine,' she said. 'Fine. I guess I'll come. Beats looking in the mirror all day for flaws.'

'So we're good, then?' asked Jay. 'Four of us looking for the Dragon's Eye?'

'I guess so. And I guess I want to know what this thing really did,' said Carlos. 'If it really *did* burn a hole in the dome and let magic into the island.'

As if in answer, the machine beeped.

Beep!

Mal nodded. 'All right, then, let's go. We've got a library to break into and a map to find.'

'Not *just* yet,' Carlos said, raising a hand. 'We can't go anywhere until my chores are done. And it's laundry day.'

chapter 18

Once Upon a Dream

Her mother was a famous beauty in a land of famous beauties, and so it was only to be expected that Princess Audrey, daughter of Aurora, was gifted with the same lilting voice, lovely thick hair, swan-like neck, and deep, dark eyes that could drown a prince in their warm embrace.

Like a kitten scenting catnip—or perhaps like an isle of banished former villains sensing magic—a young prince could hardly be expected to resist such sparkly, dimpled charms. In point of fact, Princess Audrey, like her mother before her, was exactly the sort of princess who gave princesses their rather princessy reputation—right down to her very last perfect curl and the last crystal stitched into her silken gown.

And so it was to Princess Audrey that Prince Ben went the next day, to lick his wounds and seek some comfort after the disastrous meeting of the King's Council—like the discouraged, catnip-seeking kitten he was.

'It's such a mess,' he told her as they walked around the garden of the "Cottage", as Aurora and Phillip's grand castle was nicknamed, after King Hubert had declared that the 40-room palace was a mere starter home for the royal newlyweds.

'Starter home?' Aurora had said. 'What are you possibly imagining that we'll start? A shelter for homeless giants?'

The king had not been pleased to hear it, but Aurora was a simple girl and had lived as Briar Rose for 18 years of her life in an actual cottage in the woods, so she found the castle more than spacious enough for her family. (And at least one or two stray passing giants.)

'So what happens now?' Audrey asked, looking perfectly charming with a flower in her hair. Naturally, it happened to match the silken lining of her dusty-rose bodice. 'Surely even a prince can't be expected to do everything right the very first time he tries?'

Easy for you to say, Ben thought.

A dove alighted on Audrey's shoulder, cooing sweetly. Audrey lifted one pale-pink nail, and the dove nuzzled her gentle fingertip. Ben found himself looking around for the royal portraitist.

Ben sighed.

Somehow, even the sight of his beautiful girlfriend wasn't enough to lift the prince's sombre mood. 'Dad says I have to hold another meeting to fix it. He's disappointed, of course, and he's had to send conciliatory gift baskets of his favourite cream cakes to everyone who was there, so he's not in the best mood. You know how much he likes his cream cakes.'

'Frosted or unfrosted?' Audrey asked. 'And with raisins or chocolates?'

'Both kinds,' Ben said, sighing again. 'More than a dozen each. Mum thinks it's the only way to make peace, although Dad was kind of annoyed to give away so many of his favourite treats.'

'They are rather good.' Audrey smiled. 'And everyone does love cake.'

Ben wished Audrey could be more understanding, but her life had been charmed from the beginning as the pampered princess of two doting parents—especially Aurora, who had been separated from her own mother and forced to spend her formative years in a fairy foster home, under the threat of a deadly curse. '*My* daughter will never know anything but love and beauty and peace and joy,' Aurora had declared. And she had meant it. So it wasn't hard to see now why

Audrey couldn't understand how Ben could ever disappoint his parents. *She* never had.

And she never will, he thought.

Like almost everything in Auradon, Audrey was perfectly sweet, perfectly gentle, and if Ben were honest, sometimes perfectly boring. There were other colours aside from pink and pale turquoise. There were other animals who liked to do things other than coo and cuddle. There were perhaps also other topics of interest than gowns and gardens and balls and carriages—no matter how good the custom paint job on the latest chariot was.

Weren't there?

'I don't even know what those sidekicks are so upset about,' Audrey said. 'They're so adorable, and everyone loves them. Why would they bother with things like wages and hours and—' she paused to shudder—'credit?' She stroked the dove. 'Those aren't lovely things at all.'

He looked at her. 'I don't know, exactly. I'd never thought about it before, but I can't stop thinking about it now. I'd never imagined that anyone in Auradon didn't live exactly like we do, in our castles, with our servants. And our silk sheets and breakfast trays and rose gardens.'

'I love rose gardens,' said Audrey with a smile. 'And I love the ones with topiaries shaped like adorable creatures.' She giggled in delight at the thought, and the dove on her shoulder chirped back agreeably.

'They said I was rude,' he lamented. 'And I was.'

'The elephants are my favourite. With those cute trunks.'

'But I didn't have a choice—they weren't listening to me. They also said I lost my temper.' He hung his head, ashamed of the scene he had caused.

'But also the hippos. Such lovely teeth. It's such a talent, really, to prune a bush into the shape of a hippo. Don't you think?'

'Yes, but about the meeting . . .'

Audrey laughed again, and it was a tinkle of fairy bells chiming in the wind. Ben realised then that she hadn't heard a word he was saying.

Maybe it's better this way. She doesn't understand what I'm going through, and I don't think she ever will.

Audrey must have seen the frown on his face, because she paused to take Ben's hand in her perfectly manicured fingers. 'Don't worry about it, Ben—everything will work out. It always does. You're a prince and I'm a princess. This is the land of Happy Endings, remember? You deserve nothing less than everything your heart desires. You were born to it, Ben. We all were.'

Ben stopped in his tracks. He had never thought about it like that. It was implied, certainly, in everything they did and everything that was done for them. But to hear the words themselves, from such perfectly pink lips . . .

Why us? How did we luck into this life? How is that fair? To be born into a life without a choice in the matter, without the freedom to be anyone else?

She laughed. 'Don't stop now, silly. I have something to show you. Something perfectly perfect, just like today.' He allowed himself to be pulled—like any good prince in the hands of a maiden princess—but his mind was still far away.

Is this all there is?

Is this even what I want for my life?

They had circled the garden, and now Audrey led him into a secluded patch of wildflowers. A beautiful picnic was laid out on the grass amid the blossoms, in a woodland vale filled with all manner of happy forest animals nuzzling, chirping and hopping all about. 'Isn't it amazing? I had half the groundsmen and three cooks working on it all morning.' She leaned in to nuzzle Ben's cheek. 'Just for us.'

She pulled him down to the embroidered silken blanket. Her initials, intertwined with those of her royal parents, were stitched into the fabric beneath them. The gold silken thread sparkled like sunshine in the grass.

Ben smoothed a loose curl away from the blush of her rosy cheek. 'It's lovely. And I thank you for it. But—'

'I know,' she sighed. 'I didn't bring any cream cakes. It was all I could think about when you mentioned them. I do apologise. But we can sample a good 17 sorts of other pastries.' She held up one shaped like a swan, with chocolate wings. 'This one is sweet, don't you think?'

She all but cooed at the pastry. Ben pulled away.

He shook his head. 'But don't you ever wonder if there's more to life than this?'

'What could be more than this?' asked Audrey with an uncharacteristic frown. She put down the swan. 'What else is there?'

'I don't know, but wouldn't you like to find out? Explore a little. Get out on our own and see the world? At least, see our own kingdom?'

She sucked chocolate off her finger, and even that was distractingly cute. Ben wondered if she knew it. He suspected that she did.

Then she sighed. 'You're not talking about that awful island, are you?'

He shrugged. 'Maybe. Don't you ever think about it? How weird it would be to live trapped in one place? Under a dome?'

It was, in fact, the first time Ben could ever remember seeing his princess' princessy feathers ruffled. She wasn't even pouting now. She was practically almost nearly slightly irritated.

'Perhaps, darling, *they* should have considered that before undertaking a life of evil and villainy—which could only lead to an eternity of punishment.'

Now Ben was intrigued. He had never seen her like this, and wondered for a moment if he didn't prefer it. At the very least, they were finally having a real conversation.

'You have to admit, an eternity is a rather long time.' He shook his head. 'They're captives, Audrey. At least here in

Auradon, we can travel anywhere and everywhere we please. They can't.'

Audrey smiled brightly. 'Yes, which reminds me. I told Aziz and Lonnie we would be visiting them today. Carriage picks us up in an hour.' She leaned forwards, touching his chin with her fingertip. 'Time for a new topic. Almost a whole new world, you could say.'

But Ben had a stubborn streak in him that wouldn't give it up. 'Don't try to change the subject, Audrey. Come on. Don't you wonder about them at all?'

'The villains?'

'Yeah.'

Audrey sat back, shaking her head. 'No. Good riddance. Mother says one of them tried to put her to sleep for a hundred years! After she'd already spent her entire childhood in foster care and protective custody! My own mother! And then that same horrible woman turned into a dragon who tried to kill Papa.' She shivered. Audrey must have heard the story more times than she cared to say, Ben understood, but she'd never mentioned any of it to him before today.

He didn't blame Audrey for not wanting to talk about it, and he softened his voice now, taking her hand.

'Her name is Maleficent,' said Ben, who had studied his fairy-tale history. His mother had read the old tales to him, before he could even read himself. 'She was the Mistress of Darkness, the most evil fairy who has ever lived.'

Audrey's frown deepened. 'Don't say her name here,' she whispered. It was practically a hiss, she was so upset. 'She might hear you—and curse you! She takes away everyone and everything my family loves.'

Now it was Ben's turn to smile. 'No way—that dome will hold them forever.' He leaned forwards. 'And *who* exactly does your family love?'

Audrey smiled in return. One blink, and the storm in her eyes was gone.

'My family loves all who are good and kind and deserving of such love, Your Highness.' She held up her delicate hand, and he kissed it obligingly.

I shouldn't give her such a hard time, Ben thought. *Not after everything her family has been through.*

'Dance with me, sweet prince,' she urged.

Ben stood up and bowed. 'Happy to please, my lady.' Dancing in the forest was her favourite thing to do, he knew.

Ben held her in his arms. She was beautiful. Perfect. A princess, who was in love with him. And he was in love with her . . . wasn't he?

Audrey sang softly, 'I know you, I walked with you, once upon a dream . . .'

It was their song, but this time, it caught him off guard.

With a start, Ben realised he didn't know her. Not really. He didn't know her soul, her dreams, and she didn't know his. They didn't really know each other.

And worse, he had never dreamed about her. Not once.

For Audrey, that song might be about him. But for Ben, that song wasn't about her.

No.

Not Audrey.

He had dreamed about another girl.

One with purple hair and green eyes glittering in the dark, a sly smile of mischief on her lips.

Who was she? Where was she? Would he ever meet her?

And would he ever get her out of his head?

Ben closed his eyes and tried to focus on the melody and the girl right in front of him, but the memory of the girl from his dream was too hard to forget.

chapter 19

One Hundred and One Ways to Find a Map

For the next several hours, Mal, Jay and Evie helped Carlos with the painstaking task of finishing his mother's laundry. Or, to be more specific, Jay and Evie helped Carlos, while Mal "supervised".

For a woman who lived on a semi-deserted island full of ex-villains, Cruella sure had an elaborate wardrobe, Mal thought. There were fringed scarves and silky black gloves, fishnet stockings and slinky black dresses, chunky wraps and whisper-knit cardigans, bulky coats and frilly corsets. Cruella De Vil might be exiled, but that didn't mean her clothes were going to be anything less than stunning.

Mal looked round at Evie, who was humming as she folded black-and-white towels. The blue-haired princess had been relatively easy to sway, which boded well for when they actually found the sceptre. Mal would make sure Evie would be the first one to touch it, absorbing the curse and falling asleep for a thousand years. It was the evil scheme to end all evil schemes, and Mal was looking forward to sweet revenge, as well as picking up straight Es for the semester.

Meanwhile, Jay was up to his elbows in bubbles washing a number of black-and-white sweatshirts.

'Isn't this a lot of work?' she asked, feeling exhausted just from watching everyone.

Carlos nodded, his mouth full of safety pins.

'And you do it all?' she asked Carlos. Her mother might ignore her and resent her and scold her, but at least she wasn't Maleficent's virtual slave.

Carlos nodded again. He pulled the safety pins out of his mouth and explained that he was pinning a bustier on a hanger just the way Cruella's old favourite dry-cleaner in London had. 'Yes. But you get used to it, I guess. Don't worry, we're almost done.'

'Thank goblins,' said Mal, putting her feet up on a nearby ottoman.

But just as they were putting the finishing touches on the last batch of black-and-white clothing and linens, they heard the roar of a car engine. It screeched to a stop in front of Hell Hall.

Carlos began to shake. 'It's her... Mother... she's back... she wasn't supposed to be back till tomorrow. The Spa must have dried up.'

Mal wasn't sure why Carlos was so jumpy. No-one was as scary as *her* mother after all—what on Earth could he be so freaked out about?

A car door slammed, and a heavy accent raspy from too much smoke and yelling rang through the air. 'Carlos! Carlos! My baby!' Cruella cried, her throaty voice ringing through the house.

Mal looked at Carlos. *My baby?* That didn't sound too bad, now, did it?

'My baby needs a bath!'

'She knows you're dirty from out there?' Evie asked, confused.

Carlos turned red again. 'She doesn't mean *me*,' he whispered hoarsely. 'She means her *car*. She's telling me to give it a wash.'

Evie turned away from the window with a horrified look on her face. 'But it's so filthy! It'll take hours!' The red car was splattered with dirt from driving around town, crusted black and disgusting.

'No way are we cleaning that,' muttered Jay, who couldn't be looking forward to washing one more thing.

The four of them creeped out of the laundry area and into the main room.

Cruella stopped short at the sight of three strange scraggly teenagers in her house. She still wore her hair in a frizzy black-and-white do. Her long, fur coat trailed on the floor behind her, and she was sucking on a slender black cigarette holder.

Mal gave her a disapproving glance, and Cruella shrugged. 'It's vapour. Just vapour, darling.'

Mal waved the vapour away.

'Now, enough about my baby, how is my one true love?' Cruella drawled, puffing on her long vapour wand.

The three teenagers turned to Carlos questioningly, but even he looked astounded to hear himself described in such affectionate terms. 'Your one true love?' he almost stammered.

'Why, yes, my one true love. My furs!' Cruella laughed. 'You've been taking good care of them haven't you, darling?'

'Of course,' Carlos said, reddening again.

Mal knew he was kicking himself. But what did it matter if his mother loved him or not? They'd been taught that love was for the weak, for the silly, for the *good*. Love was not for the likes of them. They were villains. The bad guys. The only thing they loved was a wicked plan.

'Who are these clowns?' Cruella demanded, waving her arms towards the group.

'Th-they're m-my . . .' Carlos stammered.

Mal knew he couldn't say *friends*, because they weren't friends, not really. She had bullied him into going with her on a quest, Evie pitied him, and Jay was there only so he could attempt to steal the chandelier.

Either Cruella didn't notice or didn't care. 'Where're Jace and Harry?' she asked.

Carlos shrugged.

'Hi, Mrs De Vil, I'm—' Evie said, offering her hand.

'I know who you are,' Cruella said dismissively.

Mal thought it was interesting that everyone knew who Evie was, even though she'd been kept in a castle for a decade.

'Hey,' said Mal.

'Oh, hello, Mal—tell your mother I send my love, darling,' Cruella said, gesturing with her vapour cigarette and then turning to glare at Jay. 'And you, tell your father he ripped me off with that lamp he sold me—the thing doesn't work.'

'Yes, ma'am.' Jay saluted.

'Well, what are you all standing here for? Didn't you hear me? My baby's dirty, darlings! It's absolutely wretched! I can't live another minute until you give my baby a bath! Now, scram!'

Evie thought they would be stuck at Cruella's forever, but at long last the car was clean, and the foursome arrived at Dragon Hall in search of a map that would hopefully show them where the Forbidden Fortress was hidden on the island. Carlos' compass would help, but if Jafar was right about the island being much bigger than they thought, they would need to be pointed in the right direction first.

Evie still wasn't sure why she had agreed to go with the group. She knew Mal was being false, but part of her was interested in the adventure. After being cooped up in a castle for 10 years, she was curious to see the rest of the island.

The school was as dead as a ghost town that Saturday afternoon; only a goblin crew had arrived to clean the halls and mow the grass around the tombstones. The four villain kids walked in and descended into the gloom of campus. The hallways were lined with overgrown ivy that seemed to be multiplying by the second, snaking round old portraits of evil villains nobody could name any more. Evie could've sworn their eyes followed her as she trotted past.

They found Dr Facilier at his desk, staring into an empty crystal ball.

'Ahh, if it isn't my least-favourite student,' he said when he saw Mal.

'Relax, Dr F, I'm not here to fill your top hat with crickets again.'

'What a relief,' he said coldly. 'How can I help you?'

'We need to get into the forbidden library,' Mal said. 'The Athenaeum of Secrets.'

'Ah, but there's a reason it's called the forbidden library—because students are expressly forbidden to enter,' he said sternly.

Evie thought Mal would give up, but instead Mal hopped up on Dr Facilier's desk, cool as Lucifer. 'Yeah, about that,' she said, plopping down a pack of tarot cards. 'Entrance fee?'

Dr F picked a few up and held them under the dim reading light beside him. 'The Major Arcana. Impressive.' He pocketed the tarot set and studied the four students in front of him. 'What exactly are you looking for in the library?'

'A map of the island,' said Mal. 'And make it quick, will you? I haven't got all day.'

The giant spider guarding the door moved away as docile as a cat when Dr Facilier tickled its belly. The door to the Library of Forbidden Secrets opened with a rusty squeak, and Dr F escorted the four of them through.

Tall, teetering bookshelves housed tattered, waterlogged leather-bound books, covered with 20 years' worth of dust, as well as beakers and vials filled with strange-looking liquids and potions. As Dr Facilier scurried down the dingy aisles before them, moving through the rows of bookshelves and muttering under his breath, they were only able to make out the faint outline of his glowing candle, casting shadows against the library walls.

'You know he's got bat droppings for brains, right? This could all be for nothing,' Jay whispered.

Mal shot him a look.

'Just saying,' said Jay.

'It's worth a try,' Evie said from behind them, stopping briefly to untangle herself from a cobweb. 'Otherwise, we'll just be wandering around in the dark, like we are now.'

'Yeah, it couldn't hurt,' agreed Carlos. He was holding his machine protectively under his jacket.

'Aha! Here we are,' Dr Facilier announced, stopping in front of a row of cases. He pulled out a yellowing rolled-up piece of parchment from one of the dusty shelves. He smoothed out the paper and placed it on a lopsided worktable while the four of them gathered round.

'Um, there's nothing there,' Evie pointed out, her voice small. It was true, the map was blank.

'Well, it was written in invisible ink, of course,' Dr Facilier said as if *everybody* knew this. 'How's a secret supposed to stay a secret, otherwise?'

Without warning, and to the shock of everyone around, Mal grabbed him by the collar and pushed him up against one of the bookcases, which caused several of the vials to fall and shatter to the floor. 'Why, you little rat, have you forgotten who my mother is and how she can have you and everyone on this filthy island . . .'

'Mal!' Evie said in a shocked tone. 'Stop it!' She put a hand on Dr Facilier's trembling arm. 'Let me handle this.'

Mal turned to her. 'Let you *what*?'

'Handle this. Easier to catch flies with honey than vinegar,' she said. 'Go on, let go, gently, gently.'

Mal slowly let go of Dr Facilier, whose knees would have given out if Evie hadn't caught him. 'Now, Dr F, there has to be a way to make the ink visible, isn't there?'

Dr Facilier mopped his sweaty brow with a raggedy silk handkerchief. 'Yes, there is.'

'Good,' said Evie. 'Now, tell us how.'

The headmaster pointed shakily to the vials that had shattered on the ground. 'The antidote was kept there. But now it's gone.'

Evie glanced at Mal, who looked stricken. Mal put her head in her hands and groaned.

'Uh, Mal?' Carlos asked softly, tapping her shoulder.

'Go away, Spotty,' she snapped.

'Listen. I know how to make the elixir. To see the ink.'

They all turned to him, including Dr Facilier. 'You can do magic?' Mal asked. 'But how?'

'No, no, it's not magic, it's just a little chemistry—you know, Weird Science,' Carlos said. 'Come on. Evie, bring the map.'

They left Dr Facilier back in his office giving himself a tarot reading and followed Carlos to the Chem Lab, where they watched him pull various bottles, beakers and powders off the shelves.

'You're sure this isn't magic?' asked Jay sceptically.

'I'm sure,' said Carlos. 'It's science. Like what humans

have to do.' Carlos mixed a few drops of liquid here, a dash of powder there . . . but then he frowned. 'Wait a minute, I can't find the binder.'

'The what?'

'Reza—he must have stolen it from the lab last week! He hates me. Ugh.' Carlos' face crumpled. 'I'm sorry, Mal. I don't think I can do it, after all. Not without the thing that puts it all together and sparks the chemical reaction.'

'Reza stole a vial from the lab?' Jay asked.

'He must have,' said Carlos. 'It's not here.'

'This vial, perhaps?' Jay grinned, holding up a small stoppered test tube filled with sparkly liquid that he had shown Mal earlier.

'Where'd you get that?!'

'From Reza's rucksack. Takes one to know one,' said Jay.

Carlos poured a few droplets into his beaker and mixed it all together. A puff of smoke blew out. 'Voilà,' he said. 'Antidote to invisible ink.' He poured the mixture over the map.

And just like magic, the Isle of the Lost began to form before their eyes, including the hidden and forbidden zones. The Forbidden Fortress appeared, a menacing-looking castle of spiky walls and twisty towers, located on the edge of the island. Right in the middle of Nowhere.

chapter 20

Goblin Wharf

Mal thought Jay's having the secret vial on hand was a pretty decent stroke of luck, which made her think that maybe they were on to something here. Maybe it was her destiny to find Maleficent's Dragon's Eye. 'Do you have the compass?' she asked Carlos.

Carlos nodded. The box beeped, as if to agree.

According to the map, they would have to walk way past the village right to the edge of the shore, and from there the path would take them to the fortress.

They set off, Carlos in front with Jay, Evie just behind, and Mal holding up the rear. She watched them walk in front of her. She knew Jay would steal the Dragon's Eye for himself at the first opportunity, that Evie was trying to get on her good side and curry favour, and that Carlos had only joined them to fulfil his curiosity.

But it didn't matter. Somehow, they all had a common goal. To find the Dragon's Eye. Better yet, she wasn't going into Nowhere alone.

Mal had her gang of thieves.

Her very own minions.

And that was progress indeed.

Her evil scheme—the big nasty one—was working.

The path away from the village and towards the shore was smooth at first, but soon became rocky. Mal began to flag. Her feet hurt in her boots, but she soldiered on grimly, now leading the way and following the directions on the map. Behind her she could hear Evie's light steps, Jay's stomping ones and Carlos' tentative ones.

'Heigh ho, heigh ho, it's off to work we go,' Carlos sang under his breath.

Evie shuddered. 'Don't.'

'What do you have against dwar—Oh, right,' he said. 'Sorry.'

'It's okay.'

'So that was your mum, huh?' said Evie.

'Yup, the one and only Cruella De Vil,' Carlos said, bypassing some poison ivy and pointing it out to the rest of the group to avoid. 'One-way ticket to crazy town, right?'

'She's not so bad,' said Evie, who ducked below a low-hanging branch of a creepy oak tree. 'At least she doesn't do this thing that my mum does, where she pretends to be a 'Magic Mirror' telling me I'm far from the fairest of the land.'

Carlos stopped in his tracks, and he and Jay looked at her, shocked. Even Mal turned round to stare at her.

'Really? But you're gorgeous,' Jay said. 'I mean, you're not my type, sweetheart, but you've got to *know* you're good-looking.'

'Do you really think so?' she asked.

'Nah, you're mum's right—you're ugly,' Jay teased.

'That sucks that she does that,' said Carlos quietly.

'Whatever,' Evie said nonchalantly. 'It's not like I care.'

'You really mean that?' asked Carlos.

'I mean, it's not like your mum is any different, right?' Evie pointed out. They were the children of the most evil villains in the world. What did they expect: love, joy, sympathy?

'I guess not.'

'And your dad, Jay? Doesn't he only care about the shop?'

Jay brooded on that. 'Yeah, of course. But what else is he supposed to care about?' he asked honestly.

Mal listened to their conversation, finding it oddly soothing to have other people around, for once. She'd never really liked companionship before, but then again,

Maleficent had always insisted that they lived apart from the pack—superior, alone and bent on revenge.

Lonely, Mal thought. *I was lonely. And so were they.*

Evie, with her beauty-obsessed mother; Carlos, with his screeching harpy of a parent; Jay, the happy-go-lucky thief with a quick wit and dashing smile, who could steal anything in the world except his father's heart.

The grey fog surrounding the edge of the shore loomed closer. Soon they would have to walk through the mist and enter Nowhere. When they did, would they also become *nobody*? Mal wondered. She cracked her knuckles. Her knees began to ache.

They trudged on in silence for a while, when a sharp whistle cut through the air. It was from Jay, who had been scouting ahead. Evie took a step and crunched twigs loudly underfoot, while Carlos looked up fearfully.

Mal whistled back.

Jay jogged over to where the three of them were huddled together.

'What is it?' Mal hissed.

'I saw something—in the shadows. Hide!' he whispered fiercely, disappearing behind a rock.

Carlos yelped and tried to climb a tree, the bark scratching his knees. Evie screamed softly and dived behind some blackberry bushes.

But Mal froze in place. She couldn't move for some

reason. At first it was because she felt annoyed to think that any daughter of Maleficent would have to hide from *anything*. But as the shadow loomed larger and approached, she worried she had made the wrong decision.

The shadow had a pair of large horns and a spiky tail. Was it a dragon? But her mother was the only dragon in these parts, and had lost the ability to transform into one, once the magic-shielding dome had been put in place.

Then there was a moan, a terrible wailing unlike anything they had ever heard.

It was a hellhound, for sure. A creature of myth and legend, a creature of tooth and fang, blood and fur.

Then the creature emitted what could only be called an adorable purr.

'Beelzebub!' Carlos cried from the tree.

The monster emerged from the shadows, and a little black cat with a wicked grin appeared on the path. The shadow had distorted its ears to look like horns and its tail to appear as if it had spikes. But it was just a little kitty.

'You know this foul beast?' asked Mal contemptuously, to hide her embarrassment at having been scared. Her heart was still beating loudly in her chest.

'It's just my cat,' Carlos said. 'I got her when I was little.' He added sheepishly, 'She's one of Lucifer's litter. She's my evil sidekick.'

'Oh, cool. I got one, too. You know, at my birthday party,' said Evie. 'Mine is Othello, a baby parrot—well, not such a baby any more. Othello's got quite the mouth on him, too. Not sure where he learned all those words.'

'Cool—you got one of Iago's babies? I got two electric eels—Lagan and Derelict. You know, from Flotsam and Jetsam. They're *huge* now. Monsters,' said Jay. 'They hardly fit in their aquarium any more.'

Carlos let the cat rub his cheek. 'Go on, Bee. Go back home, stop following us. I'll be back soon—don't worry.'

'What's your evil sidekick?' Evie asked, turning to Mal.

Mal coloured. She remembered exactly when they had each received their sidekicks—at that fabulous party long ago, to which she had not been invited. 'I don't have one,' she said shortly.

'Oh!' said Evie, and turned away, looking embarrassed.

Don't worry, thought Mal. *You'll pay soon enough.*

Finally, they stood face-to-face with the grey fog that circled the island and marked the edge of Nowhere. The mist was so thick, it was impossible to see what lay beyond it. It would entail a walk of faith to see what was on the other side. And all their lives, the four had been told to keep away from the fog, to stay back from the edge of the grey.

'Who goes first?' asked Jay.

'Not me,' said Evie.

'Nor me,' said Carlos.

'Duh,' sniffed Mal. 'As if either of you would.'

'Mal?' asked Jay. 'After you?'

Mal bit her lip. It was, after all, her quest. 'Yeah. I'll go, cowards.' She squared her shoulders and tensed. She stepped into the fog. It was like walking through a cold rain, and she shivered. She reminded herself that there was no magic on the island, and that nothing could hurt her, but even so, the grey darkness was impenetrable, and for a moment she felt like screaming.

Then she was on the other side.

Still whole.

Not disintegrated.

Not *nothing*.

She exhaled. 'It's fine,' she called. 'Get over here!'

'If she says so,' muttered Jay. Evie followed, then Carlos.

Finally, the four of them were on the other side of the fog, standing at the edge of Nowhere.

'Whoa,' said Carlos.

They all looked down. They were standing literally at the water's edge. One more step, and they would have fallen off the rocky piece of land that was the Isle of the Lost and into the deep sea below, to become an alligator's dinner.

'Holy Lucifer, what the heck are we supposed to do now?' Mal asked.

'I don't know, but this thing won't shut up,' Carlos said. It was true. The compass in his box was beeping wildly now, and the closer Carlos stepped towards the strip of rocky, foggy beach, the faster it beeped. 'It's over there. It has to be,' he said, pointing to the sea.

'Well, I forgot my swimming trunks and I don't really enjoy being eaten by reptiles, so it's all on you guys,' Jay said, backing away from the water.

'It can't be *in* the water,' Mal said, yanking out the map from her pocket. She gasped. 'Guys. Come here.' They all gathered round Mal. 'Look! There's more!' More ink had appeared, and this time, they saw that the fortress wasn't technically on the Isle of the Lost at all but was located on its own island, or rather its own piece of floating rock, which just so happened to be named the Isle of the Doomed.

'Well, that's cheery,' Carlos said.

'And just how are we supposed to get over there?' Evie asked.

Mal studied the map and pointed to a spot labelled GOBLIN WHARF.

'We'll hitch a ride from one of our friendly neighbourhood goblins to row us over, of course,' Mal said, pushing past them and starting up the muddy beach towards the docks where the goblins unloaded the Auradon barges.

'There's no such thing as a friendly goblin,' Carlos sighed, but like the rest of them, he followed Mal.

They arrived quickly at the busy port—mostly because the alligators had taken to snapping at them from the shallow water by the beach, and they'd sprinted, screaming, towards the dock.

The wharf was bustling with activity. Goblins pushed their way past the foursome, emptying cargo from the big Auradon ships that were allowed in and out of the magic dome. They placed the rotting and rotten goods on to the splintering wooden boardwalk and jumped on and off each other's makeshift rafts and boats. They hooted and hollered in their Goblin tongue, tossing bags of scraps and leftovers—clothing, food, cosmetics, electronics, everything the people on Auradon didn't want any more or had no use for, on to teetering rickshaws to sell at the market.

'We'll need to pay for passage,' Mal said. 'They're not going to take us over there for free.'

The four of them emptied their pockets to pool enough of a sum of trinkets and food to pay their way across to the Isle of the Doomed. It took some haggling—Jay did most of the talking as he spoke a bit of Goblin from having worked at the shop—but they finally secured a spot on a scrap boat. That is, a boat that collected anything and everything that fell off the Auradon rubbish barges. It was a scavenger of scavengers, the lowest of the low.

As it turned out, a goblin's boat was not constructed to hold four teenage villains. The floating wooden box creaked and groaned as Mal and the others boarded.

'If I die,' Jay said darkly, 'you still can't have any of my stuff.'

'We'll be fine,' Evie said. But she seemed to say it more for her own benefit than anyone else's.

The goblin snickered and started the ancient, rusty motor and off they went into the thick fog.

It was odd to see the Isle of the Lost from the water. It almost looked . . . pretty, Mal thought. The forest was lush and green around the edges of the island, and the rocky beach jutted out dramatically into a rolling blanket of navy-blue water. In the distance, she could see Bargain Castle. From far away, it seemed to be gleaming in the fading sunlight.

'Funny how different things look from far away, huh?' Evie said, following Mal's gaze back towards the Isle of the Lost.

'Yeah, sure, whatever,' Mal said, turning her back on Evie. That same ache was settling in her gut again, and she didn't like it. She didn't like it one bit.

Mal could only be sure they'd arrived at the Isle of the Doomed because the engine had stopped. They still couldn't see two metres in front of them. Mal scrambled blindly out of the boat and onto the rocky beach, followed quickly by the rest of the team. The goblin quickly sped off.

The fog lifted slightly as they made their way through the brush. Soon they were standing in front of a gate covered with a painful-looking bristly forest of thorns. And beyond the gate, high on a craggy mountaintop, stood a large black castle, a ruined wreck silhouetted against the night sky.

The thorns around the gate grew thick and twisted, so sharp, they would stab or scrape anyone who came near.

Worse, the thorns were covered with deadly poisonous spiders, and the whole place had a toxic and sinister air.

They stood, paralysed, unable and unwilling to figure out what to do next, while the black box in Carlos' hands kept beeping incessantly. If it was indeed communicating with the Dragon's Eye, it was clear that the sceptre was somewhere behind the thorny gates.

Mal scrunched up her face, frustrated.

It was Jay who was the first to move.

He handed Mal and Evie each a silver dagger and Carlos some insect-repellent spray. He himself hauled a red-handled machete.

'You carry an axe in your pocket?' asked Carlos.

'Who doesn't?' Jay said with a smile. 'When you steal enough things from all over the place, I find that you always arrive prepared.'

Mal had to admit that Jay's loot came in handy right then.

Jay hacked a path with his machete, and the others followed close behind. Mal slashed at a branch of thorns with her silver dagger, and the branch withered and shrank from her knife. Evie did the same on the other side, and Carlos sprayed a hairy tarantula with his spray, so that it fell off a branch, dead.

It would be hard work, but they were used to it by now. Deeper they went into the dark forest, making their way to the castle above.

chapter 21

Tale as Old as Time

Just be yourself, there are other ways to show strength than your father's kind. Ben's mother's words rang in Ben's ears as he sat down to meet with Grumpy, who had been elected to represent the dwarfs and sidekicks in their petitions.

Great. Wonderful. Just perfect. A one-on-one with Grumpy.

Ben shook his head. He suspected *anyone* else would have been a better person to negotiate with than the crabby old dwarf.

Last time they'd met, the infamous dwarf had been insulted by a sugar cookie.

These talks were doomed.

Ben wished that people would stop telling him to be *himself*. It sounded like such simple advice—and maybe it would have been, if he had had any idea who *himself* was.

But who *was* he?

Prince Ben, son of King Beast, heir to the throne of the great kingdom of Auradon?

He was certainly nothing like his father, who knew how to enforce his rule without forcing it on his subjects. Ben cringed to recall how he had stood on the table and yelled.

That wasn't who he was.

He was Prince Ben, son of King Beast *and* Queen Belle, heir to the throne of the great kingdom of Auradon.

And if, like his father, he was meant to inherit the throne—then it would be on his own terms, as his mother's son and not just as his father's heir.

Because, like his mother, Ben was quiet and gentle and loved nothing better than to disappear into a great, thick book. His childhood hadn't been about hunting or swordfighting or besting someone else on the field.

It had been spent in a library.

He shared his mother's love of reading, and he always had. Ben's fondest memories were of sitting next to Queen Belle at the hearth of her magnificent library's enormous fireplace, reading by her side. He'd be digging into a pile of books dragged from the lower shelves, while hers were always taken from the very highest. It was paradise.

Once, when his father had discovered they had spent the entire day hiding in the library and scolded them for skipping out on a royal luncheon banquet "for the sake of a story", his mother had mounted a passionate defence.

'But these aren't just stories,' she'd said. 'They're whole kingdoms. They're worlds. They're perspectives and opinions you can't offer, from lives you haven't lived. They're more valuable than any gold coin, and more important than any state luncheon. I should hope you, as king, would know that!'

King Beast's eyes had twinkled, and he had lifted Queen Belle into his powerful arms with one easy motion. 'And, as you're my queen, I should hope you would know how much I love you for that!' Then he'd gathered up his young son and the three of them had enjoyed a late lunch of cream cakes in the garden.

Of course.

Ben smiled. He hadn't thought about that day in a long time.

He found himself thinking of it still as Lumiere ushered the older dwarf into the conference room.

Grumpy nodded to him and took a seat across from the prince, his short legs swinging like a child's. 'What's this all about, young man?' He coughed. 'I'm not in the mood for any of your tantrums.' He eyed the table uneasily, as if the boy was about to leap upon it, even now. The plate of sugar cookies and the goblet of juice in front of him, he left untouched.

'Thank you for meeting me today,' said Ben. 'I thought this might be easier, if it was just the two of us talking. Since everything got a bit—loud—before.'

'Hem,' said Grumpy. 'We'll see about that. You don't plan to hop on the table again or shout like an animal, do you?'

Ben flushed. 'I apologise for my behaviour the other day. I was . . . a fool.'

'You—what?' Grumpy was caught off guard.

Ben shrugged. 'I admit it. I didn't know what I was doing, and I made a mess of everything. And I certainly don't blame you for not wanting to take me seriously now.'

Grumpy looked at him grumpily, if a little pleasantly surprised. 'Go on.'

Ben smiled. It was a start, and he'd take it.

'You see, I called you in because I read all one thousand and one pages of your complaint.'

'Really? All one thousand?' asked Grumpy, sounding impressed in spite of himself.

'And one.' Ben smiled again. He was a fast reader, and a concerned listener, and if he was truly going to be *himself*, he was going to need to use both talents in his favour to settle this complaint once and for all.

'From what I could gather, it appears that what you and your colleagues are demanding is to be heard, and to have a voice in your future. Something more than just a seat at the Council.'

'It's not that much to ask, is it?' asked Grumpy keenly.

'No, it's not,' Ben acknowledged. 'And I think we can come to a simple agreement.'

'What do you propose?'

Ben shuffled the papers. He thought about it, and about how to say it. How had his mother put it? *Perspectives and opinions I can't offer, from lives I haven't lived.*

Ben smiled. 'I propose listening to the people who know best.'

Grumpy raised an eyebrow.

Ben consulted his notes. 'Let's start with the mermaids. They should charge a silver coin for every undersea tour. And I'll talk to Ariel about giving Flounder's collecting for Ariel a break.'

Grumpy nodded. 'Sounds reasonable. Okay.'

'I've also set up a college fund for the Dalmatians—all 99 of them will be eligible for financial aid through the Puppy Grant.' Ben pushed a black-and-white-spotted folder that contained all the pertinent forms across the table.

Grumpy accepted it. 'Pongo will appreciate that,' said Grumpy. 'But what about us miners?'

'Half of everything you mine must still remain the property of the kingdom,' said Ben. He knew his father would settle for no less.

'Half? What about the rest of the diamonds? Where does that go?' asked Grumpy, sounding alarmed.

'The other half will go to a 401D Fund. A retirement fund for dwarfs, to take care of your families and your children. Tell Bashful not to worry.'

'Sounds fair enough.' Grumpy nodded, in spite of himself. 'What about the restriction of magic? Just between you and me, those three fairies make a lot of noise.'

'The three good fairies will have to take their complaint up with the Fairy Godmother. I can't do anything about it myself, I'm afraid. But I'll get them a meeting with her. That much I can do.'

'And Genie's request for unlimited travel within the kingdom?' Grumpy frowned. At this point, he looked like he was struggling to find things to still be grumpy about.

'Approved, so long as he clears his itinerary with the palace beforehand.' That was a difficult concession to make, as his father did not want the "blue-skinned-maniac popping up everywhere without notice", but he had been able to convince King Beast that as long as the subjects were warned about Genie's arrival, all would be well.

Grumpy folded his arms. 'What about the woodland creatures? They're working their paws and hooves to the bone.'

'I've had a team install dishwashers, washer-dryers and vacuum cleaners in every household. It's time we realised we're living in the twenty-first century, don't you think? Forest woodlands included?'

'Meh,' said Grumpy. 'I don't care much for modernity, but I think our furry friends will appreciate it. It's hard to do dishes by hand, without, you know, hands.'

Ben tried not to laugh.

'As for Mary and the mice, from now on, they will be well compensated with the finest cheese in the kingdom, from the king's own larders.' Ben let the last paper drop.

'Fair enough.' Grumpy nodded.

'So we have a deal?'

Grumpy put out his hand. 'Deal.'

Ben shook it. He was more relieved than he let on. (At least, he hoped he wasn't letting it on. At this point he was sweating so much, he couldn't be entirely certain.)

'You know what, young man?' huffed Grumpy with a frown.

Ben steeled himself for a grouchy comment, but none came.

'You're going to make a good king,' the dwarf said with a smile. 'Give your father my best, and send your mother my love.'

'I will,' said Ben, pleased by how well the meeting had turned out. He pushed his own chair back from the ancient table. His work was done, at least for today. *But if this is what being king is all about, then maybe it isn't as hard as I thought.*

The dwarf picked up his stocking cap and hopped down from his seat, turning towards the council-room door.

Then he paused.

'You know, son, sometimes you remind me of her.'

Queen Belle was much beloved in the kingdom.

Ben smiled. 'You know, I really hope I do.'

Grumpy shrugged, pushing open the door. 'Not nearly so pretty, though. I'll tell you that much. And your mother, she would have made sure we had a cream cake or two. And at least a few raisins in the cookies.'

Ben laughed as the door slammed shut.

chapter 22

Gargoyle Bridge

Every moment of this adventure had already proven to be a little more adventurous than Carlos had anticipated.

This revelation might have been a problem for the average man of science who didn't like to run the tombs and who kept to the labs as much as possible. Sure, Carlos had felt a little seasick on the journey over to the Isle of the Doomed, but he'd been able to hold it down, hadn't he?

If he looked at it like that, he'd already proven himself to be a better adventurer than anyone could have reasonably expected.

That's what Carlos told himself, anyway.

Then he told himself that he'd done better than anyone else in Weird Science would have. He actually laughed out loud at the thought of his classroom nemesis in this current situation, which had prompted Jay to shove him and ask if he didn't think he was taking the whole mad-scientist thing a little too literally.

'I'm not crazy,' Carlos reassured his fellow adventurers. Still, willing himself not to throw up into the churning sea itself had required more than his share of exhausting determination, and by the time the four of them were back on land and all the way clear of the thorn forest—no worse for wear save for a few scratches and itchy elbows—Carlos was more than glad to find a real path leading up to the dark castle on the hill above them.

Plain old dirt and rock had never looked so good.

Until it began to rain, and the dirt became mud, and the rock became slippery.

At least it wasn't the sea, Carlos consoled himself. And the odds of a person actually drowning in mud and rocks were incredibly slim.

Besides, his invention was now beeping at regular intervals, its sensor light flashing more brightly and more quickly with every step that drew them closer to the fortress. 'The Dragon's Eye is definitely up there,' Carlos said excitedly, feeling a scientist's enthusiasm at a working experiment. 'If this thing is right, I'm picking up on some kind of massive surge in electrical energy. If there is a hole in the dome, it's leaking magic here somehow, different from the Isle of the Lost.'

'Maybe the hole is right above this place,' said Evie.

'Yeah, I can feel it too.' Mal nodded, still moving forwards along the path. 'Do you guys?' She stopped and looked at them, shielding her eyes from the rain with one hand.

Carlos looked at her in surprise. 'Feel what? This?' He held up his box, and it beeped in her face. Mal jumped back, startled, and Jay laughed.

'Whoops,' Carlos said. 'See what I mean? The energy is surging.'

Mal looked embarrassed. 'I don't know for sure. Maybe I'm imagining it, but it almost feels like there's some kind of magnet pulling me up the path.'

'That is so creepy,' Evie said, stopping to wipe sweat off her forehead with the edge of her cape. 'Like, it's your destiny, literally, calling.'

'Well,' said Carlos, 'no, not really. If it were *literally* calling, it would be, you know, *calling* her.'

Jay laughed.

Evie glared at him. 'Okay, fine. Literally pulling like a magnet, only not really, because it's, you know, destiny. Are you happy now?'

'Literally?' Carlos raised an eyebrow.

Jay laughed again, which made Carlos feel good, though he couldn't exactly explain why, not even to himself.

'Don't you guys feel it?' Mal sounded nervous. Nobody said anything, and she sighed, turning back to the muddy path.

They'd only made it up past the next curving bend in the path when Mal stumbled and fell, sending a slide of rock down the trail behind her.

'Who-ahh,' Mal yelped, her arms flailing. The dark stones were so slick with rain that she couldn't right herself, only slipping on the rocks again.

Evie caught Mal before she tumbled headfirst down the stony path. Both girls flew backwards into Jay, who almost toppled Carlos behind him.

'I've got you,' said Evie, helping Mal find her balance.

'Yeah, and I've got you,' Jay said.

'Which is great for everyone but me,' Carlos said, barely keeping one arm around his device as the other held Jay off him. 'The human doorstop.'

'I am definitely in the wrong shoes for this,' Evie said, wincing at the sight of her own feet.

'We need flippers, not shoes. The rain has turned this whole trail into a mud river. Maybe we should all hold hands,' Jay suggested. 'We'll work better if we're all together.'

'Did you really just say that?' Mal shook her head, sounding disgusted. 'Why don't we just sing songs to cheer each other up and then weave flowers out of the mud and move to Auradon, while we're at it?'

'Come on, Mal.' Carlos tried not to smile. He knew that Mal, of all of them, had the hardest time with anything more beneficent than Maleficent.

'Do you have a better idea?' Jay looked embarrassed.

'If you wanted to hold my hand, you know, you could have just asked,' teased Evie, as she offered it to Jay, waggling her fingers.

'Well, now,' Jay winked. 'You don't say.'

Evie laughed. 'Don't worry, Jay, you're cute—but thieves aren't my style.'

'I wasn't worried,' said Jay smoothly, grasping her hand in his firm grip. 'I just don't feel like taking a mud bath today.'

'From a physics perspective, it does make sense. If you want to talk about Newton's second and third laws,' Carlos added, trying to sound reassuring. 'You know, momentum and force, and all that.'

'What he said.' Jay nodded, holding out his hand to Mal.

Carlos watched him, wondering if Jay and Evie were flirting, and if that was why Mal seemed mad. No. Mal and Jay bickered like siblings. And Jay and Evie were just trying to cover up the fact that they were scared. Jay had told him earlier that he thought Evie was cute, all right, but he thought of her like he did Mal, which meant he didn't think of her at all. Carlos thought that if the girls had been their sisters, Mal would have been their annoying, grumpy sister while Evie would have been the manipulative, pretty one. And if Jay had been his brother, he'd be the kind who was either laughing at you or punching you when he wasn't busy stealing your stuff.

The longer he thought about it, the more Carlos decided it wasn't so bad to be an only child, after all.

'Come on, Mal. Just take it. Even Newton agrees,' Jay said, wiggling his fingers at Mal, while still grasping Evie's hand tightly in his other hand.

Mal gave up with a sigh, grabbing it after only a slight hesitation. Mal then held her hand out to Carlos, who grabbed it as if it were a lifesaver, seeing as he knew his physics better than any of them.

Somewhat awkwardly, and little by little, the four of them pulled and pushed and helped each other slosh their way up the muddy path, sweaty palms and muddy ankles and cold feet and all.

Before long, the pathway curved once again, and now the thick rain cloud surrounding it seemed to part on either side of the four adventurers, revealing a sudden and dramatic vista—what appeared to be a long and slender stone bridge, half-shrouded in mist, that jutted out above a chasm in the rock directly in front of them.

'It's beautiful,' Evie said, shivering. 'In a really terrifying way.'

'It's just a bridge,' Carlos said, holding up his box. 'But we definitely have to cross it. Look—' The light was flashing so brightly and so quickly now that he covered the sensor with one hand.

'Duh,' Jay said.

'It's not just a bridge,' Mal said in a low voice, staring at the grey shape in front of her. 'It's *her* bridge. Maleficent's bridge. And it's pulling me. I have to cross it. It wants me to get to the other side.'

'It's not the bridge I'm worried about,' Carlos said, looking into the distance. 'Look!'

Beyond the bridge and mist, a black castle rose from a pillar of stone. The bridge was the only way to reach the castle, as sheer cliffs surrounded the black fortress on all other sides.

But the castle itself was so forbidding, it didn't exactly look like a place that wanted to be reached.

'That's it,' Mal breathed. 'That has to be the Forbidden Fortress.' The darkest place on their dark isle—Maleficent's old lair and ancestral home.

'Sweet,' Jay said. 'That's one sick shack.'

Evie studied it from behind him, still shivering. 'And I thought our castle was draughty.'

'I can't believe that we actually found it.' Carlos stared from his box to the castle. 'And I can't believe it was so close to the island all along.'

Mal's eyes were dark, and her expression was impossible to read. She looked almost stunned, Carlos thought. 'I guess that explains the rain. The Forbidden Fortress hides itself in a shroud of fog and mist. It's like a moat, I guess.'

Carlos examined the air around him. 'Of course it is. A defensive mechanism, built into the atmosphere itself.'

'I'm sure my mother designed it to keep everyone she didn't want out.'

She didn't say the rest, so Jay said it for her. 'Which meant, you know, *everyone*.'

Carlos found it hard to look away from the black tower on the hill. No wonder the citizens of the Isle of the Lost were told to keep away. Here was concrete proof of villainy, of the power of darkness and infamy.

Maleficent's darkness.

It wasn't just any evil. What loomed in front of them was the most powerful and most storied darkness in the kingdom.

Carlos suddenly felt it—the magnetic pull Mal had tried to describe. He could feel it thrumming in the air, in the very stones beneath his feet. Even if magic was no longer a factor, there was power here, and history.

'Feel that?' Carlos held his vibrating hand up into the air.

'I can too,' Evie said, picking up a rock from the mud. It rattled in her fingers as she held it. 'Destiny,' she announced dramatically.

Jay pointed at the lightning that crackled in the air above the black turrets. 'Me too. I guess it's time.'

Mal didn't say a word. She only stared.

'Hold on, now. We're not in any rush,' Carlos said. 'We need to do this right, or—' He didn't finish the sentence. Then he caught Mal's gaze and knew she felt the same way.

'Look,' Jay said, yanking back an armful of overgrown vines that covered the stony steps leading up to the main ramp of the bridge. He tossed them to the side.

'What are those horrible, ugly creatures?' Evie made a face. 'No, thanks. I'll stay on this side of those things.'

Because now that the vines were gone, they could see that the entire bridge appeared to be guarded by ancient stony gargoyles. The winged griffins glared down at them from where they perched, flanking the bridge on either side.

'Lovely,' Jay said.

Carlos stared. It wasn't only Mal who could see her mother's hand in every stone around them. The carved creatures sneered in exactly the same way Maleficent did, their teeth pointed, their mouths cruel.

Mal looked at them, frozen.

Then Carlos realised it was because she was paralysed by fear. 'Mal?'

She didn't answer.

She can't do this alone, Carlos thought. *None of us can.*

It's no different from pulling each other through the mud. It's just physics, if you think about it. It's science.

But then Carlos tried not to think about it, because his heart was pounding so loudly, he thought the others would hear it. He began to recite the periodic table of the elements in his head to calm himself down. Atomic numbers and electrons were always somewhat comforting in times of stress, he'd found.

And the more numbers he recited, the easier it was to put one foot in front of the other.

Which is exactly what he did.

Carlos stepped up on to the first stone paver that led to the sloping bridge. Just as he did, the stone gargoyles began to flap their wings in front of them.

'Whoa!' Jay said.

'No,' Evie said. 'Just, no.'

'How is this possible?' asked Jay. 'There's no magic on the island.'

'The hole in the dome,' said Carlos. 'It must have sparked the castle to life or something, like a chemical reaction.' It made sense—not only had Diablo been unfrozen, but the whole fortress as well.

Carlos moved his way up the next step, and then the next, until he was standing level with the main ramp of the bridge itself. Mal and Evie and Jay now followed behind him.

The creatures growled as they came to life around them, the bridge rumbling beneath their feet. The griffins' horrible eyes glowed green, illuminating the fog around them, until they were practically shining a spotlight on the four intruders. The gargoyles uncurled their hunched backs, now almost doubling themselves in height.

Evie was right, Carlos thought. They were really ugly things, with snaggly teeth and forked tongues. He couldn't look away from the hideous faces hovering over him. 'This must be residue, left over from the magical years,' he said. 'Whatever did this was probably part of the same power that sparked Diablo to life.'

'The same power?' Mal looked spellbound. 'You mean, my mother's?'

'Or the same electromagnetic wave.' Carlos thought about his last Weird Science class. 'I'm not sure how to tell the difference any more.'

Jay swallowed as a gargoyle leaned down, looking as if it could spring at Carlos at any moment. 'Right now, I'm pretty sure the difference doesn't matter.'

'Who goes there?' boomed the gargoyle to the right of Carlos.

'You cannot pass,' said the one on his left.

'Yeah? Says who?' Carlos took a step back, as did the rest of the group following behind him. They looked at each other nervously, unsure of what to do next. They hadn't known about the gargoyles, hadn't expected a fight. This was going to be more difficult than they expected, maybe even impossible.

But it didn't matter. Even Carlos knew there was no turning back now.

'You ugly things need to move!' said Mal, shouting from behind him. She glared at the griffins. 'Or I'm going to make you!'

The gargoyles growled and grimaced, flapping their stone wings as a threat.

'Any ideas?' Carlos looked over his shoulder nervously. 'We don't have weapons or magic. What would we fight with? Besides, how do we fight something made of stone?'

'There has to be a way,' Mal said. 'We have to pass!' she shouted again. 'Let us through!'

'Yeah, I'm not sure that's working.' Evie sighed.

The gargoyles glared at the children with glowing eyes, their fangs bared, their stony wings beating the wind. 'You cannot pass,' they said again in unison—and just as the creatures spoke, the thick grey clouds surrounding the long stone ramp dissipated, revealing a gap in the bridge, a 12-metre gulf with nothing below but air.

The bridge was broken, virtually impassable.

'Great,' Jay said. 'So it's over. Fine. Whatever. Can we go now?'

The others just stared.

Carlos had to admit Jay was probably right.

There was no apparent way to reach the castle. They had come all this way only to fail. Even if they could pass the gargoyles, there was no way to cross the bridge since *there was no bridge.* It was hopeless. Their journey had ended before it had truly begun.

Carlos stepped back and noticed something carved in the stones at the foot of the bridge. He sat down to read it.

'What is it?' Mal asked, kneeling next to him.

He brushed away the dirt and moss to reveal a sentence carved in the stones: *Ye who trespass the bridge must earn the right of way.*

'Great. So what are those, like, directions?' Mal looked at the others. 'What does that mean? How do we earn the right of way?'

Evie shook her head as she glanced back up at the gargoyles and the broken bridge. 'I don't know, Mal. We don't seem to have earned anything.'

'And technically, we are trespassers,' Jay said.

Evie frowned. 'I think we should go. Maybe the bridge was destroyed—maybe it's been like this for years. Maybe no-one gets in and out now.'

'No. Those words have to mean something. But is it a riddle, or a warning?' Mal asked. She looked at the gap in the bridge and pushed her way past the others, towards the edge. She was determined to figure it out.

'What are you doing?' Carlos yelled. 'Mal, wait! You're not thinking straight.'

But she couldn't wait, and she didn't stop.

He took a step back, Jay and Evie flanking him. 'Go after her,' Carlos said. 'Pull her from the break in the stone before she falls. This is crazy.'

Jay nodded and followed her.

'It's so sad,' Evie said. 'To have come this far.'

'I know. But half a bridge might as well be no bridge at all,' Carlos muttered. He put down his machine and turned it off so that he wouldn't have to listen to its beeping. The noise of the sensor—more proof of how close they'd come to finding the source of the power—only made things that much worse.

The moment Carlos killed the machine, the light in the gargoyles' eyes faded. The eerie green glow receded back into their black stone sockets.

'Wait—did you just—'

Carlos looked incredulous. 'Turn off the monsters? I don't think so.' He called out to Mal, who was now standing with Jay, just a few metres from the break in the stone ramp. 'They're like big doorbells, Mal. When we try to cross, they turn on. When we go to leave, they turn off.'

'So they're another defence mechanism?' Evie looked unconvinced.

'Maybe.' Carlos studied the bridge. 'Anything's possible. At least, that's what I'm starting to think.'

Mal came running back. 'So maybe it's just a test. Look,' she said, approaching the gargoyles, their eyes once more glowing. 'Ask me your questions!' she called up to the guardians of the bridge. 'Let us earn the right of way.'

But the gargoyles didn't answer her.

'Maybe you're not turning it on right,' Evie said.

'Maybe this is just a waste of time.' Jay sighed.

'No, it's not,' Mal said, giving them a beseeching look. 'This is my mother's castle. We've found it, and there has to be a way in. Look at the inscription on the stone—it has to be some kind of test.'

Jay spoke up. 'Carlos said they're like a doorbell. But what if they're not? What if they're like the alarm system in a house? All we would have to know to disable them is the code.' He shrugged. 'I mean, that's what I would do, if I was trying to break in.'

Of any of us, he would know, Carlos thought.

'So what's the code?' Mal turned back to the gargoyles, her eyes blazing. 'Tell me, you idiots!'

She drew herself up to her full height and spoke in a voice that Carlos knew well. It was how Cruella spoke to him, and how Maleficent spoke to her minions from the balcony. He was impressed. He'd never seen Mal so like her mother as now.

Mal did not ask the gargoyles, she commanded them.

'This is my mother's castle, and you are her servants. You will do as I bid. ASK YOUR RIDDLE AND LET US PASS!' she ordered, looking as if she were home—truly home—for the first time.

Because, as they could all now see, she was.

A moment went by.

The mists swirled, in the background, ravens cawed, and green light pulsed in the distant windows of the castle.

'Carlosssssssss,' hissed the gargoyles, in disturbingly creepy unison. 'Approaaaach usssssss.'

Hearing his name, Carlos took a step forward with an awestruck look on his face. 'Why me?'

'Maybe because you touched the step first? So the alarm is set on Carlos mode?' Jay scratched his head. 'Better you than me, man.'

'Time for the passcode.' Mal nodded. 'You got this, Carlos.'

Then the gargoyles began to hiss again. 'Carlosssssss. First quesssssstion . . .'

Carlos took a breath. It was just like school, he thought. He liked school. He liked answering questions that had answers, right? So wasn't this just another question? That needed just another answer?

'Ink spot in the snow
Or red, rough and soft
Black and wet, warm and fast
Loved and lost—what am I?'

No sooner had the gargoyles stopped speaking than rumbling began beneath their feet. 'Carlos!' Evie cried, stumbling as she tried to stand in place.

'What?' Carlos ran his hand through his hair anxiously. His mind was reeling.

Ink is black. Snow is white. What's red and rough? A steak?

Who loves a steak? We haven't had those in a while, anyway. And what does any of this have to do with me?

'Answer the question!' Mal said. The light was once more fading from the gargoyles' eyes.

'It's—' said Carlos, stalling. He was stuck.

Black. White. Spots. Red. Loved. Lost.

'The puppies. My mother's puppies, the Dalmatians. All 99 of them. All loved and all lost, by her.' He looked up at the stone faces. 'Though I think the love part is debatable.'

Silence.

'Do I need to say the names? Because I swear I can tell them to you, every last one of them.' He took a breath. 'Pongo. Perdita. Patch. Lucky. Roly Poly. Freckles. Pepper . . .' When he had finished speaking, the mist once more congealed around the bridge. Carlos let out a sigh.

It hadn't worked.

'Wait!' Mal said, pointing to the spot where the mists had congealed. 'It's doing something.' The grey mist parted, revealing a new section of the bridge, a piece that had not existed a moment ago.

The gargoyles cleared a path, and the four of them ran out on to it, hurrying to the newly formed edge, waiting for the next question.

'NEXT RIDDLE!' Mal demanded, just as a ferocious wind blew at them. Carlos was beginning to get the feeling the bridge had more than a few ways of getting rid of unwanted visitors. He swallowed.

They needed to hurry.

Or rather, he did.

'Carlosssssss. Next quessssssstion.'

He nodded.

> *'Like a rose in a blizzard*
> *It blooms like a cut*
> *A red smear*
> *Her kiss is death,'*

The gargoyles hissed in their eerie unison, turning to face them, claws raised. Their muscles flexed and their tails whipped, their forked tongues raking their fangs. It looked as if they might pounce at any moment.

Once again, the bridge began to shift beneath their feet.

'"Her kiss is death",' echoed Carlos. 'It has to be about my mother. Is that the answer? Cruella De Vil?'

The bridge began to shake even harder.

Wrong answer.

'But it *is* about your mother!' said Evie, suddenly. 'A rose in a blizzard, it blooms like a cut . . . her kiss . . . it's about what colour lipstick she wears! Cruella's signature red!'

Carlos was dumbfounded. 'It is?'

'A red smear—see? It means it's something she puts on. Oh, I know what it is!' Evie said. 'The answer is Cherries in the Snow! That has to be it; it's been everywhere this season. I mean—judging from what's been thrown away on the rubbish barges.'

Mal rolled her eyes. 'I can't believe you know that.'

The wind whipped up again, and the four of them locked hands, holding on to one another for support. They pressed their shoulders together, bracing themselves against the gale.

Evie cursed. 'It's not Cherries in the Snow? I could swear that was it. Red with a pinkish undertone. No, wait—wait—it didn't have a pink undertone; it was darker. *Redder.* A "true red"—what did the magazines call it? Frost and Flame? No—Fire and Ice! That's it! Cruella's pout is made of Fire and Ice!'

The gargoyles paused, their eyes glowing. They stood in place as the mist once more congealed around the bridge, then thinned to reveal another new section.

Carlos relaxed. Jay whooped—and even Mal clapped Evie on the back as they advanced across the bridge.

One more answered question, and the way would be clear.

'Ask your last riddle!' Mal charged them.

The gargoyles looked crafty.

'Carlosssssss. Last quesssssstion.'

He nodded.

Mal looked at him encouragingly.

Here it goes, one last time.

> *'Dark is her heart*
> *Black like the sky above*
> *Tell us, young travellers—*
> *What is her one true love?'*

The creatures hissed in unison, and as soon as they finished speaking, they walked towards the four, teeth shining, claws raised, wings flapping. The gargoyles would tear them to shreds if Carlos answered incorrectly—the four of them saw that now.

Carlos had to get it right, not just to cross the bridge but to keep them all alive. '"Dark is her heart"—they must mean Maleficent, right?' He turned to Mal. 'But it could mean any of our mothers.'

'My mother has no true love. My mother loves nothing and nobody! Not even me!' said Mal, with a slight pang that Carlos knew all too well.

'Don't look at me. I don't even *have* a mother,' Jay said.

'Beauty!' Evie called out. 'That's mine. I know . . . it's a little cliché.'

But the gargoyles were not interested in anything anyone had to say. Coming closer, parting the mists, their tails swishing: 'WHAT IS HER ONE TRUE LOVE?' they demanded, looking from Evie to Carlos to Mal to Jay.

'My *father*?' Mal ventured.

Carlos shook his head. If Maleficent was anything like Cruella, she hated Mal's father with a vengeance. Cruella had forbidden any questions about his own, no matter how curious Carlos was, how much he wanted to know. As far as Cruella was concerned, Carlos was hers alone. Maleficent had to be the same.

The gargoyles were nearly upon them. They were taller than Carlos had realised, maybe eight or nine feet. They were enormous and their weight made the bridge groan beneath their every step.

Carlos didn't think even the periodic table could help him now.

'WHAT IS HER ONE TRUE LOVE?' the gargoyles asked again, extending their massive wings. When they flapped, the mists swirled about them.

'The Dragon's Eye?' Mal guessed. 'That's all my mum cares about.'

'Being the Fairest One of All!' Evie shouted. 'Her, or me. In that order!'

Jay just shrugged. 'I can't help. I'm pretty sure the answer isn't Jafar, Prince of Pyjamas.'

At first it looked as if the gargoyles were shaking their heads, but Carlos realised it was because the bridge was rumbling so much. Everything was quaking, and the gargoyles were nearly upon them. His teeth began to chatter. Evie lost her balance and slipped, almost falling over the side, but Carlos caught her in time. Jay held on to a crumbling post and held out his hand so that Carlos could hold on to him, forming a link to Evie.

'Hurry! Somebody'd better come up with something,' Jay grunted. 'I can't hold on much longer.'

Evie screamed as she dangled off the bridge, Carlos clinging to one of her blue gloves, which she was slipping out of, one finger at a time.

'THINK, MAL! What does Maleficent love?' Carlos yelled. 'She has to love SOMETHING!'

'WHAT IS HER ONE TRUE LOVE? ANSWER THE RIDDLE OR FALL INTO DARKNESS,' the gargoyles intoned.

'Diablo?' Mal screamed. 'Is it Diablo?'

In answer, the bridge buckled under her feet and Mal slid down, only by luck managing to hold on to Jay, who was anchoring everyone. The entire castle was shaking. Stones flew down from its ramparts and the towers threatened to crumble on top of them.

The bridge began to sway dangerously.

'Wait!' screamed Jay. 'You guys! They're not talking about Maleficent! They're still talking about Cruella! Quick—Carlos—what is her one true love?'

Carlos couldn't think. He was too scared. He couldn't even put a sentence together. And he was even more frightened by what the answer *would* be.

Maybe that was why he hadn't guessed right, this time.

I can't bear to say it out loud.

Jay's voice echoed. 'CARLOS! WHAT IS YOUR MOTHER'S ONE TRUE LOVE?'

He had to say it.

He'd almost always known.

Sometimes, like this afternoon, he would think she meant him, but he really knew better.

Because she *never* meant him.

Not once. Not ever.

Carlos opened his eyes. He had to say it and he had to say it now.

'HER FURS! FUR IS HER ONE TRUE LOVE!' he yelled. She said it all the time. She had said it that afternoon in front of everyone.

'All my mother cares about is her stupid fur-coat wardrobe and everything in it!' Carlos cried. 'But you guys already know that.'

It was the truth, and like any truth, it was powerful.

In the blink of an eye, the four of them were standing on the other side of the gargoyle bridge and everything was set to rights once more. There was no more swaying or rumbling, no-one was falling over the side, and the gargoyles had all turned back to stone.

Although Carlos would swear that one of the stone gargoyles had winked at him.

They were safe, for now.

'Nice work,' said Mal, breathing heavily. 'Okay, now—where to?'

Carlos shakily looked at the beeping box in his hands. 'This way.'

chapter 23

The Wonder of It All

The Forbidden Fortress lived up to its name. Once the four adventurers had found their way in through its massive oaken doors, it was almost impossible to tell the darkness of the shadow world outside the castle from the shadow world within. Either way, it was intimidatingly dark, and the further Jay and Carlos and Evie and Mal crept inside, the more their nervous whispers echoed through the ghostly, abandoned chambers.

Jay wished he'd worn something warmer than his leather waistcoat. Mal's lips were turning blue, Carlos' breath appeared in white clouds as he spoke, and Evie's fingers felt like icicles when Jay grabbed them. (Once. Or twice. And strictly for warmth.) It was colder than Dragon Hall inside, and there was no chance of anything getting any warmer; there were no logs on the fireplace grates, no thermostats to switch on.

'That's modern castle living.' Evie sighed. 'Trade in one big, cold prison for another.' Mal nodded in agreement. Privately, Jay thought that Jafar's junk shop seemed downright cosy in comparison, but he kept that to himself.

Inside every corridor, a dense fog floated just above the black marble floor. 'That has to be magic. The fog doesn't just *do* that,' Mal said.

Carlos nodded. 'The refracted energy seems stronger here. I think we're closer to the source than we've ever been.'

As he spoke, an icy wind blew past them, whistling in through the shattered stained-glass windows high above them. Each step they took reverberated against the walls.

Even Jay the master thief was too intimidated to try to take anything, and kept his hands to himself for once.

Of course once they did find the sceptre, he'd have to man up. Jay knew that, and he'd made his peace with it— no matter how well they'd all got along on the way there.

Villains don't have friends, and neither do their children. Not when you get right down to it.

None of them had come there out of loyalty to Mal, or friendship. Jay knew what he had to do, and he'd do it.

Until then, his hands stayed in his pockets. If this haunted place was selling it, he didn't want it.

'What's that?' Jay asked, pointing. Green lights flashed through half-shattered panes of glass, but he couldn't figure out the source.

'It's what we've been tracking all along,' Carlos answered. 'That same electromagnetic energy: it's going crazy.' He shook his head at the flashing lights on his box. 'This fortress was definitely exposed to something that's left a kind of residue charge—'

'You mean, an enchantment?'

He shrugged. 'That too.'

'And so, even after all these years, this place is somehow still glowing with its own light?' Evie looked amazed.

'Cool,' Jay said.

Mal shrugged it off. 'In other words, we're getting closer to the Dragon's Eye.'

'Yep,' said Jay. Like the rest of the group, he knew what everyone else on the Isle and the kingdom knew—that the evil green light meant only one terrifying person.

Even if it probably reminded Mal of home.

Corridors led to more corridors, until they passed through dark hallways full of framed paintings shrouded in cobwebs and dust. 'It's a portrait gallery,' Evie said, straining to see the walls through the shadows. 'Every castle has one.'

'Mal, stop it—' Jay shouted, looking behind him and jumping away.

Mal reached out and tapped his shoulder. She was standing right in front of him. 'Hello? I'm not back there. I'm over here.'

'Oh, I thought that picture was you.' He pointed.

'That's not me. That's my mother,' Mal said with a sigh.

'Whoa, you really do look like her, you know,' Jay said.

'You two could be twins,' Evie agreed.

'That, my friends, is called genetics,' Carlos said with a smile.

'Gee, thanks—I look like my mother? Just what every girl wants to hear,' Mal replied. Still, Jay knew different. What Mal wanted, more than anything, *was* to be just like her mother.

Exactly like her.

Every bit as bad, and every bit as powerful.

That was what it would take for someone like Maleficent to even notice her—and Jay could tell that this portrait gallery was only making Mal want it that much more desperately.

'Now, what?' Mal asked, as if she were trying to change the subject.

Jay looked around. Before them were four corridors leading to four different parts of the fortress.

A foul draught issued from each of the paths and Jay could have sworn he heard a distant moan, but he knew it was only the wind, winding its way through the curving passages. He yanked a matchbox from his pocket and lit a match, muttering a quick 'eenie-meanie-miney-mo'.

'How scientific,' Carlos said, rolling his eyes.

'You got your way, I got mine. That one,' Jay said, pointing to the corridor directly in front of them. Just as he did, the wind blew out from that same passage, and the foul stench of something rotted or dead came along with it.

The wind snuffed the burning match out.

Evie held her nose, and Mal did the same.

'Are you sure about this?' Mal asked.

'Duh, of course not. That's why I played eenie-meanie-miney-mo! One corridor is as good as the next,' Jay said, entering the corridor and not waiting for the rest to follow. It was the first rule of breaking into an unknown castle: you never let it get to you. You always act like you know what you are doing.

Jay had a feeling this fortress was playing with them, offering them choices when really all roads probably led to the same place. It was time to take matters back into his own hands.

'No, wait—you don't know where you're going. Carlos, check your box-compass-thing,' said Mal.

Carlos brought the box up to the intersection. It beeped. 'Okay, I guess maybe Jay's right.'

'Of course I am.'

They followed Jay into the dark corridor.

Carlos held the beeping box in his hands, the sound echoing off the stony walls. It led them to a dank, cold stairway that led further downwards, deeper into darkness.

The air felt colder and damper and in the eerie silence came a distant rattle, like bones striking rock, or chains rattling in the wind.

'Because that's comforting.' Evie sighed.

'The dungeon,' said Mal. 'Or you might know it as the place where my mother encountered the lovestruck Prince Phillip.'

Evie's eyes were wide with awe. It was probably the most famous story in all of Auradon. 'Maleficent was going to lock him down here for a hundred years, right? That would have been fun.'

Carlos looked around. 'She nearly pulled it off, didn't she?'

Mal nodded. 'If not for that trio of self-righteous, busybody, blasted good fairies.' She sighed. 'End of scene. Enter Isle of the Lost.'

'I don't know about you, but I feel like we've been down here a hundred years already. Let's get on with it,' Jay said.

He was more alert than he'd been all day, because he knew he was on the job now.

It was time to get to work.

Jay found a dungeon door. Carlos held the box inside, listening for its beep. 'This is the one.'

He went ahead with the box, while Jay and Mal and Evie helped each other slowly down the steps, bracing themselves against the wall as they went. There was no rail, and the treads were coated in a black moss. Every step squished in the darkness, and it felt as if they were stepping on something living and wet.

'Suddenly the whole mud-river thing doesn't seem so bad,' said Evie.

'Seriously,' Jay said.

Mal didn't say a word. She couldn't. She was too distracted. Even the moss smelled like her mother.

It only grew thicker as they delved deeper into the dungeon. There were layer upon layer of gauzy cobwebs, a spider's tapestry woven long ago and forgotten. Every step they took pulled apart the threads, clearing a way forwards. All of them were quiet, hushed by the lingering menace in the air as their footsteps squished in the gloom.

'Here?' Mal asked, stopping in front of a rotten wooden door hanging partly off its hinges. When she touched it, the frame collapsed, sending the wood clattering against the floor. Even the heavy iron straps that had once bound the door fell against the stones and the wood, making an awful racket.

'Maybe we shouldn't touch anything,' said Carlos, scrutinising the device in his hands.

Mal rolled her eyes. 'Too late.'

'I think this is it,' Carlos said.

Jay hoped he was right, that the box had led them to the Dragon's Eye.

He couldn't imagine what Mal would do to poor Carlos

if it hadn't. And Jay himself needed to get on with the job at hand.

Mal nodded, and Jay pushed aside what was left of the door. As they entered, he couldn't help but notice that the shattered remains of the door and its frame looked like a kind of mouth—a panther's mouth—and they were stepping through its open jaws, into the mouth of the beast.

'Did any of you notice—'

'Shut up,' Evie said tensely. They had all seen the same thing, which couldn't be good. That was probably why nobody wanted to talk about it.

The four of them walked inside. The room was impossibly dark. There was not even a hint of light, not a glow from a distant window or a torch. Jay reached out, looking for a wall, something to touch.

'Maybe we should find a torch or something in Jay's pockets, before we touch any—' Carlos warned, but it was too late.

Jay struck something with his hand, and the room was suddenly filled with the deafening sounds of metal and stone colliding and grinding and tinkling all around them.

And, just as suddenly, they were bathed in the brightest light, a glow that burst from every corner of the room. The golden brilliance filled their eyes—and before they knew what was happening, the room was filling with sand.

Sand, sand everywhere . . . and they were falling into it, covered in it.

Evie screamed. Mal started to thrash. Carlos lost hold of his box. Only Jay stood perfectly still.

It wasn't a dungeon, it was a *cave*.

A cave filled with sand . . . and, from what Jay could barely make out amid the massive dunes now surrounding him . . . treasure.

He looked around at the jewels that glittered in between the dunes. Mound upon mound of gold coins shimmered in the distance, while hills of gold coins stretched as far as the eye could see. There were crowns and coronets, jewelled sceptres and goblets, emeralds the size of his fist, diamonds as brilliant as the stars, thousands of gold doubloons and silver coins. There were larger things, too: great obelisks, and coffins, lamps and urns, a pharaoh's head, a winged staff, a chalice and a sphinx made of gold.

A king's ransom, he thought. *That's what this is.*

Evie pushed the sand away and sat up, wearing a new crown on her head, quite by accident. 'What is this? Where are we?'

'I can assure you this is not part of my mother's castle,' said Mal wryly, as she spat out some sand and blew her purple fringe out of her eyes. She stood up, brushing sand off her leather jacket. 'More residue from the hole in the dome?' she asked.

Carlos nodded. 'It has to be. There's no other explanation.'

'Wait a minute, where's the sceptre?' she asked Carlos,

looking around. She sounded nervous. 'It has to be here, right? Has anyone seen it?'

Carlos removed a golden bucket that had fallen on his head and picked up his box from where it was balanced on what looked like an ancient golden sarcophagus. He blew sand from the drive and checked the machine again. 'It's still working, but I don't know. It's not beeping any more. It's like it lost the signal, or something.'

'Well, find it again!' Mal barked.

'I will, I will . . . Give me a second, here. You have no idea what sand can do to a motherboard . . .'

Meanwhile, Jay was stuffing every pocket he had with as much of the marvellous loot as he could carry.

This was the answer to his dreams . . . the stuff he had been longing for . . . heaven on Earth . . . the biggest score of his life, and his father's!

It was . . . it was . . .

It dawned on him that he knew exactly where they were.

'The Cave of Wonders!' he cried.

'Come again?' asked Mal.

'This is the place—where my father found the lamp.'

'I thought Aladdin found the lamp,' said Carlos.

'Yes, but *who* sent him there?' asked Jay with a superior smile. 'If it wasn't for Jafar, Aladdin would have never found it. Hence it was my father's lamp all along.' He looked annoyed. 'But nobody ever mentions that part, do they? And my dad said he thought there might be other things hidden in the mist—he must have suspected this might be here too.'

'Fine. Cave of Wonders. More like Basement of Sand,' said Mal. 'More important, how do we get out of here?'

'You don't,' said a deep voice.

'Excuse me?' said Mal.

'I didn't say anything,' said Jay, who was now wearing numerous gold chains round his neck and stacking diamond bracelets up his arm.

'Who was that?' asked Evie nervously.

They looked around. Nobody else seemed to be there.

'Fine. It's nothing. Now, let's find that door,' said Mal.

'You won't,' said the booming voice again. 'And you will be trapped here forever if you don't answer me correctly!'

'Great,' Jay groaned.

'Is this another riddle? This whole fortress is, like, booby-trapped or something,' Evie grumbled.

'Multiple defences—I told you,' Carlos said. 'Burglar alarm. Probably for the Dragon's Eye, don't you think?'

'Cave? Should I call you Cave?' asked Mal.

'Mouth of Wonders will do,' said the voice.

Evie made a face. 'That's a terrible name.'

Mal nodded. 'Okay, Mouth, what's the question?'

'It is but a simple one.'

'Hit us,' Mal said.

The booming voice chuckled.

Then it asked in sombre tones, 'What is the golden rule?'

'The golden rule?' Mal asked, scratching her head. She looked at her team. 'Is that some kind of jewellery thing? Jay?'

But Jay was too busy grabbing as much gold as he could get and didn't seem to hear the question.

Carlos began frantically reciting every mathematical rule he could thing of. 'Rules of logarithms? Rule of three? Rules expressed in symbols? Order of operations?'

'Is it maybe something about being nice to each other?' asked Evie tentatively. 'Do unto others what you want done unto yourself? Some kind of Auradon greeting-card nonsense?'

In answer, the cave began to fill with sand again. The Mouth of Wonders was not happy, that much was clear. Sand appeared from everywhere, filling the room, filling the spaces between the stacks of gold coins, rising like water filling a sinking ship. They would soon suffocate if they did not give the Mouth the correct answer.

'It's the Cave of Wonders, not the Fairy Godmother!' shrieked Carlos. 'The Cave doesn't care about being kind! That's not the golden rule!'

The cave continued to fill with sand.

'Come on—this way!' Mal tried to climb the stacks of gold coins—thinking she could avoid the sand by getting closer to the ceiling—but they collapsed beneath her each time she attempted to scale them, and she only ended up buried in more treasure. She tried again, and this time Evie gave her a push from behind, so that she was able to grab on to the tall statue of a sphinx.

She mounted the creature's back and reached to pull Evie up beside her, but the sand was still rising, already engulfing her leg, threatening to keep her down.

'I can't make it!' Evie shouted.

'You have to!' Mal yelled back.

But Evie had disappeared under the flood of sand.

Jay couldn't believe it when he watched her go under. 'Evie—'

'Come on—' Carlos said, feeling beneath the sand for her. 'She has to be down here. Help me find her.'

'I can't find her,' Jay shouted.

Evie popped back up, spluttering, spitting coins out of her mouth. Mal and Carlos and Jay looked relieved.

'Here—' Now Mal offered Carlos a hand to pull him up, but the sand was already at his chest. 'C'mon,' she cried, 'climb the sphinx!'

'I can't,' he said.

'What?'

'My leg is caught.'

Evie climbed up on the sphinx and tugged at his arm on one side, and Mal from the other, but no matter what they did, Carlos didn't budge an inch. He was stuck, and the sand was still rising around him. It came from the walls and from the floor, and now Evie noticed that it was coming from the ceiling too.

Mal tugged again at Carlos' arm, but instead of pulling him from the sand, she pulled him out of Evie's grasp. Evie tumbled into the ever-growing mounds of sand, crashing against chalices and crowns.

The sand covered her: first up to her knees, then her shoulders . . .

Carlos reached for her, and they held hands as the sand kept rising.

'At least I have my heels on,' Evie said, trying to sound brave. The sand was up to her neck, and Carlos could barely keep his chin above the surface now.

'JAY! WHERE'S JAY?' yelled Mal, looking around, coughing up sand as she frantically held Carlos by the arm.

'JAY!'

Jay was flailing in the sand; it was in his hair, in his eyes. He was also covered with gold doubloons. *Gold. So much gold.* He'd never seen so much gold in his life. He had all the gold in the world, it felt like.

He would die buried in gold . . .

The golden rule . . .

What is the golden rule?

Why, he knew the answer to that. He could almost hear his father whispering the answer in his ear.

Meanwhile, Carlos and Evie had disappeared beneath the sand again, and Mal herself was about to go under.

The sand was nearly at the ceiling. Soon there would be nowhere to escape to—no way to avoid the sand, and no air in the chamber. They were running out of time and out of room.

But Jay knew the answer.

Jay knew he could save them.

'WHOEVER HAS THE MOST GOLD MAKES THE RULES! THAT'S THE GOLDEN RULE!' Jay cried triumphantly, raising a fist in the air.

There was a great booming chuckle, and the sand slowly started to melt into the drains. Soon Jay and Mal and Evie and Carlos were standing right back in the fortress, out of the dungeons altogether.

The Cave of Wonders had disappeared, but then so had all its treasure.

'Fool's gold,' said Jay sadly, looking at his empty pockets. 'All of it.'

chapter 24

Funhouse Mirror

Evie thought her heart would never stop pounding. She could still taste the sand from that cave. So this was what true evil was like—like sand in the mouth and gargoyles on attack. If this was what magic did, she was glad there was a dome.

Also, she had practically lost a heel back in there.

Evie shook her head. This was the second time the Forbidden Fortress had almost got the better of them. Did Maleficent know she was sending her own daughter into a trap? And if so, did she care? Probably not: this was the feared and loathed Mistress of Darkness, after all. Evil Queen was a fool to think she could compete with someone like that, and Evie almost felt like a fool for trying to compete with the Mistress of Darkness' daughter.

Now that she thought about it, Evie almost felt sorry for Mal.

Almost.

Carlos' machine was beeping again.

The four crept through the ruined castle. Bats screamed and fluttered over their heads, and the crumbling marble floor beneath them seemed to shift and slide in order to bear their weight.

Evie stumbled. 'What *is* it with this place? Is there a fault line that runs under this island?'

'Well,' Carlos began.

'Joke. That was a joke.' Evie sighed.

There was nothing too funny about their current situation, however. It was a miracle that the surrounding ocean hadn't completely swallowed the castle and the entire mountain by now. Evie could hear the scampering of rats inside the walls, and chills ran up her spine.

Even the rats were looking for safer ground, she thought.

'This way,' Carlos said, motioning to a narrow passage in front of him.

They followed, trailing behind Carlos, the machine beeping, the sound growing louder. 'Now this way,' he said, rounding one turn, then another. Evie was right behind him as they followed, the passage growing narrower. 'And now—'

'What's going on?' asked Evie, cutting him off. 'Because I know my sizing, and I didn't just double in diameter in the last two-and-a-half minutes.'

Indeed, the passage had narrowed to nearly her shoulders' width. If it got any narrower, she would have to turn sideways. A lump formed in her throat, and her stomach began to roil—she felt as if this were no longer a corridor. It was a crack, a fissure, and it felt like it might close on them at any moment.

Mal raised her voice. 'Is it just my imagination, or are we wedged inside a mountain like—'

'A piece of string dangling down a pipe? Toothpaste squeezed inside a straw? A hangnail in this cuticle right here?' Jay said, holding out his hand. 'Dang, this one really hurts.'

'Are you describing the things you've stolen today? Because those are all terrible analogies,' Evie said, looking at Jay. 'And I'm saying that as someone who was castle-schooled by a woman who thinks the three Rs are Rouging, Reddening and Reapplying.'

'Maybe we should go back,' Carlos said, giving voice to Evie's fear. 'Except—I think I might be stuck.'

Just then, the walls shook, the castle rattled and a chip of stone fell to the floor. The shard was big enough to do damage, and it narrowly missed Evie's perfect nose.

She cried out.

Evie wanted to retreat, but she couldn't, the corridor was too narrow. 'Maybe it's some kind of trap! Let's go—it doesn't look safe!'

'No,' Carlos said. 'Look! There's another passage,' he added, wedging himself forward until he could prise first one hip and then the other out from the narrow corridor to a just-wider one.

As they followed him, Evie was so relieved that she didn't even remember to complain about her nose.

This new passage turned right, then left. The walls were further apart here, but they were oddly sloped, some tilting inward, others outward. The effect was dizzying, as even the ceiling was sloped in spots, and the corridors kept branching, splitting into two or sometimes three directions.

And, always, the rumbling continued beneath them.

'Something doesn't like us,' Jay said.

'We're not supposed to be in this place,' echoed Evie.

'We need to hurry,' Carlos said, trying to sound calm, though he had to be as scared as any of them.

Another stone broke free of the wall, shattering as it hit the floor, nearly crushing Evie's head. She jumped back this time, shuddering. 'What *is* this place?'

'We're in some kind of maze,' Mal said, thinking aloud. 'That's why the corridors keep turning, why passages keep splitting off and narrowing. It's some kind of twisted maze, and we're lost in it.'

'No, we're not. We've still got the box,' Carlos replied.

'It's the only thing that *is* keeping us from getting lost in here.'

The machine was still beeping, so they just kept following him. Evie only hoped he was right and that he knew where he was going. He must have, though, because the winding corridors soon gave way to more open spaces, and all of them breathed a sigh of relief.

Even when the hallways ran long and straight again, the castle was still rumbling, the walls still tilting, and the ceiling was even lower now where they found themselves.

'It's not random,' Carlos said, suddenly. 'It's in a rhythm.'

'You're right,' Jay said. 'Look. The rumbling seems to go along with your beeping box. When the box lights up, the walls start to move.'

Evie stared. 'You mean, he's the one doing it?'

Carlos shook his head. 'Actually, I think it's the waves. Imagine how old this castle must be. What if, each time a wave strikes the foundation, a stone falls or the floors rumble?'

Mal swallowed. 'I just hope the castle itself doesn't crumble before we find the sceptre.'

Evie bent down so her head wouldn't hit the ceiling. All of them except for Carlos had to crouch down now to avoid it.

'It's a room made for mice,' said Mal.

'Or dwarfs?' asked Evie.

'Or children?' guessed Jay.

'No,' Carlos said, quieting the others, pointing to

something in the dark distance. They followed the line of his gaze, seeing at first a pair of green glowing eyes, then another and another.

'Goblins,' said Carlos. 'This is where the goblins live. That's why the ceilings are so low and the corridors are so strange. This isn't a place for humans,' he said, and when he finished, the air filled with a terrible, raucous laughter, the sound of claws tapping and teeth grinding. The box had led them right into the goblins' den.

'Super,' Mal said.

'Yeah, good work,' Jay snorted.

Evie just glared at Carlos.

And these weren't the friendly, enterprising goblins of the wharf or the rude ones from the Slop Shop. These were horrible creatures that had lived in darkness without their mistress for 20 years. Hungry and horrible.

'What do we do?' Jay asked, cowering behind Carlos, who had flattened himself against the wall of the corridor.

'We run,' Evie and Mal cried, one after the other.

They ran towards the only open passageway, the goblin horde shrieking in the darkness, following behind them, their spears beating against the walls.

Jay shouted, 'I guess they don't get a lot of visitors.'

'Maybe they should stop eating their guests,' Carlos said, nearly tripping over what he hoped was not a bone.

'That door!' Evie said, pointing to a heavy wooden door. 'Everyone in!'

They hurried through the doorway, and Evie slammed the door after them, throwing the lock and sealing the goblins out.

'That was close,' said Mal.

'Too close,' Jay echoed. The goblins could still be heard on the far side of the door, tapping it with their spears.

'Maybe they just like to scare people?' Evie said. 'I heard they were mostly harmless.'

'Yeah, mostly,' said Carlos, sucking his hand where a spear had grazed it. 'Let's not wait around to find out.'

When it sounded as if the goblins had gone, Evie cracked open the door. She made sure they were alone before she nodded to Carlos. They continued down the narrow hallways finding nothing but empty chambers until she spied a light shining from a hidden hallway. 'Over here!' she called.

She walked towards the light excitedly, thinking it might be the Dragon's Eye glinting in the dark.

And stopped short—because she was standing in front of a mirror.

A dark, stained, cracked mirror, but a mirror nonetheless. Evie screamed.

'A monster!' she said.

'What is it?' Mal asked, following and looking over Evie's shoulder. Then Mal screamed, too.

Carlos and Jay bumped up next.

'A beast,' Evie yelled. 'A hideous beast!'

Evie was still screaming and pointing to her reflection. In the mirror, an old woman with a crooked nose and wearing a black cape pointed right back. The hag was her.

'What's happened to me?' she asked, her voice, rough and quavery. Worse, when she looked down, she saw that her formerly smooth skin was saggy, wrinkly and dotted with liver spots. She looked at her hair—white and scraggly. She was an old beggar woman, and not just in the mirror.

She wasn't the only one.

Mal was frowning at her reflection. She had a warty nose, and her head was mostly bald except for a few white strands. 'Charming. It's got to be some kind of spell.'

Jay shook his head. 'But—once again, and let's say it all together now—there's no magic on the island.'

'There was a moment—for a single second—when my machine burned a hole in the dome, and I think maybe that was what did it.'

'Did what, exactly?' Evie asked, looking spooked.

'Brought Diablo back to life, sparked the Dragon's Eye and the gargoyles and the Cave of Wonders, and probably everything that used to be magical in this fortress,' said Carlos. 'I mean, maybe. Or not.'

'I don't know, I don't think I look THAT bad,' said Jay, who grinned at his reflection. He was chubby and pasty, bearded and grey, and looked exactly like his father. He too was wearing a black cloak. 'I look like I got my hands on a whole lot of cake in my life, at least.'

'Speak for yourself,' said Carlos, who was frightened to see that in old age he resembled his mother, feature for feature: knotted neck, high cheekbones, bug-eyed glare. 'I think I'd rather face the goblins than this.'

'I'm with you.' Evie couldn't look at herself for another moment.

She began to panic; her throat was constricting. She *couldn't* look like this! She was beautiful! She was—

'Fairest,' agreed the mirror.

'Not the voice!' Evie shouted, before she realised what, exactly, she had heard. Because this time, it wasn't her mother doing her Mirror Voice, as it so often was.

It was an actual Magic Mirror. On an actual wall.

They all turned to the mirror, whose human-esque features had appeared as a ghostly presence in the reflective glass.

'Fairest you are, and fairest you will be again,
If you prove you are wise
and declare all the ingredients needed
for a pedlar's disguise,'

said the Magic Mirror.

'It's a word problem!' said Carlos, gleefully. He loved word problems.

'No, it's not. It's a spell,' Jay said, looking at him like he was crazy.

'I knew it!' said Mal.

'What's a pedlar's disguise?' asked Jay.

'Obviously—it's *this*. It's what's happened to *us*,' said Mal. 'Evie, do you know what goes into making a pedlar's disguise? It sounds like if we can name all the ingredients, we can reverse the spell.'

'Not us,' Carlos pointed out. 'Evie. It says, you know, the Fairest.' He looked at Mal, suddenly embarrassed. 'Sorry, Mal.'

'There's nothing fair about me now,' Evie said. 'But I have heard of the Pedlar's Disguise, though.' Her eyes were back on the glass, still riveted by her awful looks in the mirror.

'Of course you have. It's only your mother's most famous disguise! Remember—when she fooled Snow White into taking the apple?' said Mal impatiently.

'Don't pressure me! You're making me panic. It's like, I used to know it, but now I can't think of anything except *her*.' Evie pointed at her reflection. 'I'm paralysed.'

'I don't know. I think it's kind of cool,' Jay said. 'You could steal a whole lot of stuff, looking like that.'

Carlos nodded. 'He does have a point. You might want to give the whole get-up a test run.' Evie started to wail.

'Not helping,' Mal scolded.

Evie wailed all the more loudly.

'Evie, come on. That's not you. You know that. Don't let my mother's evil fortress get under your skin,' Mal said, sounding as passionate on the subject as Evie had ever heard her sound about anything at all.

'This is what my—I mean, Maleficent does. She finds your weaknesses and picks them off, one by one. You think it's an accident that we stumbled across this Magic Mirror, right when we happened to have the Fairest along for the ride?'

'You think it's on purpose?' Evie looked calmer, and even a little intrigued.

'I think it's a test, just like everything else in this place. Like Carlos and the gargoyles, or Jay and the Mouth.'

'Okay,' Evie said slowly, nodding at Mal. 'You really think I can do it?'

'I know you can, you loser. I mean, *Fairest* loser.' Mal grinned. Evie grinned back.

Okay, maybe she could do this. 'I have studied that spell a hundred times in my mother's grimoire.'

'That's the spirit,' Mal said, thumping her on the back.

'I can see the words of the spell as clearly as if it were before me now,' Evie said a little more loudly, standing a little straighter.

'There you go. Of course you can. It's a classic.'

'A classic,' Evie said to herself. 'That was what I called it. Remember?'

Could she?

Then she looked her old, ugly self right in the eye.

'"Mummy dust, to make me look old!"' she cried.

Suddenly, her wrinkles disappeared. Carlos whooped with joy, because his had vanished as well. And he'd hated seeing Cruella's frown lines on his face.

Evie smiled. '"To shroud my clothes, black of night!"'

In a flash, they were wearing their own clothes again.

'"To age my voice, an old hag's cackle!"' she said, and even as she said it, her real voice returned, young and melodic once again.

Jay laughed in delight, and it was no longer an old man's gruff chuckle.

'"To whiten my hair, a scream of fright!"' said Evie, watching as her hair went back to the dark, beautiful blue hue. Mal's thick purple locks returned, and the black seeped back into Carlos' white hair.

Evie was almost done now, and her voice gained confidence as she remembered the last words of the incantation. '"A blast of wind to fan my hate, a thunderbolt to mix it well, now reverse this magic spell!"'

All four of them cheered and yelled and jumped around like crazy idiots. Even Evie was grinning now.

She had never been so happy to see herself in the mirror, and now that she was herself again, she found that for once in her life, nobody even cared how she looked. Not even her.

It was like magic.

chapter 25

Dragon's Curse

As she trudged behind the others, Mal thought about what she'd said to Evie—how everything at the Forbidden Fortress had been a test.

Carlos had faced the gargoyles, and Jay, the Cave of Wonders. Evie had endured the Magic Mirror.

What about me?

What's in store for me?

Was danger—in the form of a challenge all her own—waiting for her, just behind the next castle door?

Or would it be even more like my mother to ignore me altogether? To leave me alone, and think I wasn't worthy of any kind of test at all?

She closed her eyes. She could almost hear her mother's voice now.

What is there to test, Mal? You aren't like me. You're weak, like your father. You don't even deserve your own name.

Mal opened her eyes.

Either way, nothing changed the place where they were standing.

Maleficent's home. Her lair.

Mal was on her mother's turf now, whether or not she was welcome there. And she knew that whatever happened next was about the two of them, test or not. Quest or not.

Even, Dragon's Eye or not.

Mal couldn't shake the feeling that something or someone was watching her; she'd felt it since she'd left home that morning, and the presence was even stronger in the fortress. But every time she looked over her shoulder there was nothing. Maybe she was just being paranoid.

Past the mirrored hallway, Mal and the others walked through a corridor hung with purple and gold pennants and great tapestries, depicting all the surrounding kingdoms. It was hard to tell one from the next, though, mostly because the dust was so thick. As they walked, they even made tracks across the dusty stones, as if they were instead trudging through hallways of snow.

But on they went.

The corridors bent and twisted, the floor sometimes

seeming uneven, the walls angling one way or the other, making them all feel as if they were in a dream or a funhouse or someplace that didn't really exist.

A fairy tale come to life.

A castle—only the way castles looked in nightmares.

Every wall and every stone was rendered in shades of grey and black, a faint green glow sometimes seeping through a wedge here and there.

Mother's home, Mal thought every time she noticed the green light.

The total effect was excruciating for all four of them—even for Mal.

Or, especially for Mal.

The cracked stained-glass windows were the only other source of colour. The old glass was mostly broken, and sections of the windows lay entirely in ruins, their shards dashed across the floor. Mal and the others had to step carefully to avoid slipping on the pieces. The long, window-lined corridor gave way to an even taller and wider corridor, and before long, Mal knew they were approaching some place of significance, a great chamber, perhaps even the heart of the castle itself.

Mal walked towards her fate, as Evie had said. Her destiny, if that's what it was.

Mal could feel it, the now familiar pull towards something unknown, something that perhaps belonged only to her.

It was there in front of her, buzzing and vibrating, just as it had been since the first moment she'd stepped inside the Thorn Forest. It pulled at her, beckoned her, even taunted her.

Come, it said.

Hurry.

This way.

Was it really her destiny calling to her, after all?

Or was it just another failure waiting for her in the throne room? More confirmation that she would never be her mother's daughter, no matter how hard she tried?

She stopped at a pair of doors twice the height of a grown man.

'This is it. It's here.'

She looked at Carlos, and he nodded, holding up the box. She saw that he had switched it off some time ago. 'We didn't need it any more,' he said, looking right at Mal.

Jay nodded to her. Even Evie reached for her hand, squeezing it once before she let it go again.

Mal took a breath. She felt a chill up her spine, and goosebumps all over her arm. 'This was Maleficent's throne room. I'm sure of it now. I can feel it.' She looked up at them. 'Does that sound crazy?'

They shook their heads, no.

She pushed open the doors, taking it all in.

The darkness and the power. The shadow and the light. Ceilings as high as the sky, and as black as smoke. Windows spanning whole walls, through which Maleficent could manipulate an entire world.

'Oh,' said Evie involuntarily.

Carlos looked like he wanted to bolt, but he didn't. Jay's eyes flickered across the room as if he were casing the joint.

But Mal felt like she was all alone with the ghosts.

One ghost, in particular. This was where her mother used to rage and command, where she had shot out of the ceiling as a green ball of fire to curse an entire kingdom. This was her seat of Darkness.

They pushed further inside, Mal at the front. Carlos and Jay and Evie fell like a phalanx of soldiers behind her, almost in formation.

The black stones beneath their feet were shiny and slick, and the entire room was haunted by an aura of deep malevolence. Mal could feel it; they all could.

This had been a sad, angry and unhappy home. Even now, the pain of that time burned its way through Mal, deep into her bones.

She shivered.

There was an empty place in the middle of the room where her mother's throne used to be. It had sat upon a great dais, flanked by two curving sets of stairs. The room was round and ringed with columns.

A great arc cradled the place where the throne had once sat, guarding an empty spot. The tattered remains of purple tapestries mouldered on the walls.

'There's nothing left,' Mal said, kneeling on the one dark spot that no longer held a throne. 'It's all gone.'

'You all right?' asked Jay, who was nervously blowing on his hands to warm them.

She nodded. 'It's . . .' she faltered, unable to find the words to describe what she was feeling. She had listened to all her mother's stories, but she didn't think they were *real*.

Not until now.

'Yeah,' he said. 'I know.' He shrugged, and she realised he'd probably felt the same way when they were in the Cave of Wonders. Mal knew Jafar and Iago talked about it all the time, but it was hard to imagine, hard to picture a world beyond what they knew of the Isle.

It had been, anyway.

Now everything was different.

Jay sighed. 'It's all real, isn't it?'

'I guess so,' Mal nodded. 'Every last page of every last story.' *Even the curse,* she thought, for the first time in hours.

The curse.

Someone has to touch it.

Evie has to touch it, and sleep for a thousand years.

'So, where is it?' Carlos asked, looking around the cold stone room.

'It has to be here somewhere,' said Evie, turning to look behind her.

'Maybe we should split up,' Jay said, a glint in his eye.

'Think,' Mal said. 'My mother was never without it. She held it even as she sat upon her throne.' Mal moved back to the spot where the throne no longer stood. 'Here.'

'So where would it be now?' Carlos frowned.

'It wouldn't be where anyone else could touch it,' Evie said. 'Try asking my mother if she'll let you touch any of her own Miss Fairest Everything memorabilia.'

Mal flinched at the word *touch*.

The curse was waiting for all of them—or at least, one of them—just as the Dragon's Eye was.

'But she'd want to see it, of course. From her throne,' Jay said. Mal nodded; they'd all seen Jafar orient himself in his kitchen, directly behind his stack of coins.

'Which would be—' Mal spun slowly round. She could picture her mother sitting here, clutching the staff, feeling powerful and evil and, well, like herself as she reigned over the kingdom.

She shook her head.

My mother would have no problem cursing any of the people in this room for 10,000 years, let alone one.

'There. Look!' cried Evie, spotting a tall black staff with a dim green globe at its top against the far wall.

It was, just as they had predicted, exactly in Mal's line of vision from the missing throne, but raised by some sort of magical light a good three metres into the air. Far out of the hands of any interlopers—and yes, where it could not be touched.

Of course.

There it was.

It's really here. The most powerful weapon of all Darkness. Evil lives! Indeed.

'It's right here!' Evie was closest to it and reached for it eagerly.

She shot her hand up into the air, extending her fingers. The moment she did, the Dragon's Eye began to shake, as if something about Mal herself was prising it loose from the very light and air that bound it.

Evie smiled. 'I've got it—'

Mal saw Evie's hand curl towards it, almost in slow motion. The sceptre itself seemed to glow, as if it were beckoning Evie towards it.

Everything around Mal seemed to blur until she could only see Evie's small, delicate fingers and the bewitched Dragon's Eye, just beyond her grasp.

In a split second, Mal had to make the decision: could she let Evie touch it and be cursed into a deep, death-like sleep for a thousand years?

Or would she save her?

Stop her?

Do something . . . *good?*

While betraying her own mother's wishes, and giving up on her own dream of becoming something more than a disappointment?

Was she content to remain only a Mal her entire life?

Never a Maleficent?

She froze, unable to decide.

'No!' cried Mal finally, running towards Evie. 'Don't!'

What just happened? What was she doing? Why couldn't she stop herself?

'What?' asked Evie, shocked, just as a familiar voice boomed from the Dragon's Eye.

'WHOEVER AWAKENS THE DRAGON WILL BE CURSED TO SLEEP FOR A THOUSAND YEARS!'

Maleficent's voice was coming from the staff even now, echoing and reverberating around the room.

Her mother really had left an impression behind her. What remained of her power and her energy crackled off the walls of the room, sparked to life by one accidental moment and latent until now, when it had victims to torture.

Evie's fingers brushed the air next to the staff . . . while Mal's hand closed upon it, and when it did . . . she fell to the floor, asleep.

Mal blinked her eyes. She could see herself lying on the floor of the throne room, purple hair spilling out like a stain beneath her head.

Her three companions huddled nervously round her.

So I'm sleeping, then? Or am I awake? Or maybe I'm dreaming?

Because Mal knew she was seeing something else as well.

She wasn't in the Forbidden Fortress any more.

She was in a palace, and there was good King Stefan and his queen and a baby in a cradle.

They were happy. She could see by the light in their faces, and by the way their eyes never left the child.

Almost like a magnet, Mal thought. *I know how that pull feels.*

A huge, gaily dressed crowd of courtiers and servants and guests assembled in a beautiful throne room around them. There were two good fairies hovering above the cradle, their wands making sparkles in the air. It was all so sweet, it was sickening.

Mal had never seen anything like it, not up close like this. Not in some kind of insipid storybook.

What is this?

Why am I seeing this?

Then a green ball of fire appeared in the middle of the room, and when it dispersed, Mal saw a familiar face.

Her mother.

Tall, haughty, beautiful and scorned.

Maleficent was angry.

Mal could feel the cold heat rising from her very being. She stared at her mother.

Maleficent addressed the crowd gathered around the royal family.

'Ah, I see everyone has been invited. The royalty, nobility, the gentry and the rabble. I must say, I really felt quite distressed at not receiving an invitation.'

What was her mother talking about? Then Mal realised. Maleficent had not been invited to Aurora's christening. Mal had never known this was the reason her mother hated parties and celebrations of all kinds.

But she knew exactly how her mother felt.

The hurt.

The shame.

The anger.

The desire for revenge.

Mal had felt exactly the same thing, hadn't she? When Evil Queen had thrown her party for Evie, all those years ago and kept *her* out?

Mal watched as her mother cursed the baby Princess Aurora to sleep a hundred years if she pricked her finger even once on a spindle. It was some fine spellcraft, and Mal was proud of her mother's efficiency, her power, her simple rendering. One prick of one finger could bring an entire royal house crashing down. It was a beautiful, terrible destiny. Well-woven. Deeply felt.

Mal was proud of Maleficent. She always had been, and she always would be. Maleficent had raised her daughter alone and got by as best she could. If only because there was no-one else to do it.

But her mother was made for Evil; she was good at it.

And in that very moment, and for the very first time, Mal finally understood that it wasn't just pride that she felt. It was pity. Maybe even compassion.

She was sad for her mother and that was something new.

The crowd saw a monster, a terror, a devil, a witch, cursing a beautiful princess. But Mal saw only a hurt little girl, acting out of spite and anger and insecurity.

She wanted to reach out and tell Maleficent it would be all right. She wasn't sure it was true, but they'd somehow got along this far, hadn't they?

It'll be all right, Mother.

She had to tell her.

But she woke up before she could.

Mal blinked her eyes open. She was in the throne room at the Forbidden Fortress. Jay, Carlos and Evie were standing around her nervously.

When she had fallen asleep she had been holding the Dragon's Eye sceptre in her hand. But when she woke up, it was nowhere to be seen.

chapter 26

The Girl with the Double Dragon Tattoo

'You're awake! But you're supposed to be asleep for a thousand years!' cried Evie. 'How?'

Mal rubbed her eyes. It was true—she was awake. She wasn't cursed. Why was that? Then she realised.

Prove that you are my daughter, prove that you are mine, her mother had ordered her. *Prove to me that you are the blood of the dragon. Prove you are worthy of that mark on your skin.*

The mark of the double dragon etched on her forearm. That had to be it. She held it up, showing the others.

'It couldn't hurt me,' said Mal. 'My true name is Maleficent. Like my mother, I am part dragon, and so I am immune to the Dragon's curse.'

'Lucky you,' Jay said, eyeing the impressive tat.

Mal smiled proudly down at the marking she bore.

If she had been her father's daughter, weak, human, she would be asleep by now. For a thousand years. But she wasn't. She was strong, and awake, and had proven to everyone that she was her mother's daughter.

Hadn't she?

And when she gave her mother the Dragon's Eye—

'But wait—where is it?' Mal said, looking around accusingly at the trio. 'I had it right in my hand!'

'Good question,' said Jay, sounding a little wounded himself.

'It's gone. When you grabbed it, there was a flash of light that blinded us for a second, and when we could see again, it was gone,' said Carlos. He shrugged. 'Easy come, easy go.'

The other three glared at him.

'Easy?' Evie raised an eyebrow, looking as tough as she possibly could.

Mal narrowed her eyes. 'Jay, come on, hand it over.'

'I swear, I don't have it!' said Jay, emptying his pockets to show her. 'I planned to take it. I wanted to take it. I was even going to take it out of your own hand, while you were sacked out.'

'And?'

He shrugged. 'Just didn't get around to it, I guess.'

'None of us have it,' said Evie. She folded her arms,

looking annoyed. 'And by the way, you knew the curse was on that staff and you had all of us come with you, anyway? What was up with that?'

Mal kicked a stone with her toe. 'Yeah. I didn't really work out the plan very well.'

'So why didn't you let me touch it, then? Wasn't that your evil scheme all along?'

Mal shrugged. 'What are you talking about? I just didn't want you to. It wasn't yours to touch.'

'Be honest. You were going to curse me, weren't you? You were going to let me touch that thing and end up taking the thousand-year nap?' Evie sighed.

Jay looked up. Carlos backed away instinctively. Mal knew neither one of them wanted to get anywhere near this conversation. She knew that because she felt the same way herself.

'I guess that was the plan.' Mal shrugged. *You don't have to explain yourself. Not to her.* But she found, strangely enough, that she wanted to.

'Is this still about the—you know?' Evie looked at her. 'Come on.'

Mal was embarrassed. 'I have no idea what you're talking about.'

'Sure you don't,' Jay muttered. Even Carlos laughed. Mal glared at both of them.

Evie rolled her eyes. 'The party. My party. Back when we were little kids.'

'Who can remember that far back?' Mal said, sticking out her chin stubbornly.

Evie looked tired. 'I begged my mother to invite you, you know. But she refused; she was still too angry at your mother. They've competed for everything for as long as they've known each other.'

Mal nodded again. 'I know. Because of that stupid election about who would lead this island, right?'

Evie shrugged. 'You know what they say. *Magic Mirror on the wall, who's the biggest ego of them all?*'

Mal smiled in spite of the entirely awkward nature of the conversation.

Evie looked her straight in the eye. 'Look, my mum messed up. But the party wasn't that great, really. You didn't miss much.'

'It wasn't a howler?'

'Not anything like Carlos' at all.' Evie smiled.

'That's right. I'm legendary,' Carlos said.

Mal glared at him. 'As if I didn't have to almost beat you into having that party?'

She looked back at Evie. 'Look, I didn't mean to trap you in Cruella's horrible wardrobe.' Mal glanced at Carlos, adding, 'The one she loves more than her own son.'

'Ha ha,' Carlos said, not laughing at all. Well, *sort of* not laughing. Actually, he was kind of laughing. Even Jay was having a hard time keeping a straight face.

Evie giggled as well. 'Yes, you did.'

'Okay, I did.' Mal smiled.

'It's all right.' Evie smiled back. 'I didn't get caught in any of the traps.'

'Cool,' said Mal, even as she was embarrassed by her softness.

Carlos sighed.

Jay punched him in the gut with a grin. 'Come on. At least your mum doesn't only wear tracksuits and pyjamas.'

'Let's not talk about it,' said Evie and Mal, almost in unison.

'Yeah. Enough with the violins. We got a long walk home,' Jay said. 'And I'm not all that sure that this place has a back door.'

Mal had a hard time keeping her mind on finding the way out of the fortress, though.

She was soft, and she was worried.

She had just saved someone's life, practically. Hadn't she?

What kind of self-respecting second-generation villain did anything of the sort?

What had happened to her grand evil scheme?

Why hadn't she just let Evie be cursed by Maleficent's

sceptre? Weren't princesses *meant* to sleep for years and years anyway? Didn't that basically come with the job description?

What if my mum is right?

What if Mal really *was* weak like her father—and worse, had a propensity for good somewhere in her black little heart?

Mal shuddered as she walked along behind the others.

No. If anything, being immune to the curse just proved she was definitely *not* her father's daughter. One day she too would be Maleficent.

She *had* to be.

But whether she was Maleficent's daughter or not, she had failed.

She was returning home empty-handed.

Boy, did she *not* want to be around when her mother found out.

chapter 27

The Descendants

This wasn't the victory lap Mal had imagined when she'd first set off in search of the Forbidden Fortress.

Defeated, the unlikely gang of four began to retrace their steps, just looking for the way out. They had lost everything, as usual. By any reasonable standard—or by her mother's infinitely *less* reasonable standards, Mal thought—they were utter and complete failures, every last one.

Especially her.

The moment they retreated from the throne room, though, Mal couldn't help but feel a shiver of relief at also leaving its darkness behind.

Although, oddly enough, the fortress had a different feel now, like it was dead. Mal couldn't feel the same energy it had before.

'Do you think the hole in the dome's plugged up again?' she asked Carlos. 'It feels different in here.'

'Maybe,' he said. 'Or maybe the magic it sparked is spent, now.'

Mal looked out at the sky. She had a feeling there wouldn't be any more magic on the island.

Nobody said a word as they found their way back to the hall where the Magic Mirror was now just an ordinary surface—especially not Evie, who avoided so much as a glance at it.

Nobody said a word, either, as they hurried once again over the crumbling marble floor, this time avoiding both the scampering rats and the fluttering bats—going nowhere near any goblin passages or suffocating mazes or dusty tapestry rooms or portrait halls—until they reached the vast, empty cave that had so briefly become the sand-filled Cave of Wonders.

Especially not Jay, who only quickened the pace of his own echoing footsteps until he once again found the rotting wooden door that had brought them there the first time.

And Carlos seemed in a particular hurry to get through twisting passages that led to the black-marble-floored, dark-fogged halls of the main fortress. As he pushed his way out of the front doors, the gargoyle bridge once again faced them.

Faced *him*.

When the others caught up to Carlos, they stopped and stared over the precipice where he stood. The dizzying depths of the ravine below were, well, dizzying. But he didn't seem in any hurry to step back up to the bridge this time.

'It's fine,' Evie said, encouragingly. 'We'll just do what we did before.'

'Sure. We cross one stupid bridge.' Jay nodded. 'Not very far at all.'

That was true. On the other side of the bridge, they could just make out the winding path leading its way down through the thorn forest, from the direction they'd originally come.

'We're practically home free,' Mal agreed, looking sideways at Carlos, who sighed.

He looked at Mal. 'I don't know. Do you think it looks a little more, you know, crumbly? After all those tidal earthquakes we were feeling back there? It doesn't seem like the safest plan.'

Nobody could disagree.

The problem was still the bridge. It was all in one piece this time, with no missing sections—but they all knew better than to trust anything in the fortress.

And not one of them dared set foot on it, after last time. Not after the riddles. Though they'd made it over easily enough the first time, once they'd answered the riddles, they hadn't thought about having to go back the way they'd come.

'I don't know if I can do it again,' Carlos said, taking in the faces of the once again stone gargoyles. He winced at the thought of their coming to life again.

In Mal's own mind, she hadn't got much past imagining the scene where she reclaimed her mother's missing sceptre and came home a hero. She had been a little foggy on the actual details beyond that, she supposed, and now that the whole redemption thing was off the table, she really didn't have a back-up plan.

But as she looked at Carlos, who stood there shivering, she suspected at the memory of collapsing bridges and fur coats and a mother's true love that wasn't her son, Mal figured out a way across.

Mal stepped in front of him. 'You don't have to do it again.' She took another step, and then another. 'I mean, you don't get to hog all the cool bridge action,' she said, trying to sound convincing. 'Now it's my turn.'

'What?' Carlos looked confused.

The wind picked up as Mal kept moving forward, but she didn't stop.

Mal pulled her jacket tightly round her and shouted up at the gargoyles. 'You don't scare me! I've seen worse. Where do you think I grew up, Auradon?'

The wind howled around her now. She took another step, motioning for the other three to move behind her.

'Are you crazy?' Jay shook his head, sliding behind her.

'Mal, seriously. You don't have to do this,' Carlos whispered, ducking behind Jay.

'Definitely crazy,' Evie said, from behind Carlos.

'Me, crazy?' Mal raised her voice even higher. 'How could I not be? I go to school in a graveyard and eat expired scones for breakfast. My own mother sends me to forbidden places like this, because of some old bird and a lost stick,' she scoffed. 'There's nothing you can throw at me that's worse than what I've already got going.'

As she spoke, Mal kept pressing forward. She had crossed the halfway point of the bridge now, dragging the others right behind her.

The wind roared and whipped against them, as if it would pick them up and toss them off the bridge itself, if she let it. But Mal wouldn't.

'Is that all you've got?' She stuck out her chin, that much more stubborn. 'You think a little breeze like that can get to someone like me?'

Lightning cracked overhead, and she started to run—her friends right behind her. By the time they reached the other side, the bridge had begun to rock so hard, it seemed like it would crumble again.

Only, this time it wouldn't be an illusion.

The moment Mal felt the dirt of the far cliff safely beneath her feet, she stumbled over a tree root and collapsed, bringing Carlos and Evie down with her. Jay stood there laughing.

Until he realised that he wasn't the only one laughing.

'Uh, guys?'

Mal looked up. They were surrounded by a crowd of goblins—not unlike the ones who had chased them through the goblin passages of the Forbidden Fortress. Except these particular goblins seemed to be of a friendlier variety.

'Girl,' one said.

'Brave,' said another.

'Help,' said a third.

'I don't get it,' Evie said, sitting up. Mal and Carlos scrambled to their feet. Jay took a step back.

Finally, a fourth goblin sighed. 'I think what my companions are trying to articulate is that we're incredibly impressed by that show of fortitude. The bravery. The perseverance. It's a bit unusual, in these parts.'

'Parts,' repeated the goblins.

'It talks,' Evie said.

Mal looked from one goblin to another. 'Uh, thanks?'

'Not at all,' said the goblin. The goblins around him began to grunt animatedly—although Mal thought it might be laughter, too. Carlos looked nervous. Jay just grunted back.

The fourth goblin sighed again, looking back at Mal. 'And if you'd like our assistance in any way, we'd be more than happy to help convey you to your destination.'

He looked Mal over.

She looked him over, in return. 'Our destination?'

He suddenly became flustered. 'You do seem far away from home,' he said, adding hastily: 'Not to presume. It's a conclusion I draw only from the irrefutable fact that neither you nor your friends seem, well, remotely goblin-esque.'

The goblins grunt-laughed again.

Jay stared. 'You're about two feet tall. How would a guy like you get people like us all the way back to town?'

Evie elbowed him.

'Not to be rude,' Jay said.

'Rude,' chanted the goblins, still grunt-laughing.

'I'm pretty sure that was rude,' Carlos muttered.

'Ah, there you have it. Alone, we are but a single goblin, perhaps even a brute.' The goblin smiled. 'Together, I'm afraid we are a rather brutal army. Not to mention, we pull an excellent carriage.'

'Pull!' The goblins went nuts.

An old iron carriage—like the kind you might have seen Belle and Beast ride away in, except black and burned and nothing that either the queen or king of Auradon would so much as touch—appeared in front of them.

No less than 40 goblins manned either side, fighting for a grip on the carriage itself.

'Why would you do that?' Mal said, as a good seven goblins battled the broken door open. 'Why are you being so nice?'

'A good deed. Helping a fellow adventurer. Perhaps

there's a chance for us to get off this island yet,' said the goblin. 'We have been sending messages to our dwarf kin asking King Beast for amnesty. We've been wicked for such a very long time, you know. It does get tiresome after a while. I would kill for a cream cake.'

'Raisins,' said a goblin.

'Chocolate chip,' said another.

Mal had to admit, she was starting to feel a little exhausted herself. She knew, because she slept the entire way home, without even being embarrassed that her head was resting on Evie's shoulder.

When Mal returned to the Bargain Castle, she fully expected her mother to scream invectives at her for failing in her quest. She opened the door slowly and stepped inside, as quietly as she could, keeping her eyes on the ground.

It was no use. Maleficent was on her throne. 'So, the prodigal daughter returns,' she said. Her voice sounded different.

'Mother, I have something to . . .' Mal stopped, looking up.

And stared.

And then stared some more, in about 10 different varieties of shock.

Because she found herself staring at the long black staff with the green globe at its top that her mother was holding.

The Dragon's Eye.

'Is that—' She couldn't speak.

Maleficent nodded. 'Yes, it is the Dragon's Eye. And yes, you did fail me. But thankfully, not all my servants are as useless as you.'

Mal ignored the word *servant*. 'But how?'

Maleficent laughed. 'Silly child, what do you know about quests?'

'But we found it in the Forbidden Fortress! I just touched it—an hour ago!' said Mal. 'It was in your own throne room. Suspended on the wall. Where you could see it, from where your throne used to sit.'

Her mother eyed her. Mal couldn't be certain, but it was possible, for the briefest of all split seconds, that her mother was the slightest bit impressed.

'I touched it, and that thing knocked me unconscious.'

'You touched it? You don't say,' said Maleficent. 'Well, good job, you. You really are as soft as your father.'

Mal bristled. 'I don't understand.'

'You touched the Dragon's Eye? Instead of tricking one of the others into doing it? Such weakness. I didn't want to believe the news when I heard it.' Maleficent banged her staff upon the floor next to her feet. 'How many times, Mal? How much more will you shame me?'

She rolled her eyes. 'I sent Diablo out after you to retrieve the Eye for me. He must have taken it from you while you were sleeping off the curse.' She shook her head. 'I knew you wouldn't have it in you to do what needed to be done, and I knew I couldn't take any chances. It appears I was right. Again.'

Diablo cawed proudly.

So she'd been right about feeling as if they were being followed. Of course. That was Diablo.

Mal felt like giving up. It never mattered how hard she tried, or what she did, she would never impress her mother.

Even now, her mother had eyes only for the Dragon's Eye.

'The only thing is, it's broken,' said Maleficent with a frown. 'Look at the eye, it's dead.' For a moment, she sounded like the same angry little girl who had cursed a baby over a party invitation. Mal remembered all too well, and she looked at her mother through new eyes.

'Well, the dome is still up,' said Mal, finally. 'It keeps the magic out.' It had been down for a brief moment, but there would be no magic on the island anytime soon.

'Maybe. Or maybe you broke the eye when you touched it,' Maleficent accused. 'You are such a disappointment.'

Meanwhile, at Jafar's Junk Shop, an angry Jafar was berating Jay, who had returned home empty-handed. 'So you're saying you did find the Dragon's Eye, did you? So where is it, then?'

'It disappeared!' Jay protested. 'One minute we had it, and then we lost it.'

'Right. And this had nothing to do with a certain good

deed performed by a certain daughter of evil for a certain other daughter of evil?'

Jay froze. 'Excuse me?'

The words *good* and *deed* were chilling, particularly on the Isle, and particularly when coming out of his father's mouth.

'Did you think goblins keep secrets particularly well, boy? The news is all over the island.'

'I swear. That's what really happened. I swear on a stack of stolen . . .' Jay blanked. He couldn't think of a single thing to steal at the moment.

But to be honest, for once in his life, he didn't even care.

'You are such a disappointment,' Jafar snorted.

Over at Hell Hall, Carlos was getting an earful after Cruella finally discovered her furs in disarray in her wardrobe. 'Who has been in here? It looks like a wild animal was trapped with my furs! What imbecile would do such a thing?'

'A wild one?' Carlos winced. He knew it was pointless to even try. Not when the wardrobe looked like this.

Her reply was a scream and it was bloodcurdling. Even in his mother's signature shrill octave.

'I'm sorry, Mother,' whimpered Carlos. 'It won't happen again! I know how much you love your furs.' The words were almost a whisper. He could see the faces of the gargoyles from the bridge, mocking him as he said them.

Then he could see Mal, Evie and Jay laughing at her with him, and he had to keep from secretly smiling.

Cruella sniffed. 'You are such a disappointment!'

Over at the Castle-Across-the-Way, the Evil Queen was lamenting the state of Evie's hair. 'It's like a rat's nest! What happened? You look awful.'

'I'm sorry, Mother, we ran into . . . well . . . uh . . . let's just say I couldn't find a mirror.'

I found one, she thought. *Just not the kind you want to look at.*

Not when you're supposed to be the fairest of them all.

'Just promise me these rumours I'm hearing aren't true,' her mother said. 'All this talk of a virtuous act.' She shuddered. 'The goblins are saying such horrid things about the four of you.'

'You know that goblins are horrible creatures, Mum.' Evie hid her face. She didn't know what to say. To be honest, she didn't even know what she thought. It had been a strange few days.

Not entirely bad, but strange.

The Evil Queen sighed. 'You forgot to reapply blusher again. Oh dear, sometimes, you're such a disappointment.'

Mal sat out on the balcony, hearing the sounds of laughter and mayhem from down below. Then, a shout.

'Mal!' Jay called. 'Come down!'

She ran downstairs. 'What's up?'

'Oh nothing, just trying to get away from our parents and disappointing them again,' said Carlos.

'You too, huh?' asked Mal. She turned to Jay and Evie. 'And you?'

The three of them nodded.

'Come on, let's go to the market,' said Evie. 'I need a new scarf.'

'I can get you one,' said Jay, waggling his eyebrows. 'Oh, and Evie—here you go,' he said. 'I believe this might be yours.'

'My necklace!' said Evie, putting the poison-heart charm round her neck once more, with a smile. 'Thanks, Jay.'

'I found it.'

'In his pocket,' said Mal, but even she was grinning.

With a whoop, the four descendants of the world's greatest villains ran through the crowded streets of the Isle of the Lost, causing havoc, stealing and plundering together while the citizens of the island ran the other way. They were truly rotten to the core.

Even Mal started to feel better.

And in fact, as they laughed and sang, Mal wondered if this was what happiness was like.

Because even though the four of them weren't quite friends yet, they were the closest things they had to it.

'You will join me for dinner... That's not a request!'
—Beast, Beauty and the Beast

epilogue

Sunrise Over Auradon

While the band of four villain kids was causing havoc in the streets of the Isle of the Lost, Prince Ben was looking out of the window from his high vantage point in Beast Castle, lost in a few thoughts of his own.

It was true that Grumpy the Dwarf had told him he'd make a good king, but privately Ben wondered if he was right.

More to the point, he wondered if becoming a good king was even something he cared about at all.

Did it matter? What he cared about? What he wanted?

Trapped, Ben thought, staring out over the vast expanse of the kingdom. That's what I am.

He looked up at the sky, as if it held the answers. The blue wash was bright and clear as usual, and he could see all the way to the distant horizon, where Auradon itself dissolved into nothing but misty shoreline and azure water.

No.

Not nothing.

Ben thought of his dream of the island.

The Isle of the Lost. That's what everyone called it, even his father.

He considered again what it would be like to live as they did, trapped underneath the magical dome, just as he was in his royal life.

They were prisoners, weren't they? His father tried to pretend that they were not, but even Ben knew otherwise. They were exiled to the island by order of the king.

Just as Ben was able to live in the castle because he was the king's son. *And because my father loves me,* Ben thought. *And because I was born to this.*

It was impossible to stop thinking about it.

He flinched.

'Ouch,' Ben said, as a needle poked him again in the armpit.

'Sorry, sire; forgive me, sire.' Lumiere, who was measuring him for his coronation suit, quailed.

'Quite all right,' said Ben, who looked kingly, at least

according to Lumiere, in the royal blue velvet suit with yellow piping. It had belonged to King Beast, who had worn it at his own coronation. 'It was my fault—I moved.'

'Your mind is elsewhere, sire,' said Lumiere sagely. 'As befitting a future king of Auradon.'

'Perhaps,' said Ben.

For a future king, he was surprised by how little he knew about the Isle of the Lost. How did the villains fare, beneath the dome? How did they live, eat, take care of themselves? How were their families? What were their hopes and dreams? What did they see when they stared out of the windows of their own castle or cottage or cave?

Ben remembered he had heard that a few of them had children. Some would have to be his own age by now, wouldn't they? He wondered how they dealt with living in the shadow of their infamous parents.

I imagine that for them, it's a lot like this, he thought, staring down at his royal beast-head ring. Wearing his father's suit, fitted by his father's tailor. Standing at the window of his father's castle.

We're all trapped. I'm as trapped as they are.

The more Ben thought about it, the more he knew it was true. He hadn't chosen to be born a prince and become a king, just as they hadn't chosen who their parents were. They were prisoners for a crime they themselves had not committed.

That was the greater crime, wasn't it?

It's not fair. It's not our fault. We have no say in our own lives. We're living in a fairy tale someone else wrote.

In that moment, Ben suddenly understood why it was that the sidekicks wanted more for their lives: because he found he wanted even more than *that*.

He wanted things to change, throughout Auradon.

Everything, he thought. *For everyone.*

Was that even possible? On the other hand, how could it not be? How could he possibly keep going with the way things were now?

Ben thought about it.

If he was going to be king, he would have to be himself, his mother had said. And he was different from his father. That was clear to everyone, even Lumiere. Ben would rule, but he would rule differently.

He would make different rules and proclamations.

His mind wandered again to the image of the purple-haired girl with the bright green eyes. The girl from his dream.

Who was she?

Would he ever meet her?

Was she one of them? One of the lost souls on that cursed island? He had a feeling that she was.

And just then, he had a flash of inspiration.

One that would change the fates of both Auradon and the Isle of the Lost forever.

Why not?

It's about time.

His mind was made up.

'Sire! Where are you going?' cried Lumiere as Ben suddenly leaped away from the needle and thread, a flurry of pins and bespoke chalk and measuring tape flying into the air around him.

'To find my parents! I have something to tell them and it can't wait!' said Ben. 'I've got the most brilliant idea!'

acknowledgements

When I was a little girl growing up in the Philippines, the first movie I ever saw was *Cinderella*, which had been my mother's favourite movie as a child. It was the first movie I ever watched with my daughter, and it also became *her* favourite movie. (*My* favourite is *Sleeping Beauty*.) Disney magic was a huge part of my childhood, and now it is a huge part of my daughter's. It was wonderful to watch the old movies again with her while I was writing this book, as well as share the new Disney Channel movie that inspired it. I still can't believe that I got to play in this universe and with these characters who defined my childhood. It's been a magical journey, and I owe my thanks to the people who helped me on my way. My publishing family – my editor, Emily Meehan, my publisher, Suzanne Murphy, and everyone at Disney Hyperion, especially Seale Ballenger, Mary Ann Zissimos, Simon Tasker, Elena Blanco, Kim Knueppel, Sarah Sullivan, Jackie DeLeo, Frank Bumbalo,

Jessica Harriton, Dina Sherman, Elke Villa, Andrew Sansone and Holly Nagel, who have seen me through countless books and launches, thanks for keeping the faith! Marci Senders, who put together a wickedly awesome design, and Monica Mayper, who made sure every villainous dangling participle fell into place. Disney Consumer Products grand poobahs Andrew Sugerman and Raj Murari throw the best parties. Jeanne Mosure is my hero. Big thanks to Rebecca Frazer and Jennifer Magee-Cook from Team Descendants, and all the lovely folks at the Disney Channel, especially Jennifer Rogers Doyle, Leigh Tran, Naketha Mattocks and Gary Marsh. It was a thrill to meet director Kenny Ortega, production designer Mark Hofeling and the stars of the movie, Dove Cameron, Booboo Stewart, Cameron Boyce, Sofia Carson and the inimitable Kristin Chenoweth. Screenwriters Sara Parriott and Josann McGibbon's script was hilarious and inspiring. My agent, Richard Abate, is the man. Melissa Kahn is awesome. Thanks and love to the DLC and Johnston families, especially my nephews Nicholas and Joseph Green and Sebastian de la Cruz. I get by with a little help from my friends, especially dear Margie Stohl. My husband, Mike Johnston, is a creative genius, and he and our daughter, Mattie Johnston, make everything worthwhile.

I hope you enjoyed the book and that it created a whole new set of Disney memories. You won't want to miss the movie. Thank you for reading!

xoxo

Mel

Return to the Isle of the Lost

ALSO BY MELISSA DE LA CRUZ

DESCENDANTS
The Isle of the Lost

THE BLUE BLOODS SERIES
Blue Bloods
Masquerade
Revelations
The Van Alen Legacy
Keys to the Repository
Misguided Angel
Bloody Valentine
Lost in Time
Gates of Paradise

The Ring and the Crown

Return to the Isle of the Lost

A DESCENDANTS NOVEL

#1 *NEW YORK TIMES* BEST-SELLING AUTHOR
MELISSA DE LA CRUZ

BASED ON *DESCENDANTS* WRITTEN BY
JOSANN MCGIBBON & SARA PARRIOTT

SCHOLASTIC
SYDNEY AUCKLAND NEW YORK TORONTO LONDON MEXICO CITY
NEW DELHI HONG KONG BUENOS AIRES PUERTO RICO

Copyright © 2018 Disney Enterprises, Inc. All rights reserved.
Visit www.DisneyBooks.com and DisneyDescendants.com

Published by Scholastic Australia in 2018.

Scholastic Australia Pty Limited
PO Box 579 Gosford NSW 2250
ABN 11 000 614 577
www.scholastic.com.au

Part of the Scholastic Group
Sydney • Auckland • New York • Toronto • London • Mexico City
• New Delhi • Hong Kong • Buenos Aires • Puerto Rico

Cover design by Marci Senders
Cover art by James Madsen
Hand lettering by Russ Gray

All rights reserved. No part of this publication may be reproduced or transmitted in any form or by any means, electronic or mechanical, including photocopying, recording, storage in an information retrieval system, or otherwise, without the prior written permission of the publisher, unless specifically permitted under the Australian Copyright Act 1968 as amended.

ISBN 978-1-74299-584-7

Printed in Australia by Griffin Press.

Scholastic Australia's policy, in association with Griffin Press, is to use papers that are renewable and made efficiently from wood grown in responsibly managed forests, so as to minimise its environmental footprint.

10 9 8 7 6 5 4 3 2 1   18 19 20 21 22 / 1

For Mattie,
my hero

And the

C.H. Class of 2025,

Go Vikings!

'I've got the most brilliant idea!'
—Prince Ben,
The Isle of the Lost

Disney's Descendants

Once upon a time, after all the happily-ever-afters, when all the fairy tales were supposed to have ended, came a new beginning when the teenage children of the most evil villains in the land were sent from the remote Isle of the Lost to the majestic kingdom of Auradon.

As you surely have heard, Mal, Evie, Jay and Carlos, the descendants of Maleficent, Mistress of Darkness; Evil Queen, infamous for her sleep-inducing apples; Jafar, grand vizier of avarice; and Cruella de Vil, harridan extraordinaire, were sent far from home to learn how to be good.

After childhoods spent learning to be just the opposite, the villains, being villains, had other intentions.

Mal and her friends were tasked by their evil parents to fetch Fairy Godmother's wand and use its power to return the villains to their former glory and rain vengeance on their enemies.

However, after arriving in Auradon, these young villains were soon flummoxed by the friendliness of the natives and the abundance of sugary treats in this new land. They found themselves struggling between carrying out their sinister mission and enjoying their new, deliciously cookie-filled life.

Were they falling in love with Auradon while plotting its demise? Mal was certainly falling for someone—the handsome prince of her dreams, Prince Ben, whom she'd spelled into falling in love with her, only to realise she didn't need magic to capture his heart. Ben was as smitten as she was, and there was more to him than his brilliant smile, for he also had the heart of a king.

When the time came for Mal and her friends to make their move on Fairy Godmother's wand during Prince Ben's Coronation, it was not Mal who grabbed it and caused the chaos that followed, but Fairy Godmother's own daughter, Jane. As the invisible barrier over the Isle of the Lost shattered, magic returned to the villains in full force, allowing Maleficent to escape. The evil fairy turned into a fire-breathing dragon, terrorising all of Auradon, determined to claim the wand as her own.

But Mal, Evie, Carlos and Jay stood together, and it was Mal who won the battle and wielded the wand. In the end, her power for good was far greater than her mother's talent for evil.

Mal and her friends are back at their studies at Auradon Prep . . . and Maleficent is now a tiny lizard, reduced to the size of her heart.

And this is where our story begins . . .

The 'Good' Life

'Like all dreams, well, I'm afraid this can't last forever.'
—Fairy Godmother, Cinderella

chapter 1

Tale as Old as Time

If Mal had to pick what she liked most about Auradon, it would be hard to choose just one thing. She could probably spend a whole day cataloguing everything that didn't stink about her new school. For one, it wasn't housed in a smelly, damp dungeon like Dragon Hall back on the Isle. For another, it was a surprise to find she actually enjoyed learning about a variety of subjects instead of just plotting evil schemes. She was particularly fond of her art classes, where she happily painted canvases full of mysterious foggy landscapes and gloomy dark castles instead of the peaceful sunsets and still lifes of fruit favoured by the rest of the class. Why anyone would want to paint something as boring as a bowl of fruit, Mal would never understand.

She was sitting at a long table in the great room in Auradon Prep's library, a cheerful, bright space with high ceilings and banners with the school colours hanging from the ceiling. Mal was trying to do homework for a change, but was too distracted by the people-watching as students kept filing in and out between classes. Plus, her Goodness Appreciation essay was putting her to sleep. So she looked out the floor-to-ceiling library windows instead, at the manicured lawns where she played croquet (well, made fun of people playing croquet might be more accurate) and the patch of shady oak trees where she and her friends often ate lunch together.

Yeah, life in Auradon was good; better than an unexpected makeover before midnight, or an endless feast presented by dancing plates and cutlery; better even, than being invited to a baby princess' christening.

'Happy?' a voice asked, snapping her out of her uncharacteristically dreamy reverie.

She blushed and smiled across the table at the handsome boy who smiled back at her from behind his swoop of golden-brown hair. 'What makes you say that?' she asked.

'You look . . . positively delighted,' Ben said, tapping his pencil on her nose to show he was teasing.

She raised an eyebrow. 'I was just thinking what a scream

it would be to glue a fake nose on Pin,' she said, meaning Pinocchio's son, who was a nervous first-year.

Ben chuckled, his eyes shining. He was a good sport.

Okay, so if Mal had to pick what she liked *most* about Auradon, she would probably have to admit it was the boy sitting across from her. Ben, son of Belle and Beast, was not only the kindest person she had ever met, but was easy on the eyes (um, make that *very* easy) and smart, too. More importantly, while Mal was the polar opposite of Auradon's many perfect princesses, he liked her anyway. This made her feel as warm and cozy as her favourite beat-up patchwork leather jacket, which was much more her speed than ruffles and sequins. While she'd rocked a ball gown for his Coronation, she was glad she didn't have to wear one all the time. Talk about itchy.

Ben smiled and went back to doing his homework, and Mal tried to do the same, except she kept getting interrupted by friends who came by to say hello when they saw her in the library.

'Hey, Mal! Love your outfit today!' said Lonnie with a big smile. Ever since she'd learned the truth of the villain kids' deprived childhoods on the Isle of the Lost, Mulan's daughter was especially sweet.

'Mal!' cried Jane. 'Will you stop by later and help me with my Fair Is Fair homework? I can't get the equation right.' Jane was often nervous about doing things correctly, especially after the disaster she'd caused at Ben's Coronation. It was a lot to live up to having Fairy Godmother as your mother, especially when she was also the headmistress of your school.

'Thanks, and sure!' said Mal. 'Anytime!'

'Look who's so popular,' teased Ben, when the girls were out of earshot.

Mal gave a dismissive wave. 'Everyone's just glad my mum didn't turn them all into dragon toast.' She nodded towards the guarded, double-locked doors at the end of the room that led to Maleficent's new prison. 'Not that I blame them.' Joking helped assuage some lingering guilt about her mother's behaviour; not all transfer students had to deal with things like having their parents try to destroy everyone at their new school.

Where was the new student manual for that?

'All thanks to you,' Ben said with a serious look on his face. 'We didn't stand a chance otherwise.'

'Don't worry, I'll figure out how you can all pay me back later,' Mal said airily. She couldn't help but smile. 'Although another rousing vocal performance in front of the entire school where you happen to mention your ridiculous love for me might just do the trick.'

Ben smiled broadly. 'Done! There's a tourney game this weekend for Castlecoming. I'll practise my dance moves.'

'I can't wait.' Mal laughed, tucking a strand of her bright purple locks behind her ear.

'Sure you won't be too embarrassed to be my date at the dance after?' he asked, beginning to hum the catchy melody.

'Yeah, I'll probably have to hide my face behind one of Mulan's masks,' she said, then the floor underneath their feet suddenly began to vibrate and the whole room began to shake. Mal grabbed her books before they fell to the floor, and Ben gripped the edge of the table, trying to keep it steady.

'Another earthquake,' Mal said. 'That's the third one this week!' Out of habit, she looked over her shoulder again at the door to Maleficent's prison. Until recently, Mal had only felt the ground rumble like that when a great big dragon stomped around during the Coronation attack, so Mal couldn't help but associate earthquakes with her mother.

'Heard it's happening all over, not just Auradon City,' said Ben with a frown. 'But it's a natural phenomenon, don't worry. Tectonic plates rumbling underneath the ocean and all that.'

'Well, I wish they'd stay still,' said Mal. 'They make me feel queasy.'

'At least they go away quickly,' said Ben.

Unlike some people, Mal thought, forcing herself not to look back at the prison door.

There were no aftershocks to this one thankfully, and an hour later Mal had already forgotten about it. Ben began to put his books away in his satchel and she glanced at the clock. It wasn't time for the dinner bell yet. 'Leaving already?' she asked. 'King duties?'

'Yeah, I have to cut the ribbon at the opening of the new Sidekick Recreation Centre. Don't want them to feel overlooked.' Ben shrugged into his blue blazer with the embroidered royal beast-head crest on its right-hand pocket.

'Don't you mean kick the ribbon?' Mal teased, but Ben didn't laugh back. She knew he took his royal responsibilities very seriously, and he meant to be a king for all of Auradon—sidekicks and villainy offspring included.

'Text you later?' Ben tugged at a lock of her hair.

'Not if I text you first,' she promised.

Mal did a little more work, but stopped when she heard her phone buzz in her backpack. Thinking it was Ben, she picked it up, but it was a text from an unknown number instead. Strange. She clicked it open and read the message.

Go back where you belong.

Excuse me? she sent. *What's this all about?* She looked around suspiciously, but the library was full of Auradon students diligently working on their Virtues and Values term papers on computer terminals or else absorbed in their Kindness and Decency reading. This week's assignment was Snow White's *How to Keep a Happy Home for a Family of Seven (Dwarfs Optional)*.

Mal looked back down at her phone, waiting to see what

would happen next, a pit growing in her stomach. There was no reply for a long time, then the little wand at the bottom of her screen began to show sparks, which indicated that the recipient was typing a reply. Finally, it appeared on her screen:

You must return to the Isle of the Lost at once! Before the new moon rises!

Who is this? she texted back, more irritated than scared.

You know who I am.

I'm M . . .

There was no more. Just 'M'. Who was M? Mal stared at the screen. Who demanded that she return to the Isle of the Lost? And why did she have to return before the new moon rose? And when would that be, anyway?

Mal could think of a few M's in her life, but there was only one M that mattered the most. The big one. Maleficent. Could her mother be communicating to her through text? She might be sitting in her lizard-size prison right now, but she was still the greatest evil fairy who had ever lived. Anything was possible, she supposed.

Of course Maleficent would want Mal to go home. Her mother had only planned to escape the Isle of the Lost because its invisible barrier kept her from her magic. She despised Auradon and its pretty forests and enchanted rivers. If Maleficent had succeeded in her vengeful plot, the entire kingdom would be as gloomy, dark and wretched as the Forbidden Fortress by now. In other words, darker than anything her friends at Auradon Prep could imagine . . .

That was not something she could ever let happen.

Mal read the mysterious text again, apprehension making her heart beat faster. She collected her things, determined to find her friends so they could help her figure out what was going on.

Mal had a feeling that her sweet life in Auradon was about to turn rotten.

chapter 2
Fighting Knights

Jay was used to dodging angry shopkeepers and furious bazaar merchants as they watched their precious wares disappear into the hands of the fast-moving thief in the red beanie and purple-and-yellow vest, so playing tourney was *much* easier than that. At least he didn't have to dodge rotten tomatoes and threats of dismemberment as he zigzagged his way to the goal, trying to keep away from the red-and-white-striped painted 'kill zone' in the middle of the field. It was a perfect afternoon for practise, the sky a cloudless blue, the trees bordering the field lush and green. The stands were empty save for a few students hanging out with friends or doing homework, and the cheerleaders in their yellow T-shirts and blue skirts were having their own practice by the sidelines.

When the ground beneath him began to shake, Jay ignored it and ran left, caught the puck in his stick, and ducked past the loaded cannons, tumbling as he whipped the puck right into the net. He raised his arms in victory, skidding to a stop on his knees just as the rumbling vibrations ceased. A slow, satisfied smile grew on his face. His long dark hair was plastered to his forehead and neck, and sweat drenched his uniform. Earthquakes didn't scare him; nothing could stop him from running as fast as he could towards a goal.

All his life, he'd had to use his fleet feet and lightning-quick reflexes to nab items to fill the shelves of his father's junk shop, at the expense of others. But here at Auradon Prep, his talents got him a coveted varsity spot on the tourney team, and Jay was getting so used to riding his teammates' shoulders at the end of every victory that the novelty had almost worn off. Aladdin's son, Aziz, even teased that Jay should lay off the pumpkin juice a little or else he'd get too heavy to carry.

The cheerleaders practising on the sidelines screamed Jay's name in appreciation. He jumped up and doffed his helmet to them, causing the girls to giggle and shake their pom-poms even faster.

Jay was walking over to the sidelines to grab his water from his gym bag when he noticed a crumpled piece of notebook paper among his things. What was this? He opened it up. In purple ink, someone had scrawled, *Run back to where you came from! Return to the Isle of the Lost by moon's end!*

What was that all about? And what about the moon? Huh?

'Hey, man, good play,' said Chad Charming. The golden-haired, pampered son of Cinderella usually wasn't very nice to Jay, but maybe there was more to this handsome prince than a headful of carefully coiffed hair. Chad held out his hand. Jay took it, albeit suspiciously.

'Thanks, man,' he said, stuffing the strange note in the back of his pocket.

'Then again, anyone can score off Herkie,' Chad said, squeezing Jay's palm and nodding towards Hercules' son at the goal. 'All brawn but flat feet, know what I'm saying?'

Herkie was as strong as his father and had the muscles to prove it, but he wasn't the fastest on the field. Even so, Chad was lucky he wasn't within earshot.

'You're saying you could have done it?' asked Jay, his hand still clasped in Chad's grip.

'Blindfolded,' said Chad, still shaking Jay's hand forcefully up and down and smiling through his teeth. 'See, the thing is, Jay, it's easy to dodge a cannon, but in tourney, you've got to watch out for what you never see coming.' And with his trademark sneer, Chad twisted his wrist and flipped Jay over, sending him sprawling on the ground face-first. *Oof.*

'See what I mean?' Chad smiled. 'Consider it a little coaching between friends.'

'Oh, Chad, you're too hilarious for words!' Audrey, who had come up from the sidelines to coo at her boyfriend, tittered.

'*Hilarious* isn't the word I'd use,' grumbled Jay, spitting out dirt. Did he say he was tired of being lifted on his team's shoulders? Well, he much preferred it to being thrown on the ground at the feet of an annoying prince.

'Are you okay, Jay?' Audrey asked, concerned.

'He's fine, babe,' said Chad, slinging an arm over her shoulders, the smile on his face as cloying as the pastel sweaters he usually wore. 'Come on, there's nothing to see here but garbage. Isn't that what you guys used to eat on that island? Our leftovers?'

Audrey gasped. 'The poor things, did they really? That's disgusting.'

'On Charming's honour,' said Chad, leading her away. 'Let's go, Princess, nothing to see here.'

Chad used to be one of the best players on the team, but not since Jay arrived. The prince wasn't taking his displacement from the starting lineup very well.

Jay sighed, looking up at the blue sky. He had traded a life of skulking and thievery to play good-guy at hero prep. Back on the Isle, Chad wouldn't be laughing quite so smugly if he knew how easily Jay could have swiped his watch, wallet and keys during that handshake. But Jay was in Auradon now, and they frowned on those things, so he'd left them alone, even though the temptation had been great. It would only get him and his fellow villain kids in trouble, which is what Chad really wanted.

'Are you planning on lying there forever? The dinner bell's rung,' said a voice. He looked up to see Jordan standing above him, holding out a hand.

'You came out of nowhere.'

'Genie trick.' She winked, looking down at him with a hint of a smile. She wore her dark hair up in a swoop, and her blue pantaloons were striking with her yellow leather jacket. She was soon joined by two other girls, the three of them looking concerned over his fall.

Jay took Jordan's hand and used it to help himself up. 'Thanks.'

'Don't worry about Chad, he's like that to everyone. Isn't that right, Allie?' Jordan said to the blond girl standing next to her.

The girl nodded. She wore a blue pinafore over a white blouse and had delicate features and a genteel manner. 'He's almost worse than Tweedledum and Tweedledee.'

'Definitely worse. My dad would have things to say about him, that's for sure,' said Jordan, whose father, Genie, was a famously talkative fellow. 'Are you sure you're all right, dude?'

'Nothing bruised but my pride,' Jay told them, feeling better already.

'Then he did us a favour.' The third girl laughed, fixing the tiny hat she wore sideways on her head. Freddie Facilier was one of the newer Isle kids, who had transferred over as part of the ongoing program to assimilate the villains' kids into the Auradon mainstream.

'Thanks a lot, Freddie,' grumbled Jay.

'You're welcome,' said Freddie.

'We're not all like Chad,' said Jordan. 'Some of us know that without you guys, all of Auradon would be Maleficent's minions right now.'

'Goblins,' said Jay. 'Maleficent's minions are goblins.'

'That would be awful,' said Allie. 'Green is quite a horrendous colour on me.'

The four of them walked companionably over to the dining hall, bumping into Ben, who was heading the other way. The girls swooned and curtsied at the sight of the young king.

'You missed practice,' said Jay, bumping fists with his teammate. He and Ben worked well together, Jay usually setting up the shots that Ben would then send flying into the goal.

'I know, I know, next time, I promise,' said Ben, looking harried. 'Coach is on my case.'

'Our defence is really hurting. Offence, too.'

'Yeah.' Ben sighed, craning his neck at the tourney fields longingly.

'Well, you better be back on deck when we play the Lost Boys,' Jay said. They were up against a strong Neverland team that weekend.

'I'll do my best.'

Jay nodded. It occurred to him while talking to Ben that if his father, Jafar, was in Auradon, he would probably figure out a way to smooth-talk Ben into handing over not just the crown, but the entire kingdom. Whereas Jay only wanted to play tourney and hang out. Just went to show that sometimes the apple can fall far from the tree—or maybe in his case, that the baby cobra can slink away from the nest?

He wasn't sure, but he hoped it was true.

'Hey,' Ben said, noticing Jay's face for the first time. 'Hold on. What happened at practice? Did Chad do that?'

Jay shrugged. He touched the skin around his eye and felt that it was swollen. He wasn't a tattletale, but Chad must have flipped him harder than he thought. 'Eh, it was an accident. I'm sure he didn't mean for my face to meet the ground *that* hard.'

'I'll talk to him,' said Ben, frowning.

'Nah, leave it. You've got bigger problems,' said Jay. 'I can deal with Chad.' The last thing he needed was Chad telling everyone he had to go running to Prince Ben every time he ate a little dirt.

Ben looked as if he wanted to argue. He exhaled. 'Fine.'

'Heading to dinner?' asked Jay, motioning to the dining

hall, where the tantalising smell of Mrs Potts' cooking filled the air.

'No, I've got king stuff.'

'Your loss,' Jay teased. 'What's the use of being king if you can't even stop for a decent meal?'

Ben laughed. 'Tell me about it. Catch you guys later. Take it easy.'

'Bye, Ben!' the girls called.

'Ladies?' asked Jay, leading the group to the building and opening the door for them like the gentleman he was. For a moment, he remembered the anonymous note he'd found in his gym bag earlier and wondered what that was all about. Who wanted him to return to the Isle of the Lost?

But he didn't let it bother him too much as the girls fussed over his injuries. Allie promised to brew him a cup of her favourite tea as well as ask her mother for any of the Mad Hatter's crazy cures. Jordan cheered him up with fanciful stories of travelling via carpet, and how he should really try it for longer trips sometime, and Freddie suggested ways to get even with Chad. 'I'd substitute whipped cream for a tube of his hair gel. That would show him, don't you think?'

Jay felt better already. Who cared about a cryptic note telling him he didn't belong in Auradon? And for that matter, who cared about caves full of molten gold and treasures as vast as the eye could see? As he entered the canteen in the company of his friends, Jay felt as rich as the Sultan of Agrabah.

chapter 3

Scorch in the Stone

It was true what Ben had said to Mal in the library. The kingdom's business waited for no man, not even the king. The United States of Auradon was a vast empire that held all the good kingdoms, from Triton's Bay in the west to Neverland in the east, all the way to the mountain lands up north and Belle's harbour village down south, and its governance was no small task.

After bidding goodbye to Jay and the girls outside the canteen, Ben opened his locker and exchanged his plain daytime crown for the more elaborate one he wore for official meetings of the King's Council. Okay, so it probably wasn't the best idea to keep it in a school locker—being studded with irreplaceable jewels and all—but then again, this was Auradon, and nothing bad ever happened here.

No petty theft, no grand larceny, nothing. He once lost a penny and it was returned to him immediately with a second penny for interest.

That was how Auradon rolled.

Ben also made a note to have a word with Chad. Even if he knew Jay could handle it, his black eye bothered Ben more than he cared to admit. Ben didn't expect everyone to be perfectly good all the time, but he did expect the people of Auradon to *try* to do better. Otherwise what was the point of keeping the villains separated? They might as well all live under a dome.

It had been a few weeks since his parents had left for their retirement-dream-mega-kingdom cruise. King Beast and Queen Belle had gone off in the royal yacht, leaving him to deal with everything. He passed the tourney fields on the way back to his own palace, wishing that he'd had time for practice. But most of his free time went towards his packed royal schedule now—pinning awards on heroes at fancy receptions instead of hanging out with friends, welcoming dignitaries like the Fitzherberts, who were in town this week, rather than playing video games.

Sometimes, Ben felt older than his 16 years. After presiding over the recreation centre opening and shaking hands (or was it paws?) with many furry and funny little creatures—those sidekicks were actually pretty hilarious—he hoped he wasn't too late for the meeting. Just because he was king didn't mean he wanted to take advantage of people's time.

'Ready, Sire?' Lumiere asked, standing sentry in front of the king's conference room.

Ben nodded and smoothed down his lapels.

'The King of Auradon!' Lumiere announced as he opened the door with a flourish.

'The King of Auradon!' the assembled councillors replied. 'Hail, King Ben!'

'At ease, at ease,' said Ben, settling into his chair. The throne had been built to hold his father and it still didn't quite feel like his own. He looked around the long conference table, smiling and greeting his advisers. Lumiere had placed the usual plate of sugar cookies and a pitcher of spiced tea in the middle of the table, and he waited until everyone had taken a bite to eat and had something to drink before starting.

'Hello, Doc, is it just you today?' he asked, greeting his most senior adviser in the room.

The old dwarf nodded after taking a sip from his glass. 'Grumpy sends his apologies, Sire, but he got up on the wrong side of bed and he's feeling out of sorts today.'

Ben suppressed a smile and moved on to the next councillor. 'And how are you today, Genie? I just saw Jordan on the way over.'

'Wonderful, couldn't be better, Your Highness,' said the big, blue genie, giving Ben his trademark grin. 'I'm glad the school allowed her to live in her lamp instead of the dorms. You know us genies, we need to be bottled up.'

Ben chuckled and surveyed the remaining seats at the table, and noticed several were empty. 'Is this everyone for today?' he asked.

'Yes, Sire,' said Doc. 'The Dalmatians are out touring one hundred and one colleges. Mary, Gus and Jaq are busy since Cinderella is preparing for her annual ball, and so it's just me, Genie and the three good fairies today.' Flora, Fauna and Merryweather, a trio of stout, middle-aged women in colourful pointed hats and matching dresses and capes, beamed and waved from the end of the table.

'Perfect,' Ben said.

'Shall we run through the issues and updates?' asked Doc, who peered up from his scroll, and blinked behind his spectacles.

'If you please.'

Ben leaned back in his chair, listening to the regular report on every aspect of his kingdom. After the horror of *The Incident with Maleficent*, it appeared life had returned to its regular serene rhythm. Although the kingdom's scientists had noted a few unusual weather patterns of late—not just the rash of Auradon City earthquakes, but unexpected frost in the Summerlands and unusual lightning storms in East Riding, among other unseasonal phenomena. Ben noted their concern, but as he pointed out to the council, it wasn't as if anything could be done about the weather. He yawned, and as Doc droned on, he tried to keep his eyes open, and failed. He got a few winks when Doc loudly cleared his throat.

'Ahem,' said Doc. 'Excuse me, Sire.' Having been trained by a life with Sleepy, he was well versed in all manner of waking up the suddenly asleep.

Ben sat up in his chair and blinked awake, embarrassed. 'Sorry, what did I miss?'

'I was saying, that's all we have of the regular business. But now, if you please, we have ambassadors from Camelot here to see you. They said it was an emergency, so I slotted them in. I hope that's all right,' said Doc. 'They've come a long way.'

Ben nodded. 'Of course, of course. By all means, send them in.'

Lumiere opened the door again and announced with great zeal, 'The wizard Merlin, and Artie, son of Arthur.'

Merlin, an old and wizened wizard in blue robes, and Artie, a young boy of about 12, wearing a plain tunic that marked him as a squire, walked into the King's conference room.

Artie looked around, seemingly amazed by the sight

of Genie floating next to the fairies. Camelot had its own extraordinary inhabitants, of course, but Artie probably hadn't seen someone quite like him before. Genie noticed the boy staring in awe, and pulled one of his many ridiculous faces, sending Artie into a fit of giggles.

'Arthur sends his regards,' said Merlin, bowing to the king and shooting Artie a quick glare. The boy bowed as well, but couldn't hide his smile. 'He's busy dealing with the problem right now, so he was unable to join us.'

'What seems to be the matter?' asked Ben.

'There's a monster in Camelot!' Artie interrupted.

Genie startled. 'A monster?'

'Well, I think it's a monster,' said Artie, abashed and defensive at the same time.

'What Artie is trying to say is that something is causing a lot of mayhem in town, scaring the villagers and setting fires,' Merlin said. 'It's become quite a disturbance.'

'Is that so?' asked Ben.

'Yes. It's been a few weeks now, and we've tried to catch the creature, but it keeps evading our traps, as if it has disappeared into thin air. Days will pass, then out of nowhere, it attacks again. Villagers have lost sheep and chickens. Gardens have been trampled. Whole rows of cabbages at a time.' Merlin took off his pointy hat and wiped his brow. 'It's been a real headache. Arthur decided to stay in Camelot in case it returned while we came to seek assistance.'

'How can we be of help?' Ben leaned forwards, eager to provide aid. This was so much more interesting than the news that villagers in the province his mother was from were complaining about the price of eggs once again. Singing about it, too.

Merlin shuffled his feet. 'That's why we're here, Your Highness. We've come to ask for permission to use magic to track down this creature.'

'Ah, I see,' said Ben. 'Magic.' He sat back in his throne.

'He means the real stuff too,' Doc whispered in his ear. 'Not just turning dresses a different colour or giving someone a new haircut like my nephew Doug tells me is happening at school these days.'

'Is there no other way to catch this monster?' Ben asked, frowning and tapping his pen on the table.

'We've tried everything and unfortunately, so far we haven't been successful,' said Merlin. 'We wouldn't be here otherwise.'

'And you believe that with the use of magic you will be able to catch it?' asked Flora with a stern face.

'What if it doesn't work? What then? Magic can go very wrong, you know,' added Fauna, adjusting her red hat as it slipped to the side on her curly grey hair. 'As my sisters and I have seen firsthand.'

'The consequences of using magic recklessly can certainly be very dangerous,' agreed Merryweather, her face screwing up with concern.

The rest of the table murmured its agreement.

Merlin drew himself up to his full height. He wasn't much taller than a dwarf, but he was intimidating nonetheless. He shot the King's Council a frosty glare. 'Need I remind you I am the wizard Merlin? I am well aware of the dangers of magic, and it is my belief that I will be able to use it prudently to capture this infernal creature and send it away so it cannot bother us again. You have my word.'

The council turned to its king.

'I understand, Wizard Merlin.' Ben met Merlin's glare, and tried not to show how nervous he was. He was the leader here now; his father had left the kingdom's safekeeping in his hands. 'I will consider your request, but will need to discuss it with my team before making a decision. Thank you for informing us about the situation in Camelot,' he said carefully.

The old wizard nodded gruffly. 'Come on, Artie, let's go find ourselves a chocolate-chip cookie while we wait.'

When they left the room, Ben turned to his councillors. 'Can I do that? Let Merlin use magic in such a manner?'

'You can do anything you want now that you're king,' Doc said. 'You have absolute power.'

And absolute power corrupts absolutely, Ben thought to himself. He needed to be cautious. 'When was the last time magic of this level was used in Auradon?' he asked his advisers.

'Let's see, probably the last time was when Fairy Godmother created the dome that kept magic out of the Isle of the Lost. After that, it's been your father's and Fairy Godmother's policy that we learn to live without magic, even without a dome over our heads,' said Genie. 'It was hard to adjust to at first, but we managed.'

'And we are better for it,' said Flora with a sniff. 'A little hard work never hurt anybody.'

Ben agreed. Magic wasn't expressly forbidden in Auradon—but it was discouraged, and the kingdom was more orderly for it. It would be reckless to just disregard the policies King Beast and Fairy Godmother had put into place for the sake of one issue in a faraway kingdom. Even in the hands of careful users, there had been a few incidents when magic had gone awry lately. Genie was known to accidentally grant wishes to the wrong person when he left his lamp lying around. Even the three good fairies slipped every once in a while, often letting their generosity get the best of them. They had created a massive ice castle for Ben's birthday party one year, which was dazzling until it melted and caused a flood.

Merlin was one of the most powerful magicians in the land, and if he was allowed to use magic on such a large scale, who knew where it would lead?

Ben motioned to Lumiere to send Merlin and Artie back into the room.

'I have considered the urgency of your request,' he told them.

'Thank you, Your Highness.' Merlin looked hopeful and eager to get going.

Ben held up his hand. He wasn't finished. 'But for now, I am going to reject your petition to use magic to capture this creature.'

Merlin frowned and his face turned red behind his beard. This was certainly not the news he had been hoping for, and the old wizard was clearly used to getting his way. Artie looked particularly glum. The idea of defeating a horrible creature with ancient magic had obviously been an exciting one for the young squire.

Before Merlin could object, Ben continued. 'I will travel to Camelot myself to assess the situation. I will leave with you first thing tomorrow morning.' He would have to miss a day of classes, probably two, but hopefully he would be back in Auradon by the weekend. Besides, it sounded like an adventure, and before Mal and her friends had arrived, even Ben had very few of those in Auradon.

'Very good, Sire,' said Merlin, elbowing Artie to bow like he did. 'Let's just hope Camelot is still standing when we get there.'

chapter 4

Never Read the Comments

As one who aspired to be the fairest of them all, Evie didn't need to advertise the fact by wearing the word *fairest* emblazoned all over her T-shirts, but it didn't hurt. She was seated at her desk in her and Mal's bedroom that afternoon, in front of their matching poster beds and frilly pink curtains that Mal so despised. The wood-panelled walls were decorated with the smiling portraits of Auradon's past princesses, as if to remind Evie of her goals. She brushed her long dark tresses until her blue highlights shone and pursed her lips, checking her reflection with her phone's camera. She tried out a few poses for

InstaRoyal, the latest lifestyle envy-inducer that was a big hit with the Auradon set. It was all about showing off the newest and hippest fashions in glass slippers (glass slip-ons with puffy bows were all the rage) and the plush interiors of private carriages (plump satin cushions sewn by Cinderella's hardworking mice were the most popular upgrade). Even though she'd only signed up a few weeks ago, Evie already had a lot of 'subjects' and enjoyed collecting their 'bows'.

Evie much preferred InstaRoyal to ZapChat, its grungier counterpart, which was all about sharing glimpses of Auradon's less-than-perfect side: photos of the tourney team chugging pumpkin juice, for instance, or embarrassing pictures of princesses kissing frogs—and not the type that turned into handsome princes like Prince Naveem either. She was scrolling through her royal feed when her phone began shaking in her hand as the floor rumbled with another earthquake, and she accidentally tapped on a photo. It was one that Doug had posted earlier from band practice that he'd captioned *Feeling Dopey!*

She texted him, *Hey, did you feel that? Shake, rattle and roll . . .* Unlike Mal, she'd gotten used to the occasional rumble.

Evie went back to her zapps and checked the comments on her photos to see if there were any new ones. In Auradon, the compliments were always plentiful and kind. Oooh, there was a new one on an old photo she'd posted of the four of them standing together and facing down Maleficent during the attack at the Coronation. This was the moment when they had defeated the evil fairy with the power of good.

It had run in the *Auradon Times* and it was one of Evie's favourite pictures, so she'd re-posted it to her account. There was something so inspiring about seeing them bravely standing together while facing the great dragon face of Maleficent. It reminded Evie that even if they were from the Isle of the Lost, they were just as good and courageous as the princes and princesses they went to school with, and that during Auradon's darkest hour, it was the four villain kids who had been able to keep everyone safe.

She found the new comment and read it eagerly. To her surprise, it wasn't very nice at all and had been posted by a user she didn't follow.

There's no place for you in Auradon! Go back where you belong! Return to the Isle of the Lost at once! Before the young moon shows its face!

Ouch. That was rude. And weird. What was the deal with the moon?

She was still staring at the screen when Doug appeared at her doorway. 'What's up? Ready to grab a bite?' he asked, looking adorable in a bow tie and suspenders. He made the same funny face that he'd posted to his InstaRoyal feed.

Doug was no prince, but a prince for her own heart. He was the sweetest, nicest boyfriend a girl could ever ask for, and he could dance like nobody's business.

'Sure!' Evie said cheerfully, putting away her phone for now. She was still upset by the mean comment, but a girl had to eat. Evie knew she would feel much better on a full stomach and she could show the comment to Mal later. Mal would know what to do about it; she always did.

Speaking of Mal, she entered the room just as Evie and Doug were about to leave. 'Evie! Glad I caught you. I need to show you something!'

'Oh, Mal, I have something to show you too, but we were just about to go grab dinner,' Evie said apologetically.

'No, this can't wait,' Mal said, shoving past Doug. 'Eat later.' Her green eyes were flashing dangerously and it was obvious that she was particularly annoyed. Evie hadn't seen Mal act this way since they'd first arrived in Auradon, when she'd scowled at everything. Even if she was in a rush, Mal shuddered at the sunlight streaming through the open window and closed the pink curtains once more, just like she had done on the first day.

Some things never changed.

Evie looked nervously at Doug, who had his eyebrows raised. 'Go ahead, I'll catch up later,' she told him. Somehow she'd already lost her appetite.

'Whatever it is, I can help . . .' he offered, because that was the kind of guy he was.

Mal rolled her eyes and put her hands on her hips. 'Sorry, Doug, but I have to talk to Evie privately. This isn't about *mining jewels*.'

'As you wish. See you later, Evie,' said Doug, who promptly left them alone, whistling as he went.

'So what's up?' asked Evie, turning to Mal and walking over to sit at her sewing machine. Doing something with her hands always calmed her down during stressful times.

Mal didn't answer immediately. She watched as Evie carefully pushed fabric under the needle. 'Is that your Castlecoming dress?' she asked. 'That colour is pretty.'

'Yes,' said Evie. 'You really think it's pretty?' she asked, momentarily distracted by the compliment and running a hand over the glossy fabric and smoothing out the stitches. The dress was royal blue, her favourite colour, with a deep red bodice the colour of poisoned apples.

'Very,' Mal said.

'Yours is ready, I put it in your closet. Not as many ruffles this time, like you wanted. Okay, so what did you have to talk to me about?' Evie asked.

Mal removed her phone and swiped to the screen with the strange message. 'This,' she said. 'Look.'

Evie read the message, her face growing pale as snow for a moment. 'Someone left the same message on my InstaRoyal account.' She handed Mal her phone with the offending comment on the screen. Mal studied it, frowning.

'Who do you think it's from?' asked Evie, feeling goose bumps on her arms. That had to stop. Pebbly skin was so not attractive. 'I checked and the user's anonymous and their account is private.'

'I have no idea,' said Mal, biting her lip.

'And by the way, why does it talk about the moon?' asked Evie.

'I don't know. At first, I thought the comments were only meant to be mean. But since they mentioned the moon to both of us, I wonder if there is more to it than that. Maybe they actually do want us to return by a certain time?'

Evie read the message on Mal's phone again. 'Yours says it's from M.'

'Yeah, I see that,' said Mal. 'And my mother used to count moon days rather than day days. Evil-fairy habit.'

Evie crossed her arms. In their world there was only one M that mattered. 'It can't be from her. I mean, she's a *lizard*? Lizards can't type! How can she be M?'

'I don't know. Maybe it's not her,' said Mal hopefully.

'But what if it is?' whispered Evie.

'And who else would want us to return to the Isle of the Lost so badly?' Mal said. 'It has to be from . . .'

'Our parents?' Evie squeaked. 'You really think so?'

'There's only one way to find out. You still have your Magic Mirror, don't you? Let's ask it to show us our parents. If my mother is able to get out of that pedestal and turn back into herself, maybe it'll catch her in the act.'

Evie removed the shard of the Magic Mirror that her mother had gifted to her before she left for Auradon. 'Show me Maleficent!' she demanded.

The grey clouds in the mirror's reflection parted to show

a lizard snoozing peacefully under glass. Both Mal and Evie exhaled, relieved.

'What about your mum?' Mal suggested. 'Just to make sure?'

Evie nodded. 'Show me the Evil Queen!'

But instead of showing Evil Queen happily tweezing her eyebrows or shading in the mole on her cheek, the mirror stayed cloudy. Evie tried again. 'Magic Mirror in my hand, show me my mother, I command!'

Still, the mirror's cloudy swirls remained hazy and swirly. Evie shook it a few times, and even banged it against her lap for good measure. 'This isn't good,' she said. 'It's busted. This has never happened before.'

When she asked, the mirror wouldn't show them Cruella de Vil or Jafar either, remaining stubbornly grey and fogged in.

'How about asking it to show us Evil Queen's castle, Hell Hall and the Junk Shop?' Mal suggested. 'Maybe that will work.'

Evie did so, and the mirror cooperated this time, but there was still no sign of any of the three villains. The castle was empty, Hell Hall abandoned, the Junk Shop deserted.

'That's strange,' said Evie. 'It's not like they go anywhere.' She was starting to have a dreadful feeling about all of this.

But Mal wasn't ready to give up quite yet. 'Ask it again,' she urged.

Evie tried, but no matter what, the mirror remained cloudy. 'Maybe it's broken?' she asked hopefully.

'No, it was working otherwise,' Mal pointed out. 'Something else is going on, something that might be connected to the messages we received today.'

Evie stared at Mal. 'Are you thinking what I'm thinking?'

'That Cruella, Jafar and Evil Queen are up to their old tricks on the Isle of the Lost and that Maleficent might be involved somehow? Totally,' said Mal.

Evie found she couldn't breathe for a moment. She was glad she hadn't eaten anything, or else she would seriously throw up right now.

'We don't know who sent us those messages, but here's what we do know,' said Mal, straightening her shoulders. She didn't look frightened anymore, and Evie took comfort in her friend's courage; it gave her back some of her own. 'The villains won't rest until they exact vengeance on Auradon . . .' said Mal.

'And it's possible they've hidden themselves until they can put their evil plan into action,' Evie finished.

'Evie, we've got to move fast,' said Mal.

'On it.'

'Let's go get Carlos and Jay.'

chapter 5

Tangled Web

Back in Dragon Hall, it had been school policy that the library, otherwise known as the Athenaeum of Evil, was forbidden to the average student. Carlos de Vil had never been the average student, however. Most of the reading material he'd been able to find there had consisted of last year's TV guides for shows he'd never heard of and past issues of *Carriage & Driver* magazine. Knowledge was hoarded like stolen gold and plundered treasure, and was equally hard to come by.

But at Auradon Prep, the library and its abundant resources were free and open to all. After school, Carlos could usually be found in the library, admiring the leather-bound books on every subject, from *How to Keep Yourself Busy for Sixteen Years Alone* by Rapunzel to *Genie's Blue Planet Travel Guides: See the World in Three Wishes.* He would never get tired of the place.

But today he was holed up in the room he shared with Jay, seated on his comfortable bed with the blue plaid doona around his shoulders as he stared at his laptop, ignoring the large-screen television and its many video games. The matching blue plaid curtains were drawn shut. As it turned out, like Mal, he preferred to work in a dark room. Carlos had been there all afternoon, so lost in his research that he'd missed tourney practice.

Carlos was a naturally curious boy, and when he wanted to understand how something worked, he didn't stop until he'd figured it out. For instance, when Auradon City was hit with several earthquakes in a row over the past weeks, he'd looked up the statistics and noticed that there had been more quakes in the last month than there had been in the last year. He kept meaning to bring it up with his Wonders of the Earth teacher but hadn't gotten the chance yet.

This time he wasn't merely curious, though. He was furious. Earlier that day, he had received a rather upsetting email. Unlike most kids at Auradon Prep, Carlos wasn't very active on royal media—his GraceBook account only had one old post, he never sent ZapChats. He preferred the ease of his geniemail account, which organised his emails like magic.

That morning, he logged in to see if the new video game he'd ordered (*Crown of Duty*) was on its way and discovered a new email from an unknown sender. The message, like most anonymous messages, was mean-spirited, telling him to go back where he came from and return to the Isle of the Lost by moonset. While the email itself had been annoying, it really irritated him no end that he hadn't cracked the email sender's true identity yet.

Carlos figured he was smarter than the average troll, but the only progress he'd made was to unmask the server that had routed the email, and so far he hadn't been able to hack through its security defences.

'Dalmatians,' Carlos muttered, frustrated enough to use his mother's favourite curse. 'Sorry, Dude,' he said, apologising to the dog on his lap. Dude whimpered and Carlos scratched him behind his ears.

The rapid-fire sound of knocking on the door startled him. 'Come in!' he yelled, and looked up to see Mal and Evie entering with dark looks on their faces.

He held up a hand as they crowded around his desk. He'd been expecting them for a while now. 'Don't tell me. You've both received rude messages saying to return to the Isle of the Lost, haven't you? Which is why you're here? I got an email today.'

'How did you know . . . never mind,' said Evie. Carlos was often a step ahead of them.

'Yes, we did,' said Mal, pulling up a chair, giving Carlos

the details. 'What've you found? Do you know where they're from?'

'Not yet,' he said, his fingers flying over the keys. But he was getting close, he could feel it. He'd finally breached the first security firewall; now all he had to do was figure out the password. He tried to ignore the girls so he could concentrate.

'Isn't it weird that you got an email, Evie got a comment on her InstaRoyal account and I got a text?' Mal pointed out. 'Whoever's behind it seems to know us pretty well.'

Carlos nodded. 'I'm barely on royal media, you only use your phone and everyone knows Evie's always updating her feed. Do you think they reached Jay? He's never online and he's always losing his phone.'

'I'm sure they found a way,' said Mal.

'We think the messages might be from our parents,' said Evie a little breathlessly.

That was not news he wanted to hear. 'What! Why?' Carlos twisted around, suddenly seized with the fear that his mother, Cruella de Vil, with her wild hair and trademark screech, was right behind him.

Dude whimpered.

'Relax, they're not here, at least not yet,' said Mal. Then she told him how Evie's Magic Mirror had been unable to show them the villains on the island.

'Well, call me paranoid, but lately I feel like she *is* near. Like she's watching me somehow. I can't shake the feeling,' he said, panicking as he imagined Cruella appearing at his doorway. While Maleficent might be able to turn into a dragon, Cruella *was* a dragon.

'Nah, you're just paranoid,' said Mal.

Carlos chewed on this new information. 'Maybe so, but you're saying there's really a chance they're behind these messages? Our parents? They want us to come back? But why?' he asked.

'Because they miss us and want to give us hugs?' said Evie. 'I'm kidding, I'm sure my mum only wants to know if I'm keeping up with my weekly mud masks and facial massages.'

'They want us to return so we can help them get their revenge on Auradon, of course,' said Mal. 'Defeat only makes villains try harder. I can just hear my mum now, saying *"You poor simple fools, thinking you could defeat me! Me! The mistress of all evil!"'* Then she cackled like Maleficent.

'You're scarily good at that,' said Evie, shivering.

'Thank you, I think?' said Mal.

Carlos shuddered and turned back to his computer to try out a succession of common passwords. None of them worked. He stared at the blinking cursor. 'Dalmatians,' he cursed again. Then he realised if Mal was correct and the villains were behind the messages, there was only one way to find out for sure.

C-A-V-E-O-F-W-O-N-D-E-R-S, he tried. Nothing.

M-A-K-E-U-P was his next guess. He sighed with relief

when it didn't work, and *E-V-I-L-L-I-V-E-S* turned up nothing either.

Gathering his courage, he decided to try one more password that would link the messages to their parents.

D-A-L-M-A-T-I-A-N-S, he typed.

The screen froze and for a moment Carlos was relieved that his hunch was incorrect, but after a second it came to life again, and green letters began scrolling across the screen. He'd hacked it. He was inside.

'Oh no,' he said.

'What's wrong?' asked Evie, squinting at the screen. It was a website unlike any they'd seen before. It was more primitive and crudely designed, with no pretty icons or bright colours, only windows of black screens with green letters.

'The Dark Net,' Carlos whispered, still staring at the screen, unwilling to believe it was true. 'There's a rumour going around that after the dome broke when Maleficent escaped, the Isle of the Lost was able to start up a secret online network of their own. And I'm not talking about the kind of internet where people share funny kitten videos.'

'But they don't have access to the internet on the Isle. They're cut off, remember?' said Mal.

'Maybe something happened when the dome broke open,' said Evie.

'Anything's possible,' said Carlos. 'Especially during that time when the dome let magic back onto the island.'

He looked up at them. 'Supposedly, since the Dark Net is effectively hidden from Auradon's servers, it's a way for the villains on the Isle of the Lost to communicate with each other. Think about it, on the Dark Net, they can hatch evil plots without anyone here knowing anything about it.'

'So, they use the Dark Net to send each other evil emails?' joked Mal.

'And post evil insta-messages,' Evie giggled.

'I'm serious!' said Carlos. 'It's not funny.'

'You're right, you're right,' said Mal, sobering. 'With an online network, they can organise their evil schemes more effectively.'

'Yeah, exactly, so I'm going to poke around, see what else I can find,' said Carlos.

'But, Carlos, you just said the villains are behind it!' Evie cried. 'Isn't that dangerous?'

'I would say Danger is my middle name,' said Carlos cheerfully, warming up to the task as his dog slid from his lap to nestle at his feet contentedly. Now that he had a new thing to explore, he didn't feel as frightened. He could do this. 'But my middle name is actually Oscar.'

He saw their faces and muttered as he typed, 'Hey, it could be worse, right? Mal, your middle name is Bertha.'

'Unfortunately, yes. Anyway, see what you can find,' Mal said with a crisp nod. 'But I think we have to make plans to return no matter what.'

'Return? To where?' Carlos asked, although he had a feeling he already knew the answer.

'To the Isle of the Lost, of course,' Mal said as she rolled up her sleeves.

'But why? We might be falling right into a trap,' Evie argued. 'Isn't that just what they want us to do, whoever they are?'

'Well, we can't stay here—we need to find out what the villains are up to back home,' Mal said. 'Plus, I'm not going to be intimidated by whoever's sending these messages. We have to take the risk, or something like what happened at the Coronation could happen again.'

'We sure do,' said Jay, who'd appeared at the doorway, his face bruised and one eye swollen shut, holding up a crumpled piece of paper covered in purple ink. 'Did you guys get one of these today about returning to the Isle of the Lost?'

'Old-fashioned note! Of course!' said Carlos, who couldn't help but be pleased at the cleverness of their mysterious nemesis.

'Sort of,' said Mal as the other two nodded. Jay just looked relieved.

'What happened to your eye? Are you all right?' asked Evie. 'Do you need Mal to conjure an ice-pack for that?'

'Tourney practice. It's nothing,' Jay said, waving off their concern.

'But as I was saying, we have to go back home, because

we all know the villains won't rest until Auradon is reduced to rubble and we're all minions,' Mal said fiercely, as if she would take on an army of them right now.

'Goblins,' said Jay. 'Maleficent had goblins for minions, why doesn't anyone remember that?'

chapter 6

Maleficent Dearest

After the group left Carlos to explore the Dark Net to see if he could find any more information on the villains' plans and whereabouts, Mal decided to visit her mother. It bothered her too much to think that the mysterious M in her note might actually be Maleficent and she wanted to see for herself that her mother was still a lizard. It was late when she arrived in the library, almost time for lights-out. The royal guards, trained in imperial battle tactics by Mulan, stood in front of the double-locked doors and barred her way.

'Really? You know it's me,' Mal said. 'Open up. Family

visitors are allowed under the royal decree,' she reminded them like she did every time she grudgingly visited.

The guard on the left grinned. 'Oh yes, I see the resemblance now, I think it's the forked tongue,' he joked, like he always did.

'Ha-ha,' said Mal, pushing her way inside.

The guard on the right grunted. 'You have five minutes.'

'I know,' she said as they locked the door behind her and she made her way to the pedestal in the middle of the room with a glass dome sitting on top of it.

When she was a little girl, Mal had been very frightened of her mother. Maleficent was not the help-with-homework, bake-cookies type, after all. She was more the fearsome mistress who sent you on hopeless quests—like the one to retrieve her Dragon's Eye sceptre—and she didn't take no for an answer.

Even so, these days Mal found it hard to believe she had once feared Maleficent. It was difficult to feel scared of something so small.

But the anonymous message from M had spooked her. Mal stared at her mother, who appeared to be sleeping. Under the glass dome, she looked like any other ordinary lizard, harmless, cute even. But Mal knew better. No matter how harmless the reptile looked, it was still the Mistress of Darkness at heart.

So did Maleficent have some secret talent they didn't

know about? Would she able to transform back into herself after transforming to the itty-bitty size of her heart? Was the lizard in there *really* Maleficent? What if Maleficent was already gone?

Mal stared hard at the tiny purple creature that, when awake, had green eyes just like her mother to see if she could sense something different about it. But the snoozing reptile looked exactly the same as it did the last time she'd visited.

'Hey, Mum, can I talk to you for a second?' she said, careful not to tap on the glass. She'd heard lizards didn't like that.

The lizard was still, not even a flick of her tongue.

The handful of times when she'd visited Maleficent in the past, it was like this. She never got a reaction of any sort. Mal always found it hard to accept that this small, tiny creature held the soul of the most powerful villain in all the land.

'Did you send me this?' she asked, holding up her phone with the mysterious text. 'Are you M?'

No response.

'It's only the two of us here, Mum, you can tell me if you've been changing back. In fact, it would be kind of nice to see you in your non-reptilian form,' she said. Mal still wasn't above a white lie now and then.

There was no sign that the creature even understood a word she was saying.

Mal sighed. 'I guess if you *were* planning something,

you wouldn't share it with me anyway, right? Seeing as I'm the reason you're here in the first place.' She rubbed her eyes. 'But one day I'll find a way to get you out. You just have to promise me that you won't try to destroy everything again.' Mal paused. 'Okay, fine, you can cover Sleeping Beauty's castle in thorny vines. Have a little fun.'

The lizard remained as still as the rock underneath it. The lights-out bell chimed and Mal reluctantly got ready to leave. 'Fine, don't tell me anything. I knew this was stupid. You can't even talk.'

Just then, the floor buckled underneath her from yet another earthquake. Mal swayed and struggled to keep her balance, her heart lurching in her chest. When it was over, she stared at the lizard suspiciously. 'I don't know how you're doing it, but why do I have a feeling you're behind this too?'

Someone was skulking outside the door when Mal walked out, and she immediately tensed, prepared for an ambush. But there was no surprise attack, and the stranger had a familiar face.

'Hey, Freddie,' she said, relieved to see her old friend from the Isle, and slightly embarrassed by her reaction.

'Hey, Mal, what's up?' asked Freddie, graciously pretending not to notice how rattled she seemed.

'Nothing much,' said Mal, then a thought occurred to her. 'Hey, Freddie, did you get any weird messages or emails today?'

'Weird how?' asked Freddie.

'Anonymous weird?' asked Mal. 'Like maybe from someone from the Isle of the Lost?'

Freddie shook her head. 'No. I don't think anyone even knows I'm at Auradon actually. Not our old gang back on the Isle, that's for sure. They probably all just think I'm cutting classes again.'

'Right,' said Mal. She'd only been in Auradon for a short time, but she'd almost forgotten how lax the rules had been back at Dragon Hall. But what Freddie said was interesting. Unlike the four of them, Freddie hadn't received a message to return to the island, which meant whoever had sent those notes only wanted the four original villain kids. But why?

'You got some kind of anonymous note?' asked Freddie.

Mal decided she could trust her. 'Yeah, saying I should return to the Isle of the Lost, and Jay, Carlos and Evie too. Isn't that weird?'

'Totally weird. What are you going to do about it?'

'I don't know yet,' said Mal. 'We're trying to decide.'

'Well, maybe you should . . . Go back to the island, I mean. See what's going on back there. I mean, it can't hurt, right?'

'You really think so?' asked Mal.

Freddie shrugged. 'I know if I got one I'd want to see who sent it to me.' Then she changed the subject and motioned to the heavily bolted doors and the armed guards standing sentry in front of them. 'Is that where they keep your . . . '

'Yep, that's lizard rock,' said Mal. 'The one and only home of Maleficent these days.'

'Phew, if that ever happened to my dad, you can be sure I wouldn't be sticking around just so he could yell at me when he turned back.' Freddie shook her head, her pigtails bouncing. 'And you shouldn't either. You know if she ever gets out of there, she'll come after you first.'

Mal bit her lip. 'You're not telling me anything I don't already know.'

Freddie suddenly brightened. 'But she'll probably never get out, so you'll be fine. By the way, if you do go back to the Isle, say hi to my dad for me.' She clapped Mal on the back and went on her way, casting long shadows against the walls.

chapter 7

Friends of the Round Table

Camelot Heights was located in the northern part of the kingdom, and the city of Camelot was in its centre, flanked by Sherwood Forest on one side and Eden on the other. Ben had made good on his promise and had been travelling all day with Merlin and Artie in the royal carriage, with a retinue of servants and footmen following behind in a regular coach. Ben decided not to use the usual king-size motorcade, since Camelot's roads were too rough for cars, as most of its residents travelled by horse-drawn vehicles.

As soon as they set off, the old wizard was already snoring in the backseat, but Artie was awake and excited, trying out all the features of the carriage interior and playing with the sunroof, sliding it open and closed on a whim. 'Dad won't let us update our carriage,' he explained as he put on road-cancelling headphones (carriage travel was notoriously loud due to wheel rumble) and eagerly flipped through every channel offered on the television screen installed above the back bench.

Ben settled in, amused, and let Artie have his fun.

The journey from Auradon City was a long one, taking them up to Summerlands and past Snow White's castle, where they would stop for the night before making their way into the Enchanted Wood, then across the river through acres of forest lands, and finally into Camelot. Ben tried to relax in his seat, and sent a few texts to Mal to let her know he was thinking of her. No luck, she wasn't responding, and so he closed his eyes and tried to rest.

A few hours after Ben, Merlin and Artie left Snow White's palace the next morning, King Arthur's Castle crested high on the hill, proud and tall, its red towers glowing in the sun.

'Home,' said Artie excitedly. 'Looks like they knew we were coming.' The turrets were flying both the Pendragon banner and Ben's beast-head sigil.

'I sent Archimedes ahead with the news so they could prepare,' said Merlin, meaning his pet owl. He put his rumpled wizard's hat back on his head and scratched his beard. 'What in Auradon is going on here?' he said as the castle gates opened for the royal entourage.

Ben yawned and took a look outside the window. The entire courtyard was filled with tents and crudely constructed shelters. 'Is it always this crowded here?' he asked as they disembarked.

'No,' said an irritated Merlin, stepping off the carriage and, in his haste, stumbling over his robes. 'Something must have happened.'

Artie jumped down, and Ben followed, eager to stretch his legs after the long ride. They were greeted by quite a sight—and odour. The scent of roasting meat and smoke filled the air as people huddled around unruly fire pits. The people of Camelot preferred to live as they always had, and eschewed many modern conveniences. All well and good, thought Ben, except a little deodorant never hurt anyone. It smelled like the Middle Ages in here.

'It looks like the villagers have moved from their homes to seek protection behind the castle walls,' said Merlin, frowning. 'The creature must have struck again,' he muttered under his breath.

'Make way for the king, make way,' Ben's royal guards ordered, clearing a path through the crowd to the entrance to the palace.

'King Ben!' the people cheered as men bowed their heads

and women curtsied. 'The King of Auradon has come!' he heard people whisper. 'Hope has arrived at last!'

He waved back cheerfully, trying to ignore the nerves fluttering underneath his confident smile. His subjects depended on him, and now he understood why his father had always projected strength and self-assurance. Apparently it wasn't as easy as he had made it seem.

'This way,' said Merlin when they were inside the castle proper, where the great hall was also teeming with people lying in bedrolls and hay. The castle's lord chamberlain rushed to meet them. He bowed to Ben and whispered in Merlin's ear.

'They have prepared rooms for you in the east wing,' Merlin said. 'Arthur apologises that he is not here to welcome you, but he is still out in the countryside, urging his people to head to the safety of Camelot, and expects to be delayed for quite some time. He hopes that in his place, you shall meet with his knights, who are aware of the latest developments in the situation.'

'Thank you,' said Ben. 'Please tell Arthur no apologies are necessary and I look forward to speaking with his men.'

'Sire, shall I go ahead and unpack and prepare your wardrobe?' asked Lumiere, who was travelling with Ben as his personal valet. The old Frenchman looked askance at the unwashed hordes and was probably wishing they were all back in Auradon's much more comfortable palace right about now.

'Please do,' said Ben as Merlin and Artie took their leave.

'Shall I set out the royal armour?' asked Lumiere, meaning the old-fashioned metal one that was once his father's. 'We brought it out of storage, it's polished and oiled.'

'No need, I think,' said Ben, inwardly grimacing at the thought of putting on the tin-can suit. 'I might be in Camelot, but I am the king of this century, not the twelfth.'

'Very good, Sire,' said Lumiere with a smile as bright as candlesticks in the dark.

Ben chose to wear the same royal-blue suit he'd worn to his Coronation, with the gold epaulets and Auradon's crest on the sleeves. Lumiere had polished his travelling crown, so he looked and felt very much the King of Auradon as he was welcomed to the legendary Round Table, where Camelot's knights had gathered. The room itself was rather plain, with unadorned stone walls and dim lighting, but Ben couldn't help but feel excited when he pulled up a heavy wooden chair at one of the most famous tables in history.

The knights were a good-natured, chivalrous bunch, and Ben felt right at home in their company as they chatted about the latest pro-tourney scores. But the discussion took a serious turn when Merlin called the meeting to order and talk soon became heated as they argued about how best to deal with the creature plaguing their land.

'Yesterday the thing set fire to the forest, creating such

a blaze that it almost reached Sherwood!' a young knight said indignantly. 'We need to destroy it before it destroys anything else!'

'Too many people have lost their farms and houses to this thing,' said another. 'Good that Merlin is back, he can use his magic to capture it.'

'Ahem,' said Merlin, polishing his glasses with the edge of his long sleeve. 'Unfortunately, we don't have permission from the king to do so. King Ben, I mean.'

Ben looked around the table at their distressed faces and cleared his throat. 'As you know, it is our belief that the use of magic at this level can be dangerous, and so I'm here to observe the situation before we decide to change the policies that have kept Auradon safe and peaceful for so long.'

'You know what's dangerous? The creature! That's dangerous!' cried a knight. 'Sneaks around in the dark of night, taking livestock and setting fire to everything before disappearing in a cloud of smoke!'

'Merlin tells me that no-one in Camelot has actually seen this creature?' Ben asked. 'Is that still true?'

The knights shuffled in their seats and glanced at each other nervously. 'Well . . . sort of,' said the knight on Ben's left.

'It's dark . . .' was one excuse. 'It's fast . . .' was another.

'But if we don't know what we're fighting, how can we prepare to fight against it?' Ben said. 'We can't chase after shadows and smoke. We have to know exactly what it is that's attacking your lands. You have my deepest sympathies and every resource I can offer from Auradon, but before I can allow Merlin to use magic, I need to know exactly what we're up against.'

Heads nodded around the table as the knights digested Ben's words. Merlin had Archimedes perched on his shoulder and the owl trained its bright eyes on Ben as it whispered in the wizard's ear. 'The king makes a fair point,' said Merlin, at last. 'We must lay eyes on this creature before we can conceive of how to stop it.'

Artie, who had been quietly listening in the corner until now, spoke up. 'Dad said he saw a bunch of tracks in the forest by the river's edge near Eden,' he said. 'Maybe we should set up camp there tonight and see if we can spot it.'

'Excellent idea,' said Ben, who admired the boy's pluck. 'We will camp tonight.'

The royal entourage, along with Ben, Merlin, Artie and a handful of knights, established temporary barracks in a clearing by the shore. Every night they waited for any sign of the creature, but two days passed and they didn't see smoke or fire, let alone any sort of mysterious beast emerging from the woods.

On the third evening, Ben scoured the river's shoreline, hoping that the creature would finally make an appearance. He was still unsure about allowing Merlin to use magic, and he knew the old wizard was growing impatient. King Arthur was still abroad, warning his people to find shelter, although he couldn't be too pleased to have his castle overrun by his subjects.

But Camelot's monster wasn't Ben's only problem. It was Castlecoming on Saturday at Auradon Prep and he really wanted to play the tourney game and take Mal to the dance, and he was disappointed that it looked like he wouldn't make it back in time. But that was the boy in him speaking. The king's place was here in Camelot, at the edge of the forest, waiting for a creature to appear from the shadows.

In the wee hours of the morning, Ben was asleep in his bed when he heard a boy scream.

'It's here! It's here!' cried Artie. 'It's a dragon!'

Ben dashed out of his tent and looked up at the sky, where, sure enough, a huge purple dragon was roaring, sending massive fireballs down to their camp and setting trees ablaze.

He felt his heart stop in his chest, for his worst fears had been realised. He had seen such a dragon only once before . . .

chapter 8

X Marks the What?

On Thursday, a few days after he'd first discovered the Dark Net's existence, Carlos was running across campus as fast as he could, almost as if he were still scared of dogs and had a pack of them chasing him. His teammates on the tourney field watched him run and cheered him on. 'Go, Carlos!' they yelled, thinking he was practising for Saturday's game.

When he finally arrived at the girls' dormitory and made it up to Mal and Evie's room, he threw himself at their door only to find it open already. He tripped and fell, crashing hard on the floor, just barely able to save his laptop from hitting the ground.

'Carlos!' Evie said as she and Mal helped him up. 'Are you okay?'

'Yeah, I'm okay,' he said, getting to his feet. 'I found something!'

'On the Dark Net?' asked Evie.

'Yes! Where else?' He sat on Mal's bed—which now had a purple bedspread over the white frills, and opened up his laptop to show them. 'It's not good.'

'Well, if it's on the Dark Net, we didn't think it would be,' said Mal, reasonably enough.

Once again he brought up the black screen filled with green letters and began to move through the open windows, scrolling through the threads until he found what he was looking for. 'Got it,' he said. 'Here!'

'What am I looking at exactly?' asked Evie, squinting.

'It's a forum. People go online and post things anonymously, mostly, um, complaining about things, being mean. You know what a troll is, right?'

'Yes, but I didn't think they could type,' said Evie doubtfully.

'No, not a big goblin, it's like a person on the internet who only says nasty things about people,' Carlos explained.

'Nasty things?' Evie blanched. 'Who would do that?' She had lived in Auradon too long now; she wasn't used to malice anymore.

'It's the Dark Net. The villain online underground, what do you think they'd post?' he pointed out.

'Puppies?' Mal said sarcastically.

Carlos looked ill. 'I was digging around and I found this forum about something called the Anti-Heroes movement,' he said.

Mal curled her lip. 'Anti-Heroes? I don't like the sound of that.'

'You shouldn't,' said Carlos. 'Because look at this.' He typed in a few keystrokes and a colourful picture filled the screen.

'That's us!' cried Evie.

It was a photo of the four of them, and there was a huge red *X* on all of their faces along with the words *Join the Anti-Heroes Club Today!* scrawled in spiky red letters.

'Anti-Heroes. So they're anti-us? Are we the heroes?' asked Evie. 'And the club is organised against us?'

'Looks like it,' said Carlos grimly. 'My guess is that the Anti-Heroes movement is a revolutionary group founded on the Isle of the Lost for the single goal of eradicating Auradon's heroes. They're using the Dark Net to draw members and posting incendiary pictures of us to fire up hostile sentiment. To the villains on the island, we're basically traitors. They're using what happened at the Coronation to gather numbers on their side, and when they're ready, they'll come for Auradon.'

The room went silent at Carlos' words.

'But, um, it's just a theory,' said Carlos, to try to lighten up the vibe.

'What's that?' asked Mal, pointing to the small type underneath each picture: *#AntiHeroesUnite #IRL #CAW #Yadrutas #2359 #BeThere.*

'I was about to get to that,' said Carlos. 'I cracked the code. I think it's a meeting invitation. 'IRL' is short for 'in real life,' which means it's taking place in the real world, not the online world. 'CAW' was harder, but I think it's the location.'

'*C-A-W?*' asked Evie. 'But that's—'

'The Castle Across the Way, your house, yep,' said Carlos. 'It looks like that's where it's being held.'

'But what's . . . Yadrutas?' said Mal, frowning as she tried to pronounce the strange word.

'That one took me a while, but after staring at the word for an hour, I realised there was something familiar about it. It's Saturday, spelled backwards! And two-three-five-nine is 23:59 in knight time, or 11:59 at night in royal time. So just before midnight this Saturday, there will be an Anti-Heroes meeting at the Castle Across the Way. 'Be there' is obvious. They're telling their members to be there.'

'You think?' teased Evie.

'Saturday night, right before midnight. Hold on,' said Mal. She grabbed a book from behind her desk. 'It's a moon calendar; I was using it to try to figure out what the notes were saying about the moon. Look at this—the end of the old moon, or moonset, is on Friday before midnight, and the new moon rises on Saturday at 11:59. The young moon is Sunday, which is too late. I think the notes are connected to this Anti-Heroes club. Someone wants us to go to this meeting.'

'So we were right,' said Evie. 'Evil Queen, Jafar, Cruella and Maleficent are behind it somehow. Mal said her mum goes by moon dates.'

'You guys really think it's them?' asked Carlos quietly. He had gone a bit pale again, thinking of having to face his mother. He wouldn't be able to hide behind a computer or an invention this time, and he truly wasn't looking forward to going back to being her much-maligned personal servant. He was just starting to enjoy a life that didn't revolve around fluffing furs and fixing wigs.

'Yeah, they must have sent those messages to tell us to go back to the island so they can humiliate us at this Anti-Heroes thing, don't you think?' asked Evie.

'I love how they're using our "bad example" to recruit members while also telling us to go back and join them,' said Mal.

'That sounds exactly like something they would do,' said Carlos. 'They probably have something awful planned for our homecoming.' He shivered at the thought.

'Plus, who else would be planning a meeting in Evil Queen's castle?' said Mal. 'It has to be them.'

'True. And Evil Queen probably took Maleficent's spot the second she swooped off the Isle,' said Carlos thoughtfully. 'You know they fought over who would get to lead the Isle of the Lost when they were first banished there.'

'They sure did,' said Evie. 'And that's why we were exiled to the Castle Across the Way!'

'Actually, you didn't invite me to your birthday party, and *that's* why you guys had to move,' reminded Mal. 'I was only six years old.'

'That wasn't my fault,' Evie protested. 'And you almost let me fall asleep for a thousand years!'

'What's past is past, let bygones be bygones,' said Jay, entering the room. 'What else did I miss?'

Mal nodded. 'Jay's right; sorry, Evie.'

'I'm sorry too,' said Evie. She stared at the screen again, at the giant red *X*s written across their faces. Ugh, red did not look good with her complexion.

Carlos brought Jay up to speed on what they'd discovered so far about the Anti-Heroes group on the Dark Net. They looked at the picture again.

'We need to be at that meeting so we can find out what they're planning, and that way we can stop it like we did last time,' Mal said, a serious look on her face.

'Fine, let's go, I'll start packing,' said Carlos, who was dreading it but wanted to get it over as quickly as possible. Like ripping off a Band-Aid. It would be easier to confront his mother sooner rather than later, before he had a change of heart.

'Hold on,' said Jay. 'Not so fast. Let's think it through. You know what Fairy Godmother always says.'

'Don't run in glass slippers?' joked Evie.

'Look before you leap, the slow turtle always wins the race,' said Jay. 'Oh, and it's always best to be home before midnight.'

chapter 9

Plans Within Plans

Jay smiled at his friends and rubbed his palms. He loved when a plan started to come together. It reminded him of his life back on the Isle, when he would figure out the best way to nab the least rotten banana from the fruit stands. 'We can't leave just yet,' he repeated.

'Why not?' Carlos wanted to know, even though he looked relieved to hear they didn't have to sneak out of town right then.

'For one, you and I have a tourney game on Saturday, and we can't let the team down,' he said. 'If Ben doesn't make it back from wherever he is, and we leave, they're down three starters; there's no way they have a chance against the Lost

Boys. They need us.' He looked meaningfully at Carlos. 'I know you weren't at practice today, but we're counting on you to be ready by game time.'

Carlos sighed. 'Right.'

Jay turned to Mal and Evie, who both looked sceptical. 'You guys understand, we're part of something bigger here than just us. We're part of Auradon now,' he told them. 'You know we are.'

'Yes, but—' Mal tried to argue.

'Besides,' he interrupted with an apologetic smile. 'We don't want this Anti-Heroes group to think we're onto them. What do you think will happen if news gets out that the four of us are suddenly missing from school? We need to go back, but on our own terms. We can't let them know we know.'

Mal considered it for a moment, thinking. Finally she nodded. 'Okay. Jay's right. We need to lie low,' she said. 'We'll leave Saturday after the game since everyone gets off-campus privileges on the weekend. Come back Sunday night like everyone else, be back here in time for class on Monday.'

'Now you're talking,' Jay said with a smile.

'Wait, hold on,' said Evie. 'If Jay and Carlos get to play tourney, what about the dance? I'm part of the royal committee, and I have to make sure everything's set up correctly. Otherwise, what if it looks like Wonderland threw up on everything? Plus, it's right after the game, and people will notice if we're not there, especially you, Mal. Even if Ben's not there, people will be expecting you.'

'So we go to the dance, too,' agreed Jay. 'Why not?'

Carlos made a few calculations in his head. 'The game ends by five, and the dance starts at six, we stay for an hour, maybe, to make sure everyone notices that we were there. That doesn't leave us a whole lot of time to get out of here and to the Isle by midnight, but it's doable.'

'And this way, you guys won't let down your team,' said Evie.

'And Evie gets to set up with her committee,' added Jay.

'And Mal gets to . . . dance?' said Carlos.

'We all get to dance,' said Evie, whose eyes were sparkling now.

Mal threw up her hands. 'Okay,' she said. 'We won't leave till after the game and the dance so we don't arouse suspicion, and I guess it's good to live up to our responsibilities.'

They discussed the logistics of their plan for sneaking out of Auradon: Evie would come up with disguises while Jay would figure out transportation.

'Did we miss anything?' Mal asked.

'Yes, I think so,' said Carlos after a moment. 'So far the plan can get us out of here, but wouldn't people notice that we're gone on Sunday? That would raise some alarms, don't you think? Even though we're allowed to be off campus for the weekend, people might think it's strange since we never go anywhere.'

'Oh, right,' said Jay with a sheepish smile. 'What are we going to do about that?'

Mal grimaced, thinking hard. 'We're going to be gone for less than 24 hours. How about we all pretend to catch some sort of bug that keeps us in our rooms, and we can post things online about how sick we are, when in reality we're actually running around the island. Isn't that what our online feeds are for? To convince people you're doing something that you're not?'

'I don't think that's what they're for, actually,' said Carlos.

'No, it's perfect,' said Jay. 'We all get the flu. No-one will want to be near us, then. Everyone will leave us alone.'

'Evie, can you set up our accounts so that the posts show up automatically? We won't be able to update them ourselves from the Isle,' Mal pointed out.

'Of course,' said Evie. 'I feel like I've been training my whole life for this.' She batted her eyelashes jokingly before looking serious again. 'So, we're taking off on Saturday night for sure?'

'For sure,' said Carlos, who had turned a bit green. 'What are you smiling about?' he snapped at Jay, who was leaning back, arms behind his head, looking like he hadn't a care in the world. 'Aren't you scared?'

'Totally, but I sort of expected something like this would happen,' Jay replied.

'What do you mean you expected something like this would happen?' demanded Carlos, who was practically pulling out his black-and-white hair at the roots at the thought of returning home so soon.

'I just did,' Jay said, and stopped to consider why he felt that way. He had grown up on the Isle of the Lost, scrounged for food in the garbage, survived goblin-made coffee and his favourite snack was still stale popcorn. Even after living in Auradon, he would always be a bit sceptical of happily-ever-after. And honestly, he'd been waiting for the other shoe to drop ever since the Coronation.

'I don't know, because it can't be this easy, right? We win one battle against Maleficent and it's over?' he told them. 'No way; haven't we learned by now that there are always monsters hiding under beds, or in the closet, or, um, escaping from island prisons? Monsters who are related to us even.'

'You think our parents are monsters?' Evie asked, her voice faint.

'Well, we all know mine certainly is,' said Mal. 'Fire-breathing dragon and everything.'

They all laughed. But Jay was still thinking of what he'd said about their parents. *Was* Jafar a monster? Jafar might take things to the extreme, but he was also just Jay's slightly overweight, pyjama-wearing dad, who dreamt of gold and riches beyond his wildest imagination. A man driven by greed who thought only of himself wasn't much of a monster on an island without magic. But what would happen if Jafar was able to get his magic back? Like Maleficent, Jafar had a powerful magical staff, a cobra that could hypnotise and manipulate those who came under its thrall. Who knew what he would be capable of doing then? But Jay already knew that answer. It's what had landed his father in the Isle of the Lost in the first place.

So no, Jay wasn't surprised that their parents were up to something new, and while he was frightened, he also knew that it didn't matter if all of them were scared. If it was true that this Anti-Heroes movement was growing on the Isle of the Lost, and that their errant parents—Jafar, Evil Queen and Cruella de Vil—were behind it, he and his friends were the only ones who could stop them. 'As Mal said herself, Maleficent is definitely a monster, but we took care of Maleficent, didn't we?' he said. 'So we can handle this, whatever it is.'

'But what if Maleficent is part of it, too?' said Evie worriedly. 'What if she's not completely harmless like we think she is?'

'Maleficent almost roasted us all alive,' Carlos reminded them.

'And who knows what my mum, Jafar and Cruella have in store for us,' said Evie. 'I'm not sure I want to find out.'

'Come on, guys. We can handle anything. We can handle Maleficent,' Jay said staunchly. 'Right, Mal?' He elbowed their fearless leader.

Mal elbowed Jay back, almost a shove. She was clearly just as terrified as the rest of them, but she had decided, like

Jay, to keep it under control. 'Yes, of course, Jay's right. We can handle this. We *will* handle this.' She took a deep breath and stuck out her hand, motioning to the others to do the same. One by one, they each put a hand on top of hers.

'For Auradon,' she said.

'For Auradon,' said Jay, slapping his hand down.

'For Auradon,' whispered Evie, adding hers gently.

They all turned to Carlos, waiting.

'For Auradon,' he said finally, and very reluctantly put his hand on top.

It was done. They were all afraid of their parents, but they would move forwards regardless. Mal always pulled them together and Jay could feel the relief that now filled the room.

chapter 10

Energy = Magic Squared?

Jay's plan for getting them transportation back to the island was simple. They would leave Auradon as they entered it, in the royal limousine, which also held the remote control that opened the invisible dome and let down the connecting bridge with a click of a button.

But if the four villain kids were going to leave Auradon Prep without being noticed, then they could not leave looking like themselves; that much was clear. They didn't have family or friends in the other kingdoms, so there was no reason for them to leave school before winter break. They would have to be creative. Thankfully, being creative was not a problem for Evie.

'Leave that to me,' she'd told the team the night before. 'I've got this handled. If you get the wheels, Jay, I'll make sure no-one knows it's us in the royal limousine.'

But for now, she still had time for regular life. After class, Evie headed to the grand ballroom, where tomorrow's Castlecoming dance would be held, for the last planning meeting. The annual tourney game and dance was a traditional affair, celebrating school alumni returning to their old stomping grounds, when good ol' princes and princesses regaled everyone with tales of the pranks pulled back in their day—stealing the Auradon mascot, for instance, or the time they glued the classroom furniture to the ceiling, causing Fairy Godmother to exclaim something a little more colourful than 'Bibbidi-Bobbidi-Boo!'

Evie said hello to the fellow members of the dance committee and the meeting began. Since the dance was so close, almost all the details had already been agreed upon. The menu had been approved, and Mr. and Mrs. Darling had volunteered to chaperone along with Roger and Anita Radcliffe. Lonnie was going to be the DJ, and would be bringing her own equipment. All that was left was to decide on a theme for the decorations.

'We could do an imperial banquet?' suggested Lonnie.

'How about a sultan's feast?' asked Jordan. 'We could tent the whole area!'

No-one seemed to like any of those ideas, least of all Evie, who argued that since it was Castlecoming, the theme of the decorations should reflect the school colours—royal blue and gold.

'Yes, you have a point there,' said Audrey. 'But don't you think pale pink and baby blue are so much prettier?'

'It's not a baby shower,' Evie mumbled under her breath.

'I'm sorry, did you say something?' asked Audrey, pretending not to have heard.

'I agree with Evie,' said Allie. 'But can we do something more psychedelic maybe? In Wonderland, we have the most amazing flowers of so many different hues.'

'Mmm,' said Evie, looking around at the lush, cream-coloured carpet and exquisite Auradon Prep tapestries already hung on the ballroom's walls. 'Both sound lovely, but I do think blue and gold would be best. It fits the existing colour scheme in the room.'

'If you say so.' Allie sighed. 'I suppose that is traditional.'

'So we'll go with a gold balloon banner? And blue velvet ribbons around all the columns?' asked Evie, pen poised at the ready.

'Maybe we can have bunches of violets in gold vases?' said Allie. 'Violets are actually blue.'

'Perfect!' She smiled at Allie.

'And we can trim the tables with gold leaf,' said Lonnie helpfully.

Audrey frowned. 'If you guys really think that's best.'

Evie smiled. She knew when she had won, and she could be gracious in victory. 'Audrey, Lonnie, do you want to come over and try on your ball gowns?' she asked. 'I'm pretty much done with them.'

If Mal was famous for helping with hair, Evie's talents as a fashion designer and seamstress were starting to become legendary. A number of girls had asked if she would make dresses for them for the dance, so when Mal had said they would need to leave Auradon undercover, it had given Evie an idea.

'Ooh, I can't wait!' said Audrey. 'Did you put on the swan bustle like I asked?'

'It was difficult, but I did it,' said Evie with a smile.

'I can't wait to see mine!' said Lonnie. 'Is it red and gold like we talked about?'

'You'll look like an empress,' Evie promised.

The girls followed her back to her room and Evie handed them their gowns. There was much oohing and aahing over the gorgeous dresses. Audrey's gown featured pink and blue panels that changed colour depending on how she twirled her skirt. 'It's like magic!' Audrey sighed, unable to keep her eyes off her reflection.

'I think Cinderella's mice are going to be jealous!' said Lonnie, who looked stunning in a traditional imperial column with a pretty lotus print. 'Mary's definitely going to want to hire you when you graduate from here.'

'Thanks, guys,' said Evie with a smile.

After they'd changed back into their school clothes, Audrey wandered over to Evie's vanity table, which was littered with numerous tiny glass pots filled with different colours. She stuck her finger in one. 'What's this?'

'Oh, just some batches of lip gloss I've been experimenting with in the lab. We always had to use expired cosmetics on the Isle of the Lost, so when I got here and discovered I could learn to make my own make-up, I was thrilled. I've even been able to enhance them with the right chemical compounds,' said Evie. 'Look, here's one that changes from pink to blue in the light.'

Audrey squealed. 'Can I have it?'

'It's yours,' said Evie.

Lonnie held up a clear gloss. 'What does this do?'

'Glows in the dark,' said Evie. 'I thought it would be fun when the lights go down during the dance.'

'Cool,' said Lonnie. They crowded around the vanity, picking up tubes and pots and trying every colour. Lonnie held up a purple one. 'And this?'

'Don't you hate when your lip gloss disappears in the middle of the day? So I figured out how to make one that never fades,' said Evie.

Lonnie and Audrey nodded in agreement.

'Are you sure I can have this one?' asked Audrey, holding up her blue-pink pot.

'I made it for you, of course,' said Evie. 'Which one do you want, Lonnie?'

'The glow-in-the-dark one, thanks. That way everyone can see me smiling up in the DJ booth,' said Lonnie.

'Perfect.'

The girls thanked Evie and left with their dresses. Mal walked in a few minutes later. 'All set?' she asked.

In answer, Evie opened the closet door, which held two identical dresses to the ones she had made for Audrey and Lonnie. 'Try yours on,' she said. 'I want to see if it fits.'

Evie had stayed up way too late the night before, but she had finished them. If they were going to leave Auradon, they would do so disguised as princesses. Lonnie and Audrey often left school to visit their home castles and kingdoms, and no-one would question their use of the royal limousine. Jay and Carlos would be dressed as their chauffeur and bodyguard, respectively.

'How's your mum, by the way?' asked Evie as she zipped Mal up into the replica of Audrey's dress. 'Did she tell you anything the other day?'

Mal shook her head. 'Not unless she was communicating by sleeping. I really don't see how it could be her, but who knows. We'll just have to assume the worst.' She caught her reflection. Her purple hair framed her horrified face as the dress shimmered in waves of sparkly pink and blue. 'Oh, my goblins, I look like such a princess! It's so . . . pink . . . and blue!'

Evie laughed. 'That's the point! Though I have to say, these *really* aren't your colours.'

Mal stuck her tongue out at Evie. 'Any luck with the Magic Mirror?'

'None,' said Evie. 'It works perfectly if I ask it to show me anything else. But if I ask to see my mum, Jafar or Cruella, it's just cloudy. It's like they've disappeared or something.'

'Let me see,' said Mal. 'Do you think there might be a crack in it?'

'It's already cracked,' said Evie.

'Maybe I can try a spell or two.' Mal grabbed her spell book from the shelf, the one that Maleficent had passed down to her. 'Magic Mirror at my command, heal thyself with my own hand!'

The mirror remained the same.

'Magic Mirror, do as I say, show us the villains on the Isle today!' said Mal.

Nothing changed. Evie shook her head. 'I don't think there's anything wrong with the mirror at all. I'm starting to believe they don't want to be found. They're able to hide from it somehow.'

'But the only way to do that is with magic,' said Mal. 'And there's no magic on the Isle.'

'Or maybe the Magic Mirror is weakening,' said Evie thoughtfully. 'Since we're not encouraged to do magic here, I haven't been using it as much.'

'What of it?'

'Well, what if magic is like a muscle: if you don't use it, it atrophies or tries to find somewhere else to go. Energy has to transform, right? That's what we learned in chemistry,' said Evie. 'There's no such thing as turning something into nothing. It just becomes something else, even if we don't see it.'

Mal considered this. 'You know, you might be right.'

chapter 11

A Wish Is a Dream Your Heart Makes

The biggest barrier—literally and figuratively—in their plan to return to the Isle of the Lost was the invisible dome that covered the island. There was no way in or out of the island without the king's permission. Of course, it would have been easy enough to ask for Ben's help, except he was out of town. Also, Mal didn't want the king to have to answer to his councillors and his subjects if they learned he'd allowed four villain kids to return to the Isle of the Lost, now that the borders were guarded more rigorously than ever after Maleficent's attack. The recent embargo meant most of the goblin barges that brought in supplies and leftovers to the Isle had been blocked, and the few that were allowed through were being monitored very closely.

Hence, Jay had decided on stealing the royal limousine for their escape. The only problem was how to get hold of the car without being caught.

Luckily, the one person who could help him had already issued an invitation. Jordan had asked him to stop by her lamp that afternoon. She was recording a new episode of her popular online show and planned to interview him as one of Auradon's Top Tourney players in the lead-up to the Castlecoming game that weekend.

Jay followed her directions to the lamp, which was kept on a special shelf in the residence halls. Jordan's lamp was smaller than her father's, made of rose gold with delicate filigree carvings all over its surface. Jay wondered if he should pick it up and decided not to. Instead he called down into the lamp's spout. 'Hello in there! Jordan?'

'Just rub the front and you'll pop in,' he heard Jordan yell from inside. 'No need to shout! I can hear you loud and clear!'

He did as he was told and soon found himself comfortably seated on a pink velvet footstool across from a small octagonal coffee table. Green columns painted with gold swirls circled the spacious room, and heavy blue curtains draped dramatically from the ceiling. A striking purple-and-gold Oriental rug was centred on the floor, and peacock feathers were arranged in vases all around. 'Neat,' he said. 'It's bigger than it looks.'

'Thanks, I like my space,' said Jordan, who was seated across from him on a purple footstool.

'Is it annoying that this is all the magic you can use at school?' Jay asked, picking up one of the many stuffed pillows.

'Not really,' said Jordan. 'I'm actually glad for the restrictions. Magic can be wildly unpredictable, even though it's fun, it's nice to have a break from it sometimes.'

'So no more granting wishes, huh?' he teased.

'Not today, anyway,' she said cheerfully. 'Ready for your interview?'

'Hit me,' Jay said.

Jordan snapped her fingers and the lights went on. 'Welcome to *TourneyCenter*!' she said, smiling into the camera. 'Today we have Jay, a star player on Auradon's Knights! Jay, so glad you could join us!'

'Great to be here, Jordan.'

'Are you excited about the upcoming game? Do you think the team is ready to win the tournament?' she asked.

'Very excited, and I think we're more than ready.'

'The Lost Boys have a killer defence; how do you think the Knights will succeed?'

'The way we always do: we run hard, we dodge the cannons, we make the goals.'

'You're confident.'

'I am, I know our team.'

'What about the rumours that King Ben won't be back in time to play the game? We've heard he left earlier this week on some secret official business,' Jordan said keenly. 'Can you tell us anything about that?'

'I can't speak to the rumours, but I know Ben wouldn't want to let us down. I hope he makes it back in time, but if not, we'll carry on.'

'I'm sure you will,' she said, rifling through her index cards for the next question. She smiled back up at the camera. 'One of the things we like to do on *TourneyCenter* is to get to know our players better. Can you tell us a little about yourself?'

'Well, I'm Jay, son of Jafar. I grew up on the Isle of the Lost, but I think everyone knows that by now.'

'That's right, you're one of the so-called villain kids. When did you move here?' she asked.

Jay perked up at the question. 'At the start of the school year. A big old limousine picked us up and dropped us off at Auradon Prep's front door.'

'How fancy,' said Jordan, leaning forwards with a smile.

'Sure was. The amount of candy they have in the back of that thing, I've got to tell you, Jordan, I wish I had the keys to that limo in my pocket right now,' he said, rubbing his stomach.

'Jay! You know the rules!' Jordan said, looking worried. 'You can't say the word *wish* in my lamp. Otherwise . . .

Check your pocket for the keys. You'll have to return . . .' She trailed off as the entire room went topsy-turvy, and the two of them were thrown across the lamp like rag dolls.

'Must have been another earthquake,' said Jordan, struggling to right herself and her footstool. Lamps had crashed, pillows and peacock feathers were scattered everywhere. 'They're so annoying! Every time one hits, my lamp falls on the floor. When you leave would you mind putting it back on the shelf?'

'Not at all,' said Jay with a smile, noticing she had forgotten all about the limousine keys. He felt guilty for deliberately deceiving Jordan, and tricking her into using her magic. But since it was for a good cause, maybe that was okay? The villain kids were just trying to protect Auradon from harm. He'd have to ask Fairy Godmother about it next time in Remedial Goodness class.

Jordan wrapped up the interview and thanked him for stopping by.

As Jay walked back towards campus, the keys to the royal limousine jingled in his pocket.

Chapter 12

Castlecoming Queens

Saturday morning dawned bright and early, and Mal woke up with the sun. She'd been unable to sleep the night before, thinking about the day to come. Tonight they would return to the Isle of the Lost to confront this sinister Anti-Heroes organisation most likely headed up by the biggest villains in the land. *We can do this; we have to*, she thought to herself, but a small, worried part of her was anxious just the same.

'I'm terrified too,' Evie said, when she saw the look on Mal's face as they got ready for the day. 'But like you said, we can handle it.'

'I think Jay said that.'

'Yes, but we all know you're the one who's going to make it happen,' Evie said confidently. 'And if you don't, well, at least your lip gloss won't fade.' She handed Mal a jar full of a purple tint. 'You know what my mum always says, beauty is as beauty is.'

Mal smiled at Evie and Evie smiled at Mal. It was wonderful to have supportive friends, especially when they were good at conjuring up cosmetics. Mal carefully applied the gloss, liking the way it matched her purple varsity jacket. She told Evie she'd meet her at the game and headed over to the library to check on Maleficent one last time before they left.

Her mother was curled around a rock. She looked so tiny and helpless that it was hard to imagine how she could have anything to do with the mischief that was going down on the Isle. 'If there's anything you want to say to me, if you can change back, you should let me know, Mum,' she told the tiny lizard.

But Maleficent just kept sleeping on her warm rock.

'Fine,' said Mal. 'I'll see you when I get back.'

She left the library and walked to breakfast. The entire campus was festooned with balloons and banners, a lively feeling in the air as students walked around with their parents. She saw Audrey with her mother, Aurora, pouring over the class pictures that hung in the hallways. Doug was taking a family of dwarfs on a prospective students' tour.

'This is where we have choir practice. I'm sure your kids will love singing in it,' Mal overheard him say proudly.

For a brief moment, Mal wished she could be one of those kids showing off the school to their parents, but Maleficent had never even once attended a villain–teacher conference back at Dragon Hall, and it was futile to think she would find anything to admire about Auradon Prep.

But she didn't have time to worry about feeling out of place on Castlecoming day. Friendly students mobbed her, eager to introduce her to their parents.

'Come meet my parents!' said Lonnie, introducing her to Mulan and Li Shang.

'Mother, this is Mal! I told you all about her!' said Allie, who pulled Alice away from admiring the students' artwork displayed on the walls.

Mal shook so many hands and smiled so much her dimples were starting to hurt. People in Auradon were so nice, it was a little exhausting. She wished Ben were back already. He was still out of town, and he'd let her know he was sorry, but he wouldn't make it back in time for the tourney game or the dance after all. Mal was surprised to find that she was actually quite disappointed about it, but at least she and Evie would still have fun. Mal would never admit it out loud, but dancing with her friends was nearly as good as going on a date with the King of Auradon.

'Mal, over here!' Evie called from the other end of the hall. Mal joined her side and they walked together to the tourney stadium. The band was already playing the Auradon fight song as they found their seats.

Evie handed her a piece of white silk.

'What's this for?' Mal asked, noticing that everyone else in the nearby crowd had one. The stands on the Auradon side were full of people holding the white silk streamers, waving them gaily about.

'To cheer on our knights, duh,' replied Evie, waving hers.

Mal inspected it closely. 'Hankies?'

'It's what ladies used to wave at their knights, you know, back when they had real tourneys, with horses. They used to call it "waving their colours". Don't you remember? We learned it in class.'

The Royal History of Auradon, Mal recalled now. She waved her white hankie, though really, this practice probably should have stayed behind in the Middle Ages. The crowd cheered when the Auradon Knights took the field; Mal and Evie hooted loudly when Jay and Carlos were introduced.

Carlos waved, smiling behind his helmet, and Jay gave them a thumbs-up. Chad was nowhere in the starting lineup and pouted from the bench.

The game was a close one. Without Ben to help Jay with the tourney plays, the Lost Boys nearly defeated the Knights on their home turf, but in the end Jay set up Carlos for the winning score, and the stands exploded in celebration.

'I'm glad we decided to stay for the game,' Mal told Evie. 'Jay was right, we needed to be here.'

The girls went back to their rooms to change into their dresses for the dance. 'Remember, we're only staying for a little bit, then we need to leave and change into Lonnie's and Audrey's gowns, and meet the boys in the parking lot,' said Mal as she fluffed up her lavender skirts in the mirror. The dress had just enough volume without being fussy, and the dark leather cap sleeves were embellished with tiny black crystals, which meant they shimmered in the light but didn't look princessy.

'Right,' said Evie, sounding doubtful.

'Evie!' Mal said. 'What's the matter? This is the plan.'

'But let's not go so soon, okay? Can't we have a little fun at least?' she wheedled, until Mal had to agree. 'I promised Doug we'd dance the Heigh-Ho Slide.'

'Does he know about our plan?' Mal asked. She hadn't forbidden the group to tell anyone, but had assumed they wouldn't.

'No, I didn't tell him. I don't want him to have to lie for me.' Evie straightened her tiara and took a deep breath. 'Plus, I don't want him to worry. As far as he'll know, I'll be leaving the dance with a bad stomach ache and then I'll be in my room with the flu all weekend like we agreed.'

'I'm sorry we have to go so soon,' said Mal. 'I know how much you love dances. You really do look like—'

'The Fairest?' asked Evie with a cheeky grin.

'Let's just say every princess at that dance is definitely safe from a huntsman tonight,' said Mal.

'Okay, let's do this,' said Evie. They linked arms and headed out the door.

The ballroom was festooned with so many balloons that it was hard to see the top of the ceiling. Gold bunting and blue ribbons hung everywhere.

'It's perfect.' Evie sighed.

'That is a whole lot of balloons,' Mal said.

'You think? I was worried it wouldn't be enough,' said Evie. 'I doubled the order.'

They waved to Lonnie, who was manning the turntables up at the DJ booth. The Auradon tourney team trooped in, handsome in their formal wear, and Jay and Carlos found them, exuberant and smiling. They were the stars of the evening, surrounded by a group of admiring friends and teammates, while Chad skulked by the punch. Evie left to dance with Doug, and Jay and Carlos headed for the buffet tables. Mal picked at her food and checked the clock. She was impatient to get going and was relieved when it was finally time to gather up her team.

She elbowed Jay, and he reluctantly put down the plate of desserts he was holding.

'Let's go,' she said. 'I'll grab Evie, you get Carlos and we'll meet you at the car.'

Mal felt her stomach flip as they set their plan in motion. Sure, she had faced down Maleficent and won once before. But who knew what kind of darkness awaited them this time? Alas, there was only one way to find out.

chapter 13

Ticket to Ride

Carlos had never thought of himself as much of a dancer, but during the celebration after Maleficent's defeat, when all of Auradon had danced on the school steps, he'd enjoyed shaking a leg with the group. Who knew he had it in him? And he was enjoying dancing with Jane, who looked pretty with her hair back to its original colour and neat style instead of the long, glossy mane Mal's spell had created. Carlos thought Jane's normal hair suited her better. Some people didn't really need makeovers, just more confidence.

He was spinning her around when Jay tapped on his

shoulder. 'Uh, I'm headed out,' Jay said. 'I'm not feeling too well. What about you?'

Carlos was about to say he felt great when he remembered the plan. 'Right! I, uh, I'm not feeling well either. Sorry, Jane.' He clutched his middle and pretended to double up in pain.

'Oh!' she said. 'Are you okay?'

'I'm fine, I think I just have to lie down now,' he said. 'Thanks for the dance.'

'No, thank you!' said Jane, a little wistfully.

Carlos crouch-walked out of the ballroom with Jay, who also made a show of looking ill. When they were outside the building, they straightened up and broke into a run towards the parking lot. They could still hear the music wafting from the dance as they made their way noiselessly across campus. They stopped uneasily when the ground rolled beneath them with a little tremor, but it faded away and they kept going.

Jay placed a chauffeur's cap on his head and Carlos stuck in a fake earpiece. Since they were both already wearing black suits, Evie decided that was all they needed to complete the disguise as driver and bodyguard to the royal princesses. Now all they could hope for was that no-one who saw them would know that Audrey and Lonnie were still at the dance.

They found the limousine, which had Auradon flags on each side of the hood. Jay removed the keys from his pocket and unlocked the car doors. He got in on the driver's side and Carlos climbed into the passenger seat.

'Bridge remote?' asked Jay.

'Check,' said Carlos. 'Found it in the glove compartment.'

There was a rustle of skirts from behind them, and the girls appeared out of the darkness. Mal had spelled their hair so that from far away, she and Evie really looked like Audrey and Lonnie. Actually, the disguise was so good that Carlos almost had a little panic attack thinking the real princesses were headed their way.

Mal opened the back door and they climbed in. 'Hurry,' she said. 'We need to get there before midnight.'

'Your chariot awaits, my ladies,' joked Jay, who revved up the engine.

'Um, Jay? Where did you learn to drive?' Evie asked, peeking out from the partition that separated the front of the car from the back.

'Street rats!' Jay cursed, hitting the steering wheel in frustration. 'I was hoping you'd forget that I don't, technically, know how.'

'Oh, for fur's sake,' said Carlos. 'Switch places.'

'Carlos, *you* know how to drive?' asked Mal, impressed. 'How?'

'I taught myself,' Carlos said. 'My mum has a car, remember? She would make me drive her to the Queen of Hearts's salon all the time.' He placed the chauffeur's cap on his head and handed Jay the earpiece.

'Thank goodness!' said Evie.

'I don't think goodness had anything to do with it, actually,' said Carlos with a smile. He eased the long car out of the parking lot. 'Hey, if there's any candy back there, you guys have to share.'

Mal threw him a huge lollipop that bonked him on the head, and they were off.

chapter 14

My Boyfriend's Back

They had only travelled a few metres and hadn't even left the school grounds when a flood of light covered the darkened driveway, and the limousine had to stop in its tracks. Mal squinted against the light to try to see who was blocking their way.

'It's the royal carriage!' said Evie. 'Ben must be back!'

'What do we do now?' said Carlos nervously. 'I can't go around it, it's too big.'

The royal carriage was an imposing behemoth, resembling not so much a pumpkin as a giant squash on wheels. A footman opened the door and Ben stepped out, shaded his eyes against the light, and peered into the limousine.

Carlos switched off the ignition, resigned. 'Oh, well, looks like we're not going anywhere now,' he said, trying to sound disappointed, and failing.

'Let me handle it,' said Mal, stepping out of the car to meet Ben.

'Audrey?' Ben asked, when he saw her.

'No, uh, it's me, Mal,' she said, feeling shy and a bit silly at the whole getup and embarrassed that they had been caught sneaking out of Auradon. After all their careful planning, this was a bit anti-climactic.

'Mal?' He gaped. 'What's going on? What are you wearing? Is that a dress of Audrey's? It's so pink and blue. And is that the royal limousine?'

The windows rolled down, and the rest of the group waved cheerfully at Ben. Ben waved back, a bit confused. 'Why does Evie look like Lonnie and why is Carlos driving? Does he even have a licence?'

'I can explain,' said Mal. She quickly told him about the mysterious messages they'd received, the Anti-Heroes thread on the Dark Net, and the missing villains.

Ben listened carefully, rocking back and forth on his heels, taking it all in. 'So now you're all headed back to the Isle of the Lost?'

Mal nodded. 'We have to, we have to see what's going on.'

'I see.' He wasn't frowning, which was a good sign, but he wasn't smiling either. 'And you weren't going to tell me; why?'

'We didn't want to get you in trouble—with your subjects, I mean,' said Mal. 'Everyone's a little nervous ever since the Coronation, and we didn't think it would look good for you if you knew we were going back to the Isle of the Lost, especially with the embargo and all.'

'Hmm,' said Ben. 'Okay.'

'Okay?' asked Mal. 'You're not mad?'

'No, why would I be? You're not doing anything wrong . . . well, except maybe Jay shouldn't have tricked Jordan out of the keys, you and Evie shouldn't be pretending to be Audrey and Lonnie, and Carlos shouldn't be driving without a licence,' he said mildly, but he had a hint of a smile on his face.

'But you're not going to stop us?' asked Mal.

'No. You guys should definitely check out what's happening back there. I don't know if I would have agreed to it if you had asked me beforehand, but now that I do know about it, I think it's the right thing to do,' he said. 'Tell Carlos to send me the link to the Dark Net, and I'll keep an eye on this Anti-Heroes thread in case it looks like you might need backup.'

'Definitely. And we'll be back in time for class on Monday,' she told him. 'We just wanted to check it out. Although if something is going down, we might be delayed longer. But I don't want you to worry.'

'I won't. I know you can watch out for yourself,' he said, taking her hand. 'I'm glad I caught you, though. I wanted to tell you, strange things are happening, and not just on the Isle of the Lost. In Auradon, too.'

'You mean like the earthquakes?' she asked.

He raised his eyebrows. 'Not just the earthquakes, but lately there have been unseasonal hurricanes down by the Bayou, and giant sandstorms in Agrabah.'

'What do they think is causing it?' she asked.

'We don't know yet. But that's not all.' He hesitated.

'What is it? Where were you, by the way? What's wrong?' she asked, his sombre expression making her feel anxious.

'Camelot Heights,' he said. 'It's why I took the carriage; their roads are hard on cars over there. Merlin came to the council with Artie on Monday, to ask for help with a strange creature that was attacking their town.'

'What kind of creature?' Mal asked, dreading the answer already. 'What kind of attacks?'

Ben held her gaze. 'One that was burning forests, stealing livestock and scorching farms. A real menace,' he said. 'Everyone's really scared. All of Camelot Heights is under lockdown right now.'

'Oh no,' she said. 'That's awful.'

'Mal, it was a purple dragon,' he said quietly, letting the words sink in. He told her about how he had set up camp with Camelot's knights on the edge of the forest and waited for days for the creature to appear. 'Artie was on watch that night and woke us all up. It came out of nowhere, but I saw it before it vanished. A huge purple dragon, with bright green eyes.'

'What. No. You can't think . . .' she said, her heart racing. This was madness. There was only one purple dragon in the world. Maleficent.

'I saw it,' he said. 'It looked just like her . . . I'll never forget how she looked during the Coronation. Her face was right in front of mine and she was going to roast me alive, until you stopped her. I'm telling you, it was her.'

Mal crossed her arms and kept shaking her head. 'No, just no. It can't be. I just saw her this morning. She's trapped under glass on her pedestal. Tiny. Helpless. And you know as well as I do that her Dragon's Eye sceptre is safely locked away in the museum. She's powerless and can't wield any magic without it.'

'I know what I saw,' said Ben, his face drawn. 'I know how crazy it sounds. But just in case, I'm going to place more guards in the library, and keep cameras on her 24/7. If she is getting out, we have to know how she's doing it.'

'I'm sorry I can't stay here to help you,' she said, upset to hear this new information.

Ben smiled. 'As much as I'd prefer that, I think it would be the wrong move. I'm going to stay here in Auradon to see if we can track the dragon down before it does more damage. We're keeping it off the news; I don't want to cause a panic. You guys go find out what's going on in the Isle of the Lost. Maybe this is all part of a bigger scheme. Let me know what you find, and don't be afraid to ask for help if you need it.'

'I will,' she said, giving him a tight hug. 'Thanks, Ben.'

'Is there anything else you need?' he asked.

'No, I think we're good.'

Ben hugged her one more time, then helped her into the car. The windows were still open and the four villain kids waved goodbye, nervous and hopeful expressions on their faces.

'Good luck,' Ben told them. 'And good game, by the way. Nice work. I caught the highlights on *TourneyCenter*,' he said to Jay and Carlos.

'Thanks, man,' Carlos called from the driver's seat while Jay bumped fists with Ben through the passenger window.

Ben reached for Mal's hand through her window. 'I'll see you on Monday,' he said, before reluctantly letting go. He motioned to the carriage driver to get out of the way so the limousine could pass and leave the school gates.

'Monday,' she echoed as the car pulled away. Then something occurred to her. 'Ben!' she called.

He raised his eyebrows.

'If you do catch the purple dragon . . .' She hesitated, even if she knew Ben of all people would understand.

'Yes?'

'Don't hurt it, okay?'

He nodded. 'You have my word.'

Anti-Heroes

'It's up to you how far you go. If you don't try, you'll never know.'
—Merlin, The Sword in the Stone

chapter 15

Isle Sweet Isle

The streets of Auradon were empty as the royal limousine made its way to the very edge of the coast, practically at the shoreline. They finally reached the southernmost point by the bay, where an invisible bridge connecting the island to the mainland was standing. Mal bit the edge of her thumb as she told the rest of her team what Ben had told her about the purple dragon that had been spotted in Camelot. They agreed it had to be impossible—there was no way that creature was her mother. Yet who or what else could it be? There had to be an explanation, but for now, nothing seemed to make sense.

'I sure hope we don't run into this dragon on the Isle,'

said Carlos as he steered the limousine towards the end of the road. The lights from the Isle of the Lost pierced through the fog. 'Wow, it actually looks almost pretty from here.'

'Home,' said Evie softly.

'There's no place like it,' said Jay, with forced cheer.

'Let's hope not,' said Carlos. 'One island full of villains is quite enough.'

'Well, what are we waiting for?' said Mal, who knew they had to do this before they all chickened out. 'Hit it, Jay.'

Jay removed the remote that controlled the bridge from the glove compartment and pointed it at the air in front of them. 'Here goes nothing.'

There was a spark, and through the haze, Mal could almost see the dome opening up as the bridge slowly manifested before their eyes. Carlos drove the car forwards, and the four of them pressed their faces against the windows, watching the bridge materialise in front of them as they drove over the water. Mal knew they were all thinking of the first day they'd left the island. Now they were returning, very much changed from the rotten hellions who had left not too long ago.

Just as they reached the other side, Jay turned around and zapped the remote control again, and the bridge disappeared.

'Don't drive into town,' said Mal. 'We should hide the car somewhere.'

'Good idea,' said Carlos, who veered off the main street and into one of the dusty, unfinished roads. But it was hard to steer the large car on such rocky terrain, and Carlos tried to overcompensate by turning the wheel left when he really should have turned right, and his passengers screamed as the car swerved and plunged into a ditch, sending everything flying as the limousine crashed into a copse of dead trees.

The engine died and the smoke cleared. 'Everyone okay?' Mal called from the backseat. It looked as if their seatbelts had saved them from serious injury, and Mal was thankful they had picked up the habit of wearing them in Auradon.

'Sorry, sorry!' said Carlos, coughing from the front.

Evie nodded that she was all right and Jay offered a thumbs-up from the passenger side. 'A-OK, except I think we lost the remote to the bridge,' he said. 'It must have flown out the windshield.' He pointed to the huge hole in the middle of the glass.

'We'll just have to find another way to get back,' said Mal.

'I guess we could swim?' joked Jay.

'Well, at least the crash took care of one thing. The car's definitely hidden now. No-one will find it here,' said Carlos.

They took turns changing inside the roomy back passenger area into their normal clothing and began the long walk into town. Mal checked the time. After all of their delays, they still had a few hours before the Anti-Heroes meeting was supposed to start. 'Let's meet at Evie's castle a little before midnight,' said Mal. 'For now, let's split up. Each of you, see if you can locate your parents. Once we know what they're planning, we'll figure out what to do about it.'

'What do we say if anyone from the Isle asks why we're back?' asked Evie, looking uncomfortable at the thought.

'Yeah, I bet they're not exactly going to be excited to see us,' said Carlos.

'Tell them the truth, that we're visiting our aged relatives,' suggested Jay with a grin. Soon they had reached the outskirts of town and passed Dragon Hall, following Woeful Way down to the familiar town square, cornered by shabby buildings on all sides and the Bargain Castle looming over everything.

'Don't let anyone know we know about this Anti-Heroes club,' said Mal. 'Until we find Cruella, Jafar and Evil Queen.'

The group agreed. 'Wow, this place is worse than I remember,' said Carlos, looking around. 'And what is that smell? Did you guys ever notice that before?' He made a face. 'It smells like . . .'

'Poisoned toads,' said Mal, who remembered what went into the daily coffee brew.

'Goblins,' said Jay, who seemed to have the foul creatures stuck in his mind.

'Garbage,' said Evie, who recoiled at the memory.

'Actually, it smells like a combination of all three,' Carlos decided.

Mal had to agree, even if a small part of her was happy to return to the familiar 'comforts' of home. The outdoor bazaar was closed for the day, but the Slop Shop and Ursula's Fish and Chips were doing brisk business. It was kind of sad to see how terrifically ramshackled everything looked, though. Mal used to revel in dirt and decay, but she'd been in Auradon too long, and now everything was grimier than she remembered. She really needed to chug a cup of toad coffee before she got too soft.

'Look at that,' said Jay, pointing to a poster of Maleficent pasted to the side of a wall. Someone had drawn a mustache on her face, and another person had scrawled MISTRESS OF LIZARDS over her forehead.

'Whoa,' said Carlos.

'You said it,' said Evie. 'I guess they saw the Coronation; it was broadcast live to the whole kingdom, even here.'

When Maleficent was, well, Maleficent, no-one would dare even *think* to vandalise her likeness. There were other changes too. Goblins seemed to have taken over the square. There were dozens and dozens of them, living in cardboard boxes and gathered around little trash-can fires.

'Where did they all come from?' wondered Evie, who had never seen so many.

'The Forbidden Fortress maybe?' Jay guessed. During

their quest for the Dragon's Eye sceptre, they had run into a rather large and unfriendly goblin horde.

'Nope,' grunted a goblin when he overheard their conversation. He was a stout, runty fellow, and looked as if he hadn't had a good meal in a long while. His green skin was sallow, and his yellow eyes red-rimmed. 'We used to work the barges, but with the embargo, there's a limit on how many of us can bring in supplies from the mainland now. Maleficent promised us freedom and a better life, but she got turned into a lizard, so here we are.'

'Sorry about that,' said Mal.

'You the one that did that to her?' the goblin asked.

'Sort of,' she replied as Evie pulled her away.

'Didn't your mother ever teach you not to talk to strange goblins?' her friend scolded.

'Of course not,' said Mal.

'Mine didn't either,' admitted Evie.

They walked through the streets, feeling the eyes of the island's citizens following them. Mal realised that even if they were dressed casually, they were still better dressed and much cleaner-looking than anyone else. Their clothes, unlike their former neighbours' wardrobes, weren't patched and frayed, or ill-fitting and holey. Mal felt a new wave of emotions—a little proud, a little bittersweet, a little abashed that they looked so different from everyone else. And a little scared to think what their old neighbours now thought of them. Did the people of the island now despise them like they did the fancy princes and princesses of Auradon?

In Auradon, people stared at them because they came from somewhere else, and now on the Isle of the Lost, everyone stared at them because they'd left. In a way, it was just the same. Now they were outsiders in both places. Some of the townsfolk looked at them balefully, while others were merely curious.

'Hi, Gaston, and, um, Gaston,' said Evie, seeing the burly duo across the street.

But the Gastons simply scowled.

Evie backed away. 'They used to be pretty friendly back in Dragon Hall,' she said. 'They even offered to share their lunch with me.'

'Not anymore,' said Mal. 'I bet they wouldn't even share a crumb with you at this point.'

'Let's keep going,' urged Carlos. 'Everyone's staring. I feel like they'll start throwing rotten tomatoes at us.'

'Wouldn't be the first time,' said Jay, but he looked nervous, too.

'Well, well, if isn't the heroes of Auradon.' The four of them turned at the sound of the voice and saw a girl with dark frizzy hair leaning over a balcony. She had piercing grey eyes and wore a soiled red dress with tattered golden piping at the neckline.

'There's that word again,' Evie whispered. *'Heroes.'*

'Ginny Gothel!' said Mal. 'Get down here!' Ginny had been a friendly acquaintance back in Dragon Hall, and Mal remembered with a hint of shame that they had often enjoyed making fun of smaller, weaker people together. They watched as Ginny shimmied down the edge of the building and walked towards them.

Mal wasn't sure what she was expecting when she returned to the Isle of the Lost, but it certainly wasn't to find Ginny Gothel, of all people, looking down at her.

'Don't you guys clean up nice,' Ginny sneered, crossing her arms and studying each of them in turn. 'What do you call that?' she asked, pointing at Mal's outfit.

Mal flushed. 'Preppie punk,' she explained. She was wearing a purple argyle sweater underneath her favourite jacket, along with a clean denim skirt and boots.

'Huh. I'm not sure I'm a fan, but then Auradon style is best for goody-goodies. So, what are you guys doing back here?' Ginny asked, her arms crossed and a sceptical look on her face. 'Slumming?'

'Visiting,' said Jay. 'Which reminds me, I should probably go check out the Junk Shop and let Dad know I'm here.' He waved and quickly jogged away.

'Yeah, Evie and I are gonna head over to our side of the island,' said Carlos, as they peeled away from the group.

'Going home too, are you, Mal?' asked Ginny. 'What would your mum say, I wonder, if she could talk again? To see that her nasty little girl grew up to be so good?' She shook her head. 'If you can change, I guess they're right, there's hope for all of us,' Ginny said in a soft, sweet voice, batting her eyelashes mockingly.

'Who's they?' asked Mal, but Ginny, apparently bored with the conversation, was already walking away.

chapter 16

Gothic Style

Evil Queen had been exiled to the furthest, most remote, and practically abandoned part of the island, so by the time Evie and Carlos made it past Woeful Way and turned onto Hell Street, both of them were panting from the long walk. Without the fear of Maleficent, chaos had settled upon the Isle of the Lost and it appeared even the island's mostly undependable, rinky-dink transportation system had completely broken down. The goblins had abandoned their rickshaws, which were left to rust on the side of the roads.

Everywhere they went, they were met with frowns and scowls. Evie tried not to look too nervous for Carlos' sake, since he was obviously extremely uncomfortable with all the attention.

It didn't help that she was also exhausted and her feet hurt. Evie told herself exercise was good for the skin, and wiped her forehead with her handkerchief. She was still wearing her fancy dancing shoes with the high heels, and she almost fell in relief when they finally reached the familiar tall, grey stone walls of the Evil Queen's castle. Then she remembered she was afraid to face her mother.

She knocked on the heavy fortress door. 'Mum?' she called nervously. 'Um, it's me? Evie! Are you there?'

'It looks deserted,' said Carlos, glancing askance at the cobwebs and dust.

'Oh, it always looks like this,' Evie assured him. 'Mum's big on personal maintenance, but housekeeping, not so much.

'Let me see if I can find the key,' she said, walking over to the nearest wall and feeling for a brick that had come loose. 'Here it is,' she said, holding up an ancient rusted key. 'Maybe she's out getting ready for the Anti-Heroes meeting?'

'Maybe. Wow, this place really looks like no-one's lived here for centuries,' said Carlos as they walked inside.

Evie bristled. 'It's the height of Gothic style!'

'More like the bottom of it,' said Carlos, scrunching his nose.

'Okay, fine, maybe it *is* a bit dark and dreary,' said

Evie, who had never been too bothered by the gargoyles and cobwebs until now. She looked around. Hmm. Maybe Carlos was right. It was a little dustier than she remembered. She took another step and sneezed.

'I'll wait here,' said Carlos as Evie went off to check the bedrooms.

'Mum?' she called, gingerly stepping into the Evil Queen's room. Her mother kept it the way it had always been, when she had been queen of her kingdom and bent upon destroying Snow White. There was a dark silhouette in the middle of the room where the Magic Mirror used to hang before it had been broken into pieces, and a little podium in front of it where her mother would pose and preen, as if the mirror were still there to showcase her reflection.

The closet doors were open, there were blue gowns and black capes in disarray and white ruffs strewn over the floor. Her mother's travelling trunk was missing from the topmost shelf, and from the looks of the mess, Evil Queen had packed in a hurry. That was odd; where had she gone? Didn't she have to be back in time for the meeting tonight?

Evie noticed something else. In the centre of her mother's dressing table was a large ebony box, one that Evie knew well. Her mother had schooled her in the art of beauty regimes from the pots and brushes, paints and blushes, eye make-up, foundation and mascara in that very chest.

It was strange. Her mother had left behind her most

prized possession? Where could Evil Queen have gone without her make-up?

Evie walked down the grand staircase, still sneezing from the dust. She couldn't believe they had lived this way for so long, forgotten and unloved.

Carlos was nowhere to be found. Evie got a little worried and called his name, but there was no answer. Where was he? Evie didn't scare easily, and she was in the house she had grown up in, but it was strange to be here all alone, without her mum bustling around and pressuring her to try the latest exercise fad. She didn't even know where to start looking. The castle was so big that Evie never even knew how many rooms it had. She and Evil Queen had mostly stayed in the main area in the middle.

Maybe he was outside. She walked out the front door. 'Carlos?' she yelled again.

'Over here!' he called. He was all the way on the other side of the castle, hidden by the overgrown weeds. In the moonlight, she could barely make out the tips of his black-and-white hair.

She walked over and found him standing in front of a series of stone steps that led to a cellar door. 'Well, this is the place all right,' he said, pointing to a sign that was hung on the front.

ALL ANTI-HEROES WELCOME,

MEETINGS ARE SATURDAYS NEAR MIDNIGHT

How strange, Evie thought, and for a moment she wondered nervously if Evil Queen was just out at the market buying provisions for this very mysterious gathering.

'Is anyone inside? I don't even know where that door leads,' she told him.

'No, I don't hear anything,' he told her. 'Any sign of your mum?'

'No.' Evie told him what she found in the room. 'It looks like she went away somewhere. She took her trunk, but left her make-up behind. But maybe she'll be back for the meeting?'

Carlos nodded. 'Come on, let's go check out my place. Hopefully we'll be just as lucky there.'

'But we didn't find my mum,' said Evie.

'Exactly,' said Carlos.

chapter 17

Terrible Two

Hell Hall was built in the style of an elegant Victorian mansion. Of course, since it had been transported to the Isle of the Lost, it was nothing but a rotting shell now. Carlos let them in through the side door. So far, everything was as he remembered. Cruella's mean-looking red sports car was parked in the garage, covered by a canvas sheet. The kitchen was still decorated in black and white tile, the refrigerator nearly empty. He peeked into the living room, and saw that it was exactly the same—the broken-down furniture covered with dusty white cloths, the standing knight's armour they kept in the hallway still rusty, the wallpaper still faded and there were still holes in the plaster moulding.

'Mum?' Carlos whispered.

Evie nudged him. 'She's not going to hear you that way. Louder.'

Carlos tried again. 'Mum?' he croaked.

'CRUELLA? ARE YOU HERE?' Evie yelled.

Carlos almost fell to the floor in fright. 'Don't DO that! Or at least warn me first!'

The kitchen was untidy, with dirty dishes in the sink and crusted food on the bench. Carlos began cleaning up almost automatically. It had been his job to keep house when he lived there. Cruella spent her days eating waxy old chocolate bonbons and watching the Dungeon Shopping Network.

'Doesn't look like anyone's been here in a while either,' said Evie, sniffing. 'I think I'm allergic to the Isle,' she said apologetically.

'There's only one way to find out. Wait here,' said Carlos. He steeled himself and went through the hidden passage to Cruella's treasured fur closet.

There was no way his mother would leave without her precious furs. They were all she cared about in life. He flung open the door and gasped. They were all still there—mink and ocelot, beaver and fox, rabbit and raccoon, sable and skunk. Alas, not one Dalmatian coat; Cruella's greatest regret. But he noticed that her rollers were missing from their case in her dressing room, along with the small overnight bag she often used when she went to visit the spa in Troll Town. (Apparently trolls were talented masseurs, due to their large hands.)

He walked back to the kitchen, where Evie was seated on a stool, blowing her nose. 'She's gone?' she asked.

'Looks like it,' he said, opening the cupboards for more clues. 'And the milk in the fridge expired three months ago.' He picked up the box and shook it so its contents sloshed. 'Curdled.'

'But the milk's always expired when we get it.'

'Oh, right, I forgot,' said Carlos, who wanted a huge delicious glass of fresh milk right now. Out of the corner of his eye, he saw a shadow move across the kitchen window and jumped. 'Who's there!' he called.

No answer.

'I thought I saw something,' he muttered, and not for the first time, he wished they were back home safe in Auradon. This wasn't home anymore, and it probably never had been, not really.

'She leave any clues?' Evie asked.

'No, just her furs,' said Carlos.

'Interesting. But isn't Cruella obsessed with her fur coats?' asked Evie, who had once been stuck in that very closet, until Carlos rescued her from its bear traps.

'Obsessed is putting it mildly,' said Carlos.

'Evil Queen left her make-up, and Cruella de Vil left her fur coats,' said Evie. 'But they're definitely both gone.

Maybe they thought they would be back quickly. I mean, they should be at the meeting tonight, right? Otherwise why would they leave the things that mattered to them the most?'

Carlos didn't point out how insane it was that cosmetics and furs were what mattered the most to their mothers. He was used to coming in second in Cruella's affections—make that third, after the car. Probably fourth, after the wigs, if he was being truly honest.

A twig snapped outside. This time Evie heard it too.

'Who's there?' Carlos called again, opening the door. 'Show yourself!' he said, even though he was shaking in his boots. He wished Mal was with them. Everyone was scared of Mal.

He heard snickering in the bushes, and whispering. 'It's him, it's really him. And her, I think that's her. The pretty one.' Two figures stepped out to the light. One was tall and skinny and the other was short and round.

'Harry! Jace!' Carlos said.

'Your friends?' asked Evie.

'Not exactly,' he told her. Harry and Jace were the sons of Cruella's most loyal minions, Jasper and Horace. The three of them used to hang out since their fathers were scared of Carlos' mother, and had forced their boys to befriend Carlos. They had helped decorate for the howler of a party Carlos had thrown for Mal at Hell Hall not too long ago.

'You're back!' said Harry.

'What are you doing here?' asked Jace.

'Can't a guy visit his mother?' asked Carlos. 'What's up with you guys?'

'Nothing much. We saw you on the telly,' said Harry. They sounded exactly like their fathers, down to their Cockney accents.

'At the Coronation?' Carlos said.

'Yar,' said Jace. 'When the dome broke and Maleficent zoomed out of here, fast as her dragon wings could take her, we all cheered.'

'We thought it was finally our time, that she'd take Auradon for us!' said Harry.

'Evil rules!' cheered Jace, raising a fist.

'But o'course you all had to stand up against her, eh?' Harry shook his head. 'And Mal, turning her mama into a lizard!'

'Mal's the new Big Bad, huh,' said Jace. 'She ever turn you into a lizard?'

'No,' said Carlos.

'You scared of her?' Harry wanted to know.

'Of Mal? No,' said Carlos again. 'I used to be, but not anymore. Mal's . . . changed.'

'Crikey! You mean she's a lizard too?' said Harry.

'No. Mal's not a lizard,' he told them, rolling his eyes as Evie tried not to laugh. Carlos remembered why he didn't miss hanging out with Harry and Jace. Conversation tended to go around in circles. 'Hey, do you guys know where my mother is?'

'Who?' asked Jace, affecting a blank look.

'Cruella de Vil!' yelled Carlos.

Harry and Jace exchanged shifty looks. 'Don't worry 'bout your mama, now; we're here, right?' said Harry.

'Righto, guvnor, welcome home!' said Jace, with a menacing glint in his eye.

'Shhh,' said Harry. 'Don't spoil it.'

'Spoil what?' Carlos wanted to know.

But the two junior henchmen wouldn't say and only laughed uproariously. Obviously, something was up, and it made Carlos' stomach churn. Harry and Jace had never been good at keeping evil schemes to themselves, and it sounded as if that's exactly what was about to hatch here.

chapter 18

Pirate's Booty

Jafar's Junk Shop looked as it always did, like a dilapidated dump. Through the grimy window, Jay could see the shelves filled with broken radios, lamps and chairs as well as all manner of old appliances that no-one used anymore. Jafar had filled his mind with dreams of endless riches, and Jay used to imagine that all the twisted and rusted metal and the knock-off jewellery they sold would magically turn into piles of real gold and jewels. Of course, that never happened.

Jay picked the locks on the front door (all twenty-four of them) and let himself inside, skulking around a little, afraid of what his father would say when he saw him.

'Dad?' he whispered. 'Dad? Are you here?' he asked, a little more loudly. The air was musty and stale, and a fine layer of dust covered the gadgets and trinkets on the benches. There was no answer, until a rusty squawk from the back of the room echoed, 'Dad? Dad? Dad?'

Jay ran to the private sitting area behind the shop, pushing back the heavy velvet curtains to find Iago, Jafar's loyal parrot, looking terribly scrawny and out of sorts, with molted feathers covering the newspaper at the bottom of his cage. The bird practically snorted and put his wings on his hips when he saw Jay, as if to say, *About time, kid!*

'Where's Jafar?' Jay asked.

'Gone,' said Iago. 'Gone gone gone gone gone.'

If there was one thing Jafar could be said to care about, it was his loyal sidekick. Jay didn't think his father would leave Iago to starve, so wherever he'd gone, he must have expected to return soon after. Jay changed the newspapers and refilled the bird's water and cracker supply.

'You don't know where Dad went?' Jay asked.

'Gone gone gone gone gone,' was all Iago said, stuffing his beak with crackers as fast as he could.

Jay sighed. The cranky parrot had never been much help in the past, so of course he was no help now. He checked the rest of the shop for any small clue or indication as to where Jafar could have gone, but didn't find anything helpful. Where had his father disappeared to? The only place the villains ever talked about going was Auradon; they were obsessed with returning to their true homes. Growing up, Jay recalled his father telling him how Agrabah was its most beautiful kingdom, with the Sultan's Palace and its golden domes high up north, past the Great Wall.

There was a knock on the door. 'Are you open?'

'Sure,' said Jay. 'Come in!' He figured whoever it was might be able to tell him something about his father's disappearance.

Big Murph, a young pirate who ran with Hook's crew, walked in, an eye patch over one eye, a red bandana tied around his forehead and a faded yellow vest over a dirty T-shirt and holey shorts. Like the rest of his kin, Big Murph only wore slip-ons, even when it snowed. 'Hey, Jafar, glad to see you open up again, we're out of fishing . . .'

The stout pirate stopped short when he saw Jay. 'Oh! It's you!'

'Hey, Big Murph, what's up?' Jay asked. He liked Big Murph and the pirates. The big guy was usually friendly and Captain Hook had asked Jay to join their crew a couple of times, telling him they could use a talented thief among their ranks, but he had always passed. He wasn't a big fan of scurvy.

'JAY!' Big Murph said, looking fearful as a few more people wandered into the Junk Shop to browse. He looked around the shop. 'You're really back?' he asked suspiciously.

'Yeah, I guess so.'

Big Murph continued to look askance at Jay. 'Is it

true—that Mal and Evie and Carlos are back from Auradon too?'

Jay leaned on a counter and crossed his arms, still unsure of what this was all about; the pirate was sure acting cagey. 'Yes, we're here to, um, visit our aged relatives. Do you know where my dad is, by the way?' It was still hard to believe his father wasn't at home as Jay recalled that most days Jafar was too lazy to get up from his divan.

Big Murph shook his head and wouldn't meet his eyes.

'No clue, huh?' said Jay, who was starting to feel that the big man wasn't quite telling him the whole truth.

'Nope,' said Big Murph stubbornly. 'Shop's been closed and we've been out of fishing hooks.' The pirates fished from the piers sometimes.

Jay rummaged through the nearest drawers and found a bag full of hooks. 'Here, take them,' he told Big Murph.

'How much?' the pirate asked nervously as Jafar often charged ten times the amount the stuff was actually worth.

'Just take them,' said Jay. It wasn't like he could spend those coins in Auradon anyway. His dad would scream at him for giving something away for free, but Jafar wasn't here right now, was he?

'Serious?' Big Murph asked sceptically.

'Yeah, go ahead, get out of here. Go fishing. Catch a crocodile while you're at it,' he said with a grin.

A goblin brought up his items to the register and Jay rang him up. Big Murph was still standing there. 'Guess it's true, then, what they say about you guys,' the pirate said, almost defensively.

'Who's they and what do they say about us?' asked Jay, making change for the goblin.

But Big Murph wasn't paying attention anymore, as he was too excited about the free bag of hooks. Then he checked the time on his pocket watch and jumped. 'Oh, I'll be late! Gotta run! But maybe I'll see you later?' he said meaningfully.

Then he was gone before Jay could ask him any more questions. Was Big Murph talking about the Anti-Heroes meeting? He wasn't sure, and the bad feeling he had about attending this meeting only grew. Whatever it was, it had turned a happy-go-lucky little pirate into a shifty-eyed mercenary.

Before he could think on it too much, Anthony Tremaine popped his head in the shop as well. The handsome grandson of Lady Tremaine curled his lip when he saw Jay. 'Oh, it's you,' he said, sounding terrifically bored. He had the same haughty way of speaking as his grandmother. 'I heard a nasty rumour that you and the other turncoats were back on the Isle.'

'Turncoats!'

'Isn't that what you call someone who turns against everything they used to stand for?' asked Anthony. 'That little performance at the Coronation was ever so . . . *good*, wasn't it?'

'What do you want, Anthony?' asked Jay, impatient to get rid of him.

'Jafar promised Mother a new shoe-stretcher,' Anthony said. 'I paid him but he hasn't delivered. I was hoping he was back to make good on our deal. Mother's beside herself.' Anastasia still refused to wear shoes in the right size, preferring to buy them a size smaller so she could try to expand them through rigorous and hopeless toe-straining, as if Prince Charming would still change his mind.

'Hang on,' said Jay, looking through the many shelves and drawers, but he couldn't find what he needed. 'Sorry, looks like we've run out.'

'Even if the embargo's lifted?' asked Anthony with a smirk.

'Come again?'

'If you're back, it sure looks like Auradon's sending their trash to the Isle of the Lost again, doesn't it?' Anthony laughed, pleased with his insult.

'Ha-ha,' said Jay.

'A joke,' said Anthony, with a shrug. 'What are you doing back anyway?'

'What's it to you?' asked Jay. 'Who wants to know?'

'You know what, I'm too bored to pretend to care,' said Anthony.

'Fine,' said Jay, reaching out to shake Anthony's hand.

Anthony gave him a strange look, but shook hands with Jay before leaving the shop. Now it was Jay's turn to smirk, since he'd swiped Anthony's watch for old times' sake. It was so easy, just a flick of the wrist, flip of the latch, and it was his. Oh, he'd missed this. Jay counted the seconds for the snobby boy to return. One, two, three, four . . .

Anthony reappeared at the doorway, and he sure wasn't laughing now. 'Give it back, Jay,' he said fiercely. 'Now!'

'What are you talking about?' asked Jay, the very picture of innocence even as his eyes twinkled with amusement.

'My watch. You took it.'

'No, I didn't.'

'Yes, you did!'

'I didn't take it, I swear. Maybe you just misplaced it,' said Jay with a shrug. 'You should be more careful with your things.'

'It's a wristwatch! Where else would it be but on my wrist?' Anthony glowered and stomped off, muttering darkly to himself about how Auradon should keep its trash for itself.

Jay whistled as he closed up the shop again and waved goodbye to Iago, promising to send a goblin to feed him crackers. Anthony was right, Jay had stolen his watch, but instead of keeping it, he'd hidden it in Anthony's jacket pocket. He knew Anthony would go crazy looking for it, and would be especially annoyed when he discovered Jay 'hadn't stolen it' after all.

Sometimes, even reformed villains needed to have a little fun.

chapter 19

The Mists of Auradon

While it had been hard saying goodbye to Mal and letting the four villain kids return to the Isle of the Lost, Ben knew that if anyone could get to the bottom of what was happening back there, she was the one to do it. He was glad she had her friends by her side as well. There was no point in wasting time biting his fingernails and watching the clock. He didn't realise he'd spoken out loud until Cogsworth interrupted his thoughts.

'Did you say clock, Sire?' his loyal servant asked. While Cogsworth was no longer a grandfather clock, he was still understandably sensitive when he heard about anything pertaining to timepieces. 'It is close to midnight, should you need the time.' The stalwart Englishman was overseeing the footmen as they set down Ben's trunks from the journey in the royal bedroom.

'Thank you. I didn't realise how late it was. You can leave the rest for tomorrow,' Ben said, dismissing them. He was incredibly tired, and the extra-plush mattress in his large wrought-iron four-poster bed was especially inviting after the lumpy one in Camelot. He was happy to be back in his room, with the familiar Auradon banners and exercise equipment, the huge yacht model he'd made still sitting on his desk.

'If I may . . .' said Cogsworth, pausing at the doorway. He waited for Ben to nod before continuing. 'Lumiere mentioned you had encountered a rather purple dragon in the woods. Being that my old friend is prone to flights of fancy, I thought I would ask you myself. Is it true, Sire, about the dragon?'

'I'm afraid it is,' said Ben. 'May I ask that you and the rest of the palace staff please keep this news to yourselves for now? At the right time, I shall alert the general population of the danger.'

'Of course, Sire,' said Cogsworth, who had turned grey. 'Do you think it is . . . *her*?' he asked, visibly shivering at the thought.

'Unfortunately, I can't think who or what else it could be but Maleficent,' said Ben. 'But don't worry, my friend, we'll keep Auradon safe.'

Cogsworth bowed, and when he left the room, Ben noticed that everything had been unpacked and put away in pristine order even though he'd told him to wait until tomorrow. Ben had to smile. That Cogsworth: his loyal efficiency was regular as clockwork.

Even though he was exhausted, the events of the night meant Ben found it hard to fall asleep. Deciding it was useless to keep tossing and turning, he got up to do some work instead. When he turned on his computer, he found that as promised, Carlos had sent him the link to the Dark Net. Ben clicked around till he found the photos Mal had told him about on the Anti-Heroes thread. He was taken aback to find one of himself with a red *X* over his face too. He clucked his tongue and continued to read on, steeling himself for further assault and more invectives.

The Anti-Heroes forum was lit up that night, with many of its members posting their excitement about tonight's meeting. Then Ben saw a new post that caught his eye. The message read, *Looks like four former cast-offs have washed ashore on the Isle of the Lost. Prepare Operation Welcome Home!*

Hang on.

Four former cast-offs?

That could only mean his four friends, right? Ben checked the time stamp. The message was sent an hour ago, about the same time Mal and the gang would have arrived on the island. He had to warn them that their presence had been noticed by their enemies. Ben sent texts and tried to call, then remembered that the island was cut off from the main servers. If Mal got into trouble, there was no way for him to find out until it was too late. He could send his royal troops after them right now, but since nothing had happened yet, he knew Mal would take it as an insult. Ben slammed down his laptop lid, frustrated.

He would just have to trust that she, Evie, Jay and Carlos would be able to deal even if the situation got out of hand. He forced himself to stop worrying and focus on the current problem instead—the purple dragon of Camelot. Earlier, he had sent emergency emails to his council, alerting them to the danger he'd discovered. Grumpy and the dwarfs advised they were up for battle, axes at the ready, although perhaps the best thing to do would be to destroy Maleficent while she was in her tiny lizard form in her glass dome. Others were more cautious in their response, however.

An email had arrived from the three good fairies. Merryweather, the youngest, and the most capable with modern technology, had sent their reply.

Our dearest king,

It is with great concern that we received the distressing news about Camelot's dragon. While it does seem as if none other than our old nemesis Maleficent is behind such mischief, we would like to advise caution in this arena before we jump to conclusions.

If the creature is indeed a shapeshifting evil fairy, it is best to obtain proof before we act accordingly. Perhaps it would be possible to retrieve an item linked to the dragon in question? A nail from its claw? A piece of its hide? A lock of its hair?

If you are able to recover such an item, it would be prudent to bring it to Neverland right away, the ancestral home of the fairies, so they can ascertain the identity of this dragon.

Without proof that it is indeed Maleficent, it seems imprudent to act with violence towards the lizard in the library, who might still be innocent.

Your godparents,
Flora, Fauna & Merryweather

He was glad they agreed that Maleficent should not be harmed, as he knew he could never face Mal if she returned on Monday to the news that her mother had been destroyed without a fair trial or even proof that she was the one rampaging through Camelot.

The royal technicians had set up several cameras all around Maleficent's prison, and Ben called up the screens. All of them showed a tiny lizard under glass, and so far there was no indication it was anything other than that. He closed the windows showing the security screens with a sigh.

As he was typing a grateful reply to the good fairies, there was a knock on his door. 'Enter,' he called.

'Forgive me, Sire, but Archimedes just dropped this off. From the way he was hooting, it seemed rather urgent,' said a sleepy Lumiere, handing him a letter that had beak marks around its edges.

Ben ripped open the letter, his heart pounding as he imagined what news Merlin had sent from Camelot. Had the dragon scorched the castle? Laid waste to the entire kingdom?

All well here. Purple dragon spotted off Charmington Cove, thought you should know. It appears the creature is on the move.

Not the greatest news, knowing the dragon was venturing into other areas of Auradon, but at least, not the worst news either.

Lumiere was standing at attention, awaiting orders. 'It looks like we'll have to pack up again,' Ben said. 'But I'll drive this time.'

'Very good, Sire,' said Lumiere.

'Oh, and find Chad Charming; tell him to be ready to leave with me in the morning.' It would be best to have someone who knew the lay of the land. No matter that his and Chad's friendship had cooled slightly since the villain kids had enrolled at Auradon Prep.

Ben turned back to his computer, and re-read the good fairies' words. If the purple dragon was in Charmington, he would make sure to bring a piece of it to Neverland so they could solve the mystery of the creature's identity once and for all.

chapter 20

Bargain Bin

If it could be said that the Isle of the Lost had a jewel in its crown, then Maleficent's former home, the Bargain Castle, would be it. The old place didn't look half as good these days, however, with its peeling paint, bolted doors and shuttered windows. Mal wasn't sure what she thought she would find in there, but after using a stick to pry off the panels that had nailed the door shut, discovering that the whole place was completely ransacked was a surprise. When Maleficent ruled the island, her boar-like henchmen at her command, and goblins to do her bidding, no-one would even dream of knocking on their door before a decent hour. But now . . .

Mal picked her way through the destruction. The slimy contents of their fridge were spilled on the floor, and her mother's former throne looked as if it had been raided for its upholstery, with bits and pieces of foam and feathers sticking out of the huge holes that had been ripped and torn or clawed from its seat.

The queen was dead (well, she was a lizard). But there wasn't a new queen either. The Isle had fallen further into chaos and disrepair. While its citizens feared Maleficent, she had brought a semblance of order to their hardscrabble lives, and now that she was gone, it was total anarchy.

Mal made her way to her room, wondering what she would find, and a bit anxious about the small but real treasures she had kept there. When her mother had shipped her off to Auradon, there was no expectation that she would actually stay there, and so Mal had left most of her things back home. She opened the door, expecting to see it similarly looted and plundered.

But her room was just like she had left it. Purple velvet curtains, bureau with all her little sparkly doodads, her many sketchbooks and canvases stacked neatly on the bookshelves. 'Huh,' she said. Why was her stuff left untouched?

Mal grabbed a backpack from her closet and began stuffing it with the things she wanted to bring back to Auradon: her journals and sketchbooks, a necklace with a dragon-claw charm that her mother had given her on her sixteenth birthday (in fact, it was the first—and only—gift she'd ever received from Maleficent that she'd felt like keeping). When Mal was eight her mother had gifted her with an apple core; at ten, with fingernail shavings. Maleficent explained they were part of spells, but since there was no magic on the island, it just seemed like an excuse to give her daughter trash.

'Hello?' a voice called from the main room, and Mal heard the sound of footsteps coming closer. 'Is anyone in here?'

'Who is it?' Mal asked, stepping out of her room warily.

'Mal! You're really back!' The girl who stood in the middle of the living room was tall and lanky, wearing black from head to toe, with a tight jacket and leather pants.

'Mad Maddy?' Mal said, excited to see an old friend. When they were little, Mad Maddy and Mal were practically twins since they had the same colour hair. But when they got older, Maddy liked to change it to a different shade every week. Right now it was bright aqua green to match her eyes.

'It's just Maddy now,' she said, with a witchy giggle. 'But just as mad as ever. I saw that the door was open and I thought it might be you. Everyone's saying you guys are back; news travels fast on the Isle.'

'I bet,' said Mal. 'Do you know who did this?' she asked, motioning to the gutted living room.

Maddy took a look around. 'Goblins mostly, but almost everyone came here after the Coronation. I saw Ginny Gothel wearing one of your mother's capes the other day.'

'Ugh!' said Mal. Ginny really was more rotten than she had remembered. 'Well, at least no-one touched my room; isn't that odd?'

Maddy took a seat on the broken sofa, which looked as if it had been used as a trampoline for a school of goblins, and put her booted feet up on the smashed coffee table. 'Of course not, why would they?'

'What do you mean?'

Her old friend pulled at her green hair, twirling it around her finger. 'We all saw what you did, after all.'

'What I did?'

'To your mother. You turned her into a lizard. You beat Maleficent,' said Maddy, as if the words were more than obvious.

'Is that what everyone thinks around here? That I *wanted* that to happen?' asked Mal. She'd only wanted Maleficent to stop attacking her friends, to leave the good people of Auradon alone, and she'd had no idea that by doing so her mother would be greatly reduced in size and power.

'Well, didn't you?' said Maddy, sorting through the rubble to see if she could scavenge anything worthwhile. 'It's what happened, isn't it? We all saw it.'

So that was why her room had remained untouched. The Isle no longer feared Maleficent. Now they bowed to a new ruler. They feared Mal.

'It's not what you think,' said Mal.

'Doesn't matter,' said Maddy with a shrug. 'It's what everyone thinks.'

'Well, they're wrong.' Mal kicked an overturned chair.

Maddy startled. 'Wait, what? You mean it really wasn't you? You didn't do it?'

'No, I mean, I guess I did, but it was her fault she had so little love in her heart, which is why she turned into a lizard,' explained Mal, blushing to use the word *love* in front of Maddy. They'd both grown up thinking love was for fools, morons and imbeciles, after all.

'Hmm,' said Maddy, studying Mal closely.

'What?' asked Mal.

'Nothing,' said Maddy. 'Come on, let's go get something to eat.'

chapter 21

Frenemies

They still had ample time before the meeting, so when Carlos mentioned that he was hungry, Evie suggested they walk back into town to the Slop Shop to get something to eat. After refusing to tell them any more about what they knew about Cruella's whereabouts, Harry and Jace had run off, giggling mysteriously to themselves, and she was glad to be rid of their company.

'You think they were telling us the truth? That they don't know where my mother is?' asked Carlos.

'Who knows, between those two I'll be surprised if they remember their names,' said Evie, once again cursing herself for forgetting to change into comfortable footwear.

'Where do you think they are, then?' asked Carlos, playing with the zipper on his jacket. 'Our parents, I mean.'

'My guess is they'll be at the meeting later,' said Evie. 'Don't you think?'

'What are we going to do when they tell us what their evil plan is?' said Carlos. 'I'm not sure I can stand up to Cruella the same way Mal stood up to Maleficent, you know?'

'We'll figure it out when it comes down to that,' said Evie. 'Don't worry, I'm not looking forward to seeing my mother either. I know she'll hate the way I'm doing my hair now.'

When they reached the goblin-run café, they noticed Mal in the window, laughing with a girl Evie didn't recognise. The two of them were giggling together while sharing one of the Slop specials—stale bread pudding topped with rancid banana syrup, a popular dessert on the Isle of the Lost, where extracts from rotten fruit were their only source of sugar.

'Who's that girl?' Evie asked.

'Oh, that's Mad Maddy,' said Carlos. 'She and Mal used to be tight.'

'I don't remember her from Dragon Hall,' said Evie.

'Yeah, she transferred to an all-witches school on the other side of the island in ninth grade,' said Carlos. 'Witches.

Even if you can't practice magic on the island, they still think they should teach their kids about it.'

He led them to the counter and ordered snacks. The goblin grunted and shoved two steaming-hot cakes onto paper plates.

'Ah,' said Carlos, making a face as he bit into a hard, sour scone. 'Just like I remembered.' He spat it out. 'Although I think I'll pass. I don't think I can eat this anymore.'

Evie nodded, and put hers back on its plate, untouched.

'Oh, hey, guys, come and join us,' Mal called from her table.

Evie took a seat next to Mal while Carlos pulled up a chair next to Maddy. Mal was digging into her pudding. 'Want some?'

Carlos nodded. He found a clean spoon and took a bite. 'I forgot how much I used to like these things,' he said, and took another heaped spoonful.

'You did?' Evie blanched.

'You didn't?' said Maddy, looking her over with a sardonic smile. 'Wasn't this an intrinsic part of your childhood?'

Evie returned the girl's up-and-down gaze. 'Not mine,' she said coolly. 'My mother and I hardly came into town. Actually, make that never.'

'Sorry, don't you guys know each other?' Mal asked, to make up for the awkward silence that ensued. 'Maddy, this is my friend Evie, and Evie, this is Maddy. We grew up together.'

'Yeah, Carlos told me,' Evie said.

'We liked to hex our dolls together,' said Maddy. She smiled sweetly at Carlos. 'Hey, Mal, remember when we covered Hell Hall in fake spiders?' she asked. 'Or were they real?'

'They were real and real dead,' said Mal, laughing at the memory. 'It took forever to collect so many!'

Carlos squirmed in his seat. 'Yeah, that was fun, not really,' he muttered.

'Carlos screamed so loud when he saw them, I thought he would wake up Cruella,' Maddy cackled, and put up her hand for a high five, which Mal slapped with gusto.

Mal and Maddy were still laughing over their past exploits, which Evie found highly annoying. They hadn't returned to the island to gossip with old prank-mates. Plus, they shouldn't be making fun of Carlos. Evie realised she wasn't looking at Auradon Mal. This was Dragon-Hall Mal, the sneering, scary girl who used to stomp through the island with a scowl and a can of spray paint. Evie cleared her throat to get their attention. 'So, Maddy, do you guys have any idea where my mum is? Or Carlos'? We just went home and they were nowhere to be found.'

Maddy crumpled her napkin and pushed her bowl away just as a goblin came by and grumpily reminded them that there was no lingering at the tables.

'You really don't know?' she asked coyly.

'No, we really don't,' said Evie, who had had it with this

girl's snickering innuendo. Maddy was acting as if she knew a wicked secret and wouldn't share.

'Do *you* know anything?' Mal asked Maddy.

Maddy shrugged. 'No-one knows anything about anything,' she said, a sly smile on her face.

Evie didn't like the girl, but even if she did, she knew Maddy was lying. She knew something about where Evil Queen, Jafar and Cruella de Vil had gone, that was for sure. Was she in cahoots with them and this Anti-Heroes club? Evie wouldn't put it past her.

It was almost time to head over to the Anti-Heroes meeting, and Evie felt herself breakout in a cold sweat, imagining what was in store for them. Evil Schemes was only a class taught at Dragon Hall, but Cruella de Vil, Evil Queen and Jafar could spin an evil scheme in their sleep. They lived and breathed for malice and revenge. Who knew what kind of terrible surprise their parents had cooked up for their return?

chapter 22

Needle in a Haystack

Chad Charming wasn't particularly happy to have been woken up at dawn on a Sunday, and was still complaining about it as Ben drove them down the Auradon Coast Highway that morning in the royal convertible. The handsome prince groused that he had been up late from Castlecoming festivities the night before, and what was so important that they had to leave this early?

'Really, old man, why on earth are we going to Charmington? Mum's going to freak when we get there; you know she likes to have everything sparkling clean for a royal visit,' said Chad.

'I told you, I have an early meeting with the grand duke

about the upcoming ball,' said Ben, who wasn't about to tell Chad about the dragon menace just yet. 'And you know the fastest way to get there.'

'Fine,' said Chad, leaning back in the passenger seat. 'Keep on this lane and then exit at Belle's Harbour, then we can take the back roads until you get to the Stately Chateau.'

Ben did as directed, glad that Charmington Cove wasn't stuck in the past like Camelot, and he could actually drive his own car without the burden of the full royal entourage. If he could have taken his motorbike, he would have, but the sporty coupé was fun to drive too. Plus, he'd been meaning to talk to Chad about something.

'Hey, Chad,' he said. 'What's up between you and Jay lately? Have you been giving him a hard time?'

Chad snorted. 'Those villain kids are getting big heads, don't you think? Strutting around Auradon like they own it. Someone's got to put them in their place.'

'Their place is in Auradon now,' said Ben angrily. 'Look, man, they're just trying to fit in. Give it a rest, will you?'

Chad squirmed in his seat but he nodded and said he would.

Ben relaxed his hold on the steering wheel, satisfied. As pompous a prince as Chad was, he wasn't a complete jester.

They arrived at Charming Castle by noon. Chad hollered for his parents, but was told they were out running errands for the upcoming ball and wouldn't be back till late.

While Chad went up to his room to get some more sleep,

Ben met with the grand duke, who was in charge while the royals were away. The duke was polishing his monocle in his receiving room when Ben was announced. He bowed to Ben and offered him a seat on one of the tufted red velvet chairs across the large inlaid table.

'You got my message last night?' Ben asked. 'I'm sorry for the rush.'

'Oh yes, Sire,' said the grand duke, his mustache quivering. 'As you requested, I sent messengers throughout our kingdom to see if anyone else had encountered such a creature. My men are very thorough, and they understand this is just as high a priority as Operation Glass Slipper. According to your note, we are looking for any sign of a purple dragon, am I correct?' He cupped his mouth and whispered, 'Like Maleficent?'

'Unconfirmed for now,' said Ben. 'As far as we know, she remains safely locked away in the library.'

The grand duke looked relieved. 'When she was turned into a lizard, she did seem quite harmless—cute even, if I can say so, Sire. I hear lizards make good pets.'

Ben was non-committal and the grand duke remembered the pressing business he had to communicate to Ben. He pulled up a few scrolls. 'I received this just before you arrived. Other than the report that Merlin received of a creature spotted off Charmington Cove, it appears there hasn't been any fire damage or livestock stolen, nothing of that sort. However, there was another incident this morning down by Cinderellasburg.'

'What kind of incident?'

'A creature was spotted in a chicken coop early this morning,' said the grand duke. 'However, the farmer reports that the animal did not resemble a dragon. More like a purple snake.'

Snake. Dragon. Lizard. It was all part of the reptilian family, Ben thought. 'It could still be related to what I'm looking for; let's check it out.'

Ben left Chad back at the castle, snoring away, and the grand duke and a team of his footmen accompanied him to the pretty little village that Cinderella had once called home. The farmer and his wife were expecting them, standing nervously in front of their homestead. They bowed and curtsied when they saw Ben.

'I understand you saw a strange-looking snake on your farm this morning?' he asked.

'Yes, Sire, it came out of nowhere and took three eggs from the coop!' the farmer's wife told them. 'Largest snake I've ever seen, for sure, and very purple. I screamed my head off.'

'Great fangs too,' said the farmer, shivering. 'We're lucky it didn't take a sheep . . . or a cow.'

'Would it be possible to see the coop?' Ben asked.

'Of course, Sire,' the farmer said. 'This way.' The couple

led them around the house to where a tidy-looking chicken coop stood in the middle of their backyard. Several fat fluffy chickens were pecking seeds on the ground.

The farmer opened the door to the coop and Ben knelt down to look inside. It smelled like straw and feathers, and something not entirely pleasant.

'What are you looking for?' the grand duke asked, lifting his monocle. 'I can send the footmen to search.'

'No need,' said Ben as he had spotted something glittering in the nearest nest. He picked it up with his fingertips, careful not to crush it since it was very delicate. 'I think I've found what I was looking for.'

'What is it?' asked the grand duke.

Ben stood up and held it up to the light. It was a glittering scale. Purple. The exact shade of the dragon he had seen in Camelot. He put it carefully in his handkerchief and slid it into his pocket.

'Thank you, you've been very helpful,' he told the couple. 'My staff will send you a dozen eggs for your trouble.'

'Thank you kindly, Sire,' said the farmer, tipping his hat.

'Yes, very good, very good indeed, thank you for your quick response,' said the grand duke. 'And do let us know if you see it again.'

Ben turned to leave, but the farmer's wife stopped him. 'Please, Sire, there's a rumour going around that Maleficent isn't as securely imprisoned as we think. That she's been attacking Auradon again. Might she have something to do with the snake I saw today?'

'Where did you hear that?' he asked, worried.

'My cousin lives in Camelot Heights, said there's a purple dragon over in their parts causing havoc and making a mess of everything.'

'Ah.'

'Is it Maleficent?'

In answer, Ben pulled up his phone and showed her the feed from the dozens of security cameras installed around the room that showed the tiny lizard napping on a rock. 'What do you think?'

The farmer's wife didn't look convinced. 'She could be getting out and then going back in. Crafty, she is.'

Ben had to agree with that. 'Let us know if you see the snake again, but please try not to worry. I've sent several troops of imperial soldiers to Charmington to keep it safe.'

Ben returned to the castle to pick up Chad and took his leave of the grand duke, who promised to alert him should anything else purple turn up in the area. Chad was in the kitchen patting a brown puppy from Bruno's latest litter.

'All set, old man?' he asked.

Ben nodded. 'Let's go. I'll drop you off back at school on my way.'

'Where are you going?' Chad asked as he climbed back

into the convertible. 'Maybe I'll join you. I've got nothing better to do today but homework. Now that Evie won't do mine anymore.'

'Neverland.'

Chad changed his tune. 'Right. I'll stay at Auradon Prep, if you don't mind. One of the Lost Boys is still mad that that I stole his bear costume last time they played us. He brought it up again at the game yesterday, but it wasn't my fault he never got it back!' The ragtag group was still very fond of their bear, fox, rabbit and raccoon pelts.

'But it was *your* fault that someone found it and turned it into a rug,' reminded Ben.

Chad sighed. 'Yeah, you might have a point there.'

chapter 23

Down the Rabbit Hole

Jay was hiding by the hedges that lined the road to Evil Queen's castle when he heard the voices of his friends whispering—or was that bickering?—in the darkness. 'Hey,' he said, stepping out from behind the bushes. 'About time you guys got here.' It was 11:54, only six minutes before the meeting.

'I broke a heel,' said Evie, who was limping a little. 'Sorry. I'm still wearing dance slippers, not hiking boots. I forgot how much walking we have to do on the island. But I'm okay.'

'What were you guys arguing about?' he asked.

'Evie doesn't trust Maddy,' said Mal, and filled him in

on what they'd learned so far from their brief time on the island, mostly nothing good. Evil Queen, Cruella de Vil and Jafar were still nowhere to be found.

'Mad Maddy? I wouldn't trust her either; she's pretty shady,' said Jay. 'This is the Isle of the Lost, remember? Isle of the Lost, Land of Lies.'

'Find anything at the Junk Shop?'

'Not a thing,' said Jay, who told them about how suspicious and odd Big Murph had acted, and how Anthony Tremaine had called them turncoats.

'They all hate us,' said Evie, who sounded sad about that fact.

'Yep, we're totally despised,' agreed Carlos.

'They don't *all* hate us. Some of them are really scared of me, it turns out,' said Mal.

'Everyone was always scared of you, Mal. That hasn't changed; come on,' argued Carlos.

'Okay, fine,' admitted Mal. 'But now they're even more scared!' She told them about how her room had been left pristine while the rest of the castle was ransacked. 'Apparently it's because they all think I'll turn them into lizards.'

Jay guffawed. 'You *should* turn the Isle of the Lost into the Isle of the Lizards!'

'Not funny,' said Mal, even though her lips were quirking a little. 'And we still have to find out what this Anti-Heroes club is planning.'

'Planning their revenge on us, most likely,' said Carlos.

'Do we have to go to this meeting?' asked Evie.

'Come on, let's not chicken out now. Maybe they just don't like sandwiches? Heroes? Get it?' joked Jay.

The rest of them groaned. Mal ignored his wisecracks. 'Well, from how Maddy was acting, it sounds like Jafar, Cruella and Evil Queen are definitely part of it.'

'Looked to me like Maddy is part of it, too,' said Evie.

'Oh, definitely,' said Carlos.

'Shhhh!' warned Jay. 'Someone's coming.'

The four of them melted back into the shadows, peeking out from the hedges to watch as a succession of shadowy figures made their way towards the cellar door. 'Recognise anybody?' whispered Evie.

'No,' said Jay, who had the sharpest eyesight. 'It's too far and too dark to see.'

'What do we do now?' asked Carlos, trying to push the branches aside so they didn't tickle his nose.

'We follow them in, isn't that obvious?' Mal said, mimicking the tone he'd used on them earlier.

'No bickering!' said Evie. 'And quiet, or they'll hear us!'

A few more dark silhouettes made their way down the road towards the castle, disappearing down the stone steps. After a large wave of people, the crowd trickled down to a few stragglers. 'Okay, let's go,' said Jay. 'We'll sneak in after those guys.' He scanned the area. 'I think they're the last ones.'

The four of them crept up from behind, and when the

clouds drifted from the moon, they saw that the guys they were following were Harry and Jace. Carlos shrugged his shoulders when his friends turned to him questioningly. Although Jay thought that if the sons of Cruella's most loyal minions were part of this club, then it probably meant Cruella was one of its leaders.

Harry and Jace disappeared down through the cellar door, which was left open. They waited for a beat then followed right behind. The castle dungeons were cold and damp, and as they made their way deeper and deeper into the darkness, through winding corridors and musty hallways, it grew colder and darker still.

Jay was in the lead, when he suddenly stopped short, the rest of the group piled behind him, stumbling and pushing into each other. 'Oof!' 'Ouch!' 'Watch it!'

'Where'd they go?' Carlos whispered. 'Why'd you stop?'

'I think they heard us,' Jay whispered back. 'Everyone, be quiet!' He strained to hear and squinted in the pitch-black gloom. A few moments later, he picked up the sound of Harry's heavier footsteps. 'All right, come on,' he whispered, motioning to his friends to follow him.

'Where are they going?' Mal asked Evie. 'This is your castle, right? What's down here?'

'No idea,' said Evie. 'Until today, I didn't even know we had a basement.'

The darkness abated somewhat and they saw Harry and Jace disappear into a room on the left side of the hallway.

Jay nodded and the four of them entered right after. Like the rest of the dungeon, the room was completely dark, but Jay thought he could sense people around them. What was going on? He couldn't help but feel that their sneaky entrance hadn't been so successful after all.

'Back up, back up, I have a bad feeling about this,' he said, trying to lead them the opposite way.

Too late!

The door immediately shut with a bang behind them.

'Dalmatians,' cursed Carlos. 'It's a trap!' It was just as they feared, the stuff of their nightmares.

From the darkness came a menacing voice. 'Operation Welcome Home is a go.'

chapter 24

Warm Welcome?

Carlos startled at the sound of the voice and quickly hid behind Mal. He figured it was the safest spot. He wasn't afraid to face danger, but he preferred to do it knowing Mal was in front of him. Evie gasped but managed not to scream. Jay cracked his knuckles, preparing to throw fists. Mal was calm, and her voice was even and steady when she poked Carlos and told him what to do. 'Torch, please.'

'Pardon?' he asked, before realising she meant the torchfire zapp on his phone. He turned it on, shining a blazing light into the darkness.

The four of them were illuminated by the sudden brilliance, and Carlos saw that they were surrounded on all sides by a small but excitable group of young villains. He recognised some of the faces—his cousin Diego de Vil, who raised an eyebrow in greeting; Harry and Jace with eager grins on their faces; Yzla, Hadie, Claudine Frollo and Mad Maddy, who was holding some kind of flaming weapon in her hands.

Hold on. What was that noise? What were they doing?

He couldn't be sure at first, but it looked as if the crowd was clapping, cheering even, hooting and stomping feet and calling out their names. 'They're here! They're here!' 'It's really Mal!' 'Jay's here too!' 'Yay, Carlos!' 'Evie looks fantastic!'

And hang on . . . the weapon that Maddy was holding . . . was that a cake? With way too many candles?

It was definitely a cake, and one that said WELCOME BACK, HEROES!

'I think they mean us?' said Jay, breaking into a grin.

'Definitely us,' said Evie, sounding incredibly relieved.

'Hmm, I think we had the wrong idea about this club somehow,' said Mal, nudging Carlos. 'Or maybe we're at the wrong meeting? They sure don't seem very anti-hero to me.'

But Carlos didn't notice the ribbing, he was too stunned to see a very familiar and very welcome face in the group.

'Professor!' he called, when he spotted none other than his former Magic of Science teacher, Yen Sid. He was standing right behind Maddy, the stars on his peaked sorcerer's hat reflecting the candle flames. Yen Sid was one of Dragon

Hall's most respected teachers, even if it was rumoured he wasn't any kind of villain at all, but had voluntarily relocated to the Isle of the Lost in order to help educate the villains' children.

'My boy,' said Yen Sid with a grave nod. 'Welcome.' He turned to the gathered group. 'Give them space, give them space, don't crowd them around so much,' he said gruffly. 'And I suggest you four deal with those candles before they set fire to the whole building. We wouldn't want Evil Queen returning home to a pile of ashes, now, would we.'

The four of them blew out the candles to another round of cheers. Someone turned on the lights, and Carlos realised they were in a perfectly normal-looking basement room, clean and bright. There was a chalkboard on one wall and rows of neatly arranged tables.

'Shall we begin with the cake? I had to bribe some hard-bargaining mice to sneak it out of the Auradon kitchens to the goblins earlier this week just for this,' said Yen Sid. 'Yzla, bring over the plates, please. Maddy, will you do the honours?'

'Of course, Professor,' said the young witch, and set about cutting slices.

The four of them watched in stunned silence as the group obediently and graciously moved aside and sat patiently, waiting for their slices. Carlos caught Jay's eye and shrugged.

Yen Sid motioned for them to take the nearest table. 'At

least they're not here to attack us,' said Jay, who accepted his slice with a wink.

'Unless they want to kill us with sugar,' said Mal, looking forlornly at her piece. 'I sure wish I hadn't eaten that whole stale pudding now.'

The Anti-Heroes club members, who'd never had anything remotely this good, were gobbling up the cake as fast as Maddy could slice it. It was their first taste of real sugar, and a few of them were dizzy and ecstatic from the sweetness.

Harry and Jace walked up with triumphant smiles on their faces. 'Told ye we wouldn't spoil it, and we didn't, did we?' said Jace. 'Ye had no idea, right?' asked Harry eagerly as he licked some frosting from his upper lip.

'No idea,' said Carlos, suddenly feeling much fonder of them than before. They were slow and bumbling, but often eager to please. When he had been forced to throw that party for Mal, they had helped him decorate without complaint. Jace and Harry grinned and shuffled back to their seats, satisfied.

'Professor, can we ask what this meeting is about?' said Evie as she picked daintily at her slice of cake.

'In time, in time,' replied the professor, licking frosting off his mustache. 'We have much to discuss, and it is better to do so on a full stomach.' He set his plate down on their table. 'So tell me, how were you able to return to the island?'

'I drove,' said Carlos, his mouth full of cake.

'We stole the royal limousine,' said Jay. 'It has the clicker that unlocks the dome and makes the bridge appear.'

'Clever,' said Yen Sid. 'I'm sure your talents at thievery were helpful in that area.'

Jay beamed. 'I guess so.'

'Although we ran into Prince Ben and he let us take the car anyway,' reminded Mal, rolling her eyes at Jay for taking all the credit.

'Yes, Ben was always a progressive thinker,' agreed Yen Sid. 'And you are all well, I take it? Enjoying life on Auradon?'

'Yes, sir,' said Evie. 'Very much so.'

The professor stroked his long grey beard. 'Excellent, excellent. Do give Fairy Godmother my regards when you see her next.'

Evie promised to do so. 'By the way, Professor, does my mother know you're here in our basement? Is she part of this?'

Yen Sid chuckled. 'Everything will be explained in time.'

Mal was fidgeting and looked impatient, and Carlos knew she was eager to put an end to this chitchat, but Yen Sid seemed determined to keep the conversation light.

'How are the Knights doing this season?' he asked the boys.

'So far we're five and one,' said Jay. 'We've won all our

games except a loss to a strong team from the Imperial Academy. Li Shang doesn't mess around.'

'In my day, the Olympus team was the force to be reckoned with—always difficult to beat the gods,' Yen Sid said, looking nostalgic at the memory.

'They still have a strong line-up, but a lot of the god kids are enrolled at Auradon Prep now, so maybe that's why,' said Jay.

Carlos finished his cake and was bursting with curiosity. He couldn't keep it inside anymore. 'So, Professor, come on, tell us, what is this whole Anti-Heroes thing all about?'

'I can certainly explain,' Yen Sid exclaimed jovially. 'After all, I founded it.'

chapter 25

One More Fairy Tale

In the past, the only way to get to Neverland was to fly. Just like the Isle of the Lost, there had been no usable bridge connecting the tiny island to the mainland, so the fairy court used to leave a bottle of fairy dust at the dock. Then visitors would sprinkle it on themselves while thinking happy thoughts, lifting into the air and floating to Neverland. When Ben was little, he had loved to travel by fairy dust, but when King Beast and Fairy Godmother decided that even this magic was against Auradon policy, a proper bridge was built.

Even so, Ben couldn't help feeling a bit disappointed that he wouldn't be flying anywhere that day.

He dropped Chad off at school and was in Neverland by mid-afternoon, driving across the bridge and onto the winding, curvy roads of the hilly island. He thought he was following the map correctly, but it looked like he'd taken a wrong turn somewhere, and instead of arriving at the fairy homestead, he found himself parked next to a group of tepees.

Ben left the car to ask for directions. There weren't that many other people around, and Tiger Peony, Tiger Lily's daughter, was the first person he encountered.

'Hey, Ben,' she said, when she saw him. 'Come to gloat?'

'Excuse me?' he asked, before realising she meant the tourney game that Neverland's team had lost the day before. 'Yeah, sorry about that. Lost Boys played hard.'

'Everyone's bummed,' she said. 'Mum's already sworn to train a bunch of new recruits. What are you doing here?'

'I'm headed to Fairy Vale,' Ben said, 'and I got lost. Can you show me the right way?'

'Sure,' she said. 'Are you here about the dragon?'

Ben stopped. 'How do you know?'

'Everyone knows. It's Maleficent, isn't it?'

'Actually we don't know for sure,' he said. 'That's why I'm here.'

Tiger Peony seemed to think that was a reasonable answer, and didn't ask anything more. She pointed back down to the forest. 'You just make a left at the waterfall instead of a right, and the road should take you straight to the Great Oak in the vale. They'll be waiting for you.'

The fairies lived in a thousand-year-old oak tree that was as large and roomy inside as any royal palace in the kingdom. They flitted about, their wings buzzing, excited to greet Ben, their laughter like the sound of tiny little bells ringing. Faylinn Chime, a tiny fairy who had golden hair and translucent wings, greeted Ben with a smile.

'What can we do for you, Ben?' she asked.

'The three good fairies sent me. They said you might be able to help me with a problem we're having,' he said, taking a seat at a large oak table that was carved right from the tree.

'We heard about Camelot's dragon,' she said, her voice grave. 'Is the creature still at large?'

Ben nodded. 'And if I'm right, it was just in Charmington this morning.' He removed his handkerchief and showed them the purple scale from the chicken coop. 'Do you know what this could be from?' He handed it over as gently as possible.

Faylinn picked up the scale and showed it to the other fairies. 'Looks like a serpent of some sort,' she said.

He held her gaze. 'I need to know if it's from Maleficent.'

She considered his request. 'We can check the archives. We fairies have catalogued every kind of creature across every kingdom in Auradon, so if it's from Maleficent, we'll be able to tell you for sure,' she said, putting the scale back in the handkerchief and motioning to the fairy next to her. 'Take this to Lexi Rose, and have her run a few tests to see if it matches anything we have in our database.'

'Thank you,' said Ben.

'I'm glad you're here,' said Faylinn, 'because we were just discussing whether to come to you with what we've found.'

'Oh, what's up?'

'Ben, I don't know if the three good fairies or Merlin have told you, but here in Neverland, we fairies are very sensitive to fluctuations in the atmosphere and the world around us. I've heard that in Auradon, you have been experiencing a series of earthquakes, is that right?'

'Yes, and aftershocks, too.'

'We've been having terrible weather, storms from the coast out of season, as well as giant waves crashing on our shores.'

'Yes, all around Auradon, the weather's been acting strangely. I just heard it snowed in Northern Wei, and hailed in Goodly Point,' he said. 'Scientists hope it just means winter's coming early.'

'We don't know what's really behind it yet, but I've sent letters to all the great minds of Auradon, telling them our concerns. And according to our fairy calculations, whatever this is, it started in the Isle of the Lost,' said Faylinn.

'I've already sent a team over to investigate there,' Ben

said, thinking of Mal, Evie, Jay and Carlos. 'I have confidence they'll get to the bottom of whatever is happening there.'

'Glad to hear that,' said Faylinn. 'Why don't you wait here; it shouldn't take too long to discover the origins of that scale you found. We'll get you something to eat and drink. You must be tired from driving around all day.'

'Thanks, Fay.'

He stood and she bowed to him. She began to fly away then called over her shoulder, 'By the way, when you get home, please tell Chad Charming we hope he's enjoying his bear rug.' She winked. 'And if he ever pulls something like that again, I'll fetch Captain Hook from the Isle of the Lost to teach him a lesson.'

'Will do,' Ben promised.

chapter 26

Anti-What?

When she had been a student at Dragon Hall, Mal had never been lucky enough to take one of Yen Sid's classes, and so while she knew about his mysteriously 'good' reputation, she wasn't as prepared as the others for his lighthearted demeanor. 'First of all, how did you know we would be here?' she asked.

'Well, once you received our messages, of course we began to prepare for your arrival,' said Yen Sid.

'That was you!' exclaimed Carlos.

'Of course it was. We couldn't sign them without giving ourselves away—too many bad eggs around, you know, one can never be too careful—but we hoped you would figure it out, and you did,' said the professor. 'I'm very proud of you.'

'But how were you able to reach us?' asked Jay.

'Freddie!' said Mal. 'She was the messenger, wasn't she? Because she just transferred over from the island, and so she knew how to use the Dark Net, and how best to get in touch with us.'

'You are correct,' said Yen Sid.

'What do you mean?' asked Carlos.

'I saw her at the library one night, I had a feeling she was following me. Plus, she's the only villain kid in Auradon who didn't get a message to return home,' Mal explained. 'And she must have known I'd only take it seriously if it sounded as if mine was from my mother, which is why she wrote "M".'

'But you still haven't told us what this group is all about?' asked Evie.

The old sorcerer removed his hat and scratched his bald patch. 'Before I explain further, let's clean up,' he said. 'The club knows there are different rules here, about keeping things orderly and neat. Slovenliness is a hard habit to break, but they're trying.'

'Here, let me,' said Mal, gathering the plates while Evie grabbed the cups and the boys wiped their table down with napkins.

Mal tossed the plates into the trash, and looked up to

see a group of younger kids staring at her with a worshipful look on their faces.

'What you did in Auradon, we think it was awesome,' Hadie, Hades' blue-haired son, whispered.

'It really was,' agreed Big Murph.

'So cool,' piped in Eddie, with a snaggle-toothed smile just like the one his father used when he was intent on drowning Duchess and her kittens.

Soon an admiring crowd had gathered around her, and Mal noticed similar groups were forming around Evie, Carlos and Jay as well. 'You guys really think so?' she asked them. 'That what we did at the Coronation was awesome?'

'Of course!' Hermie Bing squealed, sounding just like an elephant in her father's old circus.

For a moment, Mal believed they were all excited and impressed because she was the baddest in the land, but it soon became clear that it was just the opposite. All they wanted to talk about was how good she'd become. Mal couldn't get over how wrong she and the other villain kids had been about the club.

'Wait a minute—I thought everyone was scared of me because you guys think I'm worse than my mother,' she said, holding up her hands.

'Oh, we *are* scared,' said Harry. 'Totally scared to find out that the power of good is stronger than the power of evil!'

'Wait, so you guys aren't angry at me? You don't hate us?' she said, though she felt kind of silly even asking at this point, considering the cake and everything else.

The babble of excited voices rose in indignation. 'No!' 'Not at all!' 'We love you guys!' 'What is she talking about?' 'She's been gone, remember? She doesn't know things have changed.'

'We want to *be* you, we want to learn how to do what you did,' said Big Murph earnestly. 'We want to learn how to be good, too.'

'See, when we saw what the four of you accomplished, we realised that we don't have to do what our parents want us to do either,' said Hadie. 'Though, admittedly, it might be a little harder for me, considering. But I want to be different.'

'We choose to be good,' said Yzla forcefully, as if this statement was a rebellious act, which, considering they were in the Isle of the Lost, it truly was.

They explained that the club was formed right after Mal defeated Maleficent. The island's misfits, many of whom had already failed Lady Tremaine's Evil Schemes class and sometimes surreptitiously helped hobbled goblins cross the street rather than kicking them to the curb, realised that they were drawn to goodness rather than evil.

In a way, Carlos had been right, the Anti-Heroes movement *was* a radical group, especially since it was devoted to unravelling every tenet of the island's dearly held wicked values. Mal's actions on Auradon had sparked a revolution, one in which the new generation of villains on the Isle of the Lost were eager to follow in her footsteps. Mal had expected to find a group devoted to hating heroes, not to be the centre of hero worship. It took a while to believe that they were sincere, but eventually Mal was convinced.

Of course, the members of the club told Mal and her friends they had to practise this new inclination in secret, which is why even the villains who were at the meeting had been rude to Mal and her friends out in public. No-one could know that the members of the club were trying to be good, especially not on the Isle of the Lost. But thanks to Yen Sid, they had a place to be themselves now. Yzla explained that Yen Sid suggested the Castle Across the Way because it was far from town and had been deserted for a while. Plus, no-one would suspect that anything but the plotting of evil schemes or cosmetics lessons was under way in the home of Evil Queen.

'Wait! So she's definitely not here? Evil Queen isn't part of this group? What about Cruella or Jafar?' Mal asked.

Before anyone could answer her question, Yen Sid stepped up to the blackboard. 'Welcome to the weekly meeting of the Anti-Heroes,' he said. 'We are now formally in session.'

'Can I ask why you're called Anti-Heroes?' asked Carlos, raising his hand.

'Don't you know? Think about it,' said the professor, his eyes twinkling.

Mal scrunched her forehead, and reflected on what she had just learned from the excited group of so-called villains. 'It's called Anti-Heroes because you're hiding in plain sight,' she said.

Yen Sid smiled broadly. 'It is the only way to hide.'

To anyone who stumbled on the Anti-Heroes thread on the Dark Net, it looked as if the club despised the foursome, but of course the photos of the four of them were simply recruitment tools, subtly telling members-in-the-know that this was the place to be if they wanted to be like Mal, Evie, Jay and Carlos. Mal shared her epiphany with the group, and heads happily nodded around the class.

'That is part of it, of course, but there is another reason we are called Anti-Heroes,' said Yen Sid. 'What most people don't know is that *anti-hero* is another word for villain—or let me put it this way, an anti-hero is the villain that you root for in the story. An anti-hero is a hero who isn't perfect. An anti-hero doesn't ride up in a white horse, or have shining golden hair and wonderful manners. In fact, an anti-hero doesn't look like the typical hero of a story at all. Anti-heroes can be crude and ugly and selfish, but they are heroes nonetheless. As flawed as an anti-hero is, they're still trying to do the right thing. You are all anti-heroes, and I'm proud of you.' He beamed at them, and the group clapped and cheered.

'So just to confirm, this is a secret club to teach villains— sorry, *anti-heroes*—how to be good?' asked Carlos. Mal remembered how Ginny Gothel had said 'they' were right about Mal, and 'there was no hope for anyone'—she must have meant there was little hope for evil anymore, if even Maleficent's daughter had chosen to be good.

Mal frowned. 'Hold on, Professor. If this club is devoted to learning how to be good, am I right in assuming Evil Queen, Cruella de Vil and Jafar have nothing to do with it either?'

'With the Anti-Heroes? No, of course not, they're villains through and through, I'm afraid,' said the professor. 'But speaking of the villains, it is very fortunate you understood our message to return to the island, as we desperately need your help in locating and outwitting them.'

chapter 27

Anti-Heroes' Secret

'Wait! So they're not here? They're really gone?' asked Carlos. 'My mother, Evil Queen and Jafar?' He tried to temper his relief at the news. As much as he had convinced himself he was ready to stand up to his mother like Mal had done to hers, he was more than happy for the respite.

'And if you guys don't know where they are, does that mean they're not on the Isle of the Lost?' asked Mal.

'Not exactly on the island, no. But not exactly off it either, at least, we hope not,' said Yen Sid, remaining maddeningly obscure on the subject. 'Let me backtrack a little. It appears they vanished from the Isle of the Lost soon after Maleficent broke the dome open, but no-one knows for sure. People panicked when they saw Maleficent turned into a lizard; they feared that Auradon would seek revenge on the island. In the chaos and breakdown that ensued, it was hard to notice anything out of the ordinary since everything was out of the ordinary, especially with the goblin embargo.

'No-one thought it strange that Jafar didn't open up shop for a while, as he was often irregular in his habits, and Evil Queen and Cruella de Vil mostly keep to themselves. But then the Junk Shop remained closed, and a few weeks later, a goblin who delivered the daily basket of supplies to Evil Queen's castle reported that no-one ever took them inside. They were just piling up by the front door, and even Cruella's wigmaker remarked that she hadn't come in for her regular fitting, so we knew something was wrong.' He frowned and tugged his beard. 'I sent messengers to each of their homes, and runners across the island to see if anyone had seen them anywhere, but to no avail. They were well and truly gone.'

The rest of the group nodded, and it was clear this was old news to them. Carlos noticed that some of them were doodling in their notebooks or passing notes and whispering. Even if they were trying to be good, they were still naughty kids. He tried to ignore them and focus on what Yen Sid was saying.

'But if they're not on the Isle, where could they be?' asked Carlos with a gulp. 'You don't think they're in Auradon, do you?'

Yen Sid gazed balefully at his young pupil. 'Before I answer your question, I would like to ask a few questions of my own.'

'Shoot,' said Mal.

'Have you been experiencing a series of earthquakes in the mainland? Small tremors, vibrations? And once in a while, a real rumble?' he asked.

'Yeah, we have,' said Jay as the four of them nodded in agreement.

'Have you noticed if they are becoming stronger and more frequent?'

'They certainly are,' said Mal. 'I know Ben's council is worried about it, since it's never really happened before. Not just earthquakes, though—he mentioned that the whole kingdom is suffering from unseasonal weather: frost, hurricanes, sandstorms.'

'Then it is as I suspected,' said Yen Sid. He sighed.

'What does the weather have to do with the missing villains?' asked Mal.

But the professor was already scribbling in his notebook and ignored her question. When he looked back up at them, he had their full attention. 'I think it's time for me to tell you a little about the history of the island. As you know, when the villains were placed on the Isle of the Lost, Fairy Godmother, under King Beast's command, created the invisible dome to keep magic out of their hands so that they would never threaten Auradon's peace again.'

'I thought it was also because they were being punished for their evil deeds,' said Evie.

'In effect, it was a punishment, as they were kept here mostly to ensure the safety of the kingdom,' said Yen Sid. 'But what we didn't realise then was that keeping magic off the surface of the island created tremendous pressure in the atmosphere, and the magic that was kept out had to go somewhere else.'

'Energy transference,' said Evie knowingly, even as the rest of the club was falling asleep on their stools. It was obvious they'd all heard this before.

'Yes,' said Yen Sid, impressed. 'I warned Fairy Godmother about the risks of establishing the magical barrier, but at the time, we deemed it a better gamble than letting the villains run amok in the country with their magical powers intact.'

'Magic was pushed underground,' said Mal slowly.

'Exactly. Over the course of the 20 years since the dome was created, magic grew wild and flourished underground, where it created a system of tunnels, the Endless Catacombs of Doom, which compose a series of magical lands underneath ours,' said the professor. He looked at them somberly. 'Some say these tunnels also include an escape route out of the Isle of the Lost and straight into Auradon itself.'

'Auradon!' cried Carlos.

'Yes, and this passage must be closed before anyone

discovers it. I fear we might already be too late,' the professor said.

'A magical underground land right beneath ours that leads to Auradon,' mused Jay. 'Wild.'

The professor frowned. 'I sent a letter to King Beast explaining my conclusions, but I suspect Evil Queen, Jafar and Cruella de Vil intercepted it. Maleficent's goons used to go through my mail, and I'm certain that Evil Queen did the same thing when Maleficent was gone.'

'Ben is king now, by the way; maybe you should have written to him,' Mal chided. 'What about the tremors—the earthquakes, the weird weather we're having—are they related to this, then?'

The professor nodded. 'When Maleficent broke open the dome when she escaped, I believe that the magic that was released sparked something underneath the Isle of the Lost, which caused a ripple effect in the weather that can be felt all the way to Auradon, and has caused unusual natural phenomena.'

'Sparked something?' said Mal. 'Like what?'

The professor was about to answer when Carlos changed the subject back to his pressing worry. 'Excuse me, Professor, but they must have found out about the secret tunnel. The escape route,' he said. 'Cruella, Evil Queen and Jafar, I mean.'

'So that's why they packed light,' said Evie. 'They thought they'd be in Auradon soon, where Cruella could buy new furs and my mother could get her hands on this season's cosmetics, and Jafar probably thought he could fetch Iago back as soon as they took over Auradon.'

'But if they're in Auradon, someone would have reported them by now,' said Jay. 'I can't exactly see them blending in with the locals.'

'No, I don't believe they are in Auradon,' said Yen Sid. 'They were headed there most likely, but no, they are not there yet.'

'But you said they're not in the Isle of the Lost either,' said Carlos.

He startled when Evie suddenly straightened in her chair. 'The Magic Mirror!' she cried. 'That's why the mirror couldn't find them! Mal, remember how we were wondering if they were using some kind of powerful magic to hide themselves? And we were right—sort of—there was powerful magic, but not the way we thought.'

Yen Sid looked pleased. 'Were you ever in my class?' he asked. 'You have an extraordinary talent for logic.'

Evie flushed happily at the compliment. 'Thanks, Professor.'

Jay looked around the table. 'So where are they exactly? I don't follow.'

'They're lost in the Catacombs,' said Mal crisply. 'They were trying to get to Auradon, but they got lost somewhere along the way.'

The old wizard nodded. 'Almost. They are not lost. It

is my belief they are down there searching for something.'

'Something other than the way out?' asked Jay. 'What could be down there that they want?'

Yen Sid motioned to the group to close their books and put their maps away. He sighed heavily and looked each of them in the eye. 'Where do you think evil comes from?' he asked.

'The Isle of the Lost?' offered Carlos.

'Close.' His voice thundered in the small room. 'Evil is a real thing, it lives and breathes, it works its malice through living vessels eager to spread its vile wickedness, but villains cannot be villains without the source of their power.'

The younger members of the club began to whimper.

'Every villain has a talisman. These talismans hold the powers that were stripped from them upon their exile to the Isle of the Lost.'

'Like the Dragon's Eye sceptre,' said Mal. 'That was my mother's talisman. Are you saying there are other talismans in the Catacombs?'

'You would have been a good student in my class as well,' said Yen Sid proudly. 'Yes, the Catacombs of Doom are only one part of the equation. Like I said earlier, when Maleficent escaped, she released so much energy into the surrounding area that it sparked a magical reaction underground and caused the recent earthquakes and unseasonal weather phenomena all over Auradon. I'm afraid she's also awakened four evil talismans that have been growing in the Catacombs of Doom over the years. These talismans are growing in power, and causing havoc with our weather as they draw energy to themselves. Four of these talismans are the most dangerous right now: the Fruit of Venom, the Golden Cobra, the Ring of Envy and a new Dragon's Egg.'

An audible silence filled the room, and it was apparent that while the club knew about the Catacombs, learning of these talismans was new to the villains on the Isle of the Lost as well as the four visitors from Auradon.

'A *new* Dragon's Egg?' asked Carlos. 'What does that mean?'

'Hang on,' said Jay. 'Does this have anything to do with the Dragon's Eye staff back in Auradon? The original?'

'Yeah, that one broke when mum turned into a lizard,' said Mal. 'We found it and Ben put it away in the museum. It's useless now, so I guess this would be its replacement.'

Yen Sid nodded to show she was correct. 'Merlin wrote me about Camelot's problem, and along with the strange weather patterns worsening in Auradon, I realised I had to get you kids back to the island right away. There isn't much time, we must act, and quickly,' said the professor. 'The talismans desire to be found; they have already seduced their masters into looking for them and soon they will call others to their side. They seek to escape the darkness of the underground so they can once again bring chaos and catastrophe to our world above. You must find and disarm them before they fall into the wrong hands, then bring them back to Auradon, where they can be destroyed forever.'

'We'll go as soon as we can,' promised Mal.

'Remember how the four of you were able to defeat Maleficent?' Yen Sid asked.

They nodded.

'But what if it wasn't just Maleficent and the Dragon's Eye you were facing? What if you were facing all four villains holding their talismans? Imagine facing not just Maleficent and her sceptre, but Jafar and his Golden Cobra, Evil Queen and her poisoned apple and Cruella de Vil and her Ring of Envy?'

'Oh,' said Carlos. 'That does not sound good.'

'Used together, these four talismans for evil can overcome the power of good once and for all.'

Chapter 28

The Sorcerer's Apprentices

This was so much worse than she thought. Evie knew that this trip to the Isle of the Lost would mean they would discover that the villains were plotting yet another scheme, but she hadn't been prepared to hear about this. To think that there were four evil talismans out there, and that if their parents got ahold of them, they would be unstoppable, was too frightening to contemplate. Since Mal had defeated Maleficent, Evie felt assured that they could handle whatever happened next, and that the power of good would always prevail. But now it sounded as if they were truly in peril once more.

Thankfully, Mal still appeared calm as ever. 'At least

now we know that's where they are, underground, in the Catacombs, looking for the power that they lost.'

'Yes,' said Yen Sid. 'The four of you must find these talismans and destroy them before your parents can use them against Auradon. I'm afraid you're the only ones who will be able to outsmart them. After all, no-one knows them better than you. Mal, even if Maleficent is in no shape to retrieve the Dragon's Egg, it's still imperative that you recover it before anyone else does.'

'Great, let's go,' said Jay, already up from his seat.

'First, we must show you what we are working on.' Yen Sid nodded to the assembled group, who sat at attention now, pulling out detailed maps and charts. 'We think we are close to getting an accurate map of the underground tunnels.'

'You've been in the tunnels, then?' asked Carlos.

'No. None of us have.'

'But then how can you draw maps of somewhere you've never been?' said Carlos, confused.

'With the help of a little research,' Yen Sid told them. He nodded to the class and they raised the books they were reading. 'We stole them from the Athenaeum of Evil, of course.' *A Brief History of Evil Talismans. The Legend of the Golden Cobra. Poison Fruit from the Toxic Tree. The Dragon's Eye Sceptre: Lore and Myth.* 'According to the books, each talisman is grown by magic in its ideal habitat, and so we have been sketching their possible landscapes,' he said, as if it were as simple as learning how to plot an evil scheme, or how to trick a mark out of its money, when it was probably as difficult as teaching a jolly crew of pirates table manners.

'Great, you guys have maps to share. All right, then; just point us to the Catacombs, and we'll be on our way,' said Jay.

'Well, that's where I'll need everyone's help tonight. We haven't been able to discover the exact location of the entrance to the Catacombs,' said the professor. 'We don't have much time left, so you and the rest of the Anti-Heroes will need to scour the island until you find it.'

He began to give the members their assignments, sending them to every part of the island, from Henchman's Knob to the Blown Bridge.

'Shall we go with them?' asked Jay as the Anti-Heroes started to trickle out to search.

'Yes, but please remain where you are for now. Before I send you four off on this journey, I have a few words of advice to give each one of you. Acquiring these talismans will be very dangerous. Evil is seductive; you will have to remain strong and not fall prey to its temptations.'

He stood in front of Carlos first and placed a hand on his head. 'Carlos de Vil, you possess a keen intellect; however, do not let your head rule your heart. Learn to see what is truly in front of you.'

Evie was next, and Yen Sid did the same, resting a hand above her dark blue locks. 'Evie, remember that when you believe you are alone in the world, you are far from friendless.'

Jay bowed down and removed his beanie so the good professor could lay his hand on his head, too. 'Jay of Agrabah, a boy of many talents, open your eyes and discover that the riches of the world are all around you.'

At last he came to Mal. Yen Sid delicately touched her purple head. 'Mal, daughter of Maleficent, you are from the blood of the dragon and carry its strength and fire. However, this burden is not yours to bear alone. Rely on your friends, and let their strength carry yours as well.'

Yen Sid surveyed the young villains in front of him. 'What you are about to do is very dangerous.'

Carlos perked up. 'That's fine, my middle name is—'

'Oscar,' said Evie. 'We know.'

The group of Anti-Heroes burst into applause as Mal, Evie, Jay and Carlos shook hands with the professor and thanked him for his wisdom and guidance.

'We will collect the maps that we do have,' said Yen Sid. 'Give us a few moments.' The group began to disperse to begin their respective assignments, talking excitedly among themselves.

Carlos said goodbye to Harry and Jace, who had been tasked with searching near the Bargain Castle. Jay promised the pirates he would send them postcards from Auradon.

Evie was glad they had figured out where their parents

were, but going after them wasn't going to be easy. If Evil Queen was set on getting back her talisman of power, there was no stopping her. The woman elbowed people out of the way for a tube of concealer.

'Heading out to search?' asked Harry.

'Uh-huh,' said Evie.

'Glad you guys are the ones going after them and not me and Jace. We'd be too scared, all right. Crikey, you're all so brave.'

'I'm not, really,' said Evie. 'But sometimes you have to do the things you have to do. Thanks, though.' Before setting off, however, she had to make sure she could move properly. She inspected her broken heel. She couldn't keep going this way; the Endless Catacombs of Doom sure sounded like they would entail a lot of walking as well, and she was still wearing the wrong shoes.

'Professor,' she said, holding up her broken heel. 'Do you think you can fix this with a little magic of science or something?'

He examined her shoe. 'No, I'm afraid there is no way this can be salvaged through the magic of science.'

Evie's face fell as she resigned herself to stumbling her way through the underground, her feet blistered and callused.

'But I do have something that might help you,' said Yen Sid.

'What?'

'Tape,' he said as he deftly taped the broken heel back to its original shape.

It wasn't a pair of sneakers, but at least she wouldn't be limping anymore.

While Yen Sid went back to going over the possible locations for the entrance to the Catacombs with Jay and Carlos, and the rest of the club members waited patiently for their assignments, Evie looked around the crowded room and didn't see Mal anywhere. Where had she gone? Evie took another look and caught a glimpse of bright aqua-coloured hair swishing in the dark hallway, with Mal's purple head following behind.

At first she thought that maybe Maddy just wanted to talk to Mal privately, but when the two of them didn't return after a few minutes, she had a darker feeling about it. She peeked into the corridor and saw Maddy heading out of the basement and up the cellar stairs, with Mal following behind. Where were they going?

Already wary of Maddy's friendship with Mal, Evie decided to follow them to see what they were up to. She looked behind her to make sure the boys were still talking to Yen Sid. She wasn't spying on Mal; she was just being careful, she told herself. Mal had to have a good reason for going off with Maddy, didn't she?

Maddy was out of the basement now and heading down

the path away from the castle. Mal was following behind at some distance. They weren't walking together, Evie realised now. Mal was following Maddy, for some reason. But why? Who cared about Maddy?

They had to find the entrance to the Catacombs; there was no time for this. Cruella de Vil, Evil Queen and Jafar had a head start on them. If any one of them was able to lay their hands on their talisman, no-one in Auradon would be safe. The foursome had to get going. What was Mal doing?

Evie lagged behind, trying to put some space between them, when Maddy stopped suddenly and looked around. Mal ducked behind a tree and Evie quickly hid in the shadows as well. She wasn't sure what was going on, but she was glad she hadn't let her friend go off alone like this.

The two girls kept walking further and further away. Evie followed behind.

chapter 29

Double Trouble

When Maddy left the meeting, Mal's first thought was that her friend wanted to get a head start on walking to Troll Town, where her group was going to search. Mal wanted to take a break too, before the four of them had to embark on this journey even deeper underground. The aqua-haired girl ascended the stone steps, and Mal was about to call out to her when Maddy checked her watch, picked up the speed and disappeared into the maze of streets.

Mal also couldn't help but notice that Maddy kept looking over her shoulder nervously as she made her way through the dark alleyways. When she took off through the back way, cutting across Hell Hall's garden, going right instead of heading left for Troll Town, it became clear that she wasn't going where she'd been assigned after all. Mal watched as she ducked around a corner, and overheard bits of a whispered conversation between Maddy and an unknown stranger. Something about 'Catacombs' and 'Doom Cove'.

What was going on? Why wasn't Maddy going with her group? And who had she been talking to?

Mal's curiosity was piqued and she decided to keep following her. The group could figure out the plan with Yen Sid, but she wanted to find out what her old friend was up to.

She followed Maddy through the maze of streets, down Pain Lane and past Goblin Wharf, which was desolate and abandoned instead of the usual hive of goblin activity. Mal wished she could send her friends a text explaining where she was. She just hoped they wouldn't worry; she'd be back as soon as she found out what Maddy was doing.

Maddy led her back onto the main road, and Mal had to lag further behind so she wouldn't be caught. They passed the Bargain Castle and Maddy kept going, headed down Bitter Boulevard and right to the end of the island by the Rickety Bridge.

Maddy stepped onto the bridge and whirled around. 'Mal, you can come out now, I know you're following me.'

'You got me,' said Mal, stepping into the light and walking towards Maddy. She knew when the game was up.

'Why'd you leave the meeting so fast? Is something going on?'

Maddy peered around in the dark. As far as Mal could see, there was nothing. The waters were black and there was no-one else on the bridge. Just the sound of the waves and the light from the Shattered Lighthouse. 'Yes,' said Maddy hesitantly, as if unsure whether to trust Mal.

'What?' asked Mal.

'Before the meeting, I got an anonymous letter saying that Evil Queen, Cruella and Jafar would be returning from the Catacombs after midnight. They would be at Doom Cove.'

'But why didn't you say anything at the meeting? Why go alone, then?' asked Mal, not sure if she believed her. She'd always had fun with Mad Maddy, but Evie was right, there was something off about her. Why hadn't she seen it before? Maybe because she was having too much fun indulging in old, bad habits?

Maddy's green eyes blazed. 'Don't you see? The Anti-Heroes are the only ones who even know about the Catacombs of Doom! Yen Sid warned us that there might be double operatives in the club. I couldn't take the risk of letting them know that I knew.'

'But who could it be? Everyone seemed so sincere,' said Mal, wondering who had betrayed them.

'It could be anyone. They're a bunch of villains, Mal, come on. Do you really believe all of them would give up just like that? The professor thinks everyone is redeemable, but that can't be true,' sniffed Maddy. 'Of course there's a bad egg in the bunch. I can always smell one.'

'Who do you think it is?' asked Mal.

'My money's on Harry or Jace—their fathers are still Cruella's loyal minions.'

Mal considered this. It was hard to believe that anyone back at the meeting could be so two-faced, and Harry and Jace seemed more bumbling than malicious. 'Maybe someone else on the Isle knows that Cruella, Jafar and Evil Queen went down into the Catacombs to look for the talismans. It doesn't have to be someone in our group. If the three of them knew about it, they might have told someone before they left.'

'Maybe,' said Maddy. 'But I doubt it.'

'Who were you talking to back there?' asked Mal.

'Oh, just some goblin. I told them to find me if they catch sight of Jafar, Cruella de Vil or Evil Queen.'

'Show me the message,' said Mal.

Maddy handed her the note, written in green ink. *Doom Cove. Prepare for our return to the Isle of the Lost. Talismans acquired. Alert the troops.*

'That's Doom Cove right there,' said Maddy, pointing to the dark, sandy stretch of beach below.

'Who are the troops?' wondered Mal. 'You don't think they mean a goblin army, do you?' There weren't enough villains on the Isle to put together a real battalion, and 'troops' signified that whoever had sent the message was readying for a large-scale operation.

'Of course it means a goblin army, how else would they take down Auradon?' said Maddy.

'Are you sure you didn't tell anyone about it?' Mal asked, thinking of the conversation she'd overhead earlier.

'Duh, like I told you, of course not. No-one can know!' said Maddy.

'We need to get help. I'll go back,' said Mal, turning away. Maddy was obviously lying about telling someone and Mal figured the easiest way to handle it was to get backup.

'No! We need to stay here, in case they do arrive. What if we miss it and they slip away?' said Maddy. 'We should follow them and call for help later so we don't lose them. Don't you trust me?'

Mal understood that Maddy was testing her, and while she had a feeling that she shouldn't stay, she realised it wasn't safe to leave Maddy on her own at this point. She had to figure out what the girl was up to.

chapter 30

Seeds of Temptation

Carlos and Jay were so absorbed in their conversation with Yen Sid that they didn't notice that half of their team had absconded. The professor handed them the maps to the underground land. 'These contain all we know about the Catacombs as well as the talismans. I hope you find them useful on your journey once we find the entrance,' he said.

They thanked him, but Carlos was intent on learning as much as he could about the talismans before setting off underground. 'So can we touch them? The talismans, I mean?' he asked the professor. 'Or are they cursed? Like the Dragon's Eye?'

'Yeah, I don't look forward to falling asleep for a thousand years,' said Jay.

'I'm not certain. My hunch is that each of you should be immune to your particular talisman, as Mal was unaffected by the curse of the Dragon's Eye.'

'Anything else you can tell me about this Golden Cobra?' asked Jay.

'It should be an exact replica of your father's cobra staff. It's said that the Golden Cobras give up their freedom when they succumb to their master's power, but they are very much alive. It is a living weapon.'

'Great,' said Jay. Under his breath, he told Carlos, 'I'm sure it'll just lie down and roll over for me.'

'It's a snake, Jay, not a dog,' said Carlos. 'You should know the difference.' He turned to Yen Sid, who was erasing lines on the blackboard. 'About this Ring of Envy, what exactly does it do?'

'Your mother made everyone believe their lives were nothing compared to hers. That huge green ring that she wore was a testament to her glamour, and its size and great worth always made others feel small and useless.'

Carlos swallowed a gulp, especially since his mother had always made him feel small and useless even without the aid of a talisman. 'What about the Fruit of Venom; is it filled with poison?'

'Poisonous thoughts,' said Yen Sid. 'Taking a bite of it will fill one's mind with your deepest fears and insecurities, every kind of dark, malevolent emotion and idea, and the power to use them against other people.'

'Yikes,' Carlos said. Evie was one of the sweetest girls he knew, and he hoped she wouldn't be swayed by such a toxic influence. 'And the Dragon's Egg?'

'The most powerful talisman of all, of course, with the ability to command all the forces of evil to do its mistress' bidding. Power is its own most powerful enticement. Moreover, Mal has wielded the Dragon's Eye staff, so she has already experienced the depth of its capability for universal dominance. She must be particularly wary of succumbing to its siren song.'

'You hear that, Mal?' Carlos said, turning around, expecting to see Mal and Evie at their seats. But there was no-one there. 'Hey, where'd they go?' he asked Jay. 'Mal and Evie—they're gone.'

'That's weird, they were just here,' Jay said.

'Yeah, well, they're not here now,' said Carlos, annoyed. Most of the members had already headed out on their assignments, but Carlos ran around the room asking the remaining few if they had seen Mal and Evie.

'Yo, they bounced out with Mad Maddy,' said Yzla. 'But I don't know where they went.'

'Mad Maddy? Why would they leave with her?'

Yzla shook her head. 'Aren't Maddy and Mal friends?'

'Yes, but . . .' said Carlos, seriously agitated by now. Why had the girls taken off without telling him and Jay? It wasn't like Mal or Evie to just disappear like that. He was about to freak out when Evie burst back into the room.

'Guys!' she called.

'Where have you been!' Carlos demanded. 'And where's Mal?'

Evie caught her breath. She'd been running and her cheeks were flushed. 'If you stop yelling at me, I can tell you.'

'Sorry,' he said quickly. 'We were just worried.'

'Carlos was worried,' said Jay. 'I knew you guys would be back.'

'Mal went off with Maddy. I think they're headed towards Doom Cove. I don't know what's going on, but I have a bad feeling about this,' said Evie. 'I heard Maddy say something about the Catacombs, so I thought I'd come back and grab you guys in case something happens.'

'Let's go,' said Carlos. 'Doom Cove is a hike.'

chapter 31

The Rescuers

Jay knew all the shortcuts through town, or at least he thought he did. Thinking it was faster to stay off the little alleyways, he led them up to Mean Street instead, but soon realised his mistake. They were farther from Doom Cove than if they had just taken Pain Lane down to Goblin Wharf as Evie had suggested. 'Sorry, I thought this would be faster,' he huffed, removing his beanie and wiping his forehead with it.

'It's okay, let's just get there,' said Evie as they ran down the cobblestone streets, their heels kicking up dust as they garnered curious looks from a few townspeople. 'Hurry!'

At last they made it past the Bargain Castle and had a clear shot all the way to Rickety Bridge. 'Wait!' said Evie. 'We don't want to give ourselves away.'

'But where are they?' asked Carlos, scanning the bridge. 'I don't see them.'

'I distinctly heard Maddy say they were going to wait right here; maybe whatever they're waiting for has already happened?' Evie said, with a sinking feeling in her chest. 'I should have stayed here! Curse these shoes, they slowed me down too much.'

Jay focused on the bridge. It looked deserted and lonely in the moonlight, but at the very edge of it, he spotted two brightly coloured heads—one blue-green and one violet. 'There! I see them!'

Evie swirled to where he was pointing. 'Let's move closer,' she said, and they inched their way to the edge of the shore, as close to the bridge as they dared without giving away their presence.

'What are they doing?' asked Carlos. 'They're just looking out into the water. What are they waiting for?'

'A goblin barge maybe?' guessed Evie. 'Don't they work the graveyard shift?'

Jay scratched his forehead under his beanie. 'Explain to me again why we're sneaking around? Why don't we just tell Mal we're here?'

'No!' said Evie. 'Not just yet.'

'Why not?' asked Carlos, who looked like he thought Evie was being a little paranoid.

'Because I don't trust Maddy, and if we tell them we're here, we'll never find out what she's up to,' she told them.

'You just don't like witches,' said Jay.

'No way!' said Evie, annoyed that she wasn't being taken seriously. 'You guys seem to have forgotten I'm a witch too! Just like my mum. And I like myself just fine.'

'You're a witch?' Carlos said. 'Oh, right, you *are* a witch. I did forget.'

Evie nodded. 'It's okay, people tend to forget. Everyone just thinks I'm an evil princess.'

They watched Maddy and Mal looking intently at the dark water, and after a few minutes, the boys started to get bored. 'Come on, Evie, let's just tell Mal we're here. We need to start looking for the entrance to the Catacombs,' Jay said.

'Just a little longer,' Evie begged.

'I just don't see what the point of this is,' said Jay. The two of them were still arguing over it when Carlos nudged both of them in a panic.

'What?' said Jay, annoyed.

Carlos couldn't speak, he just pointed—and they all turned their attention back down to the Rickety Bridge, where a group of villain kids had emerged from the shadows and quickly surrounded Mal and Maddy. It was a motley group, including Anthony Tremaine, Ginny Gothel and the burly twin brothers Gaston and Gaston.

'Evie was right, this doesn't look good,' Carlos whispered.

'Shhh!' said Jay, listening intently to the group's conversation.

Anthony Tremaine's rich baritone boomed through the air. 'Look what we have here, the little heroine of the story,' he said.

'What story would that be?' said Mal.

'Oh, just a little fairy tale they're spinning in Auradon about how wonderful it is that villains can change.' He smirked. 'What a shame we don't believe in fairy tales here.'

'That's not true, there are people right on the Isle of the Lost that believe it too,' said Mal. 'Maddy, what's going on? Why are they here?' she demanded.

'Tell her, Maddy,' cackled Ginny Gothel. 'Tell her why you brought her here.'

Back where they were hiding, Carlos stood on his tiptoes since the large silhouettes of the Gastons blocked his view. 'What's going on?' he asked. 'Maybe we should go down there now.'

'Not yet!' said Evie. 'I want to hear what Maddy says.'

Maddy crossed her arms and looked Mal up and down. 'Remember how I told you there were bad eggs in the group? Looks like you just cracked one, Mal.' She laughed. 'Except I'm not the one who's going to get scrambled tonight.

Especially now that we know you don't have any powers after all.'

Evie winced.

'What?' cried Carlos. 'Are they hurting her?'

'Only with bad puns.'

'I knew it! That message was fake! You were just pretending to be good all along.' Mal's voice was clear and calm in the dark.

'Good guess, but then why are you here?' sneered Maddy.

'I had to find out for sure,' said Mal. 'I thought that maybe I still had a friend on the island.'

'Friend? Is that what you thought I was? You cut off the heads of my dolls! You put lye in my hair so I had to change its colour! You didn't like that everyone called us twins! Some friend you are! You're more delusional than your mother!' shrieked Maddy.

'Ouch,' said Evie. 'Did Mal really do all those things?'

'Um, yeah,' said Carlos. 'I mean, she is Maleficent's kid. She was pretty mean growing up.'

'And you were telling that goblin back there to fetch the rest of your crew down here so they could ambush me,' said Mal.

'Exactly,' said Maddy.

The villains crowded around Mal, so that she was pressed against the railing at the edge of the bridge.

'Okay, okay, let's go get her now,' said Evie, and they ran

out of their hiding place and headed towards the bridge, Jay in the lead.

'Okay, fine! I was a little brat! I'm sorry, okay?'

'Only suckers are sorry,' said Maddy. 'And Anti-Heroes are the biggest suckers of all!'

'Don't you get it?' Ginny Gothel asked. 'The professor's wrong! There's no hope for us and we don't want any! We're villains at heart! True villains! Not like you!' She raised her fist to the sky. 'Evil lives!'

'Evil lives,' echoed the Gastons, slapping their fists to their palms.

'When the rest of this pathetic little island discovers their hero was fed to the crocodiles, what do you think will happen to that silly little club?' asked Maddy with a crazed smile. 'Everyone will realise that there's no hope in trying to be good! Evil always triumphs! Anti-hero is just another name for villain, and we'll be villains forever!'

'You don't have to do this,' said Mal. She'd had to climb on the railing to get away from them, and Ginny was still blocking her way. 'It won't prove anything. Maddy, you're not going to get your old hair back, but maybe I can help you fix it. I'm pretty good at spells now.'

'Shut up,' said Maddy. 'And I don't have to do this. I want to!' she shrieked, and the rest of the group joined in her laughter. 'Ginny, why don't you do the honours,' she offered.

'Let's do it together,' said Ginny.

With matching grins, the two of them pushed Mal off the railing and into the bay.

Maddy leaned over the edge. 'Say hi to the crocodiles! Tell them dinner's served!'

'Jay! Carlos! Hurry!' cried Evie. 'Mal can't swim!'

chapter 32

Unfair Fight

How about that, high heels were finally useful for something, Evie discovered after hitting Ginny Gothel in the back with one. The dark-haired girl screamed and clawed at her, almost scratching her across the cheek.

'Not the face!' cried Evie, furious. 'Anywhere but the face!' Ginny lunged for her and the two of them fell to the ground, pulling each other's hair.

Jay took care of the Gastons by running between them at just the right moment so they ended up bumping heads and falling to the ground, moaning. But Mad Maddy and Anthony Tremaine kept from the fray. Carlos knew the Stepmother's grandson would shy away from a fair fight, preferring to have the deck stacked on his side, and it would be easy enough to send Anthony running if he played it right.

'What are you waiting for!' Carlos said, throwing down some judo moves he'd seen in his video games.

Anthony rolled his eyes and took off.

'Well?' Carlos said to Mad Maddy as the Gastons slunk away and Ginny ran off whimpering. 'It's only you against the three of us now.'

Maddy tossed her bright blue-green hair and sneered, her eyes wide with maniacal fury. 'You think you've won here, but I promise you, all of Auradon will burn, just like Camelot!' she said, cackling like a hag as she disappeared into the night.

Evie picked herself up off the ground and ran to the railing, scanning the dark water. 'Where's Mal?' she asked. 'I don't see her!'

'There!' said Jay, pointing to a dark purple head and arms flailing in the waves.

'Dive! What are you waiting for?' Evie asked as Jay hesitated by the rail.

'I can't swim!' he confessed. 'It's not like there were lessons on the Isle of the Lost, you know!'

Carlos ran up and began to remove his heavy jacket. 'I can dog-paddle! I'll go!'

'Wait!' said Jay. 'Crocodiles!'

Mal was surrounded by several of the large scaly beasts

snapping their jaws. She was bobbing up and down in the water and screaming for help.

'We're coming!' said Evie. 'Carlos is coming to save you!'

Carlos climbed up on the rail and stared down at the hungry crocodiles. 'Um, I am?'

'Go!' said Evie. 'Don't worry about the crocs, Jay and I will draw them away!' She gave him a little push and he dropped into the water. She saw his black-and-white head above the waves as he inched his way towards Mal.

'Great! How are we going to do that?' asked Jay.

'With bait!'

'Awesome!' he said. 'Wow, you really travel with everything you need, huh?'

Evie gave him a look.

'Hang on, are we the bait?' asked Jay with a groan.

'Yes! Hurry!' Evie threw her other heel so it bounced on the nearest crocodile's head. Then she whistled while dangling a leg over the side of the bridge. 'Over here! Yoo-hoo!'

Jay stretched his torso from the edge of the dock and began to wave his arms. 'Come on! Over here! Come and get me!' Then, seized by a sudden flash of brilliance, he began to chant. 'Tick-tock, tick-tock, tick-tock!' It was common knowledge in the Isle of the Lost that the crocodiles in its waters were no ordinary crocodiles, as they were descended from the one and only Tick-Tock himself. The sound of a ticking clock was almost a lullaby for them, and the crocodiles were hypnotised by Jay's chanting, swimming towards him and Evie.

Mal screamed one last time before disappearing under the water, but in a burst of speed, Carlos was by her side. He dived beneath the waves and hooked his arms underneath hers.

'I've got her! I've got her!' he yelled, keeping Mal's head above the water as he kicked his way back to shore, dodging the crocodiles, which were now circling Jay eagerly, entranced by his rhythmic chanting.

'Tick-tock, tick-tock . . . yeah, that's right, come on over here. Tick-tock, tick-tock,' said Jay. 'Tick-tock, tick-tock!'

Evie pulled her leg back from the edge and ran to help Carlos, and together they hauled Mal back safely on land.

chapter 33

Serpent's Scales

It was late on Sunday when a fairy tapped Ben on the shoulder and told him that Faylinn had asked that he meet her with her team of archivists in the oak tree's library. Ben had passed the time waiting by looking over the latest weather reports for the entire kingdom to see if anything had gotten worse. There hadn't been any new sightings of the purple dragon or snake in the last few hours, but who knew when it would strike next.

He followed the fairy up the winding staircase to a massive library housed in one of the topmost branches of the oak tree. Faylinn was flying in front of a huge projection screen, buzzing quietly with her team. The room was cozy and warm, with a crackling fireplace behind a grate, and long tables with pretty intertwined leaves and branches where the fairies worked.

'Ben, you're here, good,' she said, flying over to him. 'I think we've found something.'

She motioned to the images projected on the wall, which showed two blown-up photos of purple scales. Faylinn flew over and motioned to sharp ridges on one of the scales. 'Look at this,' she said. 'The ridges on your scale are almost identical to the one on the right, even though the one on the right is almost ten times its size. The one on the left is your serpent scale, and the other one is about the size of a dragon scale.'

'A match, then?' he asked.

'We think so. Either there are two different creatures, with identical ridge patterns, or these scales are from one creature that can take two different shapes. We think it is the latter, as it would be nearly impossible to find two creatures with these specific markings,' she said, buzzing between the two photographs.

'Where's the dragon scale from?' he asked, trying not to show how anxious he was. 'Is it Maleficent?'

'Not exactly,' she said, coming over to fly by his shoulder. Her voice was tiny and sharp as a wind chime.

He exhaled. 'What does that mean? What's it from?'

'The scale isn't from any creature we have in our files. As much as we tried, we couldn't find a match, actually, until Lexi Rose remembered we'd received something similar not so long ago.' Faylinn clicked to the next slide. 'As you know, fairies like to study every aspect of nature, and we ask that if anyone in Auradon discovers something new in the natural world, they send it to us so we can add it to our collection. Recently, a team of dwarfs were digging a new mine down by Faraway Cove, when they came across something unusual.'

The other fairies shifted in their seats and looked uneasy as the slide on the screen showed a group of dwarfs mugging for the camera, their wheelbarrows filled with sparkly diamond rocks. 'Look over here,' she said, flying back to the screen and flitting over the cavern floor.

Ben leaned forwards and saw that the ground was littered with the same purple scales.

'The dwarfs closed the mining operation soon after. They said they felt the tunnel was haunted even though they never saw anything, but they sensed a strange presence inside it. One of them—I think it was Doc's nephew—noticed the purple scales and sent a few to the archive.'

'Faraway Cove's pretty close to Charmington,' said Ben. 'And Camelot is directly north of it as well. The dragon must have used these mining tunnels to disappear in and out of sight, which is why Arthur's men could never catch it. I need to take a team into that mine.'

'The dwarfs sent a map, so you should be able to find the entrance easily enough,' said Faylinn. 'I'll have one copied for you.'

'Hold on, you still haven't told me—could the scales be Maleficent's?' he asked.

'I'm sorry to tell you it's because we don't know. As it turns out, we don't have a sample from Maleficent. Prince Philip's sword was wiped clean after their battle twenty years ago. But if you can send one from the lizard in your library, then we could tell you for certain.'

'Thanks. I'll have my men send over a sample as soon as I can. This has been really helpful.' He shook Faylinn's tiny hand with his thumb and forefinger and waved to the rest of the fairies.

'Ben, about this shapeshifting dragon . . . even if it isn't Maleficent, it's still incredibly dangerous. And if it is able to shift in form and size, that means it is capable of incredibly powerful magic. You must be prepared to fight it with similar enchantment. I know the rules of Auradon, so I don't give this advice lightly,' she said, buzzing worriedly.

'I won't go alone, don't worry. I'll tell Merlin to meet me at Faraway Cove as soon as possible. And he can bring his wand this time.' Ben smiled. 'I know he's been itching to use it.'

Faylinn nodded. 'I can imagine.' Seeing the sombre look on his face, she buzzed comfortingly by his shoulder.

'Remember, when in doubt, think of happy thoughts and you'll find your way.'

He smiled at the tiny fairy. The happiest thought he could think of was Mal and her friends returning safe from the Isle of the Lost. He hoped it would come true.

chapter 34

Underwater Epiphany

'Ugh, the leather is going to shrink,' said Mal, wringing her jacket and trying to dry her hair. She had already vomited up a gallon of water, and was still shaking from the near drowning, not to mention the near-crocodile-dinner experience. But Mal being Mal, of course she didn't want to show how shaken she was, so she focused on mourning her ruined jacket instead. 'What a bunch of dock rats we are,' she said with a laugh. Carlos was similarly soaked to the bone, and Evie was shoeless, her jacket torn. Her bird's-nest hair could rival any of Cruella's fright wigs.

'Speak for yourselves,' said Jay, who was dry and without a scratch.

'Don't worry about the jacket, I can make you another one,' said Evie, running a brush through her hair and trying to make herself look presentable.

'I shouldn't have run off like that,' said Mal. 'I'm sorry. I thought Maddy was my friend.'

Evie patted Mal on the shoulder; her hand made a wet, squelching sound and she withdrew it in alarm. 'Oh, uh, it's okay, we all make mistakes.'

'I didn't think she would betray me like that,' said Mal. 'I really thought she was part of the Anti-Heroes club.'

Carlos was sitting on the ground. He'd removed his shoes and socks in an effort to dry them. He pulled seaweed from his hair. 'What do you think Maddy meant when she said, 'All of Auradon will burn, just like Camelot'?'

Evie shrugged. 'Isn't that what villains do? Threaten?'

'It sounded a little more specific than that, don't you think?' said Carlos. 'How did she know about the fires in Camelot, then?'

'Hang on, she said something about Camelot?' asked Mal.

'Yeah, and didn't you say that is where that purple dragon is?' said Carlos.

Mal nodded. 'Yeah.'

'Maybe Ben put it on the news,' said Evie.

'Maybe,' said Mal. She shook out her jacket. 'Listen, I need to tell you guys something, but we should get cleaned up first, I can't think with all this wet stuff on me.' She shook her hair and droplets rained all around. 'The Junk Shop isn't far from here, so Jay and Carlos can get cleaned up over there. Evie and I will go back to the Bargain Castle across the street. Meet us there after you get changed.'

The four of them walked back into town, Mal squelching with every footstep, Evie walking in stockings, Carlos simply barefoot and holding his wet sneakers and Jay practically skipping. The boys crossed over to Pity Lane and headed for Jafar's while Mal unlocked the door to the Bargain Castle.

Mal turned to Evie with a wan smile. 'By the way, thanks for coming after me.'

'You're welcome. It's what friends do,' said Evie.

Mal nodded. 'Then thanks for being my friend. My real friend.'

Later, when the boys arrived, Carlos was dressed in a purple-and-yellow sweater and shorts that were too big for him. Evie was wearing one of Mal's old T-shirts, holey jeans and a pair of Mal's old boots. The four friends sprawled on the carpet and chairs in Mal's room. Carlos was even able to get a fire going in the fireplace. They hadn't slept all night and it was already close to sunrise.

'Mal, what did you want to tell us earlier?' said Carlos,

poking the fire with a stick. He placed his sneakers by the grate, hoping they would dry soon.

'The crocs in the bay,' said Mal. 'Aren't they usually by Hook's Inlet? Why were they all around Doom Cove all of a sudden?'

'Change of scenery?' snorted Jay.

'No, it was like they were guarding something. Something important,' she said, warming her hands by the fire. 'I think I know what it is.'

'The entrance to the Catacombs,' said Carlos promptly.

'Yeah, how'd you know?' Mal asked, looking a bit miffed that a little bit of her thunder had been stolen.

'Lucky guess,' said Carlos with a smile. 'Seriously, what else could it be?'

'Anyway, when I was underwater, I thought I saw a cave down there. The crocodiles were swimming out of it. It looked like it was their nest.'

'Hmm,' said Jay. 'If the crocodiles were coming out, there must be another entrance from the topside. Crocodiles prefer to make their homes on land, not underwater. Also, if Jafar, Evil Queen and Cruella did go down there, I doubt they swam. For one, none of them can.'

'Perfect,' said Carlos. 'Because I sure wasn't looking forward to getting wet again. My sneakers just dried.'

'We should tell the Anti-Heroes group so they can help us find it,' said Evie. 'Yen Sid told everyone to be back at the basement by sunrise, so we'll go and tell them then.'

'Good idea,' said Jay.

'It's funny,' said Mal. 'If we're right about this, and that crocodile cave down there is the entrance to the Catacombs, Maddy thought she was getting rid of me, but instead she did us a favour.'

'She helped us instead of harming us,' said Carlos, putting his dry socks back on.

'It's like Fairy Godmother always says,' said Evie, hugging a purple pillow to her chest.

'Don't let the stepsisters get you down?' said Mal.

'Goodness works in mysterious ways. Even in the deepest dark, you'll find a light to shine your way through.'

The Four Talismans

'All this has happened before, and it will all happen again.'
—Peter Pan

chapter 35

Underground Lair

The anti-heroes were a hardworking bunch, and by noon they had combed the entire beachhead, but hadn't been able to find anything. Mal was nearly ready to give up on the search for the tunnel's entrance. After all, she had basically been drowning when she saw the underwater entrance—maybe she'd hallucinated it.

But then, at the very edge of Doom Cove, in a rocky outcropping by the water's edge, Carlos, along with Big Murph, had found a small hole in the ground, about the size of a rabbit burrow.

'That can't be it. How would we fit in there?' Evie asked

doubtfully. 'And if it's not big enough for us, it's *definitely* not big enough for a crocodile.'

'We dig?' said Jay, who began to shovel away dirt with his hands. 'This is the only thing we've seen in hours. We've got to try it.' Carlos knelt down to help, and together they were able to make the hole big enough to squeeze through.

Mal knew they didn't need to worry about more crocodiles bothering them now—earlier, she'd sent Hadie to throw a bucket of rotten meat in the water on the other side of the island to draw them away. But as she looked down at the small, dark tunnel ahead, Mal wondered if they had just traded one problem for another. Still, Jay was right. They had to give it a shot.

'Thanks, you guys,' Mal called to the assembled team. 'I think we've found the entrance. We're going in!'

The sweaty group of anti-heroes cheered.

'Ladies first?' said Jay.

Mal nodded and crawled through the hole. She heard Evie struggling behind, and then the boys. After a few metres, the tunnel widened and they were able to walk upright.

'This better be it,' Mal said. 'I *really* don't want to be wandering around down here for no reason.'

But as they continued down the tunnel, Mal realised she actually felt perfectly at home. The cave was dark and wet and filled with furry things that skittered at the edge of her vision. *Why do caves get such a bad rap anyway? What's wrong with a few spiderwebs?* she wondered just as she stepped into a giant floor-to-ceiling cobweb. She struggled to push through, only to get more caught up in its lacy white stickiness.

'Don't spiders have anything else to do?' she asked aloud.

Carlos shook his head and helped pull the cobwebs away. They continued on, but stopped again when Evie shrieked at a tiny rodent that had made the mistake of crawling halfway up her pant leg.

'Just tell it to get out of the way,' Mal suggested. 'Didn't Evil Queen ever teach you how to deal with mice?'

'No, mum only cared about whether I knew how to line my eyelids properly,' said Evie, catching her breath as the small creature scampered off into the crevices.

'Oh, I forgot, I brought something from the Junk Shop,' said Jay as he removed a torch from his pocket and jiggled the batteries until they came to life. The sudden flood of light illuminated the cavern's interior—a collection of giant cool-looking spiderwebs, slimy wet puddles and an unexpected item—a gold poison-heart bracelet glittering on the ground.

Evie picked it up. 'It's my mum's!' she said excitedly. 'They must have been down here! We're going the right way!'

Walking further on, they discovered other clues. A long cigarette holder that could only be Cruella's, and a few coins that could only have fallen from Jafar's pouch. They kept going, energised by their discoveries, until the torch showed a succession of large animal footprints.

'These tracks look too big for crocodiles, right?' Jay asked, inspecting them. 'Plus, I think these are paw prints.'

'Way too big,' agreed Mal.

'Great,' said Carlos. 'Huge scary monster ahead.'

They went deeper into the cave, moving forwards cautiously.

Then, from somewhere in the darkness, a faint sound drifted through the cave, almost like the snuffling of an animal of some kind.

'Stop it, Jay!' said Mal, whirling to face him just as he was about to make that snuffling noise again.

'Couldn't resist,' said Jay.

He offered Carlos a high five, but Carlos just shook his head. 'Not cool, man. Not cool. We need to find the Poisoned Lake,' he said, studying one of the maps from Yen Sid. As far as he could tell, the body of water that surrounded the Toxic Tree with the Fruit of Venom should be the first of the underground lands they would pass. 'I wonder how the tree can grow. I mean with all this darkness, how can anything live down here?'

'Maybe it feeds on poison from the lake,' said Evie.

'For that matter, how can there be a lake underneath the ocean?'

'We're underneath the ocean floor, obviously. Plus,

everything is made by magic down here,' Mal said. 'Don't you remember?'

'Yeah, I guess so,' said Carlos as he stared at the tree on the map. 'All the books said that the magic creates the ideal location for each talisman. Okay, let's go this way.'

They followed the path as it led them further down into the earth, so steep at times that they were almost sliding. The tunnel narrowed and then widened again. Some passages were flooded, and they had to roll up their pants to cross. Eventually, the cavern grew so enormous that they could no longer see the top of the cave. They kept walking until the path split in two directions.

Just then, they heard that strange snuffling sound again. Carlos looked petrified, but Mal slapped a hand on Jay's mouth in annoyance. 'Stop!'

'Okay, okay, it's hard to resist. It's boring down here,' Jay said, his voice muffled behind her hand.

'Where to?' Mal asked Carlos.

Carlos looked down at the map. 'It doesn't say.' He studied the two tunnels in front of them. One of the paths was covered with the same large tracks they'd noticed earlier, but the other was clear. 'I don't know.'

'Hmm,' said Mal. 'The lake is poisonous, right? Whatever can live down here would know that, so instead of following its tracks, maybe we should choose the opposite direction. We need to find the one place the big guy doesn't go.'

'Sounds good to me,' said Carlos, who wasn't looking forward to meeting a large animal—or whatever it was—underground.

They set off down the undisturbed path. After walking a few metres, the torch went out, but Jay knocked it against the stone and it flickered back to life. The cave was smaller here, just big enough for them to pass through.

'I think we're close to water now,' said Mal. 'The air is damp.'

'And that smell,' said Evie. 'Talk about toxic!' Carlos was already pinching his nose and Mal and Evie did the same. Jay pulled off his beanie and held it over his face. They kept moving, until they heard the sound of water as it washed against sand. It had to be the Poisoned Lake.

They broke into a run, Jay shining the light and pointing it at the end of the cavern.

A large, deep purple lake bubbled with toxic gas. In the middle of the water was a small rocky island where one lone apple tree stood, its fruit ripe and red and luscious. The four of them stared at it, not quite believing what they were looking at. It was impossible to think that anything grew underground, and that, after all that walking, they had actually found one of the most dangerous objects in the world.

'Okay, let's figure out how to get me over there,' said

Evie, rolling up her sleeves. The fruit was her mother's talisman.

'We need to find a way to make a raft,' said Carlos. 'Maybe with some of the branches we saw back there, and anything else we can find.'

They walked back into the dark tunnel, searching for anything they could use to build a boat, when a strange sound echoed all around, distant but growing louder by the second.

Snuffle, grunt.

Mal ignored Jay. She hated it when he goofed off like that.

Grunt, snuffle.

Much louder now.

Snuffle, grunt.

The snuffling and grunting noise was so loud it was hard to concentrate. Mal had had enough. 'JAY! I SAID STOP DOING THAT!'

'Yeah, man,' said Carlos as he rolled the map back up and shoved it in his pocket. 'Lay off on the sound effects.'

'Seriously,' said Evie, with a toss of her hair. 'You're getting on my nerves.'

As they turned around to confront their friend, they realised he wasn't standing behind them anymore. His torch was on the floor. 'Jay?' Mal called uncertainly.

Jay appeared from the darkness, carrying a bunch of

dead branches in his arms. 'What?' he asked as the sound grew louder and louder. 'I left the light here for you guys.'

'Jay's not making that sound!' Evie screamed. 'RUN!'

Carlos grabbed the torch, and they sprinted back towards the lake. But something was blocking the passage. Something large and hairy with huge fanged teeth.

Snuffle, grunt.

Grunt, snuffle.

chapter 36

Fruit of Venom

The four of them ran from the creature and hid, huddling together in a nearby recess, trying not to make any noise, as whatever that thing was that was snuffling and grunting, moved away. It sounded awful, like some kind of hideous monster. Evie shivered, hoping it would move away without discovering them. She knew she was first up against her talisman, and wanted to get it over with as soon as she could.

'What is it?' Carlos whispered, shaking.

Mal stuck her head out of the hollow to see if she could see it. 'It's big and . . . pink. Like a huge cat, or a tiger—I can't tell.'

'A huge pink tiger, great; we're scared we're going to get eaten by a creature that looks like a puff of fairy floss,' said Jay.

The snuffling and grunting sound faded.

Evie exhaled. 'Okay, let's figure out a way to get across the lake.'

Carlos and Jay tried to tie the branches together to make some kind of raft, but it was clear that wasn't going to work as they didn't have anything they could use for twine. Jay kicked at the sad pile of branches dejectedly.

'Let's see how far it is, maybe there's some other way,' said Evie.

They entered the larger cavern, which was as big as a professional tourney stadium. Stalactites arched on the ceiling above them, like stars in a black sky. They stared once more at the toxic tree that stood in the middle of a tiny island surrounded by water.

'An island within the island and underwater, too. Yen Sid is right, the magic down here is wild,' said Jay.

Evie stood at the edge of the water, and a smooth rock just large and flat enough to step on appeared. She looked at her friends, who shrugged. She held her breath and jumped on it. Another rock appeared in front of her.

Stepping-stones.

Evie looked over her shoulder and smiled. 'Come on, it's like it knows I'm here.'

The talismans desire to be found, Yen Sid had told them.

Evie led the way, and the rest followed, careful to make sure they didn't fall into the poisoned water.

'Almost there,' said Evie as they stepped closer to the tiny islet holding a single toxic tree. From afar, the tree's knotted bark resembled a pattern of scowling faces.

'Creepy,' said Carlos.

'I know,' said Mal. 'We get to hang out in the coolest places.'

'Make sure your feet don't touch the water,' warned Evie, who knew a lot about poison, at least when it came to apples. She knew what they looked like, how they smelled, which ones would put you to sleep, and which ones would kill you on the spot. 'We'd melt like sugar cubes in a hot cup of tea if you tried to swim in here.'

'Nice image,' said Jay. 'I don't think we'd be as tasty, though.'

'We're here!' cried Evie, stepping ashore. She turned around and helped the rest of them onto the island.

'Great, start picking apples!' said Mal.

'Why is it called the Dark Forest,' said Jay, looking at the map that Carlos was holding open, 'when it only holds one tree?'

'Well, it *is* dark,' said Mal. 'There's that.' The only light came from Jay's torch.

'Yen Sid said the maps weren't completely accurate. They were just guesses,' Carlos reminded them. From afar, the tree looked small, but up close, it was taller than a building, its trunk as large as a house. It almost took up the entire island.

'I guess I'll have to climb it?' said Evie, staring nervously at the forbidding tree. Evie spent her days indoors, learning how to be pretty. She wasn't really one to climb trees.

The light from the torch flickered, growing dimmer by the minute, its batteries fading.

'Hurry, before our light runs out! We've still got three more talismans to recover,' said Jay.

'And whatever's out there is still out there,' said Carlos. In the distance, the sound of faint snuffling echoed in the cave. 'Hurry before it finds us.'

'All right. I'm going up,' said Evie, shaking slightly as she began to climb the tree trunk. She pulled herself up on the nearest branch and started the long, slow climb to the top, where the fruit was. Twice the thorns pricked her, but she ignored the little nicks on her legs and arms. She had work to do, and she could always get rid of them with concealer later.

Down below, her friends waited anxiously, calling up advice. 'Watch that branch—go the other way! Get a toehold on the left and lift yourself up!'

When she finally reached the top of the tree, she was stumped. There were hundreds of apples. All of them poisoned, she knew, but there was only one talisman. Only one Fruit of Venom. Which could it be?

'There are a lot of apples up here!' she called down. 'I don't know which one to pick . . . they all look alike!'

'You'll know which one!' called Carlos.

Focus! Evie told herself. Her friends were doing their best to help out, and they had to get out of here soon before that snuffling monster returned. Concentrate on the apples. There were so many of them and they were all so red and juicy.

'Which one?' she wondered aloud, and then she saw it through the highest branches.

One golden apple among all of the red ones.

She clambered up and plucked it from its branch. It was gorgeous, shiny and perfect. Evie was mesmerised by its beauty. It looked absolutely delicious, and it was practically asking to be eaten. What could it hurt, what if she just took one tiny . . .

'What are you doing!' Jay yelled from below.

Too late; Evie had already taken a bite of the apple. It *was* delicious, and for a moment she didn't regret it. Then her eyelids drooped as she yawned.

'Evie! What's happening?' asked Mal.

'I feel . . . sleepy, like the dwarf.' Evie laughed as she sat on the branch she'd been standing on, her head beginning to fog from the poison.

'Don't! Stay awake!' cried Mal.

'I'll try!' said Evie. She stood back up, fighting against the urge to sleep. She'd accidentally gobbled a poisoned apple once or twice when she was a kid, so maybe she had some kind of resistance to them. Her mother was always leaving them everywhere.

'I should have known better,' she grumbled, already growing weaker and trying to fight off the sleep that was threatening to overwhelm her. 'I'm just going to take a little nap, okay?' she called down.

'No!' Mal cried. 'No naps! No resting. Just keep moving!'

'Moving,' said Evie. 'Got to keep moving . . .' She struggled to keep her eyes open, scrunching her face into odd contortions, holding one lid open with a finger, but it fluttered shut. Evie's knees were wobbling and all she could think of was how nice it would be to lay down her head and take a brief—

'No!' Mal cried, again. Or maybe it was the third time. Evie hadn't realised that she had sat down once more. I'm in trouble, she thought. *Big trouble*.

'Get up!' called Carlos.

Jay was getting ready to climb the tree himself, but when he placed his hands on the bark, a force pushed him away and he flew to the ground.

Only Evie could climb the tree. This was her talisman.

'It says here that only by mastering the Fruit of Venom can you counter its poison,' said Carlos, reading from the map. 'Evie, don't give in! Save yourself!'

Save myself, but from what? Evie thought, before everything went black and the poison overcame her.

When she opened her eyes, she was standing in a room not unlike her mother's bedroom, on a podium in front of a Magic Mirror.

'Where am I?' she asked. 'Where are my friends?'

She was alone. Then she realised—she was alone because they had abandoned her and she had no friends. Every insecure, jealous and poisonous thought filled her mind.

She was standing before the legendary Magic Mirror, and it looked like it had before it was destroyed—whole and full of evil counsel.

'What's this?' asked Evie.

She stared at the mirror. It showed her Mal and Maddy laughing at her, pointing and screeching and mocking her.

Mal was never my friend, thought Evie. She was only pretending. The minute Mal returned to the island, she forgot about Evie.

The mirror showed another image: Mal, Jay and Carlos leaving her alone at the Poisoned Lake. They had left the minute she'd climbed the tree. They were laughing at her, and they were going to leave her to that awful grunting creature. She was alone and she would always be alone.

Mal's mother had exiled her and her mother to the Castle Across the Way. Evie had grown up with only spiderwebs for company. She had never had friends until the three of them, but maybe she'd never had friends at all.

Maybe it was all a lie. No-one liked her. Everyone was only pretending, and now that she knew the truth, she would destroy them all. She would make them *hurt*, she would make sure they never laughed like that again. She would show them what it meant to be alone, and abandoned and friendless . . .

Friendless?

Yen Sid's words echoed in her mind. *Evie, remember that when you believe you are alone in the world, you are far from friendless.*

Yen Sid had told her the total opposite of the poisonous thoughts that now filled her brain.

She stared at the mirror and the image of her friends deserting her. It wasn't true. It couldn't be true. Maddy had betrayed Mal, but Mal had never betrayed Evie. Carlos and Jay were like her brothers. The three of them would always be there for her.

'You're wrong!' she cried to the mirror. 'My friends are here! They're waiting down there! Waiting for me!'

She stepped away from the mirror, holding the apple in her hand. 'I'm not alone! I am far from friendless! I am surrounded by my friends, and I will return to them!'

The mirror shattered and Evie screamed. Suddenly, she was on the ground, looking up at the faces of her friends.

'What happened?' she asked.

'You fell,' said Carlos. 'All the way down, and we couldn't wake you.'

'We thought you were going to go to sleep forever, or at

least until we could get Doug to come and wake you up with true love's kiss.' Mal smirked.

'You okay?' said Jay, helping her up.

Evie nodded, rubbing the sleep from her eyes and tossing back her hair. 'I'm awake, at least!' she announced with considerable flair.

'Did you get it?' asked Mal. 'The talisman?'

In answer, Evie showed them the golden apple, which was whole once more, but no longer shining. 'It totally messed with my head, but I purged the poison from my body and mastered the talisman. Yen Sid was right, we've got to be careful with these things . . . they're tricky.'

'What did it do?' asked Mal, curious.

Evie shook her head and placed the apple in her handbag. 'Let's just say I knew you guys wouldn't leave me here alone.'

Mal rolled her eyes. 'Well, one more minute and we might have,' she joked. 'But then who's going to make my Auradon Prep prom dress?'

'Hey, guys,' Jay interrupted. 'Look at this.' He and Carlos were standing in front of a doorway carved into the tree trunk.

'That wasn't here before,' said Carlos.

'And look—the lake is draining!' said Evie. The tiny islet began to shake.

'Now that Evie has the Fruit of Venom, this place is self-destructing!' said Mal.

'Do we open it?' said Jay.

'I don't think we have a choice,' said Mal, looking around as the ground rumbled beneath them. It felt like the whole island was about to crumble.

'Let's go, that thing is heading over here,' said Carlos, scanning anxiously for any sign of the snuffling beast.

'Open it!' yelled Mal.

Jay threw open the door, and a blazing light shone from the darkness. 'It looks like a desert in here!' he told them, stepping inside. Evie and Carlos followed behind.

Mal waited by the entrance, her eyes on the lake, or what was left of it, ready to defend her friends from the mysterious creature in the tunnels.

But the monster never appeared, and so Mal followed her friends through the door in the tree.

chapter 37

Sand Snake

The first thing Jay noticed when he stepped through the tree was how hot it was. He had been shivering in the damp cavern, but now he was almost sweating. Instead of a wet cave, he was standing on a golden desert plain.

Evie followed, but as she crossed the threshold, her knees turned to rubber and she stumbled. Jay caught her and helped her through. 'Whoa. That poison must still be working.'

She nodded. 'I'll be fine in a minute.'

Carlos followed, blinking at the unexpected light, with Mal bringing up the rear. When they were all through, the door slammed with a bang and vanished. Carlos unrolled a new map. 'This must be the Haunted Desert,' he said. 'It says the Cobra's Cave is somewhere in the Dunes of Sorrow.'

Jay looked around. There wasn't much to see, just a whole lot of desert and wave after wave of sand dunes. 'This must be my territory. It looks a little like what my dad always told me about Agrabah. Although something tells me we won't find any magic lamps, friendly genies or flying carpets here.'

'Too bad. I'd take any of those over that weird pink thing we just avoided,' said Mal.

'Any chance the talisman is made of sand?' asked Evie as she scooped up a handful, letting the grains shift and fall between her fingers. 'Since that's all there is here.'

'Of course it's not made of sand,' said Jay.

The wind blew across the dunes, howling like a coyote. But underneath its screech was another sound: a deep, slithering hum.

'There!' said Jay, pointing to a wrinkle in the sand. 'It's moving.' The wrinkle headed towards them, and the four of them jumped away as it passed directly underneath their feet.

'Maybe your talisman *is* made of sand,' said Mal.

'It's not made of sand,' repeated Jay, exasperated now.

'That's all I see here,' said Mal, refusing to let go of the joke.

'Weren't you listening? Oh, wait, I forgot, you weren't because you were too busy running after Mad Maddy and getting yourself thrown off a bridge,' said Jay. 'Yen Sid said it was a Golden Cobra.'

He watched the movement in the sand as it slithered away—hold on . . . *slithered?* Before he could explain to his friends, Jay ran after the wriggling line. There was only one thing it could be, and when the line popped out of the dunes, he saw the Golden Cobra rear its ugly head.

The snake hissed, showing its forked tongue. It was the same golden colour as the apple Evie had picked earlier.

'I think he's found his talisman,' said Carlos as they ran to keep up with Jay, who was chasing the snake.

Jay was fast, but the snake was faster. It slithered across the sand, its golden scales shimmering in the light, while Jay kept stumbling and sinking in the dunes. Jay might be the best runner on the tourney field, but the desert definitely wasn't the ideal location for chasing an evil creature.

The cobra crested a ridge and Jay tried to follow, but when he reached the top, the snake was nowhere to be found.

'Great, it's gone,' said Mal, who, along with Evie and Carlos, had been stumbling along after Jay. 'What does the map say?'

'It says the Golden Cobra has a cave,' said Carlos. 'We could check that out, but it doesn't really say where it is.'

'Some map,' said Mal, crossing her arms across her chest.

They scanned the desert landscape, looking for any sign of the cobra, but it seemed to have disappeared completely. The heat wasn't helping either, and when the wind picked up, it blew sand at them, clouding their vision and biting their skin like little flies.

'We shouldn't have left for the Catacombs before the maps were done,' said Mal, crumpling the piece of paper in frustration.

'We didn't have a choice,' said Carlos. 'And remember, we've got to find the talismans before our parents do.'

'*My* parent is a lizard trapped in a glass-covered pedestal,' said Mal.

'Maybe,' said Carlos. 'Or your parent is a purple dragon that's been plaguing Camelot.'

'Guys, stop fighting, it's not helping with my poison headache,' said Evie as she massaged her temples.

Mal and Carlos apologised, and the four of them continued to look for any sign of the elusive cobra.

'One good thing about that toxic tree,' said Evie. 'At least it stayed still.'

'There!' Jay yelped. 'I see it! I think that's a cave!' He pointed to what looked like a pile of stones in between two dunes in the distance. He ran down the ridge, his friends following behind.

They stood in front of the rocks, which were stacked together tightly. But a small gap between two of the larger ones looked like it could be an opening into a cavern.

'Wonderful, a cave within a cave,' said Evie.

'I didn't create this world,' said Jay. 'You guys coming?'

'Hold on, we need to be careful,' said Mal. 'Evie was

almost poisoned back at the tree and who knows what that snake will do.'

'Fine,' said Jay.

'Let's go in, but we all stay together,' said Mal. 'Agreed?'

The others nodded, and they entered the cave. Jay was in the lead, his boots sliding on the sandy floor. He pulled the torch out of his pocket and hit the switch, but nothing happened. He tapped it again, and it glowed faintly, illuminating the path before them. A few minutes later, they heard that odd howling noise they'd heard when they first entered the desert.

'Do you think the cobra can make that noise?' Evie whispered.

'I don't know, but I don't really want to find out,' Carlos whispered back.

'It's called the Haunted Desert,' said Mal. 'What do you *think* it is?'

chapter 38

Golden Cobra

'Ghosts don't scare me,' Jay said as they kept walking into the darkness with only the sputtering torch to light their way. 'Hauntings aren't a big deal.'

'Oh yeah, what would you know about that?' asked Carlos, trying to get his torchlight zapp to work, but his phone was dead. There had been no time to charge it back on the Isle of the Lost.

'A ghost might try to scare you by rattling his chains or slamming a door shut, but there's nothing to be afraid of. They're basically made of air,' said Jay, still following the faint sound of rattling.

'Why do I get the feeling,' said Carlos, 'that someone is trying to convince himself of something?'

'Because *someone* is totally scared but won't admit it,' said Mal, sneaking behind Jay and yelling in his ear. 'Boo!'

Jay jumped. 'Okay, so I might be a little freaked out. But it takes a real man to admit his fears.'

'Oh, really,' said Mal with a laugh. 'It seems to me that just a moment ago you were telling us that ghosts were nothing to worry about.'

'So what? Ghosts are the worst, okay? I just wish we could leave this cave already,' Jay said.

The howling grew even louder. Carlos plugged his ears and Evie did the same. 'Maybe the ghost is deaf?' Mal said. 'Why else would it be shrieking at the top of its lungs?'

Jay sighed. 'Come on. Let's get this over with.' He started to walk faster, but stopped when they reached a sharp corner where the passage was a bit wider. The wind whistled through it, howling and screeching.

'So it's not a ghost after all,' said Jay. 'It's just the wind flying around these corners. I guess it's like a big flute that plays a note each time the wind blows through.'

'Look at Jay, getting poetic on us,' said Evie as she, Carlos and Mal tried to follow Jay into the next passage. But the same force that had pushed Jay away from the tree earlier was acting against them now.

'Wait!' said Mal. 'We can't get any further.'

Jay turned around to see his three friends standing at the corner. 'I'll meet you back outside. Don't worry about me, I've got this cobra.'

'Okay,' said Mal, scowling. 'I guess we don't really have a choice.'

'Remember what Yen Sid said,' advised Evie.

'Good luck, man,' said Carlos.

Jay promised he would see them soon, and then turned to face the empty tunnel on his own. It wound deeper and deeper into the earth, and the torch finally gave out, leaving him in darkness. The howling wind was still kind of scary, but he reminded himself that there was nothing supernatural about it.

At last, he saw a sliver of light at the end of the tunnel, and when he reached it, he discovered it was the entrance to a hidden chamber.

And not just any chamber, but one piled high with gold and treasure. A mountain of shimmering coins reached to the ceiling, so bright it cast its own light around the cavern. Jay had seen such treasure only once before, when he was in the Cave of Wonders in the Forbidden Fortress.

'This isn't real,' he said.

Oh, but it issssss, a voice hissed in the middle of all that gold, and Jay looked up to see the Golden Cobra, with its magnificent hood raised around its face, slowly unravelling from a basket. *All this is real, and it could be yours.*

'How?' asked Jay, staring straight into the red eyes of the snake.

I will be your servant, the cobra told him. *I serve the master of the sand.*

Jay was transfixed.

You see that curtain behind you?

Jay turned to see a rich, shining tapestry hanging over the passage he had just come through.

Leave your friends behind and pass through that doorway with me, and you shall have all the riches you desire.

Jay blinked, and suddenly he was seated on a raised platform, wearing a white turban on his head. He was not in the cave at all. He was the Sultan of Agrabah, the richest man in Auradon. Next to him were piles of gold and every kind of precious jewel.

A feast had been set before him with all his favourite dishes, and the people surrounding him bowed, fear in their eyes.

This was what his father had always wanted. His true place in Auradon, above everyone, above everything, and wealthy beyond reason, with all the riches of the world at his feet.

All the riches of the world . . .

He blinked against the vision, and returned to the cave, staring at the mountain of gold and the red eyes of the cobra.

What had Yen Sid told him before they had set off?

The riches of the world are all around you.

Jay didn't need much. He wasn't like his father, ruthless and cold. He just liked to play tourney and hang out with his friends. He enjoyed a good game, and good times. Good friends. He thought of how Mal had stood up to her mother rather than let Maleficent hurt any of them. And how Carlos could always be counted on to help with Maths Can Be Magic homework, and how Evie would always drop whatever she was doing to listen to him overanalyse an opposing team's play.

He had a great life, and he had wonderful friends. He was already rich beyond measure. The professor was right: the riches of the world were all around him.

'No,' he said with a smile.

No? The cobra hissed and flicked its long tongue.

'I'm taking you back to Auradon so you can be destroyed.' The cobra hissed and spat, venom arcing at Jay.

He dodged the poison, and captured the snake with his hand and held it tightly in his grip. The cobra thrashed and hissed, but Jay did not flinch or cower. 'You will submit to my will, you are mine to command! And I command you to heel!'

With those words, the cobra stiffened and froze, turning into a simple wooden stick.

When Jay finally emerged from the cave, he found his three friends waiting for him outside. Carlos was reading a book he'd brought, Mal was sketching in her journal and Evie was combing her hair.

'*That's* the Golden Cobra?' asked Mal, noticing the humble stick Jay was holding.

'It was,' said Jay with a triumphant smile. 'Okay, where next?'

In answer, the cave behind them began to rumble and disintegrate, just like the tree had done earlier. An outline of a door appeared on one of the rocks that had marked the cave's entrance. Carlos grabbed the knob and yanked the door open, blasting them with cold air. 'Let's go!' he yelled.

The three of them followed, Jay using his stick to hold the door open for the girls.

When they reached the other side, after all they had experienced so far, they were only a little surprised to find that they were in a modern city. It was time for Carlos to find his mother's talisman.

chapter 39

Metropolitan Labyrinth

Unlike Auradon City, this city was abandoned and grey instead of bustling with energy and life. Shops and streets were empty, buildings and offices shuttered. The whole place was covered in a thick dark fog, with only a few skyscrapers piercing through the heavy mist.

'Where are we?' said Carlos, his voice shaking slightly. His stomach was churning with the knowledge that this was the home of his particular talisman.

'Some kind of city,' said Evie. 'It's okay. I don't know about you guys, but I'd rather not see the inside of a cave again. Not to mention sand and snakes.'

'Hate to break it to you, but we're still underground in

the Catacombs,' said Mal, but even she looked relieved to be somewhere that resembled the real world.

'Magic created all this?' asked Evie. 'Buildings and everything? That's pretty crazy.'

Mal knocked on a brick wall. 'Yeah, and it's real, too.'

Jay turned around in a circle, looking up at the tall buildings. 'Interesting.'

'All right, enough sightseeing. We've got to keep going,' said Mal. 'What does the map say?'

'It says Cruella's talisman is in the House of Horrors,' said Carlos, checking the map.

'I thought your house was called Hell Hall?' said Evie.

'Yeah, and it sure was a house of horrors,' said Carlos. 'I think we go that way.' He headed east.

'What does the ring look like?' asked Mal.

'It's the big green one Cruella used to wear,' said Evie. 'It's pretty, actually. You think Carlos might give it to me instead?'

They walked past houses and buildings, but all of the doors were closed and the curtains were drawn. The entrance they'd used to enter this world was still open behind them. Through it, Carlos could see just a little bit of the sandy desert, and he considered running back there. Retrieving his mother's talisman wasn't exactly high on his list of favourite things to do.

The four of them walked down the centre of the road. Just like the other two worlds, this one was empty. There were no people here; the entire place was quiet, a mere façade. Not a real city at all but a place held together by magic—a home for the talisman. He led them right, then left, then two rights and he stopped, confused.

'Wait, that's the door to the desert again,' Carlos said. 'We're walking in circles.'

'No, we're not,' said Jay. 'If we had walked in circles we would have only made right turns. I definitely recall a left.'

They set off again, this time turning left, left, then right, then left, then right again. But once more, they came to the same doorway.

'Think we're in some kind of magic maze?' Mal asked. 'Let me guess: the map can't help us.'

Carlos checked, looking at the map from different angles. 'Actually, according to the map, the house should be right here, where we're standing. I'm not sure what's going on, if the landscape is shifting so it doesn't match the map, or I'm reading it wrong.'

'At least we have the door to the desert,' said Jay. 'We can always go back the way we came . . . Why are you looking at me like that?'

Carlos pointed. The door wasn't there anymore.

'We're trapped!' yelped Evie.

'And it doesn't seem to want us to find what we're looking for, and it doesn't look like there's a way out of here,' said Mal.

'Maybe it'll appear. I don't know how magic works. Let's keep walking,' said Carlos.

'In circles?' asked Jay.

'You have a better idea?' asked Mal.

'I guess not,' Jay admitted. 'Okay, carry on, circles are fine.'

'Maybe if we keep walking, we'll see something else,' said Carlos.

They kept going, looking for the house, and once again they ended up where they began. 'Hold on,' said Carlos. 'I think the map is right. The House of Horrors *is* right here.'

'But these are all regular buildings, not mansions,' said Evie. 'I don't see Hell Hall anywhere.'

'The talisman isn't in Hell Hall, I made a mistake,' said Carlos, pointing to a dusty window that had been right in front of them all along. He hadn't noticed it because he had assumed that the 'House of Horrors' was his mother's house. This was a fur shop, and in the corner was a sign that read HOUSE OF HORRORS. SALE TODAY!

'I think I'm supposed to do some shopping,' said Carlos.

'Well, go on, then,' said Jay.

'I'm going! Give me a sec,' said Carlos.

But he didn't move. He couldn't.

'Come on, man, just do it. You know you can. Go!' said Jay, giving him a little push.

Finally, Carlos opened the door and looked over his

shoulder. 'You guys probably can't come in, can you?' he asked hopefully. But sure enough, when Mal, Evie and Jay tried to follow, they were barred from entering.

'We'll wait here,' said Evie.

'Good luck,' said Mal. 'You'll need it.'

'Bring back that ring soon. I'm getting hungry,' said Jay.

Carlos swallowed his fear, squared his shoulders and walked inside.

chapter 40

The Ring of Envy

The House of Horrors didn't live up to its name at all, for when Carlos stepped inside, he found it was an elegant fur shop. The room was decorated in the manner of a fabulous salon, with racks and racks of elegant fur coats everywhere. There were fox chubbies, sable throws, mink stoles, floor-length trenches and fur-trimmed opera capes. White Mongolian vests, black goat-hair ponchos, cozy raccoon cocoon coats, cheetah-print boleros and silver-tipped mantles.

There was an elevator at the back of the store, and he walked towards it, as if drawn there by an invisible cord.

The doors opened silently and he entered, his hand pulled to the button for the topmost floor.

When Carlos stepped out of the elevator, he was no longer inside a fur shop. Instead, he was walking through a mist, a grey cloud that covered everything. In the distance, he saw a green light blinking.

He walked towards it, his heart thudding in his chest, hoping he wouldn't chicken out. The youngest of the group, Carlos was often worried that while he was smart enough, he wasn't as brave as the others were. It had taken a great force of will to enter the House of Horrors alone.

The mists parted and he saw the ring at last. It was indeed as large as a quail egg and as green as a spring meadow. And it was Cruella de Vil's ring all right, because she was wearing it.

Carlos stepped back with a yelp.

'Hello, darling,' his mother said, blowing a cloud of smoke in his face. 'Looking for this?'

'You found it?' he asked. 'You found your talisman?'

'Well, of course I did, child! It's mine!' she screeched.

He was too late, Carlos realised. Cruella already had her ring.

'Shoo, boy, don't you know when to leave your mother alone?' sneered Cruella.

Carlos backed away, petrified. He had failed his friends, and he had failed Auradon. But even as he beat himself up, he remembered Yen Sid's words. *You possess a keen intellect;*

however, do not let your head rule your heart. Learn to see what is truly in front of you.

Everything in his brain told him to run from his mother, that she had already captured the talisman. There she stood, hitching her furs across her shoulders, glaring at him.

Cruella had always haunted his nightmares, with her crazed declarations and frenzied hysterics. What was truly in front of him? What didn't he see? What was he missing?

His head screamed at him to run . . .

But his heart . . . His heart told him to stay and fight, that even if he was deathly afraid, he had to find a way to get the ring away from her. He had to prove to himself that he was brave enough, and that he *was* enough.

'Still here? Go and tell your friends to leave this place forever,' ordered Cruella.

'No,' said Carlos. 'Not without that ring.'

Gathering the last of his courage, he tackled his mother and struggled for the ring, finally pulling it off her finger and placing it on his own.

He felt the rush of power from the talisman shoot through him.

Cruella cackled with glee. 'Go ahead, then, use it on me. Destroy me. With that ring you can obliterate me forever. Tell me to throw myself off this roof and I'll do it. Isn't that what you want? Isn't that what you have always wanted?'

Carlos felt the ring throb in his hands. He could destroy

his mother, rid the world of another villain, and stop having nightmares once and for all.

'Do it!' Cruella cackled. 'Do it, boy!'

He raised his hand, pointing the ring right at her. Then he dropped his arm down with a sigh. 'No, I can't. I'm better than that,' Carlos said, turning on his heel and heading for the elevator. *I'm better than you, Mother. No matter what you've always told me.*

Suddenly he was standing outside the House of Horrors, and Jay, Mal and Evie were looking at him, concerned.

'What happened?' he asked.

'You came out of the building in a trance,' said Mal.

'The ring . . .' Carlos muttered. He opened his fist. The jewel had turned a dull green, its power abated for now. 'It wanted me to destroy her,' he said. 'But she wasn't actually there. It was just a vision, just the ring trying to scare me, to make me mad.'

'Yep, sounds about right,' said Jay. 'These talismans must get more power that way.'

Carlos nodded and put the ring away in his pocket. Three down. One Dragon's Egg to go.

They looked around for a hidden doorway, but found none. 'We could try this,' said Carlos, motioning to the revolving door that led back to the House of Horrors. 'It's the only door around here that's open. It might be the only way out of here. And from the looks of it, the city is melting!' He yelped as the sidewalk beneath them began to crack.

'Let's go!' yelled Mal. She rushed through the revolving door, and the rest of them hurriedly did the same.

chapter 41

Dragon's Nest

When she pushed through the door, Mal wasn't in the House of Horrors. She wasn't even in a city anymore. Instead, a dark, foreboding mountain loomed in the distance. Lightning crackled in the sky and vultures circled above.

'Maleficent Mountain,' she said, when the rest of the team arrived. 'Over there.' According to the map, Doom Crag lay at the very top of the mountain, where a dragon had made its nest.

'Ouch, that looks like a climb,' said Jay.

'You guys know the drill. Only I have to go,' said Mal. 'Don't worry.'

'No,' said Carlos. 'We'll all go. Remember what the professor said? You don't have to do this alone.'

'But this is my talisman,' said Mal. 'And all of you had to get yours alone.'

'We're going with you,' said Evie. 'At least until the talisman stops us. No arguments.'

'You're not getting rid of us,' said Jay. 'That's how this whole "having friends" thing works, remember?'

'Fine,' said Mal. 'Let's go, then.'

They trudged through the dead land, air thick with smoke. Sizzling green slime bubbled through cracks in the dirt, and they helped each other over the acrid puddles. Mal soldiered on as Evie groaned and complained that her head still hurt from the poison, and Jay was subdued, probably thinking of the riches he'd rejected. Carlos was definitely still shell-shocked from seeing his mother; real or not, that woman was terrifying.

They were united in their silence. The Dragon's Egg was the greatest of all the talismans and its mistress would have the forces of hell at her command.

'You know, the Dragon's Eye in the sceptre isn't an actual eye. It just looks like one. It's really a dragon's egg,' said Mal.

'Why isn't it called the Dragon's Egg sceptre, then?' asked Carlos.

'Duh, because Dragon's Eye sounds way cooler,' said Jay.

'Yeah, I guess so,' said Carlos.

'So is there a dragon here?' asked Evie, looking around fearfully.

'Let's hope not,' Carlos said.

'You guys can wait here,' said Mal. 'The mountain won't let you any closer than this.'

She began to climb, reaching for a foothold and pulling herself up.

But when Jay put a hand on the mountainside, it didn't push him away, and it didn't reject Carlos or Evie either. When Mal looked down, she was slightly disappointed to find they were climbing right behind her.

Is it because the talisman thinks I'm weak? she wondered.

With that disconcerting thought, she kept climbing, her friends right behind her.

chapter 42

Dragon's Egg

When they reached the top of Doom Crag, they discovered the dragon's nest was the size of a small boat. Its burned and blackened branches were twisted and packed tightly, and there was no sign of an egg anywhere. Mal began to search, getting down on her knees, and the rest of the team did the same, combing through every inch of the foul space.

'It's not here,' said Mal, frustrated.

'It has to be,' said Evie.

'Maybe they got here before us and found it. Cruella, Jafar and Evil Queen, I mean,' said Jay. 'They are supposed to be wandering around down here in the Catacombs, right?'

'Maybe that's why we were all able to climb the mountain,' said Mal. She'd scratched her palm on the way up, and she pinched it, trying to stop the blood. 'Because the talisman's gone.'

'No!' said Carlos. 'It has to be here. If they had found it, this mountain wouldn't be here. Remember what happened in the other places? They started to disintegrate once we recovered the talismans. Keep looking.'

Mal searched again, but bumped into Evie, who fell back on Carlos, who tripped over Jay. 'There's not enough space for all four of us,' Mal complained. 'You guys need to leave. You're not helping. Maybe it won't show itself to me because you're all here,' she said crossly.

'Are you sure?' said Evie.

'I'm sure,' said Mal.

'Fine,' said Jay. 'If she doesn't want us here, we don't need to be here. And this place gives me the creeps.'

'But the professor said . . .' Carlos began.

'He's not here now, is he? He's not the one who had to climb this mountain and look for this egg. Get out of here!' Mal shouted.

Carlos, Evie and Jay exchanged looks with each other. Mal glared at them until, one by one, they climbed out of the nest and began to make their way down the mountain.

Mal didn't need anyone, she never had. Okay, maybe the four of them had stood together when Maleficent was defeated, but come on, in the end, everyone knew that it was Mal's will that had broken her mother's and reduced the dragon to the size of a lizard.

Although Mal's heart felt small right then, thinking of her friends descending the mountain without her, she couldn't let it stop her. She covered every inch of the nest, and on the third time through the muck, she saw something out of the corner of her eye. Something small and purple.

'Aha!' she said, reaching for it. But Mal had been expecting a green egg, like in the Dragon's Eye sceptre. Why was this one purple?

Only when it hatches does it turn green, a voice answered, as if it could read her thoughts. *The Dragon's Egg does not birth a dragon, but a weapon.*

Okay, whatever, thought Mal, stuffing the egg in her jacket. At least that was done. She'd recovered her talisman just fine without anyone's help. Maybe the professor was wrong about her quest; after all, the old guy didn't know everything, right?

She stood at the edge of the nest, ready to head down, when a vulture shrieked from above. She startled, losing her balance, and fell over the edge, just barely holding onto a branch at the very bottom of the nest. Her legs kicked wildly in the air.

Great, she was about to fall off a cliff, and she'd gotten rid of the only people who could have helped her. Why did she always insist on doing everything alone?

Her hands were starting to burn.

She was an idiot, that's why, and she couldn't hold on much longer!

You've held on this long, haven't you?

She had the blood of a dragon, just like her mother.

Don't you?

Her fingers felt like they were starting to fall off.

She was Mal, daughter of Maleficent. Her mum had given her only part of her name, saying she hadn't earned the rest of it yet. But maybe she didn't want her full name at all. Maybe she didn't want to be Maleficent. Maybe she was completely fine with just being herself, being Mal.

Aren't you? Isn't that the whole point?

Who else are you supposed to be?

One hand slipped off the branch, and dirt began falling into her eyes as the roots tore off from the cliff.

Maleficent would never admit to needing or wanting anyone, and had been transformed into a lizard because she didn't have enough love in her heart. But Mal was not her mother. While she was stubborn, and way too proud, she was very different from Maleficent. And right now she wasn't ashamed to admit when she was wrong.

Now she was only holding on by one hand. The branch

was ripping out of the cliff face. She could be falling in moments.

You're wrong. You've never been more wrong—

Evie, Jay and Carlos needed to discover their own strength and so they had to face their quests for their talismans alone. Mal didn't have to be tested that way, because she already knew that she was strong. But what she didn't know until now, dangling over the edge, was that as strong as she was, she could always use a hand.

Literally.

Maybe that was my test after all—

Strength didn't have to mean facing danger alone. Strength came from trust, and friendship and loyalty. Plus, Yen Sid was right, this wasn't just her burden to bear, it was theirs too. She hoped her friends were still there.

'You guys! Help!' she yelled. 'I need help!'

She kept screaming until she saw their faces peering down at her from the nest above. 'Mal! We're coming!' said Evie.

Carlos held Evie's feet as she was lowered down, with Jay as the anchor. Ever so slowly, and ever so carefully, they dragged Mal back to safety.

Mal could barely catch her breath, and her throat still hurt from screaming. Her hands were cut and scratched.

But she was alive.

'Thanks, guys. For saving my life and everything.'

'Did you find the egg?' said Carlos, when they were all back inside the nest again.

Mal held up the purple oval that was hard as stone. 'Yep.'

'Why is it purple?'

'It still has to hatch,' said Mal. 'But let's get out of here before this mountain completely collapses or something.'

As if it heard her, the mountain began to rumble and shake, slowly disappearing back into nothingness now that its purpose had been served and its talisman taken.

chapter 43

Which Witch?

No new doorway appeared in the side of the mountain after Mal had retrieved the Dragon's Egg. She was still a bit dazed from the near-death experience as they climbed back down the mountain.

'How do we get out of here?' asked Evie nervously.

'I think we have to go through *that*,' said Carlos, motioning to a cavern at the base of the mountain after consulting the map. 'There's no way back, so we'll have to keep going forwards.'

'Great, another dark tunnel,' said Evie, who had just about had her fill of the underground catacombs.

'But I think this one leads us back home, to Auradon,' said Carlos hopefully. 'If the map is right . . .'

'Let's go,' said Mal, who'd found her voice. She held the small purple egg in her fist, unwilling to put it away in her pack just yet.

'Torch's dead, so we'll have to feel our way in the dark,' said Jay, tossing it into a bubbling green puddle with a sigh.

'Then we'll do this the only way we can,' said Mal. 'Together.' The four of them held hands and entered the foreboding cavern.

They'd travelled for a while when the path before them began to shine, and when they rounded the corner, they saw abandoned wheelbarrows and uncut rocks with diamonds still embedded in their core.

'Looks like a dwarf mine,' said Evie. She'd seen them in Doug's ZapChats.

'Abandoned,' said Jay, picking up one of the shiny rocks.

'Wonder why?' said Carlos. 'Looks like they left in a hurry.'

'Who knows,' said Mal. 'Let's keep going.'

They kept walking, until Mal suddenly stopped.

'What?' asked Carlos.

'I heard something . . . like footsteps. Can you hear it?' she asked.

Jay listened, absentmindedly pocketing one of the gems on the floor. 'Yeah.'

'There's someone else here,' said Mal.

Evie looked over her shoulder. 'Following us?'

'Maybe,' said Mal. 'Be ready.'

'You don't think it's *them* . . . ' said Carlos, who really had no desire to see his mother right now.

'Who else?' said Mal. 'Yen Sid said they're lost down here. Maybe they saw us and now they want to get their talismans back.'

'Dad!' Jay called into the darkness behind them. 'Are you there?' His voice echoed around the cavern. *Dad, Dad, Dad, Dad.*

No answer, so they kept walking, but the feeling that someone or a group of someones was in the tunnel with them remained. And their hearts dropped when they noticed a few things in the mine—a tube of red lipstick, a fluff of black-and-white fur and a discarded velvet money pouch. The villains were somewhere close by, and Mal, Evie, Jay and Carlos were ready to hear Cruella de Vil's sneer or smell Evil Queen's perfume or feel Jafar tap them on the shoulder at any moment. They tried to pretend it didn't bother them a bit, trying to act tough, even as they inadvertently huddled closer together.

'Aieee!' Carlos cried as he bumped into Jay, who yelped as he collided with Evie, who screamed as she fell on Mal.

'It's just us!' said Mal. 'Everyone calm down!'

They kept moving, until they heard the footsteps again, louder this time, along with voices. But they must have been coming from the other way—ahead of them rather than behind.

'Who's there?' called Mal while the three others huddled behind her.

'The mine starts down here,' they heard someone grumble. 'Are we sure this is necessary?'

'Let's just see how deep it goes, and where it leads. It couldn't hurt,' said another.

A sudden beam of light flooded the mine shaft, and they blinked, blinded. But even without seeing who it was, Mal knew that voice immediately.

'Ben!' she cried, running towards the group heading down the mine shaft.

'Mal? Is that you?' asked Ben, shining his torch her way.

'It is! It's all of us!' she said, appearing out of the darkness.

'You're all right!' he said, beaming as he scooped her up in his arms.

Mal closed her eyes and hugged him back tightly. There was nothing like almost rescuing an entire kingdom—and almost plunging to your death along the way—to make a person appreciate a good hug.

'What are you doing down here? Where did you come from?' she asked.

'I'll tell you everything,' he said, at the same time as she said, 'I have so much to tell you!'

They laughed as Carlos, Jay and Evie joined them, a little dirty and smudged, but whole. Ben didn't let go of Mal as he shook the boys' hands and slapped them on the back before giving Evie a quick hug. The five of them grinned at each other.

The old man behind Ben cleared his throat. 'Uh, right,' Ben said, blushing as he backed away from Mal. 'This is Merlin, and you know Grumpy.'

The wizard nodded in greeting and the dwarf grunted. 'Do you know my son, Gordon? He's at Auradon Prep with you all,' said Grumpy.

'We know Doug,' said Evie, smiling.

Grumpy huffed. 'Everyone knows Doug. Just like his father, too popular.'

Evie had to giggle at that.

Ben explained how the Neverland fairies had helped them track purple dragon scales to this deserted diamond mine. Mal's group told them about their journey to recover the talismans.

'So Yen Sid was right, the Catacombs go all the way to Auradon,' said Carlos.

'We were just at Maleficent Mountain,' said Mal. 'There was a dragon's nest on the top of Doom Crag, but we didn't see a dragon back there.'

'We're closer than we've ever been, then,' said Ben. 'The

creature must live here, and it's been getting to Auradon through this tunnel.'

Just as he spoke, a fine purple mist covered the cavern, and everyone froze.

'It's here,' said Merlin. 'The creature is here. Show yourself!' The wizard held his wand high.

'Come out, come out, wherever you are!' said Mal.

'I am King Ben of Auradon and I command you to reveal yourself to us!' said Ben.

The purple mist began to take shape . . . but instead of a fire-breathing dragon or a giant snake, there was only an old witch with purple hair standing in front of them when the mist cleared.

'Madam Mim!' exclaimed Mal, completely shocked to see Mad Maddy's grandmother, and yet something else about her was oddly familiar.

'Hello, dearie!' said Madam Mim with a cheerful wave.

'You know her?' asked Ben.

'From the Isle of the Lost,' said Mal.

'Well, I certainly know her. Hello, old friend,' said Merlin grimly. 'I thought I might see you here, Mim. Up to your old tricks, are you? I'm sorry to say that your mischief ends now.'

Madam Mim only laughed, and her cackle echoed throughout the dark cavern. 'Oh, I don't think so, you geezer, I'm having way too much fun!'

chapter 44

Wizards' Duel

As she laughed, Madam Mim turned into a large purple dragon. But unlike Maleficent's fierce dragon form, Madam Mim's looked almost comical. Her messy purple hair was still perched on top of her head, and her wings looked the size of a bird's. How on earth did Ben ever mistake this dragon for Maleficent?

'You thought this was my mother?' Mal asked him, rolling her eyes.

Ben laughed nervously. 'She was up in the sky, it was hard to see. I don't know, blame magic?'

Still, the group scrambled away as Merlin rolled up his

blue wizard sleeves. He zapped his wand at her, launching sparks, but Mim was too fast. She turned into a fox and scuttled into the darkness. Merlin sent another spell from his wand, but he was too late. Mim turned once more, this time into a raging rhinoceros.

'The boulders!' said Mal, pointing to the giant stones at the top of the mine shaft.

Jay and Carlos ran in front of the animal, pushing the rocks right into the rampaging rhino's path. But just as she was about to be crushed, Mim turned into a crafty hen and flew out of the way.

'Where'd she go?' asked Ben.

'Don't know,' panted Mal. 'But at least now we know that Camelot's dragon wasn't my mum.'

'For sure,' said Ben.

Mim must have discovered the entrance to the Catacombs, thought Mal, and she was using it to get her revenge on Merlin, who had bested her during their last battle by giving her the pox. The loony old witch was having fun wreaking havoc in Camelot and stealing food from Auradon. She must have told her granddaughter what she was doing. It's a wonder Maddy hadn't tried to escape to Auradon herself. Maybe she had been too scared about getting lost down there; she knew the dangers from being in the Anti-Heroes club.

'Mmm, you look tasty!' Mim cackled as she turned into a crocodile and opened her jaws wide.

'GAH!' yelled Carlos as they ran away from her snapping teeth. Mim reared on her hind legs, her purple hair falling into her face.

'It was you!' cried Mal. 'That pink-and-purple thing we saw in the tunnels earlier!'

'Fairy-floss tiger?' said Jay. 'I take it back, she's definitely scary!'

They barely got away from her, but Merlin soon came to their rescue. 'You're surrounded, Mim!' said Merlin, waving his wand. 'The only way out of this tunnel is through me. Your place is on the Isle of the Lost! Surrender!'

'Never!' Mim shrieked, turning back into the fat purple dragon, fire spewing from her mouth. 'I'll never go back there! You can't make me!' She shot a fireball at him, but Merlin transformed into a blue sparrow and flew away from her. But Mim deftly conjured a cage, trapping him.

'Some powerful wizard!' scoffed Mal. 'Can't he turn into something . . . I don't know . . . scarier?'

'I read the history of Camelot,' said Carlos. 'And when he battled Mim back when Arthur was a kid, Merlin did the same thing—Mim turned into ferocious creatures but Merlin fought her by turning into small and seemingly helpless animals like a rabbit and a turtle. Maybe it's the way his magic works?'

There was no time to discuss further, as Mim was headed their way, ready to spew another fireball.

'No!' cried Ben, rushing forward, but Mim swatted him

with her tail and he was thrown hard across the cavern, hitting the ground with a thump.

'BEN!' cried Mal. She started to run towards him, but Mim stomped in front of her, blocking the way. Then the dragon pushed forward, pressing Mal, Jay, Evie and Carlos against the wall.

There was nowhere else to go.

'What do we do?' cried Evie. 'She's going to roast us!'

'Talismans?' said Jay. 'If we use them to hurt someone, I have a feeling they'll come to life again! I can use my cobra staff to hypnotise her!' he said, shaking his wooden stick.

'Or my ring to make her do what we want,' said Carlos.

'Poison is always good,' said Evie, removing the golden apple from her purse.

'Mal, you've got the Dragon's Egg,' said Carlos. 'You could command all the forces of hell.'

'Not until it hatches,' said Mal. 'And the only way for it to hatch is if it sits under a dragon.'

'You mean you have to put it under Maleficent?' asked Evie.

'Maybe?' said Mal.

'Weird,' said Jay.

'But we have ours. Let's use ours,' said Carlos, rather desperately, as Mim drew closer.

'No!' said Mal. 'We can't use our talismans! Don't you see that's what the evil in them wants us to do? If we use them like this, it would only make their power stronger.

We'd be drawn to the magic . . . and we'd turn into our parents.'

'You're right,' said Evie, putting away her talisman reluctantly as the boys agreed.

'Then brace yourselves,' said Carlos, 'and prepare to be roasted.'

The four of them huddled together, seeking comfort in each other before the end, and the purple dragon reared back and opened its mouth. But before it could set them on fire, Ben appeared, holding a sword to the dragon's heart.

'Recognise this?' he asked. 'Artie loaned it to me; he thought I might need it.'

'Excalibur!' cried Carlos, who recognised the sword from Auradon's history books.

'The one and only,' said Ben, still facing Madam Mim. 'The most powerful sword in Auradon. You know what it can do.'

'So I suggest you save yourself the pain, Mim,' said Merlin, who had gotten out of the cage by turning into a caterpillar and was now back to being a wizard.

The purple dragon snorted as Ben pressed the blade against its chest. Finally, it turned into a fine purple mist, and Mim was a hag once again, her shoulders slumped. 'I'll miss Auradon so,' she said. 'The sheep were tasty.'

'But alas, Auradon is not the place for you,' said Merlin. With a wave of his wand, Madam Mim was sent back to the Isle of the Lost.

'Say hi to Maddy for me!' said Mal.

'We need to close this tunnel so that no-one else can use it to escape into Auradon,' said Ben.

'My thoughts exactly,' said Merlin, and with another wave of his wand, the passage behind them was closed forever with an impenetrable wall that no-one and no magic would ever be able to breach. 'There, it's permanently sealed. No-one from the Isle of the Lost will ever be able to use it again.'

'Let's go home,' said Ben, reaching for Mal's hand.

'Sounds like a good plan,' said Mal, squeezing Ben's hand tightly. 'You guys ready?'

The other three nodded.

'About time,' said Jay. 'We've got class tomorrow.'

'And homework tonight,' said Carlos.

'I hope our feeds updated correctly,' said Evie. 'Right now we're all supposed to be in bed, sneezing from the flu.'

'Did someone say Sneezy? I'm Grumpy,' said Grumpy.

'Merlin?' asked Ben. 'Do you mind giving us a lift? Just this once?'

'If you could send me back to the Enchanted Wood,' said Grumpy, 'it would save me a carriage ride.'

'I'll be heading back to Camelot myself,' said Merlin as he shook everyone's hands.

'You make a good king, Ben,' said Merlin. 'And you were right in the end, we didn't need magic to capture the dragon. Only diligence and courage, as you have shown.'

'Thank you,' said Ben. 'That means a lot, coming from you. Although we did need magic to send her back to the Isle of the Lost, and to close that passage. And to go home.'

'Details, details,' said Merlin with a smile. 'Who reads the fine print these days?'

'Will you give this back to Artie for me?' asked Ben, handing Merlin the sword.

'With pleasure,' said the old wizard with a smile.

'Bye, Merlin,' said Mal, and the rest of the group waved.

'Can we get going already?' asked Grumpy.

Merlin rolled up his sleeves. 'Return everyone here to where they need to be,' said the wizard. Raising his wand for the last time, he sent them all back to where they belonged.

chapter 45

Happily Ever After, for Now at Least

It was Sunday afternoon when they returned to school; the practice fields were quiet and empty, and students were taking advantage of their free time to read under the trees or lazily throw Frisbees across the lawn. Mal blinked at the sudden brightness and serenity, a stark contrast to the dark mine they'd just left. She was still holding the Dragon's Egg tightly in her hand. She was about to put it away when she noticed something—at the edge of the purple was just a hint of green.

The Dragon's Egg births a weapon. The most powerful talisman. Mal shuddered and stuffed the egg back in her pocket for now.

'Home safe,' said Ben. He thanked Mal, Jay, Carlos and Evie for all their help, but he had to go back and meet with his councillors to update them on everything that happened.

'See you in a bit,' he said, giving Mal's arm a squeeze.

'Not if I see you first,' said Mal, returning his smile.

Ben headed over to Beast Castle as they made their way back to the residence halls. It was almost impossible to believe they had been gone for less than a day, and the weekend wasn't even over yet. It felt like they'd been in the Catacombs of Doom for a lifetime.

'Well,' said Carlos. 'I guess that's it for now.'

'Not quite,' said Mal. 'We still need to figure out how we're supposed to get rid of these talismans.'

Jay nodded. 'Tomorrow.'

'I need a nap.' Evie yawned.

As they strolled back to the residence halls, they saw Audrey and Chad having a picnic under a tree while Jordan and Jane lounged on towels nearby. The Auradon kids waved when they saw them, and they stopped to say hello.

'Hey, Jay,' said Chad. 'Sorry about . . . um . . . what happened with your eye the other day. And good game yesterday.'

'No worries, man,' said Jay. The two shook hands and Mal was just a tiny bit disappointed that Jay didn't jump at the opportunity to steal Chad's rather shiny wristwatch.

'Are you feeling better?' Jane asked Carlos worriedly. 'You looked so sick at the dance last night.'

'Much better,' said Carlos, blushing. 'Thanks.'

'Oh, Jordan,' said Jay. 'About what happened in your lamp the other day, with the limousine keys. Sorry about that. I returned them to Ben, though.'

'It's all right,' said Jordan. 'I figured you must have needed them badly enough if you had to wish for them.'

'See you guys later,' said Mal. Evie looked like she was going to fall asleep standing up, and gave a limp wave with her fingers.

'I'm going to stay a bit,' said Carlos, taking a seat on a towel next to Jane.

'Me too,' said Jay, who was already lounging next to Jordan's towel.

Mal and Evie exchanged meaningful smiles, but didn't tease the boys. They'd save that for later. When they arrived in their room, both of them collapsed on their beds and slept until the alarm woke them up for school the next morning.

Before Mal headed to her classes, she had one more thing to do. She skipped breakfast and went straight to the room at the back of the library. The guards at the door didn't recognise her, and there were a lot more of them this time.

'I need to get in there to see my mother!' she demanded.

'Sorry, King Ben said absolutely no visitors.'

'But I will make an exception this time,' said Ben, who

had heard the ruckus and walked over to see what was happening.

'You're up early,' said Mal.

'Tourney practice. Playoffs are next week,' said Ben. 'What's up? You wanted to see your mum?'

'Yeah,' said Mal.

'Let her through,' said Ben.

The two of them went inside, and Mal couldn't help running ahead. She skidded to a stop in front of the domed pedestal.

Maleficent was missing.

The lizard was gone.

And there were only three people who could have taken her.

She gasped. Somehow, the villains had gotten past the guards! 'What are we going to do?'

But Ben didn't look alarmed. Instead, he looked sheepish and a bit embarrassed. 'Mal, I have to show you something,' he said. He brought up a screen on his phone, which showed a lizard in a similar domed pedestal. 'That's a live feed.'

She looked at it. 'But how? But that's . . .'

'Maleficent. When I returned from Camelot, I had her moved from the library to the museum just in case someone tried to do something funny. She's been there the whole time. She hasn't changed or transformed at all, and she's safe.'

'But all the guards?'

He looked abashed. 'They're there for show, but there's nothing to guard.'

'And mother's still just a lizard,' Mal said with a laugh.

'Just a lizard.' Ben smiled.

Later that day, Ben asked the four villain kids to meet with him to discuss the problem of the talismans. 'Obviously, we can't have them around,' he said.

'Yes, we have to neutralise them,' agreed Mal. 'But how?' Where could they find magic powerful enough to purge the talismans of evil? And she still had to figure out how to hatch her Dragon's Egg. She'd peeked at it this morning, and it was definitely starting to glow green at the edges.

'Shall we ask Merlin?' said Carlos.

'The three good fairies?' said Jay.

'Neverland, for sure,' said Evie.

But Ben surprised them. 'No, I think the person we're looking for is right here.'

'Fairy Godmother,' said Mal. 'Of course!' It was her magic that had collected all the villains of the land and trapped them in the Isle of the Lost in the first place. The most powerful sorcerer in Auradon was their chubby-cheeked middle-aged headmistress, who preferred to teach children how to live *without* magic, but she would know what to do.

'She'll be back from Cinderella's ball by the end of the

week, and we'll consult her then. For now, keep an eye on those things,' said Ben.

'We still don't know where our parents are,' reminded Jay. 'We saw signs of them in the Catacombs, but they still haven't turned up.'

But Mal had a theory about where they could be. 'Evie, will you do the honours?' she said, motioning towards the Magic Mirror.

'You think it'll really work this time?' Evie asked.

Mal nodded encouragingly.

Evie held up the Magic Mirror. 'Magic Mirror in my hand, show us where the villains stand!'

The mirror swirled, cloudy and grey, and then . . .

There they were: Evil Queen powdering her nose back at her castle, Cruella de Vil pawing through the racks of fur coats for just the right one, and Jafar inspecting a device a goblin had just brought into the shop.

'But how did they get back there?' asked Evie, who sounded as if she didn't quite believe what she was seeing.

'Merlin, right?' Ben guessed, turning to Mal. 'They must have been somewhere in the Catacombs nearby when he cast the spell.'

'Yeah, I think they were following us out of the tunnels,' said Jay. 'And they must have overheard us talking. They knew we'd found the talismans.'

Mal nodded. 'Then Merlin sent everyone back where

they belonged, and it must have returned them to the Isle of the Lost.'

'If they'd been down there for so long, I wonder why they never found the talismans?' asked Evie.

'Maybe because they didn't have a map?' said Carlos. 'Yen Sid said you could be lost down there forever. It *is* called the *Endless* Catacombs.'

'Hold on, what's that Jafar's got in his hand?' asked Mal, leaning in for a closer look.

'It's the remote that turns off the dome and lets down the bridge,' said Carlos with a groan. 'That goblin must have found it in the ditch!'

'Wait—it's broken, though, look, it's cracked in half,' said Jay.

'But once it's fixed . . .' said Evie nervously.

Once it was fixed, there was no need to explain what would happen next, thought Mal. The villains would be able to leave the island, and now that they knew who had their talismans, nothing would stop them from heading back to Auradon to take what was theirs.

More than ever, she, Evie, Jay and Carlos would have to destroy the talismans while Ben prepared the kingdom for a showdown with their enemies on the Isle of the Lost. Ben looked confident, but Mal and her friends weren't as hopeful. They knew how twisted their parents could be, and what they were capable of, and no-one would sleep well that night.

'I'm not worried,' said Ben. 'In Auradon, we can count on our heroes to protect us.'

'I don't feel like a hero,' said Carlos.

'That's okay,' said Mal with a rueful smile. 'Remember what the professor said? We're the villains you root for in the story.'

acknowledgments

Thank you to the heroic teams at Disney Hyperion, Disney Channel and Disney Consumer Products, who continue to believe that villains rule! Thanks especially to my ever-patient editors, Emily Meehan and Julie Moody, my awesome publicist, Seale Ballenger, as well as the rest of the fun-loving D-H crew who I'm proud to call my friends: Hannah Allaman, Mary Ann Zissimos, Elena Blanco, Kim Knueppel, Sarah Sullivan, Jackie De Leo, Frank Bumbalo, Dina Sherman, Elke Villa, Andrew Sansone, Holly Nagel, Marybeth Tregarthen, Sara Liebling, Martin Karlow, Dan Kaufman, Marci Senders, James Madsen and Russ Gray. Thank you to DCP grand pooh-bahs Leslie Ferraro, Andrew Sugerman, Raj Murari and my dear Jeanne Mosure. Thank you to Channel stars Jennifer Rogers-Doyle, Adam Bonnett, Naketha Mattocks, Laura Burns, Kate Reagan and Carin Davis.

Thank you to the beautiful young people who star in *Descendants*—Dove Cameron, Sofia Carson, Cameron Boyce, Booboo Stewart, Mitchell Hope, Sarah Jefferey, Brenna D'Amico, Diane Doan, Jedidiah Goodacre and Zachary Gibson—for being so inspirational, helping promote the book, and for being so nice to my kid at the premiere! Thank you, Kenny Ortega, for making such a fun movie!

Thank you to Richard Abate, Rachel Kim and everyone at 3Arts. Thank you, Colleen Wilson, for your patient dependability.

Thank you to my awesome DLC-Green-Ong-Gaisano-Torre-Ng-Lim-Johnston family. Thank you to Team A.U.: Margie Stohl and Raphael Simon for the late-night pep talks (texts?). Big love and thanks to Team Yallwest and Yallfest: Tahereh Mafi, Ransom Riggs, Marie Lu, Kami Garcia, Brendan Reichs, Sandy London, Veronica Roth, Leigh Bardugo, Holly Goldberg Sloan, Aaron Hartzler, Ally Condie, Richelle Mead, Patrick Dolan, Andria Amaral, Emily Williams, Steph Barna, Shane Pangburn, Tori Hill and Jonathan Sanchez, for the laughs and camaraderie. Thank you to my dear family of friends, especially the CH Mama Crew: Jill Lorie, Heidi McKenna, Celeste Vos, Jenni Gerber, Lindsay Nesmith, Maria Cina, Dawn Limerick, Carol Evans, Bronwyn Savasta, Gloria Jolley, Fatima Goncalves, Ava McKay, Nicole Jones, Heather Kiriakou, Kathleen Von Der Ahe, Maggie Silverberg, Dana Boyd, Dana Rees, Heidi Madzar, Angelee Reiner, Vicki Haller,

Betty Balian, Jen Kuklin, Lisa Orlando, Bridget Johnsen and Tiffany Moon. I love you and your kids and I thank you for all the support during the writing of this book and the one before it (and the one after this!).

Thank you to all the rotten little Descenders! You guys are amazing!

Thanks most to my husband, Mike Johnston, who makes every book of mine so much better and makes me feel like a queen, and to our little princess, Mattie. Thank you to my office buddy, our Maltese, Mimi, who's kept me company through every draft!

MELISSA DE LA CRUZ

(www.melissa-delacruz.com) is the author of the #1 New York Times best sellers *The Isle of the Lost* and *Return to the Isle of the Lost*, as well as many other best-selling novels, including all the books in the Blue Bloods series: *Blue Bloods, Masquerade, Revelations, The Van Alen Legacy, Keys to the Repository, Misguided Angel, Bloody Valentine, Lost in Time* and *Gates of Paradise*. She lives in Los Angeles with her husband and daughter.